## NEW PERSPECTIVES ON

# Microsoft® Excel® 2010

## INTRODUCTORY

**Important Information About This Printing**
This printing of this book was approved to meet the official standards for the Microsoft Office Specialist Excel 2010 exam. This printing includes a new Appendix C that provides:

- Information on Microsoft Office Specialist certification
- Coverage of additional skills related to the exam that are not covered in the main tutorials of this text
- A table that lists the skills for the exam and identifies where each is covered in the text

The information about the Microsoft Office Specialist exams on page ii is also new to this printing. Otherwise, the book contains the exact page-for-page content of previous printings.

D1335733

## What is the Microsoft® Office Specialist Program?

The Microsoft Office Specialist Program enables candidates to show that they have something exceptional to offer – proven expertise in certain Microsoft programs. Recognized by businesses and schools around the world, over 4 million certifications have been obtained in over 100 different countries. The Microsoft Office Specialist Program is the only Microsoft-approved certification program of its kind.

## What is the Microsoft Office Specialist Certification?

The Microsoft Office Specialist certification validates through the use of exams that you have obtained specific skill sets within the applicable Microsoft Office programs and other Microsoft programs included in the Microsoft Office Specialist Program. The candidate can choose which exam(s) they want to take according to which skills they want to validate.

The available Microsoft Office Specialist Program exams include*:

- Using Windows Vista®
- Using Microsoft® Office Word 2007
- Using Microsoft® Office Word 2007 – Expert
- Using Microsoft® Office Excel® 2007
- Using Microsoft® Office Excel® 2007 – Expert
- Using Microsoft® Office PowerPoint® 2007
- Using Microsoft® Office Access® 2007
- Using Microsoft® Office Outlook® 2007
- Using Microsoft SharePoint® 2007

The Microsoft Office Specialist Program 2010 exams will include*:

- Microsoft Word 2010
- Microsoft Word 2010 Expert
- Microsoft Excel® 2010
- Microsoft Excel® 2010 Expert
- Microsoft PowerPoint® 2010
- Microsoft Access® 2010
- Microsoft Outlook® 2010
- Microsoft SharePoint® 2010

## What does the Microsoft Office Specialist Approved Courseware logo represent?

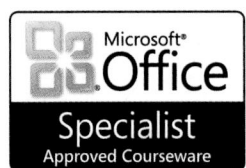

The logo indicates that this courseware has been approved by Microsoft to cover the course objectives that will be included in the relevant exam. It also means that after utilizing this courseware, you may be better prepared to pass the exams required to become a certified Microsoft Office Specialist.

## For more information:

To learn more about Microsoft Office Specialist exams, visit www.microsoft.com/learning/msbc

To learn about other Microsoft approved courseware from Cengage Learning, visit www.cengagebrain.com

The availability of Microsoft Office Specialist certification exams varies by Microsoft program, program version and language. Visit www.microsoft.com/learning for exam availability.

Microsoft, Access, Excel, the Office Logo, Outlook, PowerPoint, SharePoint, and Windows Vista are either registered trademarks or trademarks of Microsoft Corporation in the United States and/or other countries. The Microsoft Office Specialist logo and the Microsoft Office Specialist Approved Courseware logo are used under license from Microsoft Corporation.

# NEW PERSPECTIVES ON

# Microsoft® Excel® 2010

## INTRODUCTORY

June Jamrich Parsons
Dan Oja
Roy Ageloff
Patrick Carey

**COURSE TECHNOLOGY**
CENGAGE Learning™

Australia • Brazil • Japan • Korea • Mexico • Singapore • Spain • United Kingdom • United States

**COURSE TECHNOLOGY**
CENGAGE Learning™

**New Perspectives on Microsoft Excel 2010, Introductory**

Vice President, Publisher: Nicole Jones Pinard

Executive Editor: Marie L. Lee

Associate Acquisitions Editor: Brandi Shailer

Senior Product Manager: Kathy Finnegan

Product Manager: Leigh Hefferon

Associate Product Manager: Julia Leroux-Lindsey

Editorial Assistant: Jacqueline Lacaire

Director of Marketing: Cheryl Costantini

Senior Marketing Manager: Ryan DeGrote

Marketing Coordinator: Kristen Panciocco

Developmental Editor: Robin M. Romer

Senior Content Project Manager:
    Jennifer Goguen McGrail

Composition: GEX Publishing Services

Art Director: Marissa Falco

Text Designer: Althea Chen

Cover Designer: Roycroft Design

Cover Art: © David Jordan Williams/Corbis

Copyeditor: Suzanne Huizenga

Proofreader: Andrea Schein

Indexer: Alexandra Nickerson

For product information and technology assistance, contact us at
**Cengage Learning Customer & Sales Support, 1-800-354-9706**
For permission to use material from this text or product, submit all requests online at **www.cengage.com/permissions**
Further permissions questions can be emailed to
**permissionrequest@cengage.com**

Trademarks:

Some of the product names and company names used in this book have been used for identification purposes only and may be trademarks or registered trademarks of their respective manufacturers and sellers.

Microsoft and the Office logo are either registered trademarks or trademarks of Microsoft Corporation in the United States and/or other countries. Course Technology, Cengage Learning is an independent entity from the Microsoft Corporation, and not affiliated with Microsoft in any manner.

Disclaimer: Any fictional data related to persons or companies or URLs used throughout this book is intended for instructional purposes only. At the time this book was printed, any such data was fictional and not belonging to any real persons or companies.

Library of Congress Control Number: 2010930740

International Edition:

ISBN-13: 978-0-538-47069-8

ISBN-10: 0-538-47069-0

Cengage Learning International Offices

**Asia**
www.cengageasia.com
tel: (65) 6410 1200

**Australia/New Zealand**
www.cengage.com.au
tel: (61) 3 9685 4111

**Brazil**
www.cengage.com.br
tel: (55) 11 3665 9900

**India**
www.cengage.co.in
tel: (91) 11 4364 1111

**Latin America**
www.cengage.com.mx
tel: (52) 55 1500 6000

**UK/Europe/Middle East/Africa**
www.cengage.co.uk
tel: (44) 0 1264 332 424

**Represented in Canada by**
**Nelson Education, Ltd.**
tel: (416) 752 9100 / (800) 668 0671
www.nelson.com

Cengage Learning is a leading provider of customized learning solutions with office locations around the globe, including Singapore, the United Kingdom, Australia, Mexico, Brazil, and Japan. Locate your local office at: **www.cengage.com/global**

For product information: **www.cengage.com/international**
Visit your local office: **www.cengage.com/global**
Visit our corporate website: **www.cengage.com**

"AVAILABILITY OF RESOURCES MAY DIFFER BY REGION. Check with your local Cengage Learning representative for details."

Printed in the United States of America
2 3 4 5 6 7 8 9 14 13 12

# Preface

The New Perspectives Series' critical-thinking, problem-solving approach is the ideal way to prepare students to transcend point-and-click skills and take advantage of all that Microsoft Office 2010 has to offer.

In developing the New Perspectives Series, our goal was to create books that give students the software concepts and practical skills they need to succeed beyond the classroom. We've updated our proven case-based pedagogy with more practical content to make learning skills more meaningful to students.

With the New Perspectives Series, students understand *why* they are learning *what* they are learning, and are fully prepared to apply their skills to real-life situations.

*"The new Visual Overviews give students valuable insight into what they will learn in each tutorial session. Clearly seeing what's ahead will engage students from the start."*
— Diane Shingledecker
Portland Community
College

## About This Book

This book provides thorough coverage of Microsoft Excel 2010, and includes the following:
- Detailed, hands-on instruction of Excel 2010, including creating and formatting a workbook; working with formulas and functions; creating charts, tables, and PivotTables; managing multiple workbooks; and developing an Excel application
- Coverage of important spreadsheet concepts, including order of precedence in formulas, function syntax, absolute and relative cell references, what-if analysis, and data validation
- Exploration of the exciting new features in Excel 2010, including working in Backstage view, adding sparklines for compact graphing, and using a slicer to filter a PivotTable

*New for this edition!*
- Each session begins with a Visual Overview, a new two-page spread that includes colorful, enlarged screenshots with numerous callouts and key term definitions, giving students a comprehensive preview of the topics covered in the session, as well as a handy study guide.
- New ProSkills boxes provide guidance for how to use the software in real-world, professional situations, and related ProSkills exercises integrate the technology skills students learn with one or more of the following soft skills: decision making, problem solving, teamwork, verbal communication, and written communication.
- Important steps are now highlighted in yellow with attached margin notes to help students pay close attention to completing the steps correctly and avoid time-consuming rework.

## System Requirements

This book assumes a typical installation of Microsoft Excel 2010 and Microsoft Windows 7 Ultimate using an Aero theme. (You can also complete the material in this text using another version of Windows 7, such as Home Premium, or earlier versions of the Windows operating system. You will see only minor differences in how some windows look.) The browser used for any steps that require a browser is Internet Explorer 8.

www.cengage.com/ct/newperspectives

v

# The New Perspectives Approach

*"The clear step-by-step instructions, real-world data files, and helpful figures make New Perspectives texts excellent for courses taught in the classroom, the hybrid/blended format, or entirely online."*
—Sylvia Amito'elau
Coastline Community College

### Context
Each tutorial begins with a problem presented in a "real-world" case that is meaningful to students. The case sets the scene to help students understand what they will do in the tutorial.

### Hands-on Approach
Each tutorial is divided into manageable sessions that combine reading and hands-on, step-by-step work. Colorful screenshots help guide students through the steps. **Trouble?** tips anticipate common mistakes or problems to help students stay on track and continue with the tutorial.

**VISUAL OVERVIEW**

### Visual Overviews
*New for this edition!* Each session begins with a Visual Overview, a new two-page spread that includes colorful, enlarged screenshots with numerous callouts and key term definitions, giving students a comprehensive preview of the topics covered in the session, as well as a handy study guide.

**PROSKILLS**

### ProSkills Boxes and Exercises
*New for this edition!* ProSkills boxes provide guidance for how to use the software in real-world, professional situations, and related ProSkills exercises integrate the technology skills students learn with one or more of the following soft skills: decision making, problem solving, teamwork, verbal communication, and written communication.

**KEY STEP**

### Key Steps
*New for this edition!* Important steps are highlighted in yellow with attached margin notes to help students pay close attention to completing the steps correctly and avoid time-consuming rework.

**INSIGHT**

### InSight Boxes
InSight boxes offer expert advice and best practices to help students achieve a deeper understanding of the concepts behind the software features and skills.

**TIP**

### Margin Tips
Margin Tips provide helpful hints and shortcuts for more efficient use of the software. The Tips appear in the margin at key points throughout each tutorial, giving students extra information when and where they need it.

**REVIEW**
**APPLY**

### Assessment
Retention is a key component to learning. At the end of each session, a series of Quick Check questions helps students test their understanding of the material before moving on. Engaging end-of-tutorial Review Assignments and Case Problems have always been a hallmark feature of the New Perspectives Series. Colorful bars and brief descriptions accompany the exercises, making it easy to understand both the goal and level of challenge a particular assignment holds.

**REFERENCE**
**TASK REFERENCE**
**GLOSSARY/INDEX**

### Reference
Within each tutorial, Reference boxes appear before a set of steps to provide a succinct summary and preview of how to perform a task. In addition, a complete Task Reference at the back of the book provides quick access to information on how to carry out common tasks. Finally, each book includes a combination Glossary/Index to promote easy reference of material.

**www.cengage.com/ct/newperspectives**

# Our Complete System of Instruction

### Coverage To Meet Your Needs

Whether you're looking for just a small amount of coverage or enough to fill a semester-long class, we can provide you with a textbook that meets your needs.

- Brief books typically cover the essential skills in just 2 to 4 tutorials.
- Introductory books build and expand on those skills and contain an average of 5 to 8 tutorials.
- Comprehensive books are great for a full-semester class, and contain 9 to 12+ tutorials.

So if the book you're holding does not provide the right amount of coverage for you, there's probably another offering available. Go to our Web site or contact your Course Technology sales representative to find out what else we offer.

### CourseCasts – Learning on the Go. Always available…always relevant.

Want to keep up with the latest technology trends relevant to you? Visit our site to find a library of podcasts, CourseCasts, featuring a "CourseCast of the Week," and download them to your mp3 player at http://coursecasts.course.com.

Our fast-paced world is driven by technology. You know because you're an active participant—always on the go, always keeping up with technological trends, and always learning new ways to embrace technology to power your life.

Ken Baldauf, host of CourseCasts, is a faculty member of the Florida State University Computer Science Department where he is responsible for teaching technology classes to thousands of FSU students each year. Ken is an expert in the latest technology trends; he gathers and sorts through the most pertinent news and information for CourseCasts so your students can spend their time enjoying technology, rather than trying to figure it out. Open or close your lecture with a discussion based on the latest CourseCast.

Visit us at http://coursecasts.course.com to learn on the go!

### Instructor Resources

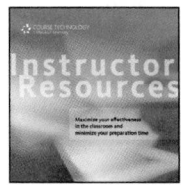

We offer more than just a book. We have all the tools you need to enhance your lectures, check students' work, and generate exams in a new, easier-to-use and completely revised package. This book's Instructor's Manual, ExamView testbank, PowerPoint presentations, data files, solution files, figure files, and a sample syllabus are all available on a single CD-ROM or for downloading at http://www.cengage.com/coursetechnology.

### SAM: Skills Assessment Manager

SAM is designed to help bring students from the classroom to the real world. It allows students to train and test on important computer skills in an active, hands-on environment.

SAM's easy-to-use system includes powerful interactive exams, training, and projects on the most commonly used Microsoft Office applications. SAM simulates the Office application environment, allowing students to demonstrate their knowledge and think through the skills by performing real-world tasks, such as bolding text or setting up slide transitions. Add in live-in-the-application projects, and students are on their way to truly learning and applying skills to business-centric documents.

Designed to be used with the New Perspectives Series, SAM includes handy page references, so students can print helpful study guides that match the New Perspectives textbooks used in class. For instructors, SAM also includes robust scheduling and reporting features.

### Content for Online Learning

WebTUTOR

Course Technology has partnered with the leading distance learning solution providers and class-management platforms today. To access this material, visit www.cengage.com/webtutor and search for your title. Instructor resources include the following: additional case projects, sample syllabi, PowerPoint presentations, and more. For students to access this material, they must have purchased a WebTutor PIN-code specific to this title and your campus platform. The resources for students might include (based on instructor preferences): topic reviews, review questions, practice tests, and more. For additional information, please contact your sales representative.

## Acknowledgments

We would like to thank the many people whose invaluable contributions made this book possible. First, sincere thanks go to our reviewers: Carol DesJardins, St. Clair County Community College; Kristen Hockman, University of Missouri–Columbia; Dana Hooper, The University of Alabama; Ahmed Kamel, Concordia College; Peter Ross, University at Albany; Diane Shingledecker, Portland Community College; Kelly Swain, Humber College; Karen Toreson, Shoreline Community College; Mary Voehl, Caldwell College; Raymond Yu, Douglas College; and Violet Zhang, George Brown College. At Course Technology we would like to thank Marie Lee, Executive Editor; Kathy Finnegan, Senior Product Manager; Brandi Shailer, Associate Acquisitions Editor; Julia Leroux-Lindsey, Associate Product Manager; Jacqueline Lacaire, Editorial Assistant; Jennifer Goguen McGrail, Senior Content Project Manager; Christian Kunciw, Manuscript Quality Assurance Supervisor; and John Freitas, Susan Pedicini, Danielle Shaw, and Susan Whalen, MQA Testers. Special thanks to Robin Romer, Developmental Editor, for her exceptional efforts, keeping us focused and providing guidance and encouragement as we worked to complete this text.

– June Jamrich Parsons
– Dan Oja
– Roy Ageloff
– Patrick Carey

# BRIEF CONTENTS

# TABLE OF CONTENTS

## GETTING STARTED WITH MICROSOFT OFFICE 2010

## EXCEL LEVEL I TUTORIALS

# Getting Started with Microsoft Office 2010

*Preparing a Meeting Agenda*

## OBJECTIVES

- Explore the programs in Microsoft Office
- Start programs and switch between them
- Explore common window elements
- Minimize, maximize, and restore windows
- Use the Ribbon, tabs, and buttons
- Use the contextual tabs, the Mini toolbar, and shortcut menus
- Save, close, and open a file
- Learn how to share files using SkyDrive
- Use the Help system
- Preview and print a file
- Exit programs

## Case | *Recycled Palette*

Recycled Palette, a company in Oregon founded by Ean Nogella in 2006, sells 100 percent recycled latex paint to both individuals and businesses in the area. The high-quality recycled paint is filtered to industry standards and tested for performance and environmental safety. The paint is available in both 1 gallon cans and 5 gallon pails, and comes in colors ranging from white to shades of brown, blue, green, and red. The demand for affordable recycled paint has been growing each year. Ean and all his employees use Microsoft Office 2010, which provides everyone in the company with the power and flexibility to store a variety of information, create consistent files, and share data. In this tutorial, you'll review how the company's employees use Microsoft Office 2010.

## STARTING DATA FILES

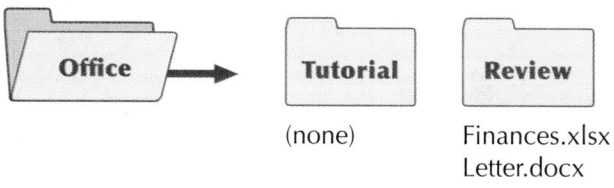

Office → Tutorial  Review

(none)  Finances.xlsx
Letter.docx

# VISUAL OVERVIEW

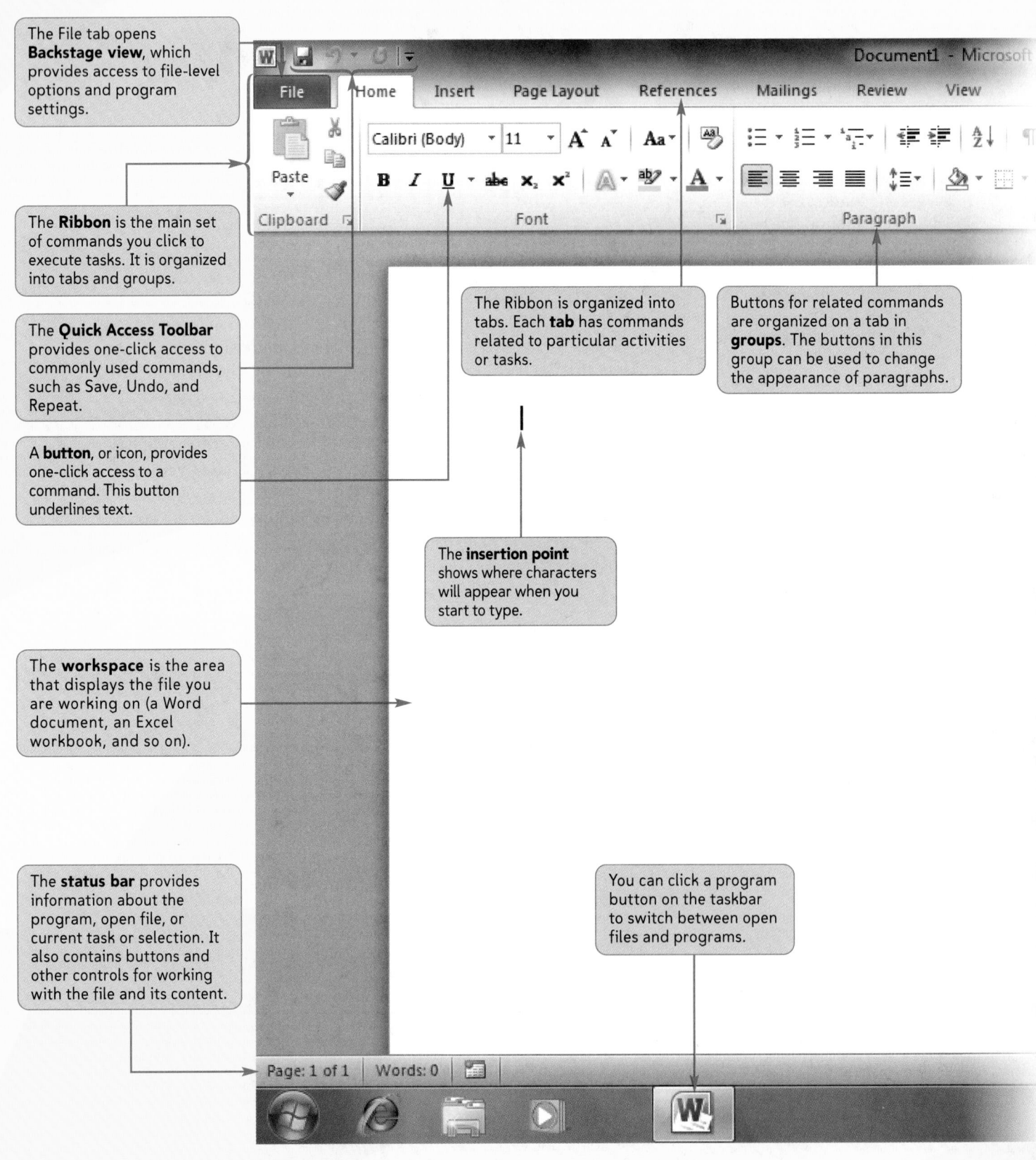

The File tab opens **Backstage view**, which provides access to file-level options and program settings.

The **Ribbon** is the main set of commands you click to execute tasks. It is organized into tabs and groups.

The **Quick Access Toolbar** provides one-click access to commonly used commands, such as Save, Undo, and Repeat.

A **button**, or icon, provides one-click access to a command. This button underlines text.

The Ribbon is organized into tabs. Each **tab** has commands related to particular activities or tasks.

Buttons for related commands are organized on a tab in **groups**. The buttons in this group can be used to change the appearance of paragraphs.

The **insertion point** shows where characters will appear when you start to type.

The **workspace** is the area that displays the file you are working on (a Word document, an Excel workbook, and so on).

The **status bar** provides information about the program, open file, or current task or selection. It also contains buttons and other controls for working with the file and its content.

You can click a program button on the taskbar to switch between open files and programs.

# COMMON WINDOW ELEMENTS

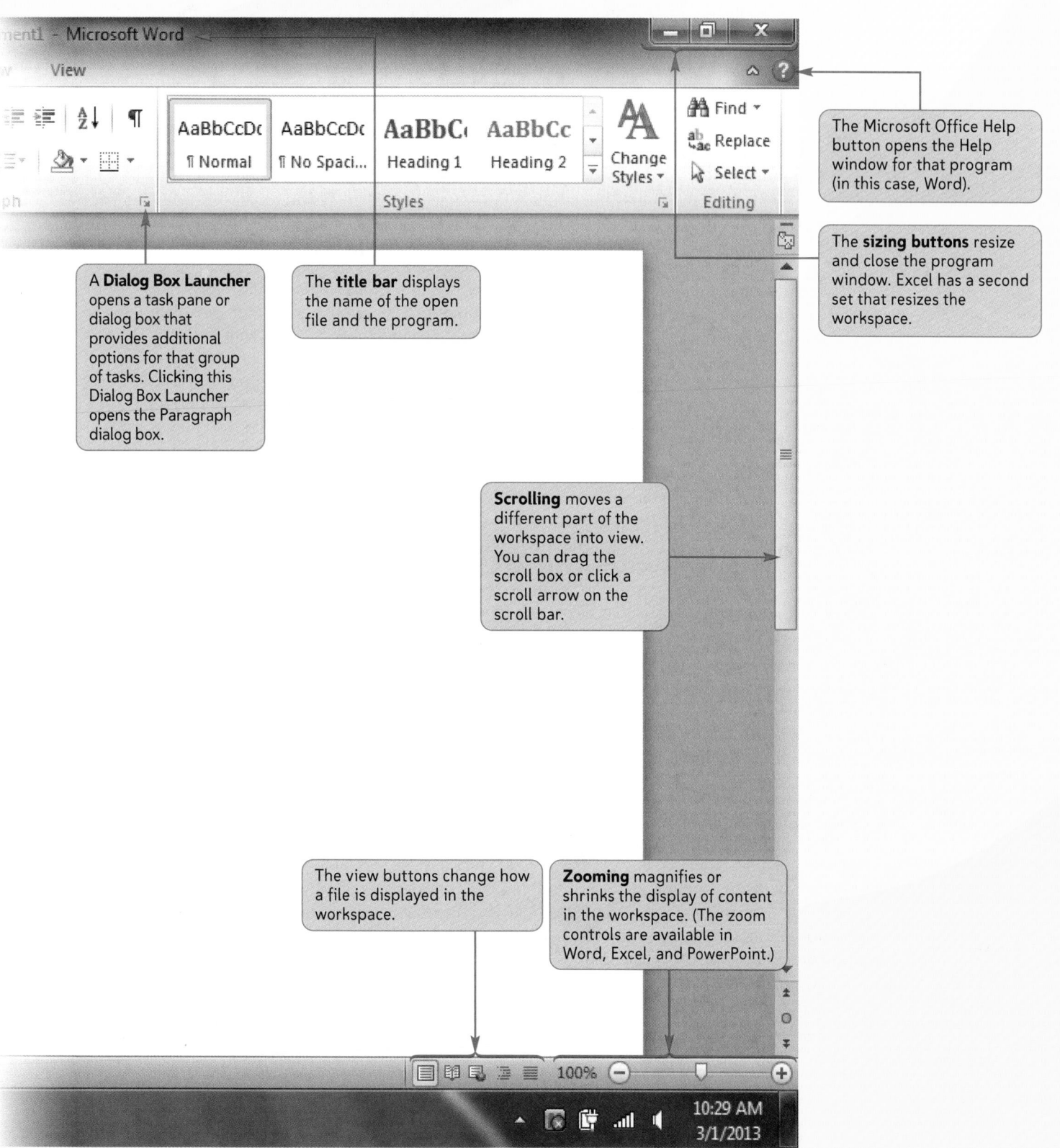

A **Dialog Box Launcher** opens a task pane or dialog box that provides additional options for that group of tasks. Clicking this Dialog Box Launcher opens the Paragraph dialog box.

The **title bar** displays the name of the open file and the program.

The Microsoft Office Help button opens the Help window for that program (in this case, Word).

The **sizing buttons** resize and close the program window. Excel has a second set that resizes the workspace.

**Scrolling** moves a different part of the workspace into view. You can drag the scroll box or click a scroll arrow on the scroll bar.

The view buttons change how a file is displayed in the workspace.

**Zooming** magnifies or shrinks the display of content in the workspace. (The zoom controls are available in Word, Excel, and PowerPoint.)

# Exploring Microsoft Office 2010

**TIP**

For additional information about the available suites, go to the Microsoft Web site.

**Microsoft Office 2010**, or **Office**, is a collection of Microsoft programs. Office is available in many suites, each of which contains a different combination of these programs. For example, the Professional suite includes Word, Excel, PowerPoint, Access, Outlook, Publisher, and OneNote. Other suites are available and can include more or fewer programs. Each Office program contains valuable tools to help you accomplish many tasks, such as composing reports, analyzing data, preparing presentations, compiling information, sending email, planning schedules, and compiling notes.

**Microsoft Word 2010**, or **Word**, is a computer program you use to enter, edit, and format text. The files you create in Word are called **documents**, although many people use the term *document* to refer to any file created on a computer. Word, often called a word-processing program, offers many special features that help you compose and update all types of documents, ranging from letters and newsletters to reports, brochures, faxes, and even books, in attractive and readable formats. You can also use Word to create, insert, and position figures, tables, and other graphics to enhance the look of your documents. For example, the Recycled Palette employees create business letters using Word.

**Microsoft Excel 2010**, or **Excel**, is a computer program you use to enter, calculate, analyze, and present numerical data. You can do some of this in Word with tables, but Excel provides many more tools for recording and formatting numbers as well as performing calculations. The graphics capabilities in Excel also enable you to display data visually. You might, for example, generate a pie chart or a bar chart to help people quickly see the significance of and the connections between information. The files you create in Excel are called **workbooks** (commonly referred to as spreadsheets), and Excel is often called a spreadsheet program. The Recycled Palette accounting department uses a line chart in an Excel workbook to visually track the company's financial performance.

**Microsoft Access 2010**, or **Access**, is a computer program used to enter, maintain, and retrieve related information (or data) in a format known as a database. The files you create in Access are called **databases**, and Access is often referred to as a database or relational database program. With Access, you can create forms to make data entry easier, and you can create professional reports to improve the readability of your data. The Recycled Palette operations department tracks the company's inventory in an Access database.

**Microsoft PowerPoint 2010**, or **PowerPoint**, is a computer program you use to create a collection of slides that can contain text, charts, pictures, sound, movies, multimedia, and so on. The files you create in PowerPoint are called **presentations**, and PowerPoint is often called a presentation graphics program. You can show these presentations on your computer monitor, project them onto a screen as a slide show, print them, share them over the Internet, or display them on the Web. You can also use PowerPoint to generate presentation-related documents such as audience handouts, outlines, and speakers' notes. The Recycled Palette marketing department uses a PowerPoint slide presentation to promote its paints.

**Microsoft Outlook 2010**, or **Outlook**, is a computer program you use to send, receive, and organize email; plan your schedule; arrange meetings; organize contacts; create a to-do list; and record notes. You can also use Outlook to print schedules, task lists, phone directories, and other documents. Outlook is often referred to as an information management program. The Recycled Palette staff members use Outlook to send and receive email, plan their schedules, and create to-do lists.

Although each Office program individually is a strong tool, their potential is even greater when used together.

### Teamwork: Integrating Office Programs

One of the main advantages of Office is **integration**, the ability to share information between programs. Integration ensures consistency and accuracy, and it saves time because you don't have to reenter the same information in several Office programs. It also means that team members can effortlessly share Office files. Team members can create files based on their skills and information that can be used by others as needed. The staff at Recycled Palette uses the integration features of Office every day, as described in the following examples:

- The accounting department created an Excel bar chart on fourth-quarter results for the previous two years, and inserted it into the quarterly financial report created in Word. The Word report includes a hyperlink that employees can click to open the Excel workbook and view the original data.
- The operations department included an Excel pie chart of sales percentages by paint colors on a PowerPoint slide, which is part of a presentation to stockholders.
- The marketing department produced a mailing to promote its recycled paints to local contractors and designers by combining a form letter created in Word with an Access database that stores the names and addresses of these potential customers.
- A sales representative merged the upcoming promotion letter that the marketing department created in Word with an Outlook contact list containing the names and addresses of prospective customers.

Even these few examples of how information from one Office program can be integrated with another illustrate how integration can save time and effort. Each team member can focus on creating files in the program best suited to convey the information he or she is responsible for. Yet, everyone can share the files, using them as needed for their specific purpose.

## Starting Office Programs

You can start any Office program from the Start menu on the taskbar. As soon as the program starts, you can immediately begin to create new files or work with existing ones.

### Starting an Office Program

- On the taskbar, click the Start button.
- On the Start menu, click All Programs, click Microsoft Office, and then click the name of the program to start.

or

- Click the name of the program to start in the left pane of the Start menu.

You'll start Word using the Start button.

### To start Word and open a new, blank document:

▶ 1. Make sure your computer is on and the Windows desktop appears on your screen.

   **Trouble?** If your screen varies slightly from those shown in the figures, your computer might be set up differently. The figures in this book were created while running Windows 7 with the Aero feature turned on, but how your screen looks depends on the version of Windows you are using, the resolution of your screen, and other settings.

▶ 2. On the taskbar, click the **Start** button 🔵, and then click **All Programs** to display the All Programs list.

▶ 3. Click **Microsoft Office**, and then point to **Microsoft Word 2010**. Depending on how your computer is set up, your desktop and menu might contain different icons and commands. See Figure 1.

| Figure 1 | Start menu with All Programs list displayed |
|---|---|

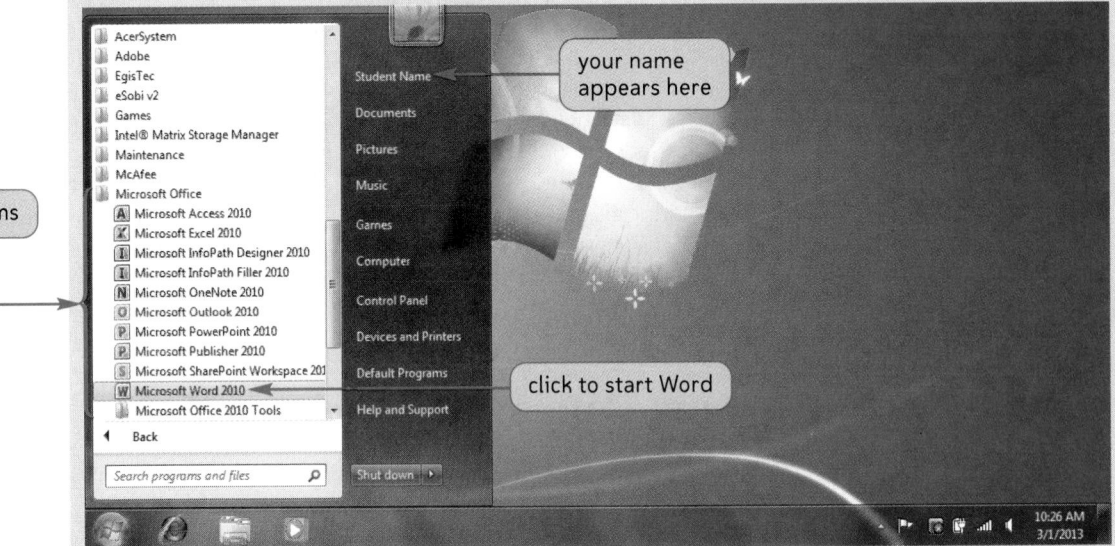

**Trouble?** If you don't see Microsoft Office on the All Programs list, point to Microsoft Word 2010 on the All Programs menu. If you still don't see Microsoft Word 2010, ask your instructor or technical support person for help.

▶ 4. Click **Microsoft Word 2010**. Word starts and a new, blank document opens. Refer to the Visual Overview to review the common program window elements.

   **Trouble?** If the Word window doesn't fill your entire screen as shown in the Visual Overview, the window is not maximized, or expanded to its full size. You'll maximize the window shortly.

You can have more than one Office program open at once. You'll use this same method to start Excel and open a new, blank workbook.

**To start Excel and open a new, blank workbook:**

▶ 1. On the taskbar, click the **Start** button ⊕, click **All Programs** to display the All Programs list, and then click **Microsoft Office**.

   **Trouble?** If you don't see Microsoft Office on the All Programs list, point to Microsoft Excel 2010 on the All Programs list. If you still don't see Microsoft Excel 2010, ask your instructor or technical support person for help.

▶ 2. Click **Microsoft Excel 2010**. Excel starts and a new, blank workbook opens. See Figure 2.

| Figure 2 | New, blank Excel workbook |

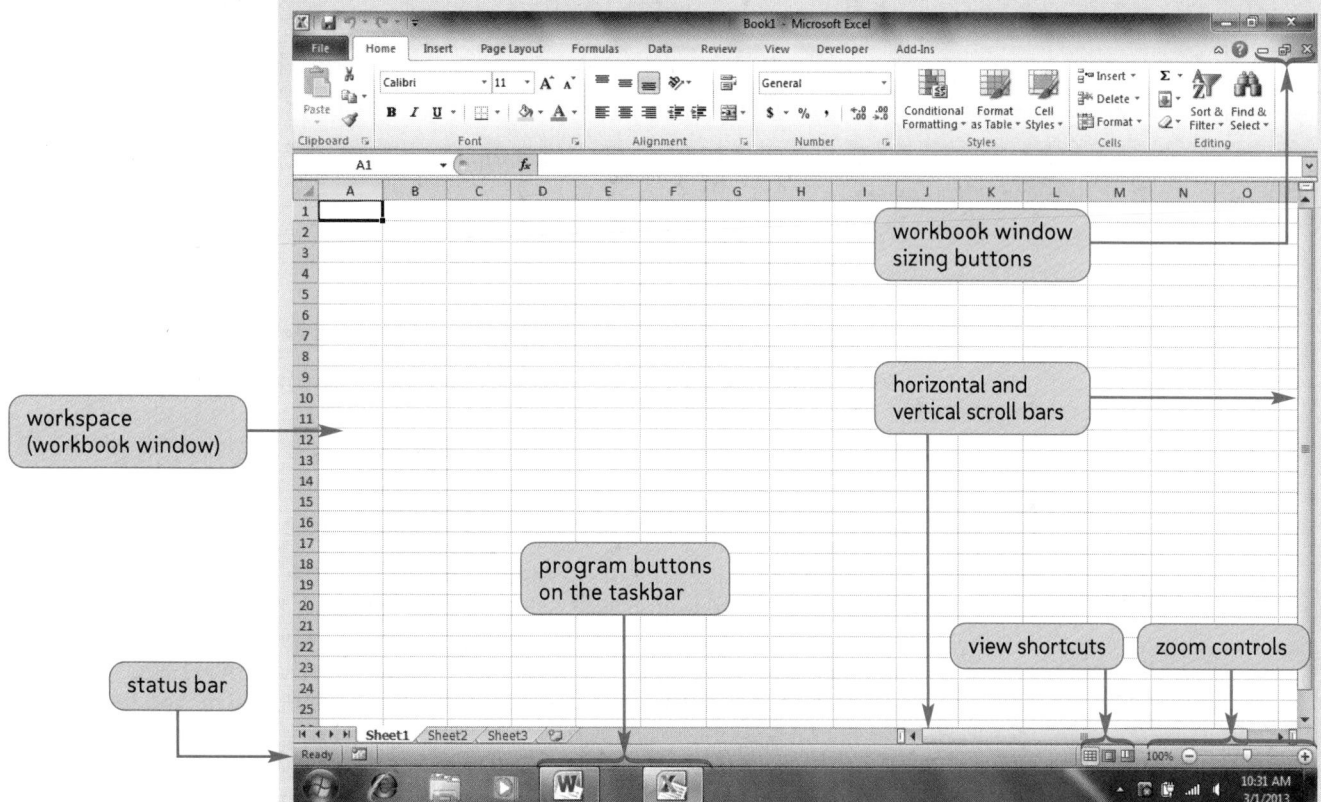

**Trouble?** If the Excel window doesn't fill your entire screen, the window is not maximized, or expanded to its full size. You'll maximize the window shortly.

## Switching Between Open Programs and Files

Two programs are running at the same time—Word and Excel. The taskbar contains buttons for both programs. When you have two or more programs running or two files within the same program open, you can click the program buttons on the taskbar to switch from one program or file to another. When you point to a program button, a thumbnail (or small picture) of each open file in that program is displayed. You can then click the thumbnail of the file you want to make active. The employees at Recycled Palette often work in several programs and files at once.

**To switch between the open Word and Excel files:**

▶ **1.** On the taskbar, point to the **Microsoft Word** program button . A thumbnail of the open Word document appears. See Figure 3.

| Figure 3 | Thumbnail of the open Word document |

click the thumbnail that appears to make the file active

point to the Word program button

Excel program button

▶ **2.** Click the **Document1 - Microsoft Word** thumbnail. The active program switches from Excel to Word.

# Exploring Common Window Elements

As you can see, many elements in both the Word and Excel program windows are the same. In fact, most Office programs have these same elements. Because these elements are the same in each program, after you've learned one program, it's easy to learn the others.

## Resizing the Program Window and Workspace

**TIP**

Excel has two sets of sizing buttons. The top set controls the program window and the bottom set controls the workspace.

There are three different sizing buttons that appear on the right side of a program window's title bar. The Minimize button ▭, which is the left button, hides a window so that only its program button is visible on the taskbar. The middle button changes name and function depending on the status of the window—the Maximize button ▭ expands the window to the full screen size or to the program window size, and the Restore Down button ▭ returns the window to a predefined size. The Close button ✕, on the right, exits the program or closes the file.

The sizing buttons give you the flexibility to arrange the program and file windows to best fit your needs. Most often, you'll want to maximize the program window and workspace to take advantage of the full screen size you have available. If you have several files open, you might want to restore down their windows so that you can see more than one window at a time, or you might want to minimize programs or files you are not working on at the moment.

**To resize the windows and workspaces:**

▶ **1.** On the Word title bar, click the **Minimize** button ▭. The Word program window is reduced to a taskbar button. The Excel program window is visible again.

▶ **2.** On the Excel title bar, click the **Maximize** button ▭ to expand the Excel program window to fill the screen, if necessary.

**3.** In the bottom set of Excel sizing buttons, click the **Restore Window** button ⊡. The workspace is resized smaller than the full program window. See Figure 4.

Figure 4    **Resized Excel window and workspace**

restored workspace (yours might be a different size or shape)

program window sizing buttons

workbook window sizing buttons

drag to resize window to a custom size

**4.** On the workbook window, click the **Maximize** button ⊡. The workspace expands to fill the program window.

**5.** On the taskbar, click the **Microsoft Word** [W] program button. The Word program window returns to its previous size.

**6.** On the Word title bar, click the **Maximize** button ⊡ if necessary to expand the Word program to fill the screen.

## Switching Views

Each program has a variety of views, or ways to display the file in the workspace. For example, Word has five views: Print Layout, Full Screen Reading, Web Layout, Outline, and Draft. The content of the file doesn't change from view to view, although the presentation of the content does. In Word, for example, Print Layout view shows how the document would appear as a printed page, whereas Web Layout view shows how the document would appear as a Web page. You'll change views in later tutorials.

## Zooming and Scrolling

You can zoom in to get a closer look at the content of an open document, worksheet, slide, or database report. Likewise, you can zoom out to see more of the content at a smaller size. You can select a specific percentage or size based on your file. The zoom percentage can range from 10 percent to 400 percent (Excel and PowerPoint) or 500 percent (Word). The figures shown in these tutorials show the workspace zoomed in to enhance readability. Zooming can shift part of the workspace out of view. To change which area of the workspace is visible in the program window, you can use the scroll bars. A scroll bar has arrow buttons that you can click to shift the workspace a small amount in the specified direction and a scroll box that you can drag to shift the workspace a larger amount in the direction you drag. Depending on the program and zoom level, you might see a vertical scroll bar, a horizontal scroll bar, or both.

### To zoom and scroll in Word and Excel:

**1.** On the Word status bar, drag the **Zoom slider** ▽ to the left until the percentage is **10%**. The document is reduced to its smallest size, which makes the entire page visible but unreadable. See Figure 5.

| Figure 5 | Word zoom level set to 10% |

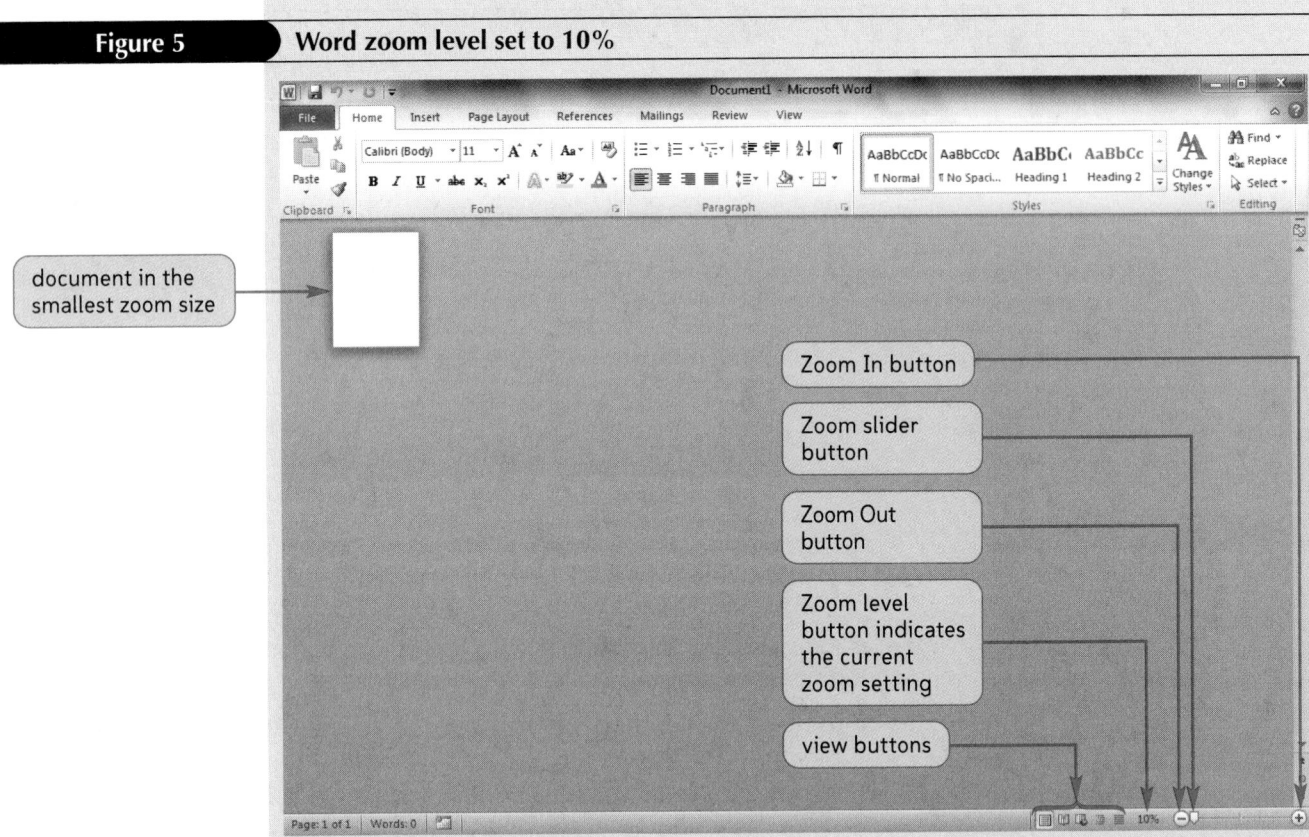

document in the smallest zoom size

Zoom In button

Zoom slider button

Zoom Out button

Zoom level button indicates the current zoom setting

view buttons

**2.** On the Word status bar, click the **Zoom level** button 10%. The Zoom dialog box opens. See Figure 6.

| Figure 6 | Zoom dialog box |

click this option button

type a custom zoom percentage

click to accept the selected zoom setting

3. Click the **Page width** option button, and then click the **OK** button. The Word document is magnified to its page width, which matches how the Word figures appear in the tutorials.

4. On the taskbar, click the **Microsoft Excel** program button. The Excel program window is displayed.

5. On the status bar, click the **Zoom In** button ⊕ twice. The worksheet is magnified to 120%, which is the zoom level that matches the Excel figures shown in the tutorials.

6. On the horizontal scroll bar, click the **right arrow** button ▶ twice. The worksheet shifts two columns to the right. Columns A and B (labeled by letter at the top of the columns) shift out of view and two other columns shift into view.

7. On the horizontal scroll bar, drag the **scroll box** all the way to the left. The worksheet shifts left to display columns A and B again.

8. On the taskbar, click the **Microsoft Word** program button. The Word program window is displayed.

# Using the Ribbon

Although the tabs on the Ribbon differ from program to program, each program has two tabs in common. The first tab on the Ribbon, the File tab, opens Backstage view. Backstage view provides access to file-level features, such as creating new files, opening existing files, saving files, printing files, and closing files, as well as the most common program options. The second tab in each program—called the Home tab—contains the commands for the most frequently performed activities, including cutting and pasting, changing fonts, and using editing tools. In addition, the Insert, Review, and View tabs appear on the Ribbon in all Office programs except Access, although the commands they include might differ from program to program. Other tabs are program specific, such as the Design tab in PowerPoint and the Datasheet Tools tab in Access.

### To use the Ribbon tabs:

1. In Word, point to the **Insert** tab on the Ribbon. The Insert tab is highlighted, though the Home tab with the options for using the Clipboard and formatting text remains visible.

2. Click the **Insert** tab. The Insert tab is displayed on the Ribbon. This tab provides access to all the options for adding objects such as shapes, pages, tables, illustrations, text, and symbols to a document. See Figure 7.

| Figure 7 | Insert tab on the Ribbon in Word |

Insert tab selected

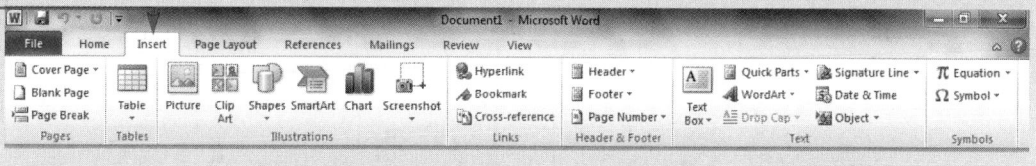

3. Click the **Home** tab. The Home tab options appear on the Ribbon.

## Clicking Buttons

For the most part, when you click a button, something happens in the file. For example, the Clipboard group on the Home tab includes the Cut, Copy, Paste, and Format Painter buttons, which you can click to move or copy text, objects, and formatting.

Buttons can be **toggles**: one click turns the feature on and the next click turns the feature off. While the feature is on, the button remains colored or highlighted. For example, on the Home tab in Word, the Show/Hide ¶ button in the Paragraph group displays the nonprinting characters when toggled on and hides them when toggled off.

Some buttons have two parts: a button that accesses a command, and an arrow that opens a menu of all the commands or options available for that task. For example, the Paste button in the Clipboard group on the Home tab includes the Paste command and an arrow to access all the Paste commands and options. To select one of these commands or options, you click the button arrow and then click the command or option.

---

**INSIGHT**

### How Buttons and Groups Appear on the Ribbon

The buttons and groups on the Ribbon change based on your monitor size, your screen resolution, and the size of the program window. With smaller monitors, lower screen resolutions, and reduced program windows, buttons can appear as icons without labels and a group can be condensed into a button that you click to display the group options. The figures in these tutorials were created using a screen resolution of 1024 × 768 and, unless otherwise specified, the program and workspace windows are maximized. If you are using a different screen resolution or window size, the buttons on the Ribbon might show more or fewer button names, and some groups might be reduced to a button.

---

You'll type text in the Word document, and then use the buttons on the Ribbon.

### To use buttons on the Ribbon:

1. Type **Meeting Agenda** and then press the **Enter** key. The text appears in the first line of the document and the insertion point moves to the second line.

   **Trouble?** If you make a typing error, press the Backspace key to delete the incorrect letters, and then retype the text.

2. In the Paragraph group on the Home tab, click the **Show/Hide ¶** button ¶. The nonprinting characters appear in the document, and the Show/Hide ¶ button remains toggled on. See Figure 8.

---

**Figure 8** | Button toggled on

Home tab selected

Paragraph group

nonprinting paragraph mark and space symbols

Show/Hide ¶ button toggled on

Meeting·Agenda¶

**Trouble?** If the nonprinting characters disappear from your screen, the Show/ Hide ¶ button was already on. Repeat Step 2 to show nonprinting characters.

3. Position the insertion point to the left of the word "Meeting," press and hold the left mouse button, drag the pointer across the text of the first line but not the paragraph mark to highlight the text, and then release the mouse button. All the text in the first line of the document (but not the paragraph mark ¶) is selected.

4. In the Clipboard group on the Home tab, click the **Copy** button. The selected text is copied to the Clipboard.

5. Press the ↓ key. The text is deselected (no longer highlighted), and the insertion point moves to the second line in the document.

6. In the Clipboard group on the Home tab, point to the top part of the **Paste** button. Both parts of the Paste button are outlined in yellow, but the icon at the top is highlighted to indicate that it will be selected if you click the mouse button.

7. Point to the **Paste button arrow**. The button is outlined and the button arrow is highlighted.

8. Click the **Paste button arrow**. The paste commands and options are displayed. See Figure 9.

| Figure 9 | Two-part Paste button |
| --- | --- |

Paste button

click the button arrow to display more options and commands

Paste commands and options

9. On the Paste Options menu, click the **Keep Text Only** button. The menu closes, and the text is duplicated in the second line of the document. The Paste Options button (Ctrl) ▾ appears below the duplicated text, providing access to the same paste commands and options.

## INSIGHT

### Using Keyboard Shortcuts and Key Tips

Keyboard shortcuts can help you work faster and more efficiently. A **keyboard shortcut** is a key or combination of keys you press to access a feature or perform a command. You can use these shortcuts to access options on the Ribbon, on the Quick Access Toolbar, and in Backstage view without removing your hands from the keyboard. To access the options on the Ribbon, press the Alt key. A label, called a Key Tip, appears over each tab. To select a tab, press the corresponding key. The tab is displayed on the Ribbon and Key Tips appear over each available button or option on that tab. Press the appropriate key or keys to select a button.

You can also press combinations of keys to perform specific commands. For example, Ctrl+S is the keyboard shortcut for the Save command (you press and hold the Ctrl key while you press the S key). This type of keyboard shortcut appears in ScreenTips next to the command's name. Not all commands have this type of keyboard shortcut. Identical commands in each Office program use the same keyboard shortcut.

## Using Galleries and Live Preview

Galleries and Live Preview let you quickly see how your file will be affected by a selection. A **gallery** is a menu or grid that shows a visual representation of the options available for a button. For example, the Bullet Library gallery in Word shows an icon of each bullet style you can select. Some galleries include a More button ⧉ that you click to expand the gallery to see all the options it contains. When you point to an option in a gallery, **Live Preview** shows the results that would occur in your file if you clicked that option. To continue the bullets example, when you point to a bullet style in the Bullet Library gallery, the selected text or the paragraph in which the insertion point is located appears with that bullet style. By moving the pointer from option to option, you can quickly see the text set with different bullet styles; you can then click the style you want.

### To use the Bullet Library gallery and Live Preview:

▶ **1.** In the Paragraph group on the Home tab, click the **Bullets button arrow** . The Bullet Library gallery opens.

▶ **2.** Point to the **check mark bullet** style ✓. Live Preview shows the selected bullet style in your document. See Figure 10.

**Figure 10** Live Preview of bullet icon

click the Bullets button arrow to open a gallery of bullet styles

Bullet Library gallery

Live Preview of the bullet style highlighted in the gallery

▶ **3.** Place the pointer over each of the remaining bullet styles and preview them in your document.

▶ **4.** Click the **check mark bullet** style ✓. The Bullet Library gallery closes, and the check mark bullet is added to the line, which is indented. The Bullets button remains toggled on when the insertion point is in the line with the bullet.

▶ **5.** On the second line, next to the check mark bullet, select **Meeting Agenda**. The two words are highlighted to indicate they are selected.

▶ **6.** Type **Brainstorm names for the new paint colors.** to replace the selected text with an agenda item.

▶ **7.** Press the **Enter** key twice to end the bulleted list.

> **TIP**
>
> You can press the Esc key to close a gallery without making a selection.

## Opening Dialog Boxes and Task Panes

The button to the right of some group names is the Dialog Box Launcher 🗔, which opens a task pane or dialog box related to that group of tasks. A **task pane** is a window that helps you navigate through a complex task or feature. For example, you can use the Clipboard task pane to paste some or all of the items that were cut or copied from any Office program during the current work session. A **dialog box** is a window from which you enter or choose settings for how you want to perform a task. For example, the Page Setup dialog box in Word contains options to change how the document looks. Some dialog boxes organize related information into tabs, and related options and settings are organized into groups, just as they are on the Ribbon. You select settings in a dialog box using option buttons, check boxes, text boxes, and lists to specify how you want to perform a task. In Excel, you'll use the Dialog Box Launcher to open the Page Setup dialog box.

### To open the Page Setup dialog box using the Dialog Box Launcher:

▶ **1.** On the taskbar, click the **Microsoft Excel** program button to switch from Word to Excel.

▶ **2.** On the Ribbon, click the **Page Layout** tab. The page layout options appear on the Ribbon.

▶ **3.** In the Page Setup group, click the **Dialog Box Launcher**. The Page Setup dialog box opens with the Page tab displayed. See Figure 11.

| Figure 11 | Page tab in the Page Setup dialog box |
|---|---|

click this Dialog Box Launcher to open the Page Setup dialog box

click a tab to view a group of related options

click an option button to select that option

click in the box and type an entry

click to accept the changes and close the dialog box

click the up or down arrow to increase or decrease the number

click the arrow and then click an option in the list

click a button to open another dialog box or window

click to close the dialog box without making changes

▶ **4.** Click the **Landscape** option button. The workbook's page orientation changes to a page wider than it is long.

▶ **5.** Click the **Sheet** tab. The dialog box displays options related to the worksheet. You can click a check box to turn an option on (checked) or off (unchecked).

▶ **6.** In the Print section of the dialog box, click the **Gridlines** check box and the **Row and column headings** check box. Check marks appear in both check boxes, indicating that these options are selected.

▶ **7.** Click the **Cancel** button. The dialog box closes without making any changes to the page setup.

**TIP**

You can check more than one check box in a group, but you can select only one option button in a group.

# Using Contextual Tools

Some tabs, toolbars, and menus come into view as you work. Because these tools become available only as you might need them, the workspace remains less cluttered. However, tools that appear and disappear as you work can take some getting used to.

## Displaying Contextual Tabs

Any object that you can select in a file has a related contextual tab. An **object** is anything that appears on your screen that can be selected and manipulated, such as a table, a picture, a shape, a chart, or an equation. A **contextual tab** is a Ribbon tab that contains commands related to the selected object so you can manipulate, edit, and format that object. Contextual tabs appear to the right of the standard Ribbon tabs just below a title label. For example, Figure 12 shows the Table Tools contextual tabs that appear when you select a table in a Word document. Although contextual tabs appear only when you select an object, they function in the same way as standard tabs on the Ribbon. Contextual tabs disappear when you click elsewhere on the screen, deselecting the object. Contextual tabs can also appear as you switch views. You'll use contextual tabs in later tutorials.

**Figure 12**    **Table Tools contextual tabs**

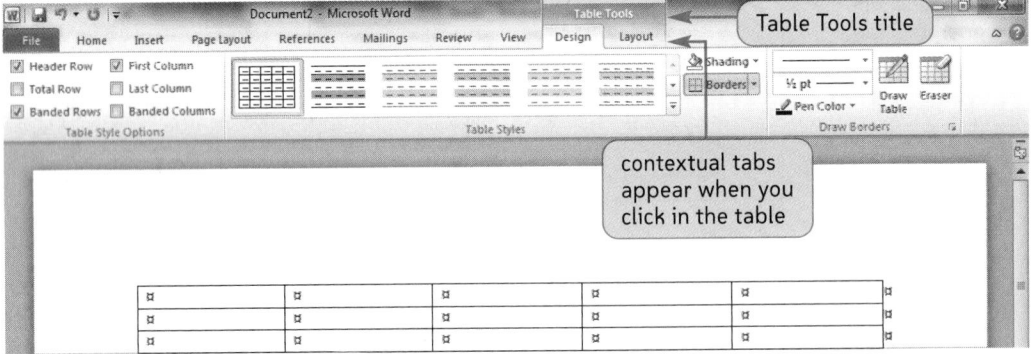

## Accessing the Mini Toolbar

The **Mini toolbar**, which appears next to the pointer whenever you select text, contains buttons for the most commonly used formatting commands, such as font, font size, styles, color, alignment, and indents. The Mini toolbar buttons differ in each program. A transparent version of the Mini toolbar appears immediately after you select text. When you move the pointer over the Mini toolbar, it comes into full view so you can click the appropriate formatting button or buttons. The Mini toolbar disappears if you move the pointer away from the toolbar, press a key, or click in the workspace. The Mini toolbar can help you format your text faster, but initially you might find that the toolbar disappears unexpectedly. All the commands on the Mini toolbar are also available on the Ribbon. Note that Live Preview does not work with the Mini toolbar.

You'll use the Mini toolbar to format text you enter in the workbook.

**To use the Mini toolbar to format text:**

1. If necessary, click cell **A1** (the rectangle in the upper-left corner of the worksheet).

2. Type **Budget**. The text appears in the cell.

3. Press the **Enter** key. The text is entered in cell A1 and cell A2 is selected.

4. Type **2013** and then press the **Enter** key. The year is entered in cell A2 and cell A3 is selected.

5. Double-click cell **A1** to place the insertion point in the cell. Now you can select the text you typed.

6. Double-click **Budget** in cell A1. The selected text appears white with a black background, and the transparent Mini toolbar appears directly above the selected text. See Figure 13.

| Figure 13 | Transparent Mini toolbar |

Mini toolbar is transparent at first

select text to display the transparent Mini toolbar

Keep the pointer directly over the Mini toolbar; otherwise, it will disappear.

7. Move the pointer over the Mini toolbar. The Mini toolbar is now completely visible, and you can click buttons.

   **Trouble?** If the Mini toolbar disappears, you probably moved the pointer to another area of the worksheet. To redisplay the Mini toolbar, repeat Steps 6 and 7, being careful to move the pointer directly over the Mini toolbar in Step 7.

8. On the Mini toolbar, click the **Bold** button **B**. The text in cell A1 is bold. The Mini toolbar remains visible so you can continue formatting the selected text. See Figure 14.

| Figure 14 | Mini toolbar with the Bold button selected |

Mini toolbar remains open for additional formatting

Bold button toggled on

bold text in cell A1

9. Press the **Enter** key. The Mini toolbar disappears, and cell A2 is selected.

## Opening Shortcut Menus

A **shortcut menu** is a list of commands related to a selection that opens when you click the right mouse button. Shortcut menus enable you to quickly access commands that you're most likely to need in the context of the task you're performing without using the tabs on the Ribbon. The shortcut menu includes commands that perform actions, commands that open dialog boxes, and galleries of options that provide Live Preview. The Mini toolbar also opens when you right-click. If you click a button on the Mini toolbar, the rest of the shortcut menu closes while the Mini toolbar remains open so you can continue formatting the selection. For example, you can right-click selected text to open a shortcut menu with a Mini toolbar; the menu will contain text-related commands such as Cut, Copy, and Paste, as well as other program-specific commands.

You'll use a shortcut menu to delete the content you entered in cell A1.

### To use a shortcut menu to delete content:

▶ **1.** Right-click cell **A1**. A shortcut menu opens, listing commands related to common tasks you'd perform in a cell, along with the Mini toolbar. See Figure 15.

**Figure 15**    **Shortcut menu with Mini toolbar**

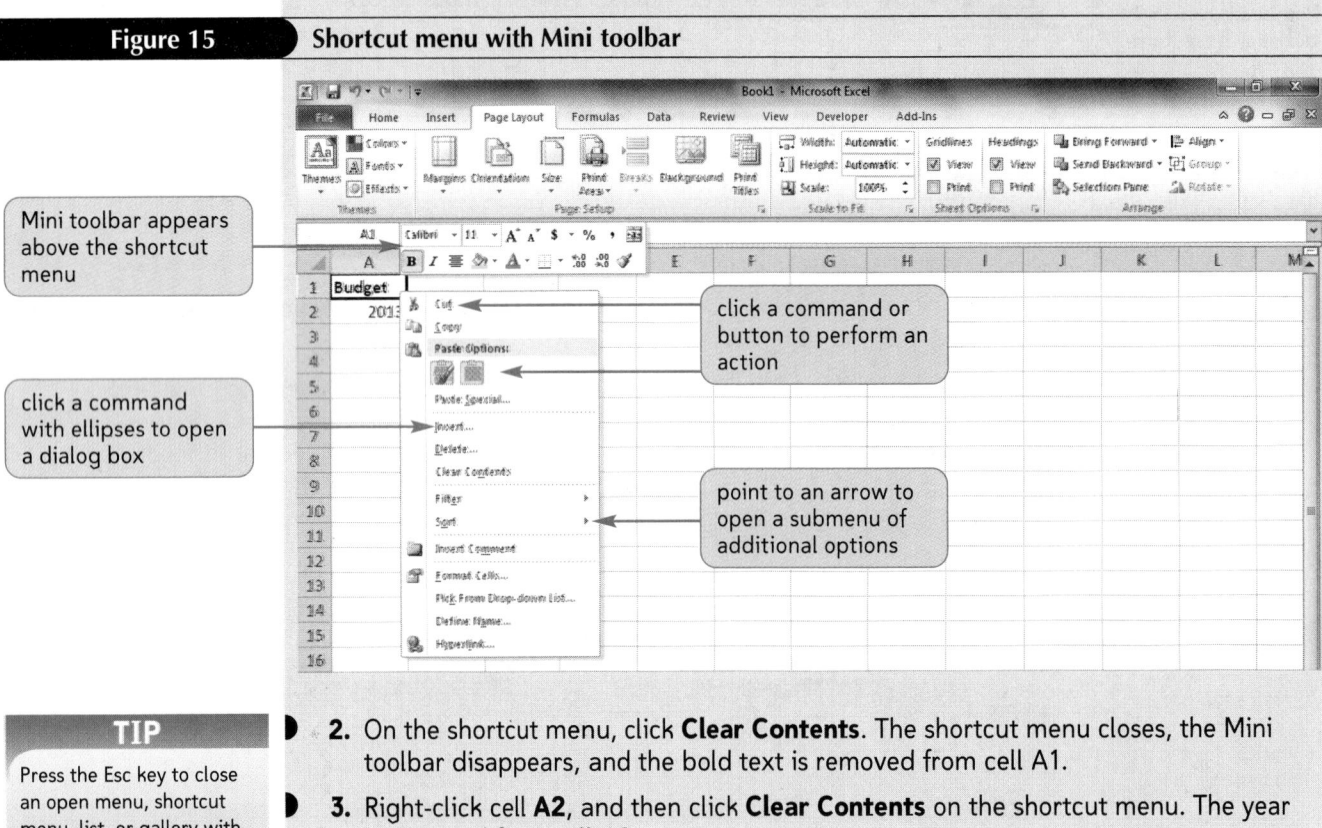

Mini toolbar appears above the shortcut menu

click a command or button to perform an action

click a command with ellipses to open a dialog box

point to an arrow to open a submenu of additional options

▶ **2.** On the shortcut menu, click **Clear Contents**. The shortcut menu closes, the Mini toolbar disappears, and the bold text is removed from cell A1.

▶ **3.** Right-click cell **A2**, and then click **Clear Contents** on the shortcut menu. The year is removed from cell A2.

## Working with Files

The most common tasks you perform in any Office program are to create, open, save, and close files. All of these tasks can be done from Backstage view, and the processes for these tasks are basically the same in all Office programs. To begin working in a program, you need to create a new file or open an existing file. When you start Word, Excel, or PowerPoint, the program opens along with a blank file—ready for you to begin working on a new document, workbook, or presentation. When you start Access, the New tab in Backstage view opens, displaying options for creating a new database or opening an existing one.

## Saving a File

As you create and modify an Office file, your work is stored only in the computer's temporary memory, not on a hard drive. If you were to exit the program without saving, turn off your computer, or experience a power failure, your work would be lost. To prevent losing work, save your file frequently—at least every 10 minutes. You can save files to the hard drive located inside your computer, an external hard drive, a network storage drive, or a portable storage drive such as a USB flash drive.

To save a file, you can click either the Save button on the Quick Access Toolbar or the Save command in Backstage view. If it is the first time you are saving a file, the Save As dialog box will open so that you can specify save options. You can also click the Save As command in Backstage view to open the Save As dialog box, in which you can name the file you are saving and specify a location to save it.

The first time you save a file, you need to name it. This **filename** includes a title you specify and a file extension assigned by Office to indicate the file type. You should specify a descriptive title that accurately reflects the content of the document, workbook, presentation, or database, such as "Shipping Options Letter" or "Fourth Quarter Financial Analysis." Your descriptive title can include uppercase and lowercase letters, numbers, hyphens, and spaces in any combination, but not the special characters ? " / \ < > * | and :. Each filename ends with a **file extension**, which is a period followed by several characters that Office adds to your descriptive title to identify the program in which that file was created. The default file extensions for Office 2010 are .docx for Word, .xlsx for Excel, .pptx for PowerPoint, and .accdb for Access. Filenames (the descriptive title and extension) can include a maximum of 255 characters. You might see file extensions depending on how Windows is set up on your computer. The figures in these tutorials do not show file extensions.

You also need to decide where to save the file—on which drive and in what folder. A **folder** is a container for your files. Just as you organize paper documents within folders stored in a filing cabinet, you can organize your files within folders stored on your computer's hard drive or on a removable drive such as a USB flash drive. Store each file in a logical location that you will remember whenever you want to use the file again. The default storage location for Office files is the Documents folder; you can create additional storage folders within that folder or navigate to a new location.

**TIP**

Office 2003 and earlier files use the extensions .doc (Word), .xls (Excel), .mdb (Access), and .ppt (PowerPoint). To save in an earlier format, click the Save as type button in the Save As dialog box and click the 97-2003 format. When you open an earlier version file in Office 2010, you can save it in the same format or the Office 2010 format.

---

**REFERENCE**

*Saving a File*

**To save a file the first time or with a new name or location:**
- Click the File tab to open Backstage view, and then click the Save As command in the navigation bar (for an unnamed file, click the Save command or click the Save button on the Quick Access Toolbar).
- In the Save As dialog box, navigate to the location where you want to save the file.
- Type a descriptive title in the File name box, and then click the Save button.

**To resave a named file to the same location with the same name:**
- On the Quick Access Toolbar, click the Save button.

---

The text you typed in the Word window needs to be saved.

**To save a file for the first time:**

1. On the taskbar, click the **Microsoft Word** program button [W]. Word becomes the active program.

2. On the Ribbon, click the **File** tab. Backstage view opens with commands and tabs for creating new files, opening existing files, and saving, printing, and closing files. See Figure 16.

| Figure 16 | Backstage view |
| --- | --- |

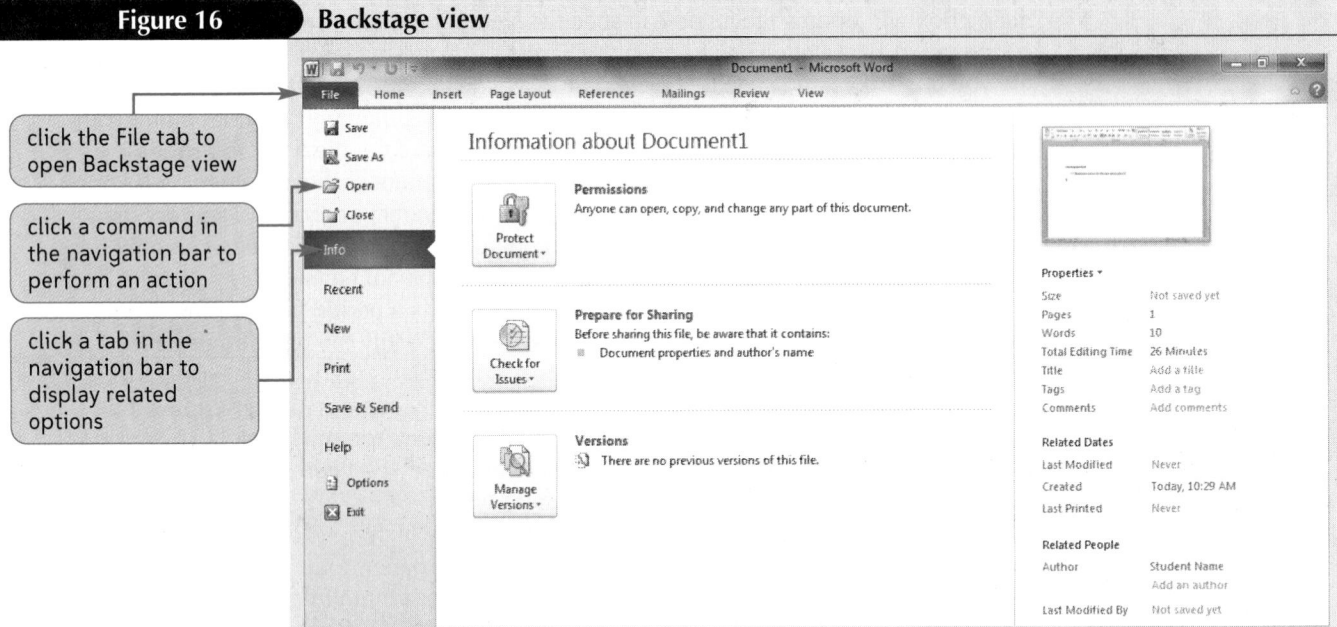

click the File tab to open Backstage view

click a command in the navigation bar to perform an action

click a tab in the navigation bar to display related options

3. In the navigation bar, click the **Save As** command. The Save As dialog box opens because you have not yet saved the file and need to specify a storage location and filename. The default location is set to the Documents folder, and the first few words of the first line appear in the File name box as a suggested title.

4. In the Navigation pane along the left side of the dialog box, click the link for the location that contains your Data Files, if necessary.

   **Trouble?** If you don't have the starting Data Files, you need to get them before you can proceed. Your instructor will either give you the Data Files or ask you to obtain them from a specified location (such as a network drive). In either case, make a backup copy of the Data Files before you start so that you will have the original files available in case you need to start over. If you have any questions about the Data Files, see your instructor or technical support person for assistance.

5. In the file list, double-click the **Office** folder, and then double-click the **Tutorial** folder. This is the location where you want to save the document.

6. Type **Agenda** in the File name box. This descriptive filename will help you more easily identify the file. See Figure 17 (your file path may differ).

**Figure 17**    Completed Save As dialog box

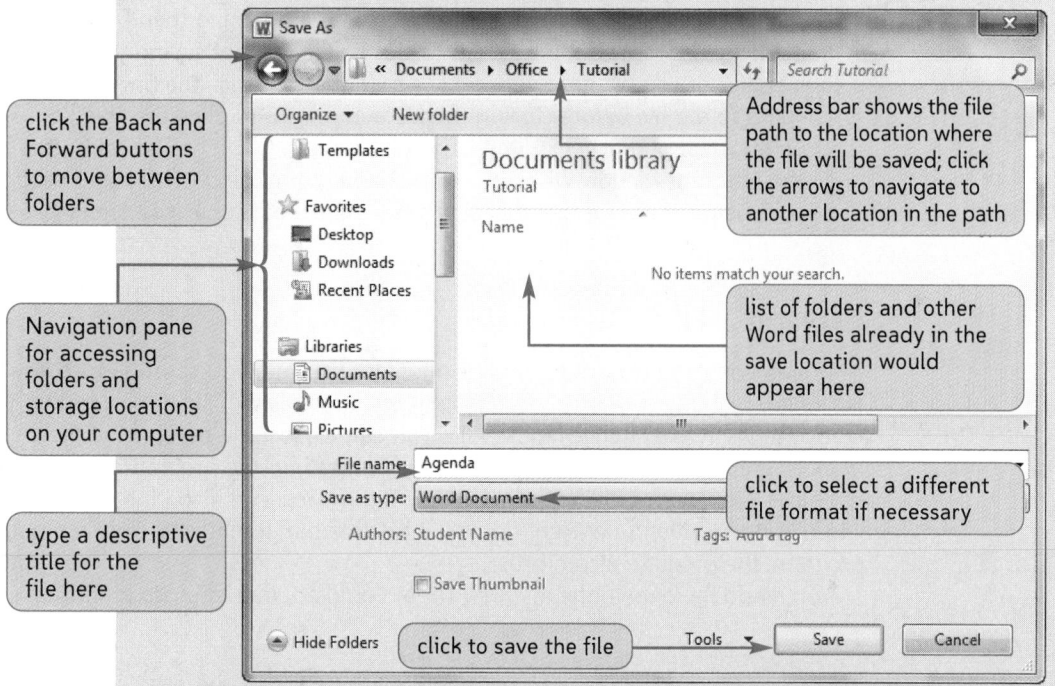

click the Back and Forward buttons to move between folders

Navigation pane for accessing folders and storage locations on your computer

type a descriptive title for the file here

Address bar shows the file path to the location where the file will be saved; click the arrows to navigate to another location in the path

list of folders and other Word files already in the save location would appear here

click to select a different file format if necessary

click to save the file

**Trouble?** If the .docx extension appears after the filename, your computer is configured to show file extensions. Continue with Step 7.

▶ **7.** Click the **Save** button. The Save As dialog box closes, and the name of your file appears in the Word window title bar.

The saved file includes everything in the document at the time you last saved it. Any new edits or additions you make to the document exist only in the computer's memory and are not saved in the file on the drive. As you work, remember to save frequently so that the file is updated to reflect the latest content.

Because you already named the document and selected a storage location, you don't need to use the Save As dialog box unless you want to save a copy of the file with a different filename or to a different location. If you do, the previous version of the file remains on your drive as well.

You need to add your name to the agenda. Then, you'll save your changes.

### To modify and save the Agenda document:

▶ **1.** Type your name, and then press the **Enter** key. The text you typed appears on the next line.

▶ **2.** On the Quick Access Toolbar, click the **Save** button 🔲. The changes you made to the document are saved in the file stored on the drive.

INSIGHT

*Saving Files Before Closing*

As a standard practice, you should save files before closing them. However, Office has an added safeguard: if you attempt to close a file without saving your changes, a dialog box opens, asking whether you want to save the file. Click the Save button to save the changes to the file before closing the file and program. Click the Don't Save button to close the file and program without saving changes. Click the Cancel button to return to the program window without saving changes or closing the file and program. This feature helps to ensure that you always save the most current version of any file.

## Closing a File

Although you can keep multiple files open at one time, you should close any file you are no longer working on to conserve system resources as well as to ensure that you don't inadvertently make changes to the file. You can close a file by clicking the Close command in Backstage view. If that's the only file open for the program, the program window remains open and no file appears in the window. You can also close a file by clicking the Close button in the upper-right corner of the title bar. If that's the only file open for the program, the program also closes.

You'll add the date to the agenda. Then, you'll attempt to close it without saving.

**To modify and close the Agenda document:**

1. Type today's date, and then press the **Enter** key. The text you typed appears below your name in the document.

2. On the Ribbon, click the **File** tab to open Backstage view, and then click the **Close** command in the navigation bar. A dialog box opens, asking whether you want to save the changes you made to the document.

3. Click the **Save** button. The current version of the document is saved to the file, and then the document closes. Word is still open, so you can create additional new files in the open program or you can open previously created and saved files.

## Opening a File

When you want to open a blank document, workbook, presentation, or database, you create a new file. When you want to work on a previously created file, you must first open it. Opening a file transfers a copy of the file from the storage location (either a hard drive or a portable drive) to the computer's memory and displays it on your screen. The file is then in your computer's memory and on the drive.

## REFERENCE

### Opening an Existing File

- Click the File tab to open Backstage view, and then click the Open command in the navigation bar.
- In the Open dialog box, navigate to the storage location of the file you want to open.
- Click the filename of the file you want to open.
- Click the Open button.
- If necessary, click the Enable Editing button in the Information Bar.

*or*

- Click the File tab, and then click the Recent tab in the navigation bar.
- Click a filename in the Recent list.

Any file you open that was downloaded from the Internet, accessed from a shared network, or received as an email attachment might open in a read-only format, called **Protected View**. In Protected View, you can see the file contents, but you cannot edit, save, or print them until you enable editing. To do so, click the Enable Editing button on the Information Bar, as shown in Figure 18.

**Figure 18**  **Protected View warning**

You need to print the meeting agenda you typed for Ean. To do that, you'll reopen the Agenda document.

### To open the Agenda document:

1. On the Ribbon, click the **File** tab to display Backstage view.

2. In the navigation bar, click the **Open** command. The Open dialog box, which works similarly to the Save As dialog box, opens.

3. In the Open dialog box, use the Navigation pane or the Address bar to navigate to the **Office\Tutorial** folder included with your Data Files. This is the location where you saved the Agenda document.

4. In the file list, click **Agenda**. See Figure 19.

**Figure 19** Open dialog box

file to open and print

folders and other Word files stored in this folder appear here

click to open the selected file

5. Click the **Open** button. The Agenda file opens in the Word program window.

# Sharing Files Using Windows Live SkyDrive

Often the purpose of creating a file is to share it with other people—sending it attached to an email message for someone else to read or use, collaborating with others on the same document, or posting it as a blog for others to review. You can do all of these things in Backstage view from the Save & Send tab.

When you send a file using email, you can attach a copy of the file, send a link to the file, or attach a copy of the file in a PDF or another file format. You can also save to online workspaces where you can make the file available to others for review and collaboration. The Save to Web option on the Save & Send tab in Backstage view gives you access to **Windows Live SkyDrive**, which is an online workspace provided by Microsoft; your personal workspace comes with a Public folder for saving files to share as well as a My Documents folder for saving files you want to keep private. (SkyDrive is not available for Access.) Figure 20 shows the Save to Web options on the Save & Send tab in Backstage view of Word. SharePoint is an online workspace set up by an organization, such as a school, business, or nonprofit group.

Files saved to an online workspace can be worked on by more than one person at the same time. The changes are recorded in the files with each author's name and the date of the change. A Web browser is used to access and edit the files. You choose who can have access to the files.

**TIP**

To use SkyDrive, you need a Windows Live ID, which you can sign up for at no cost. After you sign in, you can create new folders and save files into the folders.

**Figure 20**    Save to Web options on the Save & Send tab

**Saving a File to SkyDrive**

- Click the File tab to open Backstage view, and then click the Save & Send tab in the navigation bar.
- In the center pane, click Save to Web.
- In the right pane, click the Sign In button, and then use your Windows Live ID to log on to your Windows Live SkyDrive account.

# Getting Help

If you don't know how to perform a task or want more information about a feature, you can turn to Office itself for information on how to use it. This information is referred to simply as **Help**. You can get Help in ScreenTips and from the Help window.

## Viewing ScreenTips

ScreenTips are a fast and simple method you can use to get information about objects you see on the screen. A **ScreenTip** is a box with descriptive text about an object or button. Just point to a button or object to display its ScreenTip. In addition to the button's name, a ScreenTip might include the button's keyboard shortcut if it has one, a description of the command's function, and, in some cases, a link to more information so that you can press the F1 key while the ScreenTip is displayed to open the Help window with the relevant topic displayed.

**To view ScreenTips:**

1. Point to the **Microsoft Office Word Help** button �’. The ScreenTip shows the button's name, its keyboard shortcut, and a brief description. See Figure 21.

**Figure 21**      **ScreenTip for the Help button**

▶ **2.** Point to other buttons on the Ribbon to display their ScreenTips.

## Using the Help Window

For more detailed information, you can use the **Help window** to access all the Help topics, templates, and training installed on your computer with Office and available on Office.com. **Office.com** is a Web site maintained by Microsoft that provides access to the latest information and additional Help resources. For example, you can access current Help topics and training for Office. To connect to Office.com, you need to be able to access the Internet from your computer. Otherwise, you see only topics that are stored on your computer.

Each program has its own Help window from which you can find information about all of the Office commands and features as well as step-by-step instructions for using them. There are two ways to find Help topics—the search function and a topic list.

The Type words to search for box enables you to search the Help system for a task or a topic you need help with. You can click a link to open a Help topic with explanations and step-by-step instructions for a specific procedure. The Table of Contents pane displays the Help system content organized by subjects and topics, similar to a book's table of contents. You click main subject links to display related topic links. You click a topic link to display that Help topic in the Help window.

**REFERENCE**

*Getting Help*

- Click the Microsoft Office Help button (the button name depends on the Office program).
- Type a keyword or phrase in the Type words to search for box, click the Search button, and then click a Help topic in the search results list.
  *or*
  In the Table of Contents pane, click a "book," and then click a Help topic.
- Read the information in the Help window and then click other topics or links.
- On the Help window title bar, click the Close button.

You'll use Help to get information about printing a document in Word.

## To search Help for information about printing:

▶ **1.** Click the **Microsoft Office Word Help** button ⬛. The Word Help window opens.

▶ **2.** If the Table of Contents pane is not open on the left side of the Help window, click the **Show Table of Contents** button ☑ on the toolbar to display the pane.

▶ **3.** Click the **Type words to search for** box, if necessary, and then type **print document**. You can specify where you want to search.

▶ **4.** Click the **Search button arrow**. The Search menu shows the online and local content available.

▶ **5.** If your computer is connected to the Internet, click **All Word** in the Content from Office.com list. If your computer is not connected to the Internet, click **Word Help** in the Content from this computer list.

▶ **6.** Click the **Search** button. The Help window displays a list of topics related to the keywords "print document" in the left pane. See Figure 22.

| Figure 22 | Search results displaying Help topics |
|---|---|

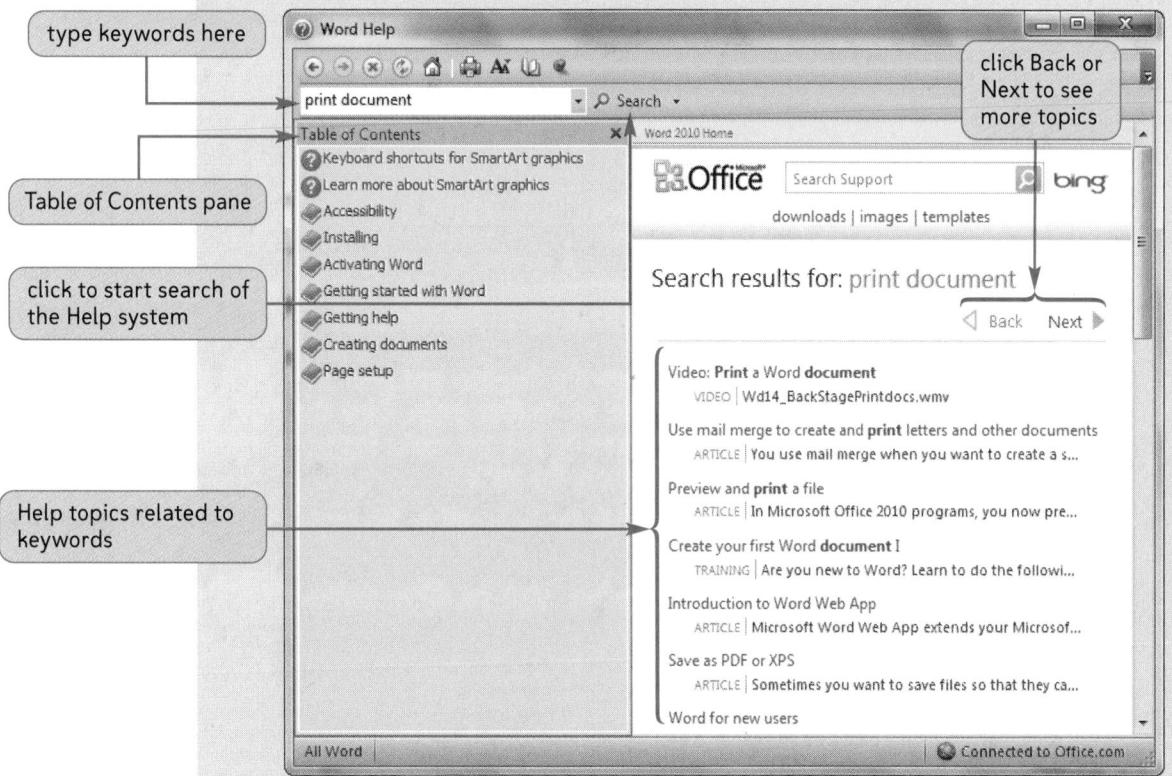

*type keywords here*

*Table of Contents pane*

*click to start search of the Help system*

*Help topics related to keywords*

*click Back or Next to see more topics*

**Trouble?** If your search results list differs from the one shown in Figure 22, your computer is not connected to the Internet or Microsoft has updated the list of available Help topics since this book was published. Continue with Step 7.

▶ **7.** Scroll through the list to review the Help topics.

▶ **8.** Click **Preview and print a file**. The topic content is displayed in the Help window so you can learn more about how to print a document. See Figure 23.

**Figure 23** Preview and print a file Help topic

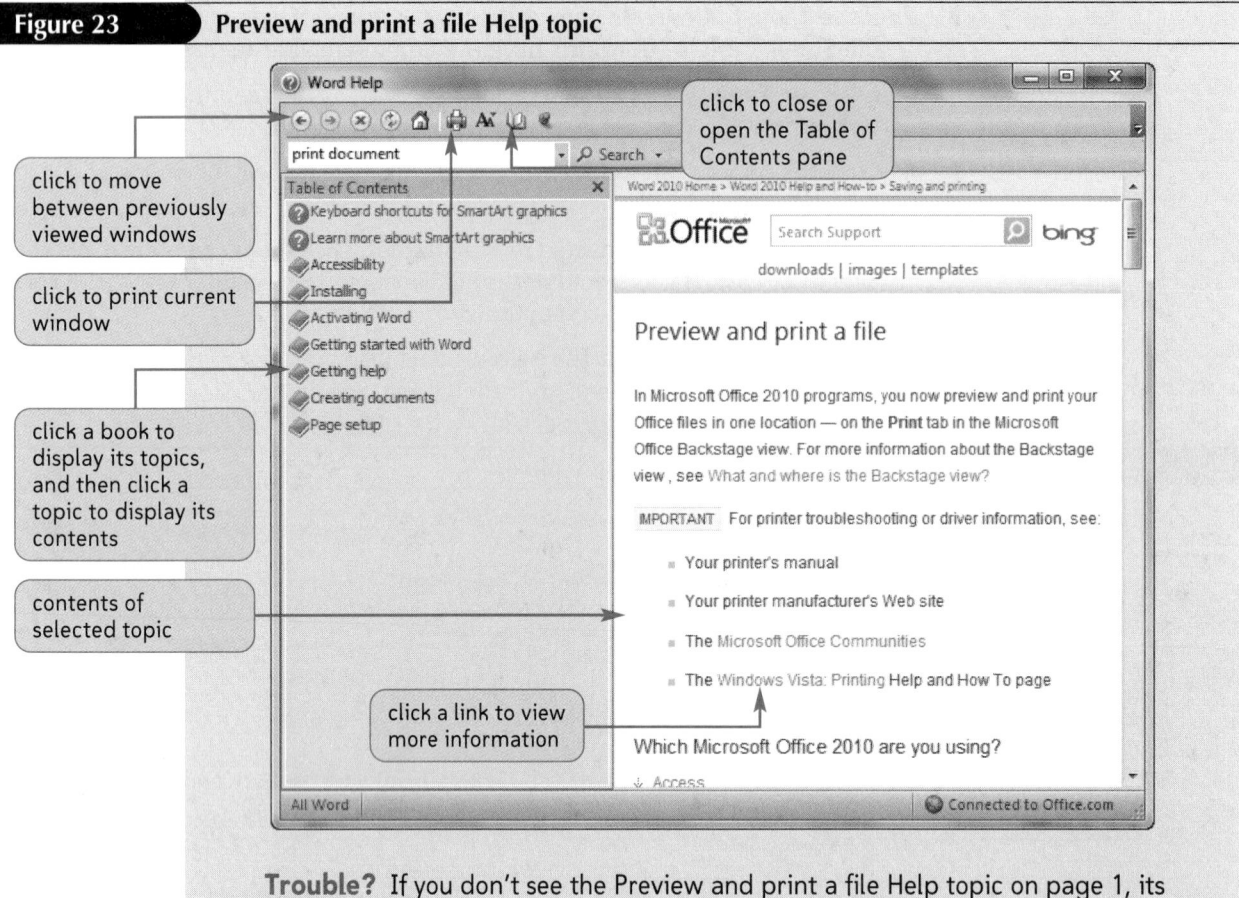

Callout labels in figure:
- click to move between previously viewed windows
- click to print current window
- click a book to display its topics, and then click a topic to display its contents
- contents of selected topic
- click to close or open the Table of Contents pane
- click a link to view more information

**Trouble?** If you don't see the Preview and print a file Help topic on page 1, its current location might be on another page. Click the Next link to move to the next page, and then scroll down to find the topic. Repeat as needed to search additional pages until you locate the topic.

9. Read the information, click the links within this topic, and then read the additional information.

10. On the Help window title bar, click the **Close** button ⊠ to close the window.

# Printing a File

At times, you'll want a paper copy of Office files. Whenever you print, you should review and adjust the printing settings as needed. You can select the number of copies to print, the printer, the portion of the file to print, and so forth; the printing settings vary slightly from program to program. You should also check the file's print preview to ensure that the file will print as you intended. This simple review will help you to avoid reprinting, which requires additional paper, ink, and energy resources.

*Printing a File*

- On the Ribbon, click the File tab to open Backstage view.
- In the navigation bar, click the Print tab.
- Verify the print settings and review the print preview.
- Click the Print button.

You will print the agenda for Ean.

## To print the Agenda document:

1. Make sure your printer is turned on and contains paper.

2. On the Ribbon, click the **File** tab to open Backstage view.

3. In the navigation bar, click the **Print** tab. The print settings and preview appear. See Figure 24.

| Figure 24 | Print tab in Backstage view |

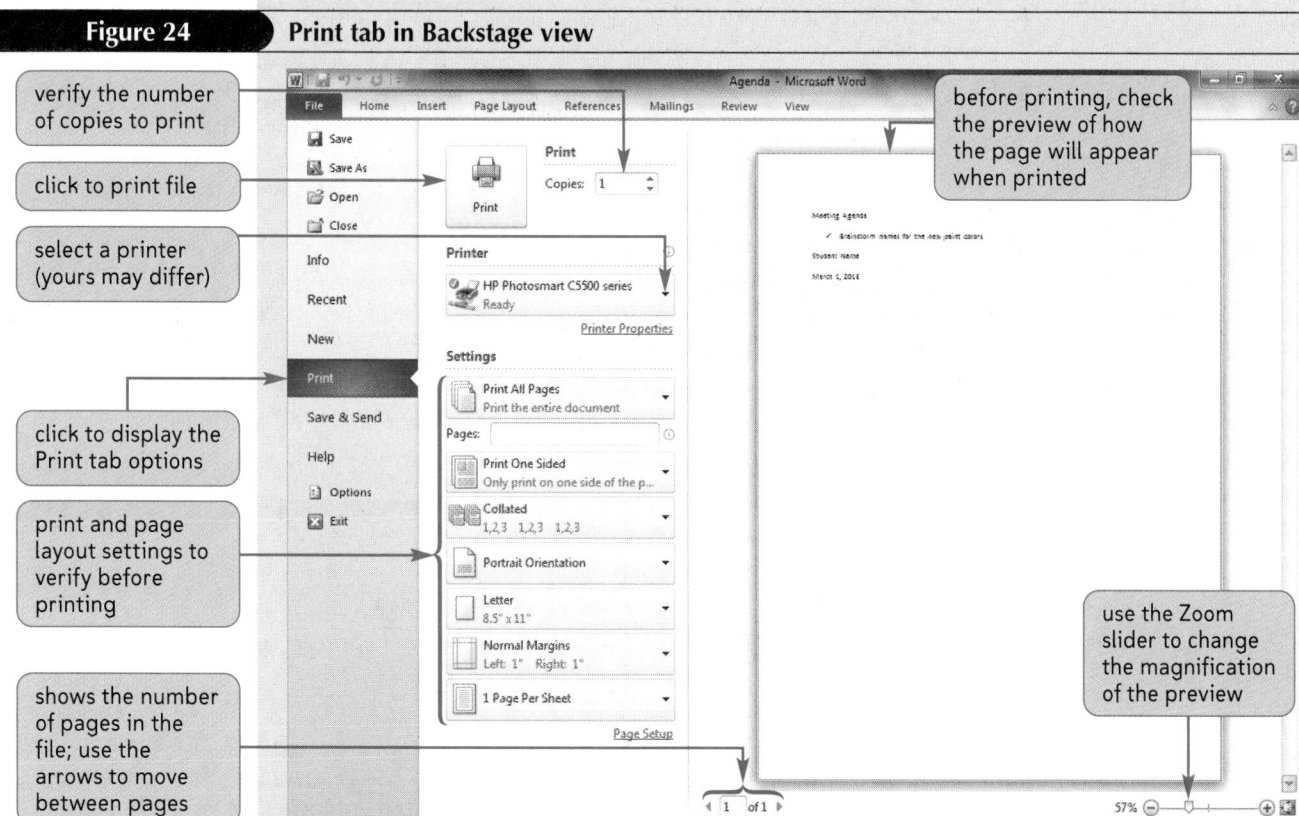

verify the number of copies to print

click to print file

select a printer (yours may differ)

click to display the Print tab options

print and page layout settings to verify before printing

shows the number of pages in the file; use the arrows to move between pages

before printing, check the preview of how the page will appear when printed

use the Zoom slider to change the magnification of the preview

4. Verify that **1** appears in the Copies box.

5. Verify that the correct printer appears on the Printer button. If it doesn't, click the **Printer** button, and then click the correct printer from the list of available printers.

6. Click the **Print** button to print the document.

**Trouble?** If the document does not print, see your instructor or technical support person for help.

# Exiting Programs

When you finish working with a program, you should exit it. As with many other aspects of Office, you can exit programs with a button or a command. You'll use both methods to exit Word and Excel. You can use the Exit command to exit a program and close an open file in one step. If you haven't saved the final version of the open file, a dialog box opens, asking whether you want to save your changes. Clicking the Save button in this dialog box saves the open file, closes the file, and then exits the program.

**To exit the Word and Excel programs:**

▶ **1.** On the Word title bar, click the **Close** button [ X ]. Both the Word document and the Word program close. The Excel window is visible again.

**Trouble?** If a dialog box opens asking if you want to save the document, you might have inadvertently made a change to the document. Click the Don't Save button.

▶ **2.** On the Ribbon, click the **File** tab to open Backstage view, and then click the **Exit** command in the navigation bar. A dialog box opens asking whether you want to save the changes you made to the workbook. If you click the Save button, the Save As dialog box opens and Excel exits after you finish saving the workbook. This time, you don't want to save the workbook.

▶ **3.** Click the **Don't Save** button. The workbook closes without saving a copy, and the Excel program closes.

Exiting programs after you are done using them keeps your Windows desktop uncluttered for the next person using the computer, frees up your system's resources, and prevents data from being lost accidentally.

## Quick Check

**REVIEW**

1. What Office program would be best to use to write a letter?
2. How do you start an Office program?
3. What is the purpose of Live Preview?
4. What is Backstage view?
5. Explain the difference between Save and Save As.
6. True or False. In Protected View, you can see file contents, but you cannot edit, save, or print them until you enable editing.
7. What happens if you open a file, make edits, and then attempt to close the file or exit the program without saving the current version of the file?
8. What are the two ways to get Help in Office?

*Practice the skills you learned in the tutorial.*

**PRACTICE**

## Review Assignments

**Data Files needed for the Review Assignments: Finances.xlsx, Letter.docx**

You need to prepare for an upcoming meeting at Recycled Palette. You'll open and print documents for the meeting. Complete the following:

1. Start PowerPoint, and then start Excel.
2. Switch to the PowerPoint window, and then close the presentation but leave the PowerPoint program open. (*Hint*: Use the Close command in Backstage view.)
3. Open a blank PowerPoint presentation from the New tab in Backstage view. (*Hint*: Make sure Blank presentation is selected in the Available Templates and Themes section, and then click the Create button.)
4. Close the PowerPoint presentation and program using the Close button on the PowerPoint title bar; do not save changes if asked.
5. Open the **Finances** workbook located in the Office\Review folder. If the workbook opens in Protected View, click the Enable Editing button.
6. Use the Save As command to save the workbook as **Recycled Palette Finances** in the Office\Review folder.
7. In cell A1, type your name, press the Enter key to insert your name at the top of the worksheet, and then save the workbook.
8. Preview and print one copy of the worksheet using the Print tab in Backstage view.
9. Exit Excel using the Exit command in Backstage view.
10. Start Word, and then open the **Letter** document located in the Office\Review folder. If the document opens in Protected View, click the Enable Editing button.
11. Use the Save As command to save the document with the filename **Recycled Palette Letter** in the Office\Review folder.
12. Press and hold the Ctrl key, press the End key, and then release both keys to move the insertion point to the end of the letter, and then type your name.
13. Use the Save button to save the change to the Recycled Palette Letter document.
14. Preview and print one copy of the document using the Print tab in Backstage view.
15. Close the document, and then exit the Word program.
16. Submit the finished files to your instructor.

**ASSESS**

## SAM: Skills Assessment Manager

For current SAM information, including versions and content details, visit SAM Central (http://samcentral.course.com). If you have a SAM user profile, you may have access to hands-on instruction, practice, and assessment of the skills covered in this tutorial. Since various versions of SAM are supported throughout the life of this text, check with your instructor for the correct instructions and URL/Web site for accessing assignments.

**ENDING DATA FILES**

Agenda.docx          Recycled Palette Finances.xlsx
                     Recycled Palette Letter.docx

# Teamwork

## Working on a Team

Teams consist of individuals who have skills, talents, and abilities that complement each other and, when joined, produce synergy—results greater than those a single individual could achieve. It is this sense of shared mission and responsibility for results that makes a team successful in its efforts to reach its goals. Teams are everywhere. In the workplace, a team might develop a presentation to introduce products. In the classroom, a team might complete a research project.

Teams meet face to face or virtually. A virtual team rarely, if ever, meets in person. Instead, technology makes it possible for members to work as if everyone was in the same room. Some common technologies used in virtual teamwork are corporate networks, email, teleconferencing, and collaboration and integration tools, such as those found in Office 2010.

Even for teams in the same location, technology is a valuable tool. For example, teams commonly collaborate on a copy of a file posted to an online shared storage space, such as SkyDrive. In addition, team members can compile data in the program that best suits the information related to their part of the project. Later, that information can be integrated into a finished report, presentation, email message, and so on.

**PROSKILLS**

### Collaborate with Others

At home, school, or work, you probably collaborate with others to complete many types of tasks—such as planning an event, creating a report, or developing a presentation. You can use Microsoft Office to streamline many of these tasks. Consider a project that you might need to work on with a team. Complete the following steps:

1. Start Word, and open a new document, if necessary.
2. In the document, type a list of all the tasks the team needs to accomplish. If you are working with a team, identify which team member would complete each task.
3. For each task, identify the type of Office file you would create to complete that task. For example, you would create a Word document to write a letter.
4. For each file, identify the Office program you would use to create that file, and explain why you would use that program.
5. Save the document with an appropriate filename in an appropriate folder location.
6. Use a Web browser to visit the Microsoft site at *www.microsoft.com* and research the different Office 2010 suites available. Determine which suite includes all the programs needed for the team to complete the tasks on the list.
7. In the document, type which Office suite you selected and a brief explanation of why.
8. Determine how the team can integrate the different programs in the Office suite you selected to create the files that complete the team's goal or task. Include this information at the end of the Word document. Save the document.
9. Develop an efficient way to organize the files that the team will create to complete the goal or task. Add this information at the end of the Word document.
10. If possible, sign in to SkyDrive, and then save a copy of the file in an appropriate subfolder within your Public folder. If you are working with a team, have your teammates access your file, review your notes, and add a paragraph with their comments and name.
11. Preview and print the finished document, and then submit it to your instructor.

## OBJECTIVES

**Session 1.1**
- Understand the use of spreadsheets and Excel
- Learn the parts of the Excel window
- Scroll through a worksheet and navigate between worksheets
- Create and save a workbook file
- Enter text, numbers, and dates into a worksheet
- Resize, insert, and remove columns and rows

**Session 1.2**
- Select and move cell ranges
- Insert formulas and functions
- Insert, delete, move, and rename worksheets
- Work with editing tools
- Preview and print a workbook

# Getting Started with Excel

*Creating an Order Report*

## Case | RipCity Digital

When Amanda Dunn purchased a DVD burner a few years ago, one of her first tasks was to convert her home videos into DVDs. After she saw how simple it was, she upgraded her hardware and software, and proceeded to create DVDs from home movies and slides for her parents and friends. Based on her success, Amanda decided to make a business out of her hobby and founded RipCity Digital, an online service specializing in creating DVDs from the home movies, photos, and slides sent to her from customers. Amanda wants to list the weekly orders from her customers, tracking the names and addresses of her clients, the number of DVDs that she creates, and finally the cost of creating and shipping the DVDs.

Amanda is so busy creating DVDs that she asks you to record her orders. You'll do this in **Microsoft Excel 2010** (or **Excel**), a computer program used to enter, analyze, and present quantitative data. You'll also enter the latest orders she received for her new business.

## STARTING DATA FILES

| Excel1 | → | Tutorial | Review | Case1 | Case2 | Case3 | Case4 |
| --- | --- | --- | --- | --- | --- | --- | --- |
| | | (none) | (none) | Altac.xlsx | Halley.xlsx | Global.xlsx | (none) |

# SESSION 1.1 VISUAL OVERVIEW

Excel stores spreadsheets in files called **workbooks**. The contents of a workbook are shown in a workbook window.

The **Name box** displays the cell reference of the active cell.

The **Select All button** is used to select all of the cells in the active worksheet.

The **formula bar** displays the value or formula entered in the active cell.

The **row headings** are the numbers along the left side of the worksheet window that identify the different rows in the worksheet. You click a row heading to select the entire worksheet row.

A workbook is made up of individual **sheets**. Each sheet is identified by a sheet name, which appears in the **sheet tab**.

The **sheet tab scrolling buttons** scroll the list of sheet tabs in the worksheet.

The sheet currently displayed in the workbook window is the **active sheet**; its sheet tab is white.

The other sheets in the workbook are not visible. The sheet tabs for these inactive sheets are gray.

# THE EXCEL WINDOW

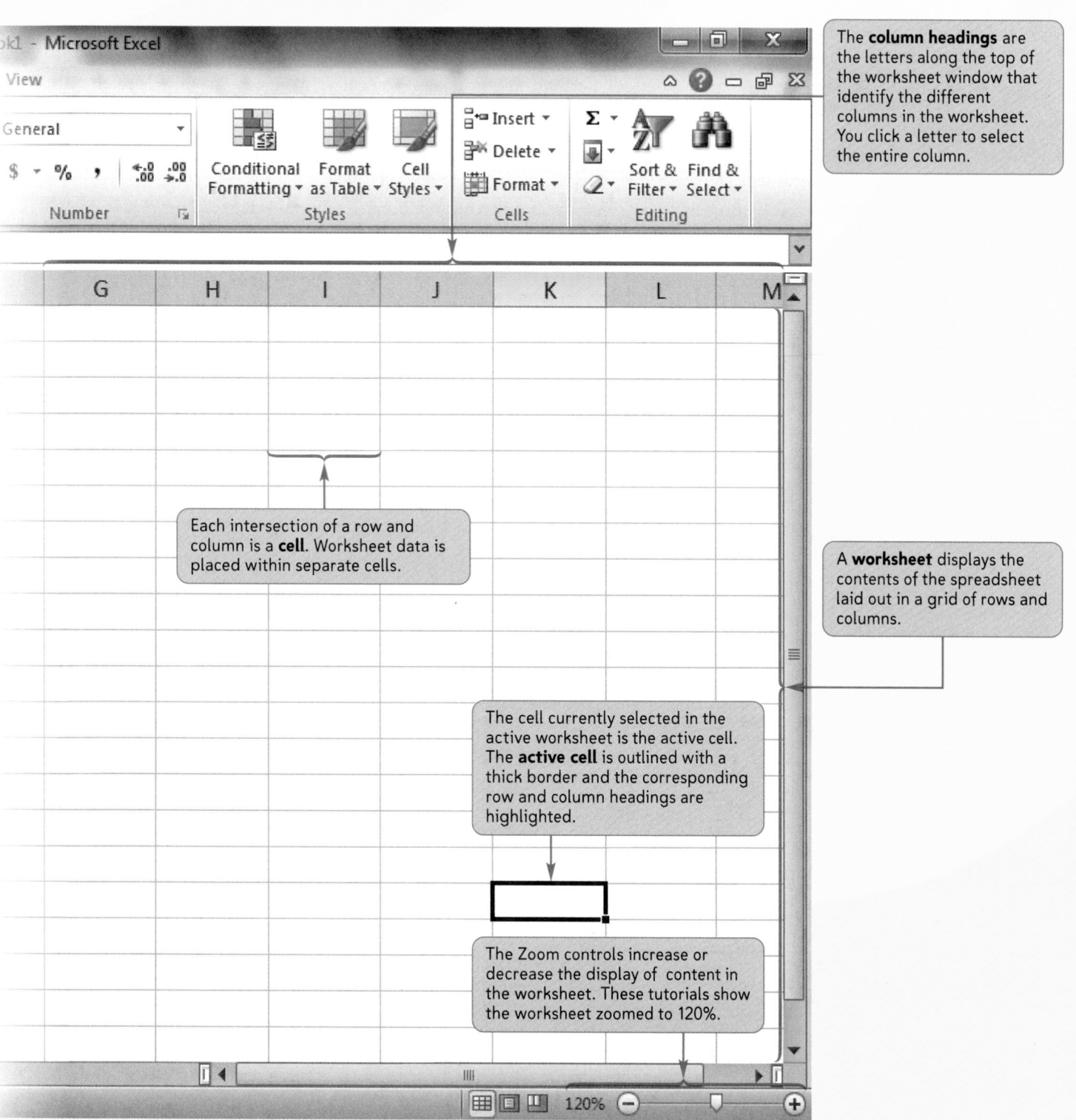

The **column headings** are the letters along the top of the worksheet window that identify the different columns in the worksheet. You click a letter to select the entire column.

Each intersection of a row and column is a **cell**. Worksheet data is placed within separate cells.

A **worksheet** displays the contents of the spreadsheet laid out in a grid of rows and columns.

The cell currently selected in the active worksheet is the active cell. The **active cell** is outlined with a thick border and the corresponding row and column headings are highlighted.

The Zoom controls increase or decrease the display of content in the worksheet. These tutorials show the worksheet zoomed to 120%.

# Introducing Excel

Before you begin working in Excel, you will review some of the features, key terms, and concepts associated with spreadsheets.

## Understanding Spreadsheets

A **spreadsheet** is a collection of text and numbers laid out in a rectangular grid. Spreadsheets are often used in business for budgeting, inventory management, and decision making. They can also be used to manage personal budgets and track household assets. Excel is a computer program used to create electronic versions of spreadsheets. For example, the spreadsheet in Figure 1-1 shows a cash flow report. The spreadsheet records the estimated and actual cash flow for the month of January. Each line, or row, displays a different value, such as the starting cash balance or cash sales for the month. Each column displays the budgeted or actual numbers, or text that describes those values. The total cash expenditures, net cash flow, and closing cash balance for the month are not entered directly, but calculated from other numbers in the spreadsheet. For example, the total cash expenditure is equal to the expenditures on advertising, wages, and supplies. This allows you to use Excel to perform a **what-if analysis** in which you change one or more values in a spreadsheet and then assess the effect those changes have on the calculated values. You can also use Excel to store data, generate reports, and analyze data values using a variety of statistical tools.

**Figure 1-1**    **Spreadsheet data in Excel**

## Exploring the Excel Window

Before entering Amanda's data, you'll review the different parts of the Excel window. The Excel window contains many of the elements that you find in other Office 2010 programs, including a title bar, the Ribbon, scroll bars, and a status bar. The Excel window also contains features that are unique to Excel.

**To start Excel:**

▶ **1.** Click the **Start** button 🪟 on the taskbar, click **All Programs**, click **Microsoft Office**, and then point to **Microsoft Excel 2010**.

**Trouble?** If you don't see Microsoft Excel 2010 on the Microsoft Office submenu, look for it on a different submenu or on the All Programs menu. If you still cannot find Microsoft Excel 2010, ask your instructor or technical support person for help.

▶ **2.** Click **Microsoft Excel 2010**. The Excel window opens.

All the figures showing the Excel window in these tutorials are zoomed to 120% for better readability. If you want to zoom your Excel window to match the figures, complete Step 3. If you prefer to work in the default zoom of 100% or at another zoom level, continue with Step 4; you might see more or less of the worksheet on your screen, but this does not affect your work in the tutorials.

▶ **3.** If you want your Excel window zoomed to match the figures, click the **Zoom In** button ⊕ on the status bar twice to increase the zoom level to 120%. The 120% magnification increases the screen size of each cell, but reduces the number of worksheet cells visible in the workbook window.

▶ **4.** If necessary, click the **Maximize** button 🔲 on the Excel window title bar. The Excel window fills the screen.

By default, Excel starts with a blank workbook maximized to fill the Excel window. The name of the active workbook, Book1, appears in the title bar. You can open more than one workbook window at a time to display the contents of different workbooks. You can also open multiple workbook windows for one workbook to display different views of the workbook's contents.

## Navigating Between Worksheets

A workbook can have two kinds of sheets: worksheets and chart sheets. A worksheet contains a grid of rows and columns into which the user enters data values and formulas. A **chart sheet** contains an Excel chart that provides a visual representation of worksheet data. Charts can also be embedded within worksheets, displaying both the data and charts in one sheet. By default, all new Excel workbooks are created with three worksheets named Sheet1, Sheet2, and Sheet3. The Sheet1 worksheet is the active sheet.

Multiple sheets enable you to better organize data in the workbook. For example, a sales report workbook might have a different worksheet for each sales region and another worksheet that summarizes the results from all the regions.

Some workbooks contain so many sheets that their sheet tabs cannot all be displayed at the same time in the workbook window. For these workbooks, you can scroll through the sheet tabs using the sheet tab scrolling buttons. Scrolling through the sheet tabs does not change the active sheet. To change the active sheet, you must click a sheet tab.

**To change the active sheet:**

▶ **1.** Click the **Sheet2** sheet tab. The Sheet2 worksheet, which is also blank, becomes the active worksheet. The Sheet2 tab is white, indicating this worksheet is active.

▶ **2.** Click the **Sheet3** sheet tab. The Sheet3 worksheet becomes the active worksheet.

▶ **3.** Click the **Sheet1** sheet tab to return to the first worksheet.

**TIP**

You can also move to the previous or next sheet by pressing the Ctrl+Page Up or Ctrl+Page Down keys.

## Navigating Within a Worksheet

Each cell within a worksheet is identified by a **cell reference**, which indicates its column and row location. For example, the cell reference B6 refers to the cell located where column B intersects row 6. The column letter always appears before the row number in any cell reference. Row numbers range from 1 to 1,048,576. The first 26 column letters range in alphabetical order from A to Z. After Z, the next column headings are labeled AA, AB, AC, and so forth. Excel allows a maximum of 16,385 columns in a worksheet (the last column has the heading XFD). When Excel starts, cell A1 is the active cell.

As you work, you'll need to change which cell is the active cell. You can use your mouse to click a cell to make it the active cell, or you can use the keyboard to move between cells, as described in Figure 1-2.

| Figure 1-2 | Excel navigation keys |
| --- | --- |

| Press | To move the active cell |
| --- | --- |
| ↑ ↓ ← → | Up, down, left, or right one cell |
| Home | To column A of the current row |
| Ctrl+Home | To cell A1 |
| Ctrl+End | To the last cell in the worksheet that contains data |
| Enter | Down one row or to the start of the next row of data |
| Shift+Enter | Up one row |
| Tab | One column to the right |
| Shift+Tab | One column to the left |
| Page Up, Page Down | Up or down one screen |
| Ctrl+Page Up, Ctrl+Page Down | To the previous or next sheet in the workbook |

You'll use both your mouse and your keyboard to change the active cell in the Sheet1 worksheet.

### To change the active cell:

1. Move your pointer over cell **A5**, and then click the mouse button. The active cell moves from cell A1 to cell A5, and the cell reference in the Name box changes from A1 to A5. The column heading for column A and the row heading for row 5 are both highlighted.

2. Press the → key on your keyboard. The active cell moves one cell to the right to cell B5.

3. Press the **Page Down** key. The active cell moves down one full screen.

4. Press the **Page Up** key. The active cell moves up one full screen, back to cell B5.

5. Press the **Ctrl+Home** keys. The active cell returns to the first cell in the worksheet, cell A1.

The mouse and keyboard provide quick ways to navigate the active worksheet. For larger worksheets that span several screens, you can move directly to a specific cell using the Go To dialog box or by typing a cell reference in the Name box. You'll try both of these methods.

**To use the Go To dialog box and Name box:**

**TIP**

You can also open the Go To dialog box by pressing the F5 key or the Ctrl+G keys.

1. Click the **Home** tab on the Ribbon, if necessary. The button to open the Go To dialog box is in the Editing group.

2. In the Editing group, click the **Find & Select** button, and then click **Go To** on the menu that opens. The Go To dialog box opens.

3. Type **C14** in the Reference box. See Figure 1-3.

**Figure 1-3** | Go To dialog box

cell reference for the cell that you want to make active

**Trouble?** If your screen varies slightly from those shown in the figures, your computer might be set up differently. The figures in this book were created while running Windows 7 using the default Windows 7 settings, but how your screen looks depends on a variety of things, including the version of Windows, background settings, monitor resolution, and so forth.

4. Click the **OK** button. Cell C14 is the active cell and its cell reference appears in the Name box. You'll use the Name box to make a different cell active.

5. Click in the **Name** box, type **A1**, and then press the **Enter** key. Cell A1 is once again the active cell.

To view more of the active worksheet, you can use the horizontal and vertical scroll bars, located at the bottom and right side of the workbook window, respectively, to move through the worksheet horizontally and vertically. You can scroll one row or column at a time, or you can scroll several rows and columns. Scrolling through the worksheet does not change the location of the active cell.

**To scroll through the worksheet:**

1. Click the **down arrow** on the vertical scroll bar three times. The worksheet scrolls down three rows, but the active cell remains cell A1.

2. Click the **right arrow** on the horizontal scroll bar twice. The worksheet scrolls two columns to the right. The active cell still remains cell A1, although that cell is scrolled out of view.

3. Drag the vertical scroll box up until you can see the first row in the worksheet.

4. Drag the horizontal scroll box to the left until you can see the first column in the worksheet.

# Planning a Workbook

Before you begin to enter data into a workbook, you should develop a plan. You can do this by using a **planning analysis sheet**, which includes the following questions that help you think about the workbook's purpose and how to achieve your desired results:

1. **What problems do I want to solve?** The answer defines the goal or purpose of the workbook.
2. **What data do I need?** The answer defines the type of data that you need to collect and enter into the workbook.
3. **What calculations do I need to enter?** The answer defines the formulas you need to apply to the data you've collected and entered.
4. **What form should my solution take?** The answer defines the appearance of the workbook content and how it should be presented to others.

Amanda carefully considered these questions and developed the following plan as a guide for entering data in her workbook:

1. I need to know contact information for each customer, how many DVDs I create for customers, how much I charge customers, and how much revenue RipCity Digital is generating.
2. I need each customer's name and contact information, the order date, the number of DVDs created for each customer, and the cost of creating each DVD.
3. I need to calculate the total charge for each order, the total number of DVDs for all orders, and the total revenue generated from all orders.
4. Customer orders should be placed in a table with each row containing data on a different customer. Information about each customer should be placed in separate columns. The last column should contain the total charge for each customer. The last row should contain the total number of DVDs created and the total revenue from all customer orders.

## PROSKILLS

### Written Communication: Creating Effective Workbooks

Workbooks convey information in written form. As with any writing, the final product creates an impression and provides an indicator of your interest, knowledge, and attention to detail. To create the best impression, all workbooks—especially those you intend to share with others such as coworkers and clients—should be well planned, well organized, and well written.

A well-designed workbook should clearly identify its overall goal and present information in an organized format. The data it includes should be accurate both in the entered values and calculated values. Developing an effective workbook includes the following steps:

- Determine the workbook's purpose, content, and organization before you start.
- Create a list of the sheets used in the workbook, making note of each sheet's purpose.
- Insert a documentation sheet that describes the workbook's purpose and organization. Include the name of the workbook author, the date the workbook was created, and any additional information that will help others to track the workbook to its source.
- Enter all of the data in the workbook. Add text to indicate what the values represent and, if possible, where they originated so others can view the source of your data.
- Enter formulas for calculated items rather than entering the calculated values into the workbook. For more complicated calculations, provide documentation explaining them.
- Test the workbook with a variety of values; edit the data and formulas to correct errors.
- Save the workbook and create a backup copy when the project is completed. Print the workbook's contents if you need to provide a hard-copy version to others or for your files.
- Maintain a history of your workbook as it goes through different versions, so that you and others can quickly see how the workbook has changed during revisions.

By including clearly written documentation, explanatory text, a logical organization, and accurate data and formulas, you'll create effective workbooks that others can use easily.

# Entering Text, Numbers, and Dates

Worksheet cells can contain text, numbers, or dates and times. **Text data** is any combination of letters, numbers, and symbols that form words and sentences. Text data is often referred to as a **text string** because it contains a string of text characters. **Number data** is any numerical value that can be used in a mathematical calculation. **Date** and **time data** are commonly recognized formats for date and time values. For example, Excel interprets the cell entry April 15, 2013 as a date and not as text. By default, text is left-aligned in cells, whereas numbers, dates, and times are right-aligned.

## Entering Text

New data values are placed into the cell that is currently active in the worksheet. As you enter data, the entry appears in both the active cell and the formula bar. Amanda wants you to enter some of the information from the planning analysis sheet into the first sheet of the workbook. This worksheet will document the workbook's purpose and content.

### To enter the text for the documentation sheet:

1. Press the **Ctrl+Home** keys to make cell A1 the active cell on the Sheet1 worksheet, if necessary.

2. Type **RipCity Digital Customer Orders** in cell A1. As you type, the text appears both in cell A1 and in the formula bar.

3. Press the **Enter** key twice. Excel enters the text into cell A1 and moves the active cell down two cells to cell A3.

4. Type **Author** in cell A3, and then press the **Tab** key. The text is entered and the active cell moves one cell to the right to cell B3.

5. Type your name in cell B3, and then press the **Enter** key. The text is entered and the active cell moves one cell down and to the left to cell A4.

6. Type **Date** in cell A4, and then press the **Tab** key. The text is entered and the active cell moves one cell to the right to cell B4, where you would enter the date you created the worksheet. For now, you'll leave the cell for the date blank.

7. Click cell **A5** to make it the active cell, type **Purpose** in the cell, and then press the **Tab** key. The active cell moves one cell to the right to cell B5.

8. Type **To record orders from RipCity Digital customers** in cell B5, and then press the **Enter** key. Figure 1-4 shows the text entered in the Sheet1 worksheet.

**Figure 1-4**    Documentation sheet

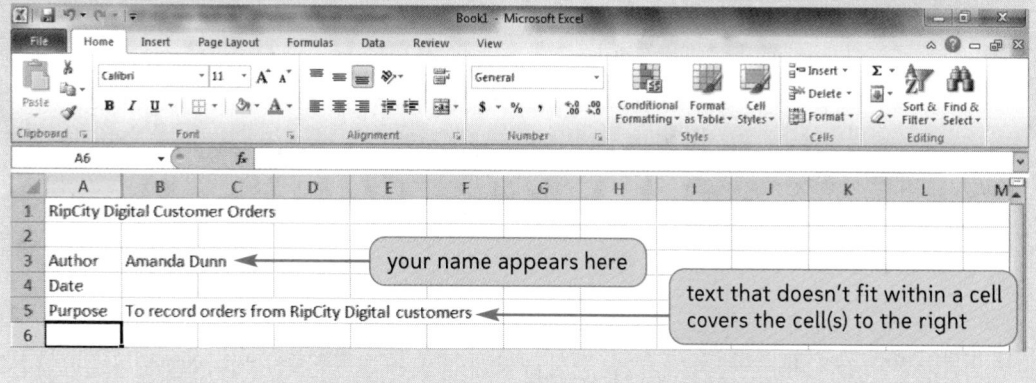

The text you entered in cell A1 is so long that it appears to flow into cells B1 and C1. The same is true for the text you entered in cells B3 and B5. Any text you enter in a cell that doesn't fit within that cell covers the adjacent cells to the right as long as they are empty. If the adjacent cells contain text or data, only the text that fits into the cell is displayed. The rest of the text entry is hidden, or **truncated**, from the view. The text itself is not affected. The complete text is still entered in the cell; it's just not displayed. To display all of the text, you must increase the cell's width, which you'll learn how to do in the next session.

Next, you'll enter the RipCity Digital customer orders. As shown in Figure 1-5, the orders will contain the name and address of each customer, the order date, the number of DVDs created from the customer's home videos, and the price per DVD. Amanda's price per DVD decreases for larger orders.

| Figure 1-5 | Customer orders |
| --- | --- |

| Last | First | Address | Date | DVDs | Price per DVD |
| --- | --- | --- | --- | --- | --- |
| Dawes | Gregory | 402 Elm St.<br>Merrill, MI 48637 | 3/13/2013 | 7 | $17.29 |
| Garcia | Susan | 1025 Drake Ave.<br>Exeter, NH 03833 | 3/14/2013 | 25 | $15.79 |
| Torbet | Dr. Lilla | 5 North Ln.<br>Oswego, NY 13126 | 3/17/2013 | 32 | $12.99 |
| Rhoden | Tony | 24 Mountain Dr.<br>Auburn, ME 04210 | 3/24/2013 | 20 | $15.79 |

You'll enter this data in the Sheet2 worksheet.

### To enter the text labels and customer names:

1. Click the **Sheet2** sheet tab. Sheet2 becomes the active worksheet. You'll enter the column labels in cells A1, B1, C1, D1, E1, and F1.

2. Type **Last** in cell A1, and then press the **Tab** key. The label is entered in cell A1 and the active cell moves to cell B1.

3. Type **First** in cell B1, and then press the **Tab** key. The label is entered in cell B1 and the active cell moves to cell C1.

4. Type **Address** in cell C1, and then press the **Tab** key.

5. Type **Date** in cell D1, and then press the **Tab** key.

6. Type **DVDs** in cell E1, press the **Tab** key, and then type **Price per DVD** in cell F1. You've typed all the labels for the customer orders.

7. Press the **Enter** key. The active cell moves to cell A2, the start of the next row where you want to begin entering the customer data.

8. Type **Dawes** in cell A2, press the **Tab** key, type **Gregory** in cell B2, and then press the **Tab** key. You've entered the first customer's name and moved the active cell to cell C2. Figure 1-6 shows the text you've entered so far.

**Figure 1-6**    Text entered for customer orders

text is left-aligned within cells

text covers the adjacent empty cell

As you type text into the active cell, Excel tries to anticipate the remaining characters by displaying text that begins with the same letters as a previous entry in the same column. This feature, known as **AutoComplete**, helps make entering repetitive text easier. To accept the suggested text, press the Tab or Enter key. To override the suggested text, continue to type the text you want to enter in the cell. AutoComplete does not work with dates or numbers, or when a blank cell is between the previous entry and the text you're typing.

## Entering Multiple Lines of Text Within a Cell

Addresses are often entered on two or more separate lines. Amanda wants you to follow that convention with her customers' addresses. To place text on separate lines within the same cell, you press and hold the Alt key while you press the Enter key. This creates a line break within the cell.

You'll enter the address for the first RipCity Digital customer, which will occupy two lines within the same cell.

### To enter multiple lines of text within a cell:

1. Type **402 Elm St.** in cell C2, but do not press the Tab or Enter key. Instead, you'll insert a new line break.

2. Hold down the **Alt** key and press the **Enter** key, and then release both keys. The insertion point moves to a new line within cell C2.

3. Type **Merrill, MI 48637** on the new line, and then press the **Tab** key. The two lines of text are entered in cell C2, and cell D2 becomes the active cell. See Figure 1-7.

> Be sure to hold down the Alt key as you press Enter; otherwise, only the first address line will be entered in cell C2.

**Figure 1-7**    Multiple lines of text entered in cell C2

text is wrapped within the cell

**TIP**

To force text that extends beyond a cell's border to fit within the cell, click the Wrap Text button in the Alignment group on the Home tab. The row height increases as needed to wrap all the text within the cell.

When you enter multiple lines of text within a cell, Excel confines the text within the cell's borders, increasing the cell's height, if necessary, to show all of the text. As you can see, the text in cell C2 appears on four lines even though you entered the address on two lines. The automatic reflow of text within a cell is referred to as wrapping. If the cell's width were increased, the text would then appear on two lines as Amanda wants. You'll do this in the next session.

## Entering Dates

You can enter dates in any of the standard date formats. For example, you can enter the date April 6, 2013 in any of the following date formats (and many others) and Excel recognizes each entry as representing the same date:

- 4/6/2013
- 4/6/13
- 4-6-2013
- April 6, 2013
- 6-Apr-13

Even though you enter a date as text, Excel stores the date as a numeric value equal to the number of days between the specified date and January 0, 1900. This means that the date January 1, 1900 has a value of 1 and so forth. Times are also entered as text and are stored as fractional parts of a 24-hour day. Storing dates and times as numeric values allows Excel to perform date and time calculations, such as determining the elapsed time between one date and another.

Based on the default date format your computer uses, Excel might alter the date format you type. For example, if you enter the date 4/6/13 into the active cell, Excel might display the date with the four-digit year value, 4/6/2013; if you enter the text April 6, 2013, Excel might convert the date format to 6-Apr-13. Changing the date or time format doesn't affect the underlying date or time value.

For Amanda's workbook, you'll enter the dates in the format $m/d/yyyy$, where $m$ is the 1- or 2-digit month number, $d$ is the 1- or 2-digit day number, and $yyyy$ is the 4-digit year number. You will enter the order date on the Sheet2 worksheet and the current date in the Sheet1 worksheet.

**To enter the dates for the customer orders:**

1. Type **3/13/2013** in cell D2, and then press the **Tab** key to move to cell E2. The date of Gregory Dawes's order appears in cell D2, and cell E2 becomes the active cell. The width of column D expands to display the full date.

2. Click the **Sheet1** sheet tab. The Sheet1 worksheet is the active worksheet.

3. Click cell **B4** to make it active, insert the current date using the format $m/d/yyyy$, and then press the **Enter** key.

4. Click the **Sheet2** sheet tab. The Sheet2 worksheet is the active worksheet, and cell E2 is still the active cell.

*International Date Formats*

As business transactions become more international in scope, you may need to adopt international standards for expressing dates, times, and currency values in your workbooks. For example, a worksheet cell might contain 06/05/12. This format could represent any of the following dates:

- The 5th of June, 2012
- The 6th of May, 2012
- The 12th of May, 2006

The date depends on which country the workbook has been designed for. You can avoid this problem by entering the full date as in the example June 5, 2012. However, this will not work with documents written in foreign languages such as Japanese that use different character symbols.

To solve this problem, many international businesses adopt ISO (International Organization for Standardization) dates in the format *yyyy-mm-dd*, where *yyyy* is the four-digit year value, *mm* is the two-digit month value, and *dd* is the two-digit day value. So, a date such as June 5, 2012 is entered as 2012/06/05. If you choose to use this international date format, make sure that people using your workbook understand this format so they do not misinterpret the dates. You can include information about the date format in the documentation sheet.

## Entering Numbers

In Excel, numbers can be integers such as 378, decimals such as 1.95, or negatives such as −5.2. In the case of currency and percentages, you can include the currency symbol and percent sign when you enter the value. Excel treats a currency value such as $87.25 as the number 87.25, and a percentage such as 95% as the decimal 0.95. Currency and percentages, like dates, are formatted in a convenient way for you to read. Excel right-aligns numbers within each cell.

You'll complete the information for Gregory Dawes's order by entering the number of DVDs Amanda created for him and the price she charged him for each DVD.

### To enter numbers for the first customer order:

1. Type **7** in cell E2, and then press the **Tab** key. The order quantity for Gregory Dawes is entered and the active cell is cell F2.

2. Type **$17.29** in cell F2, and then press the **Enter** key. The currency value is entered in cell F2. Note that Excel enters the number 17.29 in the cell and formats it as currency.

3. Click cell **A3**, which is where you want to enter the information for the next customer. See Figure 1-8.

**Figure 1-8**    **First customer order data**

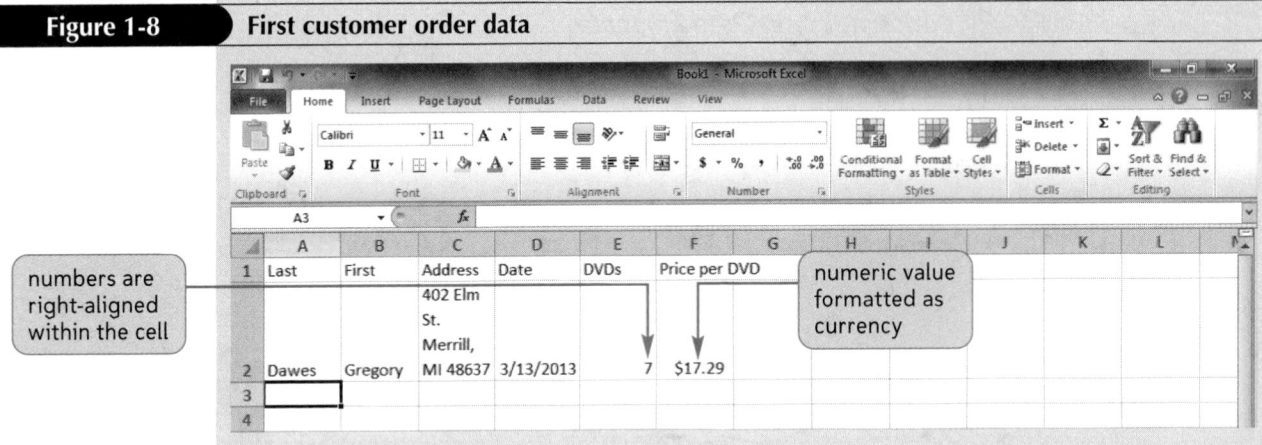

numbers are right-aligned within the cell

numeric value formatted as currency

You've completed the data entry for Amanda's first customer. You still need to enter the data for three more customers into the worksheet. You'll use the same techniques you used to enter Gregory Dawes's order to enter their data.

### To enter the remaining customer order data:

1. Type **Garcia** in cell A3, press the **Tab** key, type **Susan** in cell B3, and then press the **Tab** key. The second customer name is entered.

2. Type **1025 Drake Ave.** in cell C3, press the **Alt+Enter** keys, type **Exeter, NH 03833** on the next line, and then press the **Tab** key. The second customer's address is entered in the cell on two lines.

3. Type **3/14/2013** in cell D3, press the **Tab** key, type **25** in cell E3, press the **Tab** key, type **$15.79** in cell F3, and then press the **Enter** key. The rest of the second customer's data is entered.

4. Enter the following data for the remaining two customers in rows 4 and 5, making sure that you press the Alt+Enter keys to enter the addresses on two lines. Because column C is not wide enough to display the entire address text, it wraps within the cell and the zip code may be hidden. You'll correct this shortly. See Figure 1-9.

   **Torbet, Dr. Lilla**
   **5 North Ln.**
   **Oswego, NY 13126**
   **3/17/2013, 32, $12.99**

   **Rhoden, Tony**
   **24 Mountain Dr.**
   **Auburn, ME 04210**
   **3/24/2013, 20, $15.79**

**Figure 1-9**    Customer orders for RipCity Digital

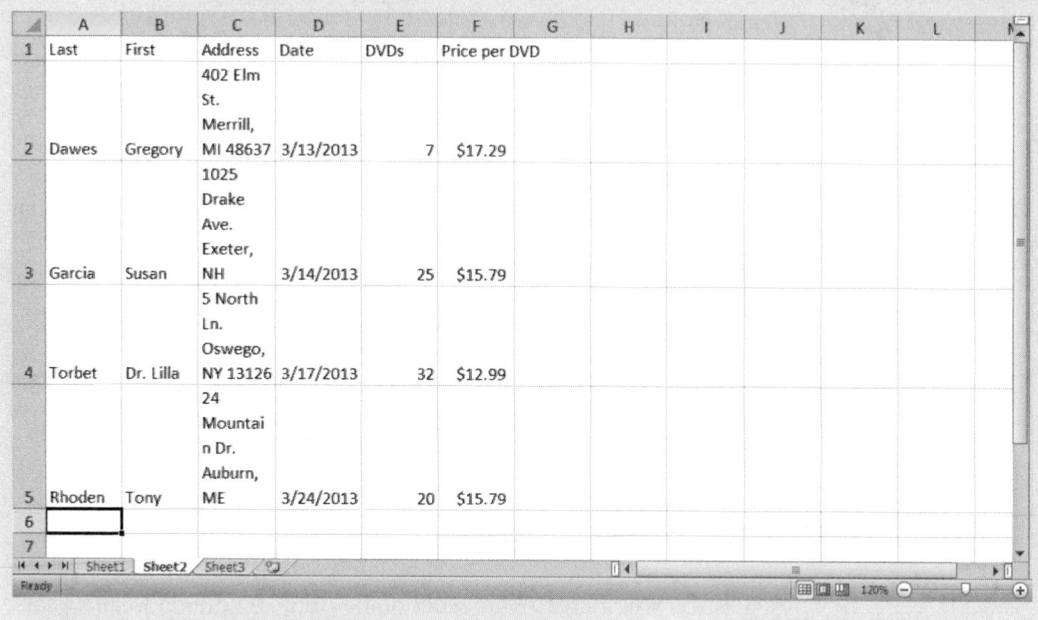

# Working with Columns and Rows

Amanda has reviewed the customer order data you entered in the worksheet. She asks you to make the data easier to read. You can do this by modifying the size of the columns and rows in the worksheet.

**REFERENCE**

*Changing the Column Width or Row Height*

- Drag the right border of the column heading left to decrease the column width or right to increase the column width.
- Drag the bottom border of the row heading up to decrease the row height or down to increase the row height.

*or*

- Double-click the right border of a column heading or the bottom border of a row heading to autofit the column or row to the cell contents (or select one or more columns or rows, click the Home tab on the Ribbon, click the Format button in the Cells group, and then click AutoFit Column Width or AutoFit Row Height).

*or*

- Select one or more columns or rows.
- Click the Home tab on the Ribbon, click the Format button in the Cells group, and then click Column Width or Row Height.
- Enter the column width or row height you want, and then click the OK button.

## Setting Column Widths

The default sizes of the columns and rows in a worksheet might not always accommodate the information you need to enter. This is what happened with the addresses you entered in the worksheet when Excel wrapped the text in ways that made the text difficult to read. Other times, long cell content might be truncated, hiding text or numeric values from the user. To make the cell content easier to read, you can resize the columns and rows in the worksheet.

Column widths are expressed in terms of the number of characters the column can contain. The default column width is 8.43 standard-sized characters. This means that, in general, you can type eight characters in a cell before that entry is truncated, overlaps the adjacent cell, or is wrapped to a new line within the cell. If the font size of the text in the cell is reduced, you can insert more characters within the cell.

Column widths are also expressed in terms of pixels. A **pixel** is a single point on a computer monitor or printout. A column width of 8.43 characters equals 64 pixels.

**INSIGHT**

### Setting Column Widths

Pixel size is based on screen resolution. As a result, cell contents that look fine on one screen might be truncated when viewed on a screen with different resolution. If you work on multiple computers or share your workbooks with others, you should set column widths based on the maximum number of characters you want to display in the cells rather than pixel size. This ensures that everyone sees the cell contents the way you intended.

You will increase the width of the Address column to allow the addresses to appear on two lines in the cells without additional line wrapping.

### To increase the width of column C:

1. Move the pointer over the right border of the column C heading until the pointer changes to ↔.

2. Click and drag to the right until the width of the column heading reaches **20** characters, but do not release the mouse button. The ScreenTip that appears as you resize the column shows the measurements of the new column width first as the number of characters and second in parentheses as pixels.

3. Release the mouse button. The width of column C expands to 20 characters and all the addresses fit on two lines with no extra line wrapping. See Figure 1-10.

**Figure 1-10** **Increased column width**

addresses fit on two lines

Amanda also wants you to increase the widths of columns A and B to 15 characters to accommodate longer names. Rather than resizing each column separately, you can select both columns and adjust their widths at the same time.

**TIP**

To select multiple columns, you can also click and drag the pointer over multiple column headings.

### To increase the widths of columns A and B:

1. Click the **column A** heading. The entire column is selected.

2. Hold down the **Ctrl** key, click the **column B** heading, and then release the **Ctrl** key. Both columns A and B are selected.

3. Move the pointer to the right border of the column B heading until the pointer changes to ┿.

4. Drag to the right until the column width changes to **15** characters, and then release the mouse button. Both columns are wide enough to display longer names.

The text in cell F1, Price per DVD, overflows the cell borders. This column would look better if you increased the width of column F to 12 characters. You can set the column width using the Format command on the Home tab. The Format command gives you precise control in setting column widths and row heights.

### To set the width of column F to 12 characters:

1. Click the **column F** heading. The entire column is selected.

2. In the Cells group on the Home tab, click the **Format** button, and then click **Column Width**. The Column Width dialog box opens.

3. Type **12** in the Column width box, and then click the **OK** button. The width of column F changes to 12 characters, placing the text in cell F1 entirely within the borders of the cell.

## Setting Row Heights

The height of an Excel row is measured in points or pixels. A **point** is approximately 1/72 of an inch. The default row height is 15 points or 20 pixels. Row heights are set in the same way as column widths. You can drag the bottom border of the row to a new row height or define a specific row height using the Format command. Another option is to autofit the row's height (or the column's width) to match its content. **Autofitting** eliminates empty space by matching the row height or column width to its tallest or longest cell entry. If the row or column is blank, Excel restores its default height or width.

The row heights didn't change after you resized the columns, which leaves a lot of blank space in the four rows of customer data. This extra blank space makes the data difficult to read and extends the content out of view. Amanda wants you to autofit the heights of these rows to remove that empty space.

### To autofit the second row to match its contents:

1. Move the pointer over the bottom border of the row 2 heading until the pointer changes to ⬩.

2. Double-click the bottom border of row 2. The height of row 2 shrinks to match the content of cell C2, which is the tallest entry in the row, with two lines of text.

You could continue to resize the remaining rows one at a time, but a quicker way is to select the rows you want to resize and then autofit all the selected rows simultaneously.

### To autofit rows 3 through 5:

1. Drag the pointer across the row headings for rows 3, 4, and 5. The contents of rows 3 through 5 are selected.

2. In the Cells group on the Home tab, click the **Format** button. A menu of commands opens.

3. Click **AutoFit Row Height**. The height of each of the three rows autofits to its contents, and all the empty space is removed.

4. Click cell **A1** to make it the active cell. The other cells in the worksheet are deselected. Figure 1-11 shows the worksheet with the revised row heights.

**Figure 1-11** Row heights after autofitting to contents

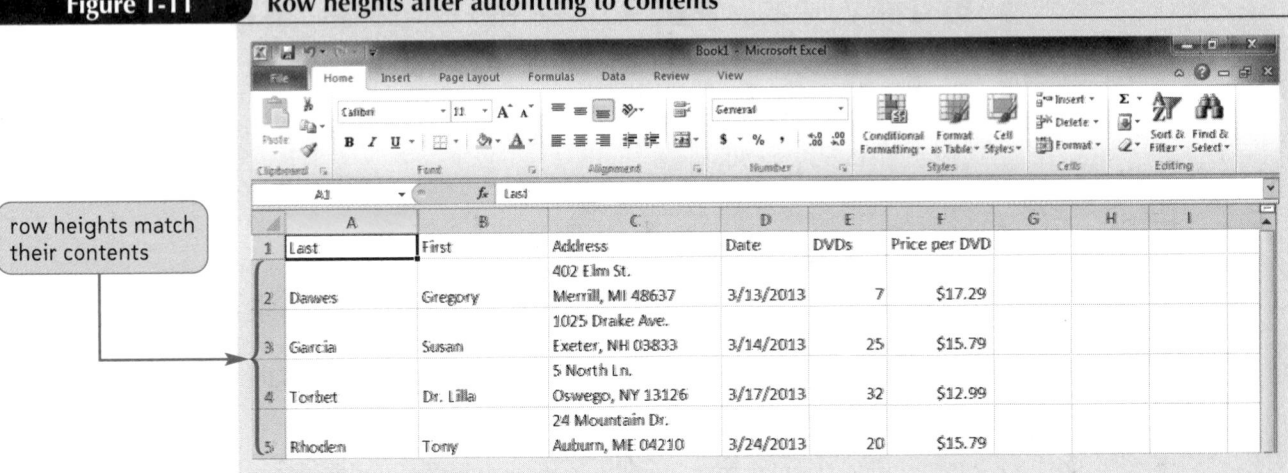

row heights match their contents

## Inserting a Column or Row

You can insert a new column or row anywhere within a worksheet. When you insert a new column, the existing columns are shifted to the right and the new column has the same width as the column directly to its left. When you insert a new row, the existing rows are shifted down and the new row has the same height as the row above it.

## Inserting a Column or Row

- Select the column(s) or row(s) where you want to insert the new column(s) or row(s); Excel will insert the same number of columns or rows as you select to the left of the selected columns or above the selected rows.
- In the Cells group on the Home tab, click the Insert button (or right-click a column or row heading or selected column and row headings, and then click Insert on the shortcut menu).

You will insert a column for customer phone numbers between the Address column and the Date column, and then enter the customer phone numbers in the new column.

### To insert the new column:

1. Click the **column D** heading to select the entire column.

2. In the Cells group on the Home tab, click the **Insert** button. A new column D is inserted into the worksheet and the rest of the columns shift to the right. The new column has the same width as column C.

3. Reduce the width of column D to **15** characters.

4. Click cell **D1** to make it the active cell, type **Phone** as the label, and then press the **Enter** key. The new column label is entered in cell D1, and cell D2 becomes the active cell.

5. Enter the phone numbers in cells D2, D3, D4, and D5, as shown in Figure 1-12, pressing the **Enter** key after each entry.

**Figure 1-12**    New column inserted into the worksheet

new column content

inserted column

existing columns shifted to the right

Amanda neglected to include a customer order. Because the customer was RipCity Digital's first customer, Amanda wants this order inserted at the top of the list. To add this new order, you need to insert a new row in the worksheet below the column labels.

**To insert the new row:**

▶ **1.** Click the **row 2** heading. The entire second row is selected.

▶ **2.** In the Cells group on the Home tab, click the **Insert** button. A new row 2 is inserted, and the remaining rows shift down.

▶ **3.** Enter the new customer order shown in Figure 1-13 into row 2.

Figure 1-13
New row inserted into the worksheet

| | A | B | C | D | E | F | G | H |
|---|---|---|---|---|---|---|---|---|
| 1 | Last | First | Address | Phone | Date | DVDs | Price per DVD | |
| 2 | Ferris | Andrew | 135 College Ave. Bar Harbor, ME 04609 | (207) 555-0101 | 3/5/2013 | 2 | $17.29 | |
| 3 | Dawes | Gregory | 402 Elm St. Merrill, MI 48637 | (989) 555-3433 | 3/13/2013 | 7 | $17.29 | |
| 4 | Garcia | Susan | 1025 Drake Ave. Exeter, NH 03833 | (603) 555-1091 | 3/14/2013 | 25 | $15.79 | |
| 5 | Torbet | Dr. Lilla | 5 North Ln. Oswego, NY 13126 | (315) 555-7823 | 3/17/2013 | 32 | $12.99 | |
| 6 | Rhoden | Tony | 24 Mountain Dr. Auburn, ME 04210 | (207) 555-9915 | 3/24/2013 | 20 | $15.79 | |

inserted row →

existing rows are shifted down →

## Deleting and Clearing a Row or Column

You can remove data in two ways: clearing and deleting. **Clearing** data from a worksheet removes the data, leaving blank cells where the data had been. **Deleting** data from the worksheet removes both the data and the cells. When a cell is deleted, the remaining cells in the worksheet shift into the deleted location. For example, when you delete a column, the columns to the right shift left to fill the vacated space. Similarly, the rows below a deleted row shift up to fill the vacated space. Note that pressing the Delete key does not *delete* the selected row or column; instead, it *clears* the contents, leaving the row or column in place.

Gregory Dawes just canceled his order. Amanda wants you to remove this order from the worksheet. You'll first clear Gregory Dawes's data from the worksheet and then delete the row that contained the data. Usually, you would do this in one step by simply deleting the row, but this will highlight the difference between clearing and deleting.

**To clear and delete the third row:**

▶ **1.** Click the **row 3** heading. The entire row 3 with Gregory Dawes's order is selected.

▶ **2.** Right-click the **row 3** heading, and then click **Clear Contents** on the shortcut menu. Excel clears the values in the third row, but leaves the blank row in that space.

▶ **3.** Verify that the third row is still selected.

▶ **4.** In the Cells group on the Home tab, click the **Delete** button. The third row is deleted, and the rows below it shift up. Only four customer orders remain in the worksheet.

Before continuing, you'll save your workbook with a descriptive name.

### To save the current workbook:

**TIP**

You can click the Save As command in the navigation bar to save a previously saved workbook with a new filename, to a different location, or in another file format.

▶ **1.** Click the **File** tab on the Ribbon to display Backstage view.

▶ **2.** Click the **Save** command in the navigation bar. The Save As dialog box opens because this is the first time you are saving this workbook.

▶ **3.** Navigate to the **Excel1\Tutorial** folder included with your Data Files.

**Trouble?** If you don't have the starting Data Files, you need to get them before you can proceed. Your instructor will either give you the Data Files or ask you to obtain them from a specified location (such as a network drive). In either case, make a backup copy of the Data Files before you start so that you will have the original files available in case you need to start over. If you have any questions about the Data Files, see your instructor or technical support person for assistance.

▶ **4.** Verify that **Excel Workbook** appears in the Save as type box.

**Trouble?** If your computer is set up to show filename extensions, you will see the Excel file extension .xlsx in the Save as type box as well.

▶ **5.** Select **Book1** in the File name box, and then type **RipCity Digital Orders**. The default filename Book1 is replaced with the name you entered.

▶ **6.** Click the **Save** button. The Save As dialog box closes and the workbook file is saved with its descriptive filename.

So far, you have entered the customer order data. In the process, you worked with rows and columns. In the next session, you'll learn how to work with individual cells and groups of cells. You will also add calculations to the worksheet to determine how much revenue Amanda will generate from these orders.

## Session 1.1 Quick Check

**REVIEW**

**1.** What are the two types of sheets used in a workbook?

**2.** List two ways of identifying the active cell in the worksheet.

**3.** What is the cell reference for the cell located in the fourth column and third row of a worksheet?

**4.** What keyboard shortcut changes the active cell to cell A1?

**5.** What is text data?

**6.** What keys do you press to start a new line of text within a cell?

**7.** Cell A4 contains May 3, 2013; why doesn't Excel consider this entry a text string?

**8.** Explain the difference between clearing a row and deleting a row.

# SESSION 1.2 VISUAL OVERVIEW

The File tab opens Backstage view, which provides access to commands for saving and printing the workbook.

The **spelling checker** verifies the words in the active worksheet against the program's dictionary. You can replace or ignore the words it flags as misspelled.

A group of cells is called a **cell range** or **range**. Ranges can be either adjacent or nonadjacent.

The status bar indicates whether you are in Ready mode or Edit mode.

The Page Layout tab provides commands to change the way worksheets appear on printed pages.

A **formula** is an expression that returns a value. This formula calculates the sum of the values in range H6:H9.

You can rename a sheet so that it has a brief description of its contents or purpose.

The Insert Worksheet tab inserts a new worksheet at the end of the workbook.

RipCity Digital Orders - Micr

File | Home | Insert | Page Layout | Formulas | Data | Review | View

Calibri | 11 | A A | Currency

B I U | $ % ,

Clipboard | Font | Alignment | Number

H10 | =SUM(H6:H9)

| | A | B | C | D |
|---|---|---|---|---|
| 1 | RipCity Digital | | | |
| 2 | Customer Orders | | | |
| 3 | 3/31/2013 | | | |
| 4 | | | | |
| 5 | Last | First | Address | Phone |
| 6 | Ferris | Andrew | 135 College Avenue Bar Harbor, ME 04609 | (207) 555-0 |
| 7 | Garcia | Susan | 1025 Drake Avenue Exeter, NH 03833 | (603) 555-10 |
| 8 | Torbet | Dr. Lila | 5 North Lane Oswego, NY 13126 | (315) 555-78 |
| 9 | Rhoden | Tony | 24 Mountain Drive Auburn, ME 04210 | (207) 555-99 |
| 10 | | | | |

Documentation | Customer Orders

Ready | Average: $12,9

# WORKSHEET DATA

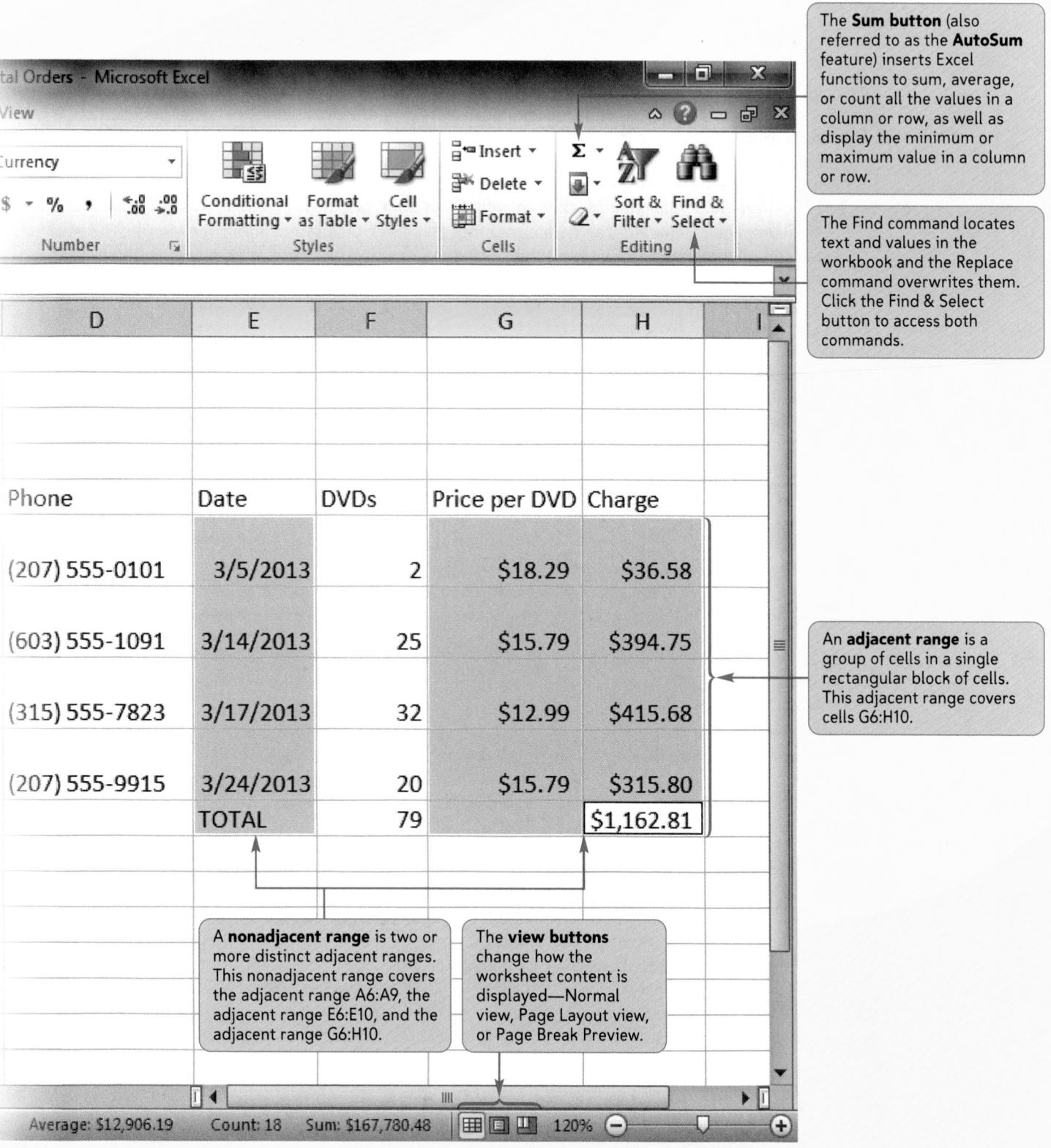

The **Sum button** (also referred to as the **AutoSum** feature) inserts Excel functions to sum, average, or count all the values in a column or row, as well as display the minimum or maximum value in a column or row.

The Find command locates text and values in the workbook and the Replace command overwrites them. Click the Find & Select button to access both commands.

An **adjacent range** is a group of cells in a single rectangular block of cells. This adjacent range covers cells G6:H10.

A **nonadjacent range** is two or more distinct adjacent ranges. This nonadjacent range covers the adjacent range A6:A9, the adjacent range E6:E10, and the adjacent range G6:H10.

The **view buttons** change how the worksheet content is displayed—Normal view, Page Layout view, or Page Break Preview.

# Working with Cells and Ranges

In the previous session, you worked with entire columns or rows of cells. In this session you'll work with groups of worksheet cells, or ranges. The customer order data you entered in cells A1 through G5 forms an adjacent range because it covers one rectangular block of cells. All the last names in cells A1 through A5 and all the numbers in cells F1 through G5 together form a nonadjacent range because they are two distinct rectangular blocks of cells.

Just as a cell reference indicates the location of an individual worksheet cell, a **range reference** indicates the location and size of a cell range. For adjacent ranges, the range reference includes the cell reference of the upper-left and lower-right cells in the rectangular block separated by a colon. For example, the range reference A1:G5 refers to all the cells in the rectangular block from cells A1 through G5. The range reference for nonadjacent ranges separates each adjacent range reference by a semicolon. For example, the cell reference A1:A5;F1:G5 references two rectangular blocks of cells: one covering cells A1 through A5 and the other covering cells F1 through G5.

## Selecting a Range

You can select adjacent and nonadjacent ranges of cells with your mouse, just as you selected individual cells. Selecting a range enables you to work with all of the cells in the range as a group. This means you can move the groups of cells, delete them, or clear all their contents at the same time.

---

**REFERENCE**

### Selecting Ranges

**To select an adjacent range:**
- Click the cell in the upper-left corner of the adjacent range, drag the pointer to the cell in the lower-right corner of the adjacent range, and then release the mouse button.

*or*
- Click the cell in the upper-left corner of the adjacent range, press the Shift key as you click the cell in the lower-right corner of the adjacent range, and then release the Shift key.

**To select a nonadjacent range of cells:**
- Select a cell or an adjacent range, press the Ctrl key as you select each additional cell or adjacent range, and then release the Ctrl key.

**To select all the cells in a worksheet:**
- Click the Select All button located at the intersection of the row and column headings (or press the Ctrl+A keys).

**To select an entire row or entire rows:**
- Click a row heading to select a single row. To select multiple rows, click and drag the pointer over multiple row headings.

**To select an entire column or entire columns:**
- Click a column heading to select a single column. To select multiple columns, click and drag the pointer over multiple column headings.

---

You'll use the pointer to select the adjacent range A1:G5, which includes all the content you entered in the orders worksheet.

### To select the adjacent range A1:G5:

1. If you took a break at the end of the previous session, make sure the RipCity Digital Orders workbook is open and the Sheet2 worksheet is active.

2. Click cell **A1** to select that cell, and then with the mouse button still pressed, drag the pointer to cell **G5**, which is the cell in the lower-right corner of the range A1:G5.

3. Release the mouse button. As shown in Figure 1-14, all the cells in the adjacent range A1:G5 are selected. The selected cells are highlighted with color and surrounded by a black border. The first cell you selected, cell A1, is still the active cell in the worksheet.

| Figure 1-14 | Selected adjacent range A1:G5 |

the active cell in the selected range is white

selected range is highlighted in the worksheet

4. Click any cell in the worksheet to deselect the range.

Next, you'll use the pointer to select the nonadjacent range A1:A5;F1:G5.

### To select the nonadjacent range A1:A5;F1:G5:

1. Select the adjacent range **A1:A5** with your mouse.

2. Hold down the **Ctrl** key, and then select the adjacent range **F1:G5**.

3. Release the **Ctrl** key. As shown in Figure 1-15, all the cells in the nonadjacent range A1:A5;F1:G5 are selected.

**Figure 1-15** Selected nonadjacent range A1:A5;F1:G5

adjacent range A1:A5

adjacent range F1:G5

▶ **4.** Click any cell in the worksheet to deselect the range.

## Moving and Copying a Range

Amanda wants you to insert titles into the worksheet that describe the customer order data you have entered. Including the company name, a descriptive title, and the current date is part of good worksheet design, enabling others to quickly see the *who*, *what*, and *when* of the data. The current worksheet has no space to add this information. You could insert several blank rows at the top of the worksheet for this information. Another option is to select and then move the customer data lower in the worksheet, freeing up the rows at the top for the new text.

**REFERENCE**

### Moving or Copying a Cell or Range

- Select the cell or range you want to move or copy.
- Move the pointer over the border of the selection until the pointer changes shape.
- To move the range, click the border and drag the selection to a new location (or to copy the range, hold down the Ctrl key and drag the selection to a new location).

*or*

- Select the cell or range you want to move or copy.
- In the Clipboard group on the Home tab, click the Cut button or the Copy button (or right-click the selection, and then click Cut or Copy on the shortcut menu).
- Select the cell or upper-left cell of the range where you want to move or copy the content.
- In the Clipboard group, click the Paste button (or right-click the selection, and then click Paste on the shortcut menu).

**TIP**

To move to a location that is not visible, drag the selection to the edge of the worksheet window until it scrolls down or across, and then drop the selection into the new location.

One way to move a cell or range is to select it, position the pointer over the bottom border of the selection, and then drag the selection to a new location. This technique is called **drag and drop** because you are dragging the range and dropping it in a new location. You can also use the drag-and-drop technique to copy cells by pressing the Ctrl key as you drag the selected range to its new location. A copy of the original range is placed in the new location without removing the original range from the worksheet.

You'll use the drag-and-drop method to move the customer order data to a new location in the worksheet.

### To drag and drop the customer order data:

1. Select the range **A1:G5**.

2. Move the pointer over the bottom border of the selected range so that the pointer changes to ⇖.

3. Press and hold the mouse button to change the pointer to ⇖, and then drag the selection down three rows. Do not release the mouse button. A ScreenTip appears, indicating the new range reference of the selected cells. See Figure 1-16.

| Figure 1-16 | Selected range being moved |

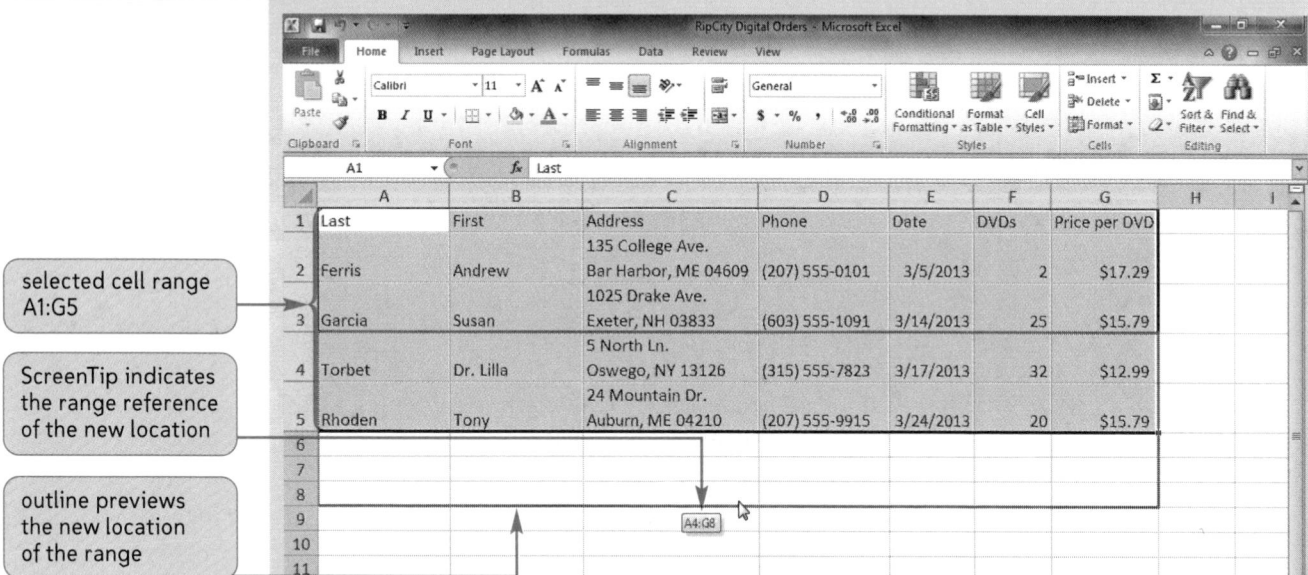

selected cell range A1:G5

ScreenTip indicates the range reference of the new location

outline previews the new location of the range

4. When the ScreenTip displays the range A4:G8, release the mouse button. The selected cells move to their new location.

5. Enter the title information shown in Figure 1-17 in the range A1:A3, pressing the **Enter** key after each entry.

**Figure 1-17** **Titles added to the worksheet**

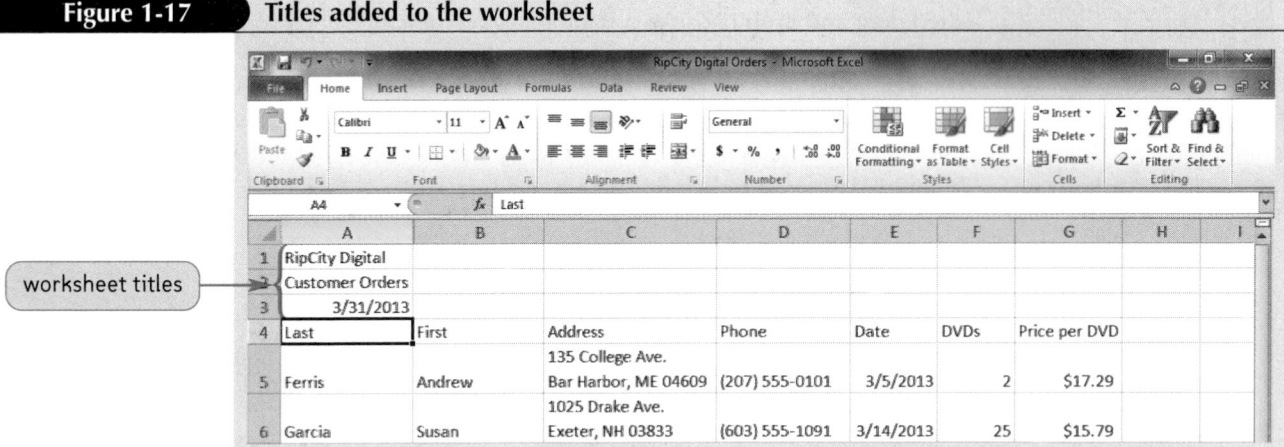

worksheet titles

Some people find dragging and dropping a difficult and awkward way to move a selection, particularly if the worksheet is large and complex. In those situations, it's often more efficient to cut and paste the cell contents. **Cutting** places the cell contents into computer memory or on the Clipboard. The contents can then be pasted from the Clipboard into a new location in the worksheet. You'll cut and paste a range now.

**To cut and paste the customer order data:**

1. Select the range **A4:G8**.

2. In the Clipboard group on the Home tab, click the **Cut** button ✂. The selected range is surrounded by a blinking border, which indicates that its contents are stored on the Clipboard.

3. Click cell **A11**. This cell is the upper-left corner of the range where you want to paste the data.

4. In the Clipboard group, click the **Paste** button. Excel pastes the contents of the range A4:G8 into the new range A11:G15. The blinking border disappears as a visual clue that the Clipboard is now empty.

5. With the range **A11:G15** still selected, click the **Cut** button ✂ in the Clipboard group.

6. Click cell **A4**, and then click the **Paste** button in the Clipboard group. The customer order data is pasted into its original location in the range A4:G8.

## Inserting and Deleting a Range

Amanda wants more space between the three title rows you just entered and the table of customer orders. You could simply move the range A4:G8 down one more row, but another way is to insert new cells between the titles and the order data.

When you insert a new range of cells with the Insert button, the existing cells shift down when the selected range is wider than it is long, and they shift right when the selected range is longer than it is wide (as shown in Figure 1-18). When you use the Insert Cells command, you specify whether the existing cells shift right or down, or whether to insert an entire row or column into the new range.

| **Figure 1-18** | **Cells being inserted into a worksheet** |

The process works in reverse when you delete a range. As with deleting a row or column, the cells adjacent to the deleted range either move up or left to fill in the space left by the deleted cells. The Delete Cells command lets you specify whether you want to shift the adjacent cells left or up, or whether to delete the entire column or row.

**REFERENCE**

*Inserting or Deleting a Range*

- Select a range that matches the range you want to insert or delete.
- In the Cells group on the Home tab, click the Insert button or the Delete button.

*or*

- Select the range that matches the range you want to insert or delete.
- In the Cells group on the Home tab, click the Insert button arrow and then click Insert Cells, or click the Delete button arrow and then click Delete Cells (or right-click the selected range, and then click Insert or Delete on the shortcut menu).
- Click the option button for the direction to shift the cells, columns, or rows.
- Click the OK button.

You will insert a blank range of cells between the worksheet titles and the table of customer orders.

**To insert the cell range:**

1. Select the range **A4:G4**. You want to insert blank cells in this range.

2. In the Cells group on the Home tab, click the **Insert button arrow**, and then click **Insert Cells**. The Insert dialog box opens.

3. Verify that the **Shift cells down** option button is selected.

4. Click the **OK** button. The existing cells shift down and the new cells are inserted into the range A4:G4.

# Working with Formulas

So far you have entered only text, numbers, and dates in the worksheet. However, the main reason for using Excel is to display values calculated from data. For example, Amanda wants the workbook to determine the number of DVDs she has to create for her customers and how much revenue these orders will generate. Such calculations are added to a worksheet using formulas and functions.

## Entering a Formula

A formula is an expression that returns a value. In most cases, this is a numeric value though it could also be a text string, a yes/no value, or a date. Every Excel formula begins with an equal sign (=) followed by an expression describing the operation that returns the value. Note that if you don't begin the formula with the equal sign, Excel assumes that you are entering text and will not treat the cell contents as a formula.

A formula is written using **operators** that combine different values, resulting in a single value that is then displayed within the cell. The most commonly used operators are **arithmetic operators** that perform addition, subtraction, multiplication, division, and exponentiation. For example, the following formula adds 5 and 7, returning a value of 12:

    =5+7

Most Excel formulas contain references to cells rather than specific values. This allows you to change the values being used in the calculation without having to modify the formula itself. For example, the following formula returns the result of adding the values stored in cells A1 and B2:

    =A1+B2

If the value 5 is stored in cell A1 and the value 7 is stored in cell B2, this formula would also return a value of 12. If you then changed the value in cell A1 to 10, the formula returns a value of 17. Figure 1-19 describes the different arithmetic operators and provides examples of formulas.

| Figure 1-19 | Excel arithmetic operators |
| --- | --- |

| Operation | Arithmetic Operator | Example | Description |
| --- | --- | --- | --- |
| Addition | + | =10+A1 | Adds 10 to the value in cell A1 |
| | | =B1+B2+B3 | Adds the values in cells B1, B2, and B3 |
| Subtraction | – | =C9–B2 | Subtracts the value in cell B2 from the value in cell C9 |
| | | =1–D2 | Subtracts the value in cell D2 from 1 |
| Multiplication | * | =C9*B9 | Multiplies the values in cells C9 and B9 |
| | | =E5*0.06 | Multiplies the value in cell E5 by 0.06 |
| Division | / | =C9/B9 | Divides the value in cell C9 by the value in cell B9 |
| | | =D15/12 | Divides the value in cell D15 by 12 |
| Exponentiation | ^ | =B5^3 | Raises the value of cell B5 to the third power |
| | | =3^B5 | Raises 3 to the value in cell B5 |

If a formula contains more than one arithmetic operator, Excel performs the calculation using the same order of precedence you might have already seen in math classes. The **order of precedence** is a set of predefined rules used to determine the sequence in which operators are applied in a calculation. Excel first calculates the value of any operation within parentheses, then it applies exponentiation (^), multiplication (*), and division (/), and finally it performs addition (+) and subtraction (−). For example, the following formula returns the value 23 because multiplying 4 by 5 takes precedence over adding 3:

=3+4*5

If a formula contains two or more operators with the same level of precedence, the operators are applied in order from left to right. In the following formula, Excel first multiplies 4 by 10 and then divides that result by 8 to return the value 5:

=4*10/8

When parentheses are used, the value inside them is calculated first. In the following formula, Excel calculates the (3+4) and then multiplies that result by 5 to return the value 35:

=(3+4)*5

Figure 1-20 shows how slight changes in a formula affect the order of precedence and the result of the formula.

**Figure 1-20**    **Order of precedence applied to Excel formulas**

| Formula | Application of the Order of Precedence | Result |
| --- | --- | --- |
| =50+10*5 | 10*5 calculated first and then 50 is added | 100 |
| =(50+10)*5 | (50+10) calculated first and then multiplied by 5 | 300 |
| =50/10–5 | 50/10 calculated first and then 5 is subtracted | 0 |
| =50/(10–5) | (10–5) calculated first and then 50 is divided by that value | 10 |
| =50/10*5 | Two operators at same precedence level, so the calculation is done left to right in the expression | 25 |
| =50/(10*5) | (10*5) calculated first and then 50 is divided by that value | 1 |

**REFERENCE**

*Inserting a Formula*

- Click the cell in which you want the formula results to appear.
- Type = and a formula that calculates a value using cell references and arithmetic operators.
- Press the Enter key or press the Tab key to complete the formula.

Amanda wants the worksheet to include the total amount she charged for creating each customer's DVDs. The charge is equal to the number of DVDs created multiplied by the price per DVD. You've already entered this information for each customer in columns F and G. You'll enter a formula to calculate the charge for each customer in column H.

## To enter the formula into the worksheet:

▶ **1.** Click cell **H5** to make it the active cell, type **Charge** for the column label, and then press the **Enter** key. The column label is entered in cell H5. Cell H6, where you want to enter the formula, is the active cell.

▶ **2.** Type **=F6*G6** (the number of DVDs created multiplied by the price per DVD). As you type the formula, a list of Excel function names appears in a ScreenTip, which provides a quick method for entering functions. The list will close when you complete the formula. You'll learn more about Excel functions shortly.

▶ **3.** Press the **Enter** key. The formula is entered in cell H6, which displays the value $34.58. The result is displayed as currency because cell G6 referenced in the formula contains a currency value.

After a formula has been entered into a cell, the worksheet displays the value returned by the formula. If the results are not what you expect, you might have entered the formula incorrectly. You can view the formula by selecting the cell and reviewing the expression displayed in the formula bar. One challenge with formulas, particularly long formulas, is interpreting the cell references. Excel makes this simpler by color coding each cell reference in the formula and its corresponding cell in the worksheet. You'll see this when you view the formula you just entered.

## To view the formula:

▶ **1.** Click cell **H6** to make it the active cell. The formula you entered appears in the formula bar, whereas the value returned by the formula appears in the cell.

▶ **2.** Click in the formula bar. Each cell used in the formula has a different colored border that matches the color of its cell reference in the formula. This provides a visual cue to the formula, so you can quickly match cell references with their locations in the worksheet. See Figure 1-21.

| Figure 1-21 | Formula in the formula bar |
| --- | --- |

formula displayed in the formula bar

cell border colors match the colors in the formula bar

formula in cell H6 multiplies the values in cells F6 and G6

For Amanda's first customer, you entered the formula by typing each cell reference in the expression. You can also insert a cell reference by clicking the cell as you type the formula. This technique reduces the possibility of error caused by typing an incorrect cell reference. You'll use this method to enter the formula to calculate the charge for the second customer.

## To enter a cell reference using the mouse:

**TIP**

Be sure to type = as the first part of the entry in any cell containing a formula; otherwise, Excel will not interpret the entry as a formula.

1. Click cell **H7** to make it the active cell, and then type =. When you type the equal sign, Excel knows that you're entering a formula. Any cell that you click from now on causes Excel to insert the cell reference of the selected cell into the formula until you complete the formula by pressing the Enter or Tab key.

2. Click cell **F7**. The cell reference is inserted into the formula in the formula bar. At this point, any cell you click changes the cell reference used in the formula. The cell reference isn't locked until you type an operator.

3. Type * to enter the multiplication operator. The cell reference for cell F7 is locked in the formula, and the next cell you click will be inserted after the operator.

4. Click cell **G7** to enter its cell reference in the formula, and then press the **Enter** key. Cell H7 displays the value $394.75, which is the total charge for the second customer.

## Copying and Pasting Formulas

Sometimes you'll need to repeat the same formula throughout your worksheet. Rather than retyping the formula, you can copy a formula from one cell and paste it into another cell. Pasting a formula is different from pasting a value. With formulas, Excel adjusts the formula's cell references to reflect the new location of the formula in the worksheet. This is because you usually want to copy the actions of a formula rather than the specific value the formula generates. In this case, the formula's action is to multiply the number of DVDs Amanda created for a customer by the price she is charging for creating each DVD. By copying and pasting the formula, you can quickly repeat that action for every customer in the worksheet.

You will see how this works as you copy the formula you just entered in cell H7 to cells H8 and H9 to calculate Amanda's charges to the two remaining customers listed in the worksheet.

## To copy and paste the formula that calculates charges:

1. Click cell **H7** to select the cell that contains the formula you want to copy.

2. In the Clipboard group on the Home tab, click the **Copy** button. Excel copies the formula to the Clipboard. The cell from which the formula was copied has a dotted border to remind you that cell is being copied.

3. Select the range **H8:H9**. These are the cells in which you want to paste the formula.

4. In the Clipboard group, click the **Paste** button. Excel pastes the formula into the selected range. A shortcut button appears below the selected range, providing options for pasting formulas and values. See Figure 1-22.

| Figure 1-22 | Formula copied and pasted |

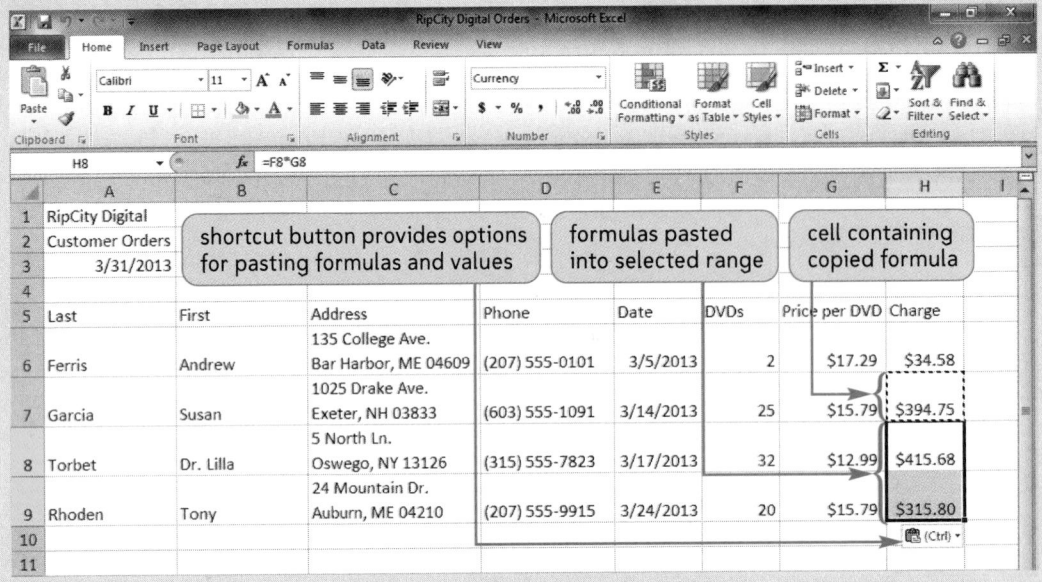

**5.** Click cell **H8** and verify that the formula =F8*G8 appears in the formula bar.

**6.** Click cell **H9** and verify that the formula =F9*G9 appears in the formula bar.

When you pasted the formulas into cells H8 and H9, Excel automatically adjusted the formulas so that the total charges calculated for the customers in rows 8 and 9 use the cell values from rows 8 and 9. By copying and pasting the formula, you have saved time and avoided potential mistakes in retyping the same formula again and again.

# Introducing Functions

In addition to cell references and operators, formulas can also contain functions. A **function** is a named operation that returns a value. Functions are used to simplify formulas, reducing what might be a long formula into a compact statement. For example, to add the values in the range A1:A10, you could enter the following long formula:

    =A1+A2+A3+A4+A5+A6+A7+A8+A9+A10

Or, you could use the SUM function to calculate the sum of cell values found within a specified range. In this case, the formula would appear as:

    =SUM(A1:A10)

In both instances, Excel adds the values in cells A1 through A10, but the SUM function is faster and simpler to enter and less prone to a typing error. You should always use a function, if one is available, in place of a long, complex formula.

Excel supports more than 300 different functions from the fields of finance, business, science, and engineering. Excel provides functions that work with numbers, text, and dates.

## Entering a Function

Amanda wants to calculate the total number of DVDs she needs to create for her customers. To do that, you'll use the SUM function to add the values in the range F6:F9.

## To enter the SUM function to add the values in the range F6:F9:

1. Click cell **E10**, type **TOTAL** in all uppercase letters as the label, and then press the **Tab** key. The label is entered in cell E10, and cell F10 is the active cell.

2. Type **=SUM(F6:F9** in cell F10. As you begin to type the function, a ScreenTip lists the names of all functions that start with the letter "S." When you type the cell references, Excel highlights all the cells in the specified range to provide a visual reminder of exactly which cells the SUM function is using. See Figure 1-23.

**TIP**

You can also insert a range reference into a function by selecting the range with the pointer.

| Figure 1-23 | SUM function being entered |

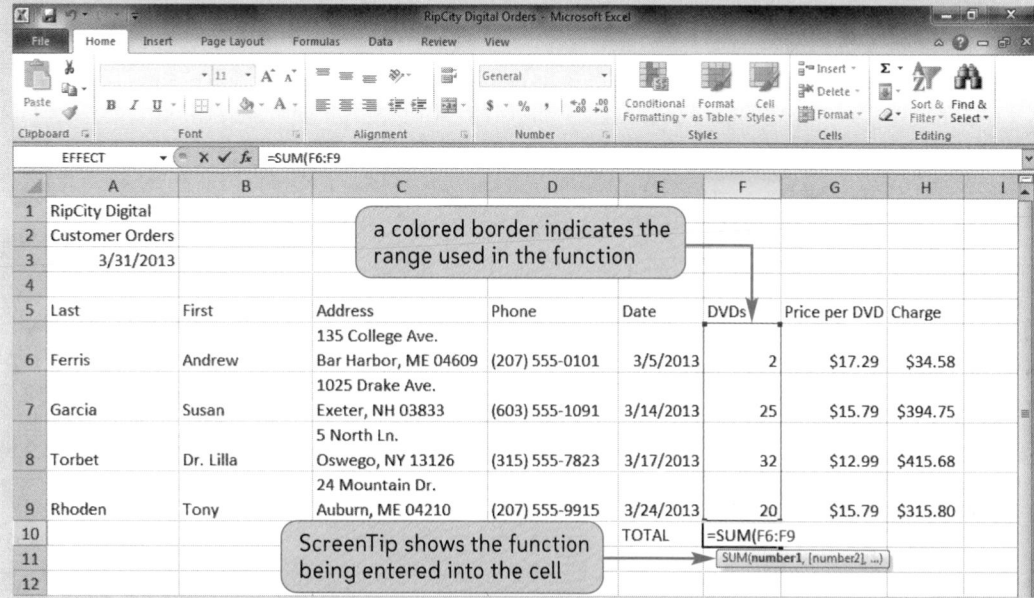

3. Type **)** to complete the function, and then press the **Tab** key. The value of the SUM function appears in cell F10, indicating that Amanda has to create 79 DVDs to complete all of her current orders.

## Entering Functions with the AutoSum Feature

A fast and convenient way to enter commonly used functions is with the AutoSum feature. The AutoSum feature includes buttons to quickly insert the SUM, AVERAGE, COUNT, MIN, and MAX functions to generate the following:

- Sum of the values in the column or row
- Average value in the column or row
- Total count of numeric values in the column or row
- Minimum value in the column or row
- Maximum value in the column or row

The Sum button automatically inserts both the function name and the range reference to the row or column of data to which the summary function is being applied.

### How AutoSum Works

Excel determines the range reference needed for the function being inserted by the AutoSum feature by examining the layout of the data and choosing what seems to be the most likely range. When you use the Sum button, Excel highlights the range it thinks you want to use. For example, if you use the Sum button in a cell that is below a column of numbers, Excel assumes that you want to summarize the values in the column. You can change that range by typing a different range reference or selecting a different range.

Make sure to always verify the range AutoSum selected, especially when a worksheet's column or row titles contain numbers. AutoSum cannot differentiate between numbers used as titles (such as years) and numbers used as data for the calculation.

Amanda wants to calculate the total revenue she'll generate after she fulfills her customer orders. You'll use the AutoSum feature to enter the SUM function.

### To calculate the total revenue using the AutoSum feature:

1. Click cell **H10** to make it the active cell.

2. In the Editing group on the Home tab, click the **Sum button arrow** $\Sigma$ ▾.
   The button's menu opens and displays five common summary functions: Sum, Average, Count Numbers, Max (for maximum), and Min (for minimum).

3. Click **Sum** to enter the SUM function. See Figure 1-24.

| Figure 1-24 | SUM function being entered with AutoSum |
| --- | --- |

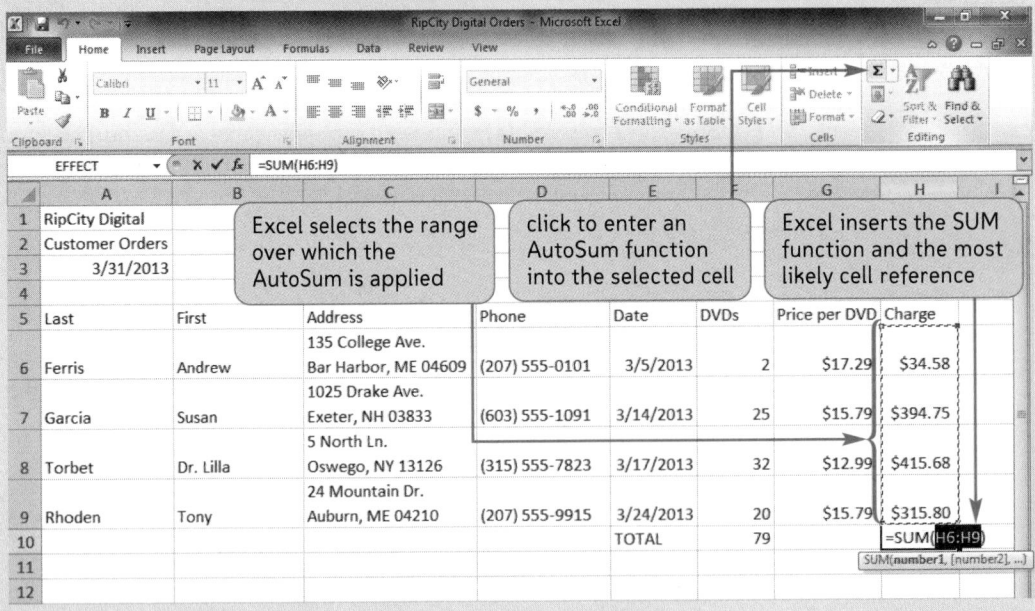

4. Verify that the range **H6:H9** appears in the SUM function and is highlighted with a dotted border. The dotted border shows what will be included in the SUM function.

5. Press the **Enter** key to accept the automatically generated formula. The total charge for all of Amanda's customers, shown in cell H10, is $1,160.81.

**PROSKILLS**

*Problem Solving: Writing Effective Formulas*

You can use formulas to quickly perform calculations and solve problems. First, identify the problem you need to solve. Then, gather the data needed to solve the problem. Finally, create accurate and effective formulas that use the data to answer or resolve the problem. Follow these guidelines:

- **Keep formulas simple.** Use functions in place of long, complex formulas whenever possible. For example, use the SUM function instead of entering a formula that adds individual cells, which makes it easier to confirm that the formula is making an accurate calculation as it provides answers needed to evaluate the problem.
- **Do not hide data values within formulas.** The worksheet displays formula results, not the actual formula. For example, to calculate a 5% interest rate on a currency value in cell A5, you could enter the formula =0.05*A5. However, this doesn't show how the value is calculated. A better approach places the value 0.05 in a cell accompanied by a descriptive label and uses the cell reference in the formula. If you place 0.05 in cell A6, the formula =A6*A5 would calculate the interest value. Other people can then easily see the interest rate as well as the resulting interest, ensuring that the formula is solving the right problem.
- **Break up formulas to show intermediate results.** When a worksheet contains complex computations, other people can more easily comprehend how the formula results are calculated when different parts of the formula are distinguished. For example, the formula =SUM(A1:A10)/SUM(B1:B10) calculates the ratio of two sums, but hides the two sum values. Instead, enter each SUM function in a separate cell, such as cells A11 and B11, and use the formula =A11/B11 to calculate the ratio. Other people can see both sums and the value of their ratio in the worksheet and better understand the final result, which makes it more likely that the best problem resolution will be selected.

Finding a solution to a problem requires accurate data and analysis. With workbooks, this means using formulas that are easy to understand, clearly show the data being used in the calculations, and demonstrate how the results are calculated. Only then can you be confident that you are choosing the best problem resolution.

# Working with Worksheets

You've seen that new workbooks are created with three initial worksheets labeled Sheet1, Sheet2, and Sheet3. If needed, you can add new worksheets to a workbook and remove unused sheets. You can also give worksheets more descriptive and meaningful names.

## Inserting or Deleting a Worksheet

When you insert a new worksheet in a workbook, the new sheet is named based on the number and names of the other sheets in the workbook. For example, if a workbook has four worksheets named Sheet1 through Sheet4, the next inserted worksheet is named Sheet5. You'll add a new, blank worksheet to the RipCity Digital Orders workbook.

**TIP**

To insert a new worksheet to the left of the active sheet, right-click a sheet tab, click Insert on the shortcut menu, select a sheet type, and then click the OK button.

**To insert a new worksheet:**

**1.** Locate the three sheet tabs in the lower-left corner of the worksheet window.

**2.** To the right of the Sheet3 sheet tab, click the **Insert Worksheet** tab ⌷. A new worksheet named Sheet4 appears at the end of the workbook and is active.

The workbook now includes two empty worksheets: Sheet3 and Sheet4. Because you don't plan to use these sheets, it's a good idea to remove them.

**To delete the Sheet3 and Sheet4 worksheets:**

▶ 1. Right-click the **Sheet3** sheet tab, and then click **Delete** on the shortcut menu. The Sheet3 worksheet is removed from the workbook.

▶ 2. If necessary, click the **Sheet4** sheet tab to make it the active sheet.

▶ 3. In the Cells group on the Home tab, click the **Delete button arrow**, and then click **Delete Sheet**. The Sheet4 worksheet is removed from the workbook.

## Renaming a Worksheet

The remaining worksheets, Sheet1 and Sheet2, do not have very descriptive names. You can rename them so that they better describe their contents. Keep in mind that sheet names cannot exceed 31 characters in length, including blank spaces. The width of the sheet tab adjusts to the length of the name you enter. You'll rename Sheet1 and Sheet2.

**To rename the two worksheets:**

▶ 1. Double-click the **Sheet2** sheet tab. The sheet name is selected in the sheet tab.

▶ 2. Type **Customer Orders** and then press the **Enter** key. The width of the sheet tab expands to match the longer sheet name.

▶ 3. Double-click the **Sheet1** sheet tab, type **Documentation**, and then press the **Enter** key. Both sheets are renamed.

## Moving and Copying a Worksheet

You can change the placement of the worksheets in a workbook. A good practice is to place the most important worksheets at the beginning of the workbook (the leftmost sheet tabs) and less important worksheets toward the end (the rightmost tabs). You'll move the Documentation sheet to the end of the workbook and then return it to the beginning.

**To move the Documentation sheet:**

▶ 1. If necessary, click the **Documentation** sheet tab to make that worksheet active.

▶ 2. Press and hold the mouse button so the pointer changes to ↳ and a small triangle appears in the upper-left corner of the tab.

▶ 3. Drag the pointer to the right of the Customer Orders sheet tab, and then release the mouse button. The Documentation worksheet is now the second sheet in the workbook.

▶ 4. Drag the **Documentation** worksheet back to be the first sheet in the workbook.

## Editing Worksheet Content

As you work, you might make mistakes that you want to correct or undo, or you might need to replace a value based on more current information. The price per DVD for Andrew Ferris's order should be $18.29, not $17.29 as entered in cell G6. You could simply clear the value in the cell and then type the correct value. However, sometimes you need to edit only a portion of an entry rather than change the entire contents of a cell, especially if the cell contains a large block of text or a complex formula. To edit the cell contents, you can work in **Edit mode**.

When you work in Edit mode, some of the keyboard shortcuts you've been using work differently because they apply only to the text within the selected cell. For example, the Home, End, Backspace, Delete, and arrow keys move the insertion point to different locations within the cell. The Home key moves the insertion point to the beginning of the cell's content. The End key moves the insertion point to the end of the cell's content. The left and right arrow keys move the insertion point backward and forward through the cell's content. The Backspace key deletes the character immediately to the left of the insertion point, and the Delete key deletes the character to the right of the insertion point. You'll change one digit of the value in cell G6 to correct the price per DVD.

### To edit the value in cell G6:

**TIP**

To change the active cell to Edit mode, press the F2 key or click in the formula bar. To cancel all changes made in Edit mode, press the Esc key or click the Cancel button in the formula bar.

1. Click the **Customer Orders** sheet tab to make it the active worksheet.

2. Double-click cell **G6**. The mode indicator on the status bar switches from Ready to Edit, indicating that you are in Edit mode.

3. Press the **End** key. The insertion point moves to the end of the cell.

4. Press the ← key three times. The insertion point moves to the right of the 7.

5. Press the **Backspace** key to delete the 7, and then type **8**. The value in cell G6 changes to 18.29. See Figure 1-25.

**Figure 1-25**    **Cell being edited in Edit mode**

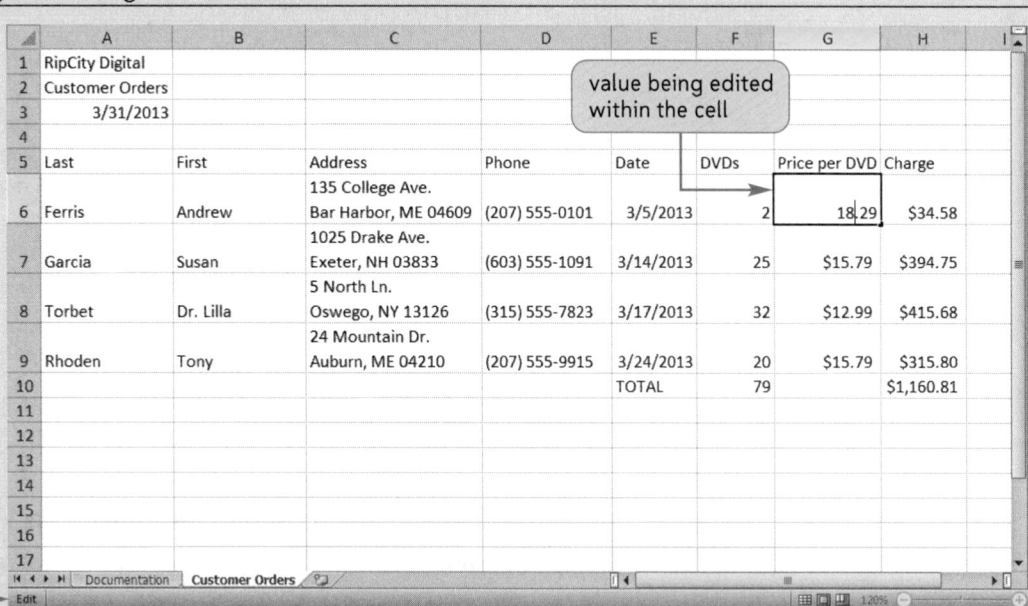

mode indicator shows that Excel is in Edit mode

6. Press the **Enter** key to accept the edit in cell G6. The value $18.29 appears in cell G6, the active cell is cell G7, and the mode indicator on the status bar changes from Edit to Ready to indicate that you are no longer in Edit mode.

## Undoing and Redoing an Action

As you revise a workbook, you might need to undo a previous action. Excel maintains a list of the actions you perform in a workbook during the current session, so you can undo most of these actions. You can reverse the most recent action or you can reverse more than one action. If you undo more than one action, all actions subsequent to the earliest action you select are also undone. You'll undo the edit to cell G6.

### To undo the edit to cell G6:

1. On the Quick Access Toolbar, click the **Undo** button ↻.

2. Verify that $17.29 appears again in cell G6, indicating that your last action—editing the value of this cell—has been undone.

If you find that you have gone too far in undoing previous actions, you can go forward in the action list and redo those actions. As with the Undo feature, you can redo more than one action at a time. You'll use Redo to restore the value of cell G6.

### To redo the edit to cell G6:

1. On the Quick Access Toolbar, click the **Redo** button ↺.

2. Verify that the value in cell G6 returns to $18.29.

## Using Find and Replace

Amanda wants you to replace all the street title abbreviations with their full names. Specifically, "Ave." should be "Avenue," "Ln." should be "Lane," and "Dr." should be "Drive." Although you could read through the worksheet to locate each occurrence, this can be time-consuming with larger workbooks. For greater speed and accuracy, you can use the Find command to locate a string of characters known as a **search string** and replace that text with a **replacement string** of new text characters.

You can limit the search to the current worksheet or search the entire workbook. You can specify whether to match the capitalization in the Find what box and whether the search text should match the entire cell contents or part of the cell contents. You can choose to review each occurrence of the search value and decide whether to replace it, or you can replace all occurrences at once.

You'll use the Find and Replace commands to replace each street title abbreviation.

### To find and replace the street title abbreviations:

1. In the Editing group on the Home tab, click the **Find & Select** button, and then click **Replace**. The Find and Replace dialog box opens.

2. Type **Ave.** in the Find what box, press the **Tab** key, and then type **Avenue** in the Replace with box.

3. Click the **Options** button. The dialog box expands to display additional Find and Replace options. See Figure 1-26.

**Figure 1-26**    **Find and Replace dialog box**

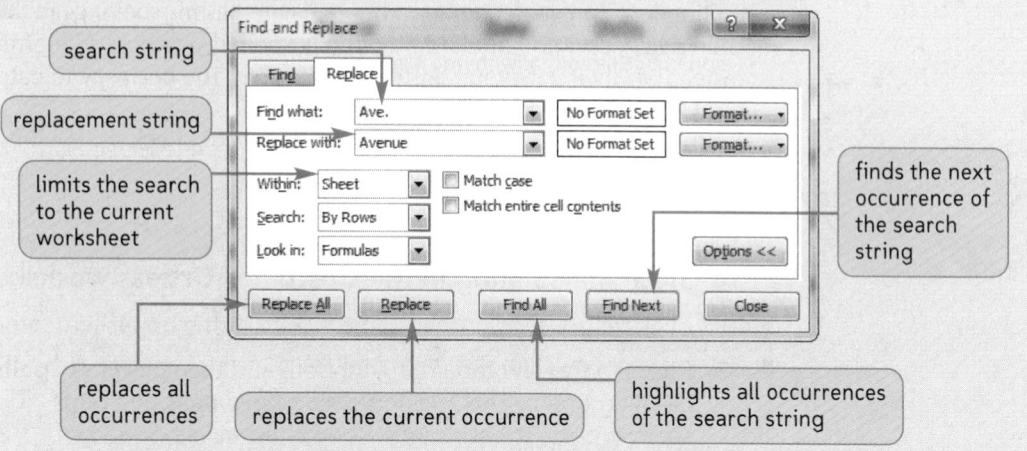

4. Verify that **Sheet** appears in the Within box to limit the find and replace to the current worksheet only.

5. Click the **Replace All** button. Excel finds and replaces the search string wherever it appears in the current worksheet. A dialog box opens, indicating that Excel has completed its search and made two replacements.

6. Click the **OK** button to close the dialog box.

7. Select the text in the Find what box, type **Ln.** as the new search string, press the **Tab** key, and then type **Lane** in the Replace with box. You want to replace all instances of this search string.

8. Click the **Replace All** button to make the replacement wherever it appears in the worksheet, and then click the **OK** button to close the dialog box that indicates Excel has completed its search and made one replacement.

9. Select the text in the Find what box, type **Dr.** as the new search string, press the **Tab** key, and then type **Drive** in the Replace with box. Because "Dr." is also the abbreviation for "Doctor," you must review each "Dr." abbreviation and replace only the ones within an address.

10. Click the **Find Next** button. The next occurrence of "Dr." in the worksheet occurs in cell B8 with the text, "Dr. Lilla."

11. Click the **Find Next** button to ignore this occurrence. The next occurrence of "Dr." is in the mailing address for Tony Rhoden.

12. Click the **Replace** button to replace this text. The only other occurrence of "Dr." in the worksheet—"Dr. Lilla"—is highlighted again. You've finished finding and replacing text in the worksheet.

13. Click the **Close** button to close the Find and Replace dialog box.

## Using the Spelling Checker

Another editing tool is the spelling checker. Although the spelling checker's dictionary includes a large number of words, as well as common first and last names and places, many words you use in workbooks might not be included. If the spelling checker finds a word that is not in its dictionary, the word appears in a dialog box along with a list of suggested replacements. You can replace the word with one from the list, or you can ignore the word and go to the next possible misspelling. You can also add words to the dictionary to prevent them from being flagged as misspellings in the future. Note that the spelling checker will not find a correctly spelled word used incorrectly, such as "there" instead of "their" or "your" instead of "you're." The best way to catch these types of errors is to proofread your worksheets.

Before giving the workbook to Amanda, you'll check the spelling in the Customer Orders worksheet.

### To check the spelling in the Customer Orders worksheet:

▶ 1. Click cell **A1** to start the spell check from the upper-left corner of the sheet.

▶ 2. Click the **Review** tab on the Ribbon, and then click the **Spelling** button in the Proofing group. The Spelling dialog box opens and flags "RipCity" as a possible spelling error. Excel suggests two alternatives. See Figure 1-27.

| Figure 1-27 | Spelling dialog box |
| --- | --- |

▶ 3. Click the **Ignore All** button. You ignored all the occurrences of this spelling because "RipCity" is the name of Amanda's company. The spelling checker flags "Torbet," a last name that is not in the program's dictionary.

▶ 4. Click the **Ignore All** button to ignore the spelling of this name. The next potential spelling error is the name "Lilla" in cell B8. The name should have been entered as "Lila," a first name that the spelling checker recognizes.

▶ 5. Click **Lila** in the Suggestions box, if necessary, and then click the **Change** button. The text is changed within the cell. The spelling checker is finished.

   **Trouble?** If the spelling checker finds another error, you might have another typing error in your worksheet. Use the spelling checker to find and correct any other errors in your workbook, and then continue with Step 6.

▶ 6. Click the **OK** button to close the Microsoft Excel dialog box.

▶ 7. Proofread the worksheet and correct any other spelling errors you find. You do not have to check the spelling in the Documentation worksheet at this time.

# Previewing and Printing a Workbook

Now that you have finished the final edit of the workbook, you are ready to print a hard copy of the customer orders list for Amanda. However, before you print the workbook, you should preview it to ensure that it will print correctly.

## Changing Worksheet Views

You can view a worksheet in three ways. **Normal view**, which you've been using throughout this tutorial, shows the contents of the worksheet. **Page Layout view** shows how the worksheet will appear when printed. **Page Break Preview** displays the location of the different page breaks within the worksheet. This is useful when a worksheet will span several printed pages and you need to control what content appears on each page.

You'll switch between these views to see how the Customer Orders worksheet will appear on printed pages.

### To switch the worksheet views:

1. Click the **Page Layout** button 🔲 on the status bar. The page layout of the worksheet appears in the program window. You want to see the rest of the data, which extends to a second page.

2. Use the Zoom slider to reduce the zoom level to **60%**. See Figure 1-28.

**Figure 1-28**    **Worksheet displayed in Page Layout view**

3. Click the **Page Break Preview** button 🔲 on the status bar. The view switches to Page Break Preview, which shows only those parts of the current worksheet that will print. A dotted blue border separates one page from another.

   **Trouble?** If the Welcome to Page Break Preview dialog box opens, this is the first time you've switched to Page Break Preview. Click the OK button to close the dialog box and continue with Step 4.

▶ **4.** Zoom the worksheet to **120%** so that you can more easily read the contents of the worksheet. See Figure 1-29.

**Figure 1-29** **Worksheet displayed in Page Break Preview**

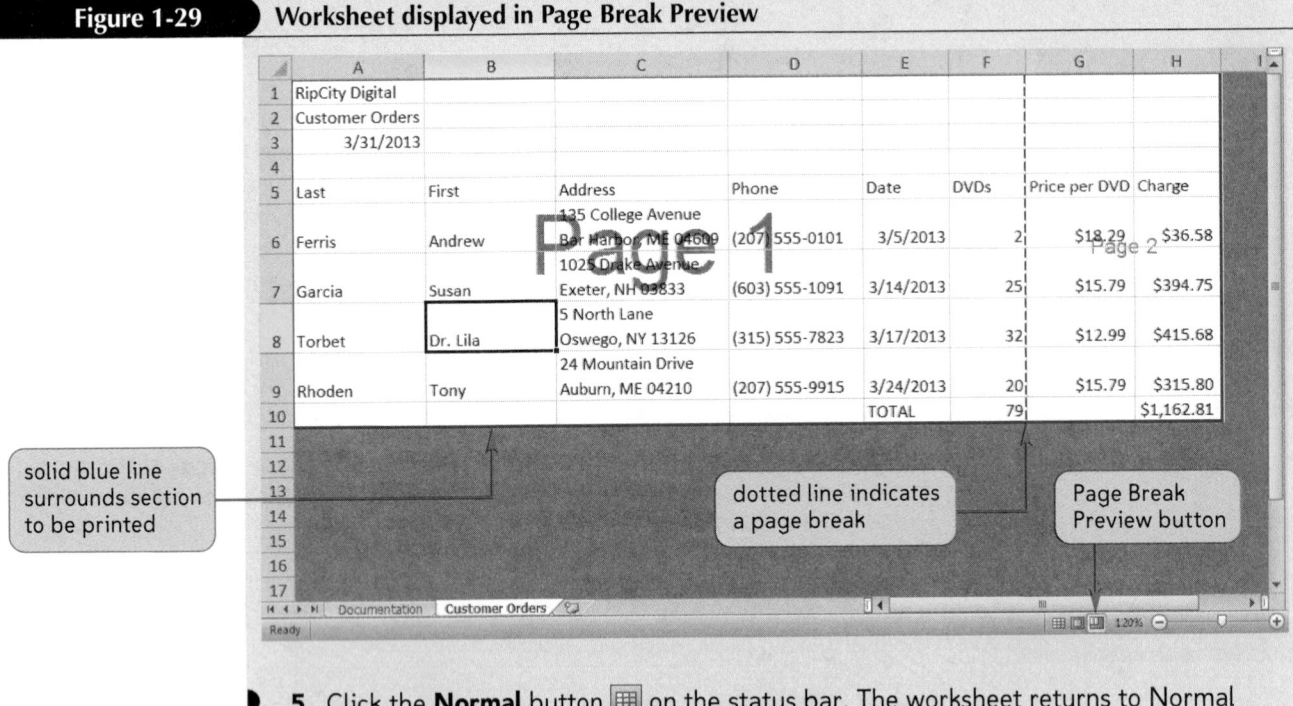

solid blue line surrounds section to be printed

dotted line indicates a page break

Page Break Preview button

▶ **5.** Click the **Normal** button ⊞ on the status bar. The worksheet returns to Normal view. A dotted black line indicates where the page break will occur.

## Working with Portrait and Landscape Orientation

As you saw in Page Layout view and Page Break Preview, the Customer Orders worksheet will print on two pages—columns A through F will print on one page and columns G and H will print on a second page. Amanda wants the entire worksheet printed on a single page. One way to accomplish this is to change the page orientation from portrait to landscape. In **portrait orientation**, the page is taller than it is wide. In **landscape orientation**, the page is wider than it is tall. By default, Excel displays pages in portrait orientation. In many cases, however, you will want to print the page in landscape orientation. Changing the page orientation affects only the active worksheet.

You'll change the orientation of the Customer Orders worksheet to landscape.

**To change the page orientation of the worksheet:**

▶ **1.** Click the **Page Layout** tab on the Ribbon.

▶ **2.** In the Page Setup group, click the **Orientation** button, and then click **Landscape**. The orientation switches to landscape, and the worksheet contents fit on one page.

▶ **3.** Click the **Page Layout** button ▢ on the status bar, and then verify that all the worksheet contents fit on one page.

▶ **4.** Click the **Documentation** sheet tab, and then click the **Page Layout** button ▢. The Documentation sheet remains in portrait orientation.

▶ **5.** Verify that the entire contents of the Documentation worksheet fit on one page.

## Printing the Workbook

You can print the contents of a workbook by using the Print tab in Backstage view. The Print tab provides options for choosing what to print and how to print. For example, you can specify the number of copies to print, which printer to use, and what to print. You can choose to print only the selected cells, the active sheets, or all worksheets in the workbook that contain data. The printout will include only the data in the worksheet. The other elements in the worksheet, such as the row and column headings and the gridlines around the worksheet cells, will not print by default. You also see a preview of the workbook so you can see exactly how printed pages will look with the settings you've chosen before you print. A good practice is to always review the print preview before printing to ensure that the printout looks exactly as you intended and avoid unnecessary reprinting.

You'll preview and print the RipCity Digital Orders workbook now.

### To preview and print the workbook:

1. Click the File tab on the Ribbon to display Backstage view.

2. Click the **Print** tab in the navigation bar to display the print options and preview of the first sheet in the workbook (the Documentation worksheet). See Figure 1-30.

**Figure 1-30**    **Print tab in Backstage view**

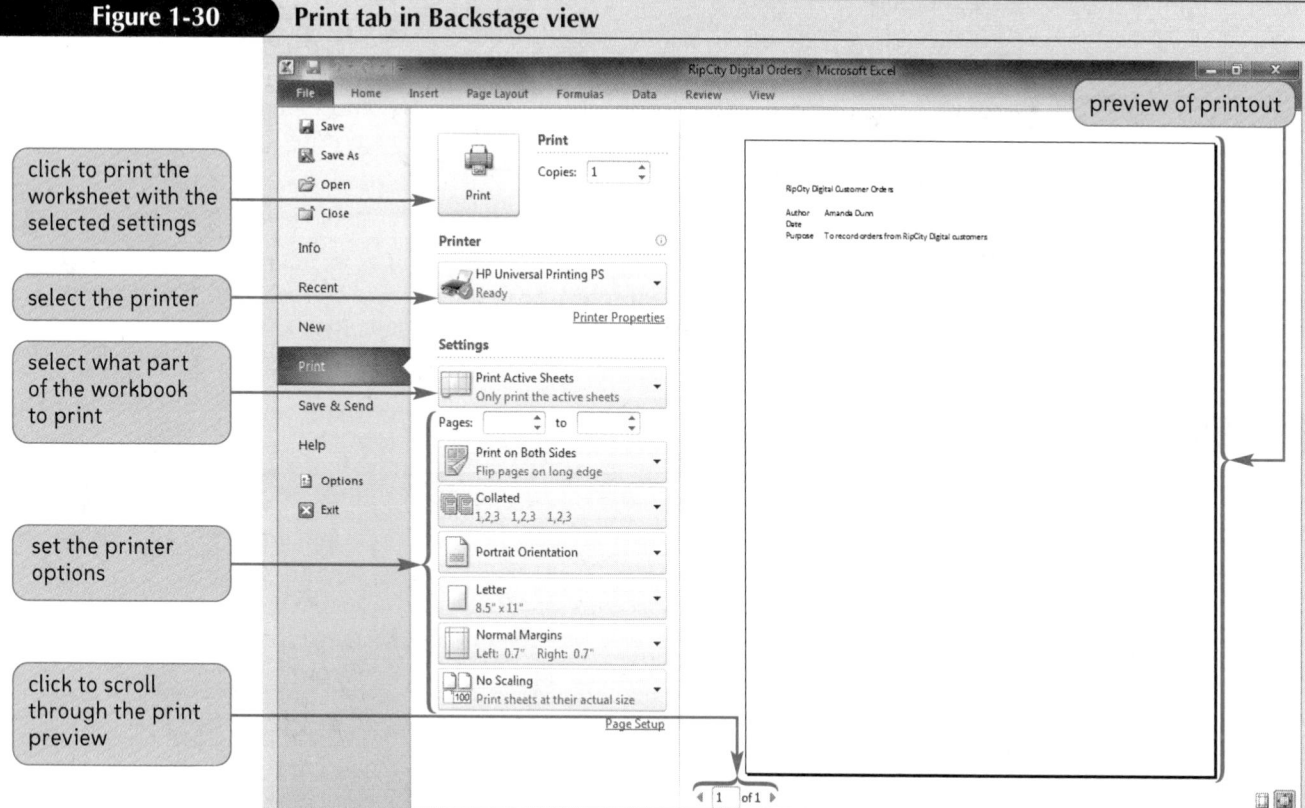

click to print the worksheet with the selected settings

select the printer

select what part of the workbook to print

set the printer options

click to scroll through the print preview

preview of printout

3. Click the **Printer** button, and then click the printer to which you want to print if it is not already selected.

4. In the Settings group, click the top button, and then click **Print Entire Workbook**. This will print both the Documentation worksheet and the Customer Orders worksheet.

5. Below the preview, click the **Next Page** button ▶. The first page of the print job contains the contents of the Documentation worksheet in portrait orientation, and the second page contains the Customer Orders worksheet in landscape orientation.

6. Click the **Print** button. The worksheet prints.

## Viewing and Printing Worksheet Formulas

The printout of the Customer Orders worksheet displays only the worksheet values and none of the formulas. Most of the time, you will be interested in only the final results of the worksheet, not the formulas used to calculate those results. However, in some cases, you might want to view the formulas used to develop the workbook. This is particularly useful when you encounter unexpected results and you want to examine the underlying formulas, or you want to discuss your formulas with a colleague. You can view the formulas in a workbook by switching to **formula view**, a view of the worksheet contents that displays formulas instead of the resulting values.

You'll look at the Customer Orders worksheet in formula view now.

### To view the formulas in the Customer Orders worksheet:

**TIP**

To toggle in and out of formula view, press the Ctrl+` keys. The ` grave accent symbol is usually located above the Tab key on your keyboard.

1. Click the **Customer Orders** sheet tab, if necessary, and then click the **Normal** button ▦ on the status bar. The Customer Orders worksheet is active and displayed in Normal view.

2. Press the **Ctrl+`** keys. The worksheet changes to formula view.

3. Scroll the worksheet to the right to view the formulas in columns F and H. The column widths are wider to display the entire formula in each cell. As long as you don't resize the column widths while in formula view, they remain unchanged in other views. See Figure 1-31.

**Figure 1-31** Worksheet in formula view

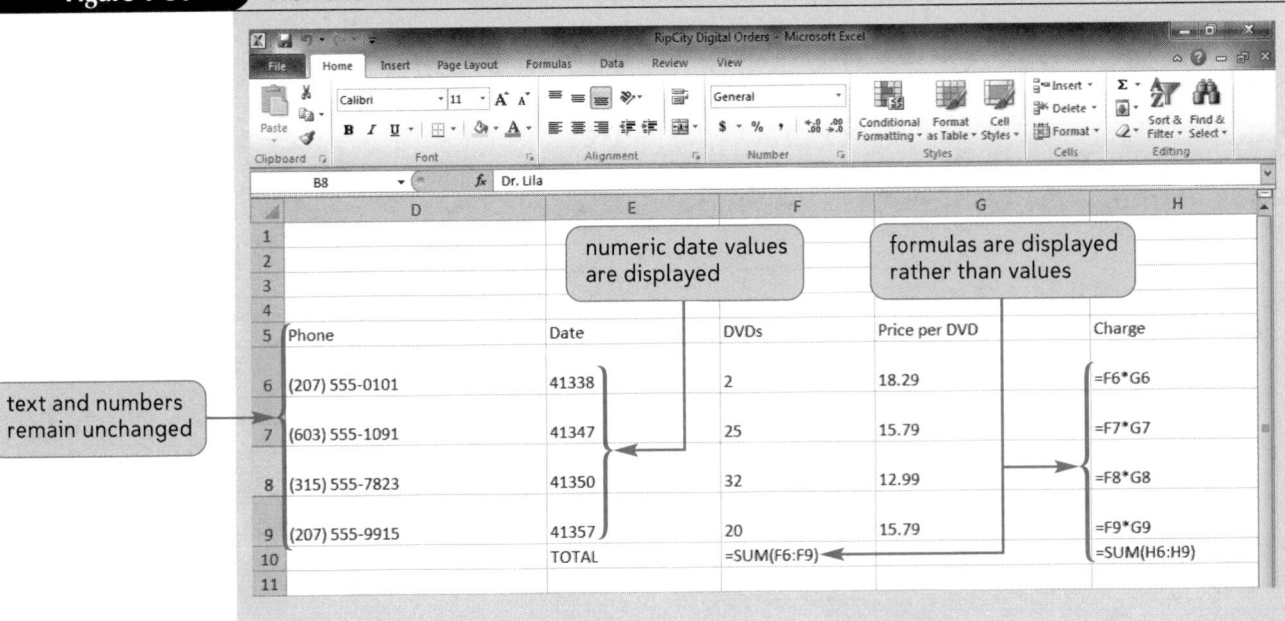

Amanda wants a printout of the formula view. The Customer Orders worksheet will not fit on one page because of the expanded column widths. You can scale the worksheet to force the contents to fit on a single page. **Scaling** a printout reduces the width and the height of the printout to fit the number of pages you specify by shrinking the text size as needed. You can also scale a printout proportionally to a percentage of its actual size. You'll scale the Customer Orders worksheet to a width and height of one page.

### To scale the worksheet formulas to print on one page:

▶ 1. Click the **Page Layout** tab on the Ribbon.

▶ 2. In the Scale to Fit group, click the **Width arrow**, and then click **1 page**.

▶ 3. In the Scale to Fit group, click the **Height arrow**, and then click **1 page**. You'll verify that the worksheet formula view fits on a single page.

▶ 4. Click the **Page Layout** button on the status bar, and then zoom the worksheet to **50%**. The formula view of the worksheet fits on one page. See Figure 1-32.

| Figure 1-32 | Printout scaled to one page |

*printout width and height set to a single page*

*text reduced to fit the worksheet on one page*

*zoom set to 50%*

▶ 5. Click the **File** tab on the Ribbon to display Backstage view, and then click the **Print** tab in the navigation bar to view the print options.

▶ 6. In the Settings group, click the top button, and then click **Print Active Sheets** to print only the Customer Orders worksheet.

▶ 7. Click the **Print** button. The active sheet, the Customer Orders worksheet, prints.

At this point, you've completed your work for Amanda. Before closing the workbook, you'll change the view of the workbook contents back to Normal view.

**To save and close the workbook:**

▶ **1.** Press the **Ctrl+`** keys to switch the worksheet out of formula view.

▶ **2.** Click the **Normal** button ⊞ on the status bar to return the worksheet to Normal view.

▶ **3.** Save your changes to the workbook, and then close it.

Amanda is pleased with the workbook you created for her. All the customers and orders appear on one worksheet, and she can easily add new customers and orders. The formulas quickly update the calculations that show her income from burning DVDs.

**REVIEW**

*Session 1.2 Quick Check*

1. Describe the two types of ranges in Excel.
2. What is the range reference for cells A3 through G5 and J3 through M5?
3. What formula would you enter to add the values in cells B4, B5, and B6? What function would you enter to achieve the same result?
4. How do you rename a worksheet?
5. Describe four ways of viewing the content of an Excel workbook.
6. How are page breaks indicated in Page Break Preview?
7. How do you display the formulas used in a worksheet?
8. Why would you scale a worksheet?

*Practice the skills you learned in the tutorial using the same case scenario.*

**PRACTICE**

## Review Assignments

**There are no Data Files needed for the Review Assignments.**

Amanda has another set of orders for you to enter on the Customer Orders worksheet. In addition to calculating the charge for creating the DVDs, Amanda also wants to include the cost of shipping in the total charged to each customer. Complete the following:

1. Open a blank workbook, and then save the workbook as **Order Report** in the Excel1\Review folder.

2. Rename the Sheet1 worksheet as **Documentation**, and then enter the following data into the specified cells:

   Cell A1: **RipCity Digital**

   Cell A3: **Author**          Cell B3: your name

   Cell A4: **Date**            Cell B4: the current date

   Cell A5: **Purpose**         Cell B5: **To track customer orders for RipCity Digital**

3. Rename the Sheet2 worksheet as **Customer Orders**.

4. Delete the Sheet3 worksheet.

5. On the Customer Orders worksheet, enter the following data into the specified cells:

   Cell A1: **RipCity Digital**

   Cell A3: **Customer Orders Report**

   Cell A4: **March 27 to April 17, 2013**

6. In cells A5 through H10, enter the column titles and data from Figure 1-33. The address text in column D should be set on two lines within each cell.

**Figure 1-33    New customer order data**

| Date | Last | First | Address | Phone | DVDs | Price per DVD | Shipping Charge |
|------|------|-------|---------|-------|------|---------------|-----------------|
| 3/27/2013 | Fleming | Doris | 25 Lee St. Bedford, VA 24523 | (540) 555-5681 | 7 | $18.29 | $7.49 |
| 4/4/2013 | Ortiz | Thomas | 28 Ridge Ln. Newfane, VT 05345 | (802) 555-7710 | 13 | $16.55 | $9.89 |
| 4/8/2013 | Dexter | Kay | 150 Main St. Greenbelt, MD 20770 | (301) 555-8823 | 25 | $15.79 | $7.23 |
| 4/9/2013 | Sisk | Norman | 250 East Maple Ln. Cranston, RI 02910 | (401) 555-3350 | 15 | $16.55 | $10.55 |
| 4/17/2013 | Romano | June | 207 Jackston Ave. Westport, IN 47283 | (812) 555-2681 | 22 | $15.79 | $13.95 |

7. Set the width of column A to 10 characters, columns B and C to 12 characters, column D to 20 characters, and columns E, G, and H to 16 characters.

8. Autofit all of the rows in the worksheet to the cell contents.

9. In cell I5, enter **Total Charge**. In cell I6, insert a formula that calculates the total charge for the first customer (the number of DVDs multiplied by the price per DVD and then added to the shipping charge). Increase the width of column I to 11 characters.

10. Copy the formula in cell I6 and paste it into the range I7:I10.

11. In cell E11, enter **Total DVDs**. In cell F11, use the SUM function to calculate the total number of DVDs created for all customers. In cell I11, use the AutoSum feature to insert the SUM function to calculate the total charges for all of the customer orders.

12. Use Edit mode to make the following corrections:

   a. In cell D6, change the street address from "25 Lee St." to **2500 Lee St.**

   b. In cell F9, change the number of DVDs from "15" to **17**.

   c. In cell H8, change the shipping charge from "$7.23" to **$8.23**.

13. Use the Find and Replace commands to replace all occurrences of "St." with **Street**, "Ln." with **Lane**, and "Ave." with **Avenue**.

14. Change the page layout of the Customer Orders worksheet to print in landscape orientation on a single page.

15. Preview and print the contents of the entire workbook.

16. Change the Customer Orders worksheet to formula view, landscape orientation, and scaled to fit on a single page. Preview and print the Customer Orders worksheet.

17. Return the view of the Customer Orders worksheet to Normal view, save your changes to the Order Report workbook, and then save the current workbook as **Revised Report** in the Excel1\Review folder. (*Hint*: Use the Save As command in Backstage view to save the existing workbook with a new name.)

18. Remove Kay Dexter's order from the Customer Orders worksheet.

19. Add the following order directly after the order placed by June Romano: date **4/22/2013**; name **Patrick Crawford**; address **200 Valley View Road, Rome, GA 30161**; phone **(706) 555-0998**; DVDs **14**; price per DVD **$16.55**; shipping charge **$12.45**.

20. Use Edit mode to change the ending date of the report in cell A4 from "April 17" to **April 22**.

21. Save the workbook, preview and print the contents and formulas of the revised Customer Orders worksheet, close the workbook, and then submit the finished workbooks and printouts to your instructor.

APPLY

## Case Problem 1

**Data File needed for this Case Problem: Altac.xlsx**

*Altac Bicycles*    Deborah York is a financial consultant for Altac Bicycles, an online seller of bicycles and bicycle equipment based in Silver City, New Mexico. She has entered some financial information in an Excel workbook for an income statement she is preparing for the company. You will enter the remaining data and formulas. Complete the following:

1. Open the **Altac** workbook located in the Excel1\Case1 folder, and then save the workbook as **Altac Bicycles** in the same folder.

2. Insert three new rows at the top of the Sheet1 worksheet, and then enter the following text on two lines within cell A1:
   **Altac Bicycles**
   **Income Statement***

3. In cell A2, enter **For the Years Ended December 31, 2011 through December 31, 2013**.

4. In the range C6:E7, enter the following net sales and cost of sales figures:

| | 2013 | 2012 | 2011 |
|---|---|---|---|
| Net Sales | 13,520 | 10,981 | 9,034 |
| Cost of Sales | 4,140 | 3,960 | 3,011 |

5. In the range C11:E14, enter the following expense figures (expand the column widths as necessary to show the text and data values):

|  | 2013 | 2012 | 2011 |
|---|---|---|---|
| Salaries and Wages | 1,632 | 1,481 | 1,392 |
| Sales and Marketing | 2,631 | 2,112 | 1,840 |
| Administrative | 521 | 410 | 375 |
| Research and Development | 501 | 404 | 281 |

6. In the nonadjacent range C18:E18;C20:E20;C24:E24, enter the following values for Other Income, Income Taxes, and Shares, pressing the Enter or Tab key to navigate from cell to cell in the selected range:

|  | 2013 | 2012 | 2011 |
|---|---|---|---|
| Other Income | 341 | 302 | 239 |
| Income Taxes | 1,225 | 1,008 | 821 |
| Shares | 3,621 | 3,001 | 2,844 |

7. In the range C8:E8, enter a formula to calculate the gross margin for each year, where the gross margin is equal to the net sales minus the cost of sales.

8. In the range C15:E15, enter the SUM function to calculate the total operating expenses for each year, where the total operating expenses equal the sum of the four expense categories.

9. In the range C17:E17, enter a formula to calculate the operating income for each year, where operating income is equal to the gross margin minus the total operating expenses.

10. In the range C19:E19, enter a formula to calculate the pretax income for each year, where pretax income is equal to the operating income plus other income.

11. In the range C22:E22, enter a formula to calculate the company's net income for each year, where net income is equal to the pretax income minus income taxes.

12. In the range C25:E25, enter a formula to calculate the earnings per share for each year, where earnings per share is equal to the net income divided by the number of shares.

13. Use the spelling checker to correct and replace any spelling errors in the worksheet. Ignore the spelling of "Altac."

14. In cell A18, use Edit mode to capitalize the word "income."

15. Increase the width of column A to 18 characters and increase the width of column B to 25 characters. Autofit the height of row 1.

16. Rename the Sheet1 worksheet as **Income Statement**, rename the Sheet2 worksheet as **Documentation** and move it to the beginning of the workbook, and then delete the Sheet3 worksheet.

17. In the Documentation worksheet, enter the following text and values:

Cell A1: **Altac Bicycles**

Cell A3: **Author**       Cell B3: your name

Cell A4: **Date**       Cell B4: the current date

Cell A5: **Purpose**       Cell B5: **Income statement for Altac Bicycles for 2011 through 2013**

18. Save the workbook, preview the workbook and make sure each worksheet in portrait orientation fits on one page in the printout, and then print the entire workbook. Close the workbook, and then submit the finished workbook and printouts to your instructor.

Use the skills
you learned
to complete a
balance sheet for
a food retailer.

**APPLY**

## Case Problem 2

**Data File needed for this Case Problem: Halley.xlsx**

*Halley Foods*   Michael Li is working on the annual financial report for Halley Foods of Norman, Oklahoma. One part of the financial report will be the company's balance sheet for the previous three years. Michael has entered some of the labels for the balance sheet. You will finish the job by entering the actual values and formulas. Complete the following:

1. Open the **Halley** workbook located in the Excel1\Case2 folder, and then save the workbook as **Halley Foods** in the same folder.

2. Rename the Sheet1 worksheet as **Balance Sheet**, and then delete the Sheet2 and Sheet3 worksheets.

3. Insert two new rows at the top of the worksheet, and then enter the following text on four lines within cell A1:

   **Halley Foods**
   **Balance Sheet**
   **As of December 31**
   **For the years 2011 through 2013**

4. Change the width of column A to 30 characters, the width of column B to 20 characters, and the width of column C to 26 characters. Autofit the height of row 1.

5. Enter the asset and liability values shown in Figure 1-34 into the corresponding cells in the Balance Sheet worksheet for each of the last three years.

| Figure 1-34 | Halley Foods assets and liabilities | | | |
|---|---|---|---|---|
| | | **2013** | **2012** | **2011** |
| Current Assets | Cash and equivalents | 806 | 589 | 423 |
| | Short-term investments | 1,194 | 1,029 | 738 |
| | Accounts receivable | 1,283 | 1,151 | 847 |
| | Net inventories | 683 | 563 | 463 |
| | Deferred taxes | 510 | 366 | 332 |
| | Other current assets | 162 | 153 | 128 |
| Other Assets | Investments | 7,077 | 5,811 | 4,330 |
| | Restricted investments | 910 | 797 | 681 |
| | Property and equipment | 779 | 696 | 420 |
| | Other assets | 1,178 | 484 | 485 |
| Current Liabilities | Accounts payable | 350 | 293 | 192 |
| | Income taxes payable | 608 | 442 | 352 |
| | Accrued payroll | 661 | 564 | 389 |
| | Other accrued liabilities | 1,397 | 1,250 | 775 |
| Minority Interest | | 44 | 43 | 36 |
| Shareholders' Equity | Preferred and common stock | 5,557 | 4837 | 3,515 |
| | Retained earnings | 5,666 | 4,007 | 3,401 |
| | Other comprehensive income | 299 | 203 | 187 |

6. Use AutoSum to calculate the total current assets, other assets, current liabilities, and shareholders' equity in the ranges D11:F11, D17:F17, D25:F25, and D33:F33, respectively, for each of the previous three years.

7. Insert a formula in the range D19:F19 to calculate the total assets (current assets plus other assets) for each year.

8. Insert a formula in the range D36:F36 to calculate the value of the total current liabilities plus the minority interest plus the total shareholders' equity for each year.

9. Use the spelling checker to correct any spelling mistakes in the Balance Sheet worksheet, and then proofread the worksheet.

10. Change the zoom level of the Balance Sheet worksheet to 70% in Normal view to view the entire contents of the sheet in the workbook window.

11. View the Balance Sheet worksheet in Page Layout view zoomed to 80%, and then scale the height and width of the worksheet to fit on one page.

12. Insert a new worksheet named **Documentation** at the beginning of the workbook.

13. In the Documentation worksheet, enter the following data:

    Cell A1: **Halley Foods**

    Cell A3: **Author**        Cell B3: your name

    Cell A4: **Date**          Cell B4: the current date

    Cell A5: **Purpose**       Cell B5: **Balance Sheet for Halley Foods for 2011 through 2013**

14. Save, preview, and then print the entire Halley Foods workbook.

15. Print the formula view of the Balance Sheet worksheet on two pages in landscape orientation. Return the Balance Sheet worksheet to Page Layout view when you're finished.

16. Save and close the workbook, and then submit the finished workbook and printouts to your instructor.

---

*Explore using AutoSum to calculate production statistics.*

**CHALLENGE**

## Case Problem 3

Data File needed for this Case Problem: Global.xlsx

***Global Site GPS***   Kevin Hodge is a production assistant at Global Site GPS, a leading manufacturer of GPS devices located in Crestwood, Missouri. One of Kevin's jobs is to monitor output at the company's five regional plants. He wants to create an Excel workbook that reports the monthly production at the five sites, including the monthly average, minimum and maximum production, and total production for the previous year. You will create the workbook that reports these statistics. Complete the following:

1. Open the **Global** workbook located in the Excel1\Case3 folder, and then save the workbook as **Global Site** in the same folder.

2. Rename the Sheet1 worksheet as **Production History**, and then insert 12 new rows at the top of the worksheet.

3. Increase the width of column A to 23 characters and the width of columns B through F to 14 characters.

4. In the range B7:F7, enter the titles **Plant1**, **Plant2**, **Plant3**, **Plant4**, and **Plant5**, respectively.

5. In the range A8:A11, enter **Total Units Produced**, **Average per Month**, **Maximum**, and **Minimum**, respectively.

✦ EXPLORE   6. Select the range B26:F26, use AutoSum to calculate the sum of the production values for each of the five plants, and then drag and drop the selected cells to the range B8:F8.

✦ EXPLORE   7. Select the range B26:F26, use AutoSum to calculate the average of the production values for each of the five plants, and then drag and drop the selected cells to the range B9:F9.

◈ EXPLORE

8. Repeat Step 7 to calculate the maximum values for each of the five plants and move those calculated values to the range B10:F10, and then repeat to calculate the minimum production values and drag and drop those calculated values to the range B11:F11.

9. In the Production History worksheet, enter the following data:

   Cell A1: **Global Site GPS**

   Cell A2: **Production Report**

   Cell A3: **Model**          Cell B3: **MapTracker 201**

   Cell A4: **Year**          Cell B4: **2013**

   Cell A5: **Total Units Produced**

10. In cell B5, use the SUM function to add the values in the range B8:F8.

11. Insert a new worksheet named **Plant Directory**, and then move it to be the first worksheet in the workbook.

12. In cells A1 and A2, enter **Global Site GPS** and **Plant Directory**, respectively, and then enter the text shown in Figure 1-35 in the range A4:D9, making sure that the address is entered on two lines within the cell.

**Figure 1-35**  Plant directory data

| Plant | Plant Manager | Address | Phone |
|-------|---------------|---------|-------|
| 1 | Karen Brookers | 300 Commerce Avenue Crestwood, MO 63126 | (314) 555-3881 |
| 2 | Daniel Gomez | 15 North Main Street Edison, NJ 08837 | (732) 555-0012 |
| 3 | Jody Hetrick | 3572 Howard Lane Weston, FL 33326 | (954) 555-4817 |
| 4 | Yong Jo | 900 South Street Kirkland, WA 98033 | (425) 555-8775 |
| 5 | Sandy Nisbett | 3771 Water Street Helena, MT 59623 | (406) 555-4114 |

13. Set the width of column B to 15 characters, the width of column C to 30 characters, and the width of column D to 16 characters. Autofit the height of each row to its content.

14. Insert a new worksheet named **Documentation**, move it to be the first worksheet in the workbook, and then enter the following data:

   Cell A1: **Global Site GPS**

   Cell A3: **Author**          Cell B3: your name

   Cell A4: **Date**          Cell B4: the current date

   Cell A5: **Purpose**          Cell B5: **Production report for Global Site GPS**

15. Switch the Production History worksheet to Page Layout view, change the orientation to landscape, and then verify that the worksheet fits on a single page.

16. Save your workbook, preview and print the workbook, close the workbook, and then submit the finished workbook and printouts to your instructor.

*Create an Excel workbook to record service calls for a lawn service agency.*

**CREATE**

## Case Problem 4

**There are no Data Files needed for this Case Problem.**

*Green Lawns*   Green Lawns provides yard service and maintenance for homes in and around Mount Vernon, Ohio. Gary Taylor manages the accounts for Green Lawns and wants to use Excel to record weekly service calls made by the company. Gary provides you with the list of service calls made in the first week of August. You will use this data to create the workbook for Gary. Complete the following:

1. Open a blank workbook, and then save it as **Green Lawns** in the Excel1\Case4 folder included with your Data Files.

2. Rename the Sheet1 worksheet as **Documentation**, and then enter information documenting the workbook. Include the name of the company, your name, the current date, and a brief description of the purpose of the workbook. The layout and appearance of the worksheet are up to you.

3. In the Sheet2 worksheet, enter the service calls shown in Figure 1-36, and then enter appropriate formulas to calculate the service charge for each customer. Green Lawns charges each customer a base fee plus a working fee that is equal to the hourly rate multiplied by the number of hours worked. Also, enter a formula to calculate the total charges for all customer calls. The layout and appearance of the page are up to you.

**Figure 1-36**   **August service calls (week 1)**

| Customer | Address | Phone | Last Service | Hours | Base Fee | Hourly Rate |
|---|---|---|---|---|---|---|
| David Lane | 391 Country Drive Mount Vernon, OH 43050 | (740) 555-4439 | 8/2/2013 | 3 | $35 | $17.50 |
| Robert Gomez | 151 Apple Lane Mount Vernon, OH 43051 | (740) 555-0988 | 8/2/2013 | 3.5 | $35 | $17.50 |
| Sandra Lee | 112 Main Street Mount Vernon, OH 43050 | (740) 555-3773 | 8/3/2013 | 1.5 | $20 | $14.50 |
| Gregory Sands | 305 Country Drive Mount Vernon, OH 43050 | (740) 555-4189 | 8/3/2013 | 5 | $35 | $21.50 |
| Betty Oaks | 205 Second Street Mount Vernon, OH 43049 | (740) 555-0088 | 8/3/2013 | 1.5 | $20 | $14.50 |

4. Rename the Sheet2 worksheet as **Service Calls**, and then delete any unused sheets from the workbook.

5. Check the spelling in the workbook, correcting any spelling errors, and then proofread the workbook.

6. Save the workbook, preview the worksheets to ensure that each fits onto a single page, and then print the entire workbook. Close the workbook, and then submit the finished workbook and printouts to your instructor.

**ENDING FILES**

Excel1 → Tutorial

RipCity Digital Orders.xlsx

Review

Order Report.xlsx
Revised Report.xlsx

Case1

Altac Bicyles.xlsx

Case2

Halley Foods.xlsx

Case3

Global Site.xlsx

Case4

Green Lawns.xlsx

# Formatting a Workbook

*Designing a Financial Report*

## Case | *ExerComp Exercise Equipment*

ExerComp, based in Mason, Ohio, manufactures electronic and computer components for fitness machines and sporting goods. At the upcoming annual sales meeting, sales managers will present reports that detail the sales history of different ExerComp products. Sales manager Tom Uhen will report on the recent sales history of the X310 heart rate monitor.

Tom has already created a workbook and entered the sales figures for the past two years. He wants you to enter formulas to calculate total sales and increases in sales. He also wants you to make the data more readable and informative. To do this, you will work with formatting tools to modify the appearance of the data in each cell, the cell itself, and the entire worksheet. Because much of Tom's data has been stored in tables, you will also use some special formatting tools designed for tables.

## OBJECTIVES

**Session 2.1**
- Format text, numbers, and dates
- Change fonts and font colors
- Add fill colors and background images
- Create formulas to add, subtract, and divide values
- Apply number formats
- Align, indent, and rotate cell contents
- Merge a range into a single cell
- Copy and paste formats

**Session 2.2**
- Apply built-in cell styles
- Change the theme of a workbook
- Create formulas to add and subtract values
- Apply a built-in table style and select table style options
- Highlight cells with conditional formats
- Hide worksheet rows
- Define the print area, insert page breaks, and add print titles
- Create headers and footers
- Select page margins

## STARTING DATA FILES

| Excel2 → | Tutorial | Review | Case1 | Case2 | Case3 | Case4 |
|---|---|---|---|---|---|---|
| | Background.jpg<br>ExerComp.xlsx | Paper.jpg<br>X410.xlsx | Frosti.xlsx | GrillRite.xlsx | Wind.xlsx | Life.xlsx |

# SESSION 2.1 VISUAL OVERVIEW

The **Format Painter** copies and pastes formatting from one cell or range to another without duplicating any data.

You can format a text string within a cell in Edit mode.

The appearance of text is determined by its **typeface**, which is the specific design of a set of characters, including letters, numbers, punctuation marks, and symbols.

Every font can be formatted with a font style such as *italic*, **bold**, or ***bold italic*** and special effects such as underline, ~~strikethrough~~, and color.

You can rotate content in the cell.

The Comma style adds a thousands separator and two decimal places to the right of the decimal point, and lines up values by their decimal points. You can change how many decimal places are displayed.

A **font** is a set of characters that employ the same typeface, such as Arial, Times New Roman, and Courier.

The Accounting style lines up currency values by their currency symbol and decimal point; negative numbers are enclosed in parentheses.

The Alignment group has buttons for setting the horizontal and vertical alignment, the orientation, indents, and text wrapping of text in a cell, as well as merging cells.

You can **merge**, or combine, several cells into one cell. This content is merged and centered across the range A4:F4.

You can set the **font size** to increase or decrease the size of the text. Font sizes are measured in **points**, where one point is approximately 1/72 of an inch.

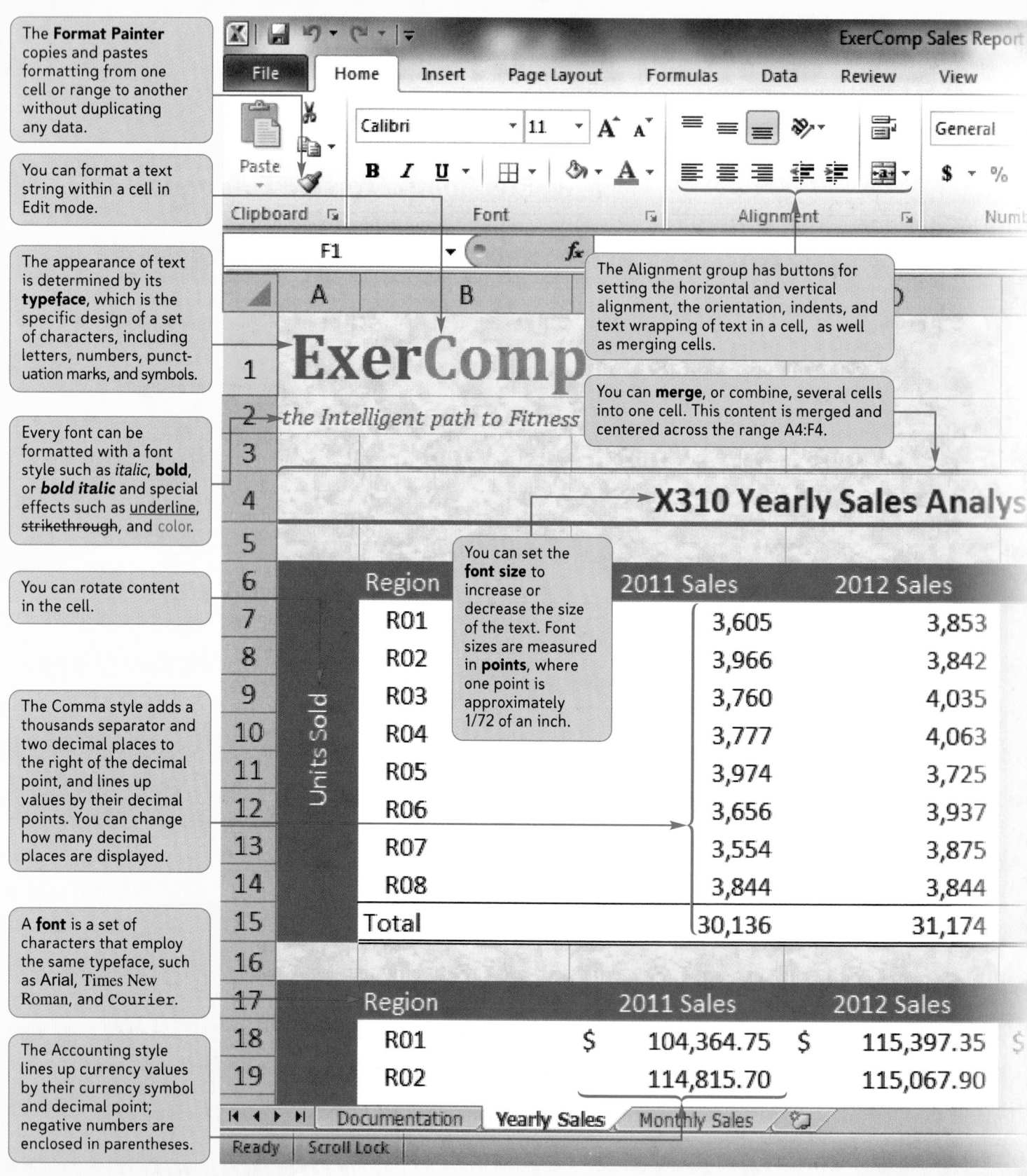

| Region | 2011 Sales | 2012 Sales |
|---|---|---|
| R01 | 3,605 | 3,853 |
| R02 | 3,966 | 3,842 |
| R03 | 3,760 | 4,035 |
| R04 | 3,777 | 4,063 |
| R05 | 3,974 | 3,725 |
| R06 | 3,656 | 3,937 |
| R07 | 3,554 | 3,875 |
| R08 | 3,844 | 3,844 |
| Total | 30,136 | 31,174 |

**X310 Yearly Sales Analys**

Units Sold

| Region | 2011 Sales | 2012 Sales |
|---|---|---|
| R01 | $ 104,364.75 | $ 115,397.35 |
| R02 | 114,815.70 | 115,067.90 |

# WORKSHEET FORMATTING

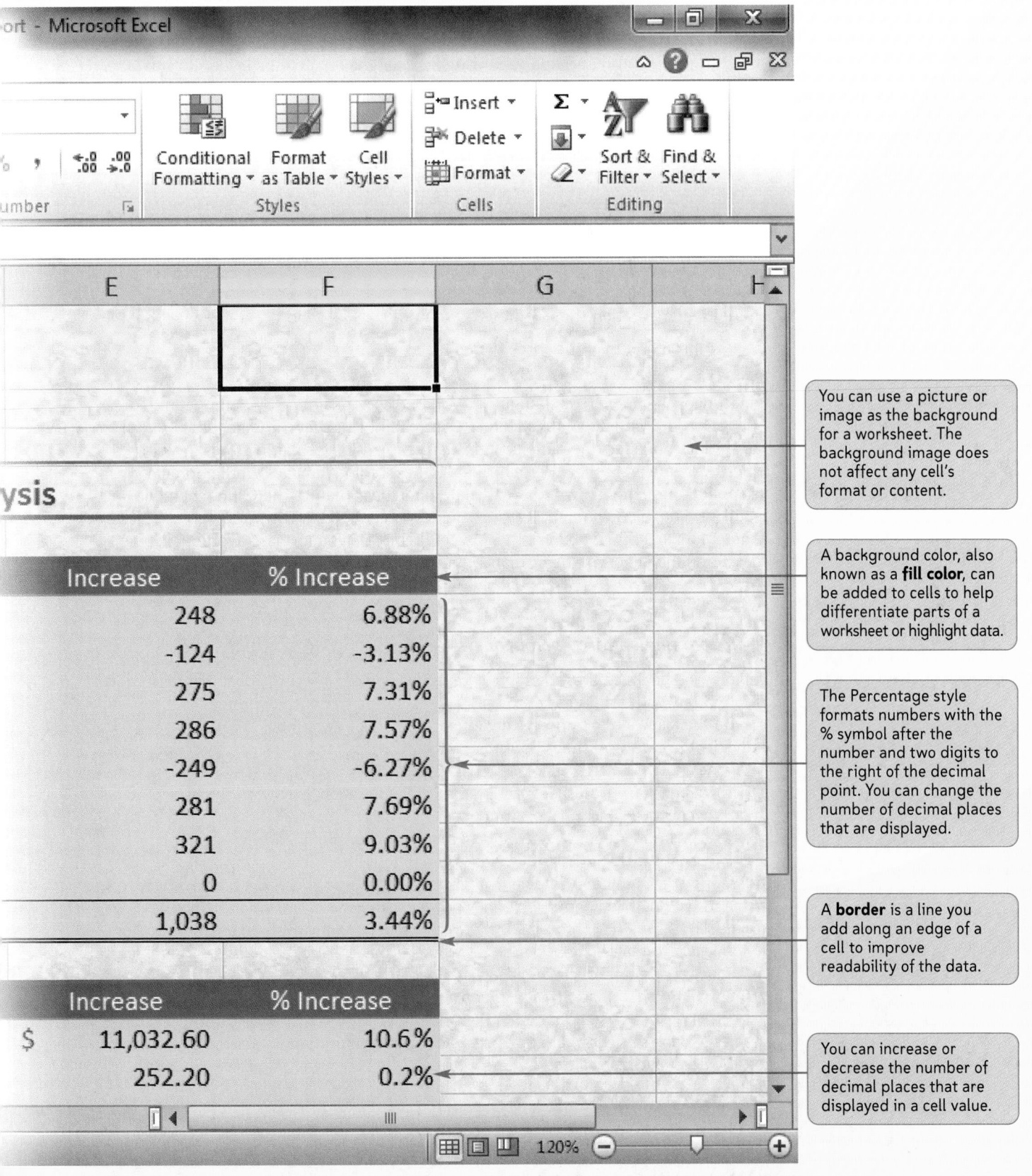

You can use a picture or image as the background for a worksheet. The background image does not affect any cell's format or content.

A background color, also known as a **fill color**, can be added to cells to help differentiate parts of a worksheet or highlight data.

The Percentage style formats numbers with the % symbol after the number and two digits to the right of the decimal point. You can change the number of decimal places that are displayed.

A **border** is a line you add along an edge of a cell to improve readability of the data.

You can increase or decrease the number of decimal places that are displayed in a cell value.

**...rt - Microsoft Excel**

Conditional Formatting ▾ | Format as Table ▾ | Cell Styles ▾

Styles

Insert ▾
Delete ▾
Format ▾

Cells

Σ ▾
Sort & Filter ▾ | Find & Select ▾

Editing

| | E | F |
|---|---|---|
| | Increase | % Increase |
| | 248 | 6.88% |
| | -124 | -3.13% |
| | 275 | 7.31% |
| | 286 | 7.57% |
| | -249 | -6.27% |
| | 281 | 7.69% |
| | 321 | 9.03% |
| | 0 | 0.00% |
| | 1,038 | 3.44% |

| | Increase | % Increase |
|---|---|---|
| $ | 11,032.60 | 10.6% |
| | 252.20 | 0.2% |

**...ysis**

120%

# Formatting Cell Text

Tom has already entered the data and some formulas in a workbook, which is only a rough draft of what he wants to submit to the company. The Documentation sheet describes the workbook's purpose and content. The Yearly Sales sheet displays the sales history of the X310 heart rate monitor including the total number of units sold per sales region (labeled R01 through R08) and the total revenue generated by those sales in the past two years. The Monthly Sales sheet also reports the number of X310 units sold by region and month. In its current form, the data is difficult to read and interpret. Tom wants you to format the workbook contents to improve its readability and visual appeal. You'll open the workbook and review its content.

## To open the workbook:

▶ **1.** Open the **ExerComp** workbook located in the **Excel2\Tutorial** folder included with your Data Files, and then save the workbook as **ExerComp Sales Report**.

▶ **2.** In the Documentation sheet, enter your name in cell B4 and the date in cell B5.

▶ **3.** Review the contents of the three worksheets.

**Formatting** is the process of changing a workbook's appearance by defining the fonts, styles, colors, and decorative features. Formatting changes only the appearance of data—it does not affect the data itself. Excel organizes its formatting tools in terms of themes. A **theme** is a collection of formats for text, colors, images, and graphical effects applied throughout a workbook. Each theme has a name. The Office theme is the default, although you can apply other themes or create your own. You can also use fonts and colors that are not part of the current theme. As you format a workbook, Live Preview shows the effects of the formats on the workbook's appearance.

**PROSKILLS**

### Written Communication: Formatting Workbooks for Readability and Appeal

Designing a workbook requires the same care as designing any written document or report. A well-formatted workbook is easier to read and establishes a sense of professionalism with readers. Do the following to improve the appearance of your workbooks:

- Clearly identify each worksheet's purpose with column or row titles and a descriptive sheet name.
- Don't crowd individual worksheets with too much information. Each worksheet should deal with only one or two topics. Place extra topics on separate sheets. Readers should be able to interpret each worksheet with a minimal amount of horizontal and vertical scrolling.
- Place worksheets containing the most important information first in the workbook. Position worksheets summarizing your findings near the front of the workbook. Position worksheets with detailed and involved analysis near the end as an appendix.
- Use consistent formatting throughout the workbook. If negative values appear in red on one worksheet, format them in the same way on all sheets. Also, be consistent in the use of thousands separators, decimal places, and percentages.
- Pay attention to the format of the printed workbook. Make sure your printouts are legible with informative headers and footers. Check that the content of the printout is scaled correctly to the page size and that page breaks divide the information into logical sections.

Excel provides many formatting tools. However, too much formatting can be intrusive, overwhelm data, and make the document difficult to read. Always remember, the goal of formatting is not simply to make a "pretty workbook," but also to accentuate important trends and relationships in the data. A well-formatted workbook should seamlessly convey your data to the reader. If the reader is thinking about how your workbook looks, it means he or she is not thinking about your data.

## Applying Fonts and Font Styles

Excel organizes fonts into theme and non-theme fonts. A **theme font** is associated with a particular theme and used for headings and body text in the workbook. These fonts change automatically when you change the theme applied to the workbook. When you don't want to apply a font associated with a particular design, you use a **non-theme font**. Text formatted with a non-theme font retains its appearance no matter what theme is used with the workbook.

Fonts appear in different character styles. **Serif fonts**, such as Times New Roman, have extra decorative strokes at the end of each character. **Sans serif fonts**, such as Arial, do not include these decorative strokes. Other fonts are purely decorative such as a font used for specialized logos.

Every font can be further formatted with a font style such as *italic*, **bold**, or ***bold italic***, and special effects such as underline, ~~strikethrough~~, and color. Finally, you can set the font size to increase or decrease the size of the text.

You'll format the company name displayed at the top of each worksheet to appear in large, bold letters using the default heading font from the Office theme. Tom wants the slogan "The Intelligent Path to Fitness" displayed below the company name to appear in the heading font, but in smaller, italicized letters.

### To format text in the Documentation worksheet:

1. Click the **Documentation** sheet tab to make it the active worksheet, and then click cell **A1** to make it the active cell.

2. In the Font group on the Home tab, click the **Font arrow** to display a list of fonts available on your computer. The first two fonts are the theme fonts for headings and body text—Cambria and Calibri. See Figure 2-1.

| Figure 2-1 | Theme and non-theme fonts in the font list |

3. Click **Cambria**. The company name in cell A1 changes to the Cambria font, the default headings font in the current theme.

**TIP**

You can also change the font size incrementally by clicking the Increase Font Size or Decrease Font Size button in the Font group on the Home tab.

4. In the Font group, click the **Font Size arrow** to display a list of font sizes, and then click **26**. The company name changes to 26 points.

5. In the Font group, click the **Bold** button **B**. The company name is boldfaced. Next, you'll format the company slogan.

6. Click cell **A2** to make it active. The slogan text is selected.

7. In the Font group, click the **Font arrow**, and then click **Cambria**. The slogan text changes to the Cambria font.

8. In the Font group, click the **Font Size arrow**, and then click **10**. The slogan text changes to 10 points.

9. In the Font group, click the **Italic** button **I**. The slogan in cell A2 is italicized.

10. Select the range **A4:A6**, click the **Bold** button **B** in the Font group, and then click cell **A7**. The column labels are bolded. The formatted text is shown in Figure 2-2.

**Figure 2-2** **Formatted cell text**

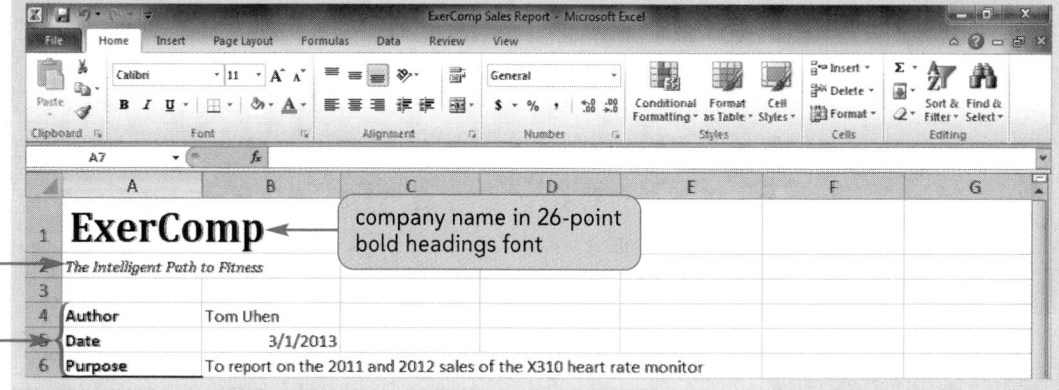

slogan in 10-point, italic, headings font

bold labels

company name in 26-point bold headings font

## Applying a Font Color

Color can transform a plain workbook filled with numbers and text into a powerful presentation that captures the user's attention and adds visual emphasis to the points you want to make. By default, Excel displays text in a black color font.

Just as it did with fonts, Excel organizes colors into theme and non-theme colors. **Theme colors** are the 12 colors that belong to the workbook's theme. Four colors are designated for text and backgrounds, six colors are used for accents and highlights, and two colors are used for hyperlinks (followed and not followed links). These 12 colors are designed to work well together and to remain readable in all combinations. Each theme color has five variations, or **accents**, in which a different tint or shading is applied to the theme color.

Ten **standard colors**—dark red, red, orange, yellow, light green, green, light blue, blue, dark blue, and purple—are always available regardless of the workbook's theme. You can also open an extended palette of 134 standard colors. You can create a **custom color** by specifying a mixture of red, blue, and green color values, making available 16.7 million custom colors—more colors than the human eye can distinguish. Some dialog boxes have an **automatic color** option that uses your Windows default text and background colors, usually black text on a white background.

Tom wants the labels in the Documentation worksheet to stand out so you will change the ExerComp title and slogan to blue.

### To change the title and slogan font color:

1. Select the range **A1:A2**.

2. In the Font group, click the **Font Color button arrow** to display the theme and standard colors. (The two colors for hyperlinked text are not shown.)

3. Point to the **Blue** color (the eighth color) in the Standard Colors section. The color name appears in a ScreenTip and you see a Live Preview of the text with the blue font color. See Figure 2-3.

**Figure 2-3**    Available font colors

Live Preview shows the text with the font color

10 theme colors (each has five variations)

standard colors

ScreenTip displays the color name

4. Click the **Blue** color. The company name and slogan change to blue.

## Formatting Text Selections

In the ExerComp logo, "Exer" appears in blue text and "Comp" appears in red text. You'll need to format part of the contents in cell A1 one way and the rest a different way. When you select text in Edit mode, you can format the selection with a different font, size, style, and color. You'll format "Comp" in a red font.

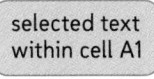

**TIP**

You can also use the buttons on the Mini toolbar to change the font, size, style, and color of selected text within a cell.

### To format the Comp text selection:

1. Double-click cell **A1** to select the cell and go into Edit mode, and then select **Comp**.

2. In the Font group on the Home tab, click the **Font Color button arrow**, and then click the **Red** color in the Standard Colors section. The text color changes. See Figure 2-4.

**Figure 2-4**    Text selection being formatted

selected text within cell A1

3. Click cell **A7** to deselect the cell. The text "ExerComp" in cell A1 is blue and red.

*Formatting Cell Content*

- To change the font, select the cell or range. In the Font group on the Home tab, click the Font arrow, and then click a font.
- To change the font size, select the cell or range. In the Font group on the Home tab, click the Font Size arrow, and then click a font size.
- To change a font style, select the cell or range. In the Font group on the Home tab, click the Bold, Italic, or Underline button.
- To change a font color, select the cell or range. In the Font group on the Home tab, click the Font Color button arrow, and then click a color.
- To format a text selection, double-click the cell to enter Edit mode, select the text to format, change the font, size, style, or color, and then press the Enter key.

# Working with Colors and Backgrounds

Another way to distinguish sections of a worksheet is by formatting the cell background. You can fill the cell background with color or an image. Tom wants you to format the Documentation worksheet by adding fill colors and background images.

## Changing a Fill Color

By default, Excel does not add any background color to worksheet cells; but background colors, also known as fill colors, can be added using the same color palette you use for font colors. The labels in the Documentation worksheet should be in a white font on a blue background. The author's name, current date, and purpose of the worksheet should be in a blue font on a white background. You will make both of these changes to the Documentation worksheet.

**To change the background fill color:**

1. Select the range **A4:A6**.

2. In the Font group on the Home tab, click the **Fill Color button arrow** , and then click the **Blue** color (the eighth color) in the Standard Colors section.

3. In the Font group, click the **Font Color button arrow** , and then click the **White** color in the Theme Colors section.

4. Select the range **B4:B6**, and then format the cells with a blue font on a white background.

5. Increase the width of column B to **55** characters.

6. Click cell **A7**. See Figure 2-5.

**Figure 2-5** Formatted labels and text in the Documentation worksheet

Fill Color button

text appears in a white font on a blue background

text appears in a blue font on a white background

## Adding a Background Image

You can use a picture or an image as the background for a worksheet. An image can give the worksheet a textured appearance, like that of granite, wood, or fibered paper. The image is repeated until it fills the entire worksheet. The background image does not affect any cell's format or content. Background colors applied to cells appear on top of the image, covering that portion of the image. Background images do not print.

Tom has provided an image for you to use as the background of the Documentation worksheet.

### To add a background image to the Documentation worksheet:

1. Click the **Page Layout** tab on the Ribbon. The page layout options appear on the Ribbon.

2. In the Page Setup group, click the **Background** button. The Sheet Background dialog box opens.

3. Navigate to the **Excel2\Tutorial** folder included with your Data Files, click the **Background** JPEG image file, and then click the **Insert** button. The image is added to the background of the Documentation worksheet. See Figure 2-6.

**Figure 2-6** Background image added to the worksheet

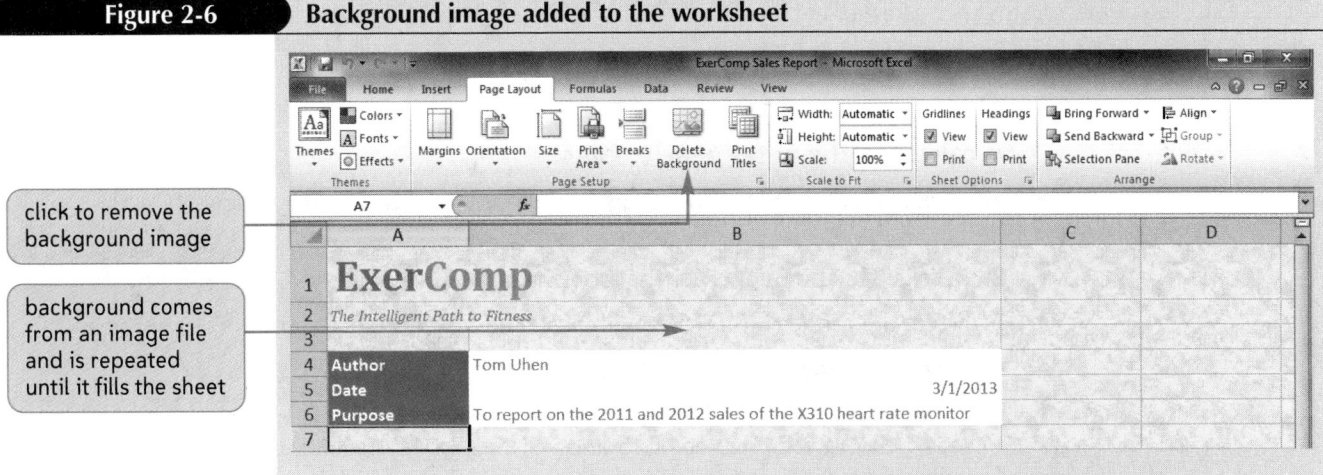

click to remove the background image

background comes from an image file and is repeated until it fills the sheet

*Using Color to Enhance a Workbook*

When used wisely, color can enhance any workbook. However, when used improperly, color can distract the user, making the workbook more difficult to read. As you format a workbook, keep in mind the following tips:

- Use colors from the same theme within a workbook to maintain a consistent look and feel across the worksheets. If the built-in themes do not fit your needs, you can create a custom theme.
- Use colors to differentiate types of cell content and to direct users where to enter data. For example, format a worksheet so that formula results appear in cells without a fill color and users enter data in cells with a light gray fill color.
- Avoid garish color combinations that can annoy the reader and be difficult to read.
- Print the workbook on both color and black-and-white printers to ensure that the printed copy is readable in both versions.
- Understand your printer's limitations and features. Colors that look good on your monitor might not look as good when printed.
- Be sensitive to your audience. About 8 percent of all men and 0.5 percent of all women have some type of color blindness and might not be able to see the text when certain color combinations are used. Red-green color blindness is the most common, so avoid using red text on a green background or green text on a red background.

# Formatting Calculated Values

When you format numeric values, the goal is to make the workbook easier for the reader to interpret (which is same goal of any formatting you apply to a workbook). For example, adding a comma as a thousands separator, controlling the number of decimal places, and using percentage and currency symbols can make a large table of numbers easier to read and understand.

For Tom's report, you'll format the values in the worksheets that contain the sales figures for the past two years.

## Creating Formulas to Add, Subtract, and Divide Values

The Yearly Sales worksheet contains the annual sales figures from 2011 and 2012 for the X310 heart rate monitor. The upper section of the worksheet displays the number of units sold in each sales region per year, and the lower section displays the revenue generated by sales region per year in dollars. You will add formulas to the worksheet to calculate the total sales for each year as well as the net and percent change in sales from one year to another.

**To calculate the total yearly sales:**

▶ **1.** Click the **Yearly Sales** sheet tab. The Yearly Sales worksheet is now the active sheet in the workbook.

▶ **2.** In cells B15 and B26, enter the label **Total**.

▶ **3.** Select the range **C15:D15**. You'll insert the SUM function in both cells at once.

▶ **4.** Click the **Home** tab on the Ribbon.

▶ **5.** In the Editing group, click the **Sum** button $\Sigma$. The formulas inserted in these cells, =SUM(C7:C14) in cell C15 and =SUM(D7:D14) in cell D15, calculate the total units sold for 2011 and 2012, which are 30136 and 31174, respectively.

▶ **6.** In the Clipboard group on the Home tab, click the **Copy** button 🗎. The formulas are copied to the Clipboard.

▶ **7.** Scroll down and select the range **C26:D26**. These are the cells in which you want to paste the copied formulas.

▶ **8.** In the Clipboard group, click the **Paste** button 🗎. The formulas to calculate the total annual revenues are pasted in the selected range, displaying totals of 872437.2 in 2011 and 933661.3 in 2012. See Figure 2-7.

| Figure 2-7 | Formulas calculate the total units sold and total revenue |

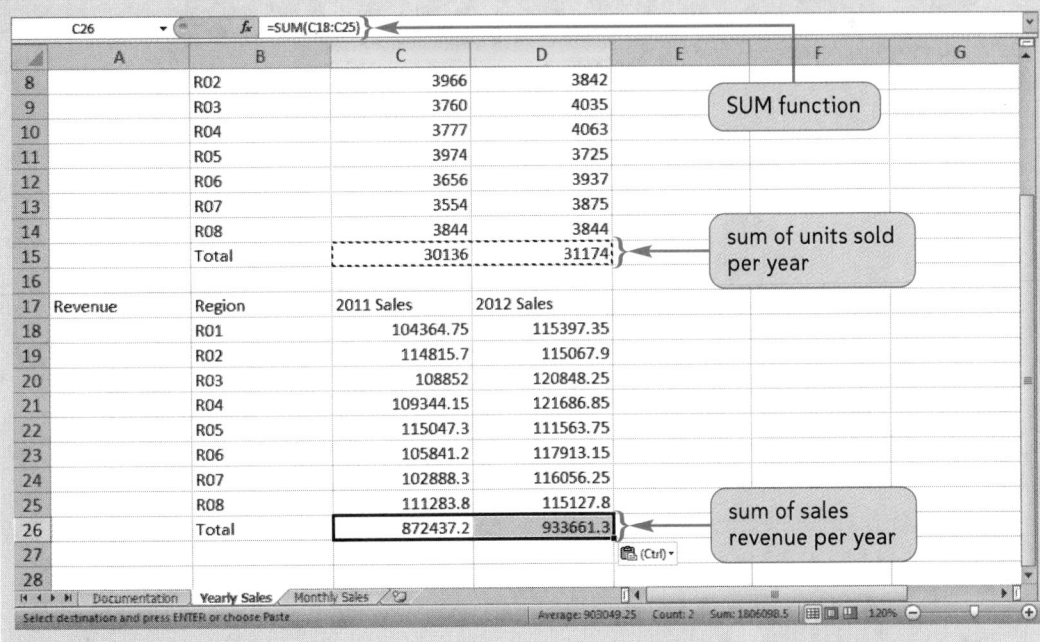

The formula results are difficult to read in their current form. You'll correct that problem shortly.

To calculate the net change in units sold and revenue from 2011 to 2012, you'll subtract the 2011 figures from the 2012 figures. To calculate the percent change, you'll divide the net change by the 2011 units sold and revenue figures for each sales region as well as across all sales regions.

### To calculate the net and percent change from 2011 to 2012:

▶ **1.** In cells E6 and E17, enter the label **Increase**, and then, in cells F6 and F17, enter the label **% Increase**.

▶ **2.** In cell E7, enter the formula **=D7–C7** to calculate the increase in units sold from 2011 to 2012.

▶ **3.** In cell F7, enter the formula **=E7/C7** to calculate the percent increase in units sold from 2011 to 2012. When calculating a percent increase, always divide the amount of increase by the starting value and not the ending value.

▶ **4.** Select the range **E7:F7**. Rather than reenter the formulas in cells E7 and F7, you'll copy and paste them into the rest of the worksheet.

▶ **5.** In the Clipboard group on the Home tab, click the **Copy** button 📋. The range is copied to the Clipboard.

▶ **6.** Select the nonadjacent range **E8:F15;E18:F26**. You want to paste the formulas in these cells.

▶ **7.** In the Clipboard group, click the **Paste** button 📋. The formulas are pasted in the selected ranges.

▶ **8.** Click cell **A6** to deselect the range. The formulas calculate the values for the net and percent increase in units sold and revenue from 2011 to 2012. See Figure 2-8.

**Figure 2-8** **Net and percent increase in sales and revenue**

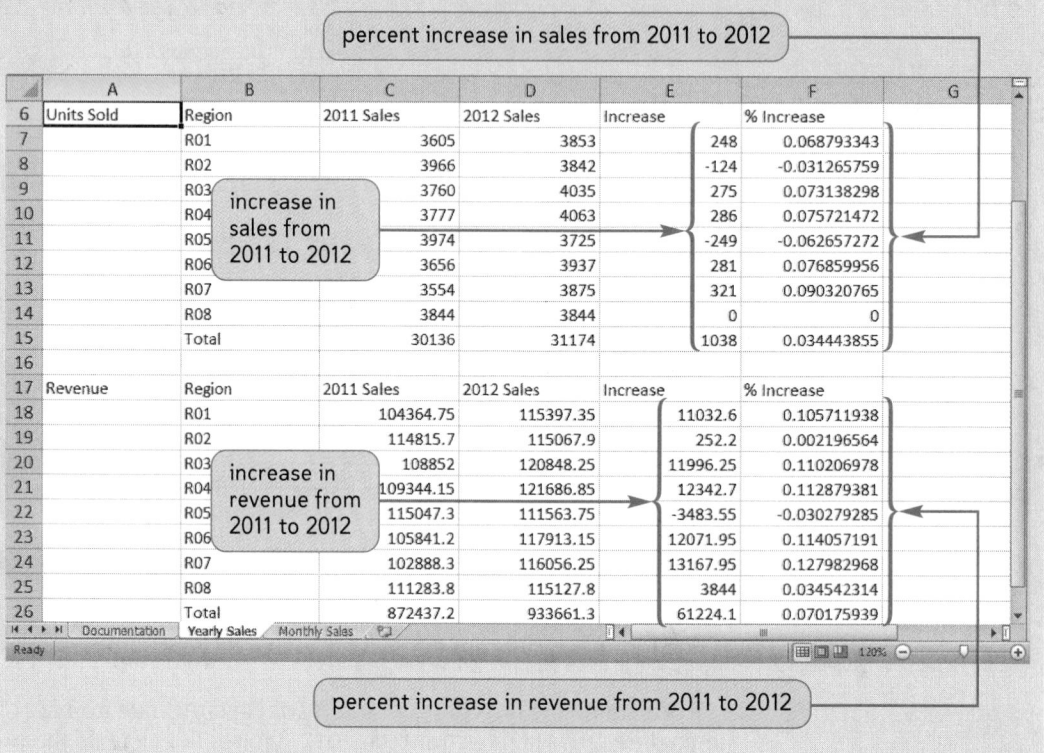

## Applying Number Formats

You can format values using a **number format**, which displays the values in a way that makes it easy for the reader to quickly understand and interpret them. You can change the number format for the displayed value without affecting the underlying stored value. Excel formats numbers by default in the **General number format**, which, for the most part, displays values exactly as they are typed by the user. If the value is calculated from a formula or function, Excel shows as many digits after the decimal point as will fit in the cell with the last displayed digit rounded. Calculated values too large to fit into the cell are displayed in scientific notation.

The General number format is good for simple calculations, but some values require additional formatting to make the numbers easier to interpret. Using Excel, you can:

- Set the number of digits displayed to the right of the decimal point
- Add commas to act as a thousands separator for large values
- Apply currency or accounting symbols to numeric values to identify the monetary unit being used
- Display percentages using the % symbol

The values in the Yearly Sales worksheet are difficult to interpret. For example, it is unclear whether a particular value represents sales revenue or units sold, and it is hard to determine, without study, whether a revenue value is expressed in millions or hundreds of thousands of dollars. You will format these values to make them easier to read.

**To apply a thousands separator to the units sold values:**

1. Select the range **C7:E15**.

2. In the Number group on the Home tab, click the **Comma Style** button. Each value in the selected range now includes a thousands separator. Two digits were also added to the right of the decimal point. Because the units sold values are expressed in integers, you will remove the digits to the right of the decimal place.

3. In the Number group, click the **Decrease Decimal** button twice. The two extra digits are removed. See Figure 2-9.

| Figure 2-9 | Units sold values formatted |
| --- | --- |

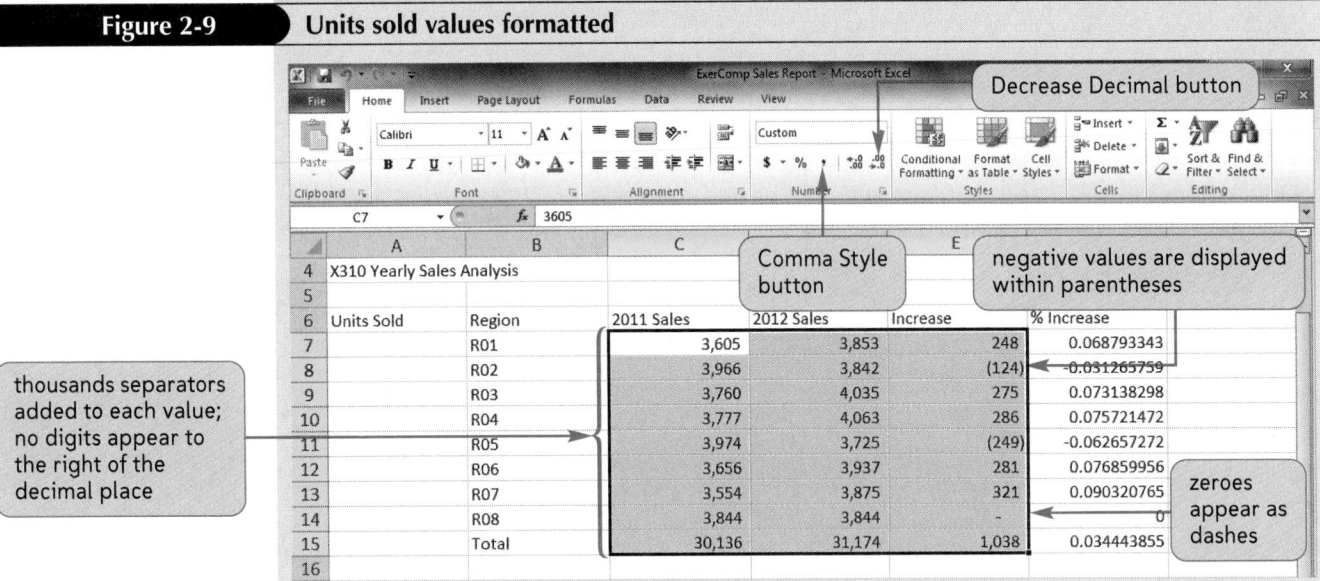

Though you used the Comma Style button to add the thousands separator, the button actually applies an accounting style used for currency values to the values in the columns. This accounting style lines up currency values within a column by the currency symbol and decimal point. When the values do not have a currency symbol, the values are aligned by the decimal point. The accounting style also encloses negative numbers, such as –124 in cell E8, within parentheses, such as (124). This is a standard format used in accounting documents. If you prefer to display negative numbers in a different way, you can modify this format. Another standard accounting practice is to add a currency symbol to only the first and last entries within a column of values.

You will display the revenue values in columns C through E using the same accounting style, but with two decimal places and with the currency symbol appearing only in rows 18 and 26.

**TIP**

For international documents, you can select other currency symbols: In the Number group on the Home tab, click the Accounting Number Format button arrow, and then click a currency symbol.

## To format the revenue values:

1. Select the range **C18:E26**.

2. In the Number group on the Home tab, click the **Comma Style** button 🔸.

3. Select the nonadjacent range **C18:E18;C26:E26**.

4. In the Number group, click the **Accounting Number Format** button 💲. As shown in Figure 2-10, $ symbols are added to the revenue values in the first and last row.

| Figure 2-10 | Revenue values formatted |
| --- | --- |

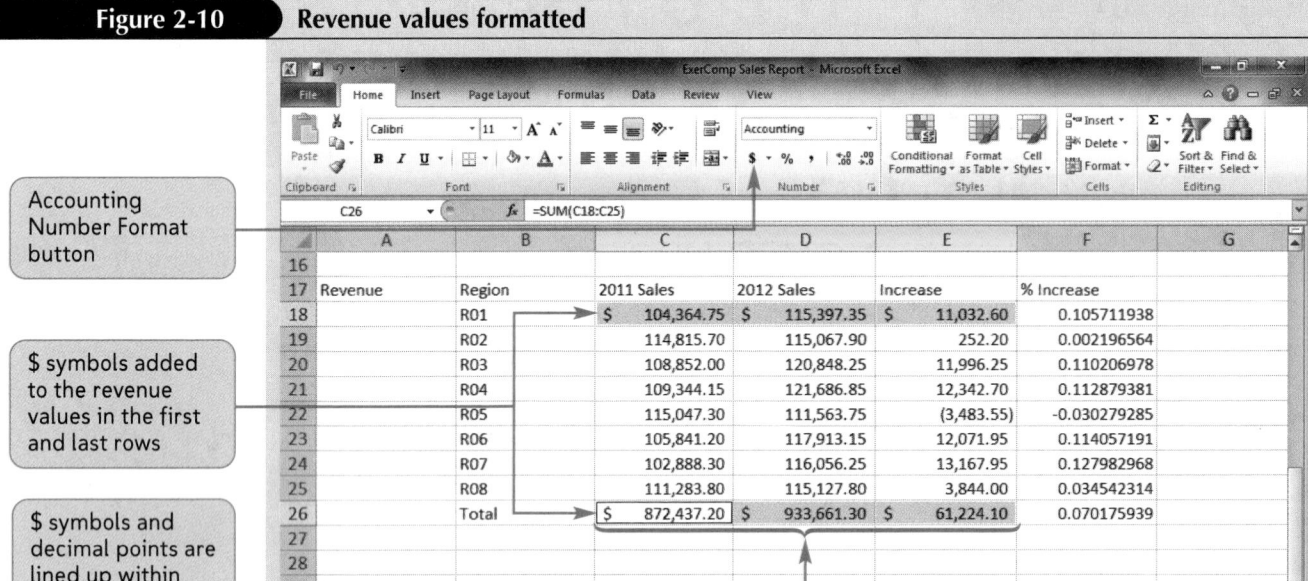

Accounting Number Format button

$ symbols added to the revenue values in the first and last rows

$ symbols and decimal points are lined up within each column

Next, you'll format the percent change values in column F. When you format values as percentages, the % symbol appears after the number and no digits appear to the right of the decimal point. You can change how many decimal places are displayed in the cell. Tom wants the percentages in column F to display the % symbol with two decimal places.

## To format the percentages in column F:

1. Select the nonadjacent range **F7:F15;F18:F26**.

2. In the Number group on the Home tab, click the **Percent Style** button %.

3. In the Number group, click the **Increase Decimal** button 🔹 twice to display the percentages to two decimal places.

4. Scroll up and click cell **A6** to deselect the range. Figure 2-11 shows the formatted numbers in the worksheet.

| Figure 2-11 | Percent increase values formatted |
|---|---|

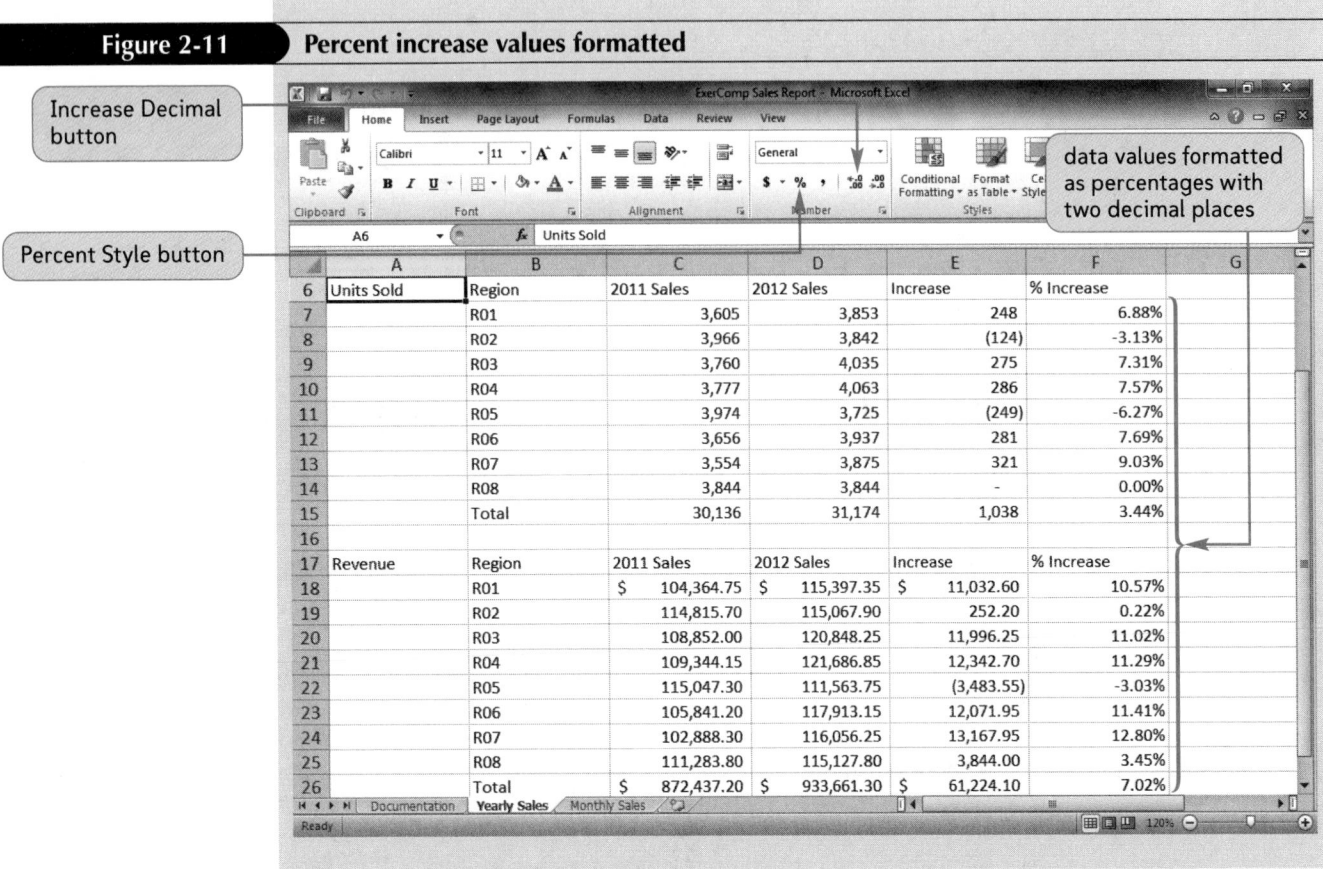

With the data reformatted, Tom can more easily see that the company sold 1038 more units in 2012 than in 2011—an increase of 3.44 percent, which increased revenue by $61,224.10, or 7.02 percent. This was not uniform across all sales regions. Total units sold and revenue for Region R05, for example, decreased between 2011 and 2012.

## Formatting Dates and Times

The date in the Documentation sheet is displayed in an abbreviated format, *mm/dd/yyyy*. Tom wants you to use an extended format that includes the day of the week, the full month name, the day, and the year.

Because Excel stores dates and times as numbers and not as text, you can apply different formats without affecting the date and time value. The abbreviated format entered into the Documentation sheet is referred to as the Short Date format. You can also apply a Long Date format that displays the day of the week and the full month name in addition to the day of the month and the year. Other built-in Excel formats include formats for displaying time values in 12- or 24-hour time.

You will change the date in the Documentation sheet to the Long Date format.

### To format the date in the Long Date format:

1. Click the **Documentation** sheet tab to make the Documentation worksheet active, and then select cell **B5**.

2. In the Number group on the Home tab, click the **Number Format** arrow, and then click **Long Date**. The date format changes to show the weekday name, month name, day, and year. See Figure 2-12.

**Figure 2-12** **Formatted date**

### Excel Dates and Times as Numeric Values

Although dates and times entered into a cell usually are displayed as text, they are actually stored by Excel as numbers measuring the interval between the specified date and time and January 1, 1900 at 12:00 a.m. For example, the date April 1, 2013 is stored as 41,365, which is the number of days between April 1, 2013 and January 1, 1900.

Times are stored as fractional parts of one day. A time of 6:00 a.m. is stored as 0.25 because that represents one-fourth of a 24-hour day (starting the day from 12:00 a.m.). Similarly, a cell containing the date and time of April 1, 2013 at 6:00 a.m. would be stored as 41,365.25.

Excel stores dates and times as numbers to make it easier to calculate time intervals. For example, to calculate the difference between one date and another, you just subtract the earlier date from the later date. If you subtract the date and time of March 30, 2013 at 12:00 p.m. from April 1, 2013 at 6:00 a.m., Excel displays 1.75—or one and three quarters of a day.

You can always view the actual date and time by selecting the cell that contains the date/time entry and applying the General number format, or by switching the workbook window to Formula view.

## Formatting Worksheet Cells

You can format the appearance of individual cells by modifying the alignment of text within the cell, indenting cell text, or adding borders of different styles and colors to individual cells or ranges. You'll make these changes to the cells in Tom's workbook.

### Aligning Cell Content

By default, cell text is aligned with the left and bottom borders of a cell and cell values are aligned with the right and bottom borders. In some cases, you might want to change the text alignment to make the text more readable or visually appealing. In general, you should center column titles, left-align other cell text, and align numbers to keep their decimal places lined up within a column. The buttons to set these alignment options are located in the Alignment group on the Home tab. Figure 2-13 describes the operations of these buttons.

| Figure 2-13 | Alignment buttons |

| Button | Description |
| --- | --- |
| ≣ | Aligns the cell content with the cell's top edge |
| ≣ | Vertically centers the cell content within the cell |
| ≣ | Aligns the cell content with the cell's bottom edge |
| ≣ | Aligns the cell content with the cell's left edge |
| ≣ | Horizontally centers the cell content within the cell |
| ≣ | Aligns the cell content with the cell's right edge |
| ≇ | Decreases the size of the indentation used in the cell |
| ≇ | Increases the size of the indentation used in the cell |
| ≫▾ | Rotates the cell content to any angle within the cell |
| ≣ | Forces the cell text to wrap within the cell borders |
| ▦ | Merges the selected cells into a single cell |

Although the date in the Documentation worksheet is formatted to display as text, it is right-aligned in the cell (because Excel treats dates and times as numbers). You'll use the Alignment group buttons to left-align the date in the Documentation worksheet and center the column titles in the Yearly Sales worksheet.

### To left-align the date and center the column titles:

1. If necessary, select cell **B5**.

2. In the Alignment group on the Home tab, click the **Align Text Left** button ≣. The date shifts to the left edge of the cell.

3. Click the **Yearly Sales** sheet tab to make that worksheet active, and then select the nonadjacent range **C6:F6;C17:F17**.

4. In the Alignment group, click the **Center** button ≣. The column titles in columns C, D, E, and F are centered.

## Indenting Cell Content

Sometimes you want a cell's content moved a few spaces from the cell left edge. This is particularly useful for entries that are considered subsections of a worksheet. For example, Tom recorded sales for eight regions and then added the totals. Each region can be considered a subsection, and Tom thinks it would look better if the region labels were indented a few spaces. You increase the indentation by roughly one character space each time you click the Increase Indent button in the Alignment group on the Home tab. To decrease or remove an indentation, click the Decrease Indent button.

You'll increase the indent for the region labels.

## To indent the region labels:

▶ **1.** Select the nonadjacent range **B7:B14;B18:B25**.

▶ **2.** In the Alignment group on the Home tab, click the **Increase Indent** button ⊞.
Each region label indents one character space.

▶ **3.** Click cell **A6** to deselect the range. See Figure 2-14.

**Figure 2-14** ▶ **Centered and indented text**

text centered in each cell

text indented one character space

| | A | B | C | D | E | F | G |
|---|---|---|---|---|---|---|---|
| 6 | Units Sold | Region | 2011 Sales | 2012 Sales | Increase | % Increase | |
| 7 | | R01 | 3,605 | 3,853 | 248 | 6.88% | |
| 8 | | R02 | 3,966 | 3,842 | (124) | -3.13% | |
| 9 | | R03 | 3,760 | 4,035 | 275 | 7.31% | |
| 10 | | R04 | 3,777 | 4,063 | 286 | 7.57% | |
| 11 | | R05 | 3,974 | 3,725 | (249) | -6.27% | |
| 12 | | R06 | 3,656 | 3,937 | 281 | 7.69% | |
| 13 | | R07 | 3,554 | 3,875 | 321 | 9.03% | |
| 14 | | R08 | 3,844 | 3,844 | - | 0.00% | |
| 15 | | Total | 30,136 | 31,174 | 1,038 | 3.44% | |
| 16 | | | | | | | |
| 17 | Revenue | Region | 2011 Sales | 2012 Sales | Increase | % Increase | |
| 18 | | R01 | $ 104,364.75 | $ 115,397.35 | $ 11,032.60 | 10.57% | |
| 19 | | R02 | 114,815.70 | 115,067.90 | 252.20 | 0.22% | |
| 20 | | R03 | 108,852.00 | 120,848.25 | 11,996.25 | 11.02% | |
| 21 | | R04 | 109,344.15 | 121,686.85 | 12,342.70 | 11.29% | |
| 22 | | R05 | 115,047.30 | 111,563.75 | (3,483.55) | -3.03% | |
| 23 | | R06 | 105,841.20 | 117,913.15 | 12,071.95 | 11.41% | |
| 24 | | R07 | 102,888.30 | 116,056.25 | 13,167.95 | 12.80% | |
| 25 | | R08 | 111,283.80 | 115,127.80 | 3,844.00 | 3.45% | |
| 26 | | Total | $ 872,437.20 | $ 933,661.30 | $ 61,224.10 | 7.02% | |

## Merging Cells

In the Yearly Sales worksheet, Tom wants the title "X310 Yearly Sales Analysis" in cell A4 centered over columns A through F. One way to align text over several columns or rows is to merge several cells into one cell. When you merge cells, only the content from the upper-left cell in the range is retained. The cell reference for the merged cell is the upper-left cell reference. So, if you merge cells A1 and A2, the merged cell reference is cell A1.

After you merge a range into a single cell, you can realign its content. The Merge button in the Alignment group on the Home tab includes the following options:

- **Merge & Center** merges the range into one cell and horizontally centers the content.
- **Merge Across** merges each of the rows in the selected range across the columns in the range.
- **Merge Cells** merges the range into a single cell, but does not horizontally center the cell content.
- **Unmerge Cells** reverses a merge, returning the merged cell back into a range of individual cells.

You will merge and center the title in cell A4 across the range A4:F4.

## To merge and center the title across a cell range:

1. Select the range **A4:F4** in the Yearly Sales worksheet.

2. In the Alignment group on the Home tab, click the **Merge & Center** button. The range A4:F4 merges into one cell with a cell reference of A4 and the text is centered within the cell.

3. Select the range **A6:A15**, and then click the **Merge & Center** button. The cells are merged vertically into a single cell, displaying the text "Units Sold" aligned with the bottom cell border.

4. Select the range **A17:A26**, and then click the **Merge & Center** button. The cells in the range are also merged vertically into a single cell.

5. Click cell **A3**. Figure 2-15 shows the merged cells in the Yearly Sales worksheet.

**Figure 2-15** Merged ranges with centered text

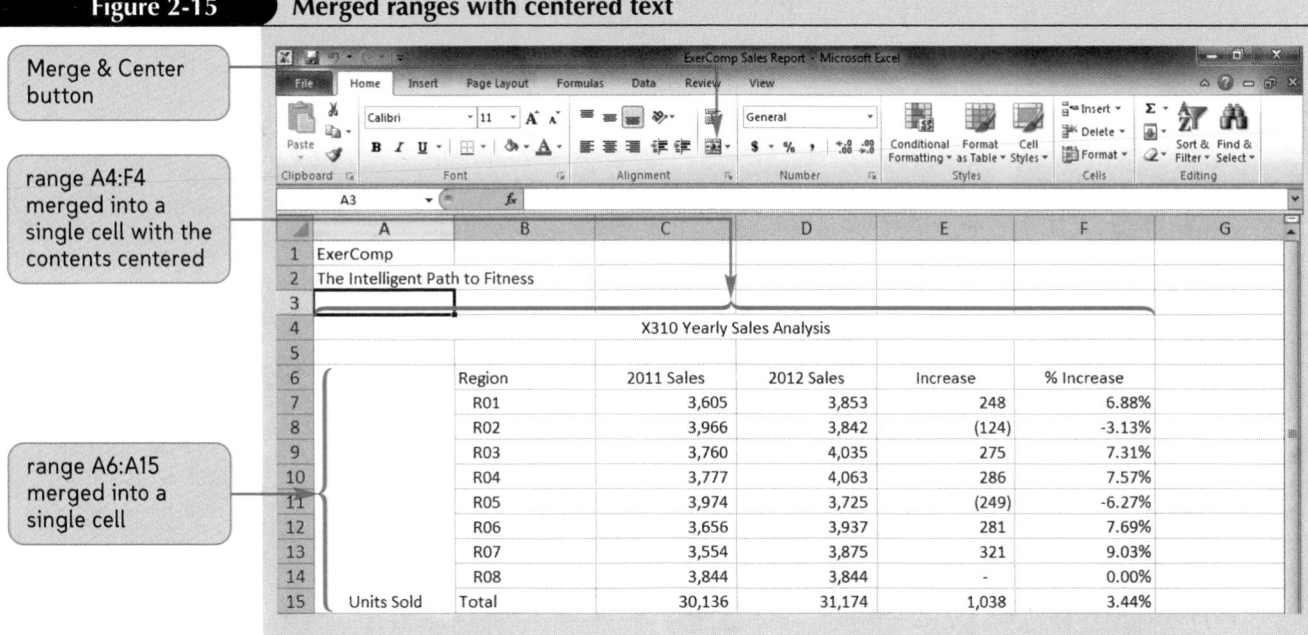

Merge & Center button

range A4:F4 merged into a single cell with the contents centered

range A6:A15 merged into a single cell

## Rotating Cell Contents

Text and numbers are displayed within cells horizontally. However, you can rotate cell text to any angle to save space or to provide visual interest to a worksheet. The Units Sold and Revenue titles were placed at the bottom of their respective merged cells, which makes them difficult to read. The titles would look better and take up less room if they were rotated vertically within their cells. You will rotate the titles.

### To rotate the titles:

1. Click the merged cell **A6** to select it.

2. In the Alignment group on the Home tab, click the **Orientation** button, and then click **Rotate Text Up**. The cell text rotates 90 degrees counterclockwise.

3. In the Alignment group, click the **Middle Align** button. The rotated text vertically aligns within the merged cell.

**4.** Click the merged cell **A17** to select it, and then repeat Steps 1 through 3 to rotate and align the text.

**5.** Reduce the width of column A to **5** characters. See Figure 2-16.

| Figure 2-16 | Rotated cell text |
|---|---|

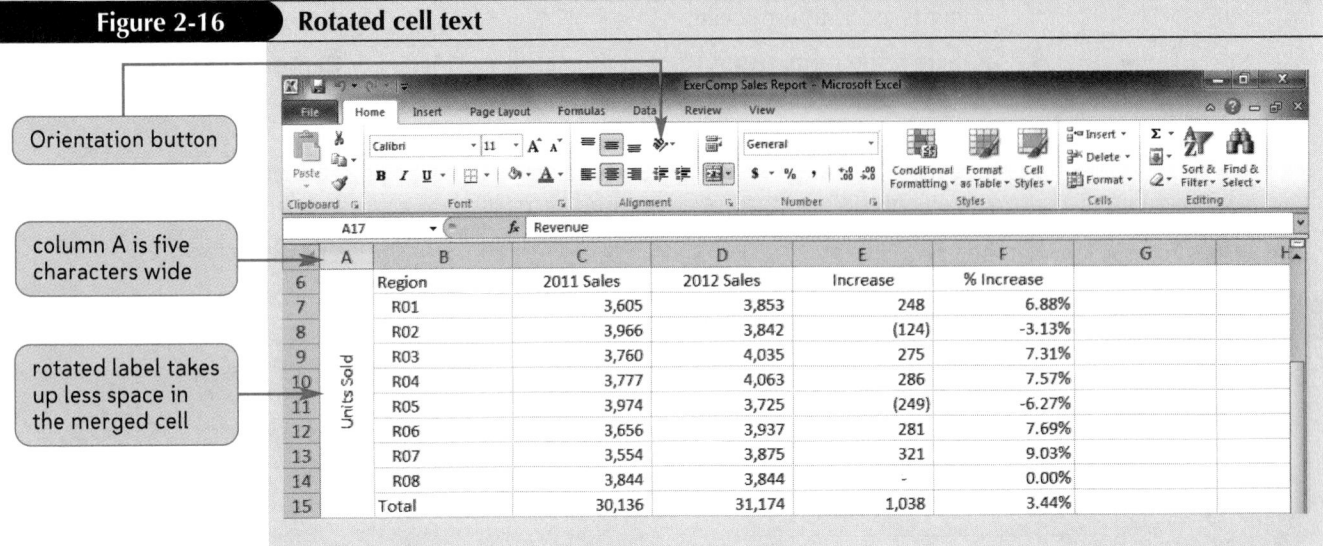

- Orientation button
- column A is five characters wide
- rotated label takes up less space in the merged cell

| | A | B | C | D | E | F | G |
|---|---|---|---|---|---|---|---|
| 6 | | Region | 2011 Sales | 2012 Sales | Increase | % Increase | |
| 7 | | R01 | 3,605 | 3,853 | 248 | 6.88% | |
| 8 | | R02 | 3,966 | 3,842 | (124) | -3.13% | |
| 9 | | R03 | 3,760 | 4,035 | 275 | 7.31% | |
| 10 | Units Sold | R04 | 3,777 | 4,063 | 286 | 7.57% | |
| 11 | | R05 | 3,974 | 3,725 | (249) | -6.27% | |
| 12 | | R06 | 3,656 | 3,937 | 281 | 7.69% | |
| 13 | | R07 | 3,554 | 3,875 | 321 | 9.03% | |
| 14 | | R08 | 3,844 | 3,844 | - | 0.00% | |
| 15 | | Total | 30,136 | 31,174 | 1,038 | 3.44% | |

## Adding Cell Borders

**TIP**

You set the gridlines or the row and column headings to print by clicking the appropriate Print check box in the Sheet Options group on the Page Layout tab.

When a worksheet is printed, the gridlines that surround the cells are not printed by default. They only appear on the worksheet as a guide. Sometimes you want to include lines along the edges of cells to enhance the readability of the rows and columns of data. One way to do this is by adding a border to a cell or range. You can add borders to the left, top, right, or bottom of a cell or range; around an entire cell; or around the outside edges of a range. You can also specify the thickness of and the number of lines in the border.

Tom wants you to add borders to the column titles and Total rows. Standard accounting practice is to add a single top border and a double bottom border to the Total rows to clearly differentiate them from financial data.

### To add cell borders to the column labels and Total rows:

**1.** Select the nonadjacent range **B6:F6;B17:F17**. You'll add a bottom border to these column labels.

**2.** In the Font group on the Home tab, click the **Border button arrow** ⊞ ▾, and then click **Bottom Border**. A border is added to the bottom of the selected cells.

**3.** Select the nonadjacent range **B15:F15;B26:F26**. You'll add top and bottom borders to these Total rows.

**4.** In the Font group, click the **Border button arrow** ⊞ ▾, and then click **Top and Double Bottom Border**. The Total rows both have a single top border and a double bottom border, following standard accounting practice.

**5.** Click cell **A5** to deselect the range. See Figure 2-17.

| Figure 2-17 | Borders added to cells |

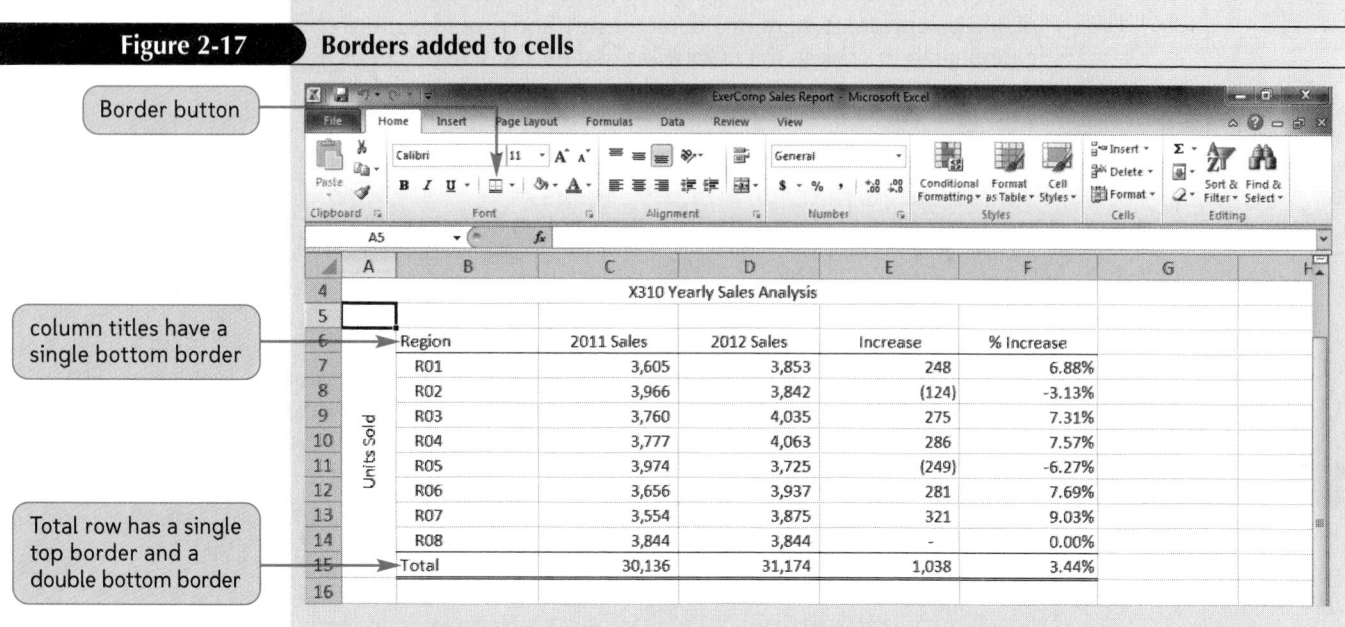

- **Border button**
- **column titles have a single bottom border**
- **Total row has a single top border and a double bottom border**

# Exploring Options in the Format Cells Dialog Box

The buttons on the Home tab provide quick access to the most commonly used formatting choices. For more options, you can use the Format Cells dialog box. For example, the numbers in cells E8 and E11 are displayed in parentheses to indicate that they are negative. Although parentheses are common in accounting to indicate negative currency values, Tom wants you to reformat the units sold numbers to display negative numbers with a minus symbol. You can do this in the Format Cells dialog box.

## To open the Format Cells dialog box:

1. Select the range **E7:E15**.

2. In the Number group on the Home tab, click the **Dialog Box Launcher**. The Format Cells dialog box opens with the Number tab active.

The Format Cells dialog box has six tabs, each focusing on a different set of formatting options, as described below. You can apply the formats in this dialog box to selected worksheet cells.

- **Number** provides options for formatting the appearance of numbers, including dates and numbers treated as text (for example, telephone or Social Security numbers).
- **Alignment** provides options for how data is aligned within a cell.
- **Font** provides options for selecting font types, sizes, styles, and other formatting attributes such as underlining and font colors.
- **Border** provides options for adding and removing cell borders as well as selecting a line style and color.
- **Fill** provides options for creating and applying background colors and patterns to cells.
- **Protection** provides options for locking or hiding cells to prevent other users from modifying their contents.

Although you've applied many of these formats from the Home tab, the Format Cells dialog box presents them in a different way and provides more choices. You'll use the Number tab to change the number format for the selected cells. Remember, modifying the number format does not affect the value stored in the workbook.

### To set the format for negative values:

▶ **1.** In the Category box on the left side of the Format Cells dialog box, click **Number**.

▶ **2.** Verify that **0** (zero) appears in the Decimal places box.

▶ **3.** Verify that the **Use 1000 Separator (,)** check box contains a check mark.

▶ **4.** In the Negative numbers box, verify that **−1,234** (the first option) is selected. See Figure 2-18.

**Figure 2-18** ▶ **Number tab in the Format Cells dialog box**

number format categories

preview of how the number in the selected cells will appear

options for displaying negative values

▶ **5.** Click the **OK** button. The Format Cells dialog box closes and the negative numbers in the range E7:E15 appear with a minus symbol, a comma as the thousands separator, and no decimal places.

Tom wants the bottom border color used for the column titles changed from black to green. You'll use the Border tab in the Format Cells dialog box to set the border line color and make this change. On the Border tab, you can select a line style ranging from thick to thin, choose double to dotted lines, and place these lines anywhere around the cells in the selected range.

### To set the border color for the column labels:

▶ **1.** Select the nonadjacent range **B6:F6;B17:F17**.

▶ **2.** In the Font group on the Home tab, click the **Borders button arrow** 🔲 ▾, and then click **More Borders**. The Format Cells dialog box opens with the Border tab active.

3. In the Line group, click the **Color arrow** to display the color palette, and then click **Green** (the sixth color) in the Standard Colors section.

4. Click the bottom border of the border preview. A green bottom border is shown in the preview. See Figure 2-19.

| Figure 2-19 | Border tab in the Format Cells dialog box |

adds a border around the entire cell or range

removes all borders

border line styles

border line color set to green

adds lines within the range

preview of the border style

5. Click the **OK** button. The dialog box closes and the cells with column titles have a green bottom border.

# Copying and Pasting Formats

You have not yet formatted the titles in cells A1 and A2 of the Yearly Sales worksheet to match the style you used for the Documentation worksheet. You could repeat the same steps to format these cells, but a quicker method is to copy those formats from the Documentation worksheet into the Yearly Sales worksheet.

## Copying Formats with the Format Painter

Using the Format Painter is a fast and efficient way of maintaining a consistent look and feel throughout a workbook. So, after you set the formatting in one cell, you can copy that formatting to another cell or range without duplicating the data.

You'll use the Format Painter to copy the cell formats from the range A1:A2 in the Documentation worksheet into the same range in the Yearly Sales worksheet.

## To copy and paste a format:

▶ 1. Click the **Documentation** sheet tab to make that worksheet active, and then select the range **A1:A2**.

▶ 2. In the Clipboard group on the Home tab, click the **Format Painter** button 🖌. The formats from the selected cells are copied to the Clipboard.

▶ 3. Click the **Yearly Sales** sheet tab to make that worksheet active, and then select the range **A1:A2**. The formatting from the Documentation worksheet is removed from the Clipboard and applied to the selected cells. Format Painter does not copy formatting applied to text selections within a cell, so the red color you applied to "Comp" was not included in the pasted formatting.

▶ 4. Double-click cell **A1** to switch to Edit mode, and then select **Comp** in the cell.

▶ 5. In the Font group on the Home tab, click the **Font Color button arrow** A ▾, and then click **Red** (the second color) in the Standard Colors section. The selected text changes to red.

▶ 6. Press the **Enter** key to exit Edit mode.

▶ 7. Select the range **A1:A2** in the Yearly Sales worksheet, and then repeat Steps 2 through 6 to copy the formatting to the range A1:A2 in the Monthly Sales worksheet.

**TIP**

You can double-click the Format Painter button to paste the same format multiple times. Click the Format Painter button again to turn it off.

## Copying Formats with the Paste Options Button

Sometimes you want to copy and paste more than a cell's formatting. When you want to paste the formatting from a copied range along with its contents, you can use the Paste Options button 📋 ▾. As shown in Figure 2-20, each time you paste, the Paste Options button appears in the lower-right corner of the pasted cell or range. When you click the Paste Options button, you can choose from a list of pasting options, such as pasting only the values or only the formatting.

**Figure 2-20** | Paste Options button

## Copying Formats with Paste Special

The Paste Special command is another way to control what you paste from the Clipboard. To use Paste Special, select and copy a range, select the range where you want to paste the Clipboard contents, click the Paste button arrow in the Clipboard group on the Home tab, and then click Paste Special to open the dialog box shown in Figure 2-21. From the Paste Special dialog box, you can control exactly how to paste the copied range.

**Figure 2-21    Paste Special dialog box**

pastes values and formats

pastes only formulas

pastes only the cell value, not the formula

pastes only the format, not the value or formula

applies the selected operation to the copied value

pastes the selected range rotated 90 degrees

So far, you have formatted cells and ranges in Tom's workbook. In the next session, you'll work with built-in styles, themes, table styles, conditional formatting, and page layout tools.

### Session 2.1 Quick Check

**REVIEW**

1. What is the difference between a serif font and a sans serif font?
2. What is the difference between a theme color and a standard color?
3. What is the General number format?
4. Why are dates right-aligned within a worksheet cell by default?
5. The range A1:C5 is merged into a single cell. What is the cell reference of this merged cell?
6. Where can you access all the formatting options for worksheet cells?
7. What are three tools you can use to copy and paste only the formatting of a cell?
8. Describe how you would use the Paste Special dialog box to multiply every value in a selected range by 2.

# SESSION 2.2 VISUAL OVERVIEW

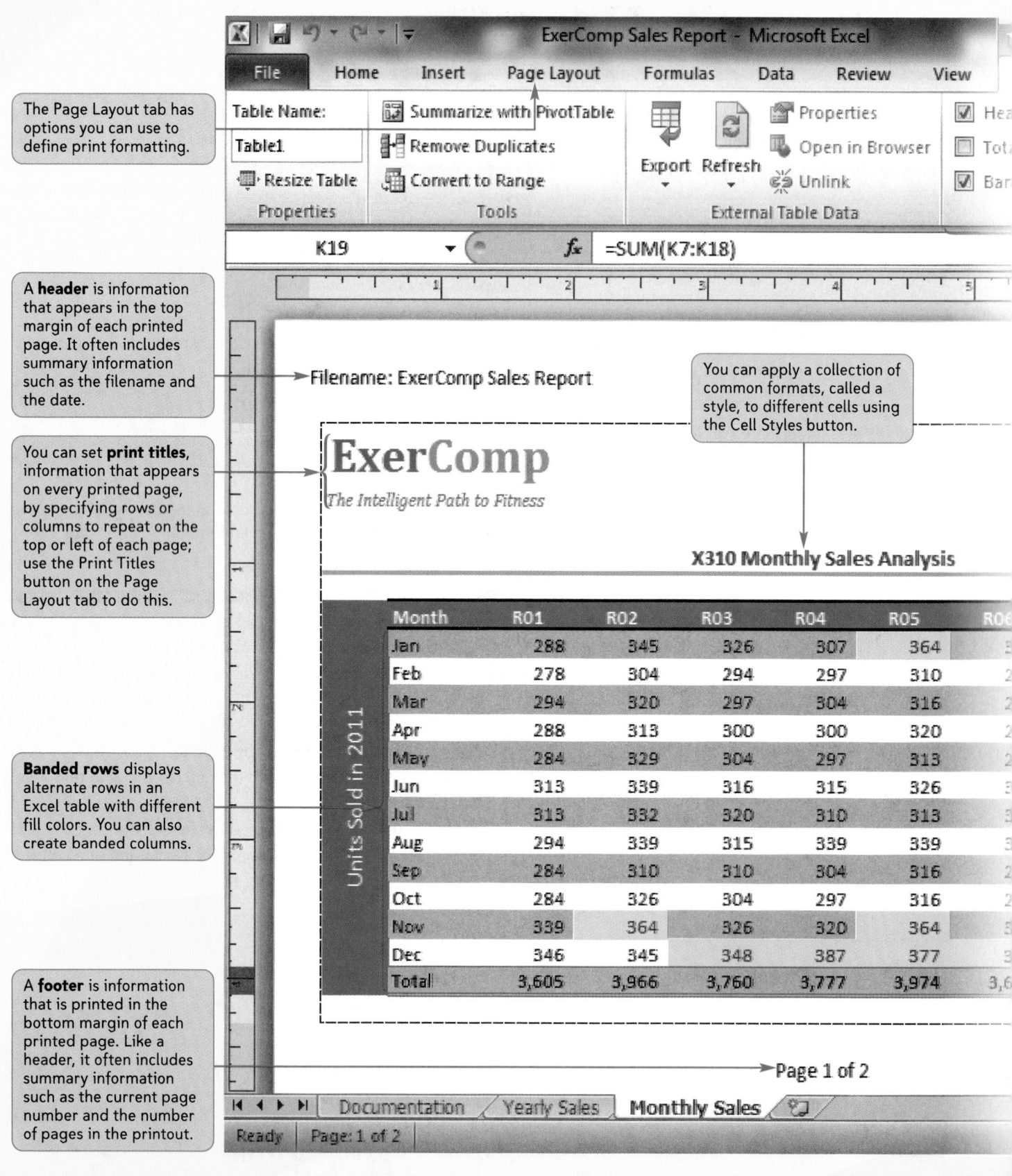

The Page Layout tab has options you can use to define print formatting.

A **header** is information that appears in the top margin of each printed page. It often includes summary information such as the filename and the date.

You can set **print titles**, information that appears on every printed page, by specifying rows or columns to repeat on the top or left of each page; use the Print Titles button on the Page Layout tab to do this.

**Banded rows** displays alternate rows in an Excel table with different fill colors. You can also create banded columns.

A **footer** is information that is printed in the bottom margin of each printed page. Like a header, it often includes summary information such as the current page number and the number of pages in the printout.

You can apply a collection of common formats, called a style, to different cells using the Cell Styles button.

ExerComp Sales Report - Microsoft Excel

| File | Home | Insert | Page Layout | Formulas | Data | Review | View |

Table Name:          Summarize with PivotTable          Properties          Hea
Table1                Remove Duplicates                  Open in Browser     Tota
Resize Table          Convert to Range    Export Refresh  Unlink             Bar
Properties                   Tools                External Table Data

K19          $f_x$    =SUM(K7:K18)

Filename: ExerComp Sales Report

# ExerComp
*The Intelligent Path to Fitness*

**X310 Monthly Sales Analysis**

Units Sold in 2011

| Month | R01 | R02 | R03 | R04 | R05 | R06 |
|-------|-----|-----|-----|-----|-----|-----|
| Jan | 288 | 345 | 326 | 307 | 364 | |
| Feb | 278 | 304 | 294 | 297 | 310 | |
| Mar | 294 | 320 | 297 | 304 | 316 | |
| Apr | 288 | 313 | 300 | 300 | 320 | |
| May | 284 | 329 | 304 | 297 | 313 | |
| Jun | 313 | 339 | 316 | 315 | 326 | |
| Jul | 313 | 332 | 320 | 310 | 313 | |
| Aug | 294 | 339 | 315 | 339 | 339 | |
| Sep | 284 | 310 | 310 | 304 | 316 | |
| Oct | 284 | 326 | 304 | 297 | 316 | |
| Nov | 339 | 364 | 326 | 320 | 364 | |
| Dec | 346 | 345 | 348 | 387 | 377 | |
| Total | 3,605 | 3,966 | 3,760 | 3,777 | 3,974 | 3,6 |

Page 1 of 2

◄ ◄ ► ►◄    Documentation    Yearly Sales    **Monthly Sales**

Ready    Page: 1 of 2

# TABLE STYLES AND PAGE FORMATTING

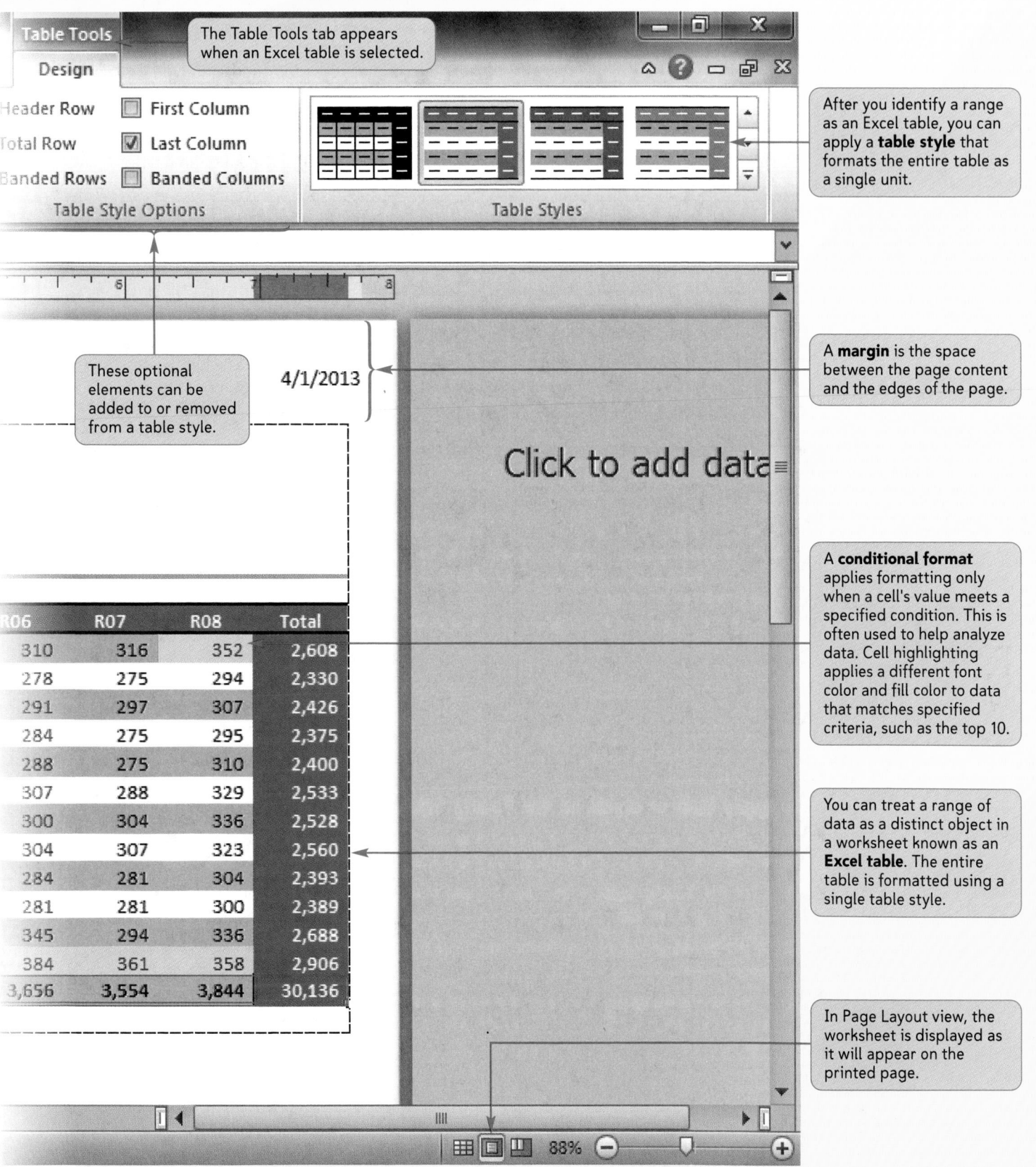

The Table Tools tab appears when an Excel table is selected.

After you identify a range as an Excel table, you can apply a **table style** that formats the entire table as a single unit.

These optional elements can be added to or removed from a table style.

A **margin** is the space between the page content and the edges of the page.

A **conditional format** applies formatting only when a cell's value meets a specified condition. This is often used to help analyze data. Cell highlighting applies a different font color and fill color to data that matches specified criteria, such as the top 10.

You can treat a range of data as a distinct object in a worksheet known as an **Excel table**. The entire table is formatted using a single table style.

In Page Layout view, the worksheet is displayed as it will appear on the printed page.

# Applying Cell Styles

A workbook often contains several cells that store the same type of data. For example, each worksheet might have a cell displaying the sheet title, or a range of financial data might have several cells containing summary totals. It's good design practice to apply the same format to worksheet cells that contain the same type of data.

One way to ensure that you are using consistent formats is to copy and paste your formats using the Format Painter. The Format Painter is effective, but it can also be time consuming if you need to copy the same format to several cells scattered across the workbook. Moreover, if you decide to modify the format, you must copy and paste the revised format all over again. Another way to ensure that cells displaying the same type of data use the same format is with styles.

A style is a selection of formatting options using a specific font and color from the current theme. For example, you can create a style to display sheet titles in a bold, white, 20-point Calibri font on a blue background. You can then apply that style to any sheet title in a workbook. If you later revise the style, the appearance of any cell formatted with that style is updated automatically. This saves you the time and effort of reformatting each cell individually.

Excel has a variety of built-in styles to format worksheet titles, column and row totals, and cells with emphasis. You used the built-in Currency and Percent styles when you formatted data in the Yearly Sales worksheet as currency and percentages. Some styles are based on the workbook's current theme and may change if the theme is changed.

**REFERENCE**

*Applying a Cell Style*

- Select the cell or range to which you want to apply a style.
- In the Styles group on the Home tab, click the Cell Styles button.
- Point to each style in the Cell Styles gallery to see a Live Preview of that style on the selected cell or range.
- Click the style you want to apply to the selected cell or range.

You will use some of the built-in styles to add more color and visual interest to the Yearly Sales worksheet.

**To apply built-in styles to the Yearly Sales worksheet:**

1. If you took a break after the previous session, open the ExerComp Sales Report workbook located in the Excel2\Tutorial folder included with your Data Files.

2. Click the **Yearly Sales** sheet tab to make that worksheet active, and then select the merged cell **A4**.

3. In the Styles group on the Home tab, click the **Cell Styles** button. The Cell Styles gallery opens.

4. Point to the **Heading 1** style in the Titles and Headings section. Live Preview shows cell A4 in a 15-point, bold font with a solid blue bottom border. See Figure 2-22.

**Figure 2-22**    Cell Styles gallery

gallery of built-in styles

Live Preview of the Heading 1 style applied to cell A4

Heading 1 selected

5. Move the pointer over different styles in the Cell Styles gallery to preview cell A4 with each style, and then click the **Heading 1** style. The style is applied to cell A4.

6. Select the nonadjacent range **B6:F6;B17:F17**, click the **Cell Styles** button, and then click the **Accent1** style in the Themed Cell Styles section. Each column heading is formatted.

7. Select the nonadjacent range **E7:F15;E18:F26**, click the **Cell Styles** button, and then click the **20% – Accent1** style in the Themed Cell Styles section. The calculated values are formatted differently from the data.

8. Click cell **F1** to deselect the range. See Figure 2-23.

**Figure 2-23**    Formatted yearly sales data

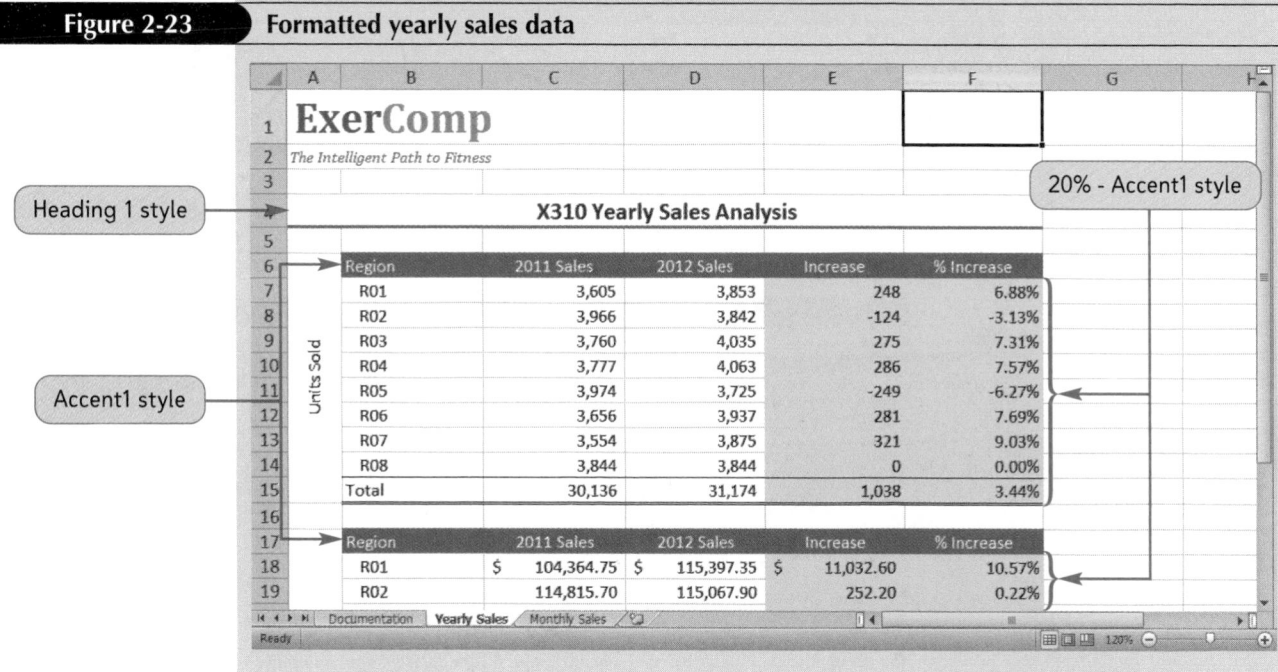

Heading 1 style

Accent1 style

20% - Accent1 style

# Working with Themes

Most of the formatting you have applied so far is based on the workbook's current theme—the default Office theme. As you've seen, fonts, colors, and cell styles are organized in theme and non-theme categories. The appearance of these fonts, colors, and cell styles depends on the workbook's current theme. If you change the theme, the formatting of these elements also changes throughout the entire workbook.

You'll change the workbook's theme to see its effect on the workbook's appearance.

### To change the workbook's theme:

1. Click the **Page Layout** tab on the Ribbon.

2. In the Themes group, click the **Themes** button. The Themes gallery opens. Office—the current theme—is the default.

3. Point to each theme in the Themes gallery. Live Preview shows how each theme changes the appearance of the Yearly Sales worksheet.

4. Click the **Apex** theme to apply that theme to the workbook. See Figure 2-24.

| Figure 2-24 | Apex theme applied to the yearly sales data |

Changing the theme made a significant difference in the worksheet's appearance. The most obvious changes are the fill colors and the fonts. Only elements directly tied to a theme change when you select a different theme. The cells you formatted with the Accent1 cell style changed because the Accent1 color is blue in the Office theme and orange in the Apex theme. The Heading 1 style you applied to the titles in cells A1 and A2 uses the Cambria typeface in the Office theme and the Lucida Sans typeface in the Apex theme. The Apex theme also uses a different font for body text, which is why the rest of the text changed size and appearance.

The logo colors in cell A1 did not change because you used two standard colors, blue and red, which are not part of a theme. Changing the theme does not affect these colors.

Tom prefers the default Office theme, so you'll reapply that theme.

### To select the Office theme:

1. In the Themes group on the Page Layout tab, click the **Themes** button, and then click the **Office** theme from the gallery of themes.

**PROSKILLS**

*Teamwork: Sharing Styles and Themes*

Using a common style and design theme for all the files you create in Microsoft Office is a simple way to give your files a consistent look and feel and project a professional image. This consistency is especially important when a team of workers is collaborating on a set of documents. When all team members work from a common set of style and design themes, readers will not be distracted by inconsistent or clashing styles.

To quickly copy the styles from one workbook to another, open the workbook with the styles you want to copy, and then open the workbook in which you want to copy those styles. In the Styles group on the Home tab, click the Cell Styles button, and then click Merge Styles. The Merge Styles dialog box opens, listing the currently open workbooks. Select the workbook with the styles you want to copy, and then click the OK button to copy those styles into the current workbook. If you modify any styles, you must copy the styles to the other workbook; Excel does not update styles between workbooks.

Because other Office files, including those created with Word or PowerPoint, use the same file format for themes, you can create one theme to use with all the Office files you create. To save a theme, in the Themes group on the Page Layout tab, click the Themes button, and then click Save Current Theme. The Save Current Theme dialog box opens. Select a save location (in a default Theme folder on your computer or another folder), type a descriptive name in the File name box, and then click the Save button. If you saved the theme file in a default Theme folder, the theme appears in the Themes gallery, and any changes made to the theme are reflected in any Office file that uses that theme.

By creating a library of styles and themes, you can create a report containing pages generated from different Office programs and those pages will still share a consistent set of design elements. Employees with expertise in page design can design a theme for the rest of the team to use. If those styles and themes are changed or modified, the new design style can be quickly applied to new and existing documents without having to reformat each document. Through careful planning, a well-designed theme can save you and your colleagues a lot of effort later on.

# Creating Formulas to Add and Subtract Values

Next, you'll work with the Monthly Sales worksheet, which contains the sales results by month for the eight sales regions over the past two years. Tom wants to use this data to identify trends. He's more interested in the "big picture" than in specific numbers. He wants to know which sales regions are performing well and which are underperforming. He also wants to explore the pattern of monthly sales throughout the year.

## Creating Formulas to Calculate Totals

The top of the worksheet contains annual sales for the previous two years. The bottom of the worksheet displays the increase in annual sales for each region and month. Tom wants you to calculate the monthly totals broken down by region. You'll start with the 2011 sales values.

**To calculate the monthly and regional totals for 2011:**

▶ **1.** Click the **Monthly Sales** sheet tab to make the worksheet active.

▶ **2.** In cells K6 and B19, enter the label **Total**.

▶ **3.** Select the nonadjacent range **K7:K18;C19:K19**. You'll add the formula to calculate the total in these cells.

▶ **4.** In the Editing group on the Home tab, click the **Sum** button $\Sigma$. The 2011 monthly and regional sales totals are entered in the selected range. See Figure 2-25.

| Figure 2-25 | Monthly and regional sales totals for 2011 |

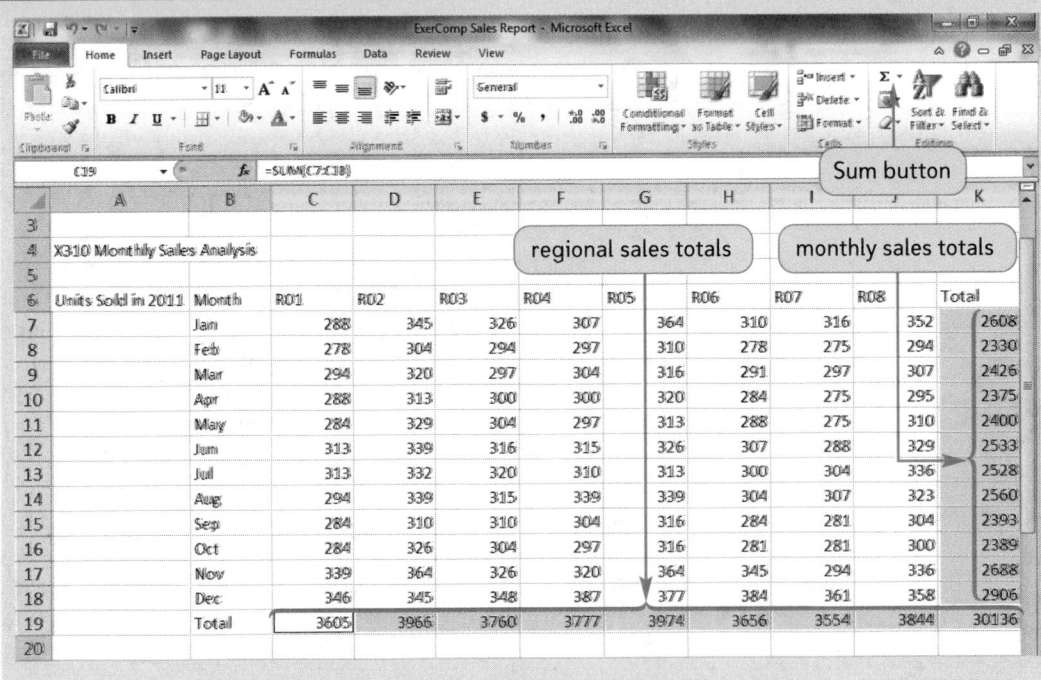

Next, you will calculate the monthly and regional sales totals for 2012. Rather than retyping the text and formulas, you can copy and paste them from 2011.

## To calculate the monthly and regional totals for 2012:

▶ **1.** Select the range **K6:K19**, and then click the **Copy** button in the Clipboard group on the Home tab. The cell contents are copied to the Clipboard.

▶ **2.** Click cell **K21**, and then click the **Paste** button. Excel inserts formulas to calculate the 2012 monthly sales totals into the range K21:K34.

▶ **3.** Select the range **B19:J19**, and then click the **Copy** button.

▶ **4.** Click cell **B34**, and then click the **Paste** button. Excel inserts formulas to calculate the 2012 regional sales totals into the range B34:J34. See Figure 2-26.

| Figure 2-26 | Monthly and regional sales totals for 2012 |
|---|---|

text and formulas to copy

monthly sales totals

regional sales totals

## Creating Formulas to Subtract Values

Tom also wants you to calculate the change in sales from one year to another, broken down by region and month. You'll use the copy and paste features to quickly add this third table to the Monthly Sales worksheet. Then you will add formulas to calculate the increase in units sold between 2011 and 2012.

## To calculate the change in sales from one year to the next:

▶ **1.** In cell A36, enter the label **Net Increase**.

▶ **2.** Copy the range **B21:K21**, and then paste it into the range **B36:K36**.

▶ **3.** Copy the range **B22:B34**, and then paste it into the range **B37:B49**.

▶ **4.** In cell C37, enter the formula **=C22–C7**. After you press the Enter key, the value 64 appears in the cell; this is the increase in January sales for region R01.

▶ **5.** Copy cell **C37**, and then paste it into the range **C37:K49**. The formula =C22–C7 is copied and pasted into the range of cells with the remaining months and regions.

▶ **6.** Click cell **A36** to deselect the range. Figure 2-27 shows the completed table.

| Figure 2-27 | Net increase in sales by region and month |

| | A | B | C | D | E | F | G | H | I | J | K |
|---|---|---|---|---|---|---|---|---|---|---|---|
| 35 | | | | | | | | | | | |
| 36 | Net Increase | Month | R01 | R02 | R03 | R04 | R05 | R06 | R07 | R08 | Total |
| 37 | | Jan | 64 | 19 | 19 | 45 | -28 | 51 | 9 | -10 | 169 |
| 38 | | Feb | 19 | 22 | 16 | 16 | -22 | 22 | 22 | 6 | 101 |
| 39 | | Mar | 13 | 13 | 29 | 12 | 0 | 25 | 13 | 9 | 114 |
| 40 | | Apr | 25 | 3 | 29 | 26 | -13 | 20 | 35 | 57 | 182 |
| 41 | | May | 26 | -6 | 22 | 29 | -9 | 25 | 38 | -10 | 115 |
| 42 | | Jun | 0 | 9 | 32 | 5 | 3 | 12 | 48 | -3 | 106 |
| 43 | | Jul | 10 | -6 | 28 | 19 | 0 | 16 | 22 | -7 | 82 |
| 44 | | Aug | 29 | -19 | 11 | 16 | -24 | 22 | 18 | -18 | 35 |
| 45 | | Sep | 16 | -13 | 16 | 22 | -19 | 26 | 26 | -11 | 63 |
| 46 | | Oct | 16 | -38 | 28 | 16 | -25 | 29 | 32 | 7 | 65 |
| 47 | | Nov | 16 | -67 | 29 | 64 | -67 | 16 | 35 | -7 | 19 |
| 48 | | Dec | 14 | -41 | 16 | 16 | -45 | 17 | 23 | -13 | -13 |
| 49 | | Total | 248 | -124 | 275 | 286 | -249 | 281 | 321 | 0 | 1038 |
| 50 | | | | | | | | | | | |

Next, you'll format the row and column titles for these tables. You'll use the formatting options on the Home tab and in the Format Cells dialog box to format the new table to match the other tables.

## To format the titles:

1. Select the range **A4:K4**, and then click the **Merge & Center** button in the Alignment group on the Home tab. The title is centered in the merged cell.

2. In the Styles group, click the **Cell Styles** button, and then click the **Heading 1** style. The Heading 1 style is applied to the title.

3. Select the range **A6:A19**, and then click the **Merge & Center** button in the Alignment group. The label is centered in the merged cell.

4. In the Alignment group, click the **Orientation** button , and then click **Rotate Text Up**. The text in the cell rotates 90 degrees.

5. In the Alignment group, click the **Middle Align** button . The text is centered both horizontally and vertically in the cells.

6. Reduce the width of column A to **5** characters.

7. Select the range **C7:K19**, and then, in the Number group on the Home tab, click the **Dialog Box Launcher**. The Format Cells dialog box opens with the Number tab displayed.

8. Click **Number** in the Category box, type **0** (a zero) in the Decimal places box, click the **Use 1000 Separator (,)** check box to insert a check mark, verify that the **−1,234** option is selected, and then click the **OK** button. The numbers display a thousands separator and use a minus symbol for negatives.

Next you'll copy this format to the two other tables on the worksheet.

9. Select the range **A6:K19**.

Be sure to double-click the Format Painter button so you can paste the copied format into multiple cells.

▶ **10.** In the Clipboard group, double-click the **Format Painter** button 🖌.

▶ **11.** Click cell **A21**. All of the formats in the range A6:K19 are applied to the cell.

▶ **12.** Click cell **A36**. Once again, all of the formats are applied to the selected cell.

▶ **13.** In the Clipboard group, click the **Format Painter** button 🖌 to turn off the Format Painter.

▶ **14.** Scroll up to the top of the worksheet and select cell **A1**. Figure 2-28 shows the formatted values for the first table.

| Figure 2-28 | Formatted table |

| | Month | R01 | R02 | R03 | R04 | R05 | R06 | R07 | R08 | Total |
|---|---|---|---|---|---|---|---|---|---|---|
| | | | | | | | | | | |
| | Jan | 288 | 345 | 326 | 307 | 364 | 310 | 316 | 352 | 2,608 |
| | Feb | 278 | 304 | 294 | 297 | 310 | 278 | 275 | 294 | 2,330 |
| | Mar | 294 | 320 | 297 | 304 | 316 | 291 | 297 | 307 | 2,426 |
| | Apr | 288 | 313 | 300 | 300 | 320 | 284 | 275 | 295 | 2,375 |
| | May | 284 | 329 | 304 | 297 | 313 | 288 | 275 | 310 | 2,400 |
| | Jun | 313 | 339 | 316 | 315 | 326 | 307 | 288 | 329 | 2,533 |
| | Jul | 313 | 332 | 320 | 310 | 313 | 300 | 304 | 336 | 2,528 |
| | Aug | 294 | 339 | 315 | 339 | 339 | 304 | 307 | 323 | 2,560 |
| | Sep | 284 | 310 | 310 | 304 | 316 | 284 | 281 | 304 | 2,393 |
| | Oct | 284 | 326 | 304 | 297 | 316 | 281 | 281 | 300 | 2,389 |
| | Nov | 339 | 364 | 326 | 320 | 364 | 345 | 294 | 336 | 2,688 |
| | Dec | 346 | 345 | 348 | 387 | 377 | 384 | 361 | 358 | 2,906 |
| | Total | 3,605 | 3,966 | 3,760 | 3,777 | 3,974 | 3,656 | 3,554 | 3,844 | 30,136 |

ExerComp — The Intelligent Path to Fitness

X310 Monthly Sales Analysis

Units Sold in 2011

# Working with Table Styles

You can identify a range as an Excel table, which makes available tools designed for analyzing tabular data, such as the ability to sort data, transfer data to and from an external file, and filter the data to show only those rows that match specified criteria. Excel tables can include optional elements such as a header row that contains titles for the different columns in the table, and a total row that contains formulas summarizing the values in the table's data. You can also apply a table style, which specifies formats such as font color, fill color, and so on for each of these elements. Formatting an entire table with a table style is more efficient than formatting individual cells in the table. (This tutorial covers only the styles associated with Excel tables.

**TIP**

Applying a table style also marks the range as an Excel table.

In addition, using a table style ensures that the table's formatting reflects any changes made to the table, such as adding or deleting table rows or columns. For example, many tables display alternate rows with different fill colors. This banded rows effect makes the data easier to read, especially in large tables with many rows. You could create the banded rows effect by applying a cell style with a background fill to every other row in the table; but if you later add or delete a row from the table, the banded rows effect might be lost. A table style, on the other hand, applies alternating row colors to the entire Excel table and adjusts the banded rows effect as needed if you add or delete rows. This is because a table style treats the table as a single object rather than a collection of cells. Figure 2-29 shows the banded rows effect applied both manually and with a table style.

**Figure 2-29** Banded rows in a table

| | A | B | C | D |
|---|---|---|---|---|
| 1 | Region | Year 1 Sales | Year 2 Sales | Difference |
| 2 | R01 | 3,605 | 3,853 | 248 |
| 3 | R02 | 3,966 | 3,842 | -124 |
| 4 | R03 | 3,760 | 4,035 | 275 |
| 5 | R04 | 3,777 | 4,063 | 286 |
| 6 | R05 | 3,974 | 3,725 | -249 |
| 7 | R06 | 3,656 | 3,937 | 281 |
| 8 | R07 | 3,554 | 3,875 | 321 |
| 9 | R08 | 3,844 | 3,844 | 0 |
| 10 | Total | 30,136 | 31,174 | 1,038 |
| 11 | | | | |

original table with banded rows

| | A | B | C | D |
|---|---|---|---|---|
| 1 | Region | Year 1 Sales | Year 2 Sales | Difference |
| 2 | R01 | 3,605 | 3,853 | 248 |
| 3 | R02 | 3,966 | 3,842 | -124 |
| 4 | R03 | 3,760 | 4,035 | 275 |
| 5 | R07 | 3,554 | 3,875 | 321 |
| 6 | R08 | 3,844 | 3,844 | 0 |
| 7 | Total | 18,729 | 19,449 | 720 |
| 8 | | | | |

after deleting a row from a table formatted manually, the banded effect is lost

| | A | B | C | D |
|---|---|---|---|---|
| 1 | Region | Year 1 Sales | Year 2 Sales | Difference |
| 2 | R01 | 3,605 | 3,853 | 248 |
| 3 | R02 | 3,966 | 3,842 | -124 |
| 4 | R03 | 3,760 | 4,035 | 275 |
| 5 | R07 | 3,554 | 3,875 | 321 |
| 6 | R08 | 3,844 | 3,844 | 0 |
| 7 | Total | 18,729 | 19,449 | 720 |
| 8 | | | | |

after deleting a row from a table formatted with a table style, the table formatting adjusts to keep banded rows

Tom wants you to format the sales data in the Monthly Sales worksheet as Excel tables. First, you'll apply a table style to the units sold in 2011 data.

**To apply a table style to the 2011 sales data:**

1. Select the range **B6:K19**.

2. In the Styles group on the Home tab, click the **Format as Table** button, and then click **Table Style Medium 2** (the second style in the first row in the Medium section). The Format As Table dialog box opens, confirming the range you selected for the table and whether the table includes header rows.

3. Verify that the range is **=$B$6:$K$19** and then verify that the **My table has headers** check box contains a check mark to include the text labels in the table.

4. Click the **OK** button to apply the table style to the selected range, and then click cell **A5** to deselect the range. See Figure 2-30.

**Figure 2-30** Range formatted with a table style

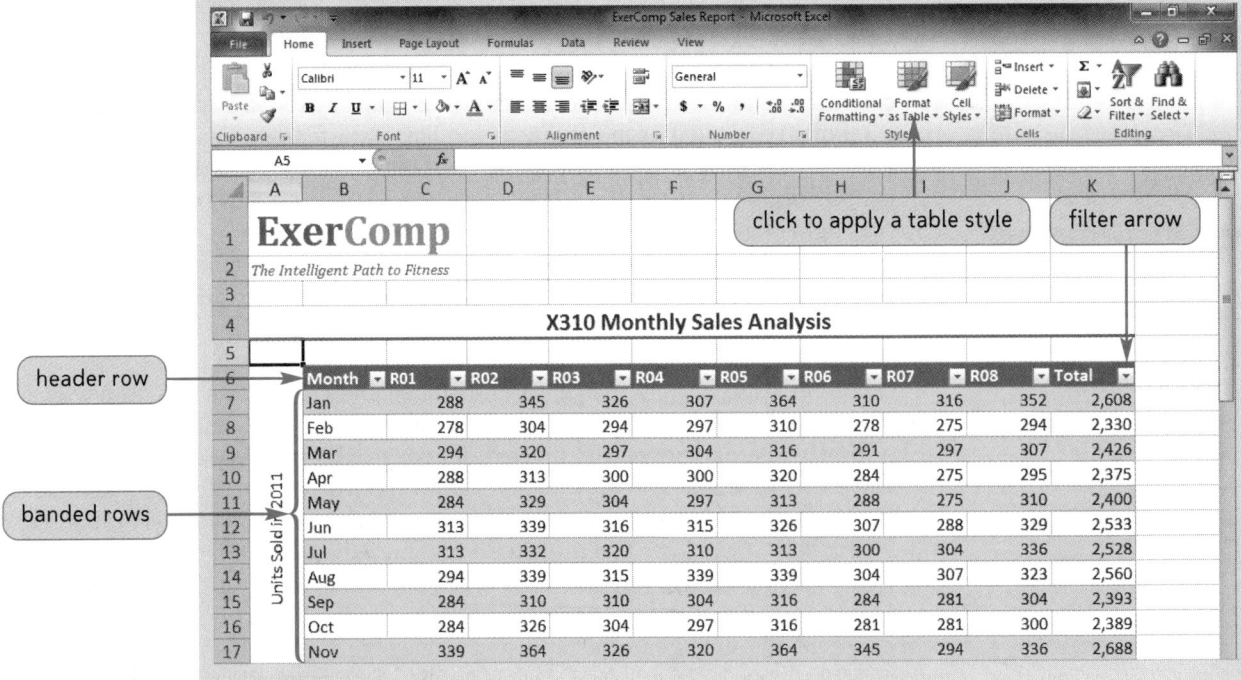

The table style treated the range as a single unit and modified its overall appearance. In this case, Table Style Medium 2 formatted the range so the header row appears in a white font on a blue fill and the remaining rows are formatted as banded rows. In addition, filter arrows appear next to the column titles in the header row. These filter arrows are applied when the user wants to hide or filter out different table rows that contain certain data.

Tom doesn't want to filter the data right now, so you will remove the arrows and work only with elements related to the table style.

**To remove the filter arrows from the table:**

▶ **1.** Click cell **B6** to make the table active.

▶ **2.** Click the **Data** tab on the Ribbon.

▶ **3.** In the Sort & Filter group, click the **Filter** button. The filter arrows disappear from the header row.

## Selecting Table Style Options

After you apply a table style, you can choose which table elements to include in the style. Table styles have the following six elements that can be turned on or off:

- **Header Row**, which formats the first row of the table
- **Total Row**, which inserts a new row at the bottom of the table that adds the column values
- **First Column**, which formats the first column of the table
- **Last Column**, which formats the last column of the table
- **Banded Rows**, which formats alternating rows in different colors
- **Banded Columns**, which formats alternating columns in different colors

For example, if you turn on the Header Row option, you can specify a format for the table's first row, which usually contains text that describes the contents of each table column. If you insert a new row at the top of the table, the new row becomes the header row and is formatted with the table style.

In the table style you just used, only the Header Row and Banded Rows options are on. Although the other elements are still part of the table structure, the current style does not format them. Tom wants you to format the table's last column and header row as well as remove the banded rows effect.

**To modify the table style:**

▶ **1.** If necessary, click cell **B6** to make the table active. The Table Tools contextual tab appears on the Ribbon.

▶ **2.** Click the **Design** tab on the Ribbon. The table design options appear on the Ribbon.

▶ **3.** In the Table Style Options group, click the **Last Column** check box to insert a check mark. The last column is formatted.

▶ **4.** In the Table Style Options group, click the **Banded Rows** check box to remove the check mark. The banded rows are removed from the table.

Only the Header Row and Last Column elements appear in the table. You'll use a built-in table style to format them.

▶ **5.** In the Table Styles group, click the **More** button ⧨. The Table Styles gallery opens.

**TIP**

You can click any cell within a table to make the table active; you do not need to select all of the table cells.

**6.** In the Medium section, click **Table Style Medium 20** (the third table style in the sixth column). The table styles in the gallery show the formatting applied to the current table elements. See Figure 2-31.

Figure 2-31 **Revised table style**

A table style might not format a table exactly the way you want. For example, Tom wants the column titles in the header row to be centered and the Total row to have a single top border and a double bottom border. Because the table style you used does not include either of these formats, you'll add these formats to the table cells. You can use cell styles and the formatting tools you've used with individual cells and ranges to format Excel tables.

### To format the header row and the Total row:

**1.** Select the range **C6:K6**. You'll change the alignment of the header row.

**2.** Click the **Home** tab on the Ribbon, and then click the **Center** button ☰ in the Alignment group. The column titles are centered.

**3.** Select the range **B19:K19**. You'll apply a different cell style to the Total row.

**4.** In the Styles group, click the **Cell Styles** button, and then click **Total** (the sixth cell style) in the Titles and Headings section.

**5.** Click cell **A5** to deselect the range. The Total row is formatted in bold with a single top border and a double bottom border.

Tom likes the formatting of the first table, and wants you to format the other two tables similarly. You cannot use the Format Painter to copy table formats, and you must format each range as a table separately.

**To format the other two tables:**

▶ 1. Select the range **B21:K34**.

▶ 2. In the Styles group on the Home tab, click the **Format as Table** button, click **Table Style Medium 6** (the sixth table style in the first row of the Medium section), and then click the **OK** button in the Format As Table dialog box. The range is formatted as a table.

▶ 3. Click the **Data** tab on the Ribbon, and then click the **Filter** button in the Sort & Filter group to turn off the filter arrows.

▶ 4. Click the **Design** tab on the Ribbon, and then, in the Table Style Options group, click the **Banded Rows** check box to remove the check mark and click the **Last Column** check box to insert a check mark. The banded rows are removed and the last column is formatted.

▶ 5. In the Table Styles group, click the **More** button, and then click **Table Style Medium 20** (the sixth table style in the third row of the Medium section). The table is quickly reformatted with a new style.

▶ 6. Select the range **C21:K21**, click the **Home** tab on the Ribbon, and then click the **Center** button ▤ in the Alignment group. The column headings are centered.

▶ 7. Select the range **B34:K34**; in the Styles group, click the **Cell Styles** button, and then click **Total** (the sixth cell style in the Titles and Headings section). The Total row is formatted.

▶ 8. Select the range **B36:K49** and repeat Steps 2 through 5, select the range **C36:K36** and repeat Step 6, and then select the range **B49:K49** and repeat Step 7. The third table is formatted to match the first two tables.

# Highlighting Cells with Conditional Formats

The formatting you have applied to the workbook has made the content more readable. However, Tom also wants this worksheet to highlight important trends and sales values of interest. For example, Tom is interested in knowing which regions and months have the highest sales or showed the highest increase between 2011 and 2012.

You can answer these kinds of questions using conditional formats, in which the format applied to a cell depends upon the value or content of the cell. For example, a conditional format can make negative numbers red and positive numbers black. Conditional formats are dynamic, so that if the cell's value changes, the cell's format also changes as needed. Each conditional format has a set of rules that define how the formatting should be applied and under what conditions the format will be changed.

*Highlighting a Cell Based on Its Value*

- Select the range in which you want to highlight cells that match a specified rule.
- In the Styles group on the Home tab, click the Conditional Formatting button, point to Highlight Cells Rules or Top/Bottom Rules, and then click the appropriate rule.
- Select the appropriate options in the dialog box, and then click the OK button.

Excel has four conditional formats—data bars, highlighting, color scales, and icon sets. In this tutorial, you will apply cell highlighting, which changes the cell's font color or background color based on the cell's value. Figure 2-32 describes some of the ways that cells can be highlighted with conditional formats.

| Figure 2-32 | Highlighting rules |
| --- | --- |

| Rule | Highlights |
| --- | --- |
| Greater Than | Cells that are greater than a specified number |
| Less Than | Cells that are less than a specified number |
| Between | Cells that are between two specified numbers |
| Equal To | Cells that are equal to a specified number |
| Text That Contains | Cells that contain specified text |
| A Date Occurring | Cells that contain a specified date |
| Duplicate Values | Cells that contain duplicate or unique values |

Tom wants to highlight sales regions that showed an increase in sales from 2011 to 2012. With all of the data on the Monthly Sales worksheet, this information can be difficult to locate. To make this data stand out, you will use a conditional format to display worksheet cells with a positive value using a different font or fill color than cells containing zero or a negative value.

### To highlight the positive sales numbers:

1. Select the range **C37:J48**. This range shows the difference in sales by region and month for 2011 and 2012.

2. In the Styles group on the Home tab, click the **Conditional Formatting** button, point to **Highlight Cells Rules**, and then click **Greater Than**. The Greater Than dialog box opens. You want to highlight those regions and months in which sales increased, which means that they are greater than zero.

3. Type **0** (a zero) in the Format cells that are GREATER THAN box, click the **with** arrow, and then click **Green Fill with Dark Green Text**. This rule formats any cells that display a number greater than zero in a green font with a green background.

4. Click the **OK** button to apply the highlighting rule.

5. Click cell **A35** to deselect the range. Cells with positive numbers are highlighted in green. See Figure 2-33.

**Figure 2-33**  **Conditional format highlights positive cell values**

positive values are highlighted in green

From the highlighting, you can tell that most regions and months had increased sales in 2012. Most of the declines occurred in regions R02, R05, and R08. Tom wonders if some months or regions had particularly strong sales increases. You'll first clear the current highlighting. Note that clearing a conditional format doesn't affect the contents of the cells.

### To clear a conditional format:

1. Select the range **C37:J48**.

2. In the Styles group on the Home tab, click the **Conditional Formatting** button, point to **Clear Rules**, and then click **Clear Rules from Selected Cells**. The current highlighting is removed.

Now add a conditional format that highlights the regions and months that rank in the top 10 percent in terms of net sales increase from 2011 to 2012.

### To highlight the top 10 percent in sales increase:

1. Make sure the range **C37:J48** is still selected.

2. In the Styles group, click the **Conditional Formatting** button, point to **Top/Bottom Rules**, and then click **Top 10 %**. The Top 10% dialog box opens.

3. Verify that **10** is entered in the % box, click the **with** arrow, and then click **Green Fill with Dark Green Text**.

4. Click the **OK** button. Cells whose sales increases for 2011 and 2012 were in the top 10 percent are highlighted in green.

5. Click cell **A35** to deselect the range. See Figure 2-34.

| Figure 2-34 | Conditional formats highlight the top 10 percent sales increases |
|---|---|

cells highlighted in green rank in the top 10 percent in sales increases

| Month | R01 | R02 | R03 | R04 | R05 | R06 | R07 | R08 | Total |
|---|---|---|---|---|---|---|---|---|---|
| Jan | 64 | 19 | 19 | 45 | -28 | 51 | 9 | -10 | 169 |
| Feb | 19 | 22 | 16 | 16 | -22 | 22 | 22 | 6 | 101 |
| Mar | 13 | 13 | 29 | 12 | 0 | 25 | 13 | 9 | 114 |
| Apr | 25 | 3 | 29 | 26 | -13 | 20 | 35 | 57 | 182 |
| May | 26 | -6 | 22 | 29 | -9 | 25 | 38 | -10 | 115 |
| Jun | 0 | 9 | 32 | 5 | 3 | 12 | 48 | -3 | 106 |
| Jul | 10 | -6 | 28 | 19 | 0 | 16 | 22 | -7 | 82 |
| Aug | 29 | -19 | 11 | 16 | -24 | 22 | 18 | -18 | 35 |
| Sep | 16 | -13 | 16 | 22 | -19 | 26 | 26 | -11 | 63 |
| Oct | 16 | -38 | 28 | 16 | -25 | 29 | 32 | 7 | 65 |
| Nov | 16 | -67 | 29 | 64 | -67 | 16 | 35 | -7 | 19 |
| Dec | 14 | -41 | 16 | 16 | -45 | 17 | 23 | -13 | -13 |
| Total | 248 | -124 | 275 | 286 | -249 | 281 | 321 | 0 | 1,038 |

*Net Increase*

The results provide Tom with some interesting information. For example, region R08, which underperformed for most of the year, had one of the largest sales increases during April (cell J40). In fact, the increase in sales during that one month compensated for the sales declines in other months; so that by the end of the year, region R08 showed no overall decline in sales. Also, region R01 had a large increase in sales during January 2012 but demonstrated the same level of increase for the rest of the year. Finally, four of the nine cells highlighted in the table are from region R07; three of those occurred during the spring months, which are traditionally slow times for the company.

Tom wonders what insights he could gain from highlighting the bottom 10 percent of the table—the regions and months that showed the lowest sales increases in 2012.

### To highlight the bottom 10 percent in sales increases:

1. Select the range **C37:J48**.

2. In the Styles group on the Home tab, click the **Conditional Formatting** button, point to **Top/Bottom Rules**, and then click **Bottom 10 %**. The Bottom 10% dialog box opens.

3. Verify that **10** is entered in the % box and **Light Red Fill with Dark Red Text** is selected in the with box.

4. Click the **OK** button. Red cells highlight the regions and months that placed in the bottom 10 percent for sales increases from 2011 to 2012.

5. Click cell **A35** to deselect the range. See Figure 2-35.

| Figure 2-35 | Conditional formats highlight the bottom 10 percent of sales increases |

ExerComp Sales Report - Microsoft Excel

| | Month | R01 | R02 | R03 | R04 | R05 | R06 | R07 | R08 | Total |
|---|---|---|---|---|---|---|---|---|---|---|
| 37 | Jan | 64 | 19 | 19 | 45 | -28 | 51 | 9 | -10 | 169 |
| 38 | Feb | 19 | 22 | 16 | 16 | -22 | 22 | 22 | 6 | 101 |
| 39 | Mar | 13 | 13 | 29 | 12 | 0 | 25 | 13 | 9 | 114 |
| 40 | Apr | 25 | 3 | 29 | 26 | -13 | 20 | 35 | 57 | 182 |
| 41 | May | 26 | -6 | 22 | 29 | -9 | 25 | 38 | -10 | 115 |
| 42 | Jun | 0 | 9 | 32 | 5 | 3 | 12 | 48 | -3 | 106 |
| 43 | Jul | 10 | -6 | 28 | 19 | 0 | 16 | 22 | -7 | 82 |
| 44 | Aug | 29 | -19 | 11 | 16 | -24 | 22 | 18 | -18 | 35 |
| 45 | Sep | 16 | -13 | 16 | 22 | -19 | 26 | 26 | -11 | 63 |
| 46 | Oct | 16 | -38 | 28 | 16 | -25 | 29 | 32 | 7 | 65 |
| 47 | Nov | 16 | -67 | 29 | 64 | -67 | 16 | 35 | -7 | 19 |
| 48 | Dec | 14 | -41 | 16 | 16 | -45 | 17 | 23 | -13 | -13 |
| 49 | Total | 248 | -124 | 275 | 286 | -249 | 281 | 321 | 0 | 1,038 |

cells highlighted in red rank in the bottom 10 percent in sales increases

Net Increase

Tom immediately sees that the bottom 10 percent come from only regions R02 and R05, and that six of the nine cells highlighted occurred in the most recent months: October, November, and December. Conditional formatting helped Tom isolate and highlight potential problem areas, which he can investigate further.

When you use conditional formatting to highlight cells in a worksheet, you should always include a **legend**, which is a key that shows each color used in the worksheet and what it means, so others know why certain cells are highlighted. You will add a legend to the Monthly Sales worksheet.

### To create a conditional formatting legend:

1. In cell D51, type **light red**, and then click cell D51 to make it the active cell. You will use a highlight rule to fill this cell with the light red color used for the bottom 10 percent sales increases.

2. In the Styles group on the Home tab, click the **Conditional Formatting** button, point to **Highlight Cells Rules**, and then click **Text that Contains**. The Text That Contains dialog box opens.

3. Verify that **light red** appears in the Format cells that contain the text box, select **Light Red Fill with Dark Red Text** in the with box, and then click the **OK** button. Cell D51 is filled with the same light red fill color used for the bottom 10 percent values.

4. In cell D52, type **light green**, and then click cell **D52** to make it the active cell. You will use a highlight rule to fill this cell with the green color used for the top 10 percent sales increases.

5. In the Styles group, click the **Conditional Formatting** button, point to **Highlight Cells Rules**, and then click **Text that Contains**. The Text That Contains dialog box opens.

▶ **6.** Verify that **light green** appears in the Format cells that contain the text box, select **Green Fill with Dark Green Text** in the with box, and then click the **OK** button. Cell D52 is filled with the same light green fill color used for the top 10 percent values.

▶ **7.** In cell E51, enter **Bottom 10% in terms of sales increase** and then, in cell E52, enter **Top 10% in terms of sales increase**.

▶ **8.** Select the range **E51:E52**. You'll format these cells with a cell style to distinguish them from the rest of the text in the worksheet.

▶ **9.** In the Styles group, click the **Cell Styles** button, and then, in the Data and Model section, click **Explanatory** (the third cell style in the first row).

▶ **10.** Click cell **A35** to deselect the range. The legend is complete. See Figure 2-36.

| Figure 2-36 | Conditional formatting legend |
| --- | --- |

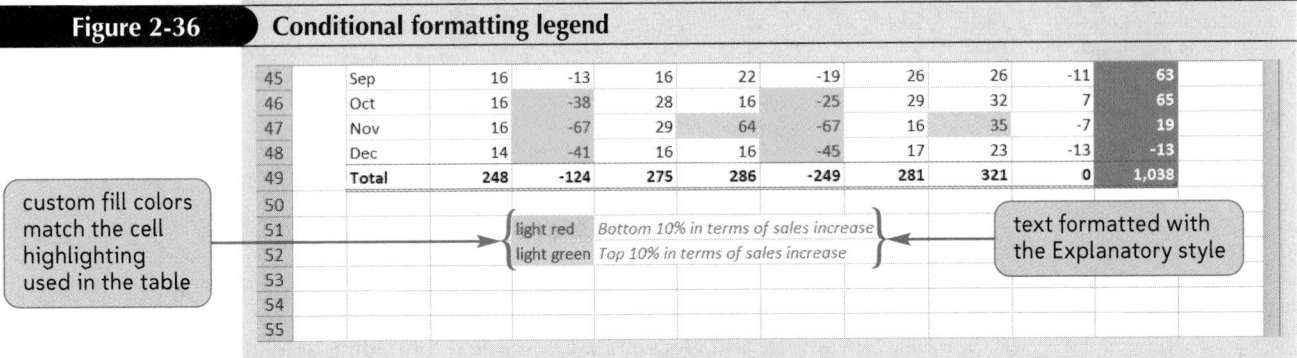

custom fill colors match the cell highlighting used in the table

text formatted with the Explanatory style

The conditional formatting in the Monthly Sales worksheet helps Tom understand how sales of the X310 heart rate monitor changed over the past two years and helps him focus on particular sales regions for additional analysis.

### Using Conditional Formatting Effectively

Conditional formatting is an excellent way to highlight important trends and data values to clients and colleagues. However, it should be used judiciously. An overuse of conditional formatting can sometimes obscure the very data values you want to emphasize. You'll need to make decisions about what to highlight and how it should be highlighted. Keep in mind the following tips as you consider the best ways to effectively communicate your findings to others:

• **Document the conditional formats you use.** If a bold, green font means that a sales number is in the top 10 percent of all sales, include that information in a legend in the worksheet.

• **Don't clutter data with too much highlighting.** Limit highlighting rules to one or two per data set. Highlights are designed to draw attention to points of interest. If you use too many, you'll end up highlighting everything—and, therefore, nothing.

• **Use color sparingly in worksheets with highlights.** It's difficult to tell a highlight color from a regular fill color, especially when fill colors are used in every cell.

• **Consider alternatives to conditional formats.** If you want to highlight the top 10 sales regions, it might be more effective to simply sort the data with the best-selling regions at the top of the list.

Remember that the goal of highlighting is to provide a strong visual clue of important data or results. Careful use of conditional formatting helps readers to focus on the important points you want to make rather than be distracted by secondary issues and facts.

# Hiding Worksheet Data

The Monthly Sales worksheet contains too much data to fit into the worksheet window without drastically reducing the zoom level, which would make the contents too small to read easily. One way to manage the contents of a large worksheet is to selectively hide (and later unhide) those rows and columns containing extraneous information, allowing you to focus your attention on only a select few data points. Hiding rows, columns, and worksheets is a good way to manage a large volume of information; but it should never be used to hide data that is crucial to understanding a workbook. Note that hiding a row or column does not affect the other formulas in the workbook. Formulas still show the correct value even if they reference a cell in a hidden row or column.

Tom wants to view only the third table, which shows the difference in sales between 2011 and 2012, but not the other tables. You'll hide the rows that contain the first two tables and then unhide those rows after Tom has looked at the third table.

### To hide and unhide worksheet rows:

1. Select row **6** through row **35** in the Monthly Sales worksheet.

2. In the Cells group on the Home tab, click the **Format** button, point to **Hide & Unhide**, and then click **Hide Rows**. Rows 6 to 35 are hidden, and the row numbers in the worksheet jump from row 5 to row 36. The data in the third table hasn't changed even though its formulas use data from the hidden tables.

3. Select row **5** and row **36**, which are the rows before and after the hidden rows.

4. In the Cells group, click the **Format** button, point to **Hide & Unhide**, and then click **Unhide Rows**. The hidden rows 6 through 35 reappear.

> **TIP**
>
> You can also hide or unhide a row or column by right-clicking the row or column header and clicking Hide or Unhide from the shortcut menu.

# Formatting the Worksheet for Printing

Your final task is to prepare the workbook for the printer. Excel supports a wealth of print options, including the ability to set the page orientation as well as specify whether the page will include headers and footers. Print settings can be applied to an entire workbook or to individual sheets. Because it is likely that other people, such as clients and colleagues, will see the printed version of your spreadsheet, you should take as much care in formatting the printed output as you do in formatting the contents of the electronic file.

Tom wants you to print the analysis of the monthly sales figures. You'll look at the Monthly Sales worksheet in Page Layout view to see how it would currently print.

### To view a worksheet in Page Layout view:

1. Click the **Page Layout** button 🔲 on the status bar. The worksheet switches to Page Layout view.

2. Change the zoom level of the worksheet to **70%** to view more of the page layout. See Figure 2-37.

Figure 2-37    **Page Layout view of the Monthly Sales worksheet**

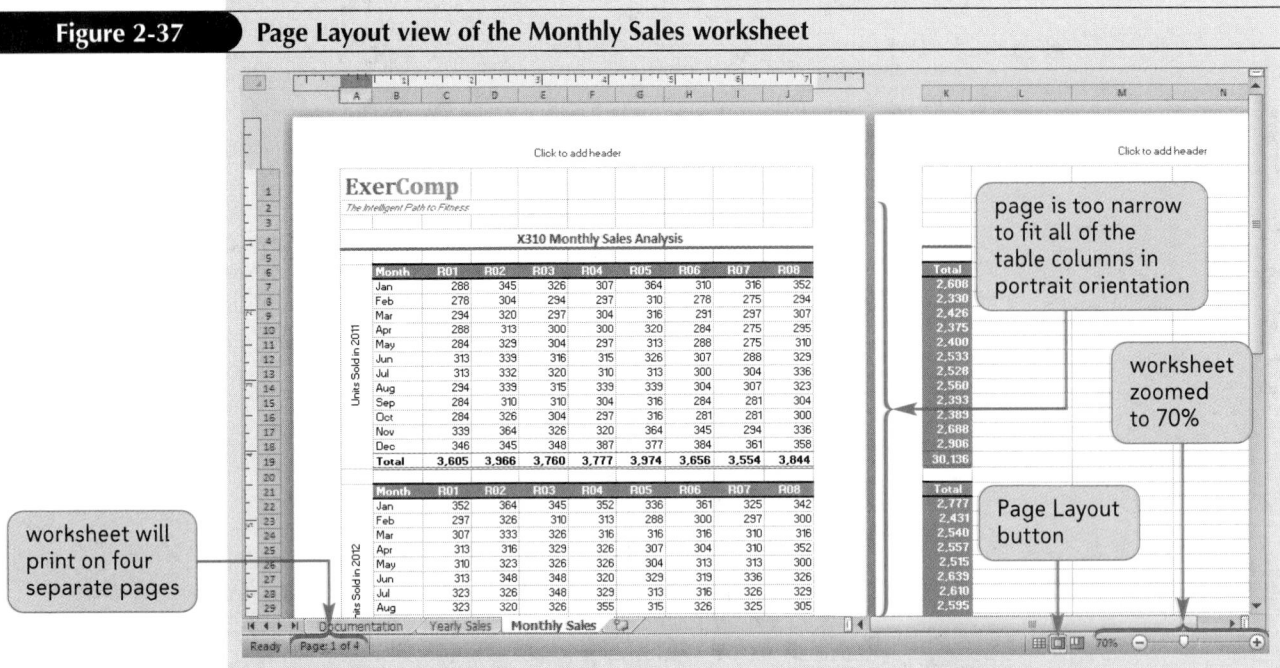

In the worksheet's current orientation, its contents do not fit on a single page and the tables break across pages. You'll change the orientation from portrait to landscape so that the page is wide enough to fit all the table columns on one page.

## To change to landscape orientation:

1. Click the **Page Layout** tab on the Ribbon.

2. In the Page Setup group, click the **Orientation** button, and then click **Landscape**. The page orientation changes to landscape, making each page wide enough to display all of the columns of each table.

## Defining the Print Area

By default, all cells in the active worksheet containing text, formulas, or values are printed. The region that is sent to the printer from the active sheet is known as the **print area**. To print part of a worksheet, you can define the print area, overriding the default setting. A print area can cover an adjacent or nonadjacent range in the current worksheet.

There are many different ways to define the print area, but it's generally easiest to set the print area in Page Break Preview. For example, if Tom wanted to print only the first table in the Monthly Sales worksheet, you could define the print area to cover that range while in Page Break Preview. You will go to Page Break Preview, and then set the print area.

## To switch to Page Break preview and set the print area:

1. Click the **Page Break Preview** button 🔲 on the status bar.

   **Trouble?** If the Welcome to Page Break Preview dialog box opens, click the OK button.

2. Change the zoom level of the worksheet to **70%**.

3. Select the range **A1:K19**, which is the range of the first table.

4. In the Page Setup group on the Page Layout tab, click the **Print Area** button, and then click **Set Print Area**. The print area changes to cover only the range A1:K19. The rest of the worksheet content is shaded to indicate that it will not be part of the printout.

5. In the Page Setup group, click the **Print Area** button, and then click **Clear Print Area**. The print area is reset to cover the entire contents of the worksheet.

## Inserting Page Breaks

Often the contents of a worksheet do not fit onto a single page. By default, Excel prints as much of the content that fits on single page without resizing the content, and then inserts **automatic page breaks** to continue printing the remaining worksheet content on successive pages. This can result in page breaks that leave a single column or row on a separate page or split worksheet content in awkward places such as within a table.

One way to fix this problem is to scale the printout by reducing the font size to fit on a single sheet of paper. However, if you have more than one or two columns or rows to fit onto the page, the resulting text is often too small to read comfortably. The better fix is usually to split the worksheet into logical segments, which you can do by inserting **manual page breaks** that specify exactly where the page breaks occur. A page break is inserted directly above and to the left of a selected cell, directly above a selected row, or to the left of a selected column.

### Inserting and Removing Page Breaks

**To insert a page break:**
- Select the first cell below the row where you want to insert a page break.
- In the Page Setup group on the Page Layout tab, click the Breaks button, and then click Insert Page Break.

**To remove a page break:**
- Select any cell below or to the right of the page break you want to remove.
- In the Page Setup group on the Page Layout tab, click the Breaks button, and then click Remove Page Break (or click Reset All Page Breaks to remove all the page breaks from the worksheet).

Tom wants the three tables in the Monthly Sales worksheet to print on separate pages. You'll insert page breaks to accomplish this.

### To insert page breaks between the tables:

1. Click cell **A20**. With this cell selected, a page break will be inserted between rows 19 and 20.

2. In the Page Setup group on the Page Layout tab, click the **Breaks** button, and then click **Insert Page Break**. A page break separates row 19 from row 20.

3. Click cell **A35**, and then repeat Step 2 to insert a page break that splits the second table from the third. The printout is now three pages. See Figure 2-38.

**Figure 2-38** Worksheet in Page Break Preview

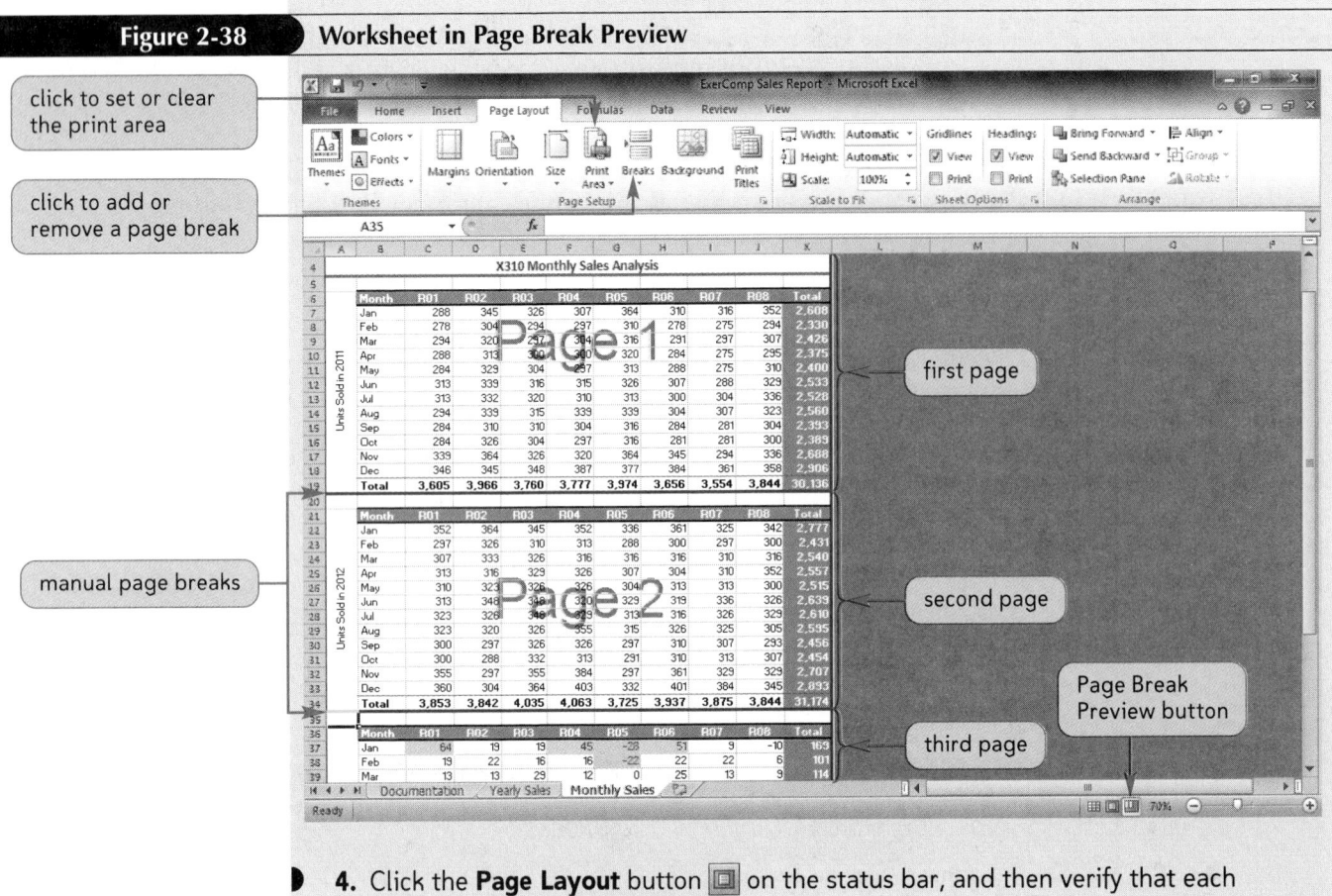

click to set or clear the print area

click to add or remove a page break

manual page breaks

first page

second page

Page Break Preview button

third page

**4.** Click the **Page Layout** button on the status bar, and then verify that each table appears on a separate page.

## Adding Print Titles

It is a good practice to include descriptive information, such as the company name, logo, and worksheet title on each page of a printout in case a page becomes separated from the other pages. You can repeat information, such as the company name, by specifying which rows or columns in the worksheet act as print titles. If a worksheet contains a large table, you can print the table's column headings and row headings on every page of your printout by designating those initial columns and rows as print titles.

In the Monthly Sales worksheet, the company name, the slogan, and the worksheet title all appear on the first page of the printout, but do not appear on the other two pages. You will define the range that includes this text as a print title. These four rows will then print on each page.

### To define the print title for the pages:

**1.** In the Page Setup group on the Page Layout tab, click the **Print Titles** button. The Page Setup dialog box opens with the Sheet tab displayed.

**2.** Click the **Rows to repeat at top** box, move your pointer over the worksheet, and then select the range **A1:A4**. A flashing border appears around the first four rows of the worksheet as a visual indicator that the contents of the first four rows will be repeated on each page of the printout. The cell reference $1:$4 appears in the Rows to repeat at top box.

3. Click the **OK** button.

4. Scroll through the second and third pages of the printout in Page Layout view to verify that the company name, slogan, and worksheet title appear on each page. See Figure 2-39.

**Figure 2-39**   **Third page of the printout**

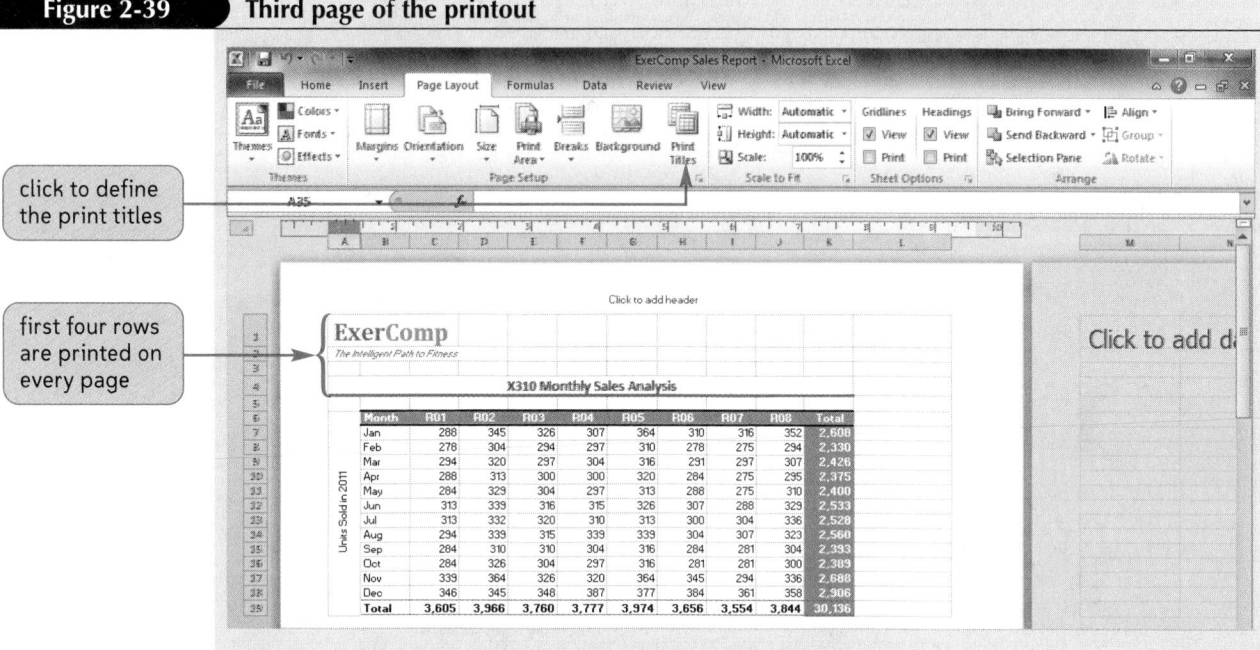

click to define the print titles

first four rows are printed on every page

The Sheet tab in the Page Setup dialog box provides other print options, such as printing the gridlines or row and column headings. You can also print the worksheet in black and white or in draft quality. For a multiple page printout, you can specify whether the pages are ordered by going down the worksheet and then across, or across first and then down.

## Creating Page Headers and Footers

Another way to repeat information on each printed page is with headers and footers. Headers and footers contain helpful and descriptive text that is usually not found within the worksheet, such as the workbook's author, the current date, or the workbook file-name. If the printout covers multiple pages, you can display the page number and the total number of pages in the printout to help ensure you and others have all the pages.

The header and footer each have three sections: a left section, a center section, and a right section. Within each section, you type the text you want to appear or insert elements such as the worksheet name or the current date and time. These header and footer elements are dynamic; if you rename the worksheet, for example, the name is automatically updated in the header or footer.

Tom wants his printouts to display the workbook's filename in the header's left section and the current date in the header's right section. He wants the center footer to display the page number and the total number of pages in the printout, and the right footer to display your name as the workbook's author.

### To insert a header and footer:

1. In Page Layout view, change the zoom level of the worksheet to **90%**.

▶ **2.** Scroll to the top of the worksheet, and then click the left section of the header directly above cell A1. The Header & Footer Tools contextual tab appears on the Ribbon.

▶ **3.** Type **Filename:** in the left section of the header, press the **spacebar**, and then, in the Header & Footer Elements group on the Design tab, click the **File Name** button. The code &[File], which displays the filename of the current workbook, is added into the left section of the header.

▶ **4.** Press the **Tab** key twice to move to the right section of the header, and then click the **Current Date** button in the Header & Footer Elements group. The code &[Date] is added into the right section of the header. See Figure 2-40.

| Figure 2-40 | Page header with content |
| --- | --- |

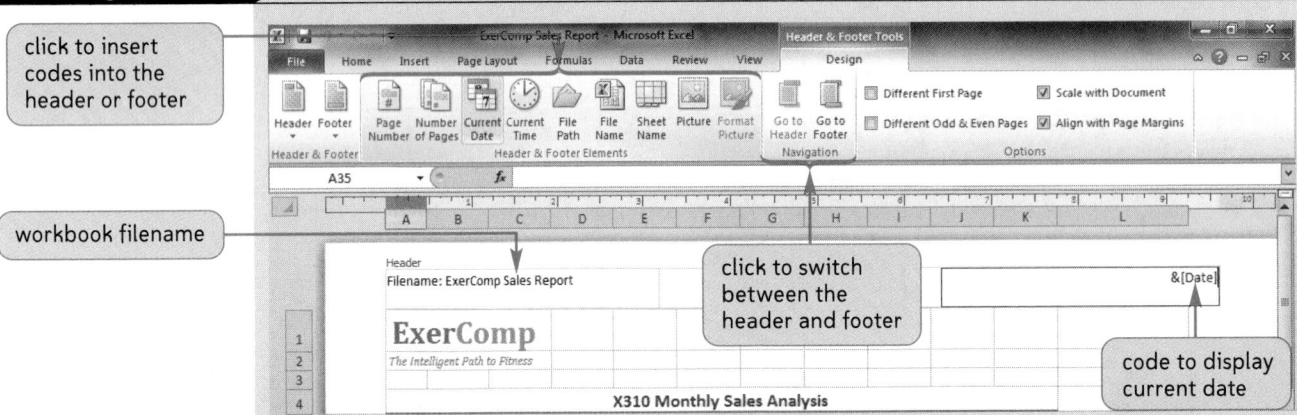

click to insert codes into the header or footer

workbook filename

click to switch between the header and footer

code to display current date

▶ **5.** In the Navigation group on the Design tab, click the **Go to Footer** button. The right section of the footer is selected.

▶ **6.** Click the center section of the footer, type **Page**, press the **spacebar**, and click the **Page Number** button in the Header & Footer Elements group.

▶ **7.** Press the **spacebar**, type **of**, press the **spacebar**, and then click the **Number of Pages** button in the Header & Footer Elements group. The text Page &[Page] of &[Pages] appears in the center section of the footer.

▶ **8.** Press the **Tab** key to move to the right section of the footer, type **Prepared by:**, press the **spacebar**, and then type your name. See Figure 2-41.

| Figure 2-41 | Page footer |
| --- | --- |

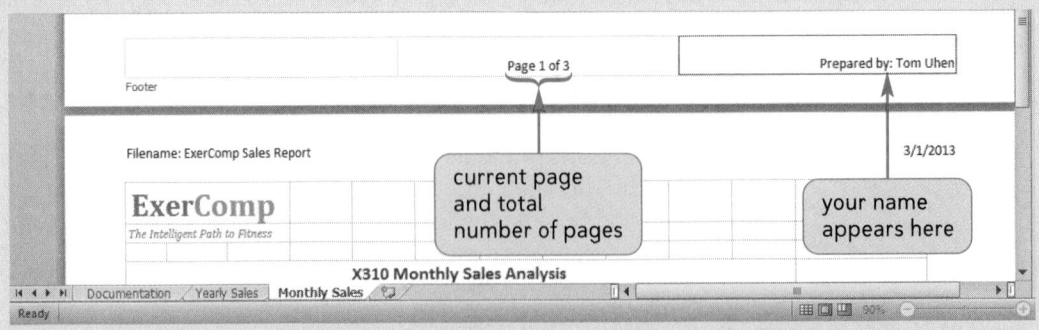

current page and total number of pages

your name appears here

▶ **9.** Click cell **A1**, and then scroll through the other two pages of the worksheet to verify that the same header appears for each page, and the center section of the footer displays the correct page number and total number of pages.

## Defining the Page Margins

Another way to fit a large worksheet on a single page is to reduce the size of the page margins. By default, Excel sets the page margins to between 0.7 and 0.75 inches, and allows for 0.3-inch margins around the page header and footer. You can reduce or increase these margins as needed by selecting from a set of predefined margin sizes or defining your own.

Tom's reports need wide margins to accommodate the page binding. You will change the default margins for the printout.

**To set the page margins:**

▶ **1.** Click the **Page Layout** tab on the Ribbon.

▶ **2.** In the Page Setup group, click the **Margins** button. A menu opens with a list of predefined margins.

▶ **3.** Click **Wide** to set 1-inch margins around the printed content with 0.5-inch margins around the header and footer. The size of the margins around the page increases, but does not affect the content. Each of the three tables and the print titles still fit on single sheets.

Tom is happy with the appearance of the worksheet and the layout of the printout. You will save the workbook, and then print the Monthly Sales worksheet.

**To save the workbook and print the worksheet:**

▶ **1.** Click the **Normal** button ⊞ on the status bar to return the Monthly Sales worksheet to Normal view.

▶ **2.** Save the workbook.

▶ **3.** Print the Monthly Sales worksheet, and then close the workbook. Each table is printed on a separate page, and the headers and footers display the filename, current date, page number and total number of pages, and your name.

Tom will distribute the finished report during the upcoming sales meeting.

**REVIEW**

### Session 2.2 Quick Check

**1.** Discuss two methods of applying the same format to different ranges.

**2.** Describe the difference between a cell style and a table style.

**3.** What are the six table style options you can turn on and off?

**4.** What is a conditional format?

**5.** How would you highlight the top five values in the range A1:C20?

**6.** How do you insert a page break into a worksheet?

**7.** What are print titles?

**8.** Describe how to add the workbook filename in the center section of the footer on every page of your printout.

*Practice the skills you learned in the tutorial using the same case scenario.*

**PRACTICE**

# Review Assignments

**Data Files needed for the Review Assignments: X410.xlsx, Paper.jpg**

ExerComp introduced another heart rate monitor, the X410, two years ago. Tom wants you to format a workbook that compares the sales of the X310 and X410 models during that time. The workbook already has a Documentation sheet, a Model Comparison sheet comparing the total units sold for each model in the eight sales regions, and a Monthly Sales sheet reporting the number of units sold per month.

In the Model Comparison sheet, you will highlight the sales regions that showed the greatest sales increases from 2011 to 2012. In the Monthly Sales sheet, you will calculate the monthly sales totals for both models during 2011 and 2012. Complete the following:

1. Open the **X410** workbook located in the Excel2\Review folder included with your Data Files, and then save the workbook as **X410 Sales Comparison**.

2. In the Documentation sheet, enter your name in cell B4 and the date in the format *mm/dd/yyyy* in cell B5.

3. In the Documentation sheet, set the font color of cells A1 and A2 to blue, format the text in cell A1 in a 26-point Times New Roman font, and then format the text in cell A2 in a 10-point italicized Times New Roman font. In cell A1, change the font color of the text "Comp" to red.

4. In the range A4:A6, set the font color to white and set the fill color to blue. In the range B4:B6, set the fill color to white. In the range A4:B6, add border lines around all of the cells.

5. In cell B5, display the date with the Long Date format and left-align it within the cell.

6. In the Documentation sheet, insert a background image using the **Paper.jpg** image file located in the Excel2\Review folder included with your Data Files.

7. Use the Format Painter to copy the format from the range A1:A2 in the Documentation sheet to the range A1:A2 in the other two sheets. In cell A1, change the font color of the text "Comp" to red.

8. Go to the Model Comparison sheet. In cells E6 and E17, enter **Increase**. In ranges E7:E14 and E18:E25, enter formulas to calculate the increase in sales for each region.

9. In cells F6 and F17, enter the text **% Increase**. In ranges F7:F14 and F18:F25, enter formulas to calculate the percent increase in sales for each region.

10. In cells B15 and B26, enter the text **Total**. In cells C15, D15, C26, and D26, enter formulas to calculate the total units sold per year for each model. In cells E15 and E26, enter formulas to calculate the total increase in sales. In cells F15 and F26, enter formulas to calculate the percent increase in total sales from 2011 to 2012.

11. Merge and center the range A6:A15, center the text vertically, and then change the orientation to vertical text. Center the text in the range C6:F6, and then indent the region labels in the range B7:B14 one character.

12. In the range C7:E15, format the numbers in a Number format using a thousands separator, no decimal places, and negative numbers displayed with a minus symbol. In the range F7:F15, format the numbers in a Percentage format with two decimal places.

13. Apply the Accent1 cell style to the range B6:F6 and the merged cell A6. Change the font of cell A6 to 18 points and bold. Apply the Total cell style to the range B15:F15.

14. In the range E7:E14, apply a conditional format that adds a Top/Bottom Rule to display the highest number in the range in dark green text with a green fill. In the range F7:F14, apply a conditional format that adds a Top/Bottom Rule to display the highest number in the range in dark red text with a light red fill.

15. Use the Format Painter to copy all of the formats from the range A6:F15 to the range A17:F26.

16. In cell D3, enter **highest**, and then apply a conditional format to cell D3 that adds a Highlight Cells Rule to format the cell that contains the text "highest" with Green Fill with Dark Green Text. In cell D4, enter **highest**, and then apply a conditional format to cell D4 that adds a Highlight Cells Rule to format the cell that contains the text "highest" with Light Red Fill with Dark Red Text.

17. In cell E3, enter **Highest increase in units sold**. In cell E4, enter **Highest % increase in units sold**. Format both cells with the Explanatory Text cell style.

18. Go to the Monthly Sales sheet. In cells D5 and I5, enter the text **All Models**. In cells A18 and F18, enter the text **Total**.

19. Enter formulas in the worksheet to calculate the total sales by month, by model, and then over all months and over both models.

20. Merge and center the range A4:D4, merge and center the range F4:I4, and then apply the Heading 1 style to both merged cells. In the range B5:D5;G5:I5, center the text.

21. In the nonadjacent range B6:D18;G6:I18, format the numbers to show a thousands separator (,) with no decimal places to the right of the decimal point.

22. Select the range A5:D18, and then apply Table Style Light 8 (the first table style in the second row of the Light section in the Table Styles gallery). Turn off the filter arrows, and then display only the header row, first column, and last column table style options. In the range A18:D18, apply the Total cell style.

23. Select the range F5:I18, and then repeat Step 22, applying the Total cell style to the range F18:I18.

24. For the Model Comparison and Monthly Sales worksheets, set the page orientation to landscape, display your name in the center section of the header, display the sheet name in the left section of the footer, display the workbook filename in the center section of the footer, and then display the current date in the right section of the footer.

25. Save and close your workbook. Submit the finished workbook to your instructor, either in printed or electronic form, as requested.

---

APPLY

**Case Problem 1**

If you have a SAM 2010 user profile, your instructor may have assigned an autogradable version of this assignment. If so, log into the SAM 2010 Web site at www.cengage.com/sam2010 to download the instructions and start files.

**Data File needed for the Case Problem: Frosti.xlsx**

*FrostiWear*    Linda Young is a sales manager for FrostiWear, a successful new store based in Hillsboro, Oregon. She's tracking the sales figures for FrostiWear's line of gloves. She created a workbook that contains the sales figures from the past year for three glove models. She wants you to help format the sales report. Complete the following:

1. Open the **Frosti** workbook located in the Excel2\Case1 folder included with your Data Files, and then save the workbook as **FrostiWear Sales Report**.

2. In the Documentation sheet, enter your name in cell B3 and the date in cell B4. Set the background color for all the cells in the worksheet to standard blue, and then set the background color for the range B3:B5 to white. Add a border line around each cell in the range B3:B5.

3. Change the font of cell A1 to the Headings font of the current theme, change the font size to 36 points, change the font color to white, and then bold the text. Change the font size of the range A3:A5 to 16 points, change the font color to white, and then bold the text.

4. Go to the Glove Sales worksheet. Add formulas to calculate the total sales for each month and region over the three glove models.

5. Merge and center the range A1:H1, apply the Title cell style, and then increase the font size to 26 points. Merge and center the range A2:H2, apply the Heading 4 cell style, and then increase the font size to 16 points.

6. Merge and center the range A3:A16, set the alignment to Middle Align, rotate the text up, apply the Accent1 cell style, increase the font size to 18 points, and then bold the text.

7. Use the Format Painter to copy the format of merged cell A3 into the two ranges A18:A31 and A33:A46.

8. Center the text in the range C3:H3. Format the range C4:H16 to include thousands separators (,) and no decimal places. Use the Format Painter to copy the formats in the range C3:H16 to the two ranges C18:H31 and C33:H46.

9. In the range B3:H16, apply the Table Style Medium 2 table style. Turn off the filter arrows, and then display the header row, first column, last column, and banded rows. In the range B16:H16, change the fill color of the Total row to standard yellow.

10. Repeat Step 9 for the other two tables in the worksheet.

11. In the Glove Sales worksheet, set the page orientation to landscape, insert manual page breaks at cells A18 and A33, and then repeat the first two rows of the worksheet on every printed page.

12. Display your name in the center header, display the filename in the left footer, display **Page** *page number* **of** *number of pages* in the center footer, and then display the current date in the right footer.

13. Save and close your workbook. Submit the finished workbook to your instructor.

*Add formulas and formatting to create a packing slip.*

**CREATE**

## Case Problem 2

**Data File needed for the Case Problem: GrillRite.xlsx**

***GrillRite Grills***    Brian Simpko is a shipping manager at GrillRite Grills in Hammond, Indiana. He uses an Excel workbook to provide shipping and order information for customer orders and deliveries. You will create and format the worksheet that Brian can use to enter information for packing slips. Complete the following:

1. Open the **GrillRite** workbook located in the Excel2\Case2 folder included with your Data Files, and then save the workbook as **GrillRite Grills Packing Slip**. In the Documentation sheet, enter your name in cell B3 and the date in cell B4.

2. Insert a new worksheet at the end of the workbook, and then rename it **Packing Slip**.

3. In the Packing Slip worksheet, select all of the cells in the worksheet. (*Hint*: Click the Select All button at the intersection of the row and column headings.) Change the font to the Body font of the current theme. For the range A1:D3, set the fill color to black and the font color to white.

4. Set the width of columns A through D to 20 characters. Set the height of row 1 to 36 characters.

5. Merge the range A1:B3, and then left- and top-align the merged cell. Merge the range C1:D3, and then right- and top-align the merged cell.

6. In cell A1, enter the following three lines of text, and then format the first line in a 26-point bold font using the Headings font of the current theme:

**GrillRite Grills**

**200 Commerce Lane**

**Hammond, Indiana 46324**

7. In cell C1, enter **Packing Slip**, and then format the text in a 26-point bold font using the Headings font of the current theme.

8. In the range A5:A7, enter the following three lines of text in a bold font, and then right-align the text and indent the text one character:

    **Order Date**

    **Order Number**

    **Purchase Order**

9. Format cell B5 in the Long Date format. Insert border lines around each of the cells in the range B5:B7.

10. In the range C5:C7, enter the following three lines of text, and then use the Format Painter to copy the formats from the range A5:B7 to the range C5:D7:

    **Date**

    **Sales Rep**

    **Account Num**

11. In cell B9, enter **Ship To**. In cell D9, enter **Bill To**. Format the text in both cells in a bold font.

12. In cell A10, enter **Address** in a bold font, right-align the text, and then indent it one character.

13. Merge the cells in the range B10:B15, left- and top-align the cell contents, and then insert a border around the merged cell. Click the Wrap Text button from the Alignment group on the Home tab to ensure that text within this cell wraps to a new line.

14. In cell C10, enter **Address**. Copy the format from the range A10:B15 into the range C10:D15.

15. Enter the following data into the worksheet:

    Cell A17: **Item**

    Cell B17: **Product No.**

    Cell C17: **Description**

    Cell D17: **Order Quantity**

    cells A18:A27: the numbers from **1** to **10**

16. For the range A17:D27, apply Table Style Medium 1, turn off the filter arrows, and display the header row, Total row, and banded rows. In cell D28, select the SUM function from the list.

17. In cell A30, enter **Comments** in a bold font.

18. Merge the range A31:D39, left- and top-align the cell contents, and then add a thick box border around the merged cell.

19. In cell D40, enter **Thank you for your business!** in an italic, 16-point font, and then right-align the cell contents.

20. Enter the packing slip data shown in Figure 2-42.

**Figure 2-42**    GrillRite Grills packing slip

21. Make sure the worksheet's page orientation is set to portrait, and then add a footer that displays your name in the left section, the filename in the center section, and the current date in the right section.

22. Save and close your workbook. Submit the finished workbook to your instructor, either in printed or electronic form, as requested.

*Apply conditional formats to create a wind speed grid.*

**CHALLENGE**

## Case Problem 3

Data File needed for the Case Problem: Wind.xlsx

*Arcadia Wind Farm*    Tara Young is a researcher at Arcadia Wind Farm, a government research center near Topeka, Kansas, involved in exploring how to create economical and efficient wind farms. One of Tara's jobs is to record wind speeds from different sectors of the wind farm. Tara has entered the wind speed data into a workbook as a table with wind speed measures laid out in a grid. Because the numbers are difficult to read and interpret, you will color code the wind speed values using a conditional format. Complete the following:

1. Open the **Wind** workbook located in the Excel2\Case3 folder included with your Data Files, and then save the workbook as **Wind Farm**. In the Documentation sheet, enter your name and the date.

2. Go to the Wind Speed Grid worksheet. Merge the range A1:V1, and then apply the Heading 1 style to the merged cell and set the font size to 20 points.

3. Select the range B3:V3, and then change the font style to white text on a black background. Copy this formatting to the grid coordinates in the range A4:A64.

4. Select the range B4:V64. The data in this range comprises the wind speed measures for different sensors in Sector 5.

**EXPLORE**

5. Create a conditional formatting that highlights cells whose value equals 18 with fill color equal to the RGB color value (99, 37, 35). (*Hint*: In the Equal To dialog box, select Custom Format in the with box to open the Format Cells dialog box. On the Fill tab, in the Background Color section, click the More Colors button, and then click the Custom tab to enter the RGB color value.)

**EXPLORE**

6. Repeat Step 5 to continue creating conditional formats that set highlight colors for the following wind speed values:

| Wind Speed | RGB Color Value |
|---|---|
| 16 m/s | (150, 54, 52) |
| 14 m/s | (218, 150, 148) |
| 12 m/s | (230, 184, 183) |
| 10 m/s | (242, 220, 219) |
| 8 m/s | (242, 242, 242) |
| 6 m/s | (255, 255, 255) |
| 4 m/s | (197, 217, 241) |
| 2 m/s | (141, 180, 226) |
| 0 m/s | (83, 141, 213) |

7. In the range B4:V64, reduce the font size of the values to 1 point.

8. Enclose each of the cells in the range B4:V64 in a light gray border.

9. Apply the conditional highlight colors specified in Steps 5 and 6 to the legend values in the cell range X3:X12.

10. Merge the range Y3:Y12, and then center the contents of the merged cell and rotate the text down. Display the text in a bold 18-point font.

11. Set the print area of the page to the range A1:Y64.

**EXPLORE**

12. On the Page Layout tab, scale the page to fit on a single page. (*Hint*: Use the Width and Height boxes in the Scale to Fit group to force the worksheet to fit on one page.)

13. Add a header to the printed page with your name in the top-left header and the filename in the top-right header.

14. Save and close your workbook. Submit the finished workbook to your instructor, either in printed or electronic form, as requested.

---

## Case Problem 4

*Format a meal-planning worksheet that highlights high-calorie and high-fat foods.*

**CREATE**

**Data File needed for the Case Problem: Life.xlsx**

*Life Managers*   Kate Dee is a dietician at Life Managers, a company in Kleinville, Michigan, that specializes in personal improvement, particularly in areas of health and fitness. Kate wants to create a meal-planning workbook for her clients who want to lose weight and improve their health. One goal of meal planning is to decrease the percentage of fat in the diet. Kate thinks it would be helpful to highlight foods that have a high percentage of fat as well as list their total fat calories. She already created an Excel work-book that contains a few sample food items and lists the number of calories and grams of fat in each item. She wants you to format this workbook. Complete the following:

1. Open the **Life** workbook located in the Excel2\Case4 folder included with your Data Files, and then save the workbook as **Life Managers Nutrition Table**. In the Documentation sheet, enter your name in cell B3 and the date in cell B4.

2. In the Meal Planner worksheet, add a column that calculates the calories from fat for each food item. Fat contains nine calories per gram.

3. Add a column that calculates the percentage of fat for each food item. This value is calculated by dividing the calories from fat by the total number of calories.

4. Display all values for calories and grams of fat with one decimal place. Display the fat percentages as percentages with one decimal place.

5. Format the rest of the Meal Planner worksheet attractively, but be sure to include at least one example of each of the following design elements:
   - A range merged into a single cell
   - Text centered and rotated within a cell
   - Cell styles applied to one or more elements
   - Borders applied to one or more elements

6. For good health, the FDA recommends that the fat percentage should not exceed 30 percent of the total calories per day. Apply a rule to the fat percentages to highlight those food items that exceed the FDA recommendation. Include a legend to document the highlighting color you used.

7. Add descriptive headers and footers to the printed document. Also insert page breaks and print titles to ensure that the printout is easily read and interpreted.

8. Save and close your workbook. Submit the finished workbook to your instructor, either in printed or electronic form, as requested.

## SAM: Skills Assessment Manager

**ASSESS**

For current SAM information, including versions and content details, visit SAM Central (http://samcentral.course.com). If you have a SAM user profile, you may have access to hands-on instruction, practice, and assessment of the skills covered in this tutorial. Because various versions of SAM are supported throughout the life of this text, check with your instructor for the correct instructions and URL/Web site for accessing assignments.

### ENDING DATA FILES

Excel2

**Tutorial**
Background.jpg
ExerComp Sales Report.xlsx

**Review**
Paper.jpg
X410 Sales Comparison.xlsx

**Case1**
FrostiWear Sales Report.xlsx

**Case2**
GrillRite Grills Packing Slip.xlsx

**Case3**
Wind Farm.xlsx

**Case4**
Life Managers Nutrition Table.xlsx

## OBJECTIVES

**Session 3.1**
- Copy formulas
- Build formulas containing relative, absolute, and mixed references
- Review function syntax
- Insert a function with the Insert Function dialog box
- Search for a function
- Type a function directly in a cell

**Session 3.2**
- Use AutoFill to fill in a formula and complete a series
- Enter the IF logical function
- Insert the date with the TODAY function
- Use the PMT financial function to calculate monthly mortgage payments

# Working with Formulas and Functions

*Developing a Family Budget*

## Case | *Drake Family Budget*

Newlyweds Diane and Glenn Drake are trying to balance career, school, and family life. The couple's income and expenses vary throughout the year. Diane works full-time as a legal assistant, but earns less in the summer months when she cuts back her work hours to attend summer courses. Glenn is in a graduate program at a nearby university where he recently was hired as a lab assistant. In the summer, Glenn takes on other work to earn additional income. The couple just moved into a new apartment, but plan to purchase a house within the next several years. Although Glenn and Diane's salaries have grown in the past few years, the couple seems to have less cash on hand. This financial shortage has prompted them to take a closer look at their finances and figure out how to best manage them.

Diane has set up an Excel workbook and entered the monthly income from their two jobs. She has identified and entered expenses the family pays on a monthly basis, such as the rent and grocery bill, as well as other expenses that occur only a few times a year, such as Glenn's tuition and vacations. She wants to calculate how much money they are bringing in and how much money they are spending. She also wants to come up with a savings plan for the down payment on a house they hope to buy in a few years.

You'll help Diane complete the workbook. You will enter formulas to perform the calculations that will provide Diane with a better overall picture of the family's finances. Diane and Glenn will be able to use this information to manage their money more effectively.

## STARTING DATA FILES

| Excel3 → | Tutorial | Review | Case1 | Case2 | Case3 | Case4 |
|---|---|---|---|---|---|---|
| | Drake.xlsx | Timov.xlsx | Chemistry.xlsx | Wizard.xlsx | Loan.xlsx | V6.xlsx |

# SESSION 3.1 VISUAL OVERVIEW

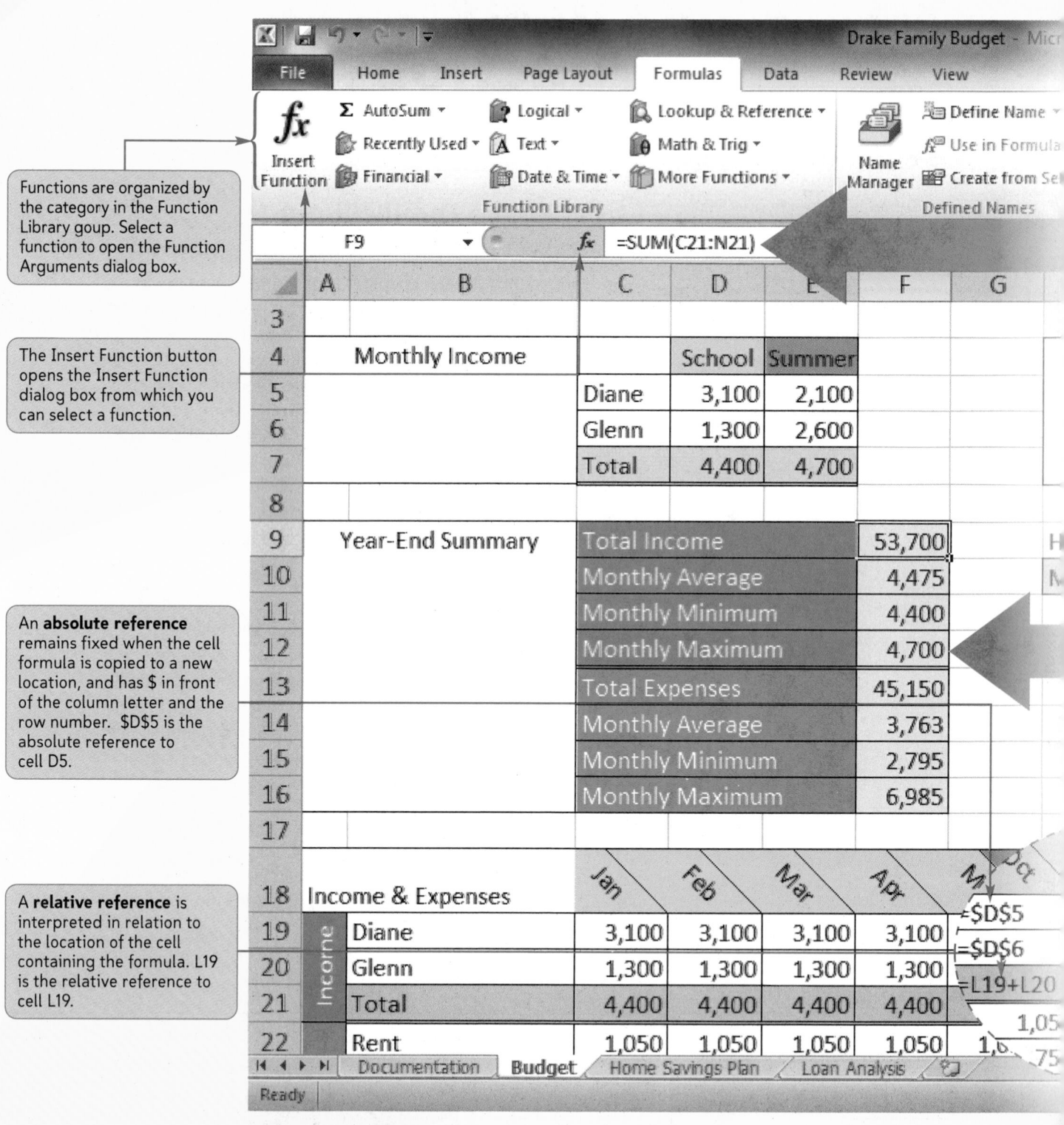

Functions are organized by the category in the Function Library goup. Select a function to open the Function Arguments dialog box.

The Insert Function button opens the Insert Function dialog box from which you can select a function.

An **absolute reference** remains fixed when the cell formula is copied to a new location, and has $ in front of the column letter and the row number. $D$5 is the absolute reference to cell D5.

A **relative reference** is interpreted in relation to the location of the cell containing the formula. L19 is the relative reference to cell L19.

# CELL REFERENCES AND EXCEL FUNCTIONS

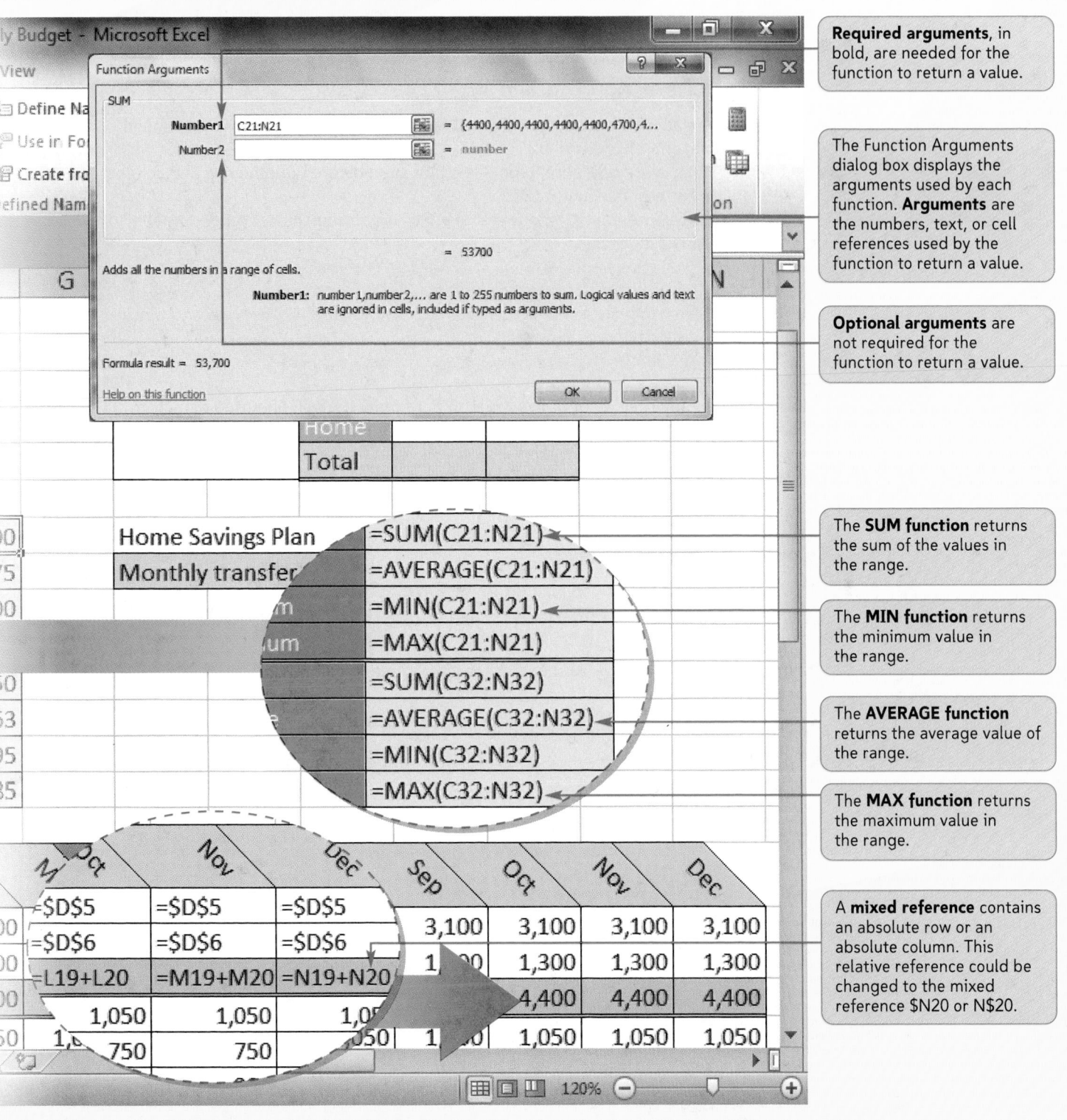

**Required arguments**, in bold, are needed for the function to return a value.

The Function Arguments dialog box displays the arguments used by each function. **Arguments** are the numbers, text, or cell references used by the function to return a value.

**Optional arguments** are not required for the function to return a value.

The **SUM function** returns the sum of the values in the range.

The **MIN function** returns the minimum value in the range.

The **AVERAGE function** returns the average value of the range.

The **MAX function** returns the maximum value in the range.

A **mixed reference** contains an absolute row or an absolute column. This relative reference could be changed to the mixed reference $N20 or N$20.

# Understanding Cell References

Most Excel workbooks are created to record and analyze data. To do this effectively, you enter data in cells in a worksheet, and then reference the cells with data in formulas that perform calculations on that data, such as adding the total of a column of numbers as part of a budget.

**REFERENCE**

## Entering Relative, Absolute, and Mixed References

- To enter a relative reference, type the cell reference as it appears in the worksheet. For example, enter B2 for cell B2.
- To enter an absolute reference, type $ (a dollar sign) before both the row and column references. For example, enter $B$2.
- To enter a mixed reference, type $ before either the row or column reference. For example, enter $B2 or B$2.

or

- Select the cell reference you want to change.
- Press the F4 key to cycle the reference from relative to absolute to mixed and then back to relative.

Diane has already done a lot of the work on her family budget. She used data from the past year to estimate the couple's monthly expenses for the upcoming year and entered this data into an Excel workbook. You will open this workbook and review her estimates of the family's monthly expenses.

### To open Diane's workbook:

1. Open the **Drake** workbook located in the **Excel3\Tutorial** folder included with your Data Files, and then save the workbook as **Drake Family Budget** in the same folder.

2. In the Documentation worksheet, enter your name in cell B3 and the date in cell B4.

3. Switch to the Budget worksheet, and then review its contents.

4. Scroll down to view the range A18:N32. This range lists Diane's estimate of her family's monthly expenses by category for the upcoming year. See Figure 3-1.

Figure 3-1    **Monthly expenses for the Drake family**

monthly expenses by category

| A | B | C | D | E | F | G | H | I | J | K | L | M | N |
|---|---|---|---|---|---|---|---|---|---|---|---|---|---|
| 17 | | | | | | | | | | | | | |
| 18 | Income & Expenses | Jan | Feb | Mar | Apr | May | Jun | Jul | Aug | Sep | Oct | Nov | Dec |
| 19 | Diane | | | | | | | | | | | | |
| 20 | Glenn | | | | | | | | | | | | |
| 21 | Total | | | | | | | | | | | | |
| 22 | Rent | 1,050 | 1,050 | 1,050 | 1,050 | 1,050 | 1,050 | 1,050 | 1,050 | 1,050 | 1,050 | 1,050 | 1,050 |
| 23 | Food | 750 | 750 | 750 | 750 | 750 | 750 | 750 | 750 | 750 | 750 | 750 | 750 |
| 24 | Utilities | 255 | 230 | 200 | 195 | 150 | 165 | 175 | 165 | 160 | 160 | 200 | 235 |
| 25 | Phone | 110 | 110 | 110 | 110 | 110 | 110 | 110 | 110 | 110 | 110 | 110 | 110 |
| 26 | Car Payments | 210 | 210 | 210 | 210 | 210 | 210 | 210 | 210 | 210 | 210 | 210 | 210 |
| 27 | Insurance | 175 | 175 | 175 | 175 | 175 | 175 | 175 | 175 | 175 | 175 | 175 | 175 |
| 28 | Tuition | 2,450 | 0 | 0 | 0 | 0 | 1,200 | 0 | 2,650 | 0 | 0 | 0 | 0 |
| 29 | Books & Supplies | 1,050 | 0 | 0 | 0 | 0 | 425 | 0 | 1,150 | 0 | 0 | 0 | 0 |
| 30 | Travel | 210 | 150 | 180 | 530 | 150 | 210 | 950 | 525 | 175 | 190 | 325 | 400 |
| 31 | Miscellaneous | 200 | 200 | 200 | 200 | 200 | 200 | 200 | 200 | 200 | 200 | 200 | 200 |
| 32 | Total | | | | | | | | | | | | |

Diane wants you to calculate the total expenses for each month. You'll start by inserting the formula to calculate the January expenses and then paste that formula into the remaining months of the year.

### To calculate the total monthly expenses:

1. In cell C32, enter the formula **=SUM(C22:C31)** to add the estimated expenses for the month of January. The value 6,460 is displayed in cell C32, indicating that Diane estimates the couple will spend $6,460 in January of the upcoming year.

2. Click cell **C32** to select it.

3. Click the **Home** tab on the Ribbon, if necessary, and then click the **Copy** button in the Clipboard group.

4. Select the range **D32:N32**, and then click the **Paste** button in the Clipboard group. The SUM function is pasted into the selected range, calculating the total expenses for the remaining months of the year. See Figure 3-2.

**Figure 3-2**    **Total monthly expenses**

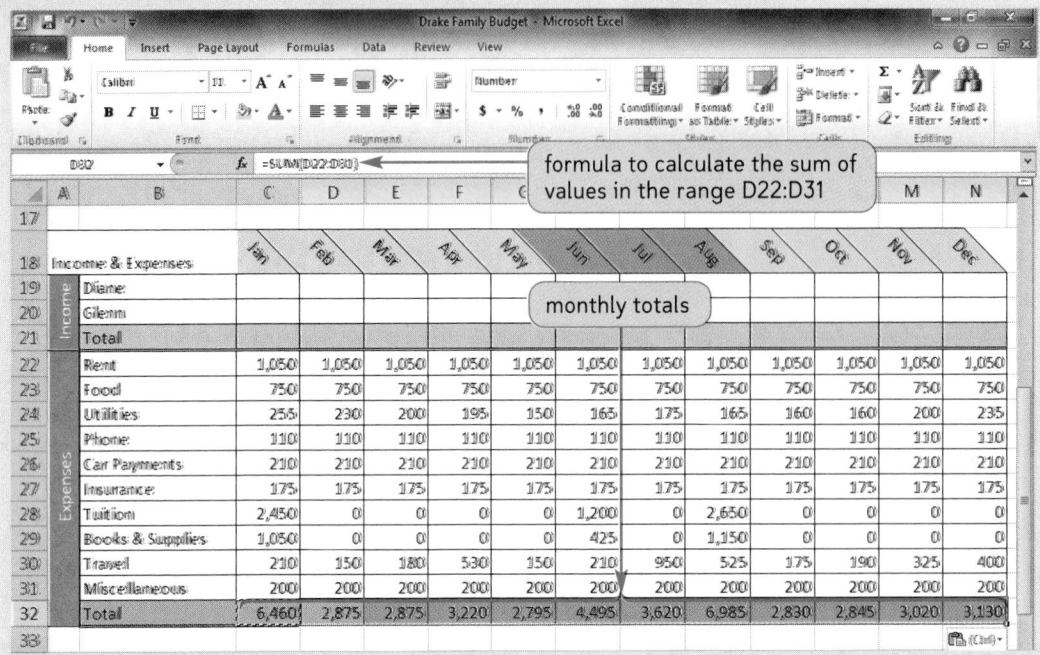

**5.** Review the total expenses for each month. January and August are particularly expensive months because Glenn has to pay tuition and purchase books for the upcoming semester.

**6.** Click each cell in the range D32:N32, reviewing the formula entered in the cell. The formulas pasted into the range D32:N32 all calculate the sums of values in different cell references. For example, the formula =SUM(D22:D31) was inserted in cell D32, the formula =SUM(E22:E31) was inserted in cell E32, and so forth.

## Using Relative References

When you entered the formula in cell C32 to sum the January expenses, Excel interprets the cell references in that formula relative to the location of cell C32. In other words, Excel interprets the formula =SUM(C22:C31) as adding the values entered in the 10 cells directly above cell C32.

Excel uses this interpretation of the cell references when the formula is pasted into other cells. For example, when you pasted the formula in cell D32, the formula changed to =SUM(D22:D31), which has a different cell reference but the same meaning: adding the values of the 10 cells directly above the active cell. The formulas in the remaining cells of the range D32:E32 were similarly adjusted so that each formula displays the total expenses for the selected month.

The cell references used in these formulas are called relative references because when Excel copies and pastes them, they are always interpreted in relation, or relative, to the location of the cell containing the formula. Figure 3-3 illustrates how a relative cell reference in a formula changes when the formula is copied to another group of cells.

**Figure 3-3**    **Formulas using a relative reference**

formula references a cell three rows up and three columns to the left of the active cell

| | A | B | C | D | E | F |
|---|---|---|---|---|---|---|
| 1 | Referenced Cells | | | | | |
| 2 | 10 | 20 | | | | |
| 3 | 30 | 40 | | | | |
| 4 | | | | Formulas with Relative References | | |
| 5 | | | | =A2 | | |
| 6 | | | | | | |
| 7 | | | | | | |
| 8 | | | | | | |

when copied to new cells, each formula still references a cell three rows up and two columns to the left

| | A | B | C | D | E | F |
|---|---|---|---|---|---|---|
| 1 | Referenced Cells | | | | | |
| 2 | 10 | 20 | | | | |
| 3 | 30 | 40 | | | | |
| 4 | | | | Formulas with Relative References | | |
| 5 | | | | =A2 | =B2 | |
| 6 | | | | =A3 | =B3 | |
| 7 | | | | | | (Ctrl) ▾ |
| 8 | | | | | | |

values returned by each formula

| | A | B | C | D | E | F |
|---|---|---|---|---|---|---|
| 1 | Referenced Cells | | | | | |
| 2 | 10 | 20 | | | | |
| 3 | 30 | 40 | | | | |
| 4 | | | | Formulas with Relative References | | |
| 5 | | | | 10 | 20 | |
| 6 | | | | 30 | 40 | |
| 7 | | | | | | (Ctrl) ▾ |
| 8 | | | | | | |

In this figure, the formula =A2 entered in cell D5 displays the value of 10, which is the value entered in cell A2. When pasted to a new location, each of the pasted formulas contains a reference to a cell that is three rows up and three rows to the left of the current cell's location. One of the great advantages of relative references is that you can quickly generate row and column totals without having to worry about revising the formulas as you copy them to new locations.

## Using Absolute References

A good practice when designing a workbook is to enter values in their own cells in one location of the worksheet, and then reference the appropriate cells in formulas throughout the worksheets. This reduces the amount of data entry when you need to use the same data in more than one location. It also makes it faster and more accurate when you need to change a data value, as all the formulas based on that cell are updated to reflect the new value.

Next, you will enter the Drakes' monthly income. The couple's income changes in the summer as Diane works fewer hours and Glenn works more. Rather than inserting these same values each month, you'll enter them in cells at the top of the worksheet and then reference those values in the income/expenses table at the bottom of the worksheet. Later, if Diane modifies the monthly income estimates, you'll need to change them in only one location rather than in 12 different locations.

## To enter the couple's estimated monthly income:

1. Scroll to the top of the worksheet, and then enter the following data in the specified cells:

   cell D5: **2800**    cell E5: **2100**
   cell D6: **1300**    cell E6: **2600**

2. Select the range **D7:E7**. You'll enter the monthly income totals in these cells.

3. In the Editing group on the Home tab, click the **Sum** button $\Sigma$. The total estimated income is calculated for the school and summer months. See Figure 3-4.

| Figure 3-4 | Monthly income estimates |
| --- | --- |

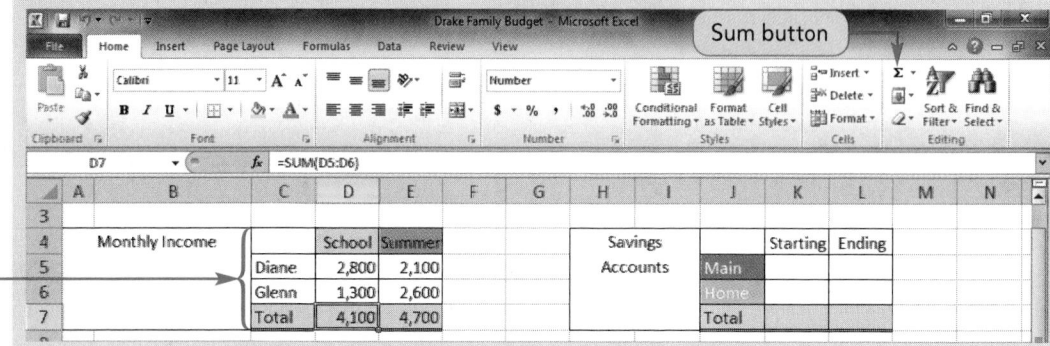

estimated income during the school and summer months

Next, you'll calculate the couple's projected income for January through May by referencing the values you just entered at the top of the worksheet. The couple will have the same income for the next four months as they did in January, so you can copy the formulas from January into February through May.

## To insert the monthly income for January through May:

1. Click cell **C19**, type **=D5**, and then press the **Enter** key. The value 2,800, Diane's income for January, appears in cell C19.

2. In cell C20, enter the formula **=D6**. The value 1,300, Glenn's income for January, appears in cell C20.

3. In cell C21, enter the formula **=C19+C20**. This formula calculates the total income for the couple in the month of January, displaying the value 4,100.

4. Select the range **C19:C21**, and then click the **Copy** button in the Clipboard group on the Home tab. The three formulas are copied to the Clipboard.

5. Select the range **D19:G21**, and then click the **Paste** button in the Clipboard group. The formulas are pasted and calculate the couple's income for January through May. See Figure 3-5.

| Figure 3-5 | Income values inserted for January through May |

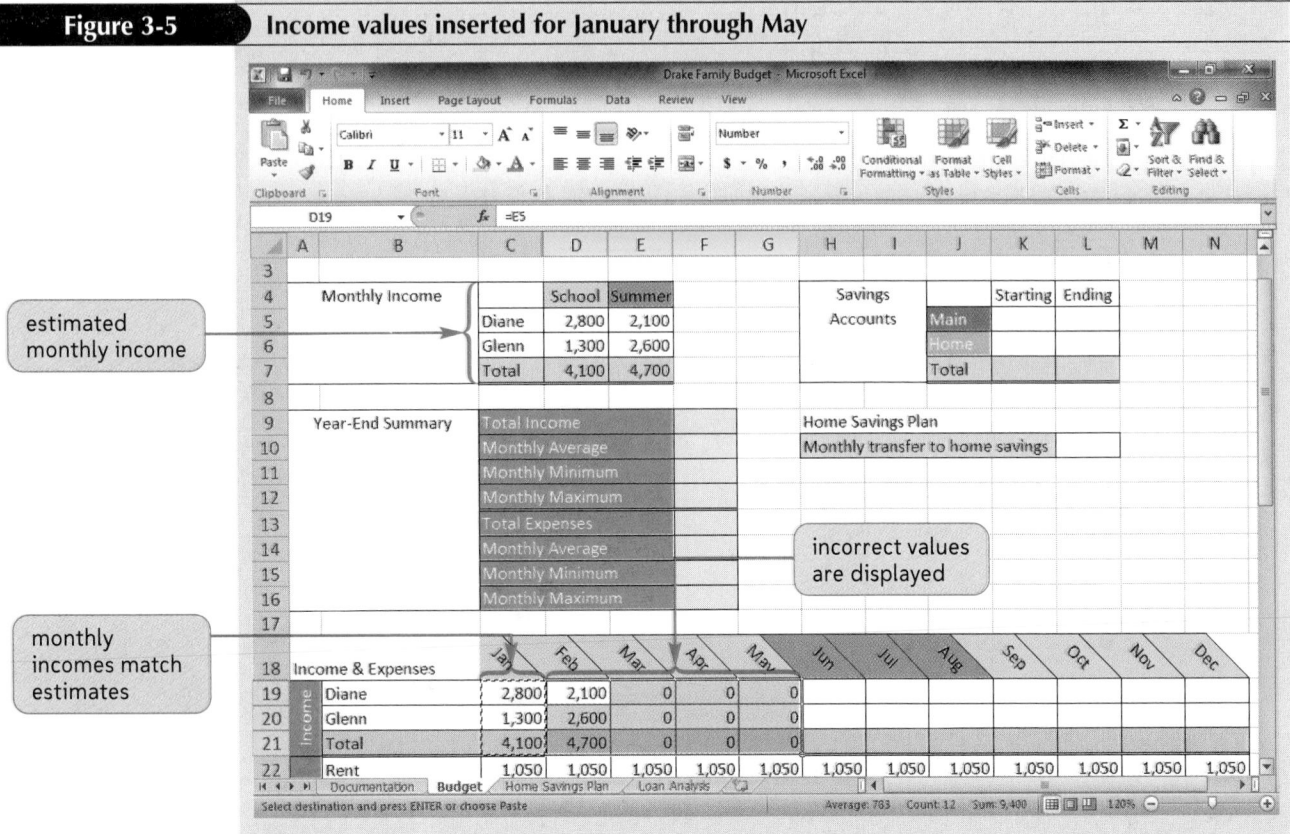

The formulas you copied and pasted from January resulted in incorrect values for February, March, April, and May. The February column show the couple's estimated monthly income for the summer, and the March, April, and May columns display the value 0. What went wrong?

The problem is that the formulas use relative references. For example, the formula in cell C19 is =D5, which references the cell located 14 rows up and 1 column to the right of the current cell. When you pasted that formula to cell G19, Excel inserted the formula =H5, which references the empty cell located 14 rows up and 1 column to the right of cell G19, so that the value displayed in the cell is 0.

Instead of using relative references, you need to use a cell reference that will remain fixed when the formula is copied to a new location. Cell references that remain fixed are called absolute references. In Excel, absolute references have a $ (dollar sign) before each column and row designation. For example, B8 is a relative reference to cell B8, whereas $B$8 is an absolute reference to cell B8. When you copy a formula that contains an absolute reference to a new location, the reference does not change. Figure 3-6 shows an example of how copying a formula with an absolute reference results in the same cell reference being pasted in different cells regardless of their location.

| Figure 3-6 | Formulas using an absolute reference |
|---|---|

formula containing an absolute reference to the sales tax rate in cell A2

| ▲ | A | B | C | D | E | F |
|---|---|---|---|---|---|---|
| 1 | Sales Tax Rate | | Purchase | Sales Tax | Total | |
| 2 | 0.05 | | $24.95 | =C2*$A$2 | =C2+D2 | |
| 3 | | | $122.35 | | | |
| 4 | | | $199.81 | | | |
| 5 | | | $45.40 | | | |
| 6 | | | | | | |
| 7 | | | | | | |

absolute reference to cell A2

relative references to cells C2 and D2

when pasted into a new location, the absolute reference remains unchanged

| ▲ | A | B | C | D | E | F |
|---|---|---|---|---|---|---|
| 1 | Sales Tax Rate | | Purchase | Sales Tax | Total | |
| 2 | 0.05 | | $24.95 | =C2*$A$2 | =C2+D2 | |
| 3 | | | $122.35 | =C3*$A$2 | =C3+D3 | |
| 4 | | | $199.81 | =C4*$A$2 | =C4+D4 | |
| 5 | | | $45.40 | =C5*$A$2 | =C5+D5 | |
| 6 | | | | | | (Ctrl) ▾ |
| 7 | | | | | | |

$A$2 continues to be referenced in the formula

relative references change based on cell location

values returned by the cell formulas

| ▲ | A | B | C | D | E | F |
|---|---|---|---|---|---|---|
| 1 | Sales Tax Rate | | Purchase | Sales Tax | Total | |
| 2 | | 5% | | $24.95 | $1.25 | $26.20 |
| 3 | | | $122.35 | $6.12 | $128.47 | |
| 4 | | | $199.81 | $9.99 | $209.80 | |
| 5 | | | $45.40 | $2.27 | $47.67 | |
| 6 | | | | | | (Ctrl) ▾ |
| 7 | | | | | | |

In this figure, the sales tax of different purchases is calculated and displayed. All items have the same 5 percent tax rate applied to the purchase, with the tax rate stored in cell A2. The sales tax and total cost of the first item are calculated in cells D2 and E2, respectively. When those formulas are copied and pasted to the remaining purchases, the relative references in the formulas are modified to point to the new location of the purchase cost; however, the sales tax rate continues to point to cell A2, regardless of the location of the selected cell.

You will modify the formulas in the Budget worksheet so that they reference Diane's income estimates using absolute rather than relative references.

### To use absolute references to display the monthly income:

▶ 1. In cell C19, enter =$D$5. This formula contains an absolute reference to cell D5, which contains Diane's monthly income during the school months.

▶ 2. In cell C20, enter =$D$6. This formula contains an absolute reference to cell D6, which contains Glenn's monthly income during the school months.

▶ 3. Copy the corrected formulas in the range C19:C20, and then paste them in the range D19:G20. As shown in Figure 3-7, the months of February through May now correctly show the monthly income values for the school months.

**Figure 3-7**     **Results of formulas with absolute references**

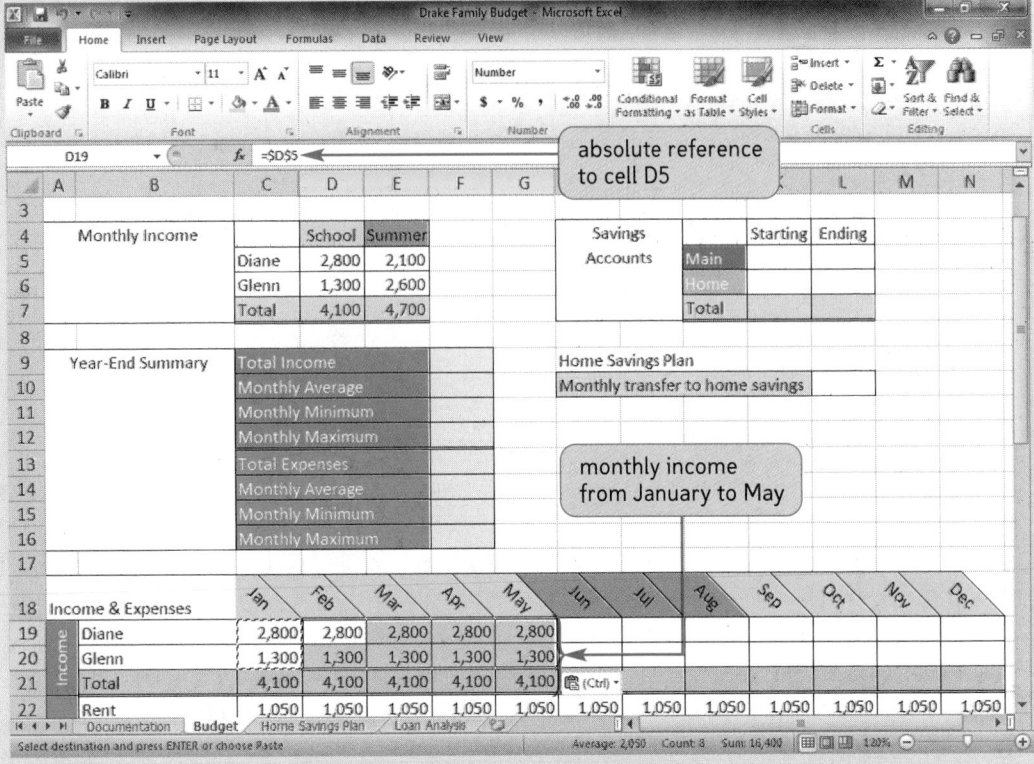

**4.** Click each cell in the range D19:G20 and verify that the formulas =$D$5 and
=$D$6 were copied into the appropriate cells.

## Using Mixed References

A formula can also include cell references that are mixed. A mixed reference contains
both relative and absolute references. For example, a mixed reference for cell A2 can
be either $A2 or A$2. In the mixed reference $A2, the column reference to column A is
absolute and the reference to row 2 is relative. In the mixed reference A$2, the column
reference is relative and the row reference is absolute. As you can see, a mixed reference
"locks" one part of the cell reference while the other part can change. When you copy
and paste a formula with a mixed reference to a new location, the absolute portion of
the cell reference remains fixed and the relative portion shifts.

Figure 3-8 shows an example of using mixed references to complete a multiplication table. The first cell in the table, cell B3, contains the formula =$A3*B$2, which
multiplies the first column entry (A3) by the first row entry (B2), returning the value 1.
When this formula is copied to another cell, the absolute portions of the cell references
remain unchanged and the relative portions of the references change. For example, if
the formula is copied to cell E6, the first mixed cell reference changes to $A6 because
the column reference is absolute and the row reference is relative, and the second cell
reference changes to E$2 because the row reference is absolute and the column refer-
ence is relative. The result is that cell E6 contains the formula =$A6*E$2 and returns the
value 16. Other cells in the multiplication table are similarly modified so that each entry
returns the multiplication of the row and column headings.

**Figure 3-8** A multiplication table using a mixed reference

original formula with a mixed cell reference that multiplies the first row by the first column

| ▲ | A | B | C | D | E | F | G |
|---|---|---|---|---|---|---|---|
| 1 | | | Multiplication Table | | | | |
| 2 | | 1 | 2 | 3 | 4 | 5 | |
| 3 | 1 | =$A3*B$2 | | | | | |
| 4 | 2 | | | | | | |
| 5 | 3 | | | | | | |
| 6 | 4 | | | | | | |
| 7 | 5 | | | | | | |
| 8 | | | | | | | |
| 9 | | | | | | | |

formula copied to the B3:F7 range with mixed ranges to multiply the first row entries by the first column entries

| ▲ | A | B | C | D | E | F | G |
|---|---|---|---|---|---|---|---|
| 1 | | | Multiplication Table | | | | |
| 2 | | 1 | 2 | 3 | 4 | 5 | |
| 3 | 1 | =$A3*B$2 | =$A3*C$2 | =$A3*D$2 | =$A3*E$2 | =$A3*F$2 | |
| 4 | 2 | =$A4*B$2 | =$A4*C$2 | =$A4*D$2 | =$A4*E$2 | =$A4*F$2 | |
| 5 | 3 | =$A5*B$2 | =$A5*C$2 | =$A5*D$2 | =$A5*E$2 | =$A5*F$2 | |
| 6 | 4 | =$A6*B$2 | =$A6*C$2 | =$A6*D$2 | =$A6*E$2 | =$A6*F$2 | |
| 7 | 5 | =$A7*B$2 | =$A7*C$2 | =$A7*D$2 | =$A7*E$2 | =$A7*F$2 | |
| 8 | | | | | | | (Ctrl) ▾ |
| 9 | | | | | | | |

values returned by each formula

| ▲ | A | B | C | D | E | F | G |
|---|---|---|---|---|---|---|---|
| 1 | | | Multiplication Table | | | | |
| 2 | | 1 | 2 | 3 | 4 | 5 | |
| 3 | 1 | 1 | 2 | 3 | 4 | 5 | |
| 4 | 2 | 2 | 4 | 6 | 8 | 10 | |
| 5 | 3 | 3 | 6 | 9 | 12 | 15 | |
| 6 | 4 | 4 | 8 | 12 | 16 | 20 | |
| 7 | 5 | 5 | 10 | 15 | 20 | 25 | |
| 8 | | | | | | | (Ctrl) ▾ |
| 9 | | | | | | | |

**INSIGHT**

### Understanding When to Use Relative, Absolute, and Mixed References

Part of effective formula writing is knowing when to use relative, absolute, and mixed references. Use relative references when you want to repeat the same formula with cells in different locations on your worksheet. Relative references are commonly used when copying a formula that sums a column of numbers or that calculates the cost of several items by multiplying the item cost by the quantity being purchased.

Use absolute references when you want different formulas to refer to the same cell. This usually occurs when a cell contains a constant value, such as a tax rate, that will be used in formulas throughout the worksheet.

Mixed references are seldom used other than when creating tables of calculated values such as a multiplication table in which the values of the formula or function can be found in the initial rows and columns of the table.

As you develop formulas and worksheets, you might want to quickly switch a cell reference from relative to absolute or mixed. Rather than retyping the formula, you can switch the reference in editing mode by selecting the cell reference and pressing the F4 key. As you press the function key, Excel cycles through the different reference types, starting by changing a relative reference to an absolute reference, then to a mixed reference with the row absolute, then to a mixed reference with the column absolute, and then finally back to a relative reference.

You'll use the F4 key to cycle through the different types of references as you enter the remaining formulas with the income for the summer months.

### To insert the remaining references to the couple's monthly income:

▶ 1. Click cell **H19**, type **=**, and then click cell **E5**. The formula =E5 appears in the cell, which remains in Edit mode. This formula enters Diane's income for the summer months.

▶ 2. Press the **F4** key. The formula changes to =$E$5, which is an absolute reference.

   **Trouble?** If the formula shows anything other than the absolute reference, you probably pressed the F4 key too many times. Continue to press the F4 key to loop through all of the cell reference types until the formula returns to =$E$5, which contains the absolute reference.

▶ 3. Press the **Enter** key. The formula is entered and 2,100 (Diane's monthly income in the summer) appears in cell H19.

▶ 4. In cell H20, enter the formula **=$E$6**. This formula uses an absolute reference to enter Glenn's monthly income in the summer.

▶ 5. In cell H21, enter the formula **=H19+H20**. This formula adds Diane and Glenn's income for June; their combined monthly income in the summer is 4,700.

▶ 6. Copy the range **H19:H21**, and then paste the copied formulas into the range **I19:J21**. The summer take-home pay values appear for the months of June through August.

   You'll complete the monthly income values for the remaining school months.

▶ 7. Copy the range **C19:C21**, and then paste it into the range **K19:N21**. The couple's monthly income is entered for all months of the year.

# Working with Functions

Excel functions provide a quick way to calculate summary data such as the total, average, minimum, and maximum values in a collection of values. You'll use these functions to summarize Diane and Glenn's income and expense data at the top of the Budget worksheet.

## Understanding Function Syntax

Every function has to follow a set of rules, or **syntax**, which specifies how the function should be written. The general syntax of all Excel functions is

```
FUNCTION(argument1, argument2, ...)
```

where *FUNCTION* is the name of the function, and *argument1*, *argument2*, and so forth are arguments, which are the numbers, text, or cell references used by the function to return a value. Arguments are always separated by a comma.

Not all functions have arguments. Some functions have optional arguments, which are not required for the function to return a value, but can be included to provide more control over how Excel calculates the returned value. If an optional argument is not included, Excel assumes a default value for it. These tutorials show optional arguments within square brackets along with the argument's default value, as follows:

```
FUNCTION(argument1, [argument2=value2, ...])
```

**TIP**

Optional arguments are always placed last in the argument list.

In this function, *argument1* is required, *argument2* is an optional argument, and *value2* is the default value used for this argument. As you learn more about individual functions, you will learn which arguments are required and which are optional, and the default values used for optional arguments.

The hundreds of available Excel functions are organized into 11 categories. Figure 3-9 describes these different categories.

**Figure 3-9**    **Excel function categories**

| Category | Functions That |
| --- | --- |
| Cube | Retrieve data from multidimensional databases involving online analytical processing or OLAP |
| Database | Retrieve and analyze data stored in databases |
| Date & Time | Analyze or create date and time values and time intervals |
| Engineering | Analyze engineering problems |
| Financial | Have financial applications |
| Information | Return information about the format, location, or contents of worksheet cells |
| Logical | Return logical (true-false) values |
| Lookup & Reference | Look up and return data matching a set of specified conditions from a range |
| Math & Trig | Have math and trigonometry applications |
| Statistical | Provide statistical analyses of a set of data |
| Text | Return text values or evaluate text |

You can learn about each function using the Help system. Figure 3-10 describes some of the more common Math, Trig, and Statistical functions used in workbooks.

| Figure 3-10 | Common Math, Trig, and Statistical functions |
| --- | --- |

| Function | Category | Description |
| --- | --- | --- |
| AVERAGE(number1 [, number2, number3, ...]) | Statistical | Calculates the average of a collection of numbers, where number1, number2, and so forth are either numbers or cell references. Only number1 is required. For more than one cell reference or to enter numbers directly into the function, use the optional arguments number2, number3, and so forth. |
| COUNT(value1 [, value2, value3, ...]) | Statistical | Counts how many cells in a range contain numbers, where value1, value2, and so forth are text, numbers, or cell references. Only value1 is required. For more than one cell reference or to enter numbers directly into the function, use the optional arguments value2, value3, and so forth. |
| COUNTA(value1 [, value2, value3, ...]) | Statistical | Counts how many cells are not empty in ranges value1, value2, and so forth, or how many numbers are listed within value1, value2, and so forth. |
| INT(number) | Math & Trig | Displays the integer portion of a number, number. |
| MAX(number1 [, number2, number3, ...]) | Statistical | Calculates the maximum value of a collection of numbers, where number1, number2, and so forth are either numbers or cell references. |
| MEDIAN(number1 [, number2, number3, ...]) | Statistical | Calculates the median, or middle, value of a collection of numbers, where number1, number2, and so forth are either numbers or cell references. |
| MIN(number1 [, number2, number3, ...]) | Statistical | Calculates the minimum value of a collection of numbers, where number1, number2, and so forth are either numbers or cell references. |
| RAND() | Math & Trig | Returns a random number between 0 and 1. |
| ROUND(number, num_digits) | Math & Trig | Rounds a number to a specified number of digits, where number is the number you want to round and num_digits specifies how many digits to which you want to round the number. |
| SUM(number1 [, number2, number3, ...]) | Math & Trig | Adds a collection of numbers, where number1, number2, and so forth are either numbers or cell references. |

For example, the AVERAGE function calculates the average value from a collection of numbers. The syntax of the AVERAGE function is

```
AVERAGE(number1 [, number2, number3, ...])
```

where number1, number2, number3, and so forth are either numbers or cell references to numbers. The following formula uses the AVERAGE function to calculate the average of 1, 2, 5, and 8, returning the value 4:

```
=AVERAGE(1, 2, 5, 8)
```

However, functions usually reference values entered in the worksheet. So, if the range A1:A4 contains the values 1, 2, 5, and 8, the following formula also returns a value of 4:

```
=AVERAGE(A1:A4)
```

The advantage of using cell references is that the values used in the function are visible to users and can be easily edited as needed. Functions can be included as part of larger formulas. For example, the following formula, which includes the MAX function, returns the maximum value from the range A1:A100, and then divides that value by 100:

`=MAX(A1:A100)/100`

Functions can also be placed inside another function, or **nested**. If a formula contains several functions, Excel starts with the innermost function and then moves outward. For example, the following formula first calculates the average of the values in the range A1:A100 using the AVERAGE function, and then extracts the integer portion of that value using the INT function:

`=INT(AVERAGE(A1:A100))`

One challenge of nesting functions is to make sure that you include all of the parentheses. You can check this by counting the number of left parentheses, and making sure that number matches the number of right parentheses. Excel will also display different levels of nested parentheses in different colors to make it easier to match the opening and closing parentheses in the formula. If the number of parentheses doesn't match, Excel will not accept the formula and will offer a suggestion for rewriting the formula so the number of left and right parentheses does match.

**PROSKILLS**

*Problem Solving: Choosing the Right Summary Function*

Problem solving involves determining how to best summarize a large sample of data into a few easy-to-use statistics. The field of statistics provides several summary measures, each with its own advantages and disadvantages.

One of the most common statistical approaches is to average the sample data. You can calculate the average in Excel with the AVERAGE function. However, determining an average is not always the best choice. Averages are susceptible to extremely large or small data values. Imagine calculating the average size of homes in a neighborhood that has one huge mansion and several small houses. In this case, the average value is heavily influenced by the size of that single mansion, and might not represent a typical neighborhood house.

When the data includes a few extremely large or extremely small values that have the potential to skew results, it's often better to use the **median**, or middle, value from the sample. For example, in a survey of nine homes, the median would be the size of the fifth largest—or middle-sized—home in the sample. You can calculate the median in Excel with the MEDIAN function.

Another approach is to calculate the most common value in the data, otherwise known as the **mode**. The mode is most often used with data that has only a few possible values, each of which might be repeated several times. Rather than using square feet, you might want to express the value in terms of the number of bedrooms each home contains. The mode would return the most common number of bedrooms in the homes included in the sample. You can calculate the mode in Excel using the MODE function.

By knowing which summary measure best fits your data, you can create useful and precise information that will aid you and others in interpreting the results.

## Inserting a Function

Functions are organized in the Function Library group on the Formulas tab on the Ribbon. In the Function Library, you can select a function from a function category or you can open the Insert Function dialog box to search for a particular function. When you select a function, the Function Arguments dialog box opens, listing all the arguments associated with that function. Required arguments are in bold type; optional arguments are in normal type.

You'll use the SUM function to add the total income and expenses for the year in Diane's proposed budget.

### To calculate annual income and expenses with the SUM function:

1. Click cell **F9** to select it.

2. Click the **Formulas** tab on the Ribbon.

3. In the Function Library group, click the **Math & Trig** button. An alphabetical listing of all the math and trigonometry functions opens.

4. Scroll down the list, and then click **SUM**. The Function Arguments dialog box opens, listing all of the arguments associated with the SUM function.

5. Click in the worksheet, and then select the range **C21:N21**. The dialog box reduces to its title bar as you select the range. The range reference, which includes all the monthly income amounts, appears as the value of the Number1 argument. See Figure 3-11.

**TIP**

You can click the Collapse Dialog Box button to shrink the Function Arguments dialog box to see more of the worksheet, select the range, and then click the Expand Dialog Box button to restore the dialog box.

| Figure 3-11 | Function Arguments dialog box |

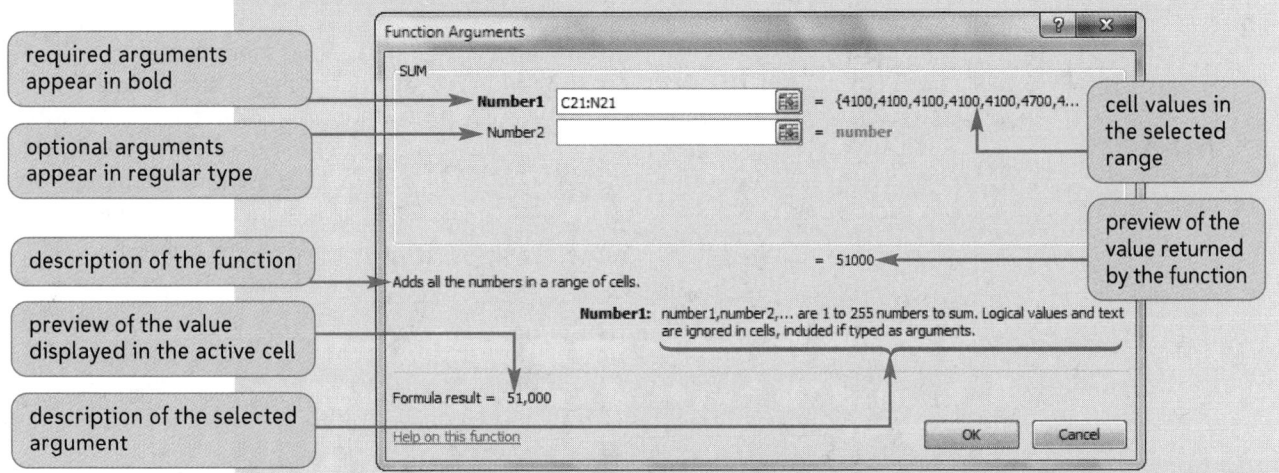

6. Click the **OK** button. The formula =SUM(C21:N21) is inserted into cell F9, which displays the value 51,000. This represents Diane and Glenn's total annual income.

7. Click cell **F13**. This is where you want the SUM function to add the monthly expenses for the year.

8. In the Function Library group on the Formulas tab, click the **Math & Trig** button, and then click **SUM**. The Function Arguments dialog box opens. You'll enter the monthly expenses stored in the range C32:N32 for the argument.

9. Click in the worksheet, and then select the range **C32:N32**.

10. In the Function Arguments dialog box, click the **OK** button. The formula =SUM(C32:N32) is inserted in cell F13, which displays the value 45,150. This represents the total projected expenses for the upcoming year. See Figure 3-12.

**Figure 3-12**    **Total annual income and expenses**

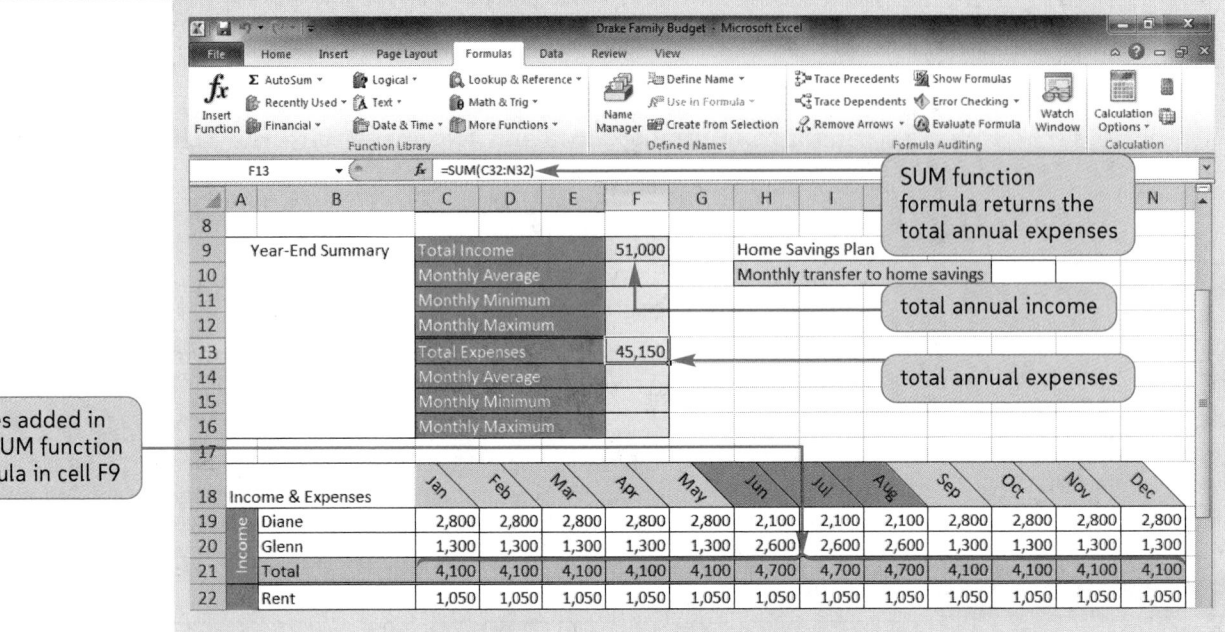

values added in the SUM function formula in cell F9

Diane projects that she and Glenn will earn roughly $6,000 more than they will spend throughout the year. It's easier for Diane to plan her budget if she knows how much, on average, the couple earns and spends each month. You can use the AVERAGE function to do this calculation using the same method you used for the SUM function.

If you aren't sure of the function's name or category, you can use the Insert Function dialog box. The Insert Function dialog box organizes all of the functions by category and includes a search feature for locating functions that perform particular calculations.

### To calculate the couple's average monthly income:

1. Click cell **F10**. This is the cell in which you want to enter the AVERAGE function formula.

2. In the Function Library group on the Formulas tab, click the **Insert Function** button. The Insert Function dialog box opens.

3. In the Search for a function box, type **Calculate an average value**, and then click the **Go** button. Functions for calculating an average appear in the Select a function box. See Figure 3-13.

**TIP**

You can also click the Insert Function button on the formula bar to open the Insert Function dialog box.

**Figure 3-13**    **Insert Function dialog box**

description of the
function

functions that match
the description (your
list might differ)

syntax and description
of the selected
function

click to access online
help about the selected
function

**4.** Verify that **AVERAGE** is selected in the Select a function box, and then click the
   **OK** button. The Function Arguments dialog box opens with the arguments for the
   AVERAGE function. A range reference for a cell directly above this cell already
   appears for the Number1 argument.

**5.** Select the range reference in the Number1 argument box, and then select the
   range **C21:N21** in the worksheet.

**6.** Click the **OK** button. The dialog box closes, and the formula =AVERAGE(C21:N21)
   is entered in cell F10, which displays the value 4,250—the couple's average
   monthly income.

How does the couple's average monthly income compare to their average monthly
expenses? To find out, you'll use the AVERAGE function again. Because the function
has already been used in your workbook, you can select it from a list of recently used
functions.

**To calculate the average monthly expenses:**

**1.** Click cell **F14**. This is the cell where you want to calculate the average monthly
   expenses.

**2.** On the formula bar, click the **Insert Function** button ![fx]. The Insert Function dialog box opens.

**3.** If necessary, click the **Or select a category** arrow, and then click **Most Recently
   Used**. The most recently used functions, sorted in order of recent use, appear
   in the Select a function box. The AVERAGE function is at the top followed by the
   SUM function.

**4.** Verify that **AVERAGE** is selected in the Select a function box, and then click the
   **OK** button.

**5.** Select the range **C32:N32** in the worksheet to insert the range reference C32:N32
   in the Number1 box.

> **6.** Click the **OK** button. The formula =AVERAGE(C32:N32) is entered in cell F14, dis-
> playing the value 3,763. This represents the average expenses per month under
> Diane's budget. See Figure 3-14.

**Figure 3-14**    **Average family income and expenses**

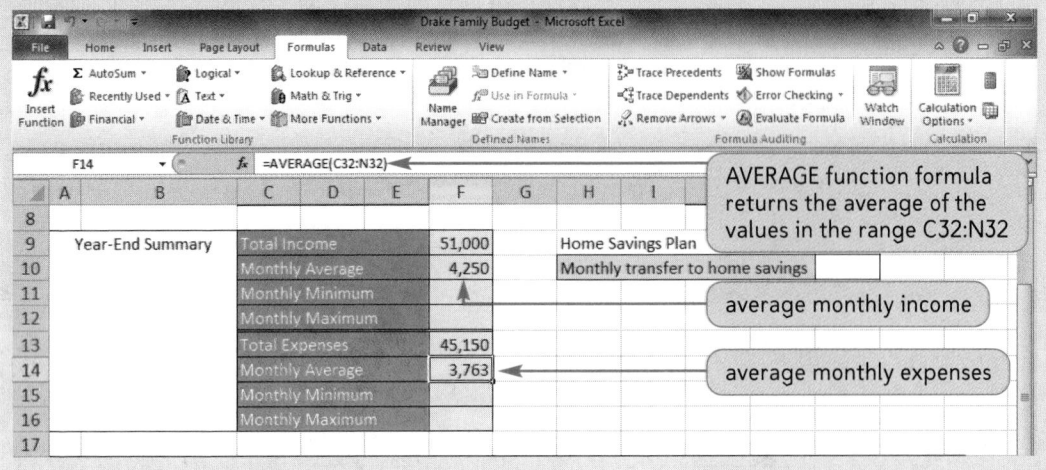

The average monthly expense, 3,763, is displayed to the nearest dollar amount. This
is because Diane has formatted the workbook to not display decimal values. The actual
value, 3,762.50, is stored in the cell although it is not displayed.

## Typing a Function

After you become more familiar with functions, it is often faster to type the functions
directly in cells rather than using the Insert Function dialog box or the Function Library.
As you begin to type a function name within a formula, a list of functions that begin with
the letters you typed appears. For example, when you type *S*, the list shows all of the
functions starting with the letter *S*; when you type *SU*, the list shows only those functions starting with the letters *SU*, and so forth. This helps to ensure that you're entering a
legitimate Excel function name.

The income and expenses averages show that the couple will bring in about $500
more than they spend each month. That does not leave much money to deal with an
unexpected expense, so Diane wants to know how much variation is in the budget.
What is the most money she could expect to take home during a single month in the
upcoming year? What is the least? And what are the highest and lowest values for the
monthly expenses? You'll use the MAX and MIN functions to calculate those values.

**To calculate the minimum value for monthly income and expenses:**

> **1.** Click cell **F11**. This is the cell in which you want to enter the monthly income.

> **2.** Type **=M**. As you type a formula, a list with function names starting with *M* opens.

> **3.** Type **I**. The list shows only those functions starting with *MI*. See Figure 3-15. As
> soon as the function you want appears in the list, you can double-click its name to
> enter it in the cell without typing the rest of its name.

| Figure 3-15 | Function being typed into a cell |

list of Excel functions starting with *MI*

ScreenTip describes the selected function

4. Double-click **MIN** in the list box. The MIN function with its opening parenthesis is inserted into cell F11 and a ScreenTip shows the syntax for the function. At this point, you can either type in the range reference or select the range with your mouse. To avoid typing errors, it's often better to use your mouse to enter range references.

5. Select the range **C21:N21**. The range reference is added to the formula.

Be sure to end this and all functions with the closing parenthesis ) to ensure that Excel interprets the formula correctly.

6. Type **)** (the closing parenthesis), and then press the **Enter** key. The formula =MIN(C21:N21) is inserted in cell F11, displaying the value 4,100. This is the minimum amount that Diane expects the couple to bring home in a single month for the upcoming year.

Next, you'll calculate the minimum monthly expense projected for the year.

7. Click cell **F15**, and then repeat Steps 2 through 6 to enter the formula **=MIN(C32:N32)** in cell F15. The cell displays the value 2,795, which is the lowest amount that Diane expects to spend in a single month in the upcoming year.

The final piece of the year-end summary is the maximum monthly value for both income and expenses. Maximum values are calculated using the MAX function.

### To calculate the maximum value for monthly income and expenses:

1. Click cell **F12**, and then enter the formula **=MAX(C21:N21)**. The value 4,700 appears in cell F12, indicating that the maximum income the couple can expect in a single month is $4,700.

   **Trouble?** If #NAME? appears in the cell, you probably mistyped the function name. Edit the formula to correct the misspelling.

2. Click cell **F16**, and then enter the formula **=MAX(C32:N32)**. The value 6,985 appears in cell F16, indicating that the maximum expenses for a single month are projected to be $6,985. See Figure 3-16.

**Figure 3-16** **Year-end summary values**

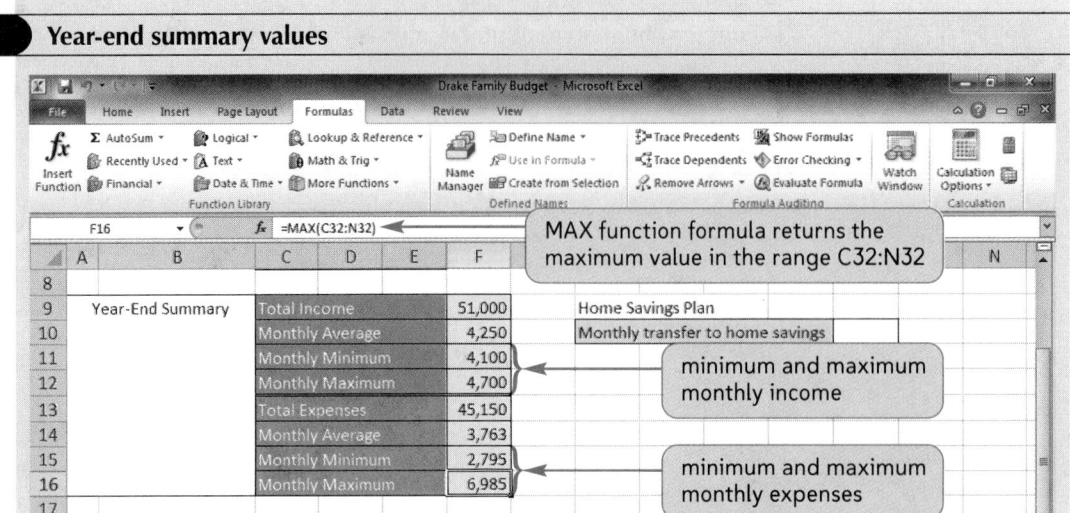

Based on the year-end summary, Diane and Glenn's monthly income will range from a minimum of $4,100 to a maximum of $4,700 with an average of $4,250. Monthly expenses, on the other hand, range from a minimum of $2,795 to a maximum of $6,985 with an average of $3,763. This budget does not have a lot of wiggle room.

Diane has just been promoted at work. Her income will increase to $3,100 per month during the school year. She wants to know how this affects the year-end summary.

### To modify Diane's estimated income:

1. In cell D5, enter the value **3100**.

2. Confirm that Diane's monthly income for January through May and September through December has been automatically updated.

3. Review how the year-end summary data has changed. See Figure 3-17.

**Figure 3-17** **Revised income projection**

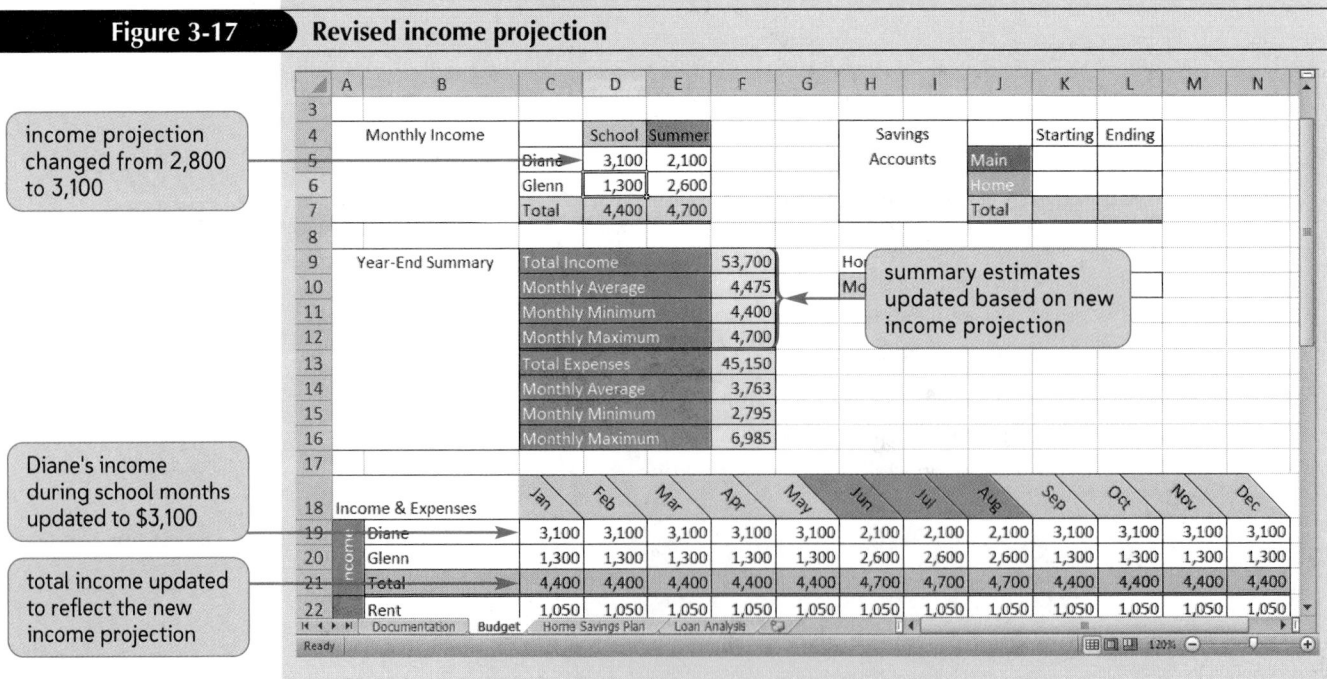

With Diane's promotion, the couple's annual income increases from $51,000 to $53,700 and the monthly average increases from $4,250 to $4,475. The couple's income should exceed their expenses by about $700 per month. The monthly income now ranges from a minimum of $4,400 up to a maximum of $4,700.

Diane now has a better picture of the family's finances for the upcoming year, and she is more confident about how to manage the couple's budget. She and Glenn hope to save enough for a down payment on a house in a few years. With the promotion, this seems like a real possibility. In the next session, you'll help Diane explore the couple's options in planning for the purchase of a house.

**REVIEW**

## Session 3.1 Quick Check

1. You need to reference cell Q57 in a formula. What is the absolute cell reference? What are the two mixed references?
2. Assume that cell R10 contains the formula =R1+R2. What formula is entered if this formula is copied and pasted into cell S20?
3. Assume that cell T10 contains the formula =$T1+T$2. What formula is entered if this formula is copied and pasted into cell U20?
4. Assume that cell V10 contains the formula =AVERAGE($U1:$U5). What formula is entered if this formula is copied and pasted into cell W20?
5. What are optional arguments? What happens if you do not include an optional argument in a function?
6. What function formula can you use to add the numbers in the range X1:X10?
7. The range of a set of values is defined as the maximum value minus the minimum value. What formula with functions can you enter to calculate the range of the values in Y1:Y10?
8. What formula with functions can you enter to calculate the ratio of the maximum value in the range Z1:Z10 to the minimum value?

# SESSION 3.2 VISUAL OVERVIEW

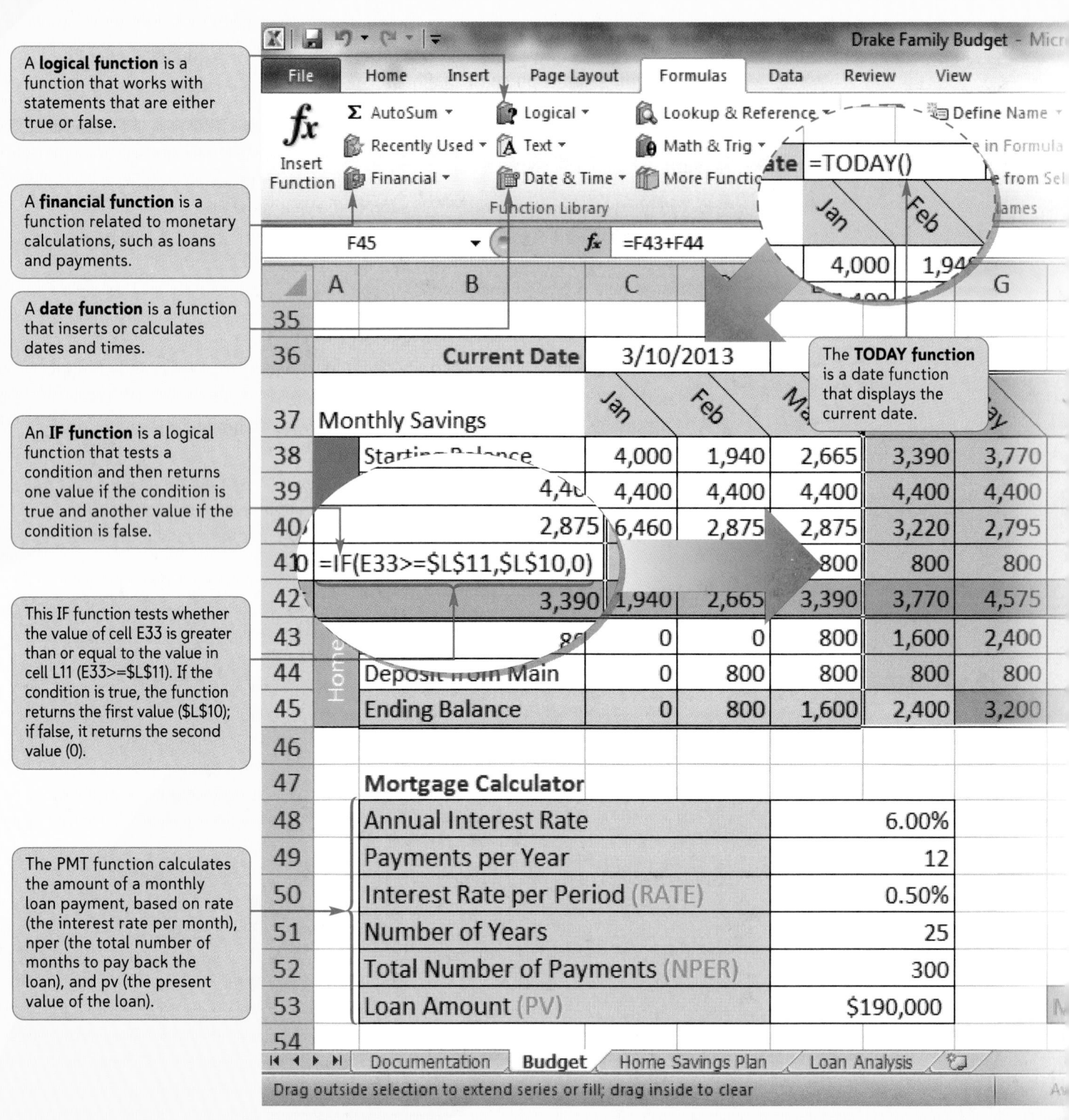

A **logical function** is a function that works with statements that are either true or false.

A **financial function** is a function related to monetary calculations, such as loans and payments.

A **date function** is a function that inserts or calculates dates and times.

An **IF function** is a logical function that tests a condition and then returns one value if the condition is true and another value if the condition is false.

This IF function tests whether the value of cell E33 is greater than or equal to the value in cell L11 (E33>=$L$11). If the condition is true, the function returns the first value ($L$10); if false, it returns the second value (0).

The PMT function calculates the amount of a monthly loan payment, based on rate (the interest rate per month), nper (the total number of months to pay back the loan), and pv (the present value of the loan).

The **TODAY function** is a date function that displays the current date.

=TODAY()

=IF(E33>=$L$11,$L$10,0)

F45    fx    =F43+F44

| | A | B | C | Jan | Feb | Mar | | |
|---|---|---|---|---|---|---|---|---|
| 35 | | | | | | | | |
| 36 | | Current Date | 3/10/2013 | | | | | |
| 37 | Monthly Savings | | | Jan | Feb | Mar | | May |
| 38 | | Starting Balance | 4,000 | 1,940 | 2,665 | 3,390 | 3,770 | |
| 39 | | | 4,400 | 4,400 | 4,400 | 4,400 | 4,400 | |
| 40 | | | 2,875 | 6,460 | 2,875 | 2,875 | 3,220 | 2,795 |
| 41 | | | | | | 800 | 800 | 800 |
| 42 | | | 3,390 | 1,940 | 2,665 | 3,390 | 3,770 | 4,575 |
| 43 | | | | 0 | 0 | 800 | 1,600 | 2,400 |
| 44 | | Deposit from Main | 0 | 800 | 800 | 800 | 800 | |
| 45 | | Ending Balance | 0 | 800 | 1,600 | 2,400 | 3,200 | |
| 46 | | | | | | | | |
| 47 | | Mortgage Calculator | | | | | | |
| 48 | | Annual Interest Rate | | | | 6.00% | | |
| 49 | | Payments per Year | | | | 12 | | |
| 50 | | Interest Rate per Period (RATE) | | | | 0.50% | | |
| 51 | | Number of Years | | | | 25 | | |
| 52 | | Total Number of Payments (NPER) | | | | 300 | | |
| 53 | | Loan Amount (PV) | | | | $190,000 | | |
| 54 | | | | | | | | |

Documentation   **Budget**   Home Savings Plan   Loan Analysis

Drag outside selection to extend series or fill; drag inside to clear

# AUTOFILL AND MORE FUNCTIONS

AutoFill can extend a series of numbers, patterned text, and dates into the new selection. In this case, AutoFill generated the abbreviations of month names.

**AutoFill** copies content and formats from a cell or range into an adjacent cell or range. The cell contents can be text, values, or formulas.

The **fill handle** appears in the lower-right corner of a selected cell or range. Dragging the fill handle over an adjacent cell or range copies the content and formatting from the original cells into the selected range.

The Auto Fill Options button appears after you complete the fill so you can select whether to copy cell content and formatting, extend the data series, fill only the cell formatting, or fill only cell content.

The **PMT function** is a financial function that calculates the monthly payment required to pay back a loan.

=PMT(E50,E52,E53)

Payments are expressed as negative numbers because they are treated as expenses.

# Entering Data and Formulas with AutoFill

Diane and Glenn hope to purchase a home in the next three years. Currently, they have $4,000 in their main savings account, and they plan to open a second account reserved for saving toward a down payment on a home. You will enter the initial balance for the main account and set up the home account with an initial balance of $0 into the Budget worksheet.

## To enter the savings account information:

1. If you took a break after the previous session, make sure the Drake Family Budget workbook is open and the Budget worksheet is active.

2. In cell K5, enter **4,000** (the starting amount in the main savings account).

3. In cell K6, enter **0** (the starting amount in the home savings account).

4. In cell K7, enter the formula **=K5+K6** to sum the total initial amount in both accounts. See Figure 3-18.

| Figure 3-18 | Savings account information |
| --- | --- |

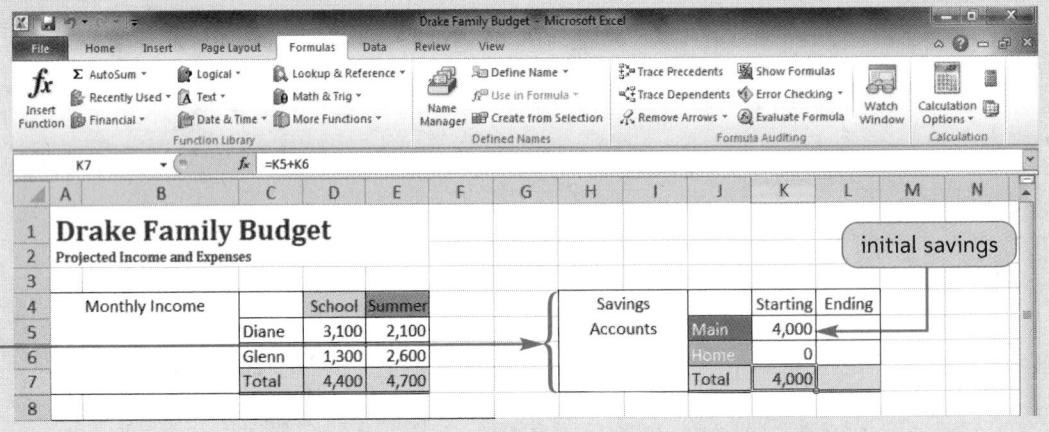

Diane wants to learn how much the couple could add to their savings accounts each month. To find out, you must first determine the couple's monthly net cash flow, which is equal to the amount of money they earn each month after paying all of their expenses. You will start by formatting the cells where you'll enter this data and calculating the net cash flow during the month of January.

## To calculate the net cash flow for January:

1. Merge and center the range **A33:B33**, and then right-align the cell contents.

2. In the merged cell A33, enter **Net Cash Flow**.

3. In cell C33, enter the formula **=C21–C32**. This formula subtracts total expenses from total income for the month of January. The resulting –2,060 indicates a projected shortfall of $2,060 for the month of January.

4. Apply conditional formatting to cell C33 to highlight the cell with a red fill and red text if the value in the cell is less than 0. Months with negative cash flow will be highlighted on the worksheet. See Figure 3-19.

## Figure 3-19    January net cash flow

Your calculations show that the couple's expenses will exceed their income by more than $2,000 in January. This is due to the cost of tuition that must be paid that month. You could copy and paste the formula and formatting from cell C33 into the rest of the row to calculate the net cash flow for the other months, as you've done before, but AutoFill is faster.

## Using the Fill Handle

After you select a range, the fill handle appears in the lower-right corner of the selection. When you drag the fill handle over an adjacent range, Excel uses AutoFill to copy the content and formats from the original cell into the adjacent range. This process is often more efficient than the two-step process of copying and pasting.

### REFERENCE

**Copying Formulas and Formats with AutoFill**

- Select the cell or range that contains the formula or formulas you want to copy.
- Drag the fill handle in the direction you want to copy the formula(s) and then release the mouse button.
- To copy only the formats or only the formulas, click the Auto Fill Options button and select the appropriate option.

*or*

- Select the cell or range that contains the formula or formulas you want to copy.
- In the Editing group on the Home tab, click the Fill button.
- Select the appropriate fill direction and fill type.

*or*

   Click Series, enter the desired fill series options, and then click the OK button.

You will use the fill handle to copy the formula and conditional formatting you entered in cell C33 into the remaining cells in the Net Cash Flow row.

## To copy the cash flow formula and formatting with the fill handle:

▶ 1. Click cell **C33** to select it, if necessary. The fill handle appears in the lower-right corner of the cell.

▶ 2. Position the pointer over the fill handle in the lower-right corner of the cell. The pointer changes to ➕.

▶ 3. Click and drag the fill handle over the range **D33:N33**. A dotted outline appears around the selected range as you move the pointer.

▶ 4. Release the mouse button. The selected range is filled in with the formula and formatting from cell C33, and the Auto Fill Options button appears in the lower-right corner of the selected cells. See Figure 3-20.

**TIP**

With AutoFill, formulas can easily be copied into the wrong range; if that happens, click the Undo button and try again.

**Figure 3-20**    **Formulas and formatting pasted with AutoFill**

▶ 5. Review the monthly net cash flows to confirm that AutoFill correctly copied the formula and conditional formatting into the selected range.

These calculations provide Diane with a better picture of how the couple's net cash flow varies from month to month. Only in January and August, when Glenn's tuition payments are due, do the couple's expenses exceed their income. In most months, their income exceeds expenses by about $1,500. In June, however, the net cash flow, while positive, is projected to be only $205.

## Using the Auto Fill Options Button

By default, AutoFill copies both the content and the formatting of the original range to the selected range. However, sometimes you might want to copy only the content or only the formatting. The Auto Fill Options button that appears after you release the mouse button lets you specify what is copied. As shown in Figure 3-21, clicking this button provides a list of Auto-Fill options. The Copy Cells option, which is the default, copies both the content and the formatting. The Fill Formatting Only option copies the formatting into the selected cells but not any content. The Fill Without Formatting option copies the content but not the formatting.

**Figure 3-21**    **Auto Fill Options button**

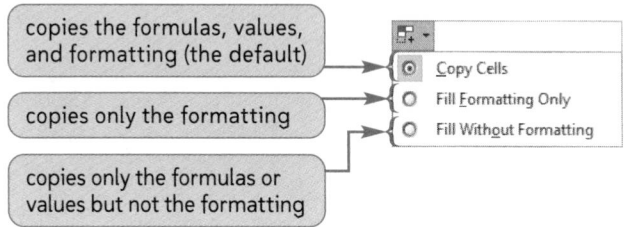

Filling a Series

## Filling a Series

AutoFill can also be used to create a series of numbers, dates, or text based on a pattern. To create a series of numbers, you enter the initial values in the series in a selected range and then use AutoFill to complete the series. Figure 3-22 shows how AutoFill can be used to insert the numbers from 1 to 10 in a selected range. You enter the first few numbers in the range A1:A3 to establish the pattern for AutoFill to use, consecutive positive integers in this example. Then, you select the range and drag the fill handle over the cells where you want the pattern continued. In Figure 3-22, the fill handle is dragged over the range A4:A10 and Excel fills in the rest of the series.

**Figure 3-22**    **AutoFill extends a numeric sequence**

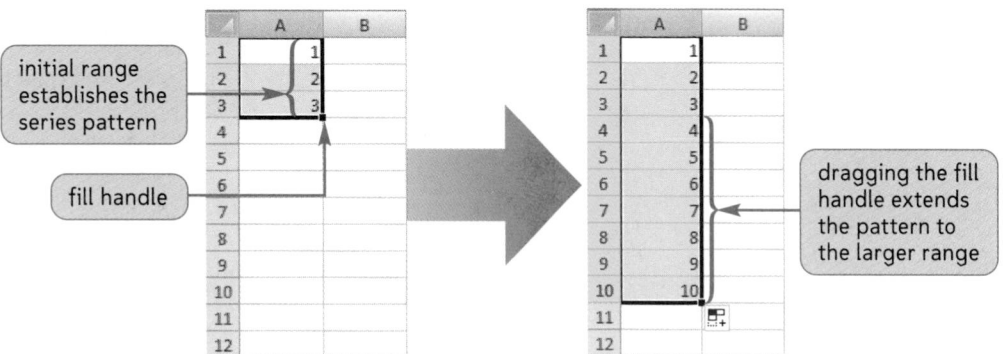

AutoFill can extend a wide variety of series, including dates and times and patterned text. Figure 3-23 shows examples of some series that AutoFill can generate. In each case, you must provide enough information for AutoFill to identify the pattern. AutoFill can recognize some patterns from only a single value, such as Jan or January, to create a series of month abbreviations or names, or Mon or Monday, to create a series of the days of the week. A text pattern that includes a text string and a number such as Region 1, Region 2, and so on can also be automatically extended using AutoFill.

**Figure 3-23** AutoFill applied to values, dates and times, and patterned text

| Type | Initial Pattern | Extended Series |
|---|---|---|
| Values | 1, 2, 3 | 4, 5, 6, ... |
| | 2, 4, 6 | 8, 10, 12, ... |
| Dates and Times | Jan | Feb, Mar, Apr, ... |
| | January | February, March, April, ... |
| | 15-Jan, 15-Feb | 15-Mar, 15-Apr, 15-May, ... |
| | 12/30/2013 | 12/31/2013, 1/1/2014, 1/2/2014, ... |
| | 12/31/2013, 1/31/2014 | 2/28/2014, 3/31/2014, 4/30/2014, ... |
| | Mon | Tue, Wed, Thu, ... |
| | Monday | Tuesday, Wednesday, Thursday, ... |
| | 11:00AM | 12:00PM, 1:00PM, 2:00PM, ... |
| Patterned Text | 1st period | 2nd period, 3rd period, 4th period, ... |
| | Region 1 | Region 2, Region 3, Region 4, ... |
| | Quarter 3 | Quarter 4, Quarter 1, Quarter 2, ... |
| | Qtr3 | Qtr4, Qtr1, Qtr2, ... |

For more complex patterns, you can use the Series dialog box. To do so, enter the first value of the series in a worksheet cell, select the entire range that will contain the series, click the Fill button in the Editing group on the Home tab, and then click Series. The Series dialog box opens. From the Series dialog box you can specify a linear or growth series for numeric values; a Date series for dates that increase by day, weekday, month, or year; or an AutoFill series for patterned text. With numeric values, you can also specify the step value (indicating how much each numeric value increases over the previous entry) and a stop value (to specify the endpoint for the entire series).

**REFERENCE**

### Creating a Series with AutoFill

- Enter the first few values of the series into a range.
- Select the range, and then drag the fill handle of the selected range over the cells you want to fill.

or

- Enter the first few values of the series into a range.
- Select the entire range into which you want to extend the series.
- In the Editing group on the Home tab, click the Fill button, and then click Down, Right, Up, Left, Series, or Justify to set the direction in which you want to extend the series.

Diane wants to see how the monthly balances in the main savings account are affected by the couple's changing income and expenses. She wants to make sure that the balance doesn't drop too low after months with particularly high expenses—such as January and August. You'll add data to the worksheet to display the monthly savings balance, starting with the month labels.

## To use AutoFill to enter a series of months:

▶ **1.** In cell C35, enter **Jan**. This is the first value in the series. Because "Jan" is a common abbreviation for January, Excel recognizes it as a month and you don't need to type "Feb" for the next month in the series.

▶ **2.** Select cell **C35**, if necessary.

▶ **3.** Drag the fill handle over the range **D35:N35**. As you drag the fill handle, ScreenTips show the month abbreviations for the selected cell.

▶ **4.** Release the mouse button. AutoFill enters the remaining three-letter abbreviations for each month of the year.

▶ **5.** Select the range **C18:N18**, and then click the **Format Painter** button 🖌 in the Clipboard group on the Home tab. You'll apply this formatting to the entries in the range C35:N35.

▶ **6.** Click cell **C35** to apply the format to the range C35:N35, and then click cell **A35** to deselect the column titles. See Figure 3-24.

| Figure 3-24 | Month labels and formatting |

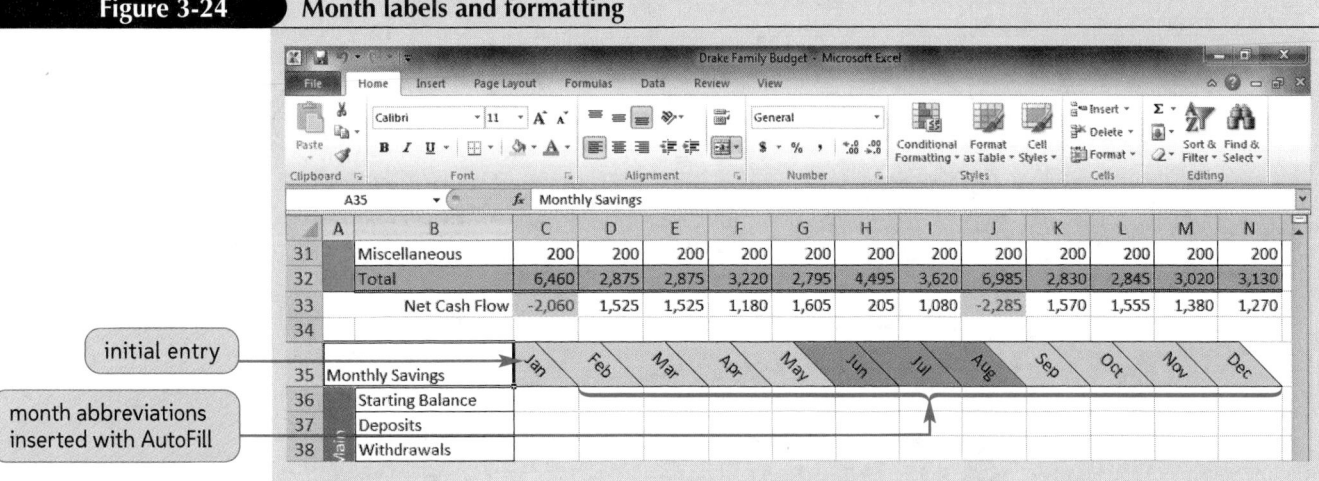

initial entry

month abbreviations inserted with AutoFill

Next, you'll enter formulas to calculate the changing balance in the couple's main savings account. The main savings account balance at the end of each month is determined by four factors:

1. The balance at the beginning of the month
2. Money deposited from the couple's paychecks at the beginning of the month
3. Money withdrawn to pay for expenses
4. Money transferred into a home savings account reserved for a down payment on a mortgage. (Diane and Glenn have not yet decided how much they want to transfer into this account, so you'll leave that value blank for now.)

You'll start by calculating the balance in the couple's account at the end of January.

## To calculate the January balance in the savings account:

▶ **1.** In cell C36, enter the formula **=K5**. The formula references the balance in the main savings account at the beginning of the year, which is stored in cell K5.

▶ **2.** In cell C37, enter **=C21** to retrieve the couple's January income. The relative reference will change when you copy the formula to other months.

3. In cell C38, enter **=C32** to retrieve the January expenses. The relative reference will change when you copy the formula to other months. You'll leave cell C39 blank because, at this point, you won't assume that any money will be transferred from the main savings account to the home savings account.

4. In cell C40, enter **=C36+C37−C38−C39**. This formula calculates the ending balance for the main savings account, which is equal to the starting balance plus any deposits minus the withdrawals and transfers. Cell C40 displays 1,940, which is the projected balance in the main savings account at the end of January.

5. Format the range C36:C39 to add borders around all of the cells.

6. Use the Format Painter to copy the formatting from cell C32 to cell **C40**, and then change the fill color to **Blue, Accent 1, Lighter 60%** (the fifth color in the third row of the Theme Colors section) to change the background color of the cell.

7. Click cell **A35**. Figure 3-25 shows the formatted January savings values.

| Figure 3-25 | January savings |

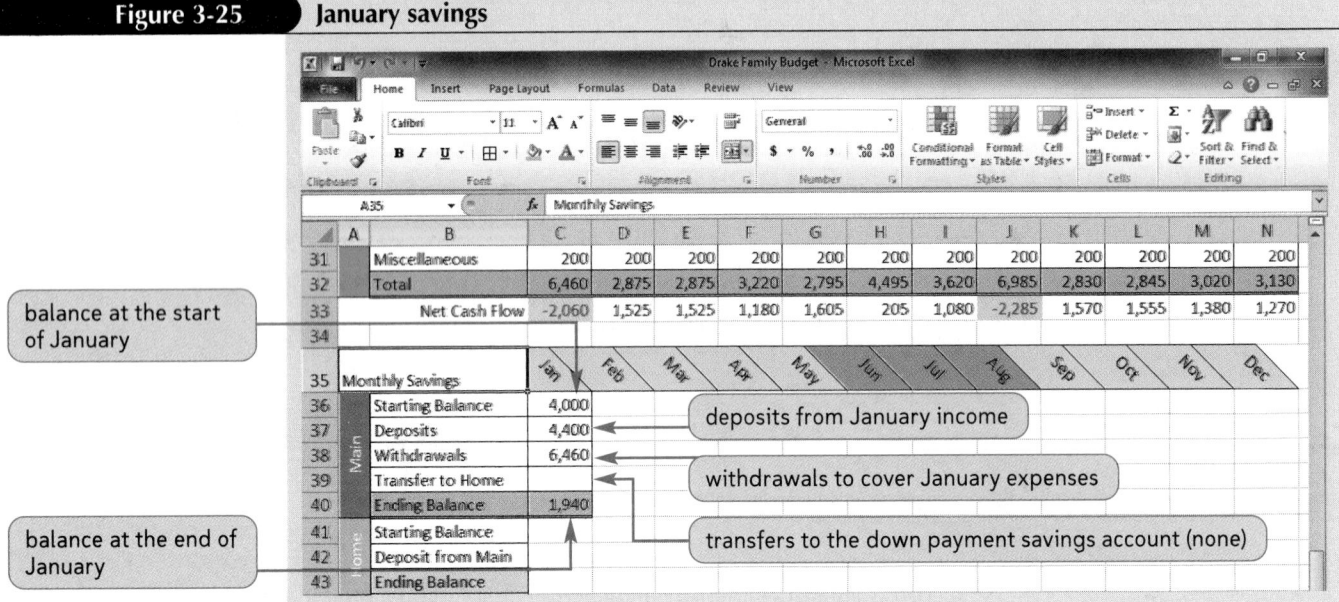

balance at the start of January

deposits from January income

withdrawals to cover January expenses

transfers to the down payment savings account (none)

balance at the end of January

At this point, the couple's projected savings at the end of January will be $1,940, which is $2,060 less than their starting balance of $4,000 at the beginning of the year. The savings formulas for the remaining months are the same as for January except that their starting balances are based on the ending balance of the previous month. You will calculate the activity in the couple's main savings account for the remaining months of the year.

### To calculate the remaining balances in the main savings account:

1. Select the range **C36:C40** and drag the fill handle over the February savings in the range **D36:D40**.

2. Change the formula in cell D36 to **=C40** so that the February starting balance for the main savings account is based on the January ending balance.

3. Select the range **D36:D40**, and then drag the fill handle over the range **E36:N40**. The formulas and formatting from February are copied into the remaining months of the year.

▶ **4.** Click cell **A35** to deselect the main savings account data. See Figure 3-26.

**Figure 3-26** | January through December savings

savings balance at the end of each month

▶ **5.** In cell L5, enter the formula **=N40**. The ending balance of the main savings account in December—12,550—appears in cell L5. Diane can quickly see that the couple's savings in the main account will increase by $8,550 in the upcoming year.

# Developing a Savings Plan

Under her current budget projections, Diane expects to have $12,550 in the main savings account at the end of the next year but nothing in the home savings account. She wants to transfer money into the home savings account each month. Because the home savings account is used for longer-term savings, Diane cannot withdraw money from it without penalty. So, she wants to make sure the main savings account always has enough money to meet monthly expenses and any unexpected bills without relying on money from the home savings account.

Diane needs to balance her desire to keep a reasonable amount in the main savings account and her desire to save enough for a down payment on a home mortgage. To achieve this balance, she needs to determine her overall savings goal and how soon she and Glenn want to meet that goal.

Diane wants to know how much money the couple can save if they transfer $500 to $1,000 into the home savings account each month for the next three years. You'll create a table that shows the total amount saved in one, two, and three years from deposits starting at $500 that increase in $100 increments through $1,000.

### To create a table for different savings plans:

▶ **1.** Go to the **Home Savings Plan** worksheet.

▶ **2.** Merge and center the range **B3:G3**, enter **Savings Deposit per Month** in the merged cell, and then format the merged cell using the **Heading 2** cell style.

▶ **3.** In cell A4, enter **Months**, and then format the cell in bold.

▶ **4.** In cell B4, enter **500** and then, in cell C4, enter **600**. You entered the first two values in the series so that you could extend the numeric series.

▶ **5.** Select the range **B4:C4**, and then drag the fill handle to cell **G4**. The values entered in the series—500, 600, 700, 800, 900, and 1000—are the different amounts the Drakes might transfer into their home savings account each month.

**Trouble?** If the number 600 was entered in each cell instead of the series, you probably did not select both cells B4 and C4 before dragging the fill handle. Repeat Step 5, being sure to select both cells before filling.

▶ **6.** In the range A5:A7, enter the values **12**, **24**, and **36**. These monthly values are equal to one year, two years, and three years, respectively. You entered the years in months because Diane and Glenn plan to deposit money into their home savings account each month. So, they would make 12 deposits in one year, they would make 24 deposits in two years, and they would make 36 deposits in three years.

▶ **7.** Format the nonadjacent range B4:G4;A5:A7 with the **Input** cell style.

Next, you'll enter formulas to calculate the amount of money saved under each plan. The amount saved is equal to the number of months of savings multiplied by the deposit per month. You'll create this table using the same formulas with mixed cell references discussed earlier in Figure 3-8.

## To enter formulas with mixed references to calculate the savings amounts:

▶ **1.** In cell **B5**, enter **=$A5*B$4**. This formula uses mixed references to calculate the amount of savings generated by saving $500 per month for 12 months. The calculated value 6000 is displayed in the cell.

▶ **2.** Select cell **B5** and drag the fill handle over the range **C5:G5** to calculate total savings over 12 months for deposits of $500 to $1,000 per month.

▶ **3.** With B5:G5 still selected, drag the fill handle down to **G7** to apply the formula to the remaining cells in the multiplication table.

▶ **4.** Format the values in the range B5:G7 using a thousands separator with no digits to the right of the decimal point, and add a border around each of the cells in the range.

▶ **5.** Click cell **B5**. Figure 3-27 shows the completed and formatted values.

**Figure 3-27** | Savings plan table

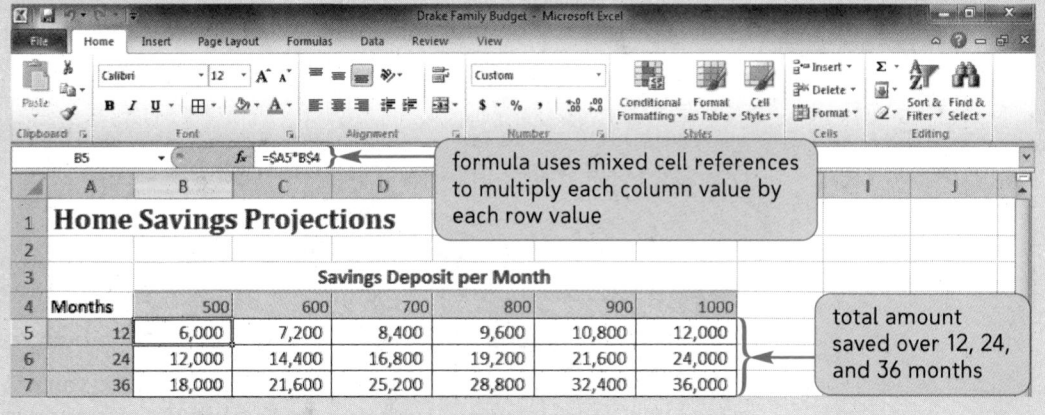

The data shows how increasing the monthly amount that Diane and Glenn save toward a down payment quickly adds up. For example, if they save $800 per month, at the end of three years (36 months), they would have saved $28,800. This is just a little less than the $30,000 they want to save for the down payment. You will add the transfer of $800 from the main savings account to the home savings account each month to the proposed budget. So that Diane can explore the impact of transferring different amounts of money per month, you'll enter the $800 value at the top of the Budget worksheet where it can be easily referenced and modified.

### To specify the $800 transfer amount:

▶ **1.** Return to the **Budget** worksheet.

▶ **2.** In cell L10, enter **800**. See Figure 3-28.

| Figure 3-28 | Home savings plan |

Next, you'll apply this monthly savings goal to Diane's proposed budget. You'll start by calculating the impact of transferring $800 on the January balances in the two savings accounts.

### To modify the January balances:

▶ **1.** In cell C39, enter the formula =**$L$10** to insert the amount of money withdrawn from the main savings account in January. The ending balance for the main account falls to $1,140. You used an absolute cell reference so that this formula continues to refer to cell L10 when you copy it into the remaining months of the year.

▶ **2.** In cell C41, enter the formula =**K6** to insert the starting balance ($0) in the home account.

▶ **3.** In cell C42, enter the formula =**C39** to insert the amount deposited from the main account into the home account.

▶ **4.** In cell C43, enter the formula =**C41+C42** to calculate the ending balance in the home account.

▶ **5.** Use the Format Painter to copy the formatting from the range **C38:C40** to the range **C41:C43**.

6. Change the fill color of cell C43 to **Orange, Accent 6, Lighter 60%** (the last color in the third row of the Theme Colors section).

7. Click cell **C43** to select it, if necessary. See Figure 3-29.

**Figure 3-29** | **Ending January balances in the Main and Home accounts**

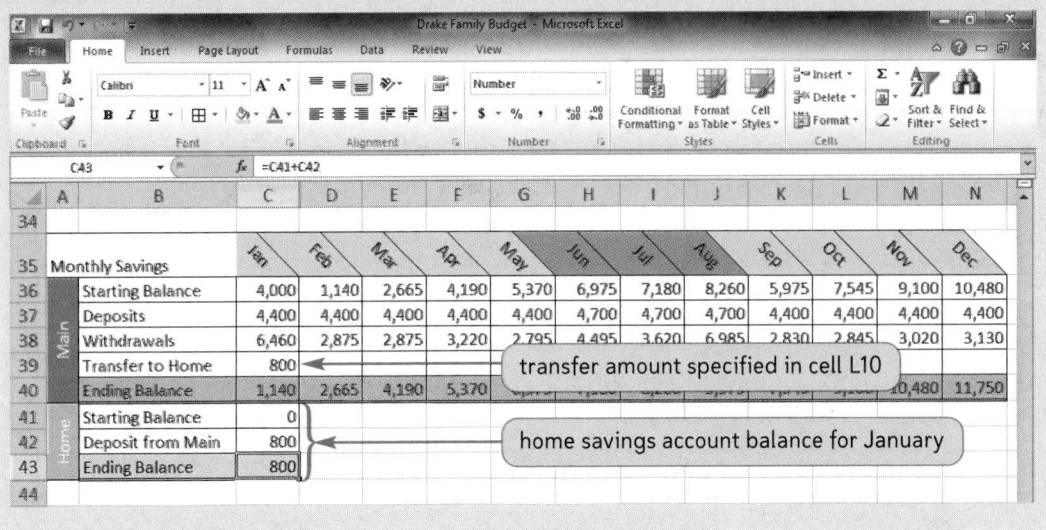

Now you'll insert the savings balances for the remaining months of the year, transferring $800 each month from the main savings account to the home savings account. As you did for the main savings account, you need to modify the formulas in row 41 so that the starting balance for February through December is taken from the ending balance of the previous month.

## To complete the formulas for the home savings account:

1. Click cell **C39**, and then drag the fill handle over the range **D39:N39**. The formula =$L$10 is inserted in each cell in the range. The ending balance for December drops to $2,950, which is the final balance in the main account after transferring $800 per month.

2. Copy the range **C41:C43**, and then paste it into the range **D41:D43**. The formulas and formatting from January are entered for February. The starting balance for February shows the initial balance in the home savings account, $0, rather than the ending balance from January, $800.

3. Change the formula in cell D41 to **=C43** so that the February starting balance is taken from the January ending balance. Cell D41 correctly shows the February starting balance of 800, and cell D43 displays the value 1,600, the ending balance for February.

4. Select the range **D41:D43**, and then drag the fill handle over the range **E41:N43**. The formulas and formatting from February are copied to the remaining months of the year.

5. Click cell **N43** to deselect the range. Figure 3-30 shows the monthly balances for both accounts from January through December.

**Figure 3-30**    **Projected monthly savings balances for the year**

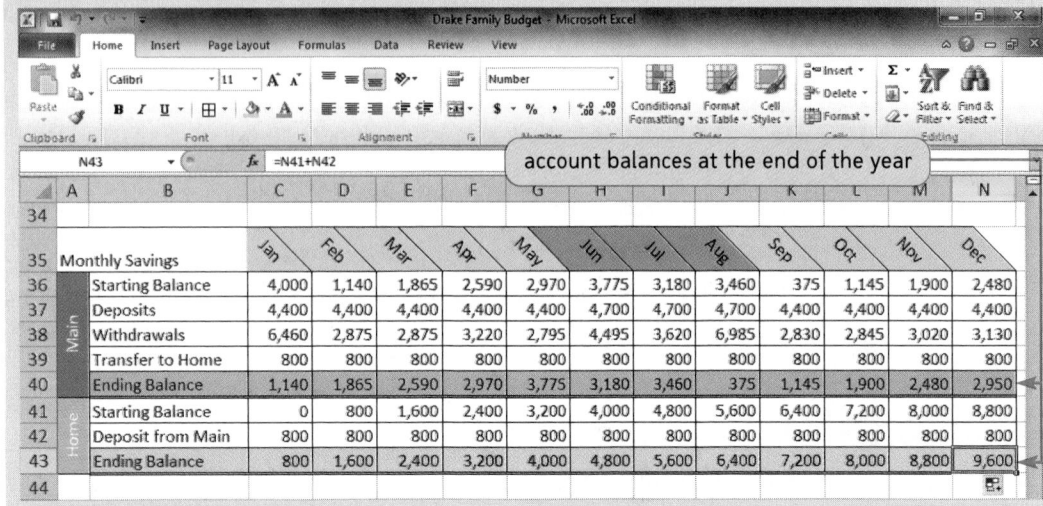

account balances at the end of the year

N43    $fx$ =N41+N42

| Monthly Savings | Jan | Feb | Mar | Apr | May | Jun | Jul | Aug | Sep | Oct | Nov | Dec |
|---|---|---|---|---|---|---|---|---|---|---|---|---|
| **Main** | | | | | | | | | | | | |
| Starting Balance | 4,000 | 1,140 | 1,865 | 2,590 | 2,970 | 3,775 | 3,180 | 3,460 | 375 | 1,145 | 1,900 | 2,480 |
| Deposits | 4,400 | 4,400 | 4,400 | 4,400 | 4,400 | 4,700 | 4,700 | 4,700 | 4,400 | 4,400 | 4,400 | 4,400 |
| Withdrawals | 6,460 | 2,875 | 2,875 | 3,220 | 2,795 | 4,495 | 3,620 | 6,985 | 2,830 | 2,845 | 3,020 | 3,130 |
| Transfer to Home | 800 | 800 | 800 | 800 | 800 | 800 | 800 | 800 | 800 | 800 | 800 | 800 |
| Ending Balance | 1,140 | 1,865 | 2,590 | 2,970 | 3,775 | 3,180 | 3,460 | 375 | 1,145 | 1,900 | 2,480 | 2,950 |
| **Home** Starting Balance | 0 | 800 | 1,600 | 2,400 | 3,200 | 4,000 | 4,800 | 5,600 | 6,400 | 7,200 | 8,000 | 8,800 |
| Deposit from Main | 800 | 800 | 800 | 800 | 800 | 800 | 800 | 800 | 800 | 800 | 800 | 800 |
| Ending Balance | 800 | 1,600 | 2,400 | 3,200 | 4,000 | 4,800 | 5,600 | 6,400 | 7,200 | 8,000 | 8,800 | 9,600 |

▶ **6.** In cell L6, enter the formula **=N43**. The savings plan table at the top of the work-sheet displays 9,600, which is the year-end balance for the home account.

▶ **7.** In cell L7, enter the formula **=L5+L6** to calculate the total savings amount from both accounts at the end of the year. Under Diane's current plan, the couple will have $2,950 in the main savings account and $9,600 in the home savings account at the end of the year.

# Working with Logical Functions

Although Diane is pleased that $9,600 will be moved into the home savings account in the next year, she's concerned about the amount of money left in the main savings account. Even more troubling are the month-to-month balances in that account. For example, the balance in the main savings account will be only $375 at the end of August and will remain well below $2,000 for several months of the year. Diane is concerned that this savings plan will leave the couple with insufficient funds in the main savings account to handle unforeseen expenses.

Part of the problem is that the couple's net cash flow is negative during several months of the year. If they continue to transfer $800 into the home savings account during those months, the main savings account might fall below an acceptable level. Diane wants to modify her savings plan so that money is not transferred into the home savings account unless the net cash flow for that month is greater than or equal to $1,000. You need a formula that can "choose" whether to transfer the funds. You can build this kind of decision-making capability into a formula through the use of a logical function.

A logical function is a function that works with statements that are either true or false. Consider a statement such as "cell A5 = 3". If cell A5 is equal to 3, this statement has a value of true; if cell A5 is not equal to 3, this statement has a value of false. Excel supports many different logical functions, one of which is the IF function.

## Using the IF Function

The IF function is a logical function that returns one value if a statement is true and returns a different value if that statement is false. The syntax of the IF function is

```
IF(logical_test, [value_if_true,] [value_if_false])
```

where *logical_test* is a statement that is either true or false, *value_if_true* is the value returned by the IF function if the statement is true, and *value_if_false* is the value returned by the function if the statement is false. For example, the following formula tests whether the value in cell A1 is equal to the value in cell B1. If it is, the formula returns a value of 100; otherwise it returns a value of 50.

```
=IF(A1=B1, 100, 50)
```

In many cases, however, you will not use values directly in the IF function. The following formula uses cell references, returning the value of cell C1 if A1 equals B1; otherwise, it returns the value of cell C2:

```
=IF(A1=B1, C1, C2)
```

The = symbol in these formulas is a comparison operator. A **comparison operator** is a symbol that indicates the relationship between two values. Figure 3-31 describes the comparison operators that can be used within a logical function.

**Figure 3-31** **Comparison operators**

| Operator | Statement | Description |
|---|---|---|
| = | A1 = B1 | Tests whether the value in cell A1 *is equal to* the value in cell B1 |
| > | A1 > B1 | Tests whether the value in cell A1 *is greater than* the value in cell B1 |
| < | A1 < B1 | Tests whether the value in cell A1 *is less than* the value in cell B1 |
| >= | A1 >= B1 | Tests whether the value in cell A1 *is greater than or equal to* the value in cell B1 |
| <= | A1 <= B1 | Tests whether the value in cell A1 *is less than or equal to* the value in cell B1 |
| <> | A1 <> B1 | Tests whether the value in cell A1 *is not equal to* the value in cell B1 |

The IF function also works with text. For example, the following formula tests whether the value of cell A1 is equal to YES. If the value of cell A1 is equal to YES, the formula returns the text DONE; otherwise, it returns the text RESTART.

```
=IF(A1="YES", "DONE", "RESTART")
```

In addition, you can nest other functions inside an IF statement. The following formula first tests whether cell A5 is equal to the maximum of values within the range A1:A100. If it is, the formula returns the text "Maximum"; otherwise, it returns no text.

```
=IF(A5=MAX(A1:A100), "Maximum","")
```

In Diane and Glenn's budget, you will use an IF function for each month to test whether the net cash flow for that month is $1,000 or greater. If it is, Diane wants to transfer some of it into the home savings account. On the other hand, if the net cash flow is less than $1,000, she does not want to transfer any of it into the home account. You'll start creating this function by entering the minimum net cash flow into the worksheet.

**To specify the minimum net cash flow:**

▶ **1.** In cell H11, enter the label **Minimum required net cash flow**.

▶ **2.** In cell L11, enter **1000**. This is the minimum cash flow amount.

▶ **3.** Use the Format Painter to copy the formatting from the range **H10:L10** to the range H11:L11.

Next, you'll enter a formula to determine how much to transfer each month. For the month of January, the formula to determine how much money is transferred is:

```
=IF(C33>=$L$11, $L$10, 0)
```

Cell C33 contains the net cash flow for the month of January, cell L11 contains the minimum net cash flow needed before Diane will transfer the money between accounts, and cell L10 contains the amount of money that Diane wants to transfer when the net cash flow meets or exceeds the minimum. For the current worksheet, this function tests whether the net cash flow for the month of January (cell C33) is greater than or equal to 1000 (cell L11). If it is, the formula returns 800 (cell L10) as the amount to transfer from the main savings account into the home savings account. Otherwise, it returns 0 and no money will be transferred that month.

This logical test uses both relative and absolute references. The C33 reference is relative because you will copy this formula into cells for the remaining months of the year. The $L$11 and $L$10 references are absolute so that the expression always references the minimum net cash flow specified in cell L11 and the amount to transfer specified in cell L10.

You'll replace the formula in cell C39 with this IF function.

### To insert the IF function to determine the monthly transfer amount:

1. Clear the contents of cell **C39**.

2. Click the **Formulas** tab on the Ribbon, if necessary.

3. In the Function Library group, click the **Logical** button, and then click **IF** in the list of logical functions. The Function Arguments dialog box for the IF function opens.

4. In the Logical_test box, enter **C33>=$L$11**. This tests whether the net cash flow for January is greater than or equal to the value in cell L11 (1000).

5. In the Value_if_true box, enter **$L$10**. If the value in cell C33 is greater than or equal to the value in cell L11, the formula returns the value in cell L10 (800).

6. In the Value_if_false box, enter **0**. If the value in cell C33 is less than the value in cell L11, the formula returns 0 and no money will be transferred from the main savings account into the home savings account that month. See Figure 3-32.

**TIP**

When you type the IF function directly in the cell, remember that the *value_if_true* argument comes before the *value_if_false* argument.

| Figure 3-32 | Function Arguments dialog box for the IF function |

test condition that is either true or false

value returned if the condition is true

value returned if the condition is false

amount to transfer to the home account if the value is true

no money is transferred if the value is false

7. Click the **OK** button. A value of 0 is displayed in cell C39. Because the net cash flow for January is –2,060, no money will be transferred from the main savings account into the home savings account that month.

8. Drag the fill handle for cell C39 over the range **D39:N39** to copy this formula with the IF function into the remaining months of Diane's proposed budget.

▶ **9.** Click cell **N40** to deselect the range. The new savings account balances are shown in Figure 3-33.

**Figure 3-33** ▶ **Monthly savings account balances**

click to view logical functions

net cash flow is >= $1,000 every month except January, June, and August

$800 is transferred every month except January, June, and August

| | A | B | C | D | E | F | G | H | I | J | K | L | M | N |
|---|---|---|---|---|---|---|---|---|---|---|---|---|---|---|
| 31 | | Miscellaneous | 200 | 200 | 200 | 200 | 200 | 200 | 200 | 200 | 200 | 200 | 200 | 200 |
| 32 | | Total | 6,460 | 2,875 | 2,875 | 3,220 | 2,795 | 4,495 | 3,620 | 6,985 | 2,830 | 2,845 | 3,020 | 3,130 |
| 33 | | Net Cash Flow | -2,060 | 1,525 | 1,525 | 1,180 | 1,605 | 205 | 1,080 | -2,285 | 1,570 | 1,555 | 1,380 | 1,270 |
| 34 | | | | | | | | | | | | | | |
| 35 | | Monthly Savings | Jan | Feb | Mar | Apr | May | Jun | Jul | Aug | Sep | Oct | Nov | Dec |
| 36 | | Starting Balance | 4,000 | 1,940 | 2,665 | 3,390 | 3,770 | 4,575 | 4,780 | 5,060 | 2,775 | 3,545 | 4,300 | 4,880 |
| 37 | | Deposits | 4,400 | 4,400 | 4,400 | 4,400 | 4,400 | 4,700 | 4,700 | 4,700 | 4,400 | 4,400 | 4,400 | 4,400 |
| 38 | Main | Withdrawals | 6,460 | 2,875 | 2,875 | 3,220 | 2,795 | 4,495 | 3,620 | 6,985 | 2,830 | 2,845 | 3,020 | 3,130 |
| 39 | | Transfer to Home | 0 | 800 | 800 | 800 | 800 | 0 | 800 | 0 | 800 | 800 | 800 | 800 |
| 40 | | Ending Balance | 1,940 | 2,665 | 3,390 | 3,770 | 4,575 | 4,780 | 5,060 | 2,775 | 3,545 | 4,300 | 4,880 | 5,350 |
| 41 | | Starting Balance | 0 | 0 | 800 | 1,600 | 2,400 | 3,200 | 3,200 | 4,000 | 4,000 | 4,800 | 5,600 | 6,400 |
| 42 | Home | Deposit from Main | 0 | 800 | 800 | 800 | 800 | 0 | 800 | 0 | 800 | 800 | 800 | 800 |
| 43 | | Ending Balance | 0 | 800 | 1,600 | 2,400 | 3,200 | 3,200 | 4,000 | 4,000 | 4,800 | 5,600 | 6,400 | 7,200 |
| 44 | | | | | | | | | | | | | | |

With this savings plan, the ending balance in the main savings account remains above $3,000 for most months of the year, and $800 is transferred from the main savings account into the home savings account in nine months of the year. Only in January, June, and August will Diane not transfer money into the home account. By the end of the year, the couple will have $5,350 in the main savings account and $7,200 in the home savings account.

Diane wants to explore what would happen if she increases the monthly transfer from $800 to $1,000. How would that affect the monthly balance of the main savings account?

**To change the conditions of Diane's savings plan:**

▶ **1.** Change the value in cell **L10** to **1000**. The end-of-year balance in the home savings account increases to $9,000 (cell L6) while the main savings account balance decreases to $3,550 (cell L5).

▶ **2.** Scroll down the worksheet and examine how the monthly balance in the main savings account changes throughout the year. Under this revised plan, the balance in the main savings account drops to $1,775 in the month of August. This is a little too low for Diane.

▶ **3.** Change the value in cell **L10** to **900**. With this savings plan, the couple will save $8,100 toward a down payment on a home, and the balance in their main savings account will remain above $2,000 every month except January, when it dips to $1,940.

Diane feels that this revised savings plan is a good compromise between the need to save money for their future home while still maintaining a decent balance in their main savings account.

PROSKILLS

*Decision Making: Using the IF Function to Explore Financial Options*

Decision making is the process of choosing between possible courses of action. No decisions should be made until after the analysis of all potential alternatives is complete.

With financial decisions, you will often explore the impact of alternative scenarios on a projected outcome. Budget planning should not be limited to a single budget projection, but instead include several possible budgets. Your decision is then based on the evaluation of these different budgets. The budget you choose should prepare you to deal with shortages in future revenue or ways to take advantage of better-than-expected revenue.

Using Excel to manage your finances allows you to quickly explore these multiple scenarios. You can quickly examine how changing one or more values will affect such outcomes as income, expenses, and cash flow. You can use logical functions such as the IF function to help you explore these what-if scenarios because you can set the outcome of one value only if certain conditions are met. Different scenarios can be coded with names such as Option1, Option2, and Option 3. By using these scenario names as input values to an IF function, you can set up the worksheet to display the results specific to each scenario. In a well-designed workbook, you can quickly switch between scenarios simply by changing a few values in the worksheet.

By applying Excel's logical functions, you can more easily plan for different outcomes, and avoid the problems associated with unexpected occurences.

# Working with Date Functions

To be effective, budgets need to be monitored and updated as conditions change. In the upcoming year, Diane plans to use this workbook to enter her and Glenn's actual salaries, expenses, and savings. This will enable Diane to track how well her projected values match the actual values. Because Diane will be updating the workbook throughout the year, she wants the worksheet to always display the current date so she can tell how far she is into her budget projections. You can accomplish this using a date function. Seven date functions supported by Excel are described in Figure 3-34. You can use these functions to help with scheduling or to determine on what days of the week certain dates occur.

**Figure 3-34**    **Date and time functions**

| Function | Description |
| --- | --- |
| DATE(*year*, *month*, *day*) | Creates a date value for the date represented by the *year*, *month*, and *day* arguments |
| DAY(*date*) | Extracts the day of the month from the *date* value |
| MONTH(*date*) | Extracts the month number from the *date* value where 1=January, 2=February, and so forth |
| YEAR(*date*) | Extracts the year number from the *date* value |
| WEEKDAY(*date*, [*return_type*]) | Calculates the day of the week from the *date* value, where 1=Sunday, 2=Monday, and so forth; to choose a different numbering scheme, set the optional *return_type* value to "1" (1=Sunday, 2=Monday, ...), "2" (1=Monday, 2=Tuesday, ...), or "3" (0=Monday, 1=Tuesday, ...) |
| NOW( ) | Displays the current date and time |
| TODAY( ) | Displays the current date |

Perhaps the most commonly used date function is the TODAY function, which returns the current date. The syntax of the TODAY function is:

=TODAY()

The TODAY function doesn't have any arguments. Neither does the NOW function, which returns both the current date and the current time. The values returned by the TODAY and NOW functions are updated automatically whenever you reopen the workbook or enter a new calculation.

Diane wants the Budget worksheet to display the current date.

### To display the current date:

1. In cell I1, enter the label **Current Date**.

2. Merge cells **I1** and **J1**, left-align the merged cell, and change the cell's fill color to **Tan, Background 2** (the third color in the first row of the Theme Colors section).

3. Click cell **K1**. You'll enter the TODAY function in this cell.

4. Click the **Formulas** tab on the Ribbon.

5. In the Function Library group, click the **Date & Time** button, and then click **TODAY** in the date functions list. The Function Arguments dialog box opens, with a description of the function and a reminder that there are no arguments for the TODAY function.

6. Click the **OK** button. The Function Arguments dialog box closes, and the =TODAY() function is inserted into cell L1.

7. Merge and center the range **K1:L1**, and then add a border around each of the cells in the range I1:L1.

8. Click cell **K1** to deselect the range. See Figure 3-35.

**Figure 3-35**    **TODAY function displays the current date**

## Working with Financial Functions

Excel provides a wide range of financial functions related to loans and interest payments. One of these is the PMT function, which can be used to calculate a payment schedule required to completely pay back a mortgage or loan. Figure 3-36 describes the PMT function and some of the other financial functions often used to develop budgets. These financial functions are the same as those widely used in business and accounting to perform various financial calculations, such as depreciation of an asset, the amount of interest paid on an investment, and the present value of an investment.

| **Figure 3-36** | **Financial functions for loans and investments** |

| Function | Description |
|---|---|
| FV(*rate, nper, pmt,* [*pv=0*] [*,type=0*]) | Calculates the future value of an investment, where *rate* is the interest rate per period, *nper* is the total number of periods, *pmt* is the payment in each period, *pv* is the present value of the investment, and *type* indicates whether payments should be made at the end of the period (0) or the beginning of the period (1) |
| PMT(*rate, nper, pv,* [*fv=0*] [*,type=0*]) | Calculates the payments required each period on a loan or investment, where *fv* is the future value of the investment |
| IPMT(*rate, per, nper, pv,* [*fv=0*] [*,type=0*]) | Calculates the amount of a loan payment devoted to paying the loan interest, where *per* is the number of the payment period |
| PPMT(*rate, per, nper, pv,* [*fv=0*] [*,type=0*]) | Calculates the amount of a loan payment devoted to paying off the principal of a loan |
| PV(*rate, nper, pmt,* [*fv=0*] [*,type=0*]) | Calculates the present value of a loan or investment based on periodic, constant payments |
| NPER(*rate, pmt, pv,* [*fv=0*] [*,type=0*]) | Calculates the number of periods required to pay off a loan or investment |
| RATE(*nper, pmt, pv,* [*fv=0*] [*,type=0*]) | Calculates the interest rate of a loan or investment based on periodic, constant payments |

The cost of a loan to the borrower is largely based on three factors: the principal, the interest, and the time required to pay back the loan. **Principal** is the amount of money being loaned, and **interest** is the amount added to the principal by the lender. You can think of interest as a kind of "user fee" because the borrower is paying for the right to use the lender's money for a period of time. A few years ago, Diane and Glenn borrowed money to buy a second car and are still repaying the bank for the principal and interest on that loan. On the other hand, Diane and Glenn have also deposited money in their main savings account and receive interest payments from the bank in return.

Interest is calculated either as simple interest or as compound interest. In **simple interest**, the interest is equal to a percentage of principal for each period that the money has been lent. For example, if Diane and Glenn deposit $1,000 at a simple interest rate of 5 percent, they will receive $50 in interest payments each year. After one year their investment will be worth $1,050, after two years it will be worth $1,100, and so forth.

With **compound interest**, the interest is applied not only to the principal but also to any accrued interest. If Diane and Glenn deposit $1,000 in a bank at 5 percent annual interest compounded every year, they will earn $50 in the first year, raising the value of the account to $1,050. If they leave that money in the bank for another year, the interest payment in the second year rises to 5 percent of $1,050 or $52.50, resulting in a total value of $1,102.50. So they earn more money the second year because they are receiving interest on their interest.

Compound interest payments are divided into the period of time in which the interest is applied. For example, an 8 percent annual interest rate compounded monthly results in 12 interest payments per year with the interest each month equal to 1/12 of 8 percent, or about 0.67 percent per month.

Another factor in calculating the cost of a loan is the length of time required to pay it back. The longer it takes to pay back a loan, the more the loan costs because the borrower is paying interest over a longer period of time. To save money, loans should be paid back quickly and in full.

*Using Functions to Manage Personal Finances*

Excel has many financial functions to manage personal finances. The following list can help you determine which function to use for the most common personal finance problems:

- To determine how much an investment will be worth after a series of monthly payments at some future time, use the FV (future value) function.
- To determine how much you have to spend each month to repay a loan or mortgage within a set period of time, use the PMT (payment) function.
- To determine how much of your monthly loan payment is used to pay the interest, use the IPMT (interest payment) function.
- To determine how much of your monthly loan payment is used for repaying the principal, use the PPMT (principal payment) function.
- To determine the largest loan or mortgage you can afford given a set monthly payment, use the PV (present value) function.
- To determine how long it will take to pay off a loan with constant monthly payments, use the NPER (number of periods) function.

   For most loan and investment calculations, you need to enter the annual interest rate divided by the number of times the interest is compounded during the year. If interest is compounded monthly, divide the annual interest rate by 12; if interest is compounded quarterly, divide the annual rate by 4. You must also convert the length of the loan or investment to the number of interest payments per year. If you will make payments monthly, multiply the number of years of the loan or investment by 12.

## Using the PMT Function

Diane and Glenn plan to purchase a house in the next several years. Diane wants to know how large of a mortgage she and Glenn could afford given their current income and expenses. To calculate the costs associated with a loan or mortgage, you need the following information:

- The amount being borrowed
- The annual interest rate
- The number of payment periods per year
- When loan payments are due
- The length of the loan in terms of the number of payment periods

   In Diane and Glenn's neighborhood, starter homes are selling for about $240,000. If Diane and Glenn can keep to their savings plan, they will have saved $8,100 by the end of the year (as shown in cell L6 in the Budget worksheet). If they save this same amount for the next three years, they will have $24,300 in their home savings account to put toward the down payment. Based on this, Diane estimates that she and Glenn will need a home loan of almost $215,000.

   Diane wants to know how much a mortgage of this size would cost in monthly payments. To determine this, you'll use the PMT function, which has the syntax

```
PMT(rate, nper, pv, [fv=0] [type=0])
```

where *rate* is the interest rate for each payment period, *nper* is the total number of payment periods required to pay off the loan, and *pv* is the present value of the loan or the amount that needs to be borrowed. For Diane and Glenn, the present value of the proposed loan is $215,000.

The PMT function has two optional arguments: *fv* and *type*. The *fv* argument is the future value of the loan. Because the intent with most loans is to pay them off completely, the future value is equal to 0 by default. The *type* argument specifies when the interest is charged on the loan, either at the end of the payment period (*type*=0), which is the default, or at the beginning of the payment period (*type*=1).

For most mortgages, the payment period is one month. This means that Diane and Glenn must make a payment on the loan every month, and interest on the loan is compounded every month. The annual interest rate on home loans in Diane and Glenn's area is 6.0 percent. To determine the interest rate per month, you divide the annual interest rate by 12. For Diane and Glenn, the interest rate each month is 6 percent divided by 12, or about 0.5 percent per month.

Diane and Glenn want to pay off their home loan in 20 years, or 240 months (20 years multiplied by 12 months per year). Putting all of this information together, you can calculate the monthly payment for the couple's home loan with the following formula:

```
=PMT(0.06/12, 20*12, 215000)
```

This formula returns a value of −$1,540.33. The value is negative because the payment is considered an expense, which Excel treats as a negative value. If you want to display this value as a positive number in a worksheet, enter a minus sign directly before the PMT function as follows:

```
=-PMT(0.06/12, 20*12, 215000)
```

Based on these calculations, Diane and Glenn would have to pay the bank $1,540.33 every month for 20 years before the loan and the interest are completely paid. Right now, the couple is spending about $1,050 per month on rent. So this home loan would be a significant increase over their current expenses.

Diane wants you to calculate the monthly payment for a home loan under other possible scenarios. You'll start by examining the costs associated with a $200,000 loan.

### To create a loan payment worksheet:

▶ **1.** Go to the **Loan Analysis** worksheet. You will do the loan calculations in this worksheet.

▶ **2.** In cell B3, enter **6.00%**. This is the annual interest rate for the loan.

▶ **3.** In cell B4, enter **12** for the number of payments per year.

▶ **4.** In cell B5, enter the formula **=B3/B4** to calculate the interest per period, which is 0.50% per month.

▶ **5.** In cell B6, enter **20** for the length of the mortgage in years.

▶ **6.** In cell B7, enter the formula **=B4*B6** to calculate the total number of monthly payments, which is 240.

▶ **7.** In cell B8, enter **$200,000** for the amount of the loan. All the values for the loan are entered.

The Loan Analysis worksheet includes all the data you need to calculate the monthly payment required to pay off the mortgage in 20 years at 6 percent interest compounded monthly. You will enter the PMT function to calculate this value.

### To use the PMT function to calculate the monthly payment:

1. Click cell **B10** to select it.

2. In the Function Library group on the Formulas tab, click the **Financial** button, and then click **PMT** in the list of financial functions. The Function Arguments dialog box opens.

3. In the Rate box, enter the cell reference **B5**, which is the cell with the interest rate per month.

4. In the Nper box, enter the cell reference **B7**, which is the cell with the total number of monthly payments required to pay back the loan.

5. In the Pv box, enter the cell reference **B8**, which is the cell with the present value of the loan. See Figure 3-37.

**TIP**

Be sure to enter the interest rate per month for the Rate argument and not the annual interest rate for any loan or investment that has monthly payments.

**Figure 3-37**    Function Arguments dialog box for the PMT function

6. Click the **OK** button. The value $1,432.86 is displayed in parentheses in cell B10 to indicate a negative currency value. See Figure 3-38.

**Figure 3-38**    **Money payments to pay back a $200,000 loan**

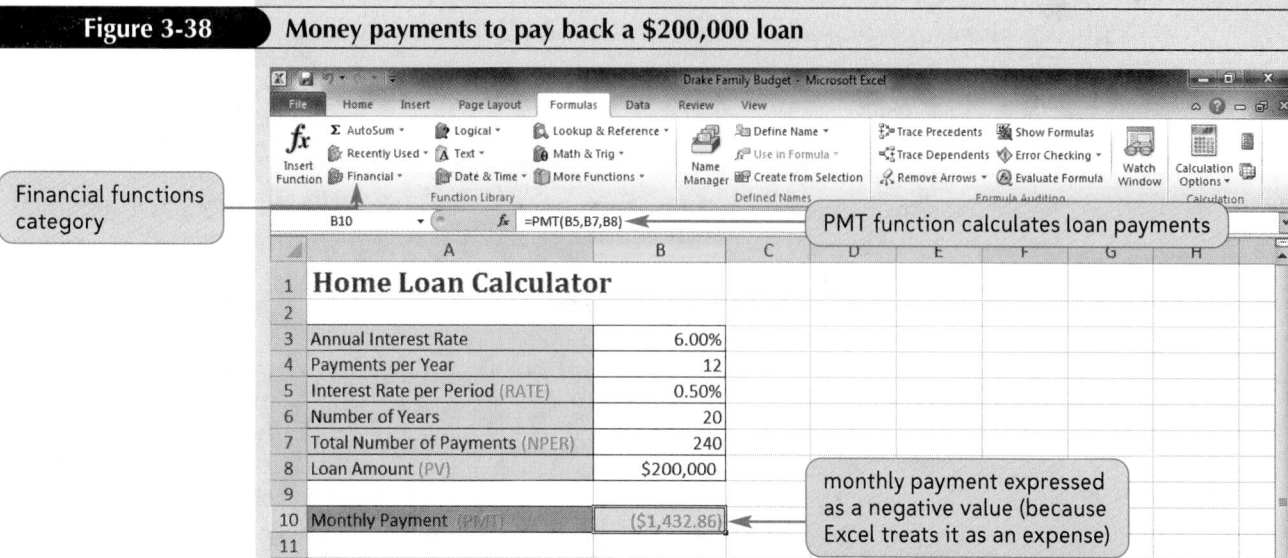

**Trouble?** If you see ##### in cell B10, the column width is too small to view the entire value. Increase the width of column B to display the monthly payment value.

Diane and Glenn would have to pay more than $1,400 per month for 20 years to repay a $200,000 loan at 6 percent interest. This is still too high. Diane is interested in other possibilities. Because you already set up the worksheet, you can quickly try other scenarios without having to reenter any formulas. Diane wonders whether extending the length of the loan would reduce the monthly payment by a sizeable margin. She asks you to calculate the monthly payment for different loan options.

### To analyze other loan options:

▶ **1.** Change the value in cell B6 to **30**. The amount of the monthly payment drops to $1,199.10, which is a decrease of $200 per month.

▶ **2.** Change the value of cell B8 to **175,000**. For this smaller home loan, the monthly payment drops even further to $1,049.21 per month. This is almost exactly equal to what the couple is currently paying in rent.

▶ **3.** Save the workbook, and then close it.

You've completed your work on Diane and Glenn's budget. Your analysis has shown Diane several important things. Her projected budget allows the couple to transfer enough money to the home savings account to make a down payment on a home in about three years. This savings plan leaves enough funds in the main savings account to cover their monthly expenses. Finally, the possible monthly mortgage payments for a loan will not be substantially more than what Diane and Glenn are currently paying in rent. So, not only will Diane and Glenn be able to save enough to make the initial down payment, their monthly income should also cover the monthly payments. Of course, all budgets must be revised periodically to meet changing expenses and income, and many different options exist in the home mortgage market. For example, Diane and Glenn could receive a mortgage with a lower interest rate or one that requires a smaller down payment. Your work has given Diane and Glenn enough information to make informed choices about their immediate financial future.

**PROSKILLS**

*Aa*

*Written Communication: Presenting a Budget*

In business, government, and personal lives, budgets play a key role in making sound financial decisions. However, a well-organized budget is only the first step. The budget must also convey information that is easily grasped by your audience or clients. Keep in mind the following guidelines as you work on budget spreadsheets:

- **Plan the budget around a few essential goals.** What is your budget trying to achieve? Be specific and focused.
- **Pick out a few important measures or "bottom lines" that can convey whether the proposed budget will meet your goals.** Are you trying to pay off a debt, raise money, or achieve a specific level of savings?
- **Look at your financial history to aid you in creating budget projections.** Search for important trends and take into account other factors such as inflation in your projections.
- **When explaining the budget, describe the results in terms of everyday examples.** Avoid the temptation of overwhelming your audience with raw facts and figures; rather, interpret what those facts and figures mean in terms of your bottom line measures.

You want your budget spreadsheet to remain current as new data and projections become available. This means continually updating the budget. But, do not just overwrite or delete the old budget spreadsheets. Keep earlier budgets easily accessible so you can access the original assumptions and goals when preparing the next budget. By keeping an audit trail of your past work, you can make your future budgets more accurate and reliable.

**REVIEW**

## Session 3.2 Quick Check

1. How do you use AutoFill to copy a set of cell values, but not the formatting?
2. If the first three selected values in a series are 3, 6, and 9, what are the next three values that will be inserted using AutoFill?
3. If cell P5 contains the text "Mon," and then you select the cell and drag the fill handle over the range P6:P8, what text will be entered into those cells?
4. If cell Q3 is greater than cell Q4, you want to display "OK"; otherwise, you want to display "RETRY". Write the formula that accomplishes this.
5. Write the formula to display the current date.
6. Write the formula to display the current date and time.
7. You want to take out a loan for $130,000. The interest on the loan is 5 percent compounded monthly. You intend to pay back the loan in 20 years. Write the formula to calculate the monthly payment required to pay off the loan under those conditions.
8. What financial function do you use to determine how many payment periods are required to pay off a loan?

## Review Assignments

**Data File needed for the Review Assignments: Timov.xlsx**

Sergei and Ava Timov, friends of Diane and Glenn, ask you to create a similar workbook for their family budget. The Timovs want to purchase a new home. They are considering two houses with different mortgages. They want the budget worksheet you create to display the impact of monthly mortgage payments on the couple's cash flow. They also want to be able to quickly switch between one mortgage plan and another to observe the impact of each plan on their budget. The couple has already designed the workbook and entered estimates of their income and expenses for the upcoming year. You need to set up the formulas. Complete the following:

1. Open the **Timov** workbook located in the Excel3\Review folder included with your Data Files, and then save the workbook as **Timov Family Budget**.
2. In the Documentation sheet, enter your name in cell B3. Use the TODAY function to display the current date in cell B4.
3. In the Family Budget worksheet, in the range C18:N18, use AutoFill to replace the month numbers with the abbreviations **Jan** through **Dec**.
4. In the range C21:N21, calculate the couple's total income. In the range C27:N27, calculate the couple's total monthly expenses. In the range C28:N28, calculate the monthly net cash flow (equal to the total income minus the total expenses).
5. In cell C7, enter a formula to calculate the sum of Sergei's monthly income for the entire year. In cell D7, calculate Sergei's average monthly income. In cell E7, calculate Sergei's maximum monthly income. In cell F7, calculate Sergei's minimum monthly income.
6. Complete the Year-End Summary table by first selecting the range C7:F7. Use AutoFill to copy the formula in the range C7:F7 into the range C7:F16. Use the Auto Fill Options button to copy only the formulas into the selected range and not both the formulas and the formats. (*Hint*: Because you haven't yet entered any mortgage payment values, cell D14 will show the value #DIV/0!, indicating that Excel cannot calculate the average mortgage payment. You'll correct that problem shortly.)
7. In the range K2:K7, enter the following loan and loan conditions of the first mortgage:
   a. In cell K2, enter **6.7%** as the annual interest rate.
   b. In cell K3, enter **12** as the number of payments per year.
   c. In cell K4, calculate the monthly interest rate.
   d. In cell K5, enter **30** as the number of years in the mortgage.
   e. In cell K6, calculate the total number of months to repay the loan.
   f. In cell K7, enter **395,000** as the loan amount.
8. In cell K8, use the PMT function to calculate the monthly payment required to repay this loan.
9. Edit the formula in cell K8, adding a minus sign directly before the PMT function to make the value returned by the formula positive rather than negative.
10. In the range K10:K15, enter the following conditions of the second mortgage plan, and calculate the monthly interest rate and the total number of months to repay the loan:
    - The annual interest rate is **6.7%**.
    - The interest rate is compounded **12** times a year (or monthly).
    - The mortgage will last **20** years.
    - The loan amount (or value of the principal) is **$300,000**.

11. In cell K16, enter the PMT function to calculate the monthly payment needed to pay off this loan, and then edit the formula to make the value displayed in the cell positive by placing a negative sign in front of the PMT function.

12. Sergei and Ava want to be able to view their monthly cash flow under both mortgage plans. The mortgage being applied to the budget will be determined by whether 1 or 2 is entered into cell E3. To switch from one mortgage to another, do the following:

    a. In cell C26, enter an IF function that tests whether cell E3 equals 1. If it does, return the value of cell K8; otherwise, return the value of cell K16. Use absolute cell references for all references in the formula.

    b. Use AutoFill to copy the formula in cell C26 into the range D26:N26.

    c. Verify that the values in the range C26:N26 match the monthly payment for the first mortgage condition. (Note that the worksheet will display the monthly payment amount to the nearest dollar.)

13. In cell E3, change the value from 1 to **2**. Verify that the monthly payment for the second mortgage appears in the range C26:N26.

14. Sergei and Ava want to maintain an average net cash flow of at least $1,000 per month. Is this achieved on either mortgage plan?

15. Save and close the workbook, and then submit the finished workbook to your instructor, either in printed or electronic form, as requested.

### Case Problem 1

If you have a SAM 2010 user profile, your instructor may have assigned an autogradable version of this assignment. If so, log into the SAM 2010 Web site at www.cengage.com/sam2010 to download the instructions and start files.

**Data File needed for this Case Problem: Chemistry.xlsx**

***Chemistry 303***    Karen Raul is a professor of chemistry at a community college in Shawnee, Kansas. She has started using Excel to calculate the final grade for students in her Chemistry 303 course. The final score is a weighted average of the scores given for three exams and the final exam. One way to calculate a weighted average is by multiplying each student's exam score by the weight given to the exam, and then totaling the results. For example, consider the following four exam scores:

Exam 1 = 84    Exam 2 = 80    Exam 3 = 83    Final Exam = 72

If the first three exams are each given a weight of 20 percent and the final exam is given a weight of 40 percent, the weighted average of the four scores is:

84*0.2 + 80*0.2 + 83*0.2 + 72*0.4 = 78.2

Karen has already entered the scores for her students and formatted much of the workbook. You will enter the formulas and highlight the top 10 overall scores in her class. Complete the following:

1. Open the **Chemistry** workbook located in the Excel3\Case1 folder included with your Data Files, and then save the workbook as **Chemistry 303 Final Scores**.

2. In the Documentation sheet, enter your name in cell B3 and the date in cell B4.

3. In the First Semester Scores worksheet, in cell F17, enter a formula to calculate the weighted average of the first student's four exams. Use the weights found in the range C8:C11, matching each weight with the corresponding exam score. Use absolute cell references for the four weights.

4. Use AutoFill to copy the formula in cell F17 into the range F18:F52.

5. In cell B5, use the COUNT function to calculate the total number of students in the class.

6. In cell D8, calculate the median score for the first exam.

7. In cell E8, calculate the maximum score for the first exam.

8. In cell F8, calculate the minimum score for the first exam.

9. In cell G8, calculate the range of scores for the first exam, which is equal to the difference between the maximum and minimum score.

10. Repeat Steps 6 through 9 for each of the other two exams, the final exam, and the overall weighted score.

11. Use conditional formatting to highlight the top 10 scores in the range F17:F52 in a light red fill with dark red text.

12. Insert a page break at cell A14, repeat the first three rows of the worksheet in any printout, and verify that the worksheet is in portrait orientation.

13. Save and close the workbook, and then submit the finished workbook to your instructor, either in printed or electronic form, as requested.

*Use formulas and functions to create an order form for a fireworks company.*

**APPLY**

## Case Problem 2

**Data File needed for this Case Problem: Wizard.xlsx**

*WizardWorks*  Andrew Howe owns and operates WizardWorks, an online seller of fireworks based in Franklin, Tennessee. Andrew wants you to help him develop an order form for his business. The form needs to contain formulas to calculate the charge for each order. The total charge is based on the quantity and type of items ordered plus the shipping charge and the 5 percent sales tax. Orders can be shipped using standard 3- to 5-day shipping for $3.99 or overnight for $10.99. Andrew is also offering a 4 percent discount for orders that exceed $200. Both the shipping option and the discount need to be calculated using formulas based on values entered into the worksheet. Complete the following:

1. Open the **Wizard** workbook located in the Excel3\Case2 folder included with your Data Files, and then save the workbook as **WizardWorks Order Form**.

2. In the Documentation sheet, enter your name in cell B3 and enter the date in cell B4.

3. In the Order Form worksheet, in cell C4, enter the customer name, **Kevin Kemper**. In cell C6, enter the order number, **28314**. In the range C9:C13, enter the following address:

Address 1:  **315 Avalon Street**
City:       **Greenfield**
State:      **IN**
Zip:        **46140**

4. In cell C5, enter a function that displays the current date.

5. In the range B20:E22, enter the following orders:

| Item | Name | Price | Qty |
|------|------|-------|-----|
| BF001 | **Bucket of Fireworks** | $45.75 | 1 |
| NAF | **Nightair Fountain** | $12.95 | 4 |
| MR20B | **Mountain Rockets (Box 20)** | $55.25 | 2 |

6. In cell C15, enter **overnight** to ship this order overnight.

**EXPLORE**

7. In cell F20, enter an IF function that tests whether the order quantity in cell E20 is greater than 0 (zero). If it is, return the value of cell E20 multiplied by cell D20; otherwise, return no text by entering **""**. AutoFill this formula into the range F21:F25.

8. In cell F27, calculate the sum of the values in the range F20:F25.

9. In cell F28, enter an IF function that tests whether cell F27 is greater than 200. If it is, return the value of cell F27 multiplied by the discount percentage in cell F12; otherwise, return the value 0 (zero).

10. In cell F29, subtract the discount value in cell F28 from the subtotal value in cell F27.

11. In cell F31, calculate the sales tax by multiplying the after discount value in cell F29 by the sales tax percentage, 0.05.

⊕ **EXPLORE**

12. In cell F32, determine the shipping charge by entering an IF function that tests whether cell C15 equals "standard". If it does, return the value in cell F9; otherwise, return the value in cell F10.

13. In cell G32, display the value of cell C15.

14. In cell F34, calculate the total of the after discount value, the sales tax, and the shipping fee.

15. Reduce the quantity of Mountain Rockets boxes from 2 to **1**, and then verify that the discount is changed to 0 for the order.

16. Change the shipping option from overnight to **standard**, and then verify that the shipping fee is changed to the fee for standard shipping.

17. Save and close the workbook, and then submit the finished workbook to your instructor, either in printed or electronic form, as requested.

*Explore how to use relative and absolute references and the PMT function to create a loan table.*

**CHALLENGE**

## Case Problem 3

Data File needed for this Case Problem: Loan.xlsx

*Eason Financial Services*    Jesse Buchmann is a finance officer at Eason Financial Services in Meridian, Idaho. She works with people who are looking for home mortgages. Most clients want mortgages they can afford, and affordability is determined by the size of the monthly payment. The monthly payment is determined by the interest rate, the total number of payments, and the size of the home loan. Jesse can't change the interest rate, but homebuyers can reduce their monthly payments by increasing the number of years to repay the loan. Jesse wants to give her clients a grid that displays combinations of loan amounts and payment periods so that they can select a loan that best meets their needs and budget. Jesse already entered much of the layout and formatting for the worksheet containing the loan payment grid. You will enter the PMT function. Complete the following:

1. Open the **Loan** workbook located in the Excel3\Case3 folder included with your Data Files, and then save the workbook as **Loan Grid**.

2. In the Documentation sheet, enter your name and the date.

3. In the Loan Calculation worksheet, in cell E3, enter a monthly payment of **$1,750**.

4. In cell E5, enter the annual interest rate of **5.75%**. In cell E6, enter **12** to indicate that the interest payment is compounded 12 times a year, or monthly.

5. In the range C10:C20, use AutoFill to enter the currency values **$250,000** through **$350,000** in increments of $10,000. In the range D9:H9, use AutoFill to enter the year values **15** through **35** in increments of 5 years.

⊕ **EXPLORE**

6. In cell D10, use the PMT function to calculate the monthly payment required to repay a **$250,000** loan in **15** years at **5.75%** interest compounded monthly. Use absolute references to cells E5 and E6 to enter the annual interest rate and number of payments per year. Use the mixed references D$9 and $C10 to cells D9 and C10, respectively, to reference the number of years to repay the loan and the loan amount. Place a minus sign before the PMT function so that the value returned by the function is positive rather than negative.

⊕ **EXPLORE**

7. Using AutoFill, copy the formula in cell D10 into the range E10:H10, and then copy that range of formulas into the range D11:H20.

⊕ **EXPLORE**

8. Conditionally format the range D10:H20 to highlight all of the values in the range that are less than the value in cell E3 in a dark green font on a green fill.

9. Add a second conditional format to the range D10:H20 to highlight all of the values in the range that are greater than the value in cell E3 in a dark red font on a red fill.

**⊕ EXPLORE**    10. Change the value in cell E3 from $1,750 to **$1,800**. If this represents the maximum affordable monthly payment, use the values in the grid to determine the largest mortgage for payment schedules lasting 15 through 35 years. Can any of the home loan values displayed in the grid be repaid in 20 years at $1,800 per month?

11. Save and close the workbook, and then submit the finished workbook to your instructor, either in printed or electronic form, as requested.

*Create a workbook that automatically grades a driving exam.*

**CREATE**

## Case Problem 4

**Data File needed for this Case Problem: V6.xlsx**

*V-6 Driving Academy*    Sebastian Villanueva owns and operates the V-6 Driving Academy, a driving school located in Pine Hills, Florida. In addition to driving, students must take multiple-choice tests offered by the Florida Department of Motor Vehicles. Students must answer at least 80 percent of the questions correctly to pass each test. Sebastian has to grade these tests himself. Sebastian could save a lot of time if the test questions were in a workbook and Excel totaled the test results. Sebastian has already entered a 20-question test into a workbook. You will format this workbook and insert the necessary functions and formulas to grade a student's answers. Complete the following:

1. Open the **V6** workbook located in the Excel3\Case4 folder included with your Data Files, and then save the workbook as **V6 Driving Test**.

2. In the Documentation sheet, enter your name in cell B3 and enter the date in cell B4.

3. In the Exam1 worksheet, format the questions and possible answers so that the worksheet is easy to read. The format is up to you. At the top of the worksheet, enter a title that describes the exam, and then enter a function that returns the current date.

4. Add a section somewhere on the Exam1 worksheet where Sebastian can enter each student's name and answers to each question. Design the workbook so that Sebastian can always go back and review any student's completed exam.

5. The answers for the 20 questions are listed below. Use this information to write functions that will grade each answer, giving 1 point for a correct answer and 0 otherwise. Assume that all answers are in lowercase letters; therefore, the function that tests the answer to the first question should check for a "c" rather than a "C".

| Question | Answer | Question | Answer | Question | Answer |
|----------|--------|----------|--------|----------|--------|
| 1 | c | 8 | a | 15 | b |
| 2 | a | 9 | c | 16 | b |
| 3 | b | 10 | b | 17 | b |
| 4 | a | 11 | c | 18 | b |
| 5 | c | 12 | b | 19 | b |
| 6 | b | 13 | b | 20 | c |
| 7 | c | 14 | a | | |

6. At the top of the worksheet, insert a formula to calculate the total number of correct answers for each student.

7. Insert another formula that divides the total number of correct answers by the total number of exam questions on the worksheet. Display this value as a percentage.

8. Enter a logical function that displays the message "PASS" on the exam if the percentage of correct answers is greater than or equal to 80 percent; otherwise, the logical function displays the message "FAIL".

9. Test your worksheet with the following student exams. Which students passed and which failed? What score did each student receive on the exam?

Juan Marquez

| Question | Answer | Question | Answer | Question | Answer |
|----------|--------|----------|--------|----------|--------|
| 1 | a | 8 | a | 15 | b |
| 2 | b | 9 | c | 16 | b |

| Question | Answer | Question | Answer | Question | Answer |
|----------|--------|----------|--------|----------|--------|
| 3 | b | 10 | b | 17 | a |
| 4 | a | 11 | c | 18 | b |
| 5 | c | 12 | b | 19 | b |
| 6 | b | 13 | a | 20 | c |
| 7 | c | 14 | a |  |  |

Kurt Bessette

| Question | Answer | Question | Answer | Question | Answer |
|----------|--------|----------|--------|----------|--------|
| 1 | a | 8 | a | 15 | c |
| 2 | a | 9 | b | 16 | b |
| 3 | b | 10 | c | 17 | a |
| 4 | a | 11 | c | 18 | b |
| 5 | c | 12 | a | 19 | a |
| 6 | b | 13 | b | 20 | c |
| 7 | c | 14 | a |  |  |

Rebecca Pena

| Question | Answer | Question | Answer | Question | Answer |
|----------|--------|----------|--------|----------|--------|
| 1 | c | 8 | a | 15 | c |
| 2 | a | 9 | c | 16 | b |
| 3 | b | 10 | a | 17 | b |
| 4 | a | 11 | c | 18 | b |
| 5 | c | 12 | b | 19 | b |
| 6 | b | 13 | b | 20 | b |
| 7 | c | 14 | a |  |  |

10. Format the worksheet so that it prints nicely with no questions crossing over a page break, and the names of the students and the name of the driving academy at the top of each page.

11. Save and close the workbook, and then submit the finished workbook to your instructor, either in printed or electronic form, as requested.

## SAM: Skills Assessment Manager

For current SAM information, including versions and content details, visit SAM Central (http://samcentral.course.com). If you have a SAM user profile, you may have access to hands-on instruction, practice, and assessment of the skills covered in this tutorial. Since various versions of SAM are supported throughout the life of this text, check with your instructor for the correct instructions and URL/Web site for accessing assignments.

**ENDING DATA FILES**

Excel3 → Tutorial
Drake Family Budget.xlsx

Review
Timov Family Budget.xlsx

Case1
Chemistry 303 Final Scores.xlsx

Case2
WizardWorks Order Form.xlsx

Case3
Loan Grid.xlsx

Case4
V6 Driving Test.xlsx

**EXCEL**

## OBJECTIVES

**Session 4.1**
- Create an embedded chart
- Create and format a pie chart
- Work with chart titles and legends
- Create and format a column chart

**Session 4.2**
- Create and format a line chart
- Modify a chart data source
- Create and format a combined chart
- Create a 3-D chart
- Create and format sparklines and data bars
- Create a chart sheet

# Enhancing a Workbook with Charts and Graphs

*Charting Financial Data*

## Case | *Seaborg Group*

Ajita Gupte is a financial assistant for the Seaborg Group, a financial consulting agency located in Providence, Rhode Island. One of her duties is to prepare financial reports on the investments the Seaborg Group makes for its clients. These reports go into a binder containing the financial status of each client's different investments. The client receives the binder at annual meetings with his or her financial advisor, and receives updates on the status of the investments periodically throughout the year.

Many of the company's clients invest in the New Century Fund, a large growth/large risk mutual fund that has been operating for the past 10 years. Ajita needs to create a report that summarizes the fund's financial holdings as well as its 10-year performance record. She already entered the financial data into an Excel workbook, but needs help finishing the report. Because many clients are overwhelmed by tables of numbers, Ajita wants to include charts and graphs in the report that display the current and past performance of the New Century Fund. You will help Ajita to create these charts.

**STARTING DATA FILES**

| Excel4 → | Tutorial | Review | Case1 | Case2 | Case3 | Case4 |
|---|---|---|---|---|---|---|
| | Fund.xlsx | Crockett.xlsx | Kenai.xlsx | Cloud.jpg<br>Tornado.xlsx | Mitchell.xlsx | Basketball.xlsx |

# SESSION 4.1 VISUAL OVERVIEW

Chart layouts provide different options for organizing chart elements.

A **chart**, or **graph**, is a visual representation of a set of data values. Charts show trends or relationships that may not be readily apparent from numbers alone.

An **embedded chart** is an object in a worksheet.

Each chart has a **data source**, which is the range that contains the data to display in the chart. The data source for the Fund Assets pie chart is the range A2:B6.

The **series name**, the first row of the data range, identifies the data series. In this case, the series name is row 9.

A data source is a collection of one or more **data series**, which is a range of values that is plotted as a single unit on the chart.

The first column of the data range is the **category values**, which are the groups or categories that the series values belong to. These categories each include three subcategories in the range A10:B21.

New Century Fund - Microsoft Excel

File | Home | Insert | Page Layout | Formulas | Data | Review | View | Design

Change Chart Type | Save As Template | Switch Row/Column | Select Data

Type | Data | Chart Layouts

Chart 1

| | A | B | C | D | E |
|---|---|---|---|---|---|
| 1 | Category | Assets | | | |
| 2 | Cash | $ 7,144 | | | |
| 3 | U.S. Stocks | $ 49,250 | | | 16 |
| 4 | Non-U.S. Stocks | $ 9,715 | | | |
| 5 | Bonds | $ 15,177 | | | 10 |
| 6 | Other Assets | $ 8,360 | | | |
| 7 | Total Assets | $ 89,646 mil | | | |
| 8 | | | | | |
| 9 | Sector Category | Sector | New Century | | |
| 10 | Information | Software | 3.80% | | 20.00% |
| 11 | | Hardware | 11.80% | | |
| 12 | | Media | 4.30% | | 15.00% |
| 13 | | Telecomm | 2.50% | | |
| 14 | Services | Healthcare | 14.40% | | 10.00% |
| 15 | | Consumer | 12.10% | | |
| 16 | | Business | 8.00% | | 5.00% |
| 17 | | Financial | 9.90% | | |
| 18 | Manufacturing | Consumer | 6.80% | | 0.00% |
| 19 | | Industrial | 9.60% | | Software |
| 20 | | Energy | 12.60% | | Hardware |
| 21 | | Utilities | 4.20% | | Info |

◄ ◄ ► ►| Fund Report

Ready

The **series values** are the data displayed in the chart. These series values are in the range C10:C21.

The **vertical**, or **value**, **axis** displays the series values from the data series.

# CHART ELEMENTS

Chart styles provide combinations of formats to customize the chart.

The **chart area** contains the chart and all of the other chart elements.

The **chart title** is a descriptive label or name for the chart.

The **plot area** is the part of the chart that contains the graphical representation of the data series.

A **legend** is a rectangular area that indicates the data markers associated with the data series.

A **data label** is text associated with an individual data marker, such as a pie slice.

**Tick marks** identify the units at regular intervals on the chart axis.

Each value in a data series is represented by a **data marker** such as a column or pie slice.

The **horizontal**, or **category**, **axis** displays the category values from each data series.

# Creating an Excel Chart

Ajita already created a workbook in which she entered and formatted data that describes the New Century Fund. In addition to the Documentation sheet, the New Century Fund workbook contains the following five worksheets:

- The Summary Report worksheet includes summary data and facts about the New Century Fund.
- The Fund History worksheet provides a table that shows how well the New Century Fund performed over the past 10 years compared to a similar fund and the S&P 500 index.
- The Assets worksheet lists the assets of the New Century Fund grouped by investment categories.
- The Sectors worksheet shows the economic sectors in which the New Century Fund invests.
- The Sector History worksheet provides a table showing how each of the economic sectors in the New Century Fund has performed in the last 10 years.

You'll begin by opening this workbook and reviewing its contents.

### To open and review Ajita's workbook:

▶ **1.** Open the **Fund** workbook located in the **Excel4\Tutorial** folder included with your Data Files, and then save the workbook as **New Century Fund** in the same folder.

▶ **2.** In the Documentation sheet, enter your name in cell B3 and the date in cell B4.

▶ **3.** Take some time to review the contents of the workbook.

Charts show trends or relationships in data that are more difficult to see by simply looking at numbers, such as the range of months in which the New Century Fund performed exceptionally well. Ajita wants financial data from the Fund History, Assets, and Sectors worksheets displayed in the Summary Report worksheet as charts, or graphs. In the summary report, she wants one chart that shows the performance of the New Century Fund compared to two similar funds, and she wants two charts that show how money in the New Century Fund is currently invested. The final Summary Report worksheet will be a single page that includes all of the information Ajita wants her clients to see.

**REFERENCE**

*Inserting a Chart*

- Select the data source with the range of data you want to chart.
- In the Charts group on the Insert tab, click a chart type, and then click a chart subtype in the Chart gallery.
- In the Location group on the Chart Tools Design tab, click the Move Chart button to place the chart in a chart sheet or embed it into a worksheet.

## Selecting a Data Source

Each chart has a data source. After you select a range to use as the chart's data source, Excel uses the first row of the selected range as the series name, the first column as the category values, and the remaining columns as the series values. If the data source is organized in rows rather than in columns, the first row contains the category values, the remaining rows contain the data values for each data series, and the first column of each series row contains the series names.

The first chart you will create is based on data in the Assets worksheet that indicates how the New Century Fund's holdings are divided among different investment categories. The data source you will select has only one data series that shows the assets for five investment categories.

### To select the data source for the assets chart:

▶ **1.** Click the **Assets** sheet tab to make the Assets worksheet active.

▶ **2.** Select the range **A3:B8**. The data source in this range has one data series, named Assets. Its category values in the range A4:A8 list the different asset categories, and its series values in the range B4:B8 contain the data to be charted. See Figure 4-1.

**Figure 4-1**    **Data source selected for the assets chart**

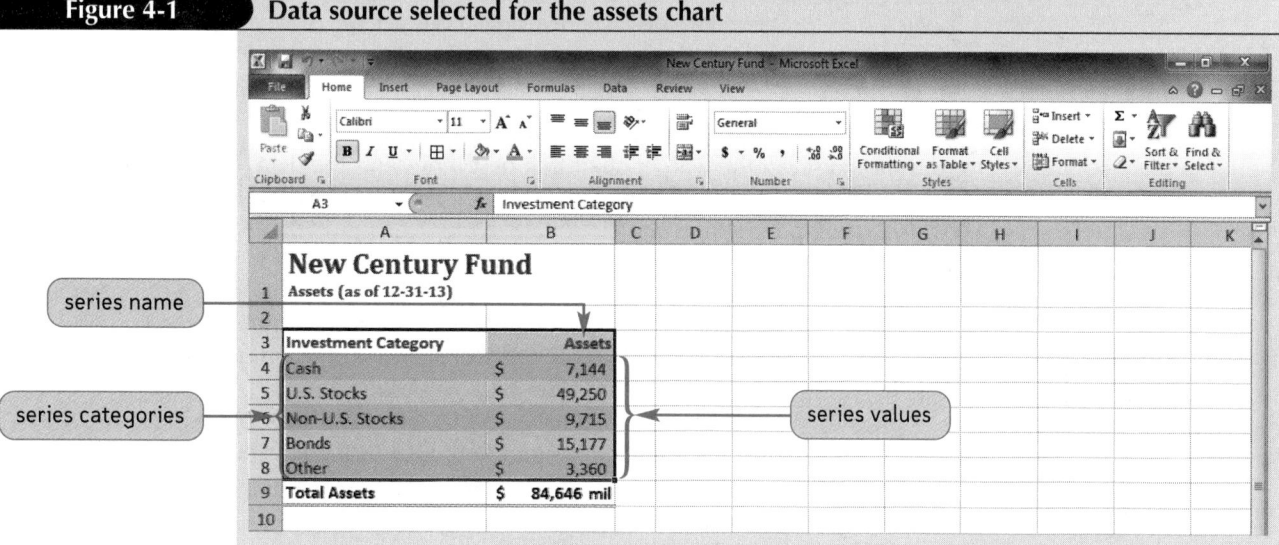

## Selecting a Chart Type

You can apply a wide variety of chart types to the selected data source. Excel supports 73 built-in charts organized into 11 categories, which are described in Figure 4-2. You can also create custom chart types based on the built-in charts.

**Figure 4-2**  Excel chart types

| Chart Type | Description |
|---|---|
| Column | Compares values from different categories. Values are indicated by the height of the columns. |
| Line | Compares values from different categories. Values are indicated by the height of the line. Often used to show trends and changes over time. |
| Pie | Compares relative values of different categories to the whole. Values are indicated by the areas of the pie slices. |
| Bar | Compares values from different categories. Values are indicated by the length of the bars. |
| Area | Compares values from different categories. Similar to the line chart except that areas under the lines contain a fill color. |
| Scatter | Shows the patterns or relationship between two or more sets of values. Often used in scientific studies and statistical analyses. |
| Stock | Displays stock market data, including the high, low, opening, and closing prices of a stock. |
| Surface | Compares three sets of values in a three-dimensional chart. |
| Doughnut | Compares relative values of different categories to the whole. Similar to the pie chart except that it can display multiple sets of data. |
| Bubble | Shows the patterns or relationship between two or more sets of values. Similar to the XY (Scatter) chart except the size of the data marker is determined by a third value. |
| Radar | Compares a collection of values from several different data sets. |

You should select the type of chart that best represents the data. For example, a pie chart provides the best way to show the breakout of the asset data you selected. A **pie chart** is a chart in the shape of a circle (like a pie) that shows data values as a percentage of the whole. Each value in the data series represents a slice of the pie. The larger the value, the larger the pie slice. For the asset data, each slice will represent the percentage of the total assets from each investment category in the New Century Fund.

Pie charts are most effective with six or fewer slices, and when each slice is large enough to view. The pie chart of the asset data will have five large slices, representing the five asset categories—Cash, U.S. Stocks, Non-U.S. Stocks, Bonds, and Other. The Total Assets row, which you did not select as part of the data source, is not an asset category and should not be included in a pie chart.

**TIP**

The data source for a pie chart should include only the category labels and data values and not row or column totals because Excel will treat those totals as another category to be graphed.

**To insert a pie chart:**

1. Click the **Insert** tab on the Ribbon. The Ribbon displays the insert options.

2. In the Charts group, click the **Pie** button. The Pie Charts gallery opens.

3. In the 2-D Pie section, click **Pie** (the first pie chart in the first row). The pie chart is inserted in the Assets sheet, and three new tabs appear on the Ribbon with a label identifying them as Chart Tools contextual tabs. See Figure 4-3.

**Figure 4-3**   **Pie chart inserted into the Assets sheet**

Each slice in the pie chart you just created is a different size based on its value in the data series. The biggest slice of the pie represents U.S. Stocks, which is the category that has the largest value in the data series. The smallest slice of the pie represents the Other category, which has the smallest value in the data series.

When you create or select a chart, three Chart Tools contextual tabs appear on the Ribbon. The Design, Layout, and Format tabs provide additional commands for working with the chart's content and appearance. On the Design tab, you set the chart's overall design. On the Layout tab, you work with individual elements of the chart, such as the chart's title. On the Format tab, you format graphic shapes found in the chart, such as the chart's border or markers placed in the chart. When you select a worksheet cell or another object that is not a chart, the Chart Tools contextual tabs disappear until you reselect the chart.

## Moving a Chart to a Different Worksheet

By default, a chart is inserted as an embedded chart. The advantage of an embedded chart is that you can display the chart alongside any text or graphics that can explain the chart's meaning and purpose. However, an embedded chart covers worksheet cells, which might contain data and formulas. You'll learn how to move and resize an embedded chart in this section.

You can move an embedded chart to a different worksheet in the workbook or you can move it into a chart sheet (a sheet that contains only the chart and no worksheet cells). Likewise, you can move a chart from a chart sheet and embed it in any worksheet you select. The Move Chart dialog box provides options for moving charts between worksheets and chart sheets. You can also cut and paste a chart to a new location in the workbook.

The assets pie chart was embedded in the Assets worksheet by default. Ajita wants the chart embedded in the Summary Report worksheet. You will move the chart.

**To move the embedded pie chart to the Summary Report worksheet:**

▶ 1. In the Location group on the Chart Tools Design tab, click the **Move Chart** button. The Move Chart dialog box opens.

**Trouble?** If you don't see the Chart Tools contextual tabs on the Ribbon, the chart is probably not selected. Click the chart in the Assets sheet to select it, and then repeat Step 1.

▶ 2. Click the **Object in** arrow to display a list of worksheets in the active workbook, and then click **Summary Report**. See Figure 4-4.

| Figure 4-4 | Move Chart dialog box |
|---|---|

moves the chart to the Chart1 chart sheet

embeds the chart in the selected worksheet

▶ 3. Click the **OK** button. The embedded pie chart moves from the Assets worksheet to the Summary Report worksheet, and remains selected.

## Moving and Resizing Charts

An embedded chart might cover other data in the worksheet or be placed in an awkward location. You can fix this by moving or resizing the embedded chart. To do so, first select the chart, which displays a **selection box**, which is a box surrounding the chart object that is used to move or resize the object. To move the chart, drag the selection box to a new location in the worksheet. To resize the chart, drag a **sizing handle**, which is a square or dot on the selection box that is used to change the object's width and height.

You will move and resize the assets pie chart so that it does not cover the data on the Summary Report worksheet.

**To move and resize the assets pie chart:**

Be sure to click the chart area; otherwise, elements in the chart might move.

▶ 1. Move the pointer over an empty area of the selected chart until the pointer changes to ✛ and the "Chart Area" ScreenTip appears.

▶ 2. Drag the chart down and to the left until its upper-left corner is in cell **A13**, and then release the mouse button. The chart moves to a new location, but it still covers some data.

**Trouble?** If the pie chart resizes or does not move to the new location, you probably didn't drag the chart from the chart area. Press the Ctrl+Z keys to undo your last action, and then repeat Steps 1 and 2, being sure to drag the pie chart from the chart area.

**TIP**

To retain the chart's proportions, hold down the Shift key as you drag the sizing handle.

▶ 3. Move the pointer over the sizing handle in the lower-right corner of the chart until the pointer changes to ↘, and then drag the sizing handle up to cell **E21**. The chart resizes to cover the range A13:E21 and remains selected. See Figure 4-5.

| Figure 4-5 | Moved and resized pie chart |

**Designing a Pie Chart**

Charts include individual elements that can be formatted, including the chart area, the chart title, the plot area, data markers, and a legend. You can choose which of these elements to include in the chart as well as how each element looks. You can make these changes using a built-in style that formats the entire chart or by selecting and formatting an individual element.

To apply formatting to an individual chart element, you can double-click that chart element to open a dialog box with format options specific to the selected element. You can also open the dialog box by clicking the appropriate element button on the Layout tab.

## Choosing a Chart Style

A chart style is similar to a cell style or a table style in that it applies several formats to the chart at one time. When you create a chart, Excel applies the default chart style for that chart type. For example, the default pie chart style applies a solid color to each slice. You can quickly change the appearance of the entire chart by selecting a different chart style in the Chart Styles gallery.

Ajita wants you to use a style that gives each pie slice a rounded, three-dimensional look.

**To apply a different chart style to the assets pie chart:**

1. Click the **Chart Tools Design** tab on the Ribbon, if necessary. The design options for charts appear on the Ribbon.

2. In the Chart Styles group, click the **More** button to open the Chart Styles gallery, and then click **Style 26** (the second style in the fourth row). Each pie slice now has a rounded, raised look. See Figure 4-6.

**Figure 4-6** | **Pie chart with the Style 26 chart style applied**

Style 26 chart style selected

click the More button to view additional chart styles

pie slices appear rounded and raised

## Choosing a Chart Layout

The built-in chart layouts specify which chart elements are displayed and how they are formatted. The chart layouts include some of the most common ways of displaying different charts. Each chart type has its own collection of layouts. Depending on the pie chart layout you choose, you can hide or display the chart title, display a chart legend or place legend labels in the pie slices, and add percentages to the pie slices.

To clarify the relationship between the pie slices in the assets pie chart, Ajita wants each slice to display its percentage of the whole. You'll do this by changing the chart layout.

**To apply the Layout 6 chart layout to the assets pie chart:**

1. In the Chart Layouts group on the Chart Tools Design tab, click the **More** button to open the Chart Layouts gallery.

2. Click **Layout 6** (the third layout in the second row). Percentages appear on or next to the slices in the pie chart, and the chart title and legend remain in their original locations. See Figure 4-7.

**TIP**

Percentages appear on pie slices large enough to fit the number; otherwise, percentages appear next to the slices in the chart area.

| Figure 4-7 | Pie chart with the Layout 6 chart layout |

**Layout 6 chart layout**

**click the More button to view additional layouts**

**percentages added to the pie slices**

**Trouble?** Depending on your monitor size and resolution, your chart might look different from that shown in Figure 4-7. This does not affect your work with the pie chart.

With the percentages displayed on the pie chart, clients can quickly see how the assets of the New Century Fund are allocated. For example, 58 percent of the New Century Fund is invested in U.S. stocks and 12 percent in non-U.S. stocks. To fit the percentages, Excel reduced the size of the pie chart in the plot area. You'll format some of the other chart elements smaller to make more space for the pie.

## Formatting the Chart Title

The chart title provides a description of the chart. By default, Excel uses the series name for the chart title. You can edit or replace the default chart title. You can also format the text of the chart title just like you can any other text in the workbook.

Ajita wants a more descriptive chart title. You'll also reduce the title's font size to make more room for the pie chart.

**TIP**

You can revise the title text rather than replacing it by double-clicking the chart title to place the insertion point in the text, and then editing the text.

### To change and resize the chart title:

1. Click the **chart title** to select it. A selection box appears around the chart title.

2. Type **Allocation of Assets**. The new chart title appears in the formula bar, but no changes are made to the title in the chart itself.

3. Press the **Enter** key. The chart title is updated with the entry and remains selected.

4. Click the **Home** tab on the Ribbon.

5. In the Font group, click the **Font Size arrow**, and then click **12**. The chart title shrinks from 18 points to 12 points, and the pie chart increases in size to fill the extra space. See Figure 4-8.

**Figure 4-8**    **Chart title updated and formatted**

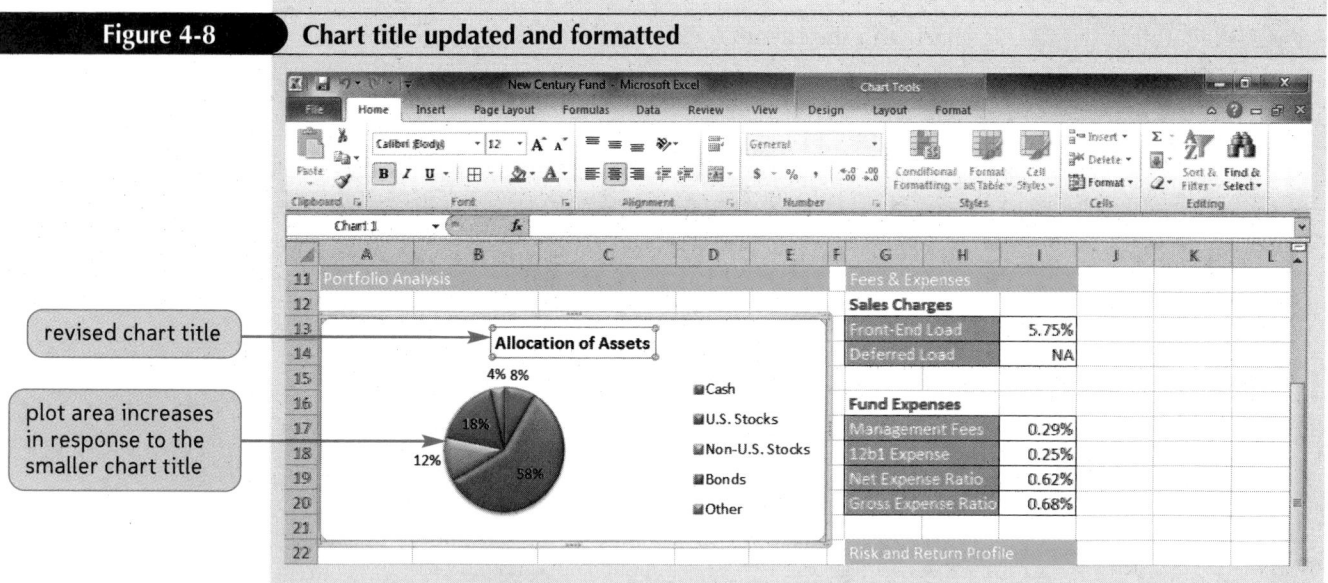

revised chart title

plot area increases in response to the smaller chart title

## Formatting the Chart Legend

The chart legend identifies each of the data series in the chart. With a pie chart, the legend shows the colors used for each slice and the corresponding category values. In this case, the category values are the different asset groups. As with the other elements, you can choose the location of the legend and format it using tools on the Chart Tools Layout tab.

Ajita wants you to move the legend to the left side of the chart and add an orange border around the legend text to distinguish it from the rest of the chart.

**To format the chart legend:**

1. Click the **Chart Tools Layout** tab on the Ribbon.

2. In the Labels group, click the **Legend** button, and then click **Show Legend at Left**. The legend moves to the left side of the chart.

3. In the Labels group, click the **Legend** button, and then click **More Legend Options**. The Format Legend dialog box opens, providing more advanced options to format the element's appearance.

4. Click **Border Color** in the list on the left side of the dialog box. The Border Color options appear on the right side of the dialog box.

5. Click the **Solid line** option button. Two options related to border colors appear in the dialog box.

6. Click the **Color** button to open the color palette, and then click **Orange, Accent 6, Lighter 40%** (the last color in the fourth row) in the Theme Colors section. See Figure 4-9.

| **Figure 4-9** | **Border Color options in the Format Legend dialog box** |

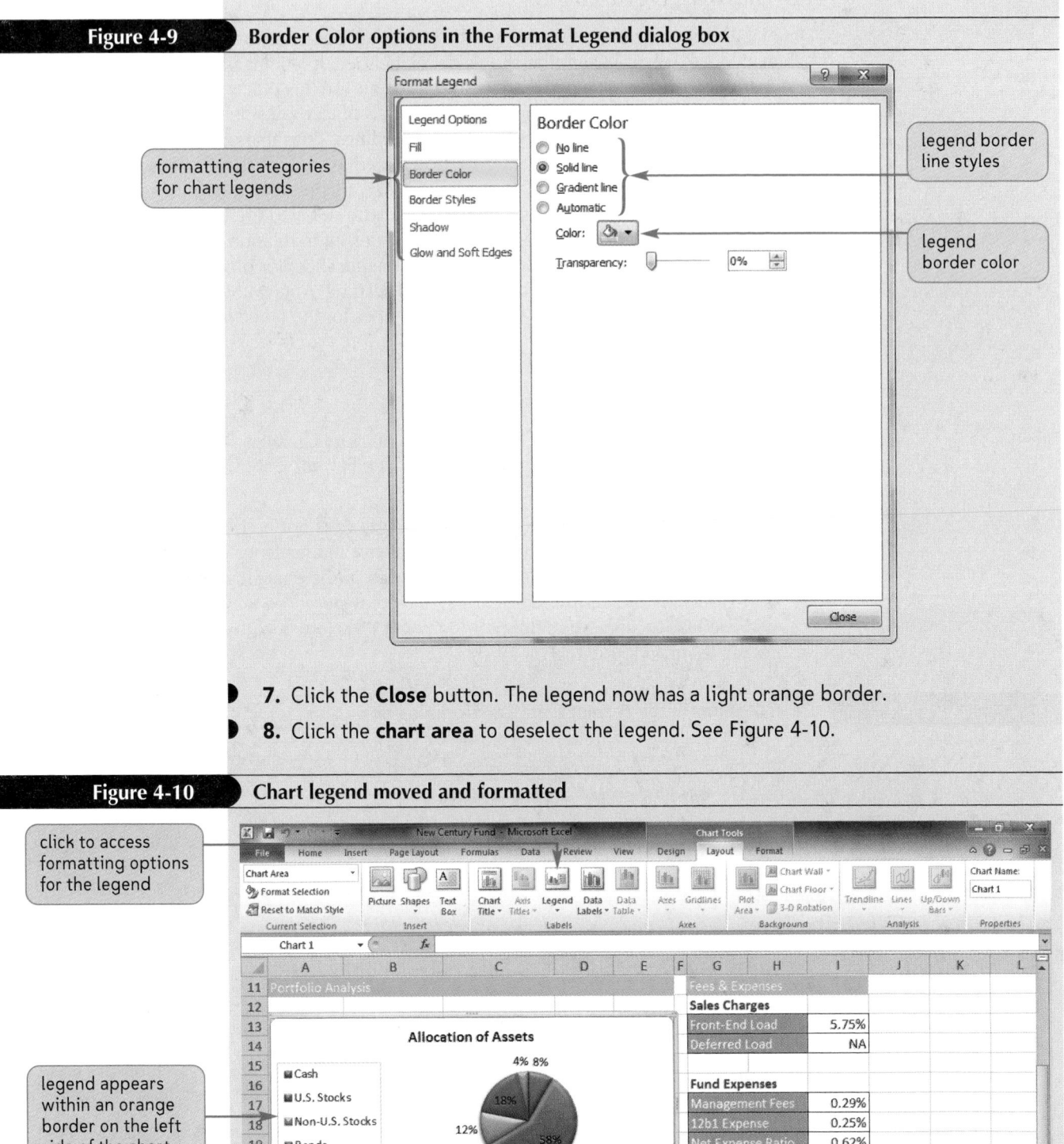

7. Click the **Close** button. The legend now has a light orange border.

8. Click the **chart area** to deselect the legend. See Figure 4-10.

| **Figure 4-10** | **Chart legend moved and formatted** |

## Formatting Data Labels

Data labels provide descriptive text for the individual data markers, such as pie slices. When you use a chart layout that shows data labels, each label is placed where it best fits—either on the pie slice or along its side. You can use this placement to specify that all data labels appear next to their pie slices. Labels placed outside of the pie might appear far from their slices. In those cases, **leader lines**, lines that connect each data label to its corresponding data marker, can be added. Note that a leader line disappears when enough space exists in the chart area to place a label next to its slice.

You added data labels to the assets chart when you selected the Layout 6 chart layout. These percentage values were placed where they best fit in relation to the pie slices. For some asset categories, the label appears within the pie slice; for others, the label appears next to the slice. For consistency and for ease of reading, Ajita wants all the data labels to appear outside the pie chart. You'll show leader lines for the labels.

### To format the pie chart's data labels:

▶ **1.** In the Labels group on the Chart Tools Layout tab, click the **Data Labels** button, and then click **More Data Label Options**. The Format Data Labels dialog box opens with the Label Options displayed.

▶ **2.** In the Label Position section, click the **Outside End** option button. In the Label Contains section, the Percentage and the Show Leader Lines check boxes are already checked because these were included in the chart layout you applied earlier. These options set the data labels to display percentages outside the pie chart and use leader lines when needed to connect the labels with their corresponding pie slices. See Figure 4-11.

**Figure 4-11    Label Options in the Format Data Labels dialog box**

options to define the number format of the data label

options to define the fill and border styles of the data label

options to define the alignment of the label text

displays the data values as percentages

shows leader lines next to the labels if necessary

places labels at the outer edge of each slice

> **3.** Click **Number** in the list on the left side of the dialog box. The options related to number formats appear in the dialog box.

> **4.** Click **Percentage** in the Category box, and then verify that **2** appears in the Decimal places box. The percentage values for each slice show two decimal places for more accuracy.

> **5.** Click the **Close** button. The data labels appear as percentages on the outer edges of the slices. Note that leader lines don't appear in the pie chart because the chart area has enough space to place the labels close to their slices. See Figure 4-12.

**Figure 4-12** ▶    **Formatted data labels**

data labels appear as percentages outside of each slice

## Changing Pie Slice Colors

Pie slice colors should be as distinct as possible to avoid confusion. Using distinct colors is especially important for adjacent slices. Depending on the printer quality or the monitor resolution, similarly colored slices might be difficult to distinguish in the final report. You can change the colors used for each slice. Because each slice in a pie chart represents a different value in the series, you must format each slice rather than the entire data series.

In the assets pie chart, the slices for Cash, Bonds, and Other have similar colors. You'll change the fill color of the Other and Cash slices.

### To select and format pie slices in the assets pie chart:

> **1.** Click the pie to select the entire data series.

> **2.** Click the light blue **Other** slice, which represents 3.97 percent of the pie. Only that value, or slice, is selected.

> **3.** Click the **Home** tab on the Ribbon.

> **4.** In the Font group, click the **Fill Color button arrow** ![fill color icon], and then click **Yellow** (the fourth color in the Standard Colors section). The Other slice and legend marker change to yellow.

> **5.** Click the dark blue **Cash** slice, which covers 8.44 percent of the pie.

▶ **6.** In the Font group, click the **Fill Color button arrow** , and then click **Light Blue** (the seventh color in the Standard Colors section). The Cash slice and legend marker change to light blue. Each slice of the pie now has a distinct color. See Figure 4-13.

**Figure 4-13** | **Pie slices with new colors**

The pie chart in the summary report clearly shows that most assets of the New Century Fund are allocated toward U.S. stocks.

---

**INSIGHT**

### Exploding a Pie Chart

Pie slices do not need to be fixed within the pie. An **exploded pie chart** moves one slice away from the others as if someone were taking the piece away from the pie. Exploded pie charts are useful for emphasizing one category above all of the others. For example, to emphasize how much of the New Century Fund is allocated toward U.S. stocks, you could explode that single slice, moving it away from the other slices in the pie.

To explode a pie slice, select that slice from the pie chart and then drag the slice away from the pie. You can also explode multiple slices by selecting each slice and dragging them away. To explode all of the slices, select the entire pie and drag the pointer away from the pie's center. Each slice will be exploded and separated from the others. Although you can explode more than one slice, the resulting pie chart is rarely effective as a visual aid to the reader.

---

## Creating a Column Chart

A **column chart** displays values in different categories as columns; the height of each column is based on its value. Related to the column chart is the **bar chart**, which is a column chart turned on its side so that the length of each bar is based on its value.

Column and bar charts are superior to pie charts when the number of categories is large or the categories are close in value. It is easier to compare height or length than area. Figure 4-14 displays the same data as a pie chart and a column chart. As you can see, it's more difficult to determine which pie slice has the largest area and by how much. This is much simpler to determine with the column chart.

| Figure 4-14 | Comparing pie charts and column charts |

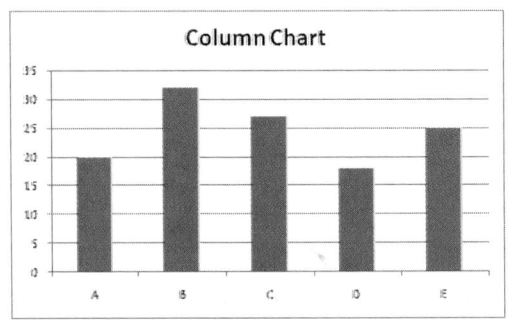

Column and bar charts can also be applied to a wider range of data than pie charts. For example, you can demonstrate how a set of values changes over time, such as the value of the New Century Fund over several years. You can also include several data series in a column or bar chart, such as the value of three funds over several years. The values from different data series are displayed in columns side by side. Pie charts usually show only one data series.

## Inserting a Column Chart

The process for creating a column chart is the same as for creating a pie chart. First, you select the data source. Then, you select the type of chart you want to create. After the chart is embedded in the worksheet, you can move and resize the chart as well as change the chart's design, layout, and format.

The next part of the summary report lists the type of stocks being purchased by the fund. Each mutual fund invests in different kinds of stocks. Some funds are heavily invested in information technology, others in the service industry, and still others in manufacturing. Diversification (the distribution of investments among a variety of companies or sectors to limit losses in the event one company or sector has an economic downturn) is important, so all funds are invested to some degree in multiple economic sectors. The New Century Fund is invested in 12 different economic sectors, organized into the categories of information, services, and manufacturing.

Ajita wants you to create a chart that shows how the New Century Fund is distributed among the 12 sectors in which it is invested. A pie chart cannot display 12 categories effectively, so you will create a column chart to display this economic sector data. The columns will represent only one data series, so you'll use the 2-D Clustered Column chart type. A clustered column chart uses vertical rectangles to compare values across categories.

### To create a column chart from the sector data:

1. Go to the **Sectors** worksheet, and then select the range **A3:C15**. This range covers the New Century Fund data that you want to include on the column chart.

2. Click the **Insert** tab on the Ribbon.

3. In the Charts group, click the **Column** button, and then click the **Clustered Column** chart (the first chart in the 2-D Column section). The column chart is inserted in the Sectors worksheet, and the Chart Tools Design tab on the Ribbon is selected.

4. In the Location group on the Chart Tools Design tab, click the **Move Chart** button. The Move Chart dialog box opens. You'll move the chart to the Summary Report worksheet.

5. Click the **Object in** arrow, click **Summary Report**, and then click the **OK** button. The column chart moves to the Summary Report worksheet.

6. In the Summary Report worksheet, click a blank spot in the chart area of the column chart to make sure the chart is selected.

7. Drag the selected column chart down so its upper-left corner is in cell **A23**.

8. Drag the sizing handle in the lower-right corner of the chart until the chart covers the range **A23:E37**. The chart is resized smaller. See Figure 4-15.

| Figure 4-15 | Column chart of investment sectors in the New Century Fund |

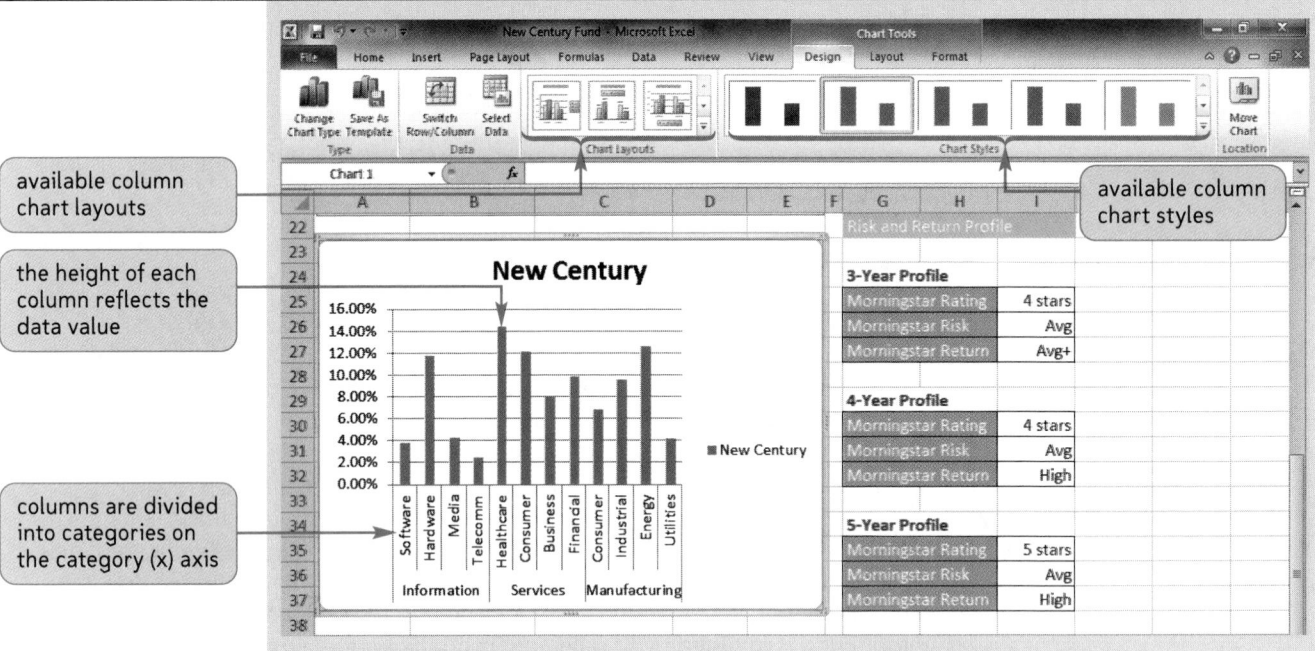

available column chart layouts

the height of each column reflects the data value

columns are divided into categories on the category (x) axis

available column chart styles

The column chart shows that the New Century Fund is most heavily invested in hardware information technology, healthcare and consumer services, and energy manufacturing. On the other hand, the fund does not invest much in software, media, and telecommunications.

## Formatting a Column Chart Title and Legend

The Design tab provides a gallery of column chart layouts and a gallery of column chart styles. As with the pie chart you created, you can design the appearance of a column chart by selecting one of the chart styles or formatting individual chart elements. The default column chart layout includes a title and legend. When a chart has only one data series—such as the column chart you just created—the chart title and legend are redundant.

You will remove the legend, and then edit and format the chart title to provide a more descriptive title.

**To remove the legend and format the chart title of the column chart:**

▶ **1.** Click the **Chart Tools Layout** tab on the Ribbon.

▶ **2.** In the Labels group, click the **Legend** button, and then click **None**. The chart legend is removed from the chart, and the column chart resizes to fill the available space.

▶ **3.** Click the chart title to select it, and then click the **Home** tab on the Ribbon.

▶ **4.** In the Font group, click the **Font Size arrow**, and then click **12**. The chart title is reduced to 12 points, and remains selected.

▶ **5.** Type **Sector Percentages** as the new chart title, and then press the **Enter** key.

## Editing the Axis Scale and Text

The vertical or value axis shows the range of series values, and the horizontal or category axis shows the category values. The range of values, or **scale**, of an axis is based on the values in the data source. The default scale usually ranges from 0 (if the data source has no negative values) up through the maximum value. If the scale includes negative values, it ranges from the minimum value up through the maximum value. Excel divides the scale into regular intervals, which are marked on the axis with tick marks and labels. For example, the scale of the vertical axis for the Sector Percentages chart ranged from 0.00 percent up to 16.00 percent in increments of 2.00 percent. Having more tick marks at smaller intervals could make the chart more difficult to read because the tick mark labels might start to overlap. Likewise, having fewer tick marks at larger intervals could make the chart less informative. Major tick marks identify the main units on the chart axis. You can also add minor tick marks to identify smaller intervals between the major tick marks. Gridlines extend the tick marks across the plot area.

Some charts involve multiple data series that have vastly different values. In those instances, you can plot one data series against a **primary axis**, which usually appears along the left side of the chart, and the other against a **secondary axis**, which is usually placed on the right side of the chart. The two axes can use different scales and labels.

By default, no titles appear next to the value and category axes. This is fine when the axis labels are self-explanatory; otherwise, you can add descriptive axis titles. In general, you should avoid adding extra chart elements such as axis titles when that information is easily understood from other parts of the chart.

Ajita thinks that the value axis scale is too crowded and wants tick marks placed at 5 percent intervals, ranging from 0 percent to 25 percent. You will modify the scale of the value axis.

**To change the scale of the vertical axis:**

▶ **1.** Click the **Chart Tools Layout** tab on the Ribbon.

▶ **2.** In the Axes group, click the **Axes** button, point to **Primary Vertical Axis**, and then click **More Primary Vertical Axis Options**. The Format Axis dialog box opens with the Axis Options displayed. The value axis options are set to Auto, which causes Excel to set the values.

▶ **3.** Next to Maximum, click the **Fixed** option button, and then type **0.25** in the box. The maximum value will be 25 percent.

▶ **4.** Next to Major Unit, click the **Fixed** option button, and then enter **0.05** in the box. The major tick marks will appear at 5 percent intervals. See Figure 4-16.

**Figure 4-16    Axis options in the Format Axis dialog box**

click to set the number format of the tick mark values

click to define the appearance of the tick mark values

click to set the alignment of the tick mark values

placement of the horizontal (category) axis

axis scale ranges from 0% to 25% in 5% increments

tick marks appear next to the axis on the outside

**5.** Click **Number** on the left side of the dialog box, make sure **Percentage** is selected in the Category box, and then type **0** in the Decimal places box. The percentage values in the vertical axis will show no decimal places.

**6.** Click the **Close** button. The percentages on the value axis range from 0 percent to 25 percent in 5 percent intervals with no decimal places.

These changes make the value axis easier to read. Ajita also thinks that the font size of both the value axis and the category axis is too large, dominating the rest of the graph. You will reduce the font size of the axes so that more of the chart area is available for the column chart itself.

### To modify the font size of the axis titles and labels:

**1.** Make sure that the vertical axis is still selected, and then click the **Home** tab on the Ribbon.

**2.** In the Font group, click the **Font Size arrow**, and then click **8**. The values displayed in the vertical axis are smaller, leaving more room for the data series.

**3.** Click anywhere within the **category axis** to select it, and then change the axis font size to **8** points. The revised column chart is easier to read. See Figure 4-17.

**Figure 4-17** **Formatted chart axes**

major tick mark values are percentages with no decimal places

vertical axis scale ranges from 0% to 25% in 5% increments

both axes have a smaller font size

## Formatting the Chart Columns

In a pie chart, each slice or data marker has a different format. In a column chart, all of the columns usually have a common format because the columns are distinguished by height, not color. (However, you can format individual columns in a data series to highlight a particular column value.) You can modify the appearance of the data markers in a column chart using a variety of formatting options.

Ajita thinks that the columns are spaced too widely and could be formatted more attractively. You will reduce the gap between the columns, and change their fill color and appearance to make the columns stand out.

**To format the chart columns:**

1. Click the **Chart Tools Layout** tab on the Ribbon, and then click the **Chart Elements arrow** in the Current Selection group. The list includes each element you can select in the column chart.

2. Click **Series "New Century"**. All the columns for the data series in the chart are selected.

3. In the Current Selection group, click the **Format Selection** button. The Format Data Series dialog box opens with the Series Options displayed.

4. Drag the Gap width slider to **50%** to reduce the gap between adjacent columns. The columns become wider to fill the space.

   **Trouble?** If you cannot drag the Gap width slider to exactly 50%, type 50 in the Gap width box below the slider.

5. Click **Fill** on the left side of the dialog box, and then click the **Gradient fill** option button to fill the columns with a gradually changing mix of colors.

**6.** Click the **Direction** button ▣▾ to open a gallery of fill directions, and then click **Linear Right** (the fourth fill direction in the first row). The columns will have a gradient fill that blends to the right. See Figure 4-18.

---

**Figure 4-18**    **Fill options in the Format Data Series dialog box**

apply a gradient color fill

select the fill direction

---

**7.** Click the **Close** button, and then click cell **A38** to deselect the chart. See Figure 4-19.

---

**Figure 4-19**    **Formatted chart columns**

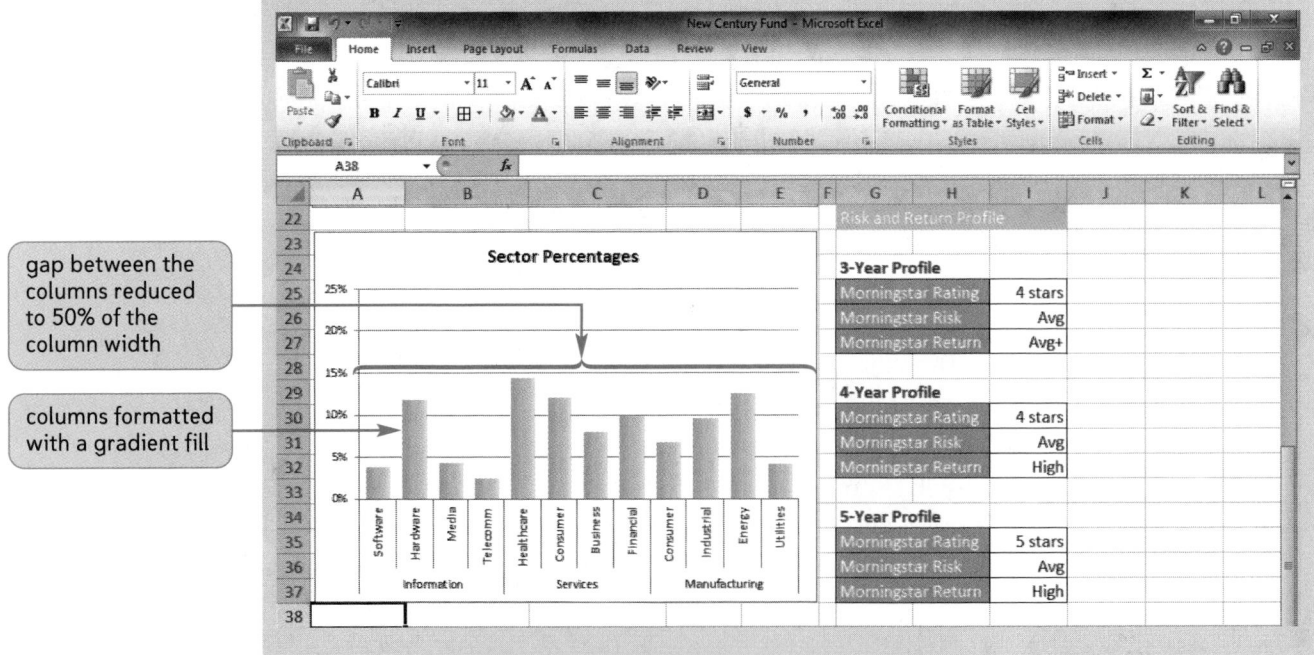

gap between the columns reduced to 50% of the column width

columns formatted with a gradient fill

**PROSKILLS**

## Written Communication: Communicating Effectively with Charts

Studies show that people interpret information easier in a graphic form than in a tabular format. As a result, charts can help communicate the real story underlying the facts and figures you present to colleagues and clients. A well-designed chart can illuminate the bigger picture that might be hidden by viewing only the numbers. However, poorly designed charts can mislead readers and make it more difficult to interpret data.

To create effective and useful charts, keep in mind the following tips as you design charts:

- **Keep it simple.** Do not clutter a chart with too many graphic elements. Focus attention on the data rather than on decorative elements that do not inform.
- **Focus on the message.** Design the chart to highlight the points you want to convey to readers.
- **Limit the number of data series used in the chart.** Line charts and column charts should display no more than three or four data series. Pie charts should have no more than six slices.
- **Use gridlines in moderation.** Gridlines should be used to provide only approximate values for the data markers. Having too many gridlines can obscure the data being graphed.
- **Choose colors carefully.** Display different data series in contrasting colors to make it easier to distinguish one series from another. Modify the default colors as needed to make them distinct on the screen and in the printed copy.
- **Limit your chart to a few text styles.** Use a maximum of two or three different text styles in the same chart. Having too many text styles in one chart can distract attention from the data.

The goal of written communication is always to inform the reader in the simplest, most accurate, and most direct way possible. When creating worksheets and charts, everything in the workbook should be directed toward that end.

Ajita is pleased with the two charts you've created and formatted. In the next session, you'll create a line chart and you'll explore options for creating 3-D charts, chart sheets, and sparklines.

**REVIEW**

### Session 4.1 Quick Check

1. What are the three components of a data series?
2. In what two locations can a chart be placed?
3. What is the difference between the chart area and the plot area?
4. A data series contains values divided into 10 categories. Would this data be better displayed as a pie chart or a column chart? Why?
5. What are major tick marks, minor tick marks, and gridlines?
6. What is a bar chart?
7. How do you change the scale of a chart axis?

# SESSION 4.2 VISUAL OVERVIEW

A **sparkline** is a graph that is displayed within a cell. You can create line, column, and win/loss sparklines.

Line sparklines can contain data markers to identify the high and low points (as shown here), negative points, first and last point, and all points.

A **data bar** is a conditional format that adds a horizontal bar to the background of a cell proportional in length to the cell's value.

A **line chart** displays data values using a connected line rather than columns or bars.

You can create custom label units; the value axis entries are displayed with the thousands unit.

When the axis labels are date values, you can create a custom date format, such as *yyyy*, to display the four-digit year value shown here.

# CHARTS, SPARKLINES, AND DATA BARS

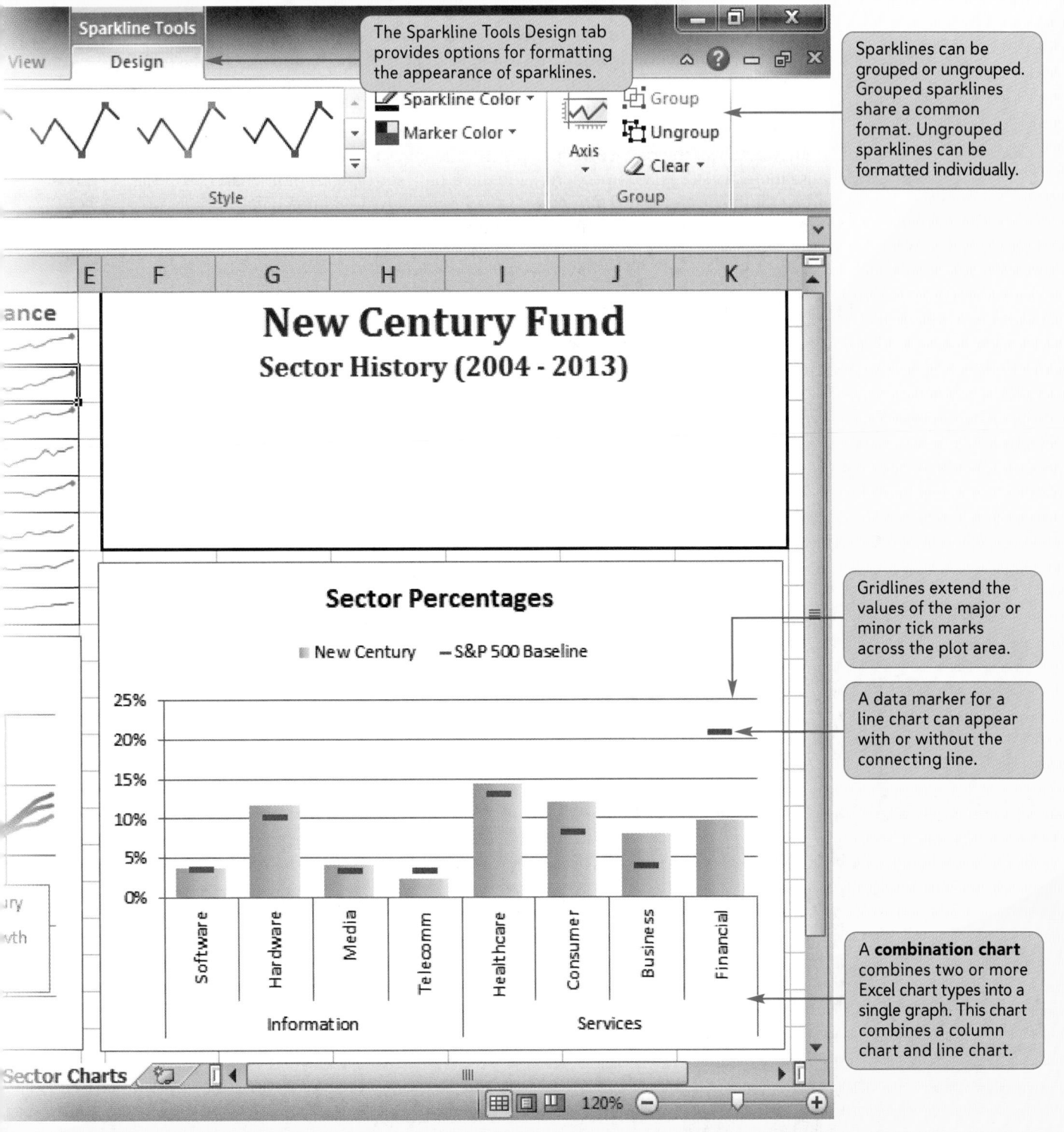

The Sparkline Tools Design tab provides options for formatting the appearance of sparklines.

Sparklines can be grouped or ungrouped. Grouped sparklines share a common format. Ungrouped sparklines can be formatted individually.

Gridlines extend the values of the major or minor tick marks across the plot area.

A data marker for a line chart can appear with or without the connecting line.

A **combination chart** combines two or more Excel chart types into a single graph. This chart combines a column chart and line chart.

**New Century Fund**
**Sector History (2004 - 2013)**

**Sector Percentages**

■ New Century    — S&P 500 Baseline

# Creating a Line Chart

Line charts are typically used when the data consists of values drawn from categories that follow a sequential order at evenly spaced intervals, as with historical data in which the data values are recorded periodically such as monthly, quarterly, or yearly.

Ajita wants the summary report to include a chart of the performance history of the New Century Fund against two other investments: a large growth fund and the S&P 500. (The Standard and Poor's 500 is an index of 500 blue chip stocks that is commonly used to measure the performance of stocks and funds.)

Ajita has already entered this data in the Fund History worksheet. She calculated the quarterly value over the past 10 years of a $10,000 investment in each of the three funds. Because there are 40 data points across the three data series, a column chart of this data would be difficult to read and interpret. Instead, you'll create a line chart for the New Century Fund performance, plotting the value of the three investments against time.

### To create the fund history line chart:

▶ 1. If you took a break at the end of the previous session, make sure that the New Century Fund workbook is open.

▶ 2. Go to the **Fund History** worksheet, and then select the range **A4:D44**. This range contains the data for the value of the New Century Fund, the average value of large growth funds, and the value of the S&P 500 for each quarter of 2004 through 2013.

▶ 3. Click the **Insert** tab on the Ribbon.

▶ 4. In the Charts group, click the **Line** button, and then click the **Line** chart (the first chart in the 2-D Line section). A line chart is embedded in the Fund History worksheet.

▶ 5. In the Location group on the Chart Tools Design tab, click the **Move Chart** button. The Move Chart dialog box opens.

▶ 6. Click the **Object in** arrow, and then click **Summary Report**.

▶ 7. Click the **OK** button. The line chart moves to the Summary Report worksheet.

▶ 8. Move and resize the chart to cover the range **D1:I9**. See Figure 4-20.

**Figure 4-20    Line chart moved and resized**

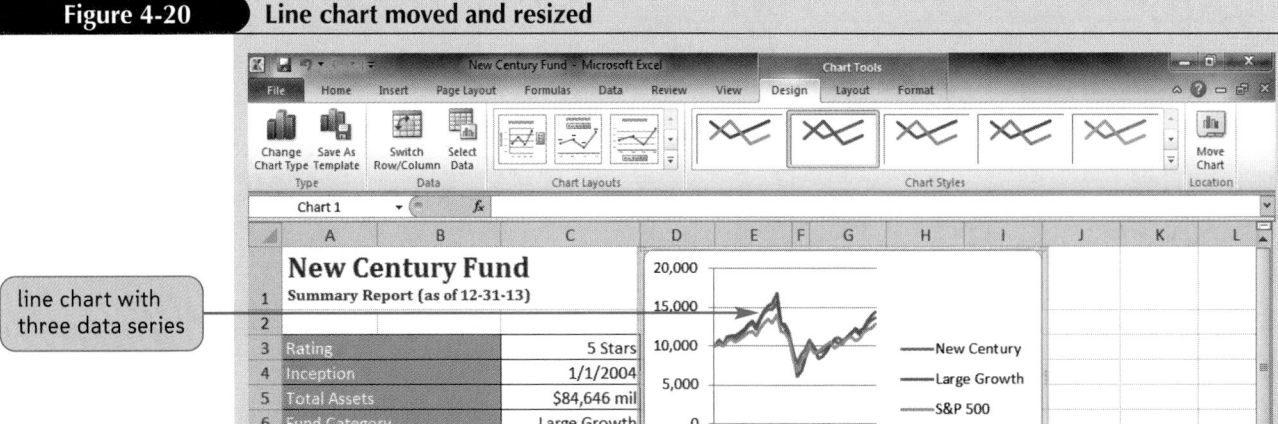

line chart with three data series

The line chart includes three data series—the New Century Fund, a competing large growth fund, and the S&P 500. Each series has a different line color. The line chart is crowded by the default size of the legend and axis labels. You'll reduce the font size of the axis and legend, and then add a chart title that describes the chart's content.

**To edit the fund history line chart:**

▶ 1. Click the **Chart Tools Layout** tab on the Ribbon.

▶ 2. In the Labels group, click the **Chart Title** button, and then click **Above Chart**. A chart title appears above the line chart surrounded by a selection box.

▶ 3. Type **Fund History**, and then press the **Enter** key. The new, descriptive title appears above the chart.

▶ 4. Click the **Home** tab on the Ribbon.

▶ 5. In the Font group, click the **Font Size arrow**, and then click **10**. The chart title is reduced to 10 points.

▶ 6. Click the **value axis** to select it, and then set its font size to **8** points.

▶ 7. Click the **category axis** to select it, and then set its font size to **8** points.

▶ 8. Click the **chart legend** to select it, and then set its font size to **8** points. The line chart resizes to fill the space left by the smaller chart titles, axes, and chart legend.

Next, you will change the scale used in the value axis so that the values range from $0 to $20,000 in $5,000 increments.

**To modify the value axis scale:**

▶ 1. Double-click the **value axis** to open the Format Axis dialog box.

▶ 2. Next to Maximum, click the **Fixed** option button, and then type **20000** in the box.

▶ 3. Next to Major Unit, click the **Fixed** option button, and then type **5000** in the box.

▶ 4. Click the **Close** button. The scale of the vertical axis ranges from $0 to $20,000 in $5,000 increments.

## Formatting Date Labels

In addition to numbers, a scale can be based on dates, as the category axis in the Fund History line chart is. As with numerical scales, you can set the minimum and maximum dates to use in the scale's range. You can also set the major and minor units as days, months, or years to use for the scale's interval.

Ajita is more interested in the general trend from year to year than the exact dates on which the fund values were calculated. Because of this, she wants the scale of the category axis to show only years. You can save space by showing the labels every other year. To do this, you'll set the major tick marks to appear at two-year intervals, and then set the minor tick marks to appear at one-year intervals, even though you won't display the minor tick marks on the chart until later.

## To format the category axis labels:

▶ **1.** Double-click the **category axis** to open the Format Axis dialog box with the Axis Options displayed.

▶ **2.** Next to Major unit, click the **Fixed** option button, type **2** in the box, and then select **Years** in the list. The major tick marks are set to every two years.

▶ **3.** Next to Minor unit, click the **Fixed** option button, type **1** in the box, if necessary, and then select **Years** in the list. The minor tick marks are set to every year. See Figure 4-21.

**Figure 4-21** Date intervals for tick marks

Next, you'll format the category labels to show the four-digit year value rather than the complete date. Excel does not have a built-in format to display only four-digit year values, but you can create a custom format to accomplish this.

Custom date formats use combinations of the letters "m", "d", and "y" for months, days, and years, respectively. The number of letters controls how Excel displays the date, as follows:

- With months, *m* or *mm* displays the one- or two-digit month number, *mmm* displays the month's three-letter abbreviation, and *mmmm* displays the month's full name.
- With days, *d* or *dd* displays the one- or two-digit day value and *dddd* displays the day's full name.
- With years, *yyyy* displays the four-digit year value.

For example, a custom format of *mmm-dd* displays a three-letter month abbreviation followed by a hyphen and a two-digit day number (such as Apr-05). The current date format used in the category axis is *m/d/yyyy*, which—for example—displays March 14, 2013 as 3/14/2013.

You'll create a custom format for the category axis that displays only the four-digit year.

### To create a custom format for the four-digit year:

▶ **1.** Click **Number** on the left side of the Format Axis dialog box.

▶ **2.** Type **yyyy** in the Format Code box, which is the code for displaying only years. See Figure 4-22.

| **Figure 4-22** | **Custom date format** |

built-in date formats

custom format to display the four-digit year

▶ **3.** Click the **Add** button. The four-digit year format code is added to the list of custom formats and is selected.

▶ **4.** Click the **Close** button. The Format Axis dialog box closes, and the category axis labels show values for every other year on the major tick marks. See Figure 4-23.

**Figure 4-23**  **Rescaled vertical and horizontal axes**

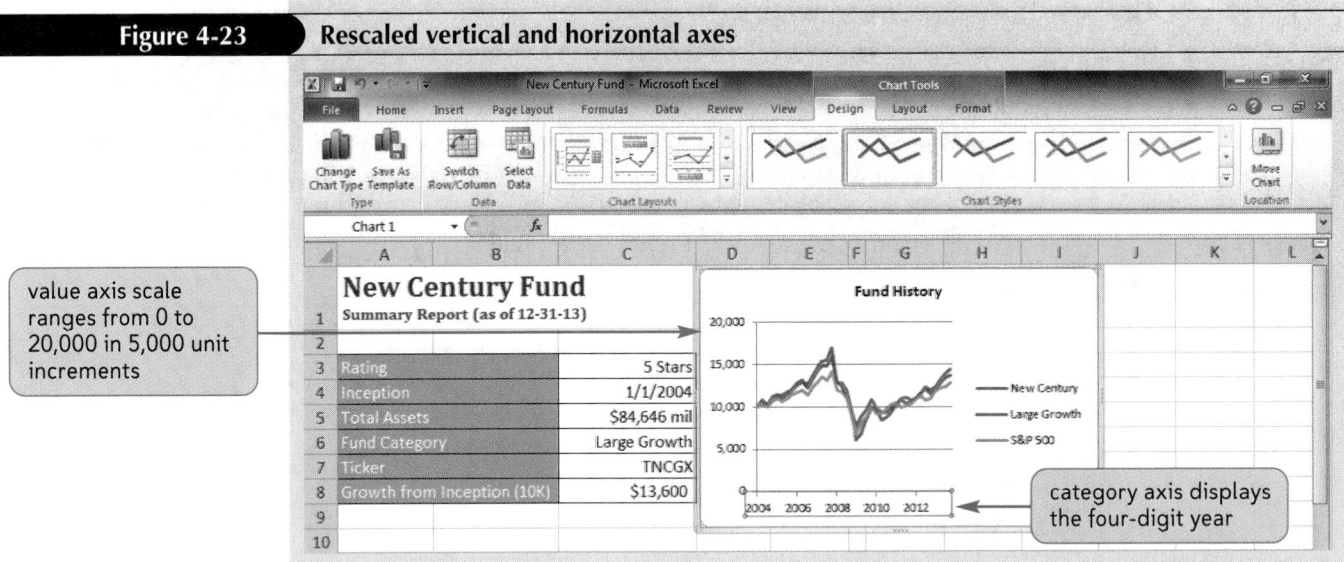

value axis scale ranges from 0 to 20,000 in 5,000 unit increments

category axis displays the four-digit year

The category axis shows four-digit year values for 2004, 2006, 2008, 2010, and 2012. Because fewer years are included on the axis, there is enough room to display the labels horizontally instead of vertically.

## Setting Label Units

When a chart involves large numbers, the axis labels can take up a lot of the available chart area and be difficult to read. You can simplify the chart's appearance by displaying units of measure more appropriate to the data values. For example, you can display the value 20 to represent 20,000 or 20,000,000. This is particularly useful when space is at a premium, such as in an embedded chart confined to a small area of the worksheet. When you select the display units, such as Thousands, you can choose to show the display unit in the axis title.

The Fund History line chart displays data in tens of thousands of dollars. Rather than displaying a large value such as 20,000, Ajita wants to save space by displaying numbers in units of thousands. You will change the display units for the value axis but not show the units in the axis title.

### To set the display unit for the value axis:

1. Double-click the **value axis** to open the Format Axis dialog box with the Axis Options displayed.

2. Click the **Display units** arrow, and then click **Thousands**.

3. Move the dialog box so you can see the line chart's value axis. The scale of the value axis changed from 0 to 20,000 in intervals of 5,000 to 0 through 20 in intervals of 5. The axis title "Thousands" indicates that the values are expressed in units of 1000. To save space, you'll remove this title from the chart.

4. Click the **Show display units label on chart** check box to remove the check mark. The axis title is removed from the chart.

You can apply custom formats to numbers just as you did earlier with dates. One application of custom formats is to add text to a number. This is often used to include the units of measure alongside the value, such as 10k to indicate 10,000. To add text to a value, you use the custom format *value*"*text*", where *value* is the number format applied to the value and *text* is the text to include next to the value. The text must be placed within quotation marks.

**TIP**

Use Excel Help to learn more about custom format codes.

Without the Thousands title, the Fund History line chart provides no indication of what the value axis numbers mean. Ajita suggests you add the letter "k" to each number, displaying the values as 10k, 20k, and so forth. To do this, you'll create a custom format. Excel uses the format #,##0 to display integers, so you'll change this format to #,##0"k" to display the letter "k" at the end of the value.

### To create a custom format showing the thousands unit:

1. Click **Number** on the left side of the Format Axis dialog box.

2. Click in the Format Code box after the number format, and then type **"k"** to make the format code #,##0"k".

3. Click the **Add** button. This format code is added to the list of custom formats in the Type box.

4. Click the **Close** button. The Format Axis dialog box closes, and the value axis labels are revised, with the letter "k" added after each value. See Figure 4-24.

**Figure 4-24**    Custom value axis label units

value axis labels use the letter "k" to represent thousands as the display units

## Overlaying a Chart Legend

Chart elements, such as titles and legends, overlay the chart area, which means they are placed on top of the chart. Overlaying chart elements is a way to make more space for the plot area because the chart does not resize to make room for that element. After you overlay an element, you might want to format it to make it easier to read.

Ajita thinks the legend takes up too much space on the right side of the chart. You will overlay the legend, leaving more room in the chart area for the chart itself, and then format it.

## To overlay and format the chart legend:

1. Double-click the **legend** to open the Format Legend dialog box.

2. Click the **Show the legend without overlapping the chart** check box to remove the check mark. The size of the chart increases, and the legend is now overlaying the chart. The plot and the legend intersect, and the plot area shows through the legend.

3. Click **Fill** on the left side of the Format Legend dialog box, and then click the **Solid fill** option button.

4. Click the **Color** button ⬛▾, and then click **white** (the first color in the Theme Colors section). The legend now has a solid white background, making it easier to read.

5. Click **Border Color** on the left side of the Format Legend dialog box, and then click the **Solid line** option button.

6. Click the **Color** button ⬛▾, and then click **Blue** (the eighth color in the Standard Colors section).

7. Click the **Close** button. The Format Legend dialog box closes, and the reformatted legend overlays the chart.

An overlaid chart element floats in the chart area and is not fixed to a particular position. This means that you can drag the chart element to a new location. This is helpful because when you overlay a chart element, it might overlap some of the chart contents, as the legend does. You'll drag the overlaid legend down a bit so that it doesn't obscure any of the data in the line chart.

## To move the chart legend:

1. Position the pointer over a blank spot in the chart legend so the pointer changes to ⬚ and "Legend" appears in a ScreenTip.

2. Drag the legend to the lower-right corner of the plot area so the bottom of the legend is on the horizontal axis.

3. Click and drag the upper-left sizing handle of the legend down a few pixels until the legend no longer overlaps the lines on the chart. See Figure 4-25.

**Figure 4-25**    Legend overlaid, moved, and resized

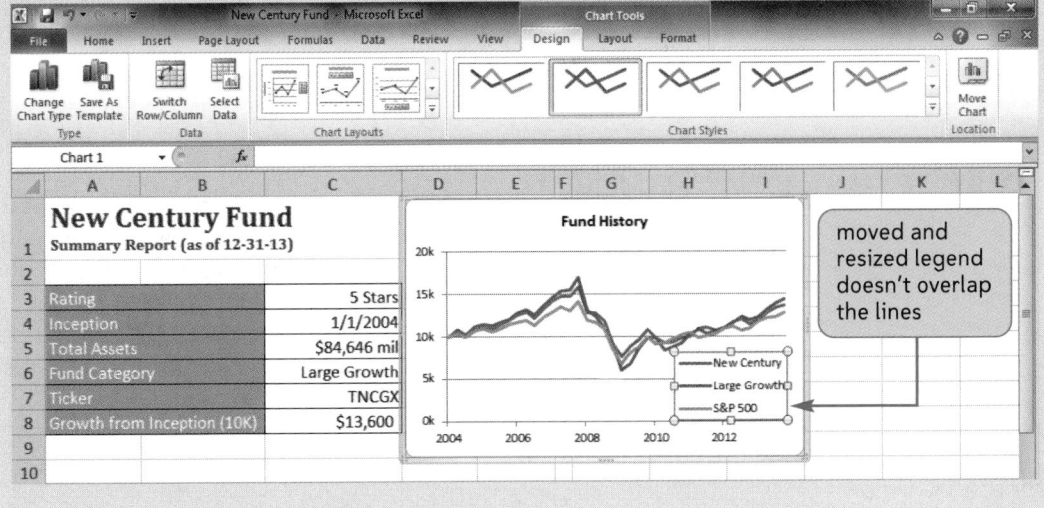

## Adding Gridlines

By default, Excel places horizontal gridlines on line charts and column charts. Each gridline is aligned with a major tick mark on the value axis. You can change the gridlines so that they appear for only the minor units, appear for both the major and minor units, or do not appear at all. The category axis has these same gridline options.

Ajita wants you to add vertical gridlines at the minor tick marks on the category axis.

**To add vertical gridlines to the chart:**

▶ **1.** Click the **Chart Tools Layout** tab on the Ribbon.

▶ **2.** In the Axes group, click the **Gridlines** button.

▶ **3.** Point to **Primary Vertical Gridlines**, and then click **Minor Gridlines**. Vertical gridlines appear on the chart at each minor tick mark (in this case, every year).

## Adding an Axis Title

An axis title is descriptive text that appears next to the axis values. An axis title can provide additional information that is not covered in the chart title. It can include information about the source of the data and the units in which the data is measured.

The values in the chart represent the return that the investor would have enjoyed from a $10,000 investment starting in 2004. Because this fact is not obvious from the chart, Ajita wants you to add the title "Return on $10K Investment" to the vertical axis.

**To add a title to the vertical axis:**

▶ **1.** In the Labels group on the Chart Tools Layout tab, click **Axis Titles**, point to **Primary Vertical Axis Title**, and then click **Rotated Title**. A title rotated 90 degrees is added to the axis.

▶ **2.** Type **Return on $10K Investment**, and then press the **Enter** key. The descriptive title is entered, but doesn't fit well in the chart area.

▶ **3.** Click the **Home** tab on the Ribbon.

▶ **4.** In the Font group, click the **Font Size button arrow**, and then click **8**. The font size is reduced to 8 points.

▶ **5.** In the Font group, click the **Bold** button **B** to remove the boldface from the axis title.

▶ **6.** Click cell **A9** to deselect the chart. The final version of the line chart is easier to read than the unformatted version, and highlights how the New Century Fund has performed over the past 10 years compared to the two benchmarks. See Figure 4-26.

**Figure 4-26** **Final line chart**

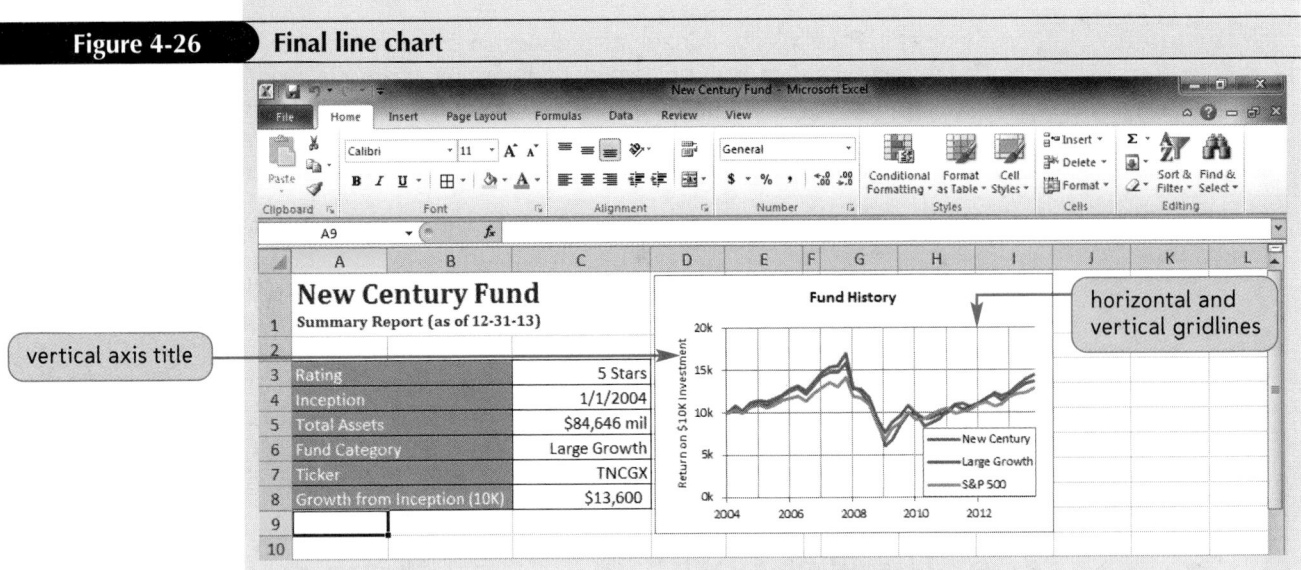

# Editing and Revising Chart Data

Chart data can be edited and revised at any time. You do this by modifying the data range that the chart is based on, not by directly modifying the data in the chart. The change can be as simple as updating a specific value within the data source. Or it can be as involved as adding another data series to the chart.

## Changing a Data Value

Charts remain linked or connected to their data sources, even if they appear in different worksheets. If you change any values or labels in the data source, the chart is automatically updated to show the new content. One advantage of Excel charts is that you can quickly see how changing one or more values affects a graph.

Ajita found a data entry error in the Assets worksheet—the amount of assets in the Other category entered in cell B8 should be $8,360, not $3,360. She also wants the label "Other" to be changed to "Other Assets." This change also needs to be reflected in the Allocation of Assets pie chart you created based on this data. Because both the asset values and the asset labels are linked to the pie chart, when you make these changes in the Assets worksheet, they will automatically be reflected in the pie chart.

### To edit the data source for the assets pie chart:

▶ **1.** Go to the **Assets** worksheet.

▶ **2.** In cell A8, edit the text to **Other Assets**.

▶ **3.** In cell B8, change the value to **8360**.

▶ **4.** Go to the **Summary Report** worksheet, and then verify that the pie chart was updated with the new data value and category name. Note that the percentage values for each category were recalculated based on the new data. As a result, the Other Assets slice increased in size to reflect its larger percentage of the whole, and the remaining slices decreased in size. See Figure 4-27.

**Figure 4-27**    Revised pie chart

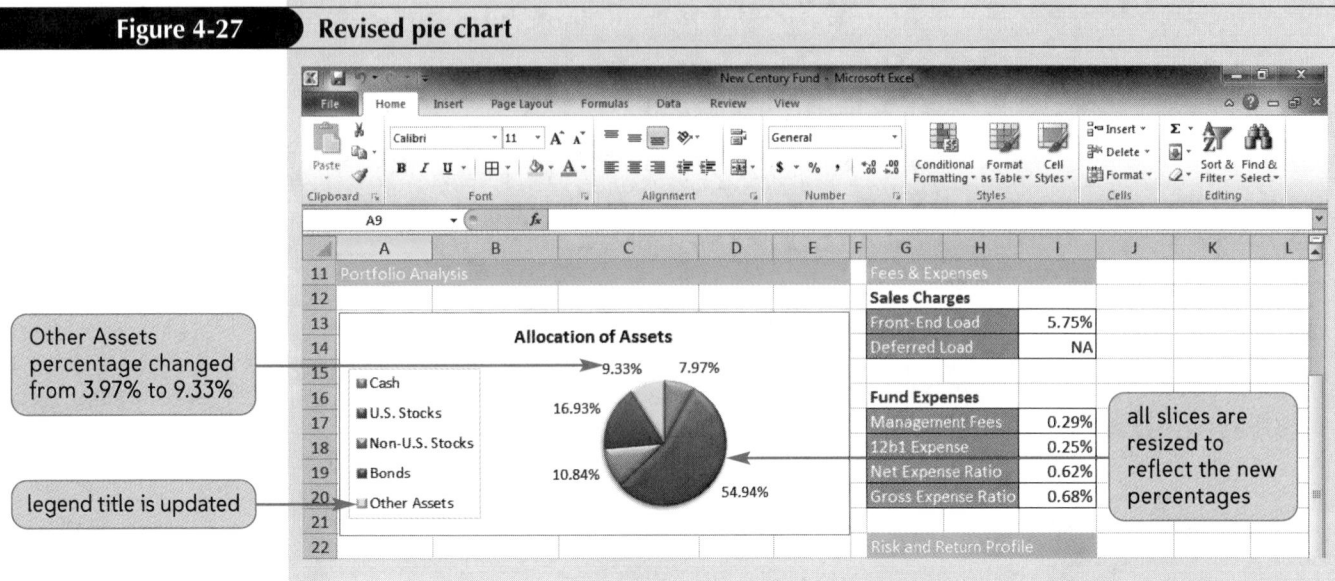

Other Assets percentage changed from 3.97% to 9.33%

legend title is updated

all slices are resized to reflect the new percentages

Occasionally, you will want a chart to show a "snapshot" of the data at a certain time. Before updating the values in the data source, copy and paste the chart as a picture. Select the chart, copy it as usual, click the Paste button arrow, and then click Picture. The chart is pasted as a picture without any connection to its data source.

## Adding a Data Series to an Existing Chart

You can also modify a chart by adding a new data series. The new data series appears in the chart with a different set of data markers in the same way that the line chart you created had different data markers for each of the three different series.

**REFERENCE**

### Adding a Data Series to a Chart

- Select the chart to which you want to add a data series.
- In the Data group on the Chart Tools Design tab, click the Select Data button.
- Click the Add button in the Select Data Source dialog box.
- Select the range with the series name and series values you want for the new data series.
- Click the OK button in each dialog box.

The column chart you created shows the distribution of stocks in the New Century Fund. Ajita wonders how this distribution compares to the distribution in the S&P 500 index. For example, does the New Century Fund invest more in the information sector, and is that why it outperformed the S&P 500 for the past 10 years? Ajita included the sector percentages for the S&P 500 in the Sectors worksheet. You will add this information to the column chart you've already created.

### To add a data series to the existing column chart:

1. Click the **Sector Percentages** column chart to select it.

2. Click the **Chart Tools Design** tab on the Ribbon, and then, in the Data group, click the **Select Data** button. The Select Data Source dialog box opens. The left side lists all of the data series displayed in the chart. The right side lists the category axis labels associated with each data series. You can add, edit, or remove any of these data series from the chart.

3. Click the **Add** button. The Edit Series dialog box opens. In this dialog box, you specify the name of the new data series and its range of data values.

4. With the insertion point in the Series name box, click the **Sectors** sheet tab, click cell **D3**, and then press the **Tab** key. The cell with the series name is entered and the insertion point moves to the Series values box.

5. Select the range **D4:D15**. See Figure 4-28.

---

**Figure 4-28**    **Edit Series dialog box**

reference for the cell containing the series name

reference for the range containing the series values

---

6. Click the **OK** button. The Select Data Source dialog box reappears with the S&P 500 data added to the list of data series in the chart. See Figure 4-29.

---

**Figure 4-29**    **Select Data Source dialog box**

click to add a new data series to the chart

data series in the column chart

---

7. Click the **OK** button. The S&P 500 sector values appear as red columns in the chart. See Figure 4-30.

**Figure 4-30** Column chart with added data series

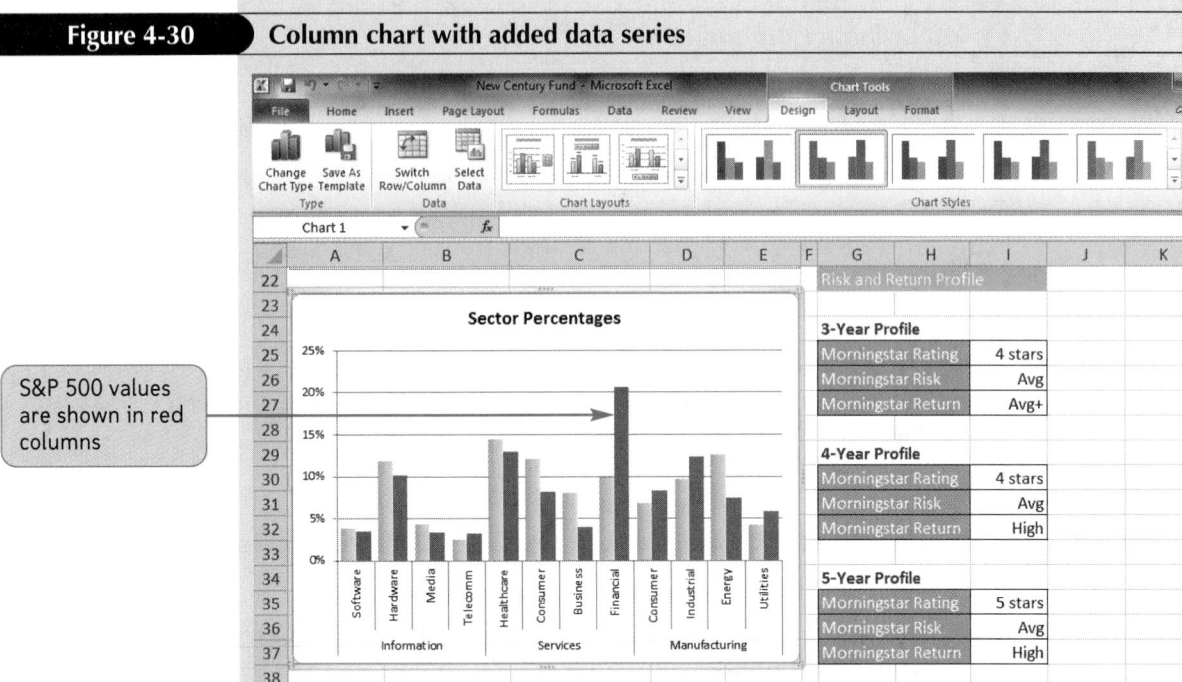

S&P 500 values are shown in red columns

## Understanding the Series Function

**INSIGHT**

If you select a chart's series and look at the formula bar, the formula being displayed uses the SERIES function. The SERIES function describes the content of a chart data series and has the syntax

```
=SERIES(name, categories, values, order)
```

where *name* is the name that appears in the chart, *categories* are the labels that appear on the category axis of the chart, *values* are the values that Excel plots for the data series, and *order* is the order in which the series appears in the chart. For example, a data series might be represented by the following SERIES function:

```
=SERIES(Sheet1!$D$1,Sheet1!$A$2:$A$9,Sheet1!$D$2:$D$9,3)
```

In this function, the name of the series is in cell D1 of the Sheet1 worksheet, the labels are in the range A2:A9 in the Sheet1 worksheet, the data values are in the range D2:D9 in the Sheet1 worksheet, and the series is the third data series in the chart.

Note that although you can edit the SERIES function within the formula bar to make quick changes to your chart, the function is tied to an existing chart. It cannot be used within a worksheet cell or referenced from another Excel formula.

# Creating a Combination Chart

A combination chart is a chart that combines two or more chart types in a single graph, such as a column chart and a line chart. To create a combination chart, you select a data series in an existing chart, and then apply a new chart type to that series, leaving the other data series in its original format.

## Creating a Combination Chart

- Select a data series in an existing chart that you want to appear as another chart type.
- In the Type group on the Chart Tools Design tab, click the Change Chart Type button, and then click the chart type you want.
- Click the OK button.

With so many columns in the Sector Percentages column chart, the data is difficult to read and interpret. Ajita suggests you separate the S&P 500 values from the New Century Fund values by plotting them as lines rather than columns. To do that, you'll create a chart that is a combination of a column and a line chart.

### To apply the line chart type to the S&P 500 data series:

1. Click the **Chart Tools Layout** tab on the Ribbon.

2. In the Current Selection group, click the **Chart Elements arrow**, and then click **Series "S&P 500 Baseline"** to select the data series.

3. Click the **Chart Tools Design** tab on the Ribbon, and then click the **Change Chart Type** button in the Type group. The Change Chart Type dialog box opens.

4. In the Line section, click **Line with Markers** (the fourth Line chart type).

5. Click the **OK** button. The S&P 500 values change to a line chart with markers. See Figure 4-31.

| Figure 4-31 | Combination chart |

New Century Fund values displayed as columns

S&P 500 values displayed as a line with markers

As noted earlier, line charts are appropriate when the categories can be ordered sequentially such as the Fund History line chart in which the categories represented dates. In Figure 4-31, the sector categories do not have a sequential order and the lines connecting the different categories have no meaning. You'll remove these lines from the chart to avoid confusing Ajita's clients. Also, you'll change the square markers to horizontal line markers at each data point.

### To remove the lines and edit the markers in the line chart:

1. Click the line for the S&P 500 data series to select it, if necessary.

2. Click the **Chart Tools Layout** tab on the Ribbon, and then click **Format Selection** in the Current Selection group. The Format Data Series dialog box opens.

3. Click **Line Color** on the left side of the dialog box, and then click the **No line** option button to remove the line from the line chart.

4. Click **Marker Options** on the left side of the dialog box, and then click the **Built-in** option button. You can now select the type and size of the marker.

5. Click the **Type arrow**, and then click the horizontal line marker (the seventh marker in the list).

6. Click the **Size** up arrow until 10 appears in the box. See Figure 4-32.

**Figure 4-32** | **Marker Options in the Format Data Series dialog box**

7. Click the **Close** button. The S&P 500 values appear only as data markers.

Because the chart now has two data series, you'll add a legend to the top of the chart to identify them.

### To add a legend to the combination chart:

▶ **1.** In the Labels group on the Chart Tools Layout tab, click the **Legend** button, and then click **Show Legend at Top**. The legend appears above the chart.

▶ **2.** Click the **legend** to select it.

▶ **3.** Click the **Home** tab on the Ribbon, and then reduce the font size of the legend to **8** points.

▶ **4.** Click cell **A38** to deselect the chart. See Figure 4-33.

**Figure 4-33** **Completed combination chart**

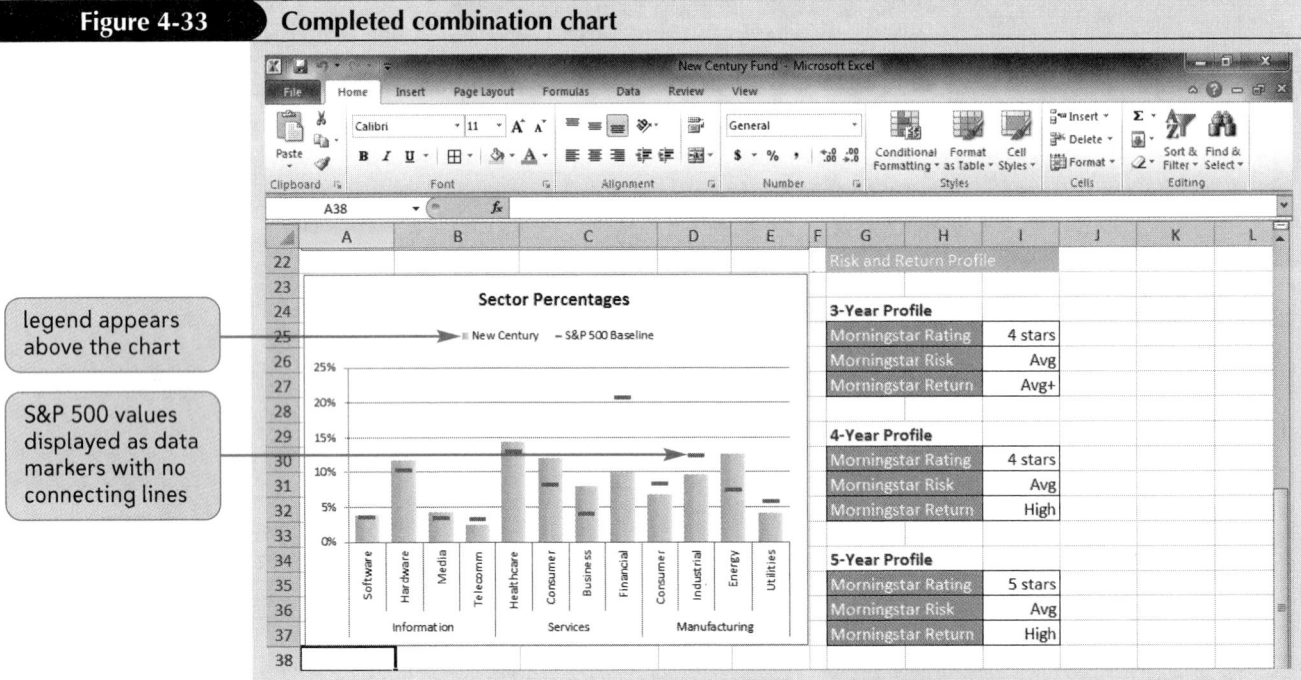

legend appears above the chart

S&P 500 values displayed as data markers with no connecting lines

The combination chart effectively shows that the New Century Fund invests less than the S&P 500 in sectors from the financial service industry, and invests more in other sectors such as energy, consumer services, and hardware. This might account for the higher performance of the New Century Fund.

**PROSKILLS**

*Decision Making: Choosing the Right Chart*

Excel supports a wide variety of charts and chart styles. Deciding which type of chart to use requires evaluating your data and determining the ultimate purpose or goal of the chart. Consider how your data will appear with each type of chart before making a final decision.

In general, pie charts should be used only when the number of categories is small and the relative sizes of the different slices can be easily distinguished. If you have several categories, use a column or bar chart.

Line charts are best for categories that follow a sequential order. Be aware, however, that the time intervals must be a constant length if used in a line chart. Line charts will distort data that occurs in irregular time intervals, making it appear that the data values occurred at regular intervals when they did not.

Pie, column, bar, and line charts assume that numbers are plotted against categories. In science and engineering applications, you will often want to plot two numeric values against one another. For that data, use **XY scatter charts**, which show the patterns or relationship between two or more sets of values. XY scatter charts are also useful for data recorded at irregular time intervals.

If you still can't find the right chart to meet your needs, you can create a custom chart based on the built-in chart types. Third-party vendors also sell software to allow Excel to create charts not built into the software.

Choosing the right chart and chart style can make your presentation more effective and informative.

# Creating a 3-D Chart

You can add visual interest to charts by using 3-D (three dimensional) effects. The 3-D effects provide the illusion of depth and distance, which makes the charts appear to stand out on the page. You'll change the format of the Allocation of Assets pie chart to a 3-D style.

**To change the assets pie chart to 3-D:**

▶ **1.** Click the **Allocation of Assets pie chart**, and then click the **Chart Tools Design** tab on the Ribbon.

▶ **2.** In the Type group, click the **Change Chart Type** button. The Change Chart Type dialog box opens.

▶ **3.** In the Pie section, click **Pie in 3-D** (the second Pie chart type).

▶ **4.** Click the **OK** button. The pie chart is now a 3-D chart, and has a slight shadow along its lower edge.

To create a 3-D effect, Excel adds three spatial dimensions to the chart, which it labels the x-, y-, and z-axes. The **x-axis** represents the length of the object. The **y-axis** represents the height of the object. The **z-axis** represents the object's depth. These Excel definitions of the x-, y-, and z-axes might not match what you have learned in math classes about 3-D charting.

Currently, the 3-D pie chart does not look very different from the 2-D version because you are looking straight down on the chart from "above," directly along the y-axis. To increase the 3-D effect, you need to rotate the chart. You can only rotate the chart horizontally or vertically. Increasing the rotation horizontally spins the chart clockwise (as seen from above); increasing the rotation vertically raises the user's viewpoint higher above the chart. Often you'll need to experiment to find the right angles for a 3-D chart by rotating the chart in different directions until it looks good without distorting the data.

Excel charts cannot be rotated around the z- or depth axis, but you can specify the chart's depth. Depth values can range from 0 to 2000 units. The larger the value, the thicker or deeper the chart appears to extend away from the viewer. You can also change the chart's **perspective**, which controls how fast the chart appears to recede from the viewer's eye. Perspective values range from 0 degrees to 90 degrees. A 90 degree perspective value exaggerates the 3-D effect, making distant objects appear very small, whereas perspective values near 0 degrees minimize this effect. Excel immediately applies your choices for depth and perspective, so you can try different depth and perspective values to determine which work best for your chart.

You'll rotate the Allocation of Assets pie chart along the horizontal axis so that the largest slice is on the left side of the pie. You'll also orient the chart so that the viewer's eye level is slightly above the chart. You will not change the chart's perspective or depth.

### To rotate and reorient the 3-D pie chart:

1. Click the **Chart Tools Layout** tab on the Ribbon.

2. In the Background group, click the **3-D Rotation** button. The Format Chart Area dialog box opens with the 3-D Rotation options displayed.

3. In the Rotation section, type **90** in the X box, and then type **20** in the Y box. See Figure 4-34.

**Figure 4-34** **Format Chart Area dialog box with 3-D Rotation options**

4. Click the **Close** button. The pie chart rotates based on the new x-axis and y-axis values. See Figure 4-35.

| Figure 4-35 | Rotated 3-D pie chart |
| --- | --- |

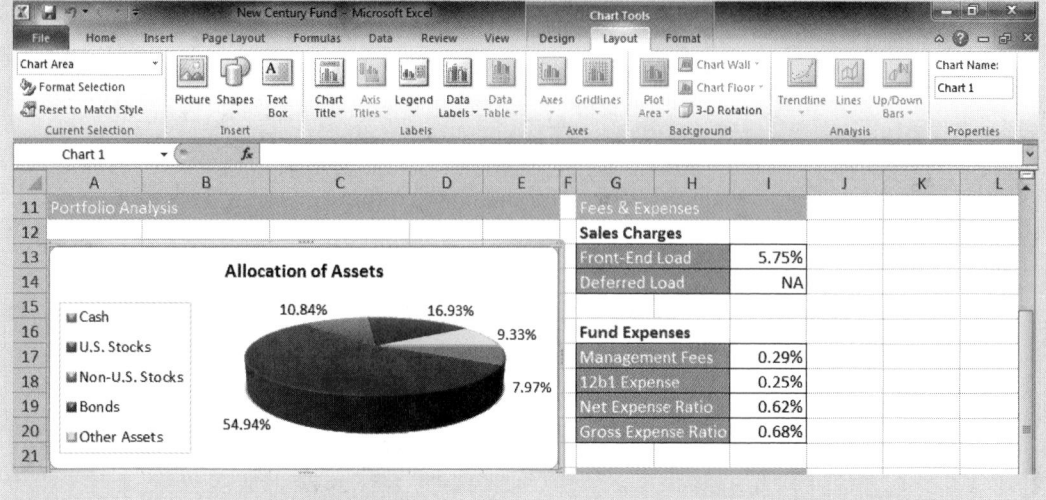

The horizontal and vertical rotation has a significant impact on the way the chart looks. The pie chart was rotated clockwise one-quarter of the way around the circle so that the largest slice, the red U.S Stocks slice, is in the front. The vertical rotation turned the pie chart so that the viewer is looking down on the chart at a lower angle above the horizontal axis. Ajita is pleased with the 3-D effect you added.

## INSIGHT

### Creating Effective 3-D Charts

Although 3-D charts are visually attractive, they can obscure the relationship between the values in the chart. This is especially true when an exaggerated perspective obscures the relative sizes of different chart elements, such as pie slices.

Because of the visual distortion that can result with 3-D representations, you should include data labels with all 3-D charts. Also, try to avoid extreme viewing angles that elongate chart elements and might cause the viewer to misread the data. Although 3-D charts can be eye-catching, do not use this effect if it overrides the main purpose of a chart, which is data interpretation.

# Adding Sparklines and Data Bars

For more compact graphing, you can insert charts within worksheet cells. Excel provides two tools to do this—sparklines and data bars. Both convey graphical information about worksheet data without occupying a lot of space.

## Creating Sparklines

A sparkline is a mini chart that is displayed within a worksheet cell. Because sparklines are compact in size, they don't include chart elements such as legends, titles, gridlines, or axes. The goal of a sparkline is to convey the maximum amount of graphical information within a very small space. As a result, sparklines are useful when you don't want charts to overwhelm the rest of your worksheet or take up valuable page space.

Excel supports the following three types of sparklines:

- A line sparkline for highlighting trends
- A column sparkline used for column charts
- A win/loss sparkline for highlighting positive and negative values

Figure 4-36 shows examples of each type of sparkline. The line sparklines show the sales history of each department and all four departments for a computer manufacturer. From glancing at the sparklines, you can quickly see the recent sales history within and across departments. Notice that although total sales rose steadily during the year, peripheral sales lagged for the first two-thirds of the year before increasing in the final third.

**Figure 4-36**    **Types of sparklines**

The column sparklines present a record of monthly temperature averages for four cities. Temperatures above 0°C are presented in blue columns; temperatures below 0°C are presented in red columns that extend downward.

Finally, the win/loss sparklines reveal a snapshot of the season results for four sports teams. Wins are displayed in blue; losses are in red. From the sparklines, you can quickly see that the Cutler Tigers finished their 10-2 season with six straight wins and the Liddleton Lions finished their 3-9 season with four straight losses.

To create a set of sparklines, you first select a data range containing the data you want to graph, and then you select a location range where you want the sparklines to appear. Note that the cells in which you insert the sparklines need not be blank. Sparklines are added as part of the cell background and do not replace any cell content.

*Creating and Editing Sparklines*

- In the Sparklines group on the Insert tab, click the Line, Column, or Win/Loss button.
- In the Data Range box, enter the range for the data source of the sparkline.
- In the Location Range box, enter the range into which to place the sparkline.
- Click the OK button.
- To edit a sparkline's appearance, click the Sparkline Tools Design tab.
- In the Show group, click the appropriate check boxes to specify which markers to display on the sparkline.
- In the Group group, click the Axis button, and then click Show Axis to add an axis to the sparkline.

Ajita wants to add graphs to the Sectors worksheet to indicate how each of the 12 investment sectors performed during the last 10 years. Rather than create a separate chart for each sector, you'll conserve space in the worksheet by creating sparklines.

### To insert sparklines in the Sectors worksheet:

1. Go to the **Sectors** worksheet.

2. In cell E3, enter **10-Year History**, and then apply the **Heading 4** cell style to the cell and center the text within the cell.

3. Select the range **E4:E15**. This is the location range, the cells in which you want to insert the sparklines.

4. Click the **Insert** tab on the Ribbon, and then click the **Line** button in the Sparklines group. The Create Sparklines dialog box opens. The location range is already entered because you selected it before opening the dialog box.

5. With the insertion point in the Data Range box, click the **Sector History** sheet tab, and then select the data in the range **B6:M45**. This is the range that contains the data you want to chart in the sparklines. See Figure 4-37.

| Figure 4-37 | Create Sparklines dialog box |

the range B6:M45 on the Sector History worksheet contains the data for the sparklines

the range E4:E15 on the current worksheet is the location to place the sparklines

6. Click the **OK** button. Sparklines are inserted into each cell in the selected range. See Figure 4-38.

**Figure 4-38**          **Line sparklines created for each sector**

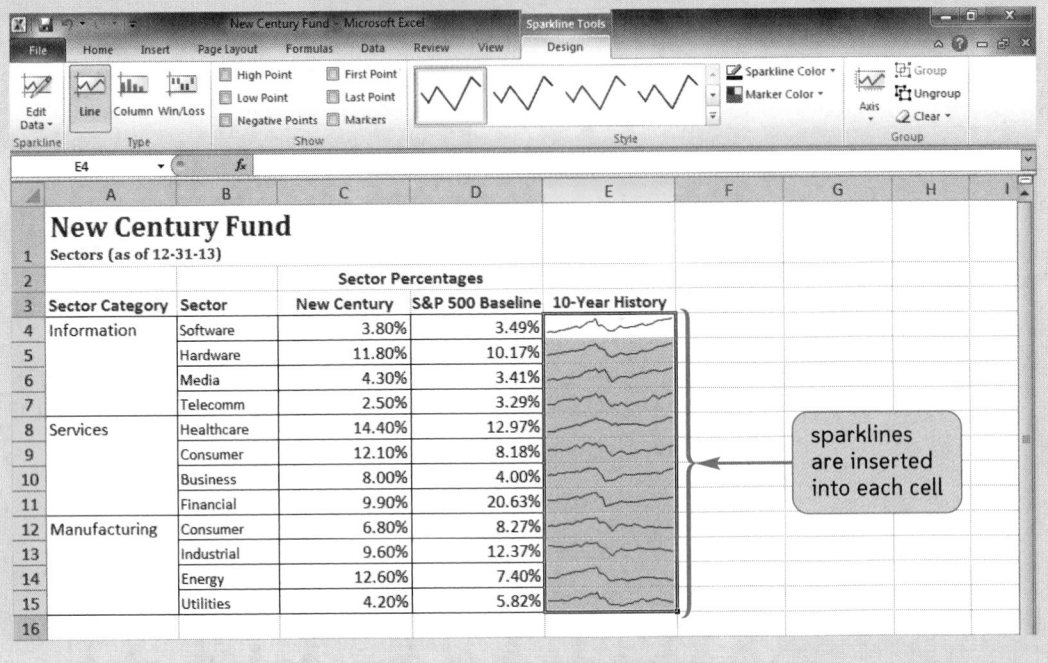

Ajita quickly notices from the sparklines that all of the investment sectors experienced a sharp decline mid-way through the previous decade. The stocks in the information sector category recovered from that loss to post gains during the second half of the decade. However, the manufacturing stocks showed little or no increase after that mid-decade decline. The stocks in the service category showed a moderate increase in the second half of the decade.

## Adding and Formatting Sparkline Markers

As with other charts, Excel provides built-in styles for sparklines. Because of the compactness of sparklines, you can specify only the line color and the marker color. For line sparklines, you can create markers for the following points: the highest value, the lowest value, all the negative values, the first value, and the last value. You can also create markers for all data points regardless of their value or position in the data source.

Ajita wants you to add data markers for the high and low points within each sparkline so that she can more easily track the progress each sector made during the decade and locate the decade's maximum and minimum values.

### To add high and low markers to the sparklines:

1. Click the **Sparkline Tools Design** tab on the Ribbon, if necessary. The tab contains options associated with the selected sparklines—in this case, line sparklines.

2. In the Show group, click the **High Point** and **Low Point** check boxes to display markers for the high and low points within each sparkline.

3. In the Style group, click the **More** button to open the Style gallery, and then click **Sparkline Style Colorful #2** (the second style in the last row). The color of the high and low point markers changes to reflect the selection. See Figure 4-39.

**TIP**

You can change the sparkline color by clicking the Sparkline Color button in the Style group on the Sparkline Tools Design tab. You can change the marker color by clicking the Marker Color button.

**Figure 4-39**    **Data markers added to sparklines**

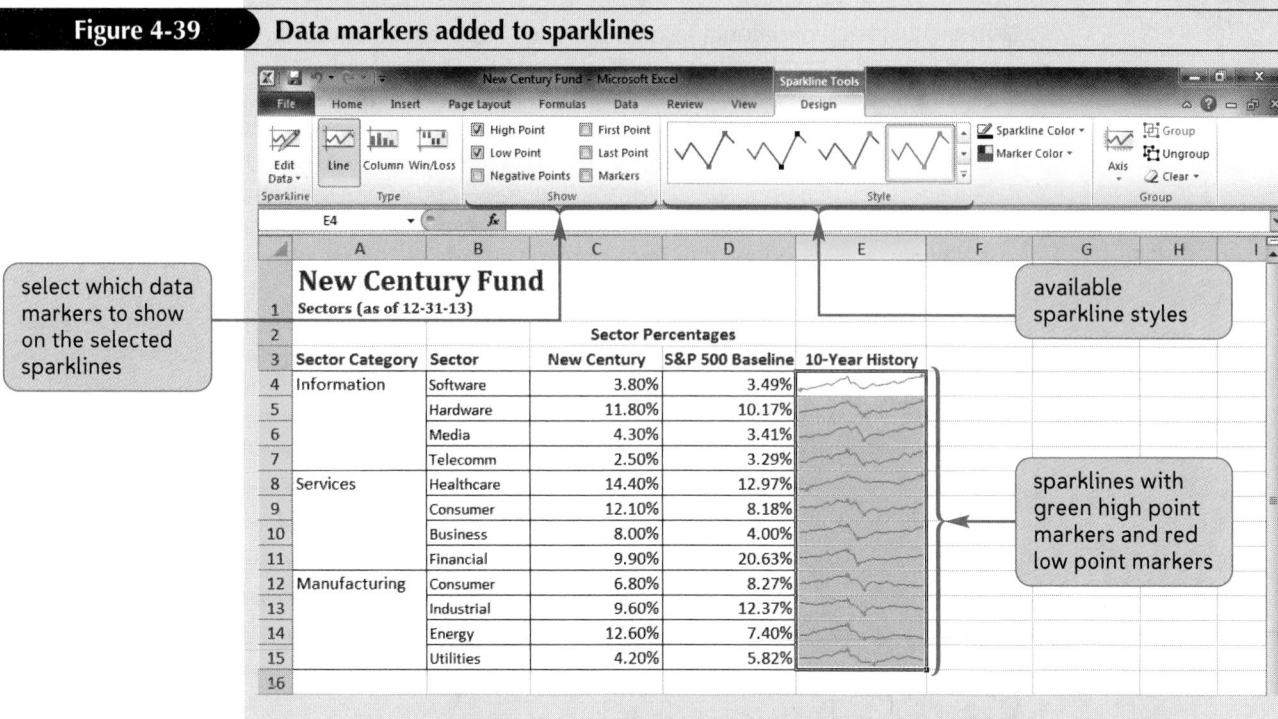

select which data markers to show on the selected sparklines

available sparkline styles

sparklines with green high point markers and red low point markers

> **4.** Click cell **A2** to deselect the location range containing the sparklines. You can more clearly see that the formatted sparklines use a green marker for the high points and a red marker for the low points.

The only other feature you can add to a sparkline is an axis. The sparkline axis is simply a horizontal line that separates positive values from negative values. To add an axis to a sparkline, click the Axis button in the Group group on the Sparkline Tools Design tab, and then click Show Axis. You won't add an axis to the 10-Year History sparklines because all of the fund values are positive and an axis would not add any information to the charts.

**INSIGHT**

## Sparkline Groups

When you create sparklines, all the sparklines in the location range are part of a single group. Clicking any cell in the location range selects all of the sparklines in the group. Similarly, any formatting you apply affects all the sparklines in the group. This ensures that all the sparklines for related data are formatted consistently.

In some instances, you might want to differentiate one sparkline from others in its group. You can do this by applying a different format to that sparkline. To format an individual sparkline, select the sparkline you want to format, and then click the Ungroup button in the Group group on the Sparkline Tools Design tab. The selected sparkline is split from the rest of the sparklines in the group. You can then apply a unique format to the selected sparkline. To regroup the sparklines, select all of the cells in the location range containing sparklines, and then click the Group button in the Group group.

One advantage of breaking up a sparkline group is that Excel can display each sparkline based on the maximum and minimum values associated with the individual sparkline's data series. This becomes an important consideration if your data source contains multiple data series covering vastly different ranges.

## Creating Data Bars

A data bar is a conditional format that adds a horizontal bar to the background of a cell containing a numeric value. When applied to a range of cells, the data bars have the same appearance as a bar chart with each cell containing one bar.

The lengths of data bars are based on the value of each cell in the selected range. Cells with larger values have longer bars; cells with smaller values have shorter bars. Data bars are dynamic, which means that if one cell's value changes, the lengths of the data bars in the selected range are automatically updated.

Data bars differ from sparklines in that the bars are always placed in the cells containing the value they represent and each cell represents only a single bar from the bar chart. By contrast, a column sparkline can be inserted anywhere within the workbook and can represent data from several rows or columns. However, like sparklines, data bars can be used to create compact graphs that can be easily integrated alongside the text and values stored in your worksheet cells.

Ajita wants you to add data bars to the sector percentage values in the Sectors worksheet. The data bars will provide a visual picture of how the New Century Fund and the S&P 500 compare in their investments in different sectors.

**To add data bars to the sector percentages:**

1. In the Sectors worksheet, select the range **C4:D15**.

2. Click the **Home** tab on the Ribbon.

3. In the Styles group, click the **Conditional Formatting** button, and then point to **Data Bars** to display the Data Bars gallery.

4. In the Solid Fill group, click **Blue Data Bar** (the first data bar style). The data bars are added to the selected cells.

5. Click cell **A2** to deselect the sector percentages range. See Figure 4-40.

**Figure 4-40**    **Data bars added to the Sectors worksheet**

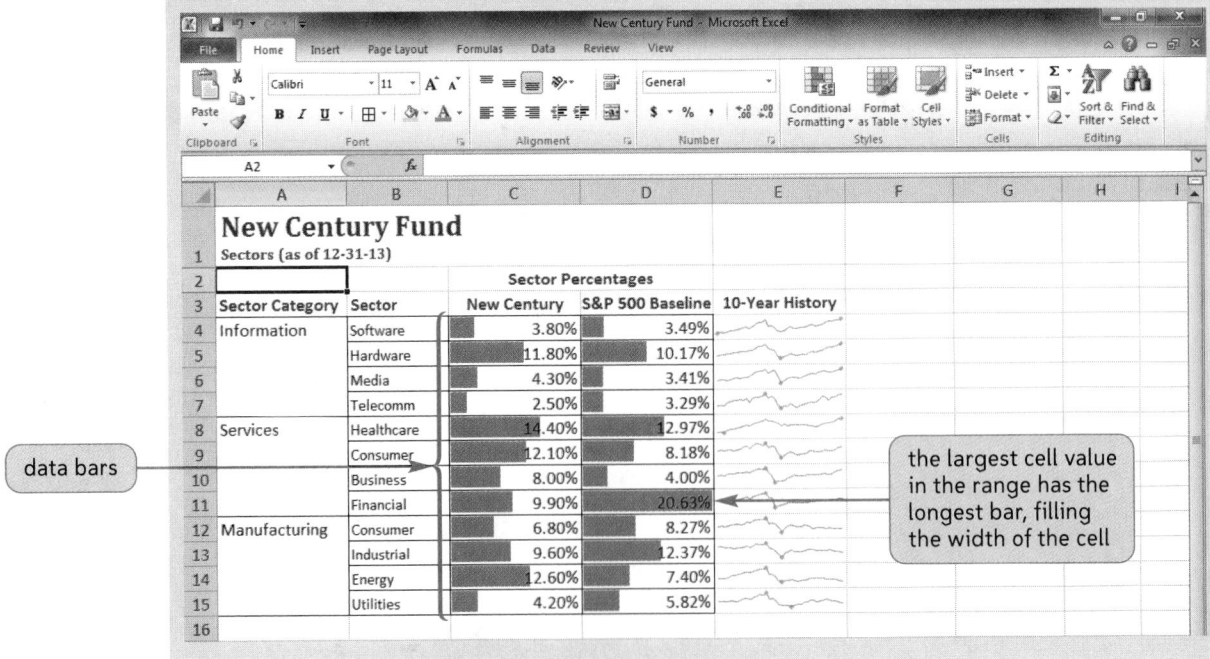

The data bars shown in Figure 4-40 present essentially the same information as the combination column and line chart you created earlier. However, the data bars have the advantage of being compact in size and integrated with the values in the Sector Percentages table.

## Modifying a Data Bar Rule

The lengths of the data bars are determined based on the values in the selected range. The cell with the largest value contains a data bar that extends across the entire width of the cell, and the lengths of the other bars in the selected range are determined relative to that bar. In some cases, this means that the longest data overlaps the cell's data value, making it difficult to read. You can modify the length of the data bars by altering the rules of the conditional format.

In the Sector Percentages data, cell D11 contains the largest value (20.63 percent) in the range C4:D15 and has the longest data bar. The data bar in cell D5, representing 10.17 percent, fills only half the cell width by comparison. Ajita does not want data bars to overlap the cell values. You will modify the data bar rule to proportionally reduce the lengths of the data bars so that the longest of them only fills less than half of a cell rather than an entire cell.

### To modify the data bar rule:

1. Select the range **C4:D15**, which contains the data bars.

2. In the Styles group on the Home tab, click the **Conditional Formatting** button, and then click **Manage Rules**. The Conditional Formatting Rules Manager dialog box opens, displaying all the rules applied to any conditional format in the workbook.

3. Make sure **Current Selection** appears in the Show formatting rules for box. You'll edit the rule applied to the current selection, the data bars in the Sectors worksheet.

4. Click the **Edit Rule** button. The Edit Formatting Rule dialog box opens. You want to modify this rule so that the maximum value for the data bar is set to 0.40, or 40 percent. All data bar lengths will then be defined relative to this value.

5. In the Type row, click the **Maximum** arrow, and then click **Number**.

6. In the Value row, type **0.40** in the Maximum box. See Figure 4-41.

**Figure 4-41**    Edit Formatting Rule dialog box

**Edit Formatting Rule**

**Select a Rule Type:**
▶ Format all cells based on their values
▶ Format only cells that contain
▶ Format only top or bottom ranked values
▶ Format only values that are above or below average
▶ Format only unique or duplicate values
▶ Use a formula to determine which cells to format

**Edit the Rule Description:**

**Format all cells based on their values:**

Format Style: Data Bar  ☐ Show Bar Only → *hides the cell value, showing only the data bar*

*defines the value used for the shortest data bar* →

Minimum          Maximum ← *defines the value used for the longest data bar*

Type: Automatic          Number

Value: (Automatic)          0.4

*sets the fill and border colors of the data bars* →

**Bar Appearance:**

Fill          Color          Border          Color
Solid Fill                    No Border

*click to define how negative values will be presented in the data bars* →

Negative Value and Axis...    Bar Direction: Context

Preview:

OK    Cancel

**7.** Click the **OK** button in each dialog box, and then click cell **A2**. The lengths of the data bars are reduced so that the longest bar covers less than half the cell width. See Figure 4-42.

**Figure 4-42**    Revised data bars

*data bar lengths are expressed relative to a maximum value of 40%*

*the longest data bar covers less than half of the cell and doesn't overlap the cell value*

*Edward Tufte and Chart Design Theory*

Any serious study of chart design will include the works of Edward Tufte, who pioneered the field of information design. One of Tufte's most important works is *The Visual Display of Quantitative Information* in which he laid out several principles for the design of charts and graphics.

Tufte was concerned with what he termed as "chart junk," in which a proliferation of chart elements—chosen because they look "nice"—confuse and distract the reader. One measure of chart junk is Tufte's data-ink ratio, which is the amount of "ink" used to display quantitative information compared to the total ink required by the chart. Tufte advocated limiting the use of non-data ink. Non-data ink is any part of the chart that does not convey information about the data. One way of measuring the data-ink ratio is to determine how much of the chart you can erase without affecting the user's ability to interpret the chart. Tufte would argue for high data-ink ratios with a minimum of extraneous elements and graphics.

To this end, Tufte helped developed sparklines, which convey information with a high data-ink ratio within a compact space. Tufte believed that charts that can be viewed and comprehended at a glance have a greater impact on the reader than large and cluttered graphs, no matter how attractive they might be.

# Creating a Chart Sheet

**TIP**

You can also embed charts in a chart sheet, enabling you to display several charts in a single chart sheet.

Chart sheets are helpful for detailed charts that need more space to be seen clearly or when you want to show a chart without any worksheet text or data. Some reports require large expansive charts rather than compact graphs to provide more detail and make them easier to view and share. In those situations, you may want to devote an entire sheet to a graph rather than embed it within a worksheet. To create a larger version of a chart that covers an entire sheet, you move the chart to a chart sheet. Chart sheets are used for graphic elements like charts and images, and do not contain worksheet cells for calculating numeric values.

Ajita asks you to create a chart sheet for the workbook that shows a 3-D image of the performance of the New Century Fund over the past 10 years. In this case, the chart sheet is purely decorative; Ajita plans to use it as a cover page for the New Century Fund report.

**To create the chart sheet for the New Century Fund report:**

▶ **1.** Go to the **Fund History** worksheet, and then select the range **A4:B44**. This range contains the data you want to use in the chart.

▶ **2.** Click the **Insert** tab on the Ribbon.

▶ **3.** In the Charts group, click the **Line** button, and then click the **3-D Line** chart type. The 3-D line chart is embedded in the Fund History worksheet. You'll move this chart to a chart sheet.

▶ **4.** In the Location group on the Chart Tools Design tab, click the **Move Chart** button. The Move Chart dialog box opens.

▶ **5.** Click the **New sheet** option button, and then type **Cover Sheet** in the box as the name for the new chart sheet.

▶ **6.** Click the **OK** button. A chart sheet named "Cover Sheet" that contains the 3-D line chart is inserted in the workbook.

**7.** Drag the **Cover Sheet** sheet tab to the right of the Documentation sheet tab. The Cover Sheet appears before the Summary Report worksheet and the worksheets that contain the detailed data used to create the summary report. See Figure 4-43.

**Figure 4-43** ▶ **3-D chart in a chart sheet**

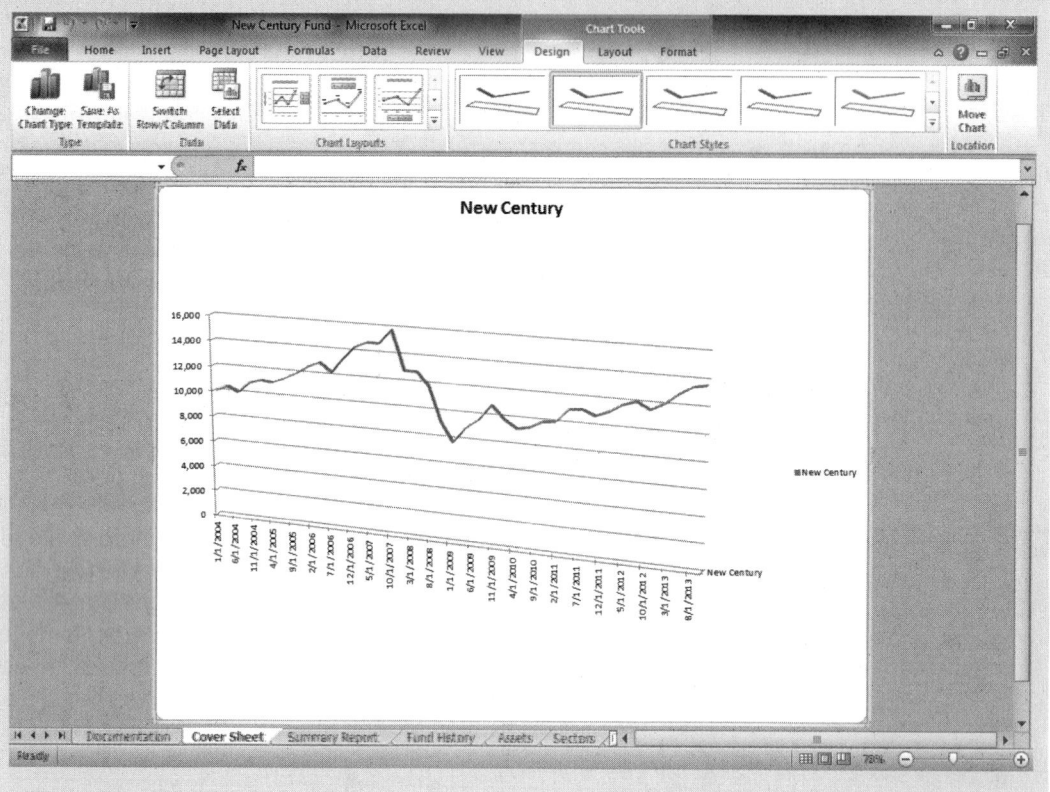

You can format a chart in a chart sheet using all the same options and tools as you do to format a chart embedded in a worksheet. You'll remove the axis labels and legend from the chart and rotate the chart in three dimensions. To increase the 3-D effect, you'll widen the chart's base from 100 to 1000 points.

**To format the chart in the chart sheet:**

**1.** In the Chart Styles group on the Chart Tools Design tab, click the **More** button, and then click **Style 40** (the last style in the fifth row in the Chart Styles gallery).

**2.** Click the **Chart Tools Layout** tab on the Ribbon.

**3.** In the Labels group, click the **Legend** button, and then click **None** to turn off the legend.

**4.** In the Axes group, click the **Axes** button, point to **Primary Horizontal Axis**, and then click **None** to remove the horizontal axis.

**5.** In the Axes group, click the **Axes** button, point to **Primary Vertical Axis**, and then click **None** to remove the vertical axis from the chart.

**6.** In the Axes group, click the **Axes** button, point to **Depth Axis**, and then click **None** to remove the depth axis.

▶ **7.** In the Background section, click the **3-D Rotation** button. The Format Chart Area dialog box opens, displaying the 3-D Rotation options.

▶ **8.** In the Rotation section, change the X value to **60°**, change the Y value to **20°**, and then change the Perspective value to **80°**. These settings rotate the chart.

▶ **9.** In the Chart Scale section, change the Depth (% of base) value to **1000**. This setting exaggerates the 3-D effect, making the chart appear thicker.

▶ **10.** Click **Fill** on the left side of the dialog box, and then click the **Gradient fill** option button. The background color of the chart area is set to a gradient fill.

▶ **11.** Click the **Preset colors** button ▣ ▾, and then click **Daybreak** (the fourth color in the first row).

▶ **12.** Click the **Direction** button ▣ ▾, and then click **Linear Down** (the second direction in the first row).

▶ **13.** Click the **Close** button to return to the chart sheet. See Figure 4-44.

| Figure 4-44 | Rotated 3-D chart with exaggerated perspective |

all axes removed from the chart

Daybreak color fill gradient applied to the chart area background

click to define the rotation and perspective of the 3-D chart

To complete the chart sheet, you'll overlay the chart title "The New Century Fund" over the chart and format it in a 48-point white font.

### To overlay and format the chart title:

▶ **1.** In the Labels group on the Chart Tools Layout tab, click the **Chart Title** button, and then click **Centered Overlay Title**. The chart title is overlaid above the chart. The chart expands to fill the extra space in the chart area.

▶ **2.** Type **The New Century Fund**, and then press the **Enter** key. The new title is entered.

**3.** Click the **Home** tab on the Ribbon, and then change the font size to **36** points and the font color to **white**.

**4.** Click outside of the chart to deselect it. The cover sheet is final. See Figure 4-45.

**Figure 4-45**    **Final cover sheet**

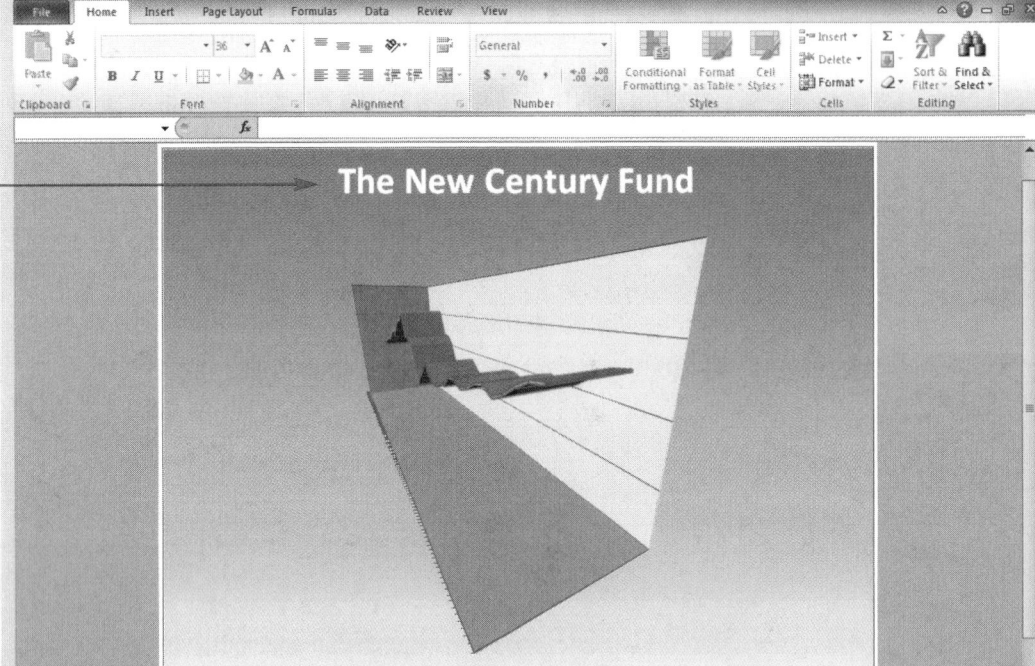

formatted chart title is overlaid above the chart area

**5.** Save the workbook, and then close it.

Ajita is pleased with the work you've done adding charts and graphics to the workbook. She will present the workbook with all of its different charts to her clients to provide them a concise report on the performance of the New Century Fund.

## Session 4.2 Quick Check

**REVIEW**

**1.** When should you use a line chart in place of a column chart?

**2.** How do you overlay a chart legend?

**3.** How do you add a data series to an already existing chart?

**4.** What is a combination chart? Describe how to create a combination chart.

**5.** Explain how 3-D charts can lead to a false interpretation of the data. What can you do to correct this problem?

**6.** What are sparklines? Describe the three types of sparklines.

**7.** What are data bars? Describe how data bars differ from sparklines.

**8.** How do you create a chart sheet?

*Practice the skills you learned in the tutorial using the same case scenario.*

**PRACTICE**

## Review Assignments

**Data File needed for the Review Assignments: Crockett.xlsx**

Ajita has to create a report on the investment portfolio for Brian and Tammy Crockett. She wants to add charts that display where the couple's money is currently being invested and how their portfolio has performed in recent years. She's already entered the data. You will complete the report by adding the charts and a decorative cover sheet. Complete the following:

1. Open the **Crockett** workbook located in the Excel4\Review folder included with your Data Files, and then save the workbook as **Crockett Portfolio**. In the Documentation sheet, enter your name in cell B3 and the date in cell B4.

2. In the Composition worksheet, select the range A3:B8, and then insert the first 2-D pie chart. Move and resize the embedded pie chart to cover the range D1:G9 in the Portfolio Report worksheet.

3. Move the legend to the left side of the chart area. Change the chart title to **Investment Categories** and set its font size to 11 points. Change the fill color of the Cash slice to yellow. Add data labels that show the percentage of each pie slice to two decimal places outside of the pie chart, and then set the font size of the labels to 8 points.

4. Change the pie chart to a 3-D pie chart and set the 3-D rotation of the x-axis to 230° and the y-axis to 40°.

5. In the Sectors worksheet, select the range A3:D15, and then insert a 2-D clustered column chart. Move and resize the embedded chart to cover the range A12:D25 in the Portfolio Report worksheet.

6. Change the font size of the axis labels and legend to 8 points. Insert the chart title **Sector Percentages** above the plot and set its font size to 11 points. Change the format of the percentages in the vertical axis to display no decimal places. Overlay the legend at the top of the chart, and then change its fill color to white and insert a solid border around the legend.

7. Change the chart type of the S&P 500 series to a line chart, remove the line connecting the markers in the chart, and then change the marker type to a solid horizontal line of size 10.

8. Change the fill color of the columns for the Portfolio data series to the theme color Purple, Accent 4, Lighter 60%. Set the gap width of the columns in the Portfolio data series to 30%.

9. In the Portfolio History worksheet, select the range A3:B127, and then insert a line chart. Move and resize the chart to cover the range D29:G37 in the Portfolio Report worksheet. (*Hint*: Scroll down the Portfolio Report worksheet to locate the embedded chart.)

10. Remove the chart legend. Set the font size of the chart title to 11 points, and then set the font size of the axis labels to 8 points.

11. Set the major tick mark interval for the category axis at two years and the minor tick mark interval at one year. Use a custom format that displays the category axis date values as four-digit year values. Insert vertical gridlines for the minor tick marks.

12. Change the scale of the value axis to range from $200,000 to $350,000. Add major tick marks every $50,000. Add minor tick marks every $25,000. Insert horizontal gridlines for every minor tick mark.

13. In cell B32, insert a line sparkline for the data range C4:C127 of the Portfolio History worksheet to describe the growth of the portfolio over consecutive three-month periods. Mark the high point and the low point with green and red markers, respectively.

14. In cell B37, insert a line sparkline for the data range D4:D127 of the Portfolio worksheet to show the growth of the portfolio over consecutive one-year periods. Add high/low data markers and an axis to this sparkline to match the first sparkline.

15. In cell B42, insert a line sparkline showing the growth of the portfolio over con-secutive three-year periods using the data range E4:E127 of the Portfolio worksheet. Format the sparkline to match the other two sparklines.

16. Add solid blue data bars to the values in the range G13:G20. Modify the data bar rule so that the maximum length of the data bar corresponds to a number value of 1.8. Repeat to create data bars for the area values in the range G23:G25.

17. Select the range A3:B127 in the Portfolio History worksheet, and insert a line chart. Move the embedded chart to a new chart sheet named **Cover Sheet**. Move the Cover Sheet worksheet directly after the Documentation sheet.

18. Change the chart style to Style 34 (the second style in the fifth row of the Chart Styles gallery). Remove the display of the horizontal, vertical, and depth axes. Remove the chart legend.

19. For the 3-D rotation, set the x-axis to 60°, the y-axis to 10°, the perspective to 15°, and the depth of the base to 2000.

20. Change the chart title to **Crockett Family Portfolio**. Set the font size of the chart title to 40 points.

21. Save and close your workbook, and then submit the finished workbook to your instructor, either in printed or electronic form, as requested.

**Case Problem 1**

**APPLY**

**Data File needed for this Case Problem: Kenai.xlsx**

**Kenai Fjords National Park**    Maria Sanford is the chief of interpretation at Kenai Fjords National Park. Part of her job is to report on park usage at the visitor centers. She wants to create a chart sheet that displays the park usage data. She has recorded last year's usage data in an Excel workbook. She asks you to present this data in a 3-D column chart for an upcoming meeting with her supervisor. She wants the chart to show the monthly usage totals organized by visitor center. She also wants a 3-D pie chart superim-posed on the column chart and a table of park usage data. Complete the following:

1. Open the **Kenai** workbook located in the Excel4\Case1 folder included with your Data Files, and then save the workbook as **Kenai Fjords Park**. In the Documentation sheet, enter your name in cell B3 and the date in cell B4.

2. In the Park Usage Data worksheet, select the range A3:D15, and then insert the 3-D Column chart (the last chart in the 3-D Column section in the Charts gallery).

3. Move the chart to a chart sheet named **Monthly Visits**. Place the Monthly Visits chart sheet directly after the Documentation sheet.

4. Change the style of the chart to Style 42 (the second style in the sixth row in the Chart Styles gallery).

5. Insert a chart title using the centered overlay title format, change the title to **Kenai Fjords National Park 2013 Census**, and then set its font size to 24 points. Remove the legend from the chart.

6. Add the title **Monthly Visitors** to the vertical axis. Rotate the title 90° and set the font size to 14 points.

7. Rotate the 3-D chart using the following parameters: x-axis rotation 30°, y-axis rotation 20°, perspective 25°, and depth 130. (*Hint*: Uncheck the Right Angle Axes check box in the Chart Scale section to make the Perspective box active.)

⊕ **EXPLORE**    8. Modify the depth axis so that the values are displayed in reverse order. (*Hint*: Use the Axes button in the Axes group on the Chart Tools Layout tab to modify the depth axis.)

⊕ **EXPLORE**    9. Insert a data table without legend keys below the 3-D chart to provide the data val-ues for the different columns. (*Hint*: Use the Data Table button in the Labels group on the Chart Tools Layout tab.)

10. Change the fill color of the Visitor Center series to orange.

11. In the Park Usage Data worksheet, select the range B3:D3;B16:D16, and then insert a 3-D pie chart.

12. Move the embedded chart to the Monthly Visits chart sheet.

13. Insert the chart title **Total Visits** above the pie chart, and set its font size to 16 points and its color to white.

14. Change the color of the Visitor Center slice to orange.

15. Remove the chart legend from the pie chart.

16. Add data labels to the inside of each slice, displaying the slice's value.

17. Change the fill color of the chart area to none (removing the fill color) and change the border color to no line (removing the border). Resize the embedded pie chart and move it to the lower-left of the column chart.

18. Go to the Park Usage Data worksheet, and then add data bars to the range B4:D15. Modify the rule for the data bars so that the maximum data bar length matches a value of 100,000.

19. Save and close your workbook, and then submit the finished workbook to your instructor, either in printed or electronic form, as requested.

*Create a combination chart describing tornado events.*

**APPLY**

## Case Problem 2

**Data Files needed for this Case Problem: Tornado.xlsx, Cloud.jpg**

***Midwest Tornado Institute*** Joyce Bishop is a meteorologist at the Midwest Tornado Institute located in Decatur, Illinois. Joyce is preparing for a talk she is giving to a local civic group on the possible effects of global warming on tornados. She has collected data on minor, moderate, and major tornado sightings in five-year periods during the second half of the twentieth century and wants you to create a graph for her talk showing her data. She's already entered this data into an Excel workbook. Complete the following:

1. Open the **Tornado** workbook located in the Excel4\Case2 folder included with your Data Files, and then save the workbook as **Tornado Sightings**. In the Documentation sheet, enter your name in cell B3 and the date in cell B4.

2. In the Sightings History worksheet, select the range A3:E13, and then insert a 2-D clustered column chart. Move the embedded chart to a chart sheet named **Sightings Chart**.

3. Change the chart style to Style 32 (the last chart style in the fourth row of the Chart Styles gallery).

4. Insert the chart title **Tornado Sightings: 1950–1999** at the top of the chart, and then change the font size to 24 points.

5. Add the vertical axis title **Sightings** in a 14-point font with horizontal orientation. Add the horizontal axis title **Years** in a 14-point font.

6. Move the legend to the bottom of the chart, and then set its font size to 14 points.

**EXPLORE** 7. Change the line style of the horizontal gridline from a solid line to a dashed line. (*Hint*: Use the Dash type button in the Line Style options in the Format Major Gridlines dialog box.)

8. Add vertical gridlines to the major tick marks in the chart. Display the gridlines as dashed lines.

9. Change the chart type of the All data series from a column chart to a 2-D line chart. Change the color of the line to standard blue.

**EXPLORE** 10. Select the plot area and change the fill to a picture fill, using the **Cloud.jpg** file located in the Excel4\Case2 folder included with your Data Files. (*Hint*: Open the Format Plot Area dialog box. In the Fill options, click the Picture or texture fill option button, click the File button, and then locate and select the picture file.)

11. Go to the Sightings History worksheet, and then insert orange data bars in the range B4:D13. Insert blue data bars in the range E4:E13. Note that the meaning of the lengths of the two sets of data bars is different because they are applied to different ranges.

12. In cell B2, insert a sparkline for the data in the range B4:B13 (do *not* include the total in cell B14). Repeat to insert a sparkline in each cell in the range C2:E2.

13. Save and close your workbook, and then submit the finished workbook to your instructor, either in printed or electronic form, as requested.

*Explore how to use Excel to chart stock market data.*

**CHALLENGE**

## Case Problem 3

Data File needed for this Case Problem: Mitchell.xlsx

***Hardin Financial***   Kurt Lee is a financial analyst for Hardin Financial, a consulting firm in Owatonna, Minnesota. As part of his job, he records stock market activity in Excel workbooks. One workbook contains the recent stock market activity of Mitchell Oil. He wants your help in creating a chart displaying the stock values. The chart should display the stock's opening, high, low, and closing values, and the number of shares traded for each day of the past few weeks. The volume of shares traded should be expressed in terms of millions of shares. Complete the following:

1. Open the **Mitchell** workbook located in the Excel4\Case3 folder included with your Data Files, and then save the workbook as **Mitchell Oil**. In the Documentation sheet, enter your name in cell B3 and the date in cell B4.

⊕ EXPLORE   2. In the Stock Values worksheet, select the range A3:F33, and then insert a Volume-Open-High-Low-Close stock chart. (*Hint:* Click the Other Charts button in the Charts group on the Insert tab to locate the stock charts.) Move the embedded chart to the chart sheet named **Stock History**.

3. Insert the chart title **Mitchell Oil** above the chart area, and then set the font size of the chart title to 18 points. Remove the chart legend.

4. Add the title **Date** to the primary horizontal axis, and then set its font size to 14 points. Add the title **Shares Traded** to the primary vertical axis, set its font size to 14 points, and then rotate the title 270°.

⊕ EXPLORE   5. Add the title **Stock Value** to the secondary vertical axis, set its font size to 14 points, and rotate the title 90°. (*Hint:* Open the Format Axis Title dialog box for the secondary vertical axis and use the Text direction button found in the Alignment category.)

6. Set the font size of all axis values to 12 points.

7. Display the horizontal and vertical gridlines using a dashed line style. Set the interval between major tick marks on the primary horizontal axis to 7 days.

8. For the primary vertical axis, display the values in units of one million, change the number format to two decimal place accuracy, and then set the maximum value of the axis scale to 2,000,000.

9. For the secondary vertical axis, set the minimum value of the scale to 10.

10. Decrease the gap width between the columns in the plot to 30% and change the fill color to light blue.

11. Change the fill color of the plot area to light yellow.

⊕ EXPLORE   12. In a stock market chart, the daily chart values will show either an increase or a decrease from the previous day. Increases are shown with an up bar displayed in white and decreases are shown with a down bar displayed in black. Select the data series for the up bars and change their fill colors to light green. Select the data series for the down bars and change their fill colors to red.

⊕ **EXPLORE** 13. Go to the Stock Values worksheet. Add a column sparkline to cell B2 to display the Shares Traded values in the range B4:B33.

14. Add a line sparkline to cell F2 to display the closing values of the stock over the range F4:F33.

15. In the range G3:G33, create a new column of values named **Difference** that is equal to the difference between the stock's closing value and its opening value on each day. Display the difference values using the same format as in column F.

⊕ **EXPLORE** 16. Add a win/loss sparkline to cell G2 that indicates the days that the stock gained value and the days that the stock lost value.

17. Save and close your workbook, and then submit the finished workbook to your instructor, either in printed or electronic form, as requested.

*Create an Excel workbook to provide a report on a sporting event.*

**CREATE**

## Case Problem 4

**Data File needed for this Case Problem: Basketball.xlsx**

***Blowout Sports*** Steve Eagan is the owner and operator of Blowout Sports, a sports information and scouting company located in Lexington, Kentucky. One of Steve's jobs is to provide detailed graphical reports and analysis of college basketball games for the media, coaches, and interested fans. Steve has been placing box score data and game logs into an Excel workbook. He wants to summarize this data in one worksheet using charts and graphs. He's asked you to help develop the workbook. Steve has a sample workbook containing the results of a recent basketball game for you to work on. Complete the following:

1. Open the **Basketball** workbook located in the Excel4\Case4 folder included with your Data Files, and then save the workbook as **Basketball Report**. In the Documentation sheet, enter your name in cell B3 and the date in cell B4.

2. The Game Log worksheet contains the minute-by-minute score of the game. Use the data in this worksheet to create a line chart describing the ebb and flow of the game that is embedded in the Game Report worksheet. The format of the chart is up to you, but it should include titles for the chart and the axes, a chart legend overlay, vertical gridlines spaced at 4-minute intervals, and horizontal gridlines at 5-point intervals. (*Hint*: To display vertical gridlines at 4-minute intervals, you must turn off the multi-level category labels.)

3. The Box Score worksheet contains statistical summaries of the game. Use the data in this worksheet to create two column charts describing the points scored by each player on the two teams. Embed the charts in the Game Report worksheet. The format of the charts is up to you, but it should include titles for the chart and axes, and gradient fill colors for the columns.

4. The Box Score worksheet also contains team statistics. Use this data to create several pie charts that compare the two teams. Embed the pie charts in the Game Report worksheet. The final pie charts should include data labels for the pie slices and slice colors that match the team's colors (red for Wisconsin, gold for Iowa).

5. The Season Record worksheet contains a record of each team's season including wins and losses. Use this data to create a win/loss sparkline displayed on the Game Report worksheet alongside each team's season record.

6. Create a chart sheet for the report that will be a cover sheet. The cover sheet should include a 3-D chart of some of the data in the workbook. The format of the chart and chart sheet is up to you.

7. Save and close your workbook, and then submit the finished workbook to your instructor, either in printed or electronic form, as requested.

### SAM: Skills Assessment Manager

For current SAM information, including versions and content details, visit SAM Central (http://samcentral.course.com). If you have a SAM user profile, you may have access to hands-on instruction, practice, and assessment of the skills covered in this tutorial. Since various versions of SAM are supported throughout the life of this text, check with your instructor for the correct instructions and URL/Web site for accessing assignments.

**ENDING DATA FILES**

Decision Making

# Creating a Budget Worksheet to Make Financial Decisions

Decision making is the process of choosing between alternative courses of action, usually in response to a problem that needs to be solved. Having an understanding of decision-making processes will lead to better decisions and greater confidence in carrying out those decisions. This is especially important when making financial decisions.

## Gather Relevant Information

Begin by collecting data and information related to the decision you need to make. This information can include data expressed as currency or numbers, as well as data that cannot be measured numerically. For example, when creating a budget, numerical data includes your income and expenses, current savings, future savings and purchases, and so on. Other data might include the amount of savings you need to feel comfortable before making a large purchase, such as buying a car or paying tuition.

## Evaluate the Gathered Information and Develop Alternatives

Evaluate the data you collected and determine potential alternatives. Excel workbooks are well suited to evaluating numerical data. You can also use workbooks to evaluate potential outcomes based on other data by assigning numerical weights to them. For example, you can enter your monthly income and fixed expenses into a worksheet along with variable expenses to determine your cash flow. You can then consider this information along with your current savings to determine how much money to contribute to savings or earmark for a purchase. Based on these results, you can develop alternatives for how to distribute your available money among variable expenses (such as entertainment), savings, and a large purchase.

## Select the Best Alternative

Carefully evaluate the alternatives you developed based on your analysis. Before making a decision, be sure to take into account all factors. Consider such questions as:

- Does this alternative make sense for the long term? For example, does this budget allow you to achieve all your financial goals?
- Can you realistically carry out this alternative? For example, does this budget provide enough for necessities such as food and housing as well as for luxuries such as entertainment?
- Will this alternative be acceptable even if its outcome is not perfect or some unconsidered factors emerge? For example, will this budget cover unforeseen expenses such as car repair or an unexpected trip?
- How comfortable are you with this decision? For example, does this budget relieve or add stress about managing your finances?

After analyzing all the factors, one alternative should begin to emerge as the best alternative. If it doesn't, you might need to develop additional alternatives.

ProSkills

# Prepare an Action Plan

After making a decision, you need to plan how to implement that decision. Consider what steps you need to take to achieve the final outcome. For example, do you need to open a bank account or change services to reduce expenses (such as switching to a less expensive cell phone plan)? Determine a reasonable time table. When do you want start? How long will each task take? What tasks must be completed before others start? Can tasks be performed at the same time? Develop milestones to track the success of your plan. For example, one milestone might be to see your savings increase by 10 percent in three months. Finally, identify what resources you need to be successful. For example, do you need to talk to a financial advisor at your bank?

# Take Action and Monitor the Results

After you develop the action plan, the actual plan begins. For example, you can open bank accounts, change telephone services, and so forth as outlined in your action plan. Be sure to check off completed tasks and assess how well those actions produce the desired outcome. For example, is the budget achieving the financial goals you set? If so, then continue to follow the established plan. If not, you may need to modify the action plan or reevaluate your decision.

**PROSKILLS**

## Develop a Budget Worksheet

Excel is valuable to a wide audience of users: from accountants of *Fortune 500* companies to homeowners managing their budgets. An Excel workbook can be a complex document, recording data from thousands of financial transactions, or it can track a few monthly household expenses. Anyone who has to balance a budget, track expenses, or project future income can use the financial tools in Excel to help them make good financial decisions about their financing and future expenditures.

In this exercise, you will use Excel to create a sample budget workbook that will contain information of your choice, using Excel skills and features presented in Tutorials 1 through 4. Use the following steps as a guide to completing your workbook.

**Note:** Please be sure *not* to include any personal information of a sensitive nature in any workbooks you create to be submitted to your instructor for this exercise. Later, you can update the workbooks with such information for your personal use.

1. Gather the data related to your monthly cash inflows and outflows. For example, how much do you take home in your paychecks each month? What other sources of income do you have? What expenses do you have—rent, utilities, gas, insurance, groceries, entertainment, car payments, and so on?

2. Create a new workbook for the sample financial data. Use the first worksheet as a documentation sheet that includes your name, the date on which you start creating the workbook, and a brief description of the workbook's purpose.

3. Plan the structure of the second worksheet, which will contain the budget. Include a section to enter values that remain consistent from month to month, such as monthly income and expenses. As you develop the budget worksheet, reference these cells in formulas that require those values. Later, you can update any of these values and see the changes immediately reflected throughout the budget.

ProSkills

4. In the budget worksheet, enter realistic monthly earnings for each month of the year. Use formulas to calculate the total earnings each month, the average monthly earnings, and the total earnings for the entire year.

5. In the budget worksheet, enter realistic personal expenses for each month. Divide the expenses into at least three categories, providing subtotals for each category and a grand total of all the monthly expenses. Calculate the average monthly expenses and total expenses for the year.

6. Calculate the monthly net cash flow (the value of total income minus total expenses).

7. Use the cash flow values to track the savings throughout the year. Use a realistic amount for savings at the beginning of the year. Use the monthly net cash flow values to add or subtract from this value. Project the end-of-year balance in the savings account under your proposed budget.

8. Format the worksheet's contents using appropriate text and number formats. Add colors and line borders to make the content easier to read and interpret. Use cell styles and themes to provide your worksheet with a uniform appearance.

9. Use conditional formatting to automatically highlight negative net cash flow months.

10. Insert a pie chart that compares the monthly expenses for the categories.

11. Insert a column chart that charts all of the monthly expenses regardless of the category.

12. Insert a line chart or sparkline that shows the change in the savings balance throughout the 12 months of the year.

13. Insert new rows at the top of the worksheet and enter titles that describe the worksheet's contents.

14. Examine your assumptions. How likely are certain events to occur? Perform several what-if analyses on your budget, providing the impact of (a) reducing income with expenses remaining constant, (b) increasing expenses with income remaining constant, (c) reducing income and expenses, and (d) increasing income and expenses. Discuss the different scenarios you explored. How much cushion does your projected income give you if expenses increase? What are some things you can do in your budget to accommodate this scenario?

15. Think of a major purchase you might want to make—for example, a car or a computer. Determine the amount of the purchase and the current annual interest rate charged by your local bank. Provide a reasonable length of time to repay the loan, such as five years for a car loan or 20 to 30 years for a home loan. Use the PMT function to determine how much you would have to spend each month on the payments for your purchase. You can do these calculations in a separate worksheet

16. Add the loan information to your monthly budget and evaluate the purchase of this item on your budget. Is it affordable? Examine other possible loans you might pursue and evaluate their impact on your budget. Come up with the most realistic way of paying off the loan while still maintaining a reasonable monthly cash flow and a cushion against unexpected expenses. If the payment exceeds your budget, reduce the estimated price of the item you're thinking of purchasing until you determine the monthly payment you can afford under the conditions of the loan.

17. After settling on a budget and the terms of a loan that you can afford, develop an action plan for putting your budget into place. What are some potential pitfalls that will prohibit you from following through on your proposed budget? How can you increase the likelihood that you will follow the budget? Be specific, and write down a list of goals and benchmarks that you'll use to monitor your progress in following your financial plan.

18. With the worksheet set up and your budget in place, you can take action and monitor your results. You will want to update your worksheet each month as income or expense items change to be sure you remain on track to meet your goals. You will also want to confirm that you made a good decision. If not, evaluate your budget and determine what new action you need to take to get yourself back on track.

19. Format the worksheets for your printer. Include headers and footers that display the workbook filename, the workbook's author, and the date on which the report is printed. If the report extends across several pages, repeat appropriate print titles on all of the pages and include page numbers and the total number of pages on every printed page.

20. Save and close your workbook, and then submit the completed workbook to your instructor, in printed or electronic form, as requested.

TUTORIAL 5

## OBJECTIVES

**Session 5.1**
- Explore a structured range of data
- Freeze rows and columns
- Plan and create an Excel table
- Rename and format an Excel table
- Add, edit, and delete records in an Excel table
- Sort data

**Session 5.2**
- Filter data
- Insert a Total row to summarize an Excel table
- Split a worksheet into two panes
- Insert subtotals into a range of data
- Use the Outline buttons to show or hide details

**Session 5.3**
- Create and modify a PivotTable
- Apply PivotTable styles and formatting
- Filter and sort a PivotTable
- Insert a slicer to filter a PivotTable
- Group PivotTable items
- Create a PivotChart

# Working with Excel Tables, PivotTables, and PivotCharts

*Tracking Museum Art Objects*

## Case | LaFouch Museum

Henry LaFouch, a rancher in Missoula, Montana, amassed a huge collection of North American art, particularly art of the West. Henry was a well-respected, active member of the community, and he often donated art to the town. Similarly, he loaned the town artwork to place in public locations and community centers. Upon his death, Henry donated his art collection to the town of Missoula and its people. They established an art museum in his name.

Mary Littlefield was recently hired as the curator and director of the LaFouch Museum. She is responsible for assessing the current holdings and using the endowment set aside by Henry to purchase additional art in keeping with his vision for the collection. One of Mary's first tasks was to establish an accurate inventory of the museum's holdings. For each piece of artwork, she identified the title, the artist, the date acquired, the type of art, and other pertinent facts such as its location in the museum, its condition, and its appraised value. Then, she entered all this data in an Excel worksheet.

You will help Mary maintain this data so she can provide current and accurate information to the administration and board of directors about the art objects. You'll work with the data using Excel table features. You will sort the data and add, modify, and delete the data to ensure it is current. You'll also filter the information to display only data that meets certain criteria. Finally, you'll summarize the data using a PivotTable and a PivotChart.

## STARTING DATA FILES

| Excel5 → | Tutorial | Review | Case1 | Case2 | Case3 | Case4 |
|---|---|---|---|---|---|---|
| | Museum.xlsx | Art.xlsx | Pledges.xlsx | Ring.xlsx | CustLoans.xlsx | Bowls.xlsx |

# SESSION 5.1 VISUAL OVERVIEW

Every Excel table has a table name, which you can change to a descriptive name.

Each column represents a **field**, which describes some characteristic of a person, place, or thing such as a last name, address, city, or state.

The first row of the range contains field names called the **header row**. Although the header row often is row 1, it can begin in any row.

Each row represents a **record**, which is a collection of related fields that are grouped together.

You can rearrange, or **sort**, the records in a table or range based on one or more fields.

LaFouch Museum - Microsoft Excel

Table Name: ArtObjects

| | A | B | C | D |
|---|---|---|---|---|
| 1 | ArtID | Artist | Title | Date Acquired |
| 2 | 21 | Aserty | Bead Wall | 9/10/2007 |
| 3 | 83 | Roman | Untitled | 9/17/2008 |
| 4 | 13 | Aserty | Superstitions | 3/10/2012 |
| 5 | 53 | Bindner | Blue Eyed Indian | 1/10/2012 |
| 6 | 66 | Waid | Untitled (still life) | 4/13/2011 |
| 7 | 4 | Roman | Seeking Shelter | 8/8/2008 |
| 8 | 104 | Acconci | Trail End | 9/10/2006 |
| 9 | 55 | Budd | Starlit Evening | 1/10/2007 |
| 10 | 97 | Cardenas | Ceremonial Sticks | 7/23/2007 |
| 11 | 103 | Cox | Crying Hats | 7/11/2007 |
| 12 | 59 | Dawson | Dwelling | 3/16/2007 |
| 13 | 5 | DiGrigoro | The Hang | 7/16/2007 |
| 14 | 110 | Fratt | Friends | 10/18/2007 |
| 15 | 72 | Garin | Funnel | 5/18/2007 |
| 16 | 113 | Gonzales | Dark Canyon | 3/16/2007 |
| 17 | 41 | Hamend | Night Version | 1/16/2007 |
| 18 | 29 | Hofmann | Horseshoe Falls | 8/16/2007 |
| 19 | 31 | Ingraham | Inside/Out | 12/16/2007 |

# AN EXCEL TABLE

Table styles provide a way to quickly format an entire table using a preset style definition.

A **field name**, or **column header**, is a unique label that describes the contents of the data in a column.

The filter arrow changes to a sort icon as a reminder that the data is sorted by that field.

You can click a filter arrow to sort the table by data in that column.

An Excel table is a range of related data that is managed independently from data in other rows and columns in the worksheet.

The fields that you use to order data are called **sort fields**. This data is sorted by Location, the sort field.

You can create a custom list to sort data in the order you specify, such as art objects by their condition rankings: Excellent, Good, Fair, and Poor.

| Category | Condition | Location | Appraised Value |
|----------|-----------|----------|-----------------|
| Installation | Excellent | Courtyard | $ 14,000 |
| Installation | Good | Courtyard | $ 2,500 |
| Painting | Excellent | Courtyard | $ 78,000 |
| Painting | Excellent | Courtyard | $ 40,000 |
| Painting | Excellent | Courtyard | $ 19,500 |
| Sculpture | Excellent | Courtyard | $ 52,000 |
| Painting | Excellent | East Pavilion | $ 8,000 |
| Painting | Excellent | East Pavilion | $ 9,500 |
| Painting | Excellent | East Pavilion | $ 15,000 |
| Painting | Excellent | East Pavilion | $ 10,000 |
| Painting | Excellent | East Pavilion | $ 16,000 |
| Painting | Excellent | East Pavilion | $ 8,000 |
| Painting | Excellent | East Pavilion | $ 16,000 |
| Painting | Excellent | East Pavilion | $ 4,500 |
| Painting | Excellent | East Pavilion | $ 8,000 |
| Painting | Excellent | East Pavilion | $ 3,800 |
| Painting | Excellent | East Pavilion | $ 15,000 |
| Painting | Excellent | East Pavilion | $ 3,500 |

# Planning a Structured Range of Data

One of the more common uses of a worksheet is to manage data, such as lists of clients, products, and transactions. Using Excel, you can store and update data, sort data, search for and retrieve subsets of data, summarize data, and create reports. In Excel, a collection of similar data can be structured in a range of columns and rows, representing fields and records, respectively.

Figure 5-1 shows a portion of the data Mary compiled for the LaFouch Museum's art objects. In this data, the ArtID, Artist, and Title columns are the first three fields. Each row is a record that stores the data for each art object—art ID, artist name, title, date acquired, category, condition, location, and appraised value. All the art object records make up the *structured range of data*. A structured range of data is commonly referred to as a list or table.

| Figure 5-1 | LaFouch Museum art objects data |
| --- | --- |

## Decision Making: The Importance of Planning

Before you create a structured range of data, be sure to create a plan. Planning involves gathering relevant information about the data and deciding your goals. The end results you want to achieve will help you determine the kind of data to include in each record and how to divide that data into fields. Specifically, do the following to create an effective plan:

- Spend time thinking about how you will use the data.
- Consider what reports you want to create for different audiences (supervisors, customers, directors, and so forth) and the fields needed to produce those reports.
- Think about the various questions, or *queries*, you want answered and the fields needed to create these results.

Careful and thorough planning will help you avoid having to redesign a structured range of data later.

Before creating the list of art objects, Mary carefully planned what information she needs and how she wants to use it. Mary plans to use the data to track where each art object is located in the museum, its condition, the date it was acquired, its art category, and its appraised value. She wants to be able to create reports that show specific lists of art objects, such as all the objects by a specific artist or all the objects that are paintings. Based on her needs, Mary developed a **data definition table**, which is documentation that lists the fields to be maintained for each record (in this case, each art object) and a description of the information each field will include. Figure 5-2 shows Mary's completed data definition table.

| Figure 5-2 | Data definition table for the art objects |
|---|---|

| Field | Description |
|---|---|
| ArtID | Unique number |
| Artist | Name of artist |
| Title | Title of art object |
| Date Acquired | Date of purchase or donation of art object |
| Category | Painting, Sculpture, Installation, Textile |
| Condition | Excellent, Good, Fair, Poor |
| Location | Location of art object |
| Appraised Value | Current value of art object |

After you determine the fields and records you need, you can enter the data in a blank worksheet or use a range of data that is already entered in a worksheet. You can then work with the data in many ways, including the following common operations:

- Add, edit, and delete data in the range.
- Sort the data range.
- Filter to display only rows that meet specified criteria.
- Insert formulas to calculate subtotals.
- Create summary tables based on the data in the range (usually with PivotTables).

You'll perform many of these operations on the art objects data.

You'll open the workbook in which Mary entered the art objects data according to the data definition table.

## To open and review the Museum workbook:

1. Open the **Museum** workbook located in the Excel5\Tutorial folder included with your Data Files, and then save the workbook as **LaFouch Museum**.

2. In the Documentation sheet, enter your name in cell B3 and the date in cell B4.

▶ **3.** Switch to the **Art Collection** worksheet. This worksheet (which was shown in Figure 5-1) contains data about the museum's art objects. Currently, the worksheet lists 115 art objects. Each art object record is a separate row (rows 2 through 116) and contains eight fields (columns A through H). The top row, the header row, contains labels that describe the data in each column.

▶ **4.** Scroll the worksheet to row **116**, the last record. The column headers, in the top row, are no longer visible.

▶ **5.** Press the **Ctrl+Home** keys to return to cell A1.

## Freezing Rows and Columns

You want to see the column headers as you scroll the art objects data. Without the column headers visible, it is difficult to know what the data entered in each column represents. You can select rows and columns to remain visible in the workbook window as you scroll around the worksheet. **Freezing** a row or column lets you keep headings visible as you work with the data in a large worksheet. As you scroll the data, the first row remains on the screen so the column headers are visible, making it easier to identify the data in each record.

You'll freeze the first row, which contains the column headers.

### To freeze the top row in the worksheet:

▶ **1.** Click the **View** tab on the Ribbon. The Ribbon displays the View options.

▶ **2.** In the Window group, click the **Freeze Panes** button, and then click **Freeze Top Row**. A dark, horizontal line appears below the column headers to indicate which row is frozen.

▶ **3.** Scroll the worksheet to row **99**. This time, the column headers remain visible as you scroll. See Figure 5-3.

| Figure 5-3 | Top row of the worksheet is frozen |

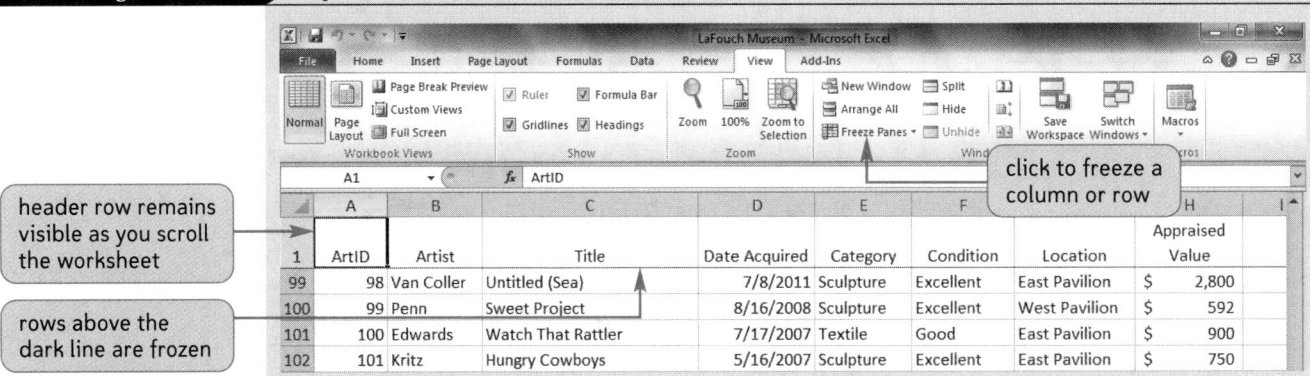

header row remains visible as you scroll the worksheet

rows above the dark line are frozen

click to freeze a column or row

▶ **4.** Press the **Ctrl+Home** keys to return to cell A2, the cell directly below the frozen row.

After you freeze panes, the first option on the Freeze Panes menu changes to Unfreeze Panes. This option releases the frozen headers, which means that all the columns and rows in worksheet shift when you scroll the worksheet. You will use a different method to keep the column headers visible, so you will unfreeze the top row of the worksheet.

**To unfreeze the top row of the worksheet:**

▶ **1.** In the Window group on the View tab, click the **Freeze Panes** button. The first Freeze Panes option is now Unfreeze Panes.

▶ **2.** Click **Unfreeze Panes**. The headers are no longer frozen and the dark, horizontal line below the column headers is removed. You can now scroll all the rows and columns in the worksheet.

# Creating an Excel Table

You can convert a structured range of data, such as the art objects data in the range A1:H116, to an Excel table. An Excel table makes it easier to identify, manage, and analyze the groups of related data. You can create more than one Excel table in a worksheet. Although you can perform all of the tasks in this section without creating an Excel table, there are many advantages to creating a table rather than leaving the art collection data as a range of data.

*Saving Time with Excel Table Features*

Excel tables provide many advantages to structured ranges of data. When you create an Excel table, you can perform the same operations as you can for a structured range of data. In addition, you can use Excel tables to do the following to be more productive and reduce the chance of error:

- Format the Excel table quickly using a table style.
- Add new rows and columns to the Excel table that automatically expand the range.
- Add a Total row to calculate the summary function you select, such as SUM, AVERAGE, COUNT, MIN, and MAX.
- Enter a formula in one table cell that is automatically copied to all other cells in that table column.
- Create formulas that reference cells in a table by using table and column names instead of cell addresses.

These Excel table features let you focus on analyzing and understanding the data, leaving the more time-consuming tasks for the program to perform.

Next, you'll create an Excel table from the art objects data in the Art Collection worksheet. By doing so, you'll be able to take advantage of the many features and tools for working with Excel tables to analyze data effectively.

**To create an Excel table from the art objects data:**

▶ **1.** Verify that the active cell is cell **A2**, which is in the range of art objects data.

▶ **2.** Click the **Insert** tab on the Ribbon. The Ribbon displays the Insert options.

▶ **3.** In the Tables group, click the **Table** button. The Create Table dialog box opens. The range of data for the table is entered in the dialog box.

**4.** Click the **OK** button. The dialog box closes, and the range of data is converted to an Excel table. Filter arrows appear in the header row, the table is formatted with a predefined table style, and the Table Tools Design contextual tab appears on the Ribbon. See Figure 5-4.

| Figure 5-4 | Excel table created for the art objects data |

contextual tab appears on the Ribbon

table style applied

filter arrows appear in the header row

**5.** Scroll the table down. The text of the header row replaces the standard lettered column headings (A, B, C, and so on) as you scroll so that you don't need to freeze panes to keep the header row visible. See Figure 5-5.

| Figure 5-5 | Art objects table scrolled |

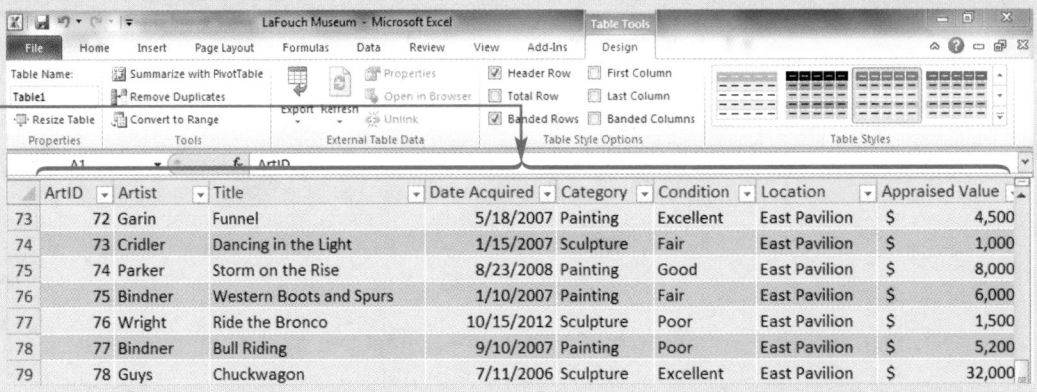

header row replaces the letters in the column headers

**6.** Press the **Ctrl+Home** keys to make cell A1 active. The column headings return to the standard display, and the header row scrolls back into view as row 1.

## Renaming an Excel Table

Excel assigns the name Table1 to the first Excel table created in a workbook. Any additional Excel tables you create in the workbook are named consecutively, Table2, Table3, and so forth. You can assign a more descriptive name to a table, making it easier to identify a particular table by its content. Descriptive names are especially useful when you create more than one Excel table in the same workbook. Table names must start with a letter or an underscore and can use any combination of letters, numbers, and underscores for the rest of the name. Table names cannot include spaces.

You will change the name of the Excel table you just created from the art objects data.

**To rename the Table1 table:**

▶ **1.** In the Properties group on the Design tab, select **Table1** in the Table Name box. See Figure 5-6.

| Figure 5-6 | Table Name box |

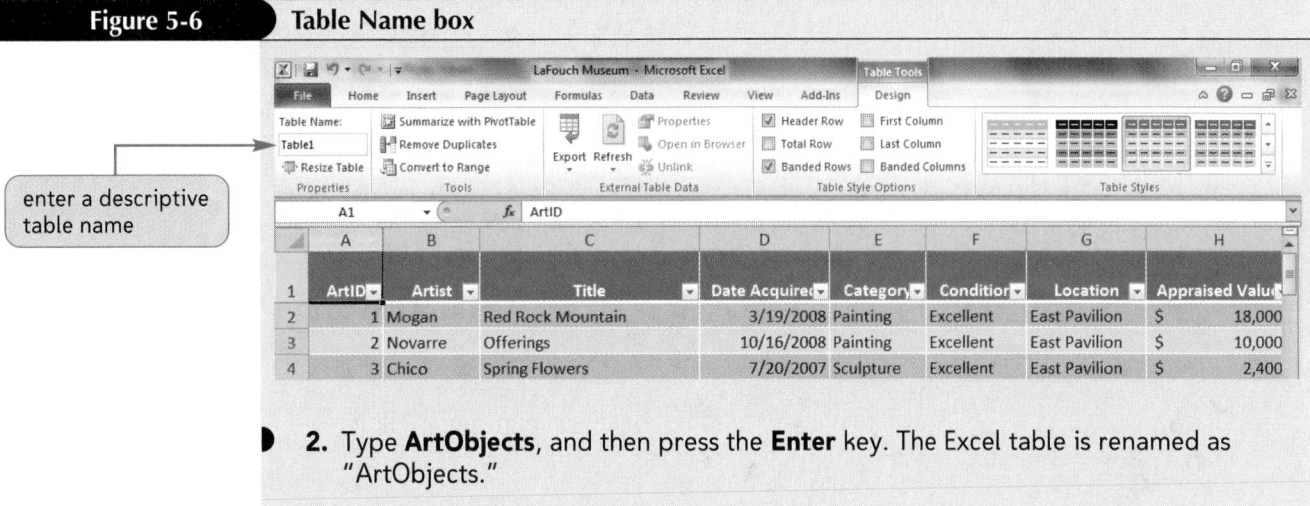

enter a descriptive table name

▶ **2.** Type **ArtObjects**, and then press the **Enter** key. The Excel table is renamed as "ArtObjects."

## Formatting an Excel Table

The check boxes in the Table Style Options group on the Design tab enable you to quickly and easily add or remove table elements or change the table's formatting. For example, you can display or hide the header row and select whether to format the table with banded rows, banded columns, or neither. You can also apply a table style.

You will format the table by selecting which table style options are applied to the Excel table.

**To format the ArtObjects table:**

▶ **1.** In the Table Style group on the Table Tools Design tab, click the **More** button ⏷. A gallery of table styles opens.

▶ **2.** In the Table Styles gallery, click **Table Style Medium 4**. The table now has a green theme.

▶ **3.** Change the width of column D to **12** characters. The width of the Date Acquired column better fits the dates.

▶ **4.** Change the width of columns E, F, and H to **12** characters.

▶ **5.** If cell A1 is not already the active cell, click cell **A1**.

## Maintaining Data in an Excel Table

Mary has several changes you need to make to the data in the ArtObjects table. First, the museum acquired a new painting and received a sculpture from an anonymous donor; both art objects need to be added to the table. Second, the condition of the Moonlight painting has deteriorated and requires repairs; its condition needs to be changed from "Fair" to "Poor." Finally, one of the paintings has been sold to raise money for new acquisitions; the record for this art object needs to be deleted from the table. You will update the ArtObjects table to reflect these changes.

# Adding Records

As you maintain data in an Excel table, you often need to add new records. You add a record to an Excel table in a blank row. The simplest and most convenient way to add a record to an Excel table is to enter the data in the first blank row below the last record. You can then sort the data to arrange the table in the order you want. If you want the record in a specific location, you can also insert a row within the table for the new record.

### Adding a Record to an Excel Table

- Click in the row below the last row of the Excel table.
- Type the values for the new record, pressing the Tab key to move from field to field.
- Press the Tab key to create another new record.

  *or*

  Press the Enter key if this is the last record.

Next, you'll add records for the new painting and sculpture to the ArtObjects table.

### To add two records to the ArtObjects table:

1. Press the **End+↓** keys to make cell A116 the active cell. This cell is in the last row of the table.

2. Press the **↓** key to move the active cell to cell A117. This is the first blank row below the table.

3. In cell A117, type **116**, and then press the **Tab** key. Cell B117 in the Artist column becomes the active cell. The table expands to include a new row in the table structure with the same formatting as the rest of the table. The AutoCorrect Options button appears so you can undo the table formatting if you hadn't intended the new data to be part of the existing table. The sizing handle in the lower-right corner of the table indicates the last row and column in the table. You can use the sizing handle to add columns or rows to the Excel table to expand it, or remove them to make the table smaller. See Figure 5-7.

**Figure 5-7** New row added to the ArtObjects table

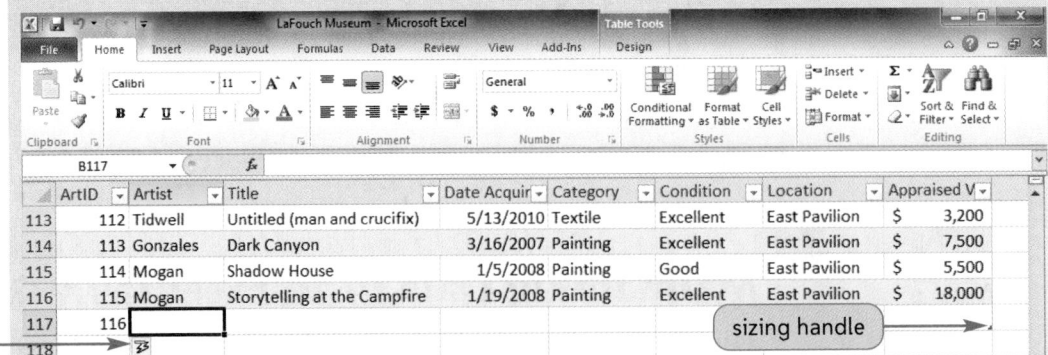

**Trouble?** If cell A118 is the active cell, you probably pressed the Enter key instead of the Tab key. Click cell B117 and then continue entering the data in Step 4.

**TIP**

As you type in a cell, AutoComplete displays any existing entry in the column that matches the characters you typed. Press the Tab key to accept the entry; continue typing to replace it.

4. In the range B117:H117, enter **Giama** for the artist, **Starry Night** for the title, **4/3/2013** for the date acquired, **Painting** for the category, **Excellent** for the condition, **South Pavilion** for the location, and **8500** for the appraised value, pressing the **Tab** key after each entry. Cell A118 becomes the active cell and the table expands to incorporate row 118.

5. In the range A118:H118, enter **117** for the art ID, **Higgins** for the artist, **Apache Warrior** for the title, **4/5/2013** for the date acquired, **Sculpture** for the category, **Excellent** for the condition, **Garden** for the location, and **23000** for the appraised value, press the **Enter** key, and then click cell **A119** after the last entry. The record for the sculpture is added to the table. See Figure 5-8.

**Figure 5-8**    **Records added to the ArtObjects table**

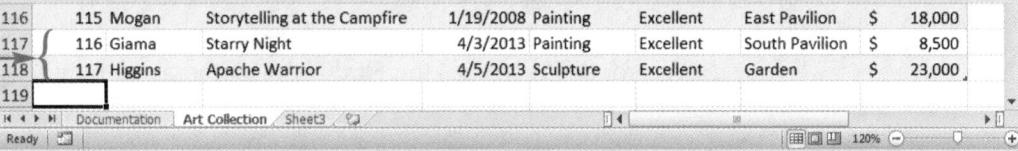

two new records

| 116 | 115 | Mogan | Storytelling at the Campfire | 1/19/2008 | Painting | Excellent | East Pavilion | $ | 18,000 |
| 117 | 116 | Giama | Starry Night | 4/3/2013 | Painting | Excellent | South Pavilion | $ | 8,500 |
| 118 | 117 | Higgins | Apache Warrior | 4/5/2013 | Sculpture | Excellent | Garden | $ | 23,000 |
| 119 | | | | | | | | | |

H ◀ ▶ H   Documentation   Art Collection   Sheet3   ⏎

Ready 🔲                                                           ⊞ ▣ ▥ 120% ⊖ ⸺ ⊕

**Trouble?**  If a new row is added to the table, you probably pressed the Tab key instead of the Enter key after the last entry in the record. On the Quick Access Toolbar, click the Undo button 🔄 to remove the extra row.

## Finding and Editing Records

You need to update the condition for the art object with the title "Moonlight." Although you can manually scroll through the table to find a specific record, a quicker and more accurate way to locate a record is to use the Find command. You edit the data in a field the same way as you edit data in a worksheet cell. You'll use the Find command to locate the record for the Moonlight painting, which has deteriorated to poor condition. Then, you'll edit the record in the table to change the condition to "Poor."

### To find and edit the record for the Moonlight painting:

1. Press the **Ctrl+Home** keys to move to the top of the worksheet, and then click cell **C2** to make it the active cell.

2. In the Editing group on the Home tab, click the **Find & Select** button, and then click **Find**. The Find and Replace dialog box opens.

3. Type **Moonlight** in the Find what box, and then click the **Find Next** button. Cell C69, which contains the title "Moonlight," is selected. This is the record you want. If it wasn't, you would click the Find Next button again to display the next record that meets the search criteria.

4. Click the **Close** button. The Find and Replace dialog box closes.

5. Press the **Tab** key three times to move the active cell to the Condition column, and then type **P**. AutoComplete displays "Poor" in the cell, which is the condition text you want to enter.

6. Press the **Tab** key to enter the AutoComplete entry. The painting's condition is changed in the table.

7. Press the **Ctrl+Home** keys to make cell A1 active.

## Deleting a Record

The final update you need to make to the ArtObjects table is to delete the record for the Trappers painting (ArtID 90), which was sold. You'll use the Find command to locate the painting's record. Then, you'll delete the record from the table.

**To find and delete the Trappers painting record:**

1. In the Editing group on the Home tab, click the **Find & Select** button, and then click **Find**. The Find and Replace dialog box opens.

2. Type **90** in the Find what box, and then click the **Find Next** button. Because Excel searches the entire worksheet (not just the current column), and because it finds the search value even if it is part of another value, the appraised value $1,900 is selected. This is not the record you want to delete.

3. Click the **Find Next** button to highlight the appraised value $1,900 for a different record, and then click the **Find Next** button again to highlight the value 90 in the ArtID column. This is the record you need to delete.

4. Click the **Close** button. The Find and Replace dialog box closes.

5. In the Cells group on the Home tab, click the **Delete button arrow**, and then click **Delete Table Rows**. The record for the Trappers painting is deleted from the table.

   **Trouble?** If a different record was deleted, the active cell was not in the record for the Trappers painting. On the Quick Access Toolbar, click the Undo button to restore the record, and then repeat Steps 1 through 5.

6. Press the **Ctrl+Home** keys to make cell A1 active.

# Sorting Data

The records in the ArtObjects table appear in the order that Mary entered them. As you work, however, you'll want to view the same records in a different order, such as by the artist name or by the art object's location in the museum. For example, if you want to arrange the art objects by artist name, you can sort the data using the Artist column as the sort field.

You can sort data in ascending or descending order. **Ascending order** arranges text alphabetically from A to Z, numbers from smallest to largest, and dates from oldest to newest. **Descending order** arranges text in reverse alphabetical order from Z to A, numbers from largest to smallest, and dates from newest to oldest. In both ascending and descending order, blank fields are placed at the end of the table.

## Sorting One Column Using the Sort Buttons

You can quickly sort data with one sort field using the Sort A to Z button or the Sort Z to A button. Mary wants you to sort the art objects in ascending order by the artist. This will rearrange the table data so that the records appear in alphabetical order by the artist name.

**To sort the ArtObjects table in ascending order by the artist name:**

1. Click any cell in the Artist column. You do not need to select the entire ArtObjects table, which consists of the range A1:H117. Excel determines the table's range when you click any cell in the table.

2. Click the **Data** tab on the Ribbon. The Data options appear on the Ribbon.

**3.** In the Sort & Filter group, click the **Sort A to Z** button $\boxed{\text{A↓}}$. The data is sorted in ascending order by Artist. The Artist filter arrow indicates the data is sorted by that column. See Figure 5-9.

| Figure 5-9 | ArtObjects table sorted by Artist |
|---|---|

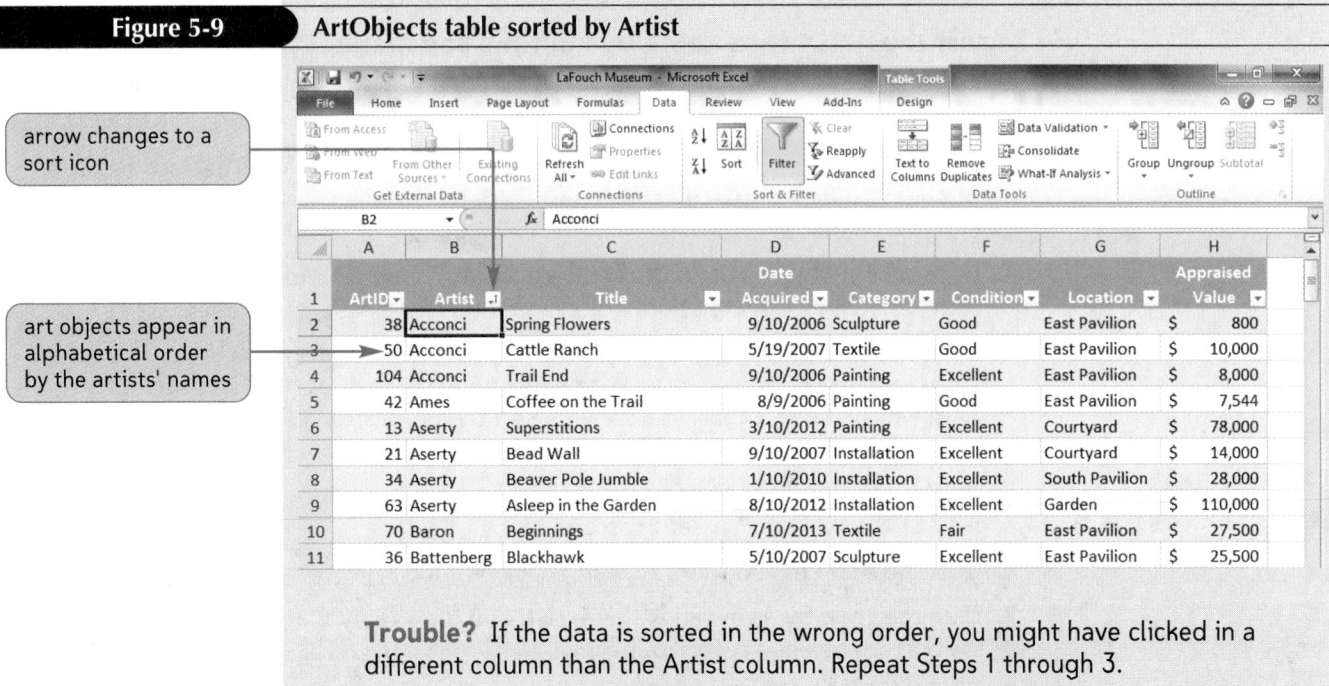

arrow changes to a sort icon

art objects appear in alphabetical order by the artists' names

**Trouble?** If the data is sorted in the wrong order, you might have clicked in a different column than the Artist column. Repeat Steps 1 through 3.

## Sorting Multiple Columns Using the Sort Dialog Box

Sometimes, sorting by one sort field is not adequate for your needs. For example, Mary wants you to arrange the ArtObjects table so that all the art objects in each location are together, and then all the objects for each artist within each location are together, and then each artist's work is arranged by the date acquired. You must sort on more than one column to accomplish this. The first sort field is called the **primary sort field**, the second sort field is called the **secondary sort field**, and so forth. You can use up to 64 sort fields in a single sort, although you most typically will use one to three sort fields. In this case, the Location field is the primary sort field, the Artist field is the secondary sort field, and the Date Acquired field is the tertiary sort field. When you have more than one sort field, you should use the Sort dialog box to specify the sort criteria.

**REFERENCE**

*Sorting Data Using Multiple Sort Fields*

- Click any cell in a table or range.
- In the Sort & Filter group on the Data tab, click the Sort button.
- If necessary, click the Add Level button to insert the Sort by row.
- Click the Sort by arrow, select the column heading for the primary sort field, click the Sort On arrow to select the type of data, and then click the Order arrow to select the sort order.
- To sort by a second column, click the Add Level button. Click the Then by arrow, select the column heading for the secondary sort field, click the Sort On arrow to select the type of data, and then click the Order arrow to select the sort order.
- To sort by additional columns, click the Add Level button and select appropriate Then by, Sort On, and Order values.
- Click the OK button.

You will sort the art objects by location, and then within location by artist, and then within artist by date acquired, with the most recently acquired objects for the artist appearing before the older ones. This will make it faster for Mary to find information about the location and the creator of the art objects in each location.

### To sort the ArtObjects table by multiple sort fields:

▶ **1.** Click cell **A1** in the ArtObjects table. Cell A1 is the active cell, although you can click any cell in the table to sort the table data.

▶ **2.** In the Sort & Filter group on the Data tab, click the **Sort** button. The Sort dialog box opens. Any sort specifications (sort field, type of data sorted on, and sort order) from the last sort appear in the dialog box.

▶ **3.** Click the **Sort by** arrow to display the list of the column headers in the ArtObjects table, and then click **Location**. The primary sort field is set to Location.

▶ **4.** If necessary, click the **Sort On** arrow to display the type of sort, and then click **Values**. Typically, you want to sort by the numbers, text, or dates stored in the cells, which are all values. You can also sort by formats such as cell color, font color, and cell icon (a graphic that appears in a cell due to a conditional format).

▶ **5.** If necessary, click the **Order** arrow to display sort order options, and then click **A to Z**. The sort order is set to ascending.

▶ **6.** Click the **Add Level** button. A Then by row is added below the primary sort field.

▶ **7.** Click the **Then by** arrow and click **Artist**, and then verify that **Values** appears in the Sort On box and **A to Z** appears in the Order box.

▶ **8.** Click the **Add Level** button to add a second Then by row.

▶ **9.** Click the second **Then by** arrow, click **Date Acquired**, verify that **Values** appears in the Sort On box, click the **Order** arrow, and then click **Newest to Oldest** to specify a descending sort order for the Date Acquired values. See Figure 5-10.

| Figure 5-10 | Sort dialog box with complete sort specifications |

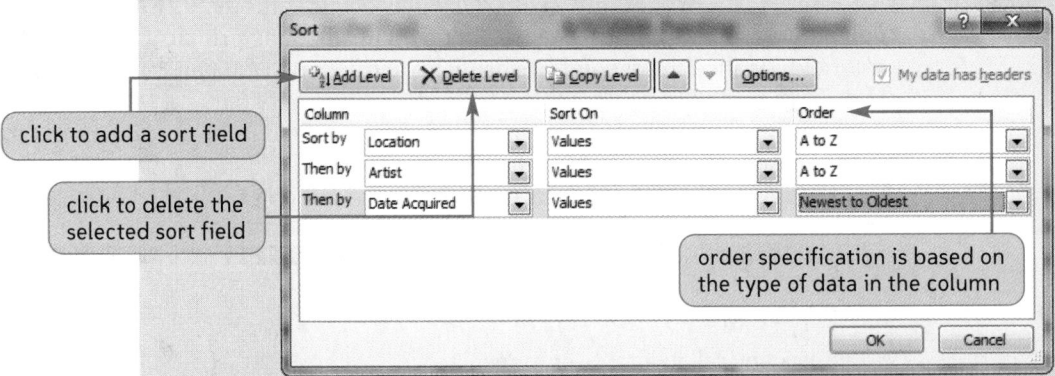

click to add a sort field

click to delete the selected sort field

order specification is based on the type of data in the column

▶ **10.** Click the **OK** button. Excel sorts the table records first in ascending order by the Location field, then within each location by the Artist field (again, in ascending order), and then within each artist by the Date Acquired field. For example, notice the three works by Acconci located in the East Pavilion; the works are arranged in descending order by the value in the Date Acquired column, so that the newer works appear before the older works. See Figure 5-11.

| Figure 5-11 | Art objects sorted by Location, then by Artist, and then by Date Acquired |

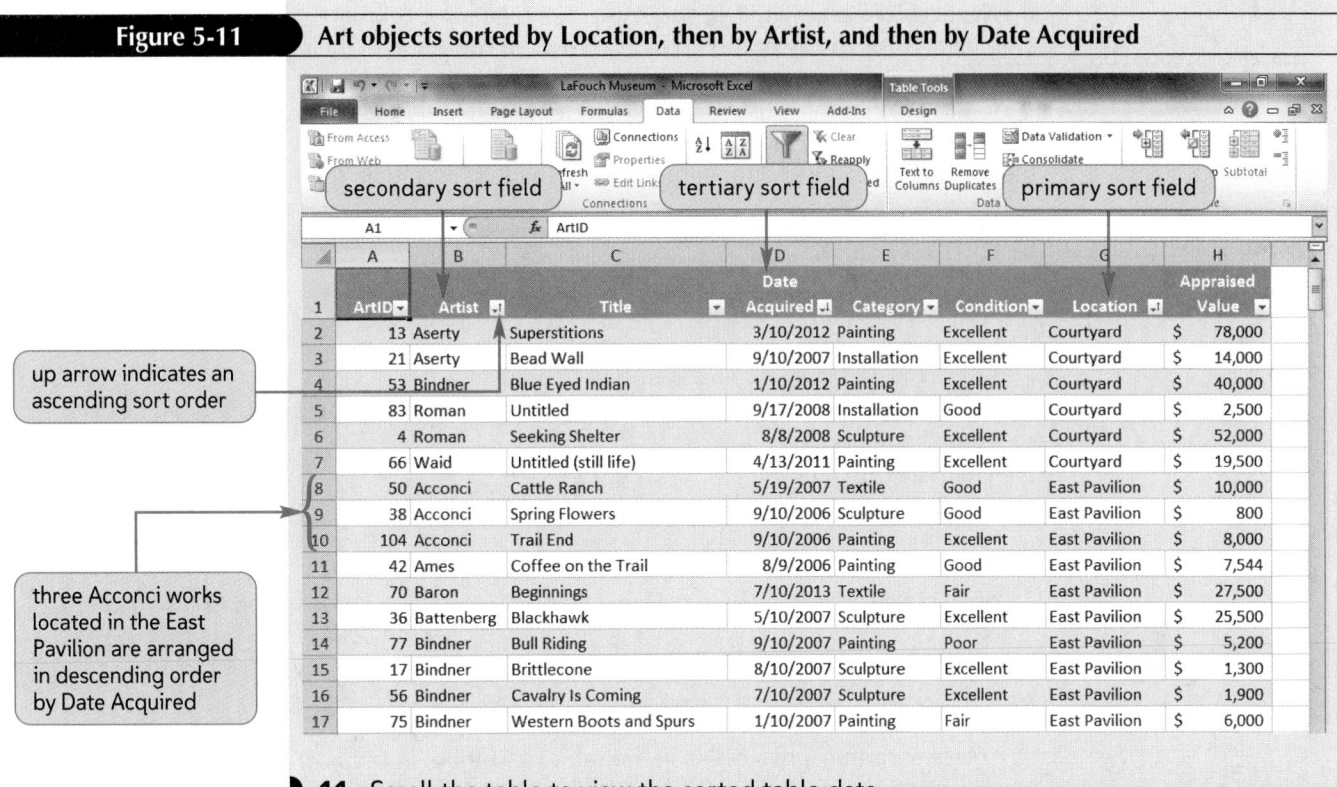

up arrow indicates an ascending sort order

three Acconci works located in the East Pavilion are arranged in descending order by Date Acquired

> **11.** Scroll the table to view the sorted table data.

Mary wants to review the condition of each art object to determine how many objects need repairs. It is easier to do this with the objects sorted by their condition. Because you need to sort by only one field, you'll use the Sort A to Z button.

## To sort the art objects by condition:

> **1.** Click any cell in the **Condition** column.

> **2.** In the Sort & Filter group on the Data tab, click the **Sort A to Z** button ⇵. The previous sort is removed and the art objects are now sorted in ascending order by condition.

> **3.** Scroll the table to see the reordered art objects.

The table data is sorted in alphabetical order by the condition of the art objects: Excellent, Fair, Good, and Poor. This default sort order for fields with text values is not appropriate for the condition ratings. Instead, Mary wants you to base the sort on quality ranking rather than alphabetical order. You'll use a custom sort list to set up the sort order Mary wants.

## Sorting Using a Custom List

Text is sorted in ascending or descending alphabetical order unless you specify a different order using a custom list. A **custom list** indicates the sequence in which you want data ordered. Excel provides four predefined custom sort lists. Two days-of-the-week custom lists (Sun, Mon, Tues, ... and Sunday, Monday, Tuesday, ...) and two months-of-the-year custom lists (Jan, Feb, Mar, Apr, ... and January, February, March, April, ...). If a column consists of day or month labels, you can sort them in their correct chronological order using one of these predefined custom lists.

You can also create custom lists to sort records in a sequence you define. In this case, you want to create a custom list to arrange the art objects based on their condition, with the top quality condition appearing first, as follows: Excellent, Good, Fair, Poor.

### REFERENCE

### Creating a Custom List

- In the Sort & Filter group on the Data tab, click the Sort button.
- Click the Order arrow, and then click Custom List.
- In the List entries box, type each entry for the custom list, pressing the Enter key after each entry.
- Click the Add button.
- Click the OK button.

You'll create a custom list that Mary can use to sort the records by the Condition field.

### To create the custom list based on the Condition field:

1. Make sure the active cell is in the table, and then, in the Sort & Filter group on the Data tab, click the **Sort** button. The Sort dialog box opens, showing the sort specifications from the previous sort.

2. If necessary, click the **Sort by** arrow, click **Condition** to select the sort field (if necessary), and then verify that **Values** appears in the Sort On box.

3. Click the **Order** arrow to display the sort order options, and then click **Custom List**. The Custom Lists dialog box opens.

4. In the Custom lists box, click **NEW LIST** to place the insertion point in the List entries box.

   Next, you'll enter the condition values in the order you want them sorted. You must press the Enter key after each entry.

**TIP**

You can also use commas to separate entries in a custom list.

5. Type **Excellent**, press the **Enter** key to move the insertion point to the next line, type **Good**, press the **Enter** key, type **Fair**, press the **Enter** key, type **Poor**, and then press the **Enter** key. The four items appear in the List entries box.

6. Click the **Add** button. The custom list entries are added to the Custom lists box. See Figure 5-12.

**Figure 5-12**    **Custom Lists dialog box with custom list defined**

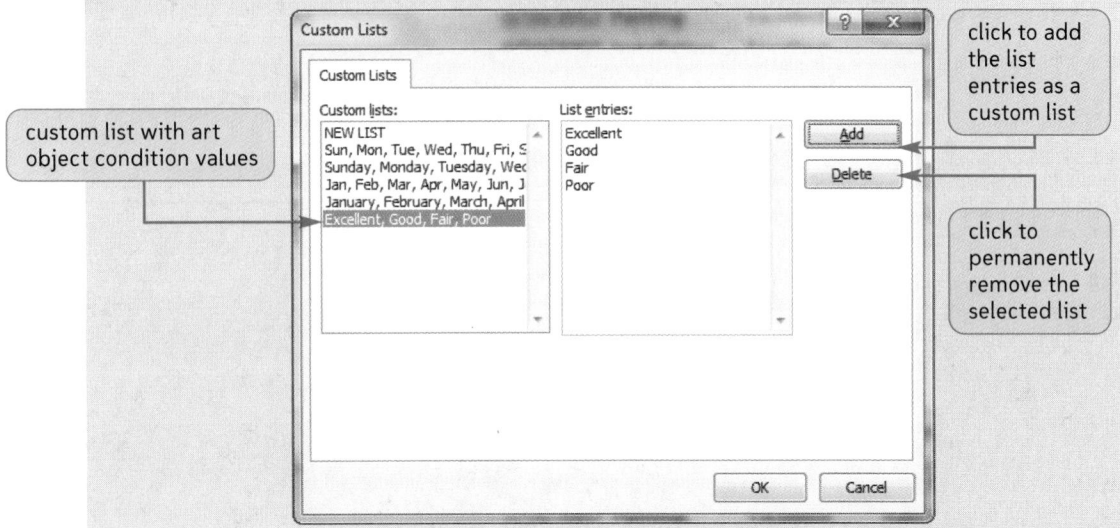

custom list with art object condition values

click to add the list entries as a custom list

click to permanently remove the selected list

▶ **7.** Click the **OK** button to return to the Sort dialog box. The custom sort list—Excellent, Good, Fair, Poor—appears in the Order box.

▶ **8.** Click the **OK** button. The table is sorted based on the custom list.

▶ **9.** Scroll the sorted table to verify that the art objects are sorted by their condition rankings: Excellent, Good, Fair, and Poor. Six art objects are in poor condition.

So far, you created an Excel table for the art objects, and then named and formatted the table. You updated the table by adding, editing, and deleting records. You also sorted the records and created a custom list to sort the Condition field by its quality ratings. In the next session, you will filter the ArtObjects table to retrieve specific information on some of the art objects.

## Session 5.1 Quick Check

**REVIEW**

1. What is the purpose of the Freeze Panes button in the Window group on the View tab? Why is this feature helpful?

2. What three elements indicate an Excel table is created in the worksheet?

3. A field that you use to order data is referred to as a(n) _____ field.

4. An Excel table of college students tracks each student's first name, last name, major, and year of graduation. How can you order the table so that students graduating in the same year appear together in alphabetical order by the student's last name?

5. How do you enter a new record in an Excel table?

6. An Excel table of faculty data includes the Rank field with the values Full, Associate, Assistant, and Instructor. How can you sort the data by rank in the following order: Full, Associate, Assistant, and Instructor?

7. If you sort table data from the most recent purchase date to the oldest purchase date, in what order have you sorted the data?

# SESSION 5.2 VISUAL OVERVIEW

Check box to display or hide the Total row.

Button to convert an Excel table to a range.

As a reminder that the records are filtered, only the row numbers of the records that match the filter appear (leaving gaps in the consecutive numbering) and are blue.

The **Total row** is used to calculate summary statistics (including sum, average, count, maximum, and minimum) for any column in an Excel table.

The status bar indicates that the table is filtered.

The selection list displays the unique items in the selected column. You can select one item or multiple items from the list to filter the table by.

LaFouch Museum - Microsoft Excel

File    Home    Insert    Page Layout    Formulas    Data    Review    View    Add-In

Table Name:    Summarize with PivotTable    Properties    ☑ Header Ro
ArtObjects    Remove Duplicates    Open in Browser    ☑ Total Row
Resize Table    Convert to Range    Export  Refresh    Unlink    ☑ Banded R
Properties    Tools    External Table Data    Tab

C4    fx    Asleep in the Garden

| | A | B | C | Date |
|---|---|---|---|---|
| 1 | ArtID▾ | Artist ▾ | Title ▾ | Acquired ▾ |
| 4 | 63 | Aserty | Asleep in the Garden | |
| 5 | 13 | Aserty | Superstitions | |
| 6 | 4 | Roman | Seeking Shelter | |
| 7 | 53 | Bindner | Blue Eyed Indian | |
| 8 | 78 | Guys | Chuckwagon | |
| 9 | 34 | Aserty | Beaver Pole Jumble | |
| 10 | 70 | Baron | Beginnings | |
| 11 | 36 | Battenberg | Blackhawk | |
| 12 | 95 | Lerman | Life Is Sweet | |
| 19 | 117 | Higgins | Apache Warrior | |
| 20 | 82 | Hamend | Spring Flowers | |
| 24 | 96 | Reed | The Spirit | |
| 25 | 87 | Yasami | Three Woman | |
| 31 | 85 | Rogers | Traces | |
| 118 | **Total** | 32 | | |
| 119 | | | | |
| 120 | | | | |
| 121 | | | | |

A↓ Sort A to Z
Z↓ Sort Z to A
Sort by Color
Clear Filter From "Category"
Filter by Color
Text Filters
Search
☑ (Select All)
☑ Installation
☑ Painting
☑ Sculpture
☑ Textile

OK

Documentation    Art Collection    Sheet3

Ready    Filter Mode

# FILTERING TABLE DATA

The filter arrow opens the Filter menu, which includes options to sort and filter the table based on the data in that column.

**Filtering** is the process of displaying a subset of rows in an Excel table that meets the criteria you specify. In this case, the table is filtered to show art objects in with an appraised value of $20,000 or higher.

To view different areas of a large worksheet, you can split the window into two or four resizable areas. Each area is called a **pane**.

Each pane has its own set of scroll bars for shifting different parts of the worksheet into view in each pane.

The **split bar** indicates the division between the panes. You can drag the split bar to resize the panes.

# Filtering Data

Mary needs to determine which art objects the museum can afford to repair this year. She asks you to prepare a list of all paintings in poor condition. Although you could sort the list of paintings by condition to group those in poor condition, you are still working with the entire table. A better solution is to display only the specific records you want. Filtering the data temporarily hides any records that do not meet the specified criteria. After data is filtered, you can sort, copy, format, chart, and print it.

## Filtering Using One Column

When you create an Excel table, a filter arrow appears in each column header. You click a filter arrow to open the AutoFilter menu for that field. You can use options on the AutoFilter menu to create three types of filters. You can filter a column of data by its cell colors or font colors; by a specific text, number, or date filter, although the choices depend on the type of data in the column; or by selecting the exact values by which you want to filter in the column. After you filter a column, the Clear Filter command becomes available so you can remove the filter and redisplay all the records.

Mary wants to see only paintings in poor condition. First, you'll filter the ArtObjects table to show only those records with the value "Paintings" in the Category column.

### To filter the ArtObjects table to show only paintings:

1. If you took a break after the previous session, make sure the LaFouch Museum workbook is open, the Art Collection worksheet is active, and the ArtObjects table is active.

2. Click the **Category filter arrow**. The AutoFilter menu opens, as shown in Figure 5-13, listing the unique entries in the Category column: Installation, Painting, Sculpture, and Textile. All the items are selected initially, but you can set which items to use to filter the data. In this case, you want to select the Painting item.

**Figure 5-13    Filter menu for the Category column**

If the list is long you can enter the item you want to find in the Search box

unique items in the Category column

3. Click the (**Select All**) check box to remove the check marks from all the Category items, and then click the **Painting** check box to insert a check mark. The filter will show only those records that match the checked item and hide records that contain the unchecked items.

4. Click the **OK** button. The filter is applied. The status bar lists the number of paintings found in the entire table. Fifty-seven of the 116 records in the table are displayed. See Figure 5-14.

| Figure 5-14 | ArtObjects table filtered to show only paintings |

icon indicates that this column is being used to filter the table

row numbers of the filtered records are blue

only records with a category value of "Painting" are displayed

status bar indicates the number of records displayed

5. Review the records to verify that only records with a value equal to "Painting" in the Category column are visible. All records that do not have the value "Painting" in this column are hidden, leaving gaps in the row numbers.

6. Point to the **Category filter arrow**. A ScreenTip—Category: Equals "Painting"— describes the filter applied to the column.

The AutoFilter menu includes options to Sort by Color and Filter by Color. These options enable you to filter and sort data using color, one of many cell attributes. Suppose that Mary used specific cell background colors for certain works of art in the ArtObjects table. For example, she might want to highlight the works given to the museum by its two most generous donors, using yellow for one and red for the other. So the cells in the Title column for the two donors would be formatted with these colors. You could then click the Sort by Color option in the AutoFilter menu to display a list of available colors by which to sort, and then click the specific color so that all the records for the first donor (formatted with yellow) would appear together, and all the records for the second donor (formatted with red) would appear together. Similarly, you could click the Filter by Color option to display a submenu with the available colors by which to filter, and then click a color. In this example, if you selected yellow, only the records for the first donor would be displayed in the table, allowing you to focus on just those records.

**INSIGHT**

### Exploring Text Filters

You can use different text filters to display the records you want. If you know only part of a text value or if you want to match a certain pattern, you can use the Begins With, Ends With, and Contains operators to filter a text field to match the pattern you specify.

The following examples are based on a student directory table that includes First Name, Last Name, Address, City, State, and Zip fields:

- To find a student named Smith, Smithe, or Smythe, create a text filter using the Begins With operator. In this example, use "Begins With Sm" to display all records that have "Sm" at the beginning of the text value.
- To Find anyone whose Last Name ends in "son" (such as Robertson, Anderson, Dawson, Gibson, and so forth), create a text filter using the Ends With operator. In this example, use "Ends With son" to display all records that have "son" as the last characters in the text value.
- To find anyone whose street address includes "Central" (such as 101 Central Ave., 1024 Central Road, or 457 Avenue De Central), create a text filter using the Contains operator. In this example, use "Contains Central" to display all records that have "Central" anywhere in the text value.

When you create a text filter, think about the results you want. Then, consider what text filter you can use to best achieve those results.

## Filtering Using Multiple Columns

If you need to further restrict the records that appear in a filtered table, you can filter by one or more of the other columns. Each additional filter is applied to the currently filtered data and further reduces the records that are displayed. Mary wants to see only paintings that are in poor condition, rather than all the paintings in the ArtObjects table. To do this, you need to filter the painting records to display only those with the value "Poor" in the Condition column. You'll use the filter arrow in the Condition column to add this second filter criterion to the filtered data.

### To filter the painting records to show only those in poor condition:

1. Click the **Condition filter arrow**. The AutoFilter menu opens.

2. Click the **Excellent**, **Fair**, and **Good** check boxes to remove the check marks. The Poor check box remains checked, so only paintings in poor condition will be displayed.

3. Click the **OK** button. The ArtObjects table is further filtered and shows the three paintings that are in poor condition. See Figure 5-15.

| Figure 5-15 | ArtObjects table filtered to show only paintings in poor condition |

three paintings are in poor condition

## Clearing Filters

When you want to redisplay all of the data in a filtered table, you need to **clear** (or remove) the filters. When you clear a filter from a column, any other filters are still applied. For example, in the ArtObjects table, you would see all the paintings in the table if you cleared the filter from the Condition field, or you would see all the art objects in poor condition if you cleared the filter from the Category field. To redisplay all the art objects in the table, you need to clear both the Condition filter and the Category filter. You will do this now to redisplay the entire table of art objects.

### To clear the filters to show all the records in the ArtObjects table:

▶ 1. Click the **Condition filter arrow**, and then click **Clear Filter From "Condition"**. The Condition filter is removed from the table. The table shows only paintings because the Category filter is still in effect.

▶ 2. Click the **Category filter arrow**, and then click **Clear Filter From "Category"**. The Category condition is removed, and all the records in the ArtObjects table are displayed again.

## Selecting Multiple Filter Items

You can often find the information you need by selecting a single filter item from a list of filter items. Sometimes, however, you need to specify a more complex set of criteria to find the records you want. Earlier, you selected one filter item for the Category column and one filter item for the Condition column to display the records whose Category field value equals Painting AND whose Condition field value equals Poor. The records had to contain both values to be displayed. The AND condition requires that all of the selected criteria be true for the record to be displayed.

Now you want to select two filter items for the Category column to display records whose Category field value equals Installation OR whose Category field value equals Sculpture. The records must have at least one of these values to be displayed. A filter that selects more than one item from the list of items in a single column uses the OR condition, which requires that only one of the selected criteria true for a record to be displayed. For example, if you check the Installation and Sculpture check boxes in the Category filter items, you create the filter condition "Category equals Installation" OR "Category equals Sculpture."

The museum's board of directors wants a list of all installations or sculptures valued at more than $20,000. You will create a list of these holdings.

**To select multiple filter items:**

▶ 1. Click the **Category filter arrow**, and then click the **Painting** and **Textile** check boxes to remove the check marks.

▶ 2. Verify that the **Installation** and **Sculpture** check boxes remain checked. When you select more than one item, you create a multiselect filter.

▶ 3. Click the **OK** button. The ArtObjects table is filtered, and the status bar indicates that 51 out of 116 records are either an installation or a sculpture.

## Creating Criteria Filters to Specify More Complex Criteria

Filter items enable you to filter a range of data or an Excel table based on exact values in a column. However, many times you need broader criteria. **Criteria filters** enable you to specify various conditions in addition to those that are based on an "equals" criterion. For example, you might want to find all art objects with an appraised value greater than $20,000 or those that were acquired after 7/1/2011. You use criteria filters to create these conditions.

The type of criteria filters available change depending on whether the data in a column contains text, numbers, or dates. Figure 5-16 shows some of the options for text, number, and date criteria filters.

**Figure 5-16** Options for text, number, and date criteria filters

| Filter | Criteria | Records Displayed |
|---|---|---|
| Text | Equals | Exactly match the specified text string |
| | Does Not Equal | Do not exactly match the specified text string |
| | Begins With | Begin with the specified text string |
| | Ends With | End with the specified text string |
| | Contains | Have the specified text string anywhere |
| | Does Not Contain | Do not have the specified text string anywhere |
| Number | Equals | Exactly match the specified number |
| | Greater Than or Equal to | Are greater than or equal to the specified number |
| | Less Than | Are less than the specified number |
| | Between | Are greater than or equal to *and* less than or equal to the specified numbers |
| | Top 10 | Are the top or bottom 10 (or the specified number) |
| | Above Average | Are greater than the average |
| Date | Today | Have the current date |
| | Last Week | Are in the prior week |
| | Next Month | Are in the month following the current month |
| | Last Quarter | Are in the previous quarter of the year (quarters defined Jan, Feb, Mar; Apr, May, June; and so on) |
| | Year to Date | Are since January 1 of the current year to the current date |
| | Last Year | Are in the previous year (based on the current date) |

**PROSKILLS**

## Problem Solving: Using Filters to Find Appropriate Data

Problem solving often requires finding information from a set of data to answer specific questions. When you're working with a range of data or an Excel table that contains hundreds or thousands of records, filters help you find that information without having to review each record in the table. For example, a human resources manager can use a filter to narrow the search for a specific employee of the 2,500 working at the company knowing only that the employee's first name is Elliot.

Filtering limits the data to display only the specific records that meet the criteria you set, enabling you to more effectively analyze the data. The following examples further illustrate how filtering can help people to quickly locate the data they need to answer a particular question:

- A customer representative can use a filter to search a list of 10,000 products to find all products priced between $500 and $1,000.
- A donations coordinator can use a filter to prepare a report that shows the donations received during the first quarter of the current year.
- A professor who has 300 students in a psychology class can use a filter to develop a list of potential student assistants for next semester from the names the professor has high-lighted in blue because their work was impressive. Filtering by the blue color generates a list of students to interview.
- The author of a guide to celebrity autographs can use a filter to determine whether an entry for a specific celebrity already exists in an Excel table and, if it does, determine whether the entry needs to be updated. If the entry does not exist, the author will know to add the autograph data to the autograph price table.

As these example show, filtering is a useful tool for locating the answers to a wide variety of questions. You then can use this information to help you resolve problems.

You will modify the filtered ArtObjects table to add a criteria filter that includes only objects that have values greater than $20,000.

### To create a number filter:

▶ 1. Click the **Appraised Value filter arrow**, and then point to **Number Filters**. A menu opens, displaying the comparison operators available for columns of numbers.

▶ 2. Click **Greater Than**. The Custom AutoFilter dialog box opens. The upper-left box lists *is greater than*, the comparison operator you want to use to filter the Appraised Value column. You enter the value you want to use for the filter criteria in the upper-right box, which, in this case, is $20,000.

▶ 3. Type **20000** in the upper-right box. See Figure 5-17. You use the lower set of boxes if you want the filter to meet a second condition. You click the And option button to display rows that meet both criteria. You click the Or option button to display rows that meet either of the two criteria. You only want to set one criterion for this filter, so you'll leave the lower boxes empty.

| Figure 5-17 | Custom AutoFilter dialog box |
| --- | --- |

operator for the first condition

criterion for the first condition

boxes to specify a second condition for the list

▶ **4.** Click the **OK** button. The status bar indicates that 7 of 116 records were found. The seven records that appear in the ArtObjects table are either installations or sculptures and have an appraised value greater than $20,000.

Before Mary sends this list to the board of directors, you'll sort the filtered data to show the largest appraised value first. Although you can sort the data using Sort buttons, as you did earlier, these sort options are also available on the AutoFilter menu for your convenience. If you want to perform a more complex sort, you still need to use the Sort dialog box.

### To sort the filtered table data:

▶ **1.** Click the **Appraised Value filter arrow**. The AutoFilter menu opens. The sort options are at the top of the menu.

▶ **2.** Click **Sort Largest to Smallest**. The filtered table now displays installations and sculptures with an appraised valued greater than $20,000 sorted in descending order. See Figure 5-18.

| Figure 5-18 | Filtered ArtObjects table |
| --- | --- |

icon shows that this column is filtered

icon shows that this column is filtered and sorted

installations and sculptures with values greater than $20,000 sorted in descending order

Mary will send this list to the board of directors. You need to restore the entire table of art objects, which you can do by clearing all the filters at one time.

**To clear all the filters from the ArtObjects table:**

▶ **1.** Click the **Data** tab on the Ribbon, if necessary.

▶ **2.** In the Sort & Filter group, click the **Clear** button. All the records appear in the table.

# Using the Total Row to Calculate Summary Statistics

You can calculate summary statistics (including sum, average, count, maximum, and minimum) on all the columns in an Excel table or on a filtered table in a Total row, which you can display at the end of the table. When you click in each cell in the Total row, an arrow appears that you can click to open a list of the most commonly used functions.

Mary is creating a brochure for an upcoming fund-raising event, and wants to know the number and value of the items in the current museum collection, excluding art objects in poor condition. You will filter the table to display art objects that are in excellent, good, and fair condition (art objects in poor condition will not be displayed). Then, you will display the Total row for the ArtObjects table to count the number of art objects in excellent, good, and fair condition, and add their total appraised value.

**To add a Total row and select summary statistics:**

▶ **1.** Click the **Condition filter arrow**, click the **Poor** check box to remove the check mark, and then click the **OK** button. The ArtObjects table displays objects that are in excellent, good, or fair condition. The status bar indicates that 110 of 116 records remain in the filtered table.

▶ **2.** Click the **Table Tools Design** tab on the Ribbon, and then click the **Total Row** check box in the Table Style Options group to insert a check mark.

▶ **3.** Scroll to the end of the table. The Total row is the last row of the table, the word "Total" appears in the far-left cell, and the total appraised value $1,118,723 appears in the far-right cell. By default, the Total row adds the numbers in the last column of the Excel table or counts the number of records if the data in the last column contains text. See Figure 5-19.

| Figure 5-19 | Total row added to the ArtObjects table |

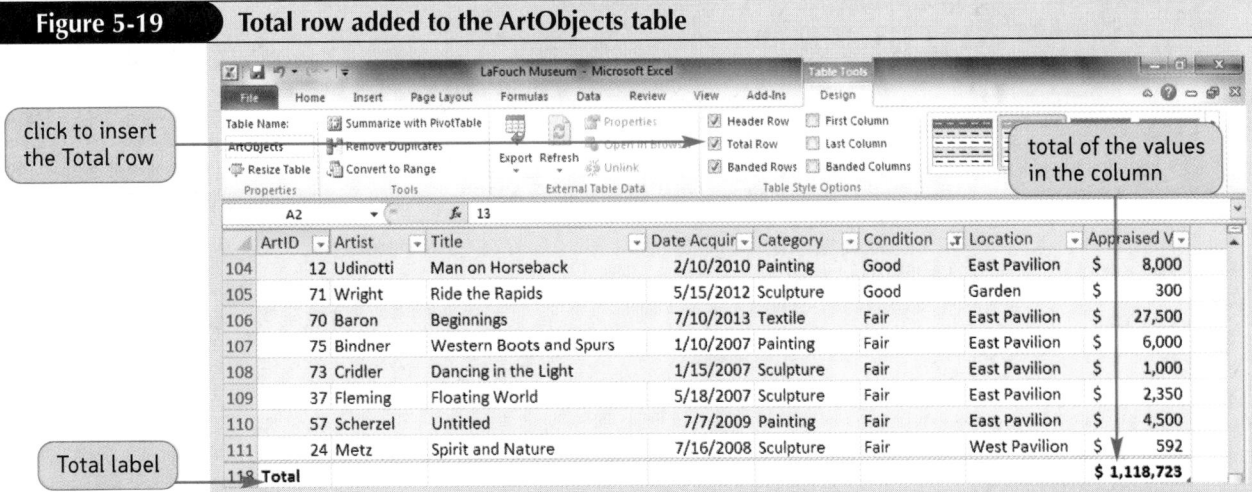

In the Artist cell of the Total row, you want to count the number of records whose appraised values were added in the last column.

4. Click cell **B118** (the Artist cell in the Total row), and then click the **arrow button** to display a list of functions. "None" is the default function in all columns except the last column. See Figure 5-20.

**Figure 5-20** | **Total row functions**

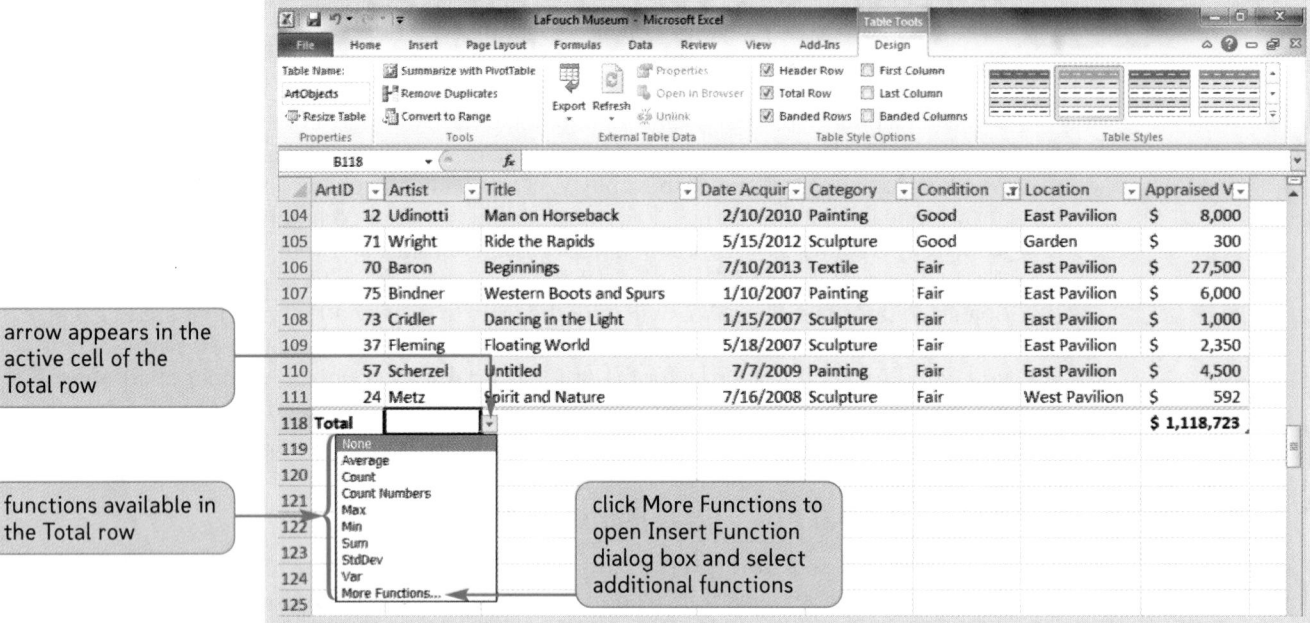

arrow appears in the active cell of the Total row

functions available in the Total row

click More Functions to open Insert Function dialog box and select additional functions

5. Click **Count**. The number 110, which is the number of records in the filtered ArtObjects table, appears in the cell. See Figure 5-21.

**Figure 5-21** | **Count of records in the filtered table**

number of records displayed

## Splitting the Worksheet Window into Panes

You can split the worksheet window into two or four separate panes. This allows you to easily view data from several areas of the worksheet at the same time. Each pane has its own scroll bars so you can navigate easily within one pane or display different parts of the worksheet. You can move between panes using the mouse. To create two panes, select a cell in row 1 or column A; to create four panes, select any other cell.

Mary wants to view the art collection summary totals at the same time she views the data on individual art objects. You will divide the worksheet into two horizontal panes to view the art object records in the top pane and the totals in the bottom pane.

### To split the Art Collection worksheet window into panes:

1. Press the **Ctrl+Home** keys to jump to the top of the table, and then click cell **A17**.

2. Click the **View** tab on the Ribbon, and then click the **Split** button in the Window group. The worksheet window splits into two panes. Each pane has its own set of scroll bars. See Figure 5-22.

| Figure 5-22 | Worksheet split into two panes |

3. If necessary, click cell **A17** to activate the bottom pane.

4. Using the lower scroll bar, scroll down until row 118, the Total row, appears immediately below the split bar. See Figure 5-23.

**Figure 5-23**    Total row displayed in the bottom pane

A popular painting named "Dark Canyon" had a new appraisal. Its value is now $8,000. You will change the appraised value of this painting.

### To update the appraised value of the Dark Canyon painting:

1. Click any cell in the top pane.

2. Use the Find command to locate the art object with ArtID **113**.

3. In the Appraised Value cell, enter **8000**. The total appraised value in the bottom pane changed from $1,118,723 to $1,119,223.

Next, you will remove the split panes from the worksheet window.

### To remove the split panes from the Art Collection worksheet window:

1. If necessary, click the **View** tab on the Ribbon.

2. In the Window group, click the **Split** button. The split bar is removed, and the worksheet is again a single window.

**TIP**

You can also double-click the split bar to remove the panes.

Now, you will remove the Total row and clear the filter.

**To remove the Total row and clear the filter from the ArtObjects table:**

▶ **1.** Click the **Table Tools Design** tab on the Ribbon.

▶ **2.** In the Table Style Options group, click the **Total Row** check box to remove the check mark. The Total row is no longer visible.

▶ **3.** Click the **Condition filter arrow**, and then click **Clear Filter From "Condition"**. The ArtObjects table displays all the art objects.

▶ **4.** Press the **Ctrl+Home** keys to return to cell A1.

**TIP**

If you redisplay the Total row, the functions you last used will appear even after you save, close, and then reopen the file.

The board of directors asked Mary to create a report that shows all the museum's art objects sorted by Category with the total appraised value of the art objects in each category. The board also wants to see the total appraised value for each category after the last item of that category. Although you could use the Total row in the Excel table to calculate the results, you would need to filter, total, and print the data for each category separately. A faster way to provide the information Mary needs is to use the Subtotal command.

# Inserting Subtotals

You can summarize data in a range by inserting subtotals. The Subtotal command offers many kinds of summary information, including counts, sums, averages, minimums, and maximums. The Subtotal command inserts a subtotal row into the range for each group of data and adds a grand total row below the last row of data. Because Excel inserts subtotals whenever the value in a specified field changes, you need to sort the data so that records with the same value in a specified field are grouped together *before* you use the Subtotal command. The Subtotal command cannot be used in an Excel table, so you must first convert the Excel table to a range.

**REFERENCE**

*Calculating Subtotals for a Range of Data*

- Sort the data by the column for which you want a subtotal.
- If the data is in an Excel table, in the Tools group on the Table Tools Design tab, click the Convert to Range button, and then click the Yes button to convert the Excel table to a range.
- In the Outline group on the Data tab, click the Subtotal button.
- Click the At each change in arrow, and then click the column that contains the group you want to subtotal.
- Click the Use function arrow, and then click the function you want to use to summarize the data.
- In the Add subtotal to box, click the check box for each column that contains the values you want to summarize.
- To calculate another category of subtotals, click the Replace current subtotals check box to remove the check mark, and then repeat the previous three steps.
- Click the OK button.

To produce the results Mary needs, you will sort the art objects by category and calculate subtotals in the Appraised Value column for each category grouping. You will also convert the Excel table to a normal range.

### To sort the art objects and convert the table to a range:

1. Click the **Category filter arrow**, and then click **Sort A to Z** on the AutoFilter menu. The ArtObjects table is sorted in ascending order by the Category field. This ensures one subtotal is created for each category.

2. In the Tools group on the Table Tools Design tab, click the **Convert to Range** button. A dialog box opens, asking if you want to convert the table to a normal range.

3. Click the **Yes** button. The Excel table is converted to a range. You can tell this because the filter arrows and the Table Tools Design tab disappear, and the Home tab on the Ribbon is selected.

Next, you'll calculate the subtotals.

### To calculate appraised values subtotals for each category of art object:

1. Click the **Data** tab on the Ribbon, and then, in the Outline group, click the **Subtotal** button. The Subtotal dialog box opens. See Figure 5-24.

**Figure 5-24** Subtotal dialog box

2. Click the **At each change in** arrow, and then click **Category**. This is the column you want Excel to use to determine where to insert the subtotals; it's the column you sorted. A subtotal will be calculated at every change in the Category value.

3. If necessary, click the **Use function** arrow, and then click **Sum**. The Use function list provides several options for subtotaling data, including counts, averages, minimums, maximums, and products.

4. In the Add subtotal to list box, make sure only the **Appraised Value** check box is checked. This specifies the Appraised Value field as the field to be subtotaled. If the data already included subtotals, you would check the Replace current subtotals check box to replace the existing subtotals or uncheck the option to display the new subtotals on separate rows above the existing subtotals. Because the data has no subtotals, it makes no difference whether you select this option.

5. Make sure the **Summary below data** check box is checked. This option places the subtotals below each group of data, instead of above the first entry in each group, and places the grand total at the end of the data, instead of at the top of the column just below the row of column headings.

6. Click the **OK** button. Excel inserts rows below each category group and displays the subtotals for the appraised value of each art category. A series of Outline buttons appears to the left of the worksheet so you can display or hide the detail rows within each subtotal.

   **Trouble?** If each item has a subtotal following it, you probably forgot to sort the data by Category. Click the Undo button 🔄 on the Quick Access Toolbar, sort the data by Category, and then repeat Steps 1 through 6.

7. Scroll through the data to see the subtotals below each category and the grand total at the end of the data. See Figure 5-25.

| Figure 5-25 | Subtotals and grand total added to the art objects data |

Outline buttons

## Using the Subtotal Outline View

In addition to displaying subtotals, the Subtotal feature "outlines" your worksheet so you can control the level of detail that is displayed. The three Outline buttons at the top of the outline area, as shown in Figure 5-25, allow you to show or hide different levels of detail in the worksheet. By default, the highest level is active; in this case, Level 3. Level 3 displays the most detail—the individual art object records, the subtotals, and the grand total. Level 2 displays the subtotals and the grand total, but not the individual records. Level 1 displays only the grand total.

The subtotals are useful, but Mary wants you to isolate the different subtotal sections so that she can focus on them individually. You will use the Outline buttons to prepare a report for Mary that includes only subtotals and the grand total.

### To use the Outline buttons to hide records:

1. Click the **Level 2 Outline** button, and then scroll up to view all the category subtotals, if necessary. The individual art object records are hidden, and you see only the subtotals for each category and the grand total. See Figure 5-26.

| Figure 5-26 | Table displaying only subtotals and grand total |

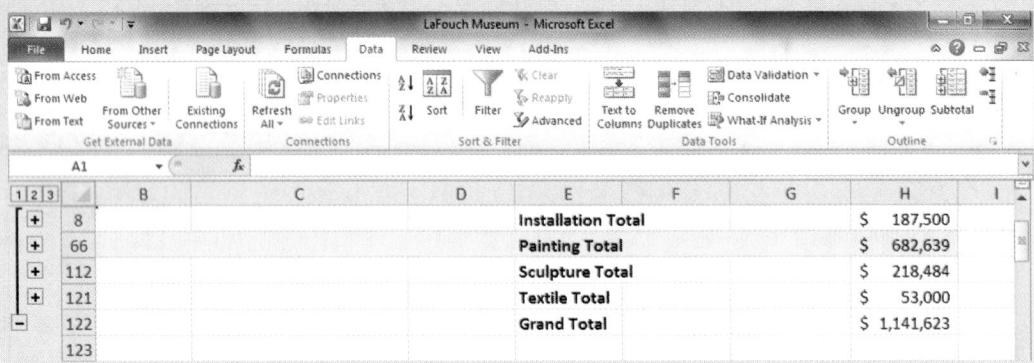

**Trouble?** If necessary, scroll the worksheet up to see the complete Level 2 list.

2. Click the **Level 1 Outline** button. The individual art object records and the subtotals for each category are hidden. Only the grand total remains visible.

3. Click the **Level 3 Outline** button. Scroll to the top. All the records along with the subtotals and the grand total are visible.

Mary has all the information she needs for her meeting with the board to review financial plans for the next fiscal cycle. So you can remove the subtotals from the data.

### To remove the subtotals from the art objects data:

1. In the Outline group on the Data tab, click the **Subtotal** button. The Subtotal dialog box opens.

2. Click the **Remove All** button. The subtotals are removed from the data, and only the records appear in the worksheet.

   You'll reset the art objects data as an Excel table.

3. Make sure the active cell is a cell within the structured range of data.

▶  **4.** Click the **Insert** tab on the Ribbon, and then click the **Table** button in the Tables group. The Create Table dialog box opens.

▶  **5.** Click the **OK** button to create the Excel table, and then click any cell in the table. The table structure is active.

▶  **6.** In the Properties group on the Table Tools Design tab, type **ArtObjects** in the Table Name box, and then press the **Enter** key. The Excel table is again named "ArtObjects."

In this session, you filtered the table data and determined totals and subtotals for the data. Mary needs to generate information for a board meeting about the appraised values of the museum's art objects. You will work with PivotTables and PivotCharts in the next session to gather the information that Mary needs.

## Session 5.2 Quick Check

**REVIEW**

1. Explain the relationship between the Sort and Subtotal commands.
2. An Excel table includes records for 500 employees. What can you use to calculate the average salary of employees in the finance department?
3. How can you display a list of marketing majors with a GPA of 3.0 or greater from an Excel table with records for 300 students?
4. After you display subtotals, how can you change the amount of detail displayed?
5. True or False. The COUNT function is a valid subtotal function when using the Subtotal command.
6. An Excel table of Major League Baseball players includes the column Position (pitchers, catchers, infielders, outfielders, and so forth). What feature can you use to display only pitchers and catchers in the table?
7. If you have a list of employees that includes fields for gender and salary, among others, how can you determine the average salary for females using the Total row feature?

# SESSION 5.3 VISUAL OVERVIEW

A **PivotTable** is an interactive table used to group and summarize either a range of data or an Excel table into a concise, tabular format for easier reporting and analysis.

This PivotTable uses the data from the Category field as column labels.

This PivotTable uses the data from the Location field as row labels.

You can add many levels of subtotals and totals to a PivotTable.

**Values fields** are the fields that contain summary data in a PivotTable. This PivotTable uses the total of the Appraised Value as the values field.

A **PivotChart** is a graphical representation of the data in a PivotTable.

Button to filter the PivotChart.

# PIVOTTABLE AND PIVOTCHART

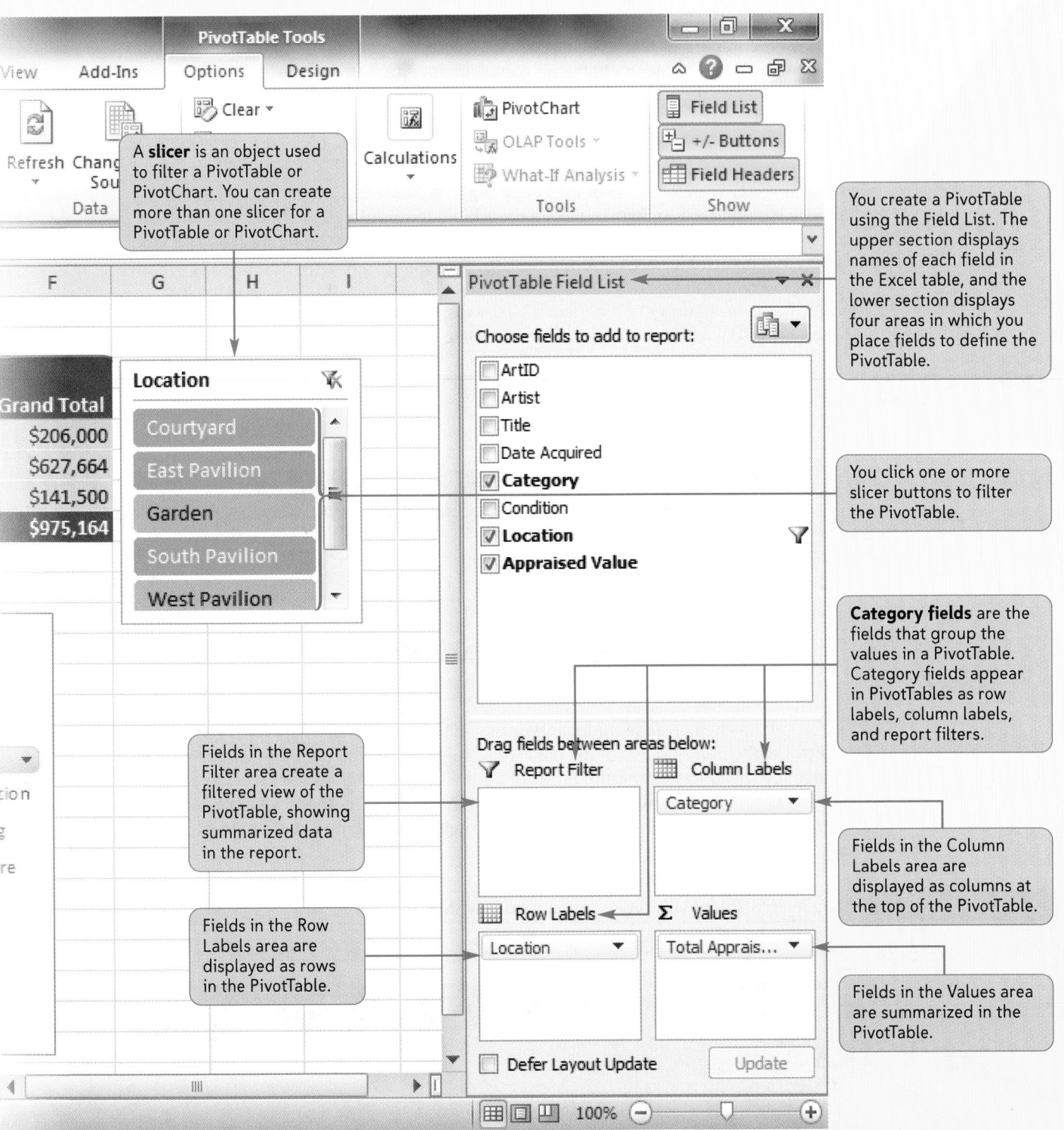

# Analyzing Data with PivotTables

An Excel table can contain a wealth of information. However, the large amounts of detailed data it contains often make it difficult to form a clear, overall view of that information. You can use a PivotTable to help organize the data into a meaningful summary. A PivotTable summarizes data into categories using functions such as COUNT, SUM, AVERAGE, MAX, and MIN. For example, Mary is preparing a presentation for the museum's board of directors that will include a report of the appraised value of the museum's art objects by location, category, and condition. Although there are several ways to generate the information Mary needs, a PivotTable can generate this information quickly and concisely.

To create a PivotTable report, you need to specify which fields in the data source to summarize. In the ArtObjects table, the Appraised Value field is the most likely field to summarize. In other applications, fields such as salaries, sales, and costs are frequently summarized in PivotTables. In PivotTable terminology, the fields that contain summary data are known as values fields. Category fields are the fields that group the values in a PivotTable, such as condition, location, and year acquired. Category fields appear in PivotTables as row labels, column labels, and report filters, which allows you to focus on a subset of the PivotTable by displaying one, several, or all items. Figure 5-27 shows the PivotTable you will create.

**Figure 5-27**    **Sample PivotTable**

| | A | B | C | D | E | F |
|---|---|---|---|---|---|---|
| 2 | | | | | | |
| 3 | Total Appraised Value | | | | | |
| 4 | | Installation | Painting | Sculpture | Textile | Grand Total |
| 5 | East Pavilion | | $436,639 | $141,525 | $53,000 | $631,164 |
| 6 | Courtyard | $16,500 | $137,500 | $52,000 | | $206,000 |
| 7 | Garden | $118,000 | | $24,100 | | $142,100 |
| 8 | South Pavilion | $53,000 | $88,500 | | | $141,500 |
| 9 | West Pavilion | | $20,000 | $3,859 | | $23,859 |
| 10 | Grand Total | $187,500 | $682,639 | $221,484 | $53,000 | $1,144,623 |

You can easily rearrange, hide, and display different category fields in the PivotTable to provide alternative views of the data. This ability to "pivot" the table—for example, change row headings to column positions and vice versa—gives the PivotTable its name and makes it a powerful analytical tool. In Figure 5-28, the PivotTable is rearranged so that the Category items appear as row labels and the Location items appear as column labels.

**Figure 5-28**    **Sample PivotTable with rows and columns pivoted**

| | A | B | C | D | E | F | G |
|---|---|---|---|---|---|---|---|
| 1 | | | | | | | |
| 2 | Total Appraised Value | | | | | | |
| 3 | | Courtyard | East Pavilion | Garden | South Pavilion | West Pavilion | Grand Total |
| 4 | Installation | $ 16,500 | | $ 118,000 | $ 53,000 | | $ 187,500 |
| 5 | Painting | $ 137,500 | $ 436,639 | | $ 88,500 | $ 20,000 | $ 682,639 |
| 6 | Sculpture | $ 52,000 | $ 141,525 | $ 24,100 | | $ 3,859 | $ 221,484 |
| 7 | Textile | | $ 53,000 | | | | $ 53,000 |
| 8 | Grand Total | $ 206,000 | $ 631,164 | $142,100 | $ 141,500 | $ 23,859 | $1,144,623 |

To conceptualize the layout of a PivotTable and convey your ideas to others who might implement them, a useful first step in creating a PivotTable is to sketch its layout. Mary's sketch, shown in Figure 5-29, illustrates the PivotTable you will create to show the appraised value of the art objects organized by location, category, and condition.

**Figure 5-29**    PivotTable sketch

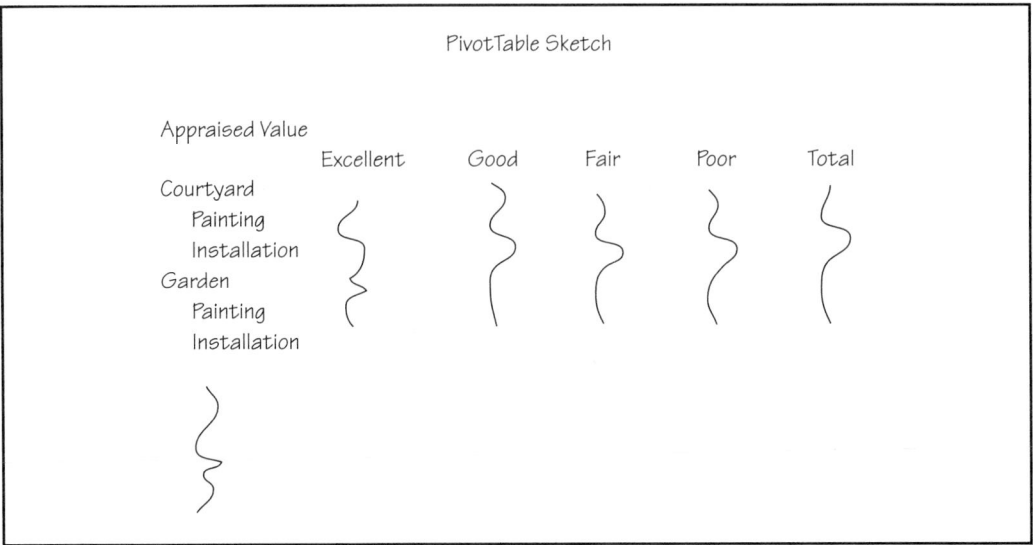

You are ready to create a PivotTable summarizing the total appraised value of art objects by location, category, and condition.

**PROSKILLS**

## Written Communication: Summarizing Data with a PivotTable

PivotTables are a great way to summarize data from selected fields of an Excel table or range, which can help you back up or support specific points in written documents. The PivotTable omits all the detailed data, enabling readers to focus on the bigger picture. This makes it easier for readers to understand the results and gain insights about the topic.

You can show summaries in written documents based on function results in PivotTables. The SUM function is probably the most frequently used function. For example, you might show the total sales for a region. However, you can use many other functions to summarize the data, including COUNT, AVERAGE, MIN, MAX, PRODUCT, COUNT NUMBERS, STDEV, STDEVP, VAR, and VARP. For example, you might show the average sales for a region, the minimum price of a product, or a count of the number of products sold.

When you write a report, you want supporting data to be presented in the way that best communicates your points. With PivotTables, you display the values in different views. For example, to compare one item to another item in the PivotTable, you can show the values as a percentage of a total. You can display the data in each row as a percentage of the total for the row. You can also display the data in each column as a percentage of the total for the column or display the data as a percentage of the grand total of all the data in the PivotTable. Viewing data as a percentage of the total is useful for analyses such as comparing product sales with total sales within a region or comparing expense categories to total expenses for the year

As you can see, PivotTables provide great flexibility in how you analyze and display data. This makes it easier to present data in a way that highlights and supports the points you are communicating, making your written documents much more effective.

# Creating a PivotTable

To create the PivotTable that will provide the information Mary needs, you will use the PivotTable dialog box to select the data to analyze and the location of the PivotTable report. Often when creating a PivotTable, you begin with data stored in a worksheet, although a PivotTable can also be created using data stored in an external database file such as one in Access. In this case, you will use the ArtObjects table to create the PivotTable and place the PivotTable in a new worksheet.

### Creating a PivotTable

- Click in the Excel table or select the range of data for the PivotTable.
- In the Tables group on the Insert tab, click the PivotTable button.
- Click the Select a table or range option button and verify the reference in the Table/Range box.
- Click the New Worksheet option button or click the Existing Worksheet option button and specify a cell.
- Click the OK button.
- Click the check boxes for the fields you want to add to the PivotTable (or drag fields to the appropriate box in the layout section).
- If needed, drag fields to different boxes in the layout section.

When you create a PivotTable, you need to specify where to find the data for the PivotTable. The data can be in an Excel table or range in the current workbook or an external data source such as an Access database file. You also specify whether to place the PivotTable in a new or an existing worksheet. If you place the PivotTable in an existing worksheet, you must also specify the cell in which you want the upper-left corner of the PivotTable to appear. For the appraised value PivotTable report, you will use the ArtObjects table and place the PivotTable in a new worksheet.

### To create a PivotTable using the ArtObjects table:

1. If you took a break after the previous session, make sure the LaFouch Museum workbook is open, the Art Collection worksheet is active, and the Excel table is active.

2. Click the **Insert** tab on the Ribbon, and then, in the Tables group, click the **PivotTable** button. The Create PivotTable dialog box opens. See Figure 5-30.

**Figure 5-30**    **Create PivotTable dialog box**

> **3.** Make sure the **Select a table or range** option button is selected and **ArtObjects** appears in the Table/Range box.

> **4.** Click the **New Worksheet** option button, if necessary. This sets the PivotTable report to be placed in a new worksheet.

> **5.** Click the **OK** button. A new worksheet, Sheet1, is inserted to the left of the Art Collection worksheet. The empty PivotTable report area is where the finished PivotTable will be placed. You use the PivotTable Field List to build the PivotTable by adding, removing, and arranging fields, or columns. The PivotTable Tools contextual tabs appear on the Ribbon. See Figure 5-31.

| Figure 5-31 | PivotTable report area and PivotTable Field List |
|---|---|

The PivotTable Field List is divided into two sections. The upper field list section displays the names of each field in the ArtObjects table. You check a field check box to add that field to the PivotTable. The lower layout section includes boxes for the four areas in which you can place fields: Report Filter, Row Labels, Column Labels, and Values. Figure 5-32 describes the function of each area.

**Figure 5-32** | **Layout areas for a PivotTable**

| Layout Area | Description |
|---|---|
| Row Labels | The fields you want to display as the rows in the PivotTable. One row is displayed for each unique item in this area. You can have nested row fields. |
| Column Labels | The fields you want to display as columns at the top of the PivotTable. One column is displayed for each unique item in this area. You can have nested column fields. |
| Report Filter | A field used to filter the report by selecting one or more items, enabling you to display a subset of data in a PivotTable report. |
| Values | The fields you want to summarize. |

Initially, selected fields with numeric data are placed in the Values area and the SUM function is used to summarize the PivotTable. Fields with nonnumeric data are placed in the Row Labels area. You can change these default placements of fields.

## Adding Fields to a PivotTable

You need to calculate the total appraised value of art objects by location, within location by category, and within category by condition. In the PivotTable, you'll begin by adding the Location, Category, and Condition fields to appear as row labels, and the data in the Appraised Value field to be summarized. First, you will create a PivotTable summarizing the appraised value by location.

### To add fields to the PivotTable:

1. In the PivotTable Field List, click the **Location** check box. The Location field is added to the Row Labels box and the unique values in the Location field—Courtyard, East Pavilion, Garden, South Pavilion, and West Pavilion—appear in the PivotTable report area. See Figure 5-33.

**Figure 5-33** | **PivotTable with the Location field items as row labels**

Location field values entered as the row labels in the PivotTable

click the Location check box

Location field entered in the Row Labels box because its field values are text

▶ **2.** In the PivotTable Field List, click the **Appraised Value** check box. The Sum of Appraised Value button appears in the Values box. The PivotTable groups the items from the ArtObjects table by location, and calculates the total appraised value for each location. The grand total appears at the bottom of the PivotTable. See Figure 5-34.

| Figure 5-34 | PivotTable of the appraised value of art objects by location |
| --- | --- |

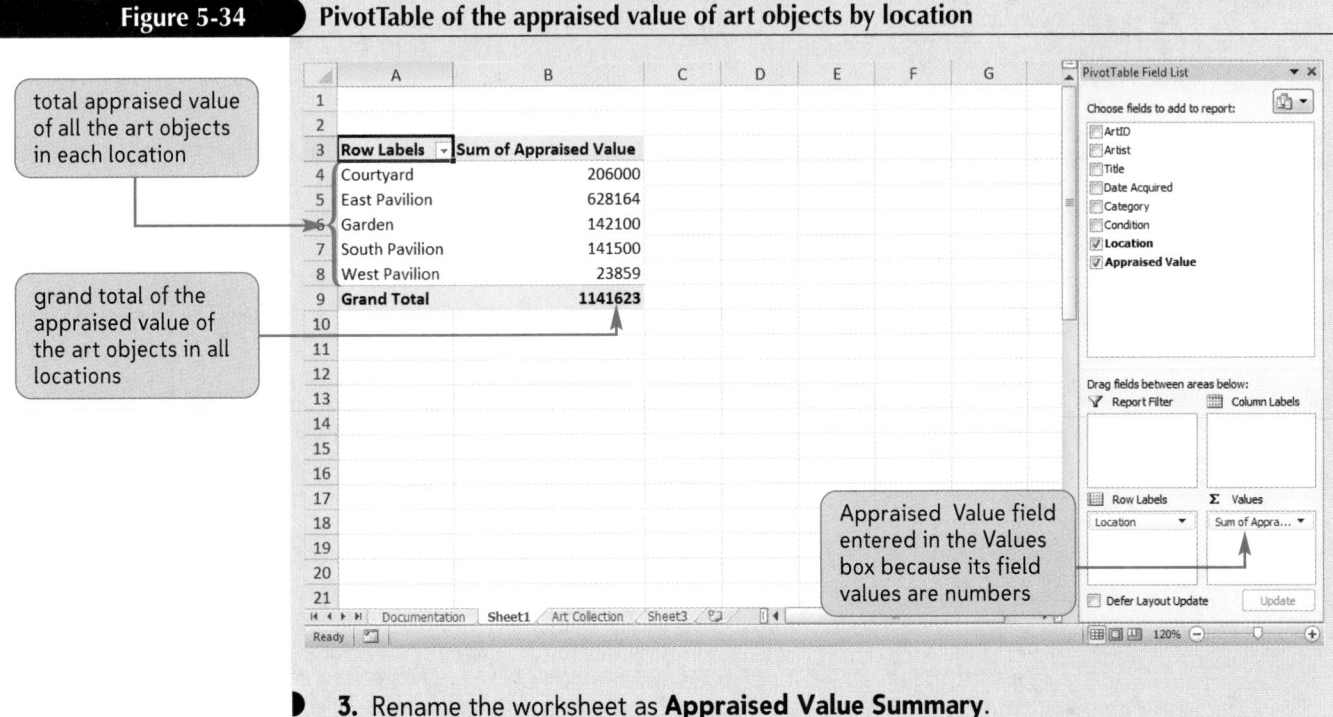

total appraised value of all the art objects in each location

grand total of the appraised value of the art objects in all locations

Appraised Value field entered in the Values box because its field values are numbers

▶ **3.** Rename the worksheet as **Appraised Value Summary**.

By default, the PivotTable report uses the SUM function for numbers in the Values area and the COUNT function for text and other nonnumeric values. If you want a different summary function, such as AVERAGE, MAX, or MIN, click the appropriate button in the Values box (in this case, the button is called "Sum of Appraised Value") in the PivotTable Field List, and then click Value Field Settings. The Value Field Settings dialog box opens. You can then select the type of calculation you want from the list of available functions, and then click the OK button.

Next, you'll add the Category and Condition fields to the PivotTable.

## To add the Category and Condition fields to the PivotTable:

▶ **1.** In the PivotTable Field List, click the **Category** check box. The Category field appears in the Row Labels box below the Location field, and the unique items in the Category field are indented below each location field item in the PivotTable.

**Trouble?** If the PivotTable Field List is not visible, the active cell is probably not in the PivotTable. Click any cell within the PivotTable to redisplay the PivotTable Field List.

▶ **2.** In the PivotTable Field List, click the **Condition** check box. The Condition field appears in the Row Labels box below the Category field, and its unique items are indented below the Location and Category fields already in the PivotTable. See Figure 5-35.

| Figure 5-35 | PivotTable with Location, Category, and Condition field items as row labels |

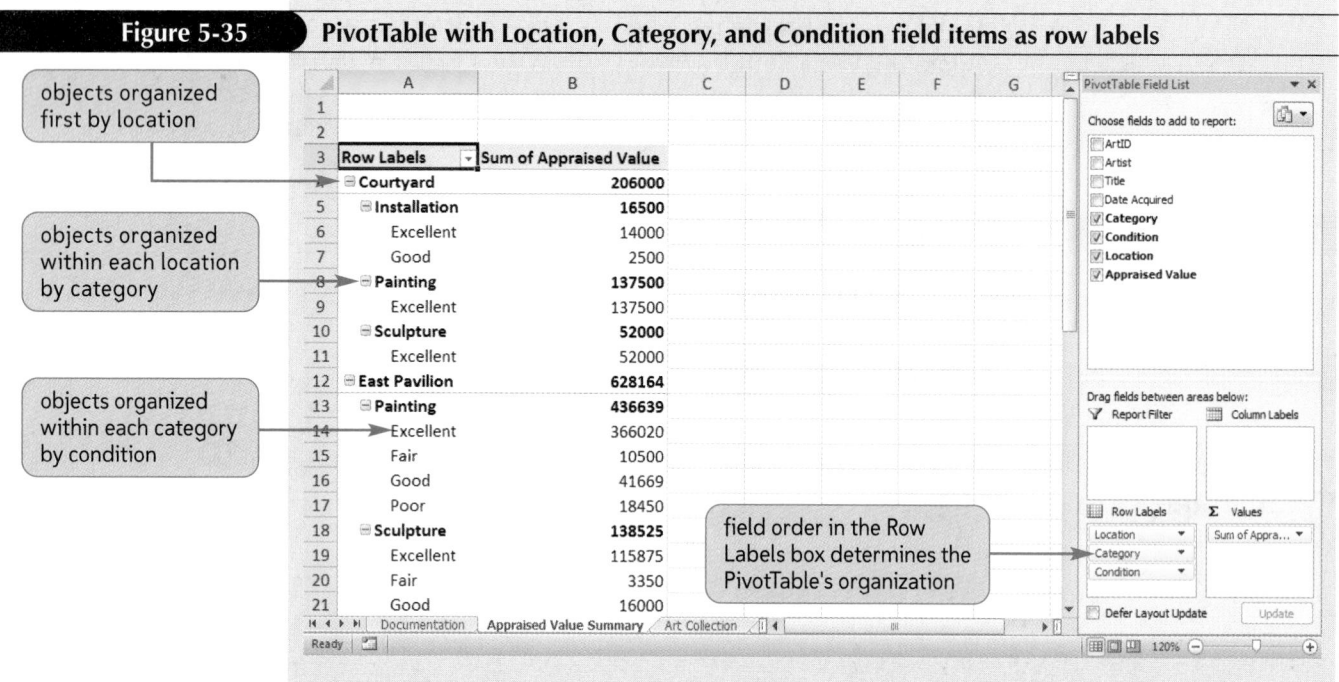

objects organized first by location

objects organized within each location by category

objects organized within each category by condition

field order in the Row Labels box determines the PivotTable's organization

## Applying PivotTable Styles

As with worksheet cells and Excel tables, you can quickly format a PivotTable report using a preset style. You can choose from a gallery of PivotTable styles similar to the gallery of Table styles. You can point to any style in the gallery to see a Live Preview of the PivotTable with that style applied. You also can modify the appearance of PivotTables by adding or removing banded rows, banded columns, row headers, and column headers.

You will apply the Dark 4 style, which makes each group in the PivotTable stand out and subtotals in the report easier to find.

### To apply a PivotTable style to the PivotTable report:

1. Make sure the active cell is in the PivotTable, and then click the **PivotTable Tools Design** tab on the Ribbon.

2. In the PivotTable Styles group, click the **More** button to open the PivotTable Styles gallery.

3. Move the pointer over each style to see the Live Preview of the PivotTable report with that style.

4. Click the **Pivot Style Dark 4** style (the fourth style in the Dark section). The style is applied to the PivotTable.

## Formatting PivotTable Values Fields

Applying PivotTable styles does not change the numeric formatting in the PivotTable. Mary wants the numbers in the PivotTable to be quickly recognized as currency. You can format cells in a PivotTable the same way as you do cells in the worksheet. You'll change the total appraised values in the PivotTable to Currency style.

## To format the appraised value numbers in the PivotTable:

1. Click any cell in the **Sum of Appraised Value** column of the PivotTable report.

2. Click the **PivotTable Tools Options** tab on the Ribbon, and then click the **Field Settings** button in the Active Field group. The Value Field Settings dialog box opens. See Figure 5-36.

**Figure 5-36**    Value Field Settings dialog box

settings in dialog box affect this component of the PivotTable

select a summary calculation

click to format the PivotTable values

enter the label you want to appear on the PivotTable

click to see other ways to view the values

3. Click the **Number Format** button. The Format Cells dialog box opens. This is the same dialog box you've used before to format numbers in worksheet cells.

4. Click **Currency** in the Category box, and then type 0 in the Decimal places box.

5. Click the **OK** button. The numbers in the PivotTable will be formatted as currency with no decimal places.

6. In the **Custom Name** box, replace "Sum Of Appraised Value" with **Total Appraised Value**.

7. Click the **OK** button. The Value Field Settings dialog box closes, and the name used to describe the calculations in the PivotTable report is changed to the custom name you entered.

**TIP**

You can use the Summarize Values By tab to change the SUM function to a different summary function, such as AVERAGE. The name is updated to reflect your selection.

## Rearranging a PivotTable

You can add, remove, and rearrange fields to change the PivotTable's layout. Recall that the benefit of a PivotTable is that it summarizes large amounts of data into a readable format. After you create a PivotTable, you can view the same data in different ways. The PivotTable Field List enables you to change, or pivot, the view of the data in the PivotTable by dragging the field buttons to different areas in the layout section.

Refer back to Mary's PivotTable sketch in Figure 5-29. As illustrated in the sketch, the Condition field items should be positioned as column labels instead of row labels in the PivotTable. You'll move the Condition field now to produce the format Mary wants.

## To move the Condition field:

1. In the layout section of the PivotTable Field List, locate the Condition field button in the Row Labels box.

▸ **2.** Drag the **Condition** field button from the Row Labels box to the Column Labels box. The PivotTable is rearranged so that the Condition field is a column label instead of a row label. See Figure 5-37. Each time you make a change in the PivotTable Field List, the PivotTable layout is rearranged.

| Figure 5-37 | **PivotTable rearranged with Condition as a column label** |

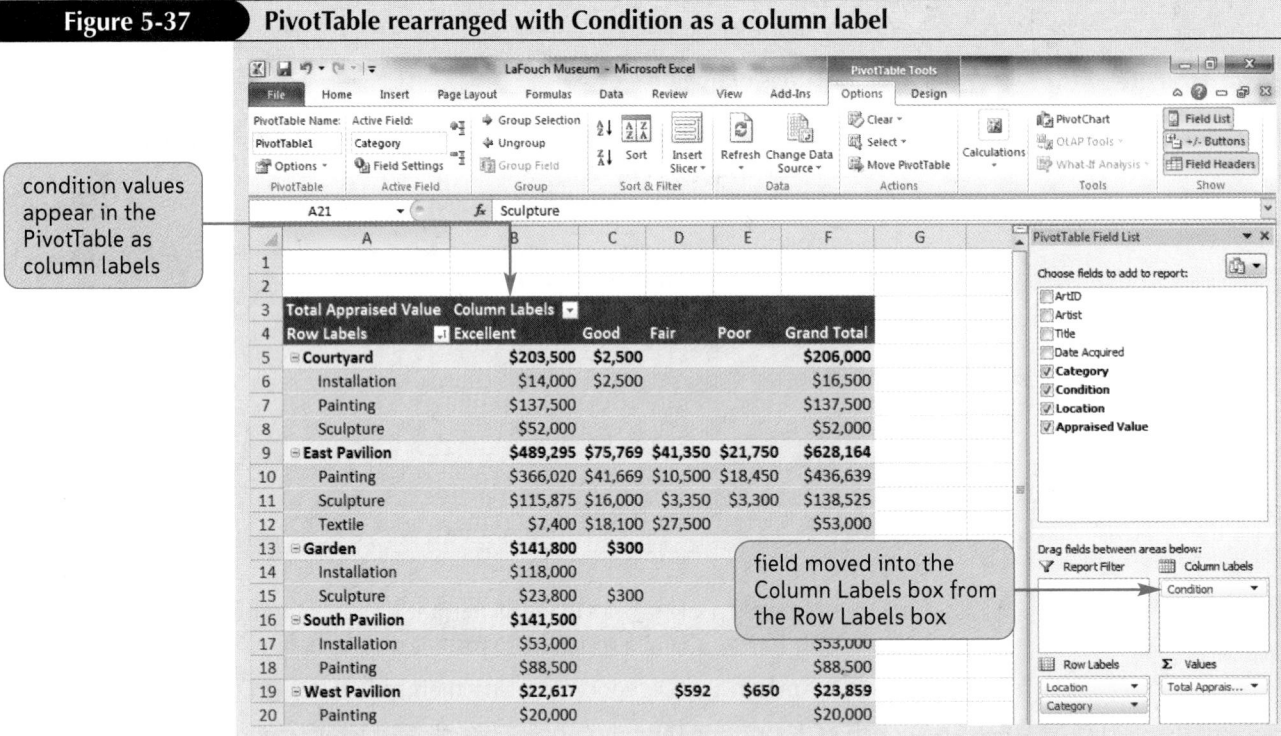

## Changing the PivotTable Report Layout Options

The Compact report layout, shown in Figure 5-37, places all fields from the row area in a single column and indents the items from each field below the outer fields. This is the default layout for PivotTable reports. You can choose two other layouts. In the Outline report layout, each field in the row area takes a column in the PivotTable. By default, the outline form shows the subtotals for each group at the top of every group. The Tabular report layout displays one column for each field and leaves space for column headers. A total for each group appears at the bottom of each group. You can find these report layout options on the PivotTable Tools Design tab in the Layout group.

You will see how the PivotTable looks in these alternative layouts.

**To display the PivotTable in Outline and Tabular layouts:**

▸ **1.** Click the **PivotTable Tools Design** tab on the Ribbon.

▸ **2.** In the Layout group, click the **Report Layout** button, and then click **Show in Outline Form**. The PivotTable layout changes to the Outline report layout. See Figure 5-38.

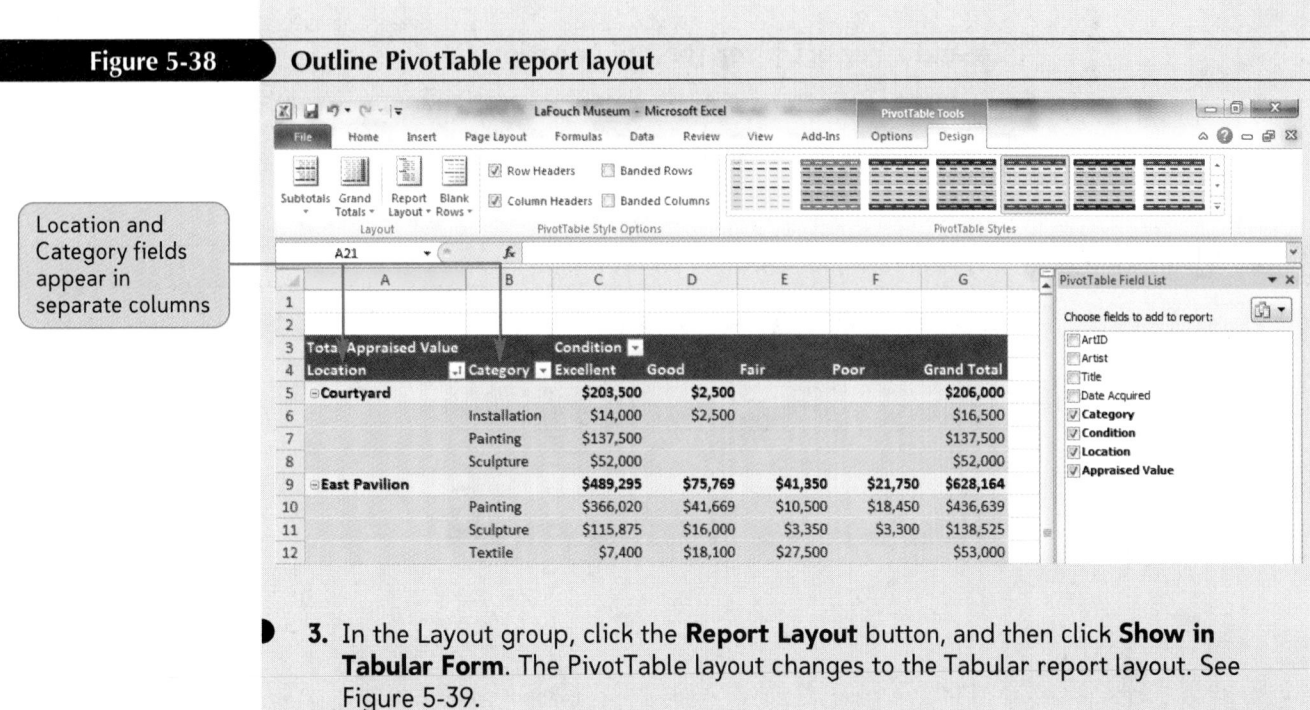

| Figure 5-38 | Outline PivotTable report layout |

Location and Category fields appear in separate columns

3. In the Layout group, click the **Report Layout** button, and then click **Show in Tabular Form**. The PivotTable layout changes to the Tabular report layout. See Figure 5-39.

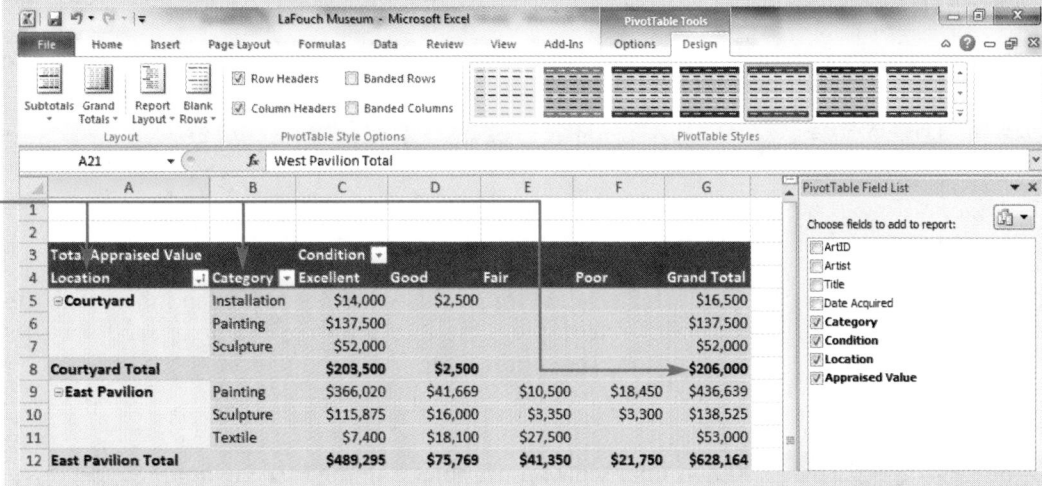

| Figure 5-39 | Tabular PivotTable report layout |

Location and Category fields appear in separate columns, and totals appear below each location grouping

4. In the Layout group, click the **Report Layout** button, and then click **Show in Compact Form**. The PivotTable returns to the original layout, the Compact form.

## Adding a Report Filter to a PivotTable

You can drag a field to the Report Filter area to create a filtered view of the PivotTable report. A report filter is used to filter the PivotTable to display summarized data for one or more field items or all field items in the Report Filter area. For example, creating a report filter for the Location field allows you to view or print the total appraised value for all locations or for specific locations such as the Courtyard.

You will add a report filter for the Location field to see if displaying the information in this way adds value to the report.

## To add a report filter for the Location field:

**1.** In the PivotTable Field List, drag the **Location** button from the Row Labels box to the Report Filter box. The Report Filter field item shows "All" to indicate that the PivotTable report displays all the summarized data associated with the Location field. See Figure 5-40.

**Figure 5-40** | **PivotTable with the Location report filter applied**

PivotTable shows all the values in the Location field

field moved into the Report Filter box

Next, you'll change the summarized report to show only art objects in the East Pavilion.

**2.** Click the **report filter arrow** in cell B1. The AutoFilter menu opens, showing the field items displayed.

**3.** Click **East Pavilion** in the AutoFilter menu, and then click the **OK** button. The PivotTable displays the total appraised value of art objects located only in the East Pavilion. The report filter arrow changes to an icon to indicate the PivotTable is currently filtered. See Figure 5-41.

**TIP**

To filter more than one location at a time, click the Select Multiple Items check box in the AutoFilter menu to add a check mark next to each item, and then uncheck items you don't want to include.

**Figure 5-41** | **Report filter view for art objects in the East Pavilion**

filtered PivotTable shows the appraised values of art objects located in the East Pavilion

**4.** In the PivotTable Field List, drag the **Location** button from the Report Filter box to the top of the Row Labels box. The Location field is positioned above the Category field, and the PivotTable returns to its previous layout.

**Trouble?** If the PivotTable report is arranged differently, the Location field is not the top field in the Row Labels box. Drag the Location button in the Row Labels box above the Category button.

## Filtering PivotTable Fields

Filtering a field lets you focus on a subset of items in that field. You can filter field items in the PivotTable by clicking the field arrow button in the PivotTable that represents the data you want to hide, and then uncheck the check box for each item you want to hide. To show hidden items, you click the field arrow button and check the check box for the item you want to show.

Mary wants to focus her analysis on art objects in excellent, good, and fair condition. She asks you to remove art objects in poor condition from the PivotTable. You will hide the art objects in poor condition from the PivotTable report.

### To filter the Condition field items from the PivotTable:

**1.** In the PivotTable, click the **Column Labels filter arrow**. The AutoFilter menu displays the list of items in the Condition field.

**2.** Click the **Poor** check box to remove the check mark. The Select All check box is deselected as well.

**3.** Click the **OK** button. The Poor column is removed from the PivotTable. The PivotTable includes only art objects in excellent, good, and fair condition. See Figure 5-42. You can show the hidden objects by clicking the Column Labels arrow and checking the Poor check box.

**Figure 5-42**   **PivotTable report filtered by condition**

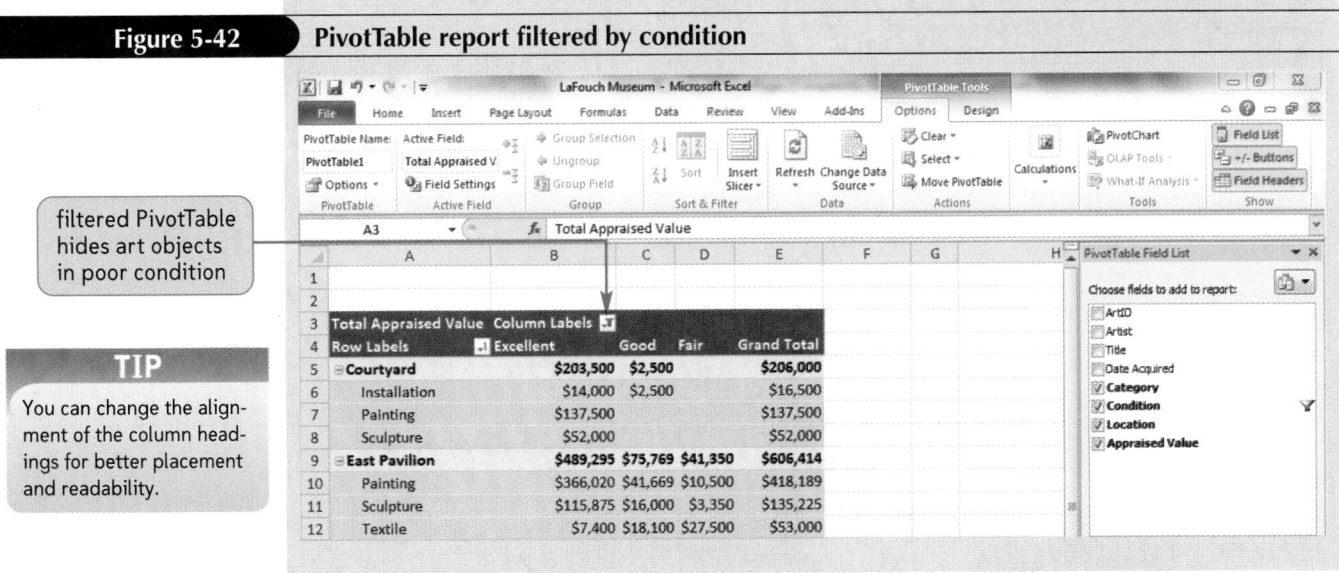

filtered PivotTable hides art objects in poor condition

**TIP**

You can change the alignment of the column headings for better placement and readability.

## Collapsing and Expanding Items

You can expand and collapse items in the row labels of the PivotTable to view fields at different levels of detail. The Expand and Collapse buttons identify where more details exist. The Expand button ⊞ indicates you can show more details for that item, and the Collapse button ⊟ indicates you can hide details for that item. The lowest level of the hierarchy does not have Expand and Collapse buttons because there is no data to expand or collapse. These buttons are helpful when you have complex PivotTables where you want to switch quickly between a detailed view and an overview.

Mary wants to see the total appraised value for each location without the Category items in the PivotTable. You will collapse the level of detail so that only the Location items are showing. Currently, all items are expanded.

### To collapse the Courtyard items in the PivotTable:

▶ 1. Point to the **Collapse** button ⊟ next to Courtyard until the pointer changes to ▷.

▶ 2. Click the **Collapse** button ⊟ next to Courtyard. The detail items below Courtyard are hidden, and the Collapse button changes to an Expand button.

▶ 3. Click the **Collapse** button ⊟ next to East Pavilion, Garden, South Pavilion, and West Pavilion. The details for these four locations are hidden, and only the Location items are displayed. The PivotTable provides a higher level summary without displaying the Category details. See Figure 5-43.

| Figure 5-43 | PivotTable with all locations collapsed and categories hidden |

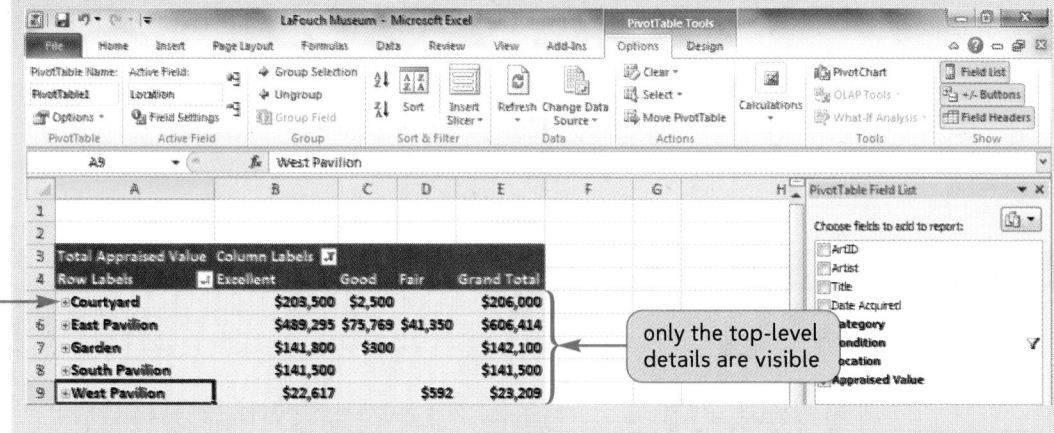

click to display the hidden details

only the top-level details are visible

You can collapse or expand all level of detail in a PivotTable at one time. You'll do this to return to the original level of detail.

### To expand all items in the PivotTable:

▶ 1. Click the **PivotTable Tools Options** tab on the Ribbon.

▶ 2. In the Active Field group, click the **Expand Entire Field** button. The detail items for all levels reappear. The lowest level of the hierarchy does not have Expand and Collapse buttons.

## Sorting PivotTable Fields

You can sort a PivotTable field either by its own items—for example, alphabetizing fields such as Location and Category—or by the values in the body of the PivotTable. To sort a PivotTable field, you can use any of the Sort buttons on the Options tab to sort the information in a PivotTable report. These options are similar to the sort options you used earlier in the tutorial.

The PivotTable might be more informative if the appraised values in each location were sorted in descending order. You will sort the PivotTable so that the location with the highest total appraised value is displayed first.

### To sort the PivotTable:

1. Click cell **E5**, which contains the Grand Total for Courtyard. This is the field total you want to sort.

2. In the Sort & Filter group on the PivotTable Tools Options tab, click the **Sort Largest to Smallest** button. The Location field is sorted based on the total appraised value for each location. For example, the East Pavilion location appears first in the PivotTable because it has the highest total appraised value, $606,414. The Courtyard location appears next because it has the second highest total appraised value, $206,000, and so on. See Figure 5-44.

**Figure 5-44** ▸ **PivotTable results sorted by location**

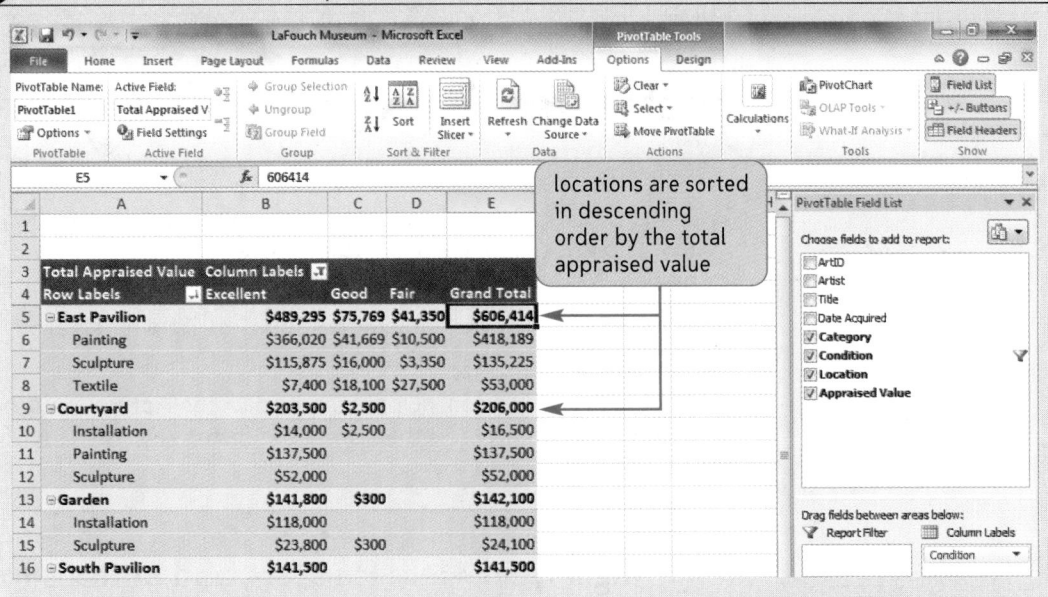

## Adding a Second Values Field to a PivotTable

You can expand a PivotTable to create a more informative table by adding fields to the Values layout area. For example, Mary believes that a more accurate presentation of the art objects would include the number of objects corresponding to the total value in each cell of the PivotTable. Adding the Title field to the Values box would count the number of art objects in each location-category-condition combination (because the title is a non-numeric field). You will add the Title field to the PivotTable.

### To add the Title field to the Values box:

1. In the PivotTable Field List, drag **Title** from the field area to immediately below the Total Appraised Value button in the Values box. The PivotTable displays the number of art objects as well as the total appraised value. The Values box in the layout area includes a second button, Count of Title, and fields from the Values box are added to the Column Labels box. See Figure 5-45.

| Figure 5-45 | Count of art objects added to the PivotTable |
| --- | --- |

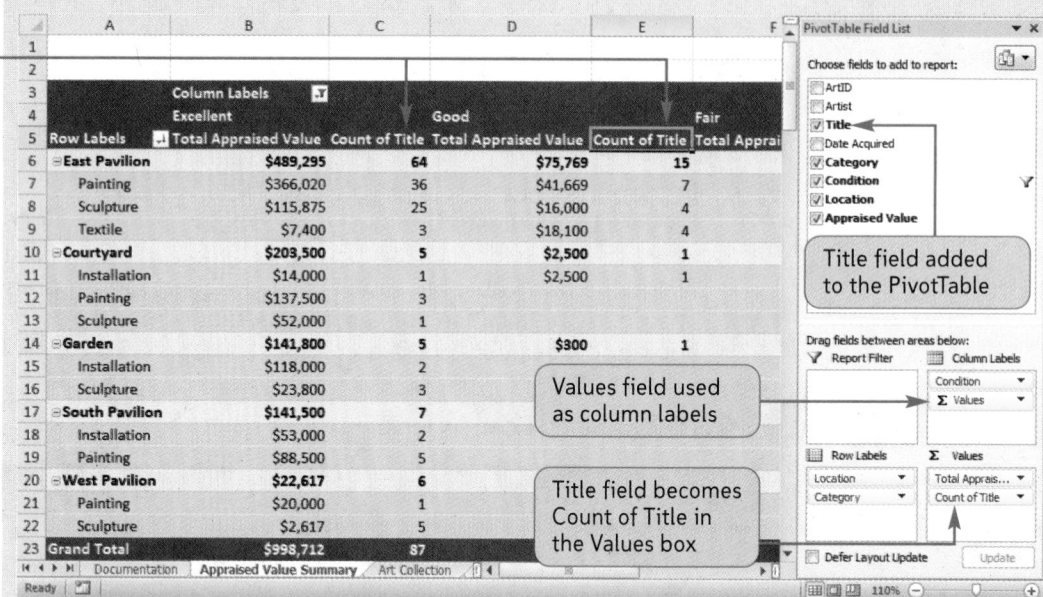

Count of Title column appears for each condition

Title field added to the PivotTable

Values field used as column labels

Title field becomes Count of Title in the Values box

2. In the Show group on the PivotTable Tools Options tab, click the **Field List** button. The PivotTable Field List closes, so a section of the PivotTable is no longer hidden. More of the PivotTable is now visible.

3. In the PivotTable, click any of the **Count of Title** labels. You want to change the "Count of Title" label to "Count."

4. On the PivotTable Tools Options tab, click the **Active Field** box in the Active Field group, type **Count**, and then press the **Enter** key. The Count label replaces the Count of Title label.

## Removing a Field, Field Headers, and Buttons from a PivotTable

The PivotTable report with the Count column looks cluttered and is difficult to read. You will remove the Title field from the PivotTable. Removing a field from the PivotTable has no effect on the underlying Excel table.

### To remove the Title field from the PivotTable:

1. In the Show group on the PivotTable Tools Options tab, click the **Field List** button to display the PivotTable Field List.

2. In the PivotTable Field List, click the **Title** check box in the field area. The Count column is removed from the PivotTable, which returns to its previous layout. The Title field is still in the ArtObjects table.

The PivotTable is almost complete. Mary wants you to improve the appearance of the PivotTable by removing the field headers (Row Labels and Column Labels) and hiding the Expand/Collapse buttons.

### To remove the field headers and hide the Expand/Collapse buttons:

▶ **1.** In the Show group on the PivotTable Tools Options tab, click the **+/- Buttons** button. The Expand/Collapse buttons disappear from the PivotTable.

▶ **2.** In the Show group, click the **Field Headers** button. The Column Labels and Row Labels headers are hidden. See Figure 5-46.

| Figure 5-46 | PivotTable without field headers and the Expand/Collapse buttons |
|---|---|

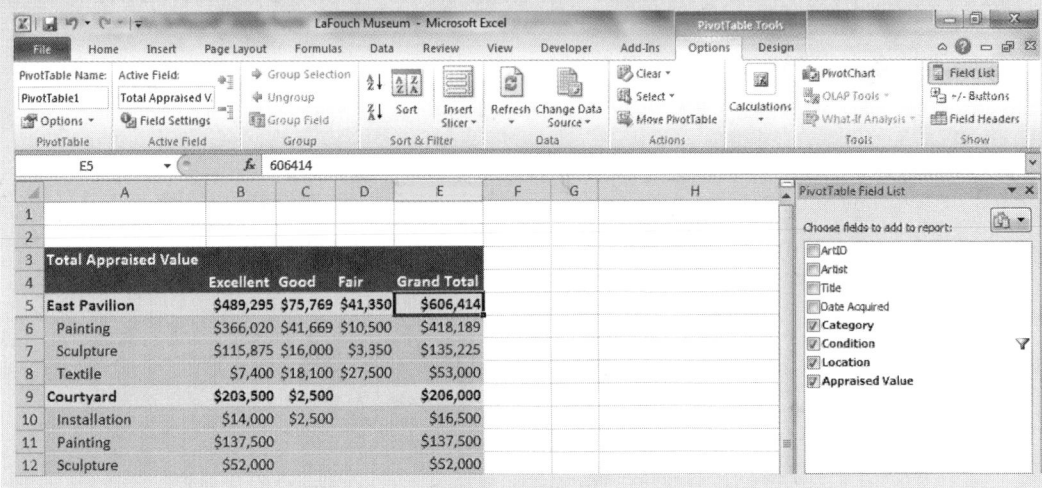

## Using a Slicer to Filter a PivotTable

Although you can filter a PivotTable using the report filter arrow, column label arrows, and row label arrows, a slicer provides a quicker and easier way to filter a PivotTable or PivotChart. You can create a slicer for any field in a range or an Excel table. Every slicer consists of an object that contains a button for each unique value in that field. You can format the slicer and its buttons, changing its style, height, and width. You also can create more than one slicer at a time. For example, you can have a slicer for Category that has a button for each unique category value and a second slicer for Condition. This allows you to filter a PivotTable report so that it displays the results for all paintings in Excellent or Good condition by clicking the corresponding slicer buttons.

You will add a Location slicer to the current PivotTable so that Mary can have more flexibility in making changes to the PivotTable.

### To add the Location slicer to the PivotTable:

▶ **1.** Set the width of column F to **8**.

▶ **2.** In the Sort & Filter group on the PivotTable Tools Options tab, click the **Insert Slicer** button. The Insert Slicers dialog box opens, displaying a list of available PivotTable fields. You can select any or all of the fields.

▶ **3.** Click the **Location** check box to insert a check mark, and then click the **OK** button. The Location slicer control appears on the worksheet.

▶ **4.** Drag the **Location slicer control** to the right of the PivotTable, placing its upper-left corner in cell G3.

▶ **5.** If necessary, click the **Location** slicer to select the slicer object. The Slicer Tools Options tab appears on the Ribbon.

▶ **6.** In the Size group on the Slicer Tools Options tab, change the height to **1.9"** and change the width to **1.3"**. The slicer object is resized, eliminating the extra space below the buttons and to the right of the labels.

▶ **7.** In the Slicer Styles group, click the **More** button ⊽, and then click **Slicer Style Dark 3**. The slicer colors now match the PivotTable. See Figure 5-47.

| Figure 5-47 | Location slicer control |
| --- | --- |

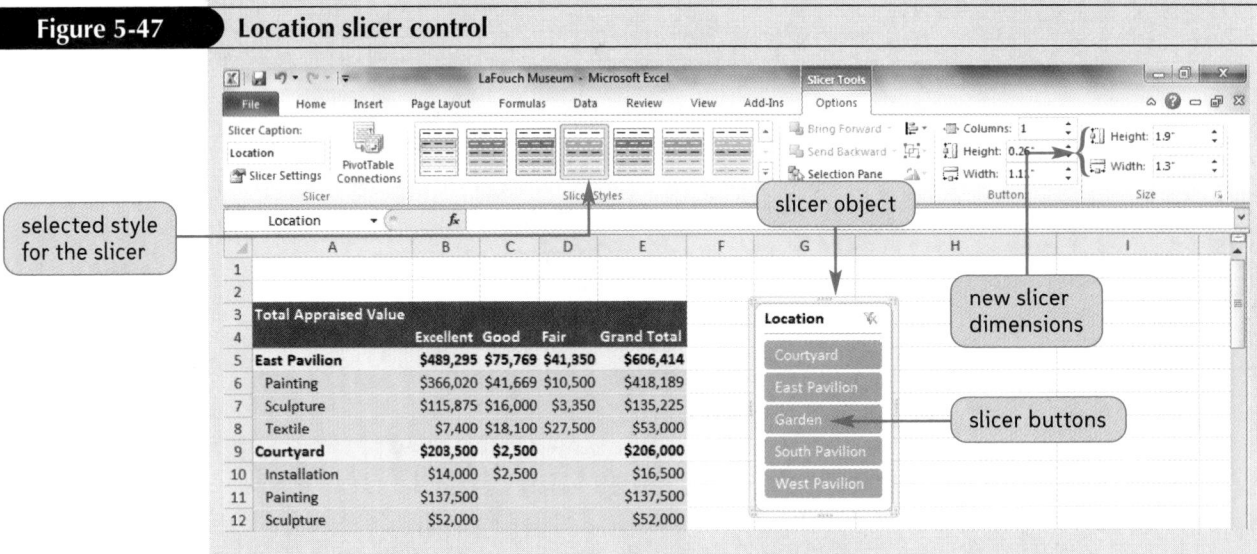

Mary wants you to display the results of the PivotTable for all the pavilion rooms—East, South, and West. You can do this quickly using the Location slicer.

### To filter the PivotTable using the Location slicer:

▶ **1.** In the Location slicer control, click the **East Pavilion** button. The PivotTable is filtered to display only the results for the East Pavilion. The other slicer buttons are gray because those locations have been filtered and are not part of the report.

▶ **2.** Press and hold the **Ctrl** key, click the **South Pavilion** button, and then release the Ctrl key. The South Pavilion data also appears in the PivotTable.

▶ **3.** Press and hold the **Ctrl** key, click the **West Pavilion** button, and then release the Ctrl key. The West Pavilion data is added to the PivotTable. See Figure 5-48.

| Figure 5-48 | Location slicer used to filter the PivotTable |

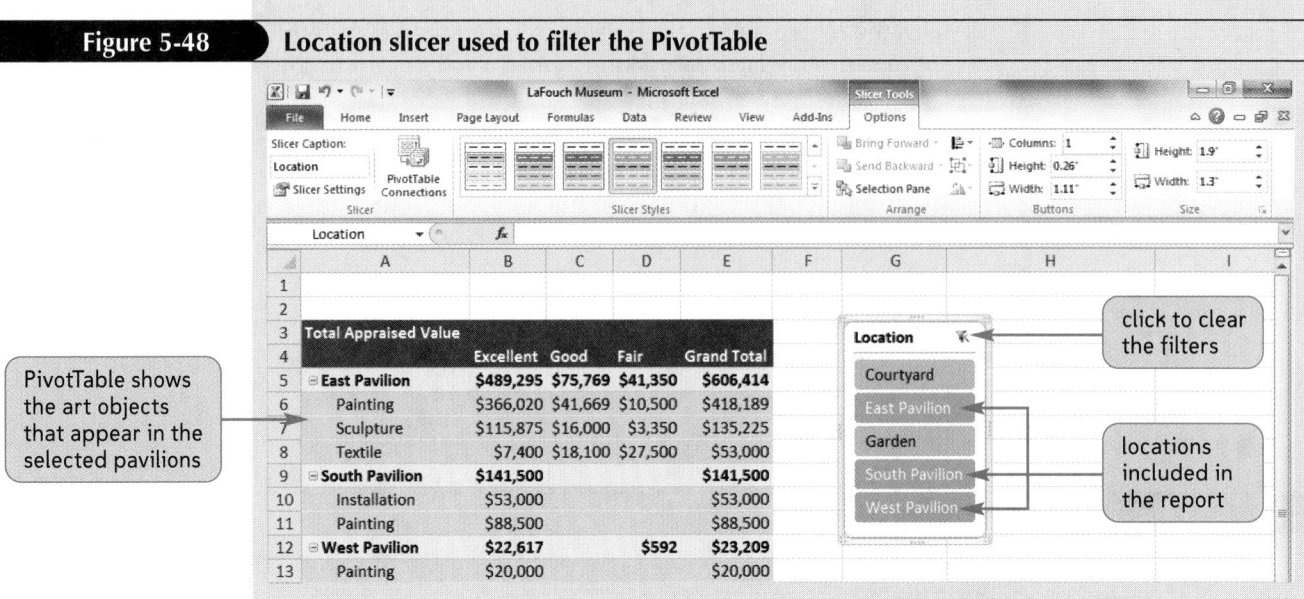

PivotTable shows the art objects that appear in the selected pavilions

click to clear the filters

locations included in the report

Next, you will remove all the filters so that Mary can view the PivotTable with all locations.

### To remove the filters from the PivotTable:

1. In the Location slicer, click the **Clear Filter** button 🔏. The filters are removed and all locations appear in the PivotTable.

2. In the Location slicer, notice that all the buttons are deselected, indicating that no filters are being used.

## Refreshing a PivotTable

The art object titled "Dancing in the Light" by Cridler has been reappraised and is now valued at $4,000 (not $1,000 as indicated in its current listing). You cannot change data directly in the PivotTable. Instead, you must edit the Excel table, and then **refresh**, or update, the PivotTable to reflect the updated data—in this case, the current state of the art objects list.

You'll edit the record for Dancing in the Light in the ArtObjects table. This sculpture is located in the East Pavilion and is in fair condition. This one change will affect the PivotTable in several locations. For example, currently the Total value of objects in the East Pavilion is $606,414; the sculptures in the East Pavilion are valued at $135,225; and sculptures in the East Pavilion in fair condition are valued at $3,350. After you update the appraised value of this art object in the Excel table, all these values in the PivotTable will increase by $3,000.

### To update the ArtObjects table:

1. Switch to the **Art Collection** worksheet, and then find **Cridler**, **Dancing in the Light** (ArtID 73).

> **2.** Click the record's Appraised Value cell, and then enter **4000**. The sculpture's appraised value is updated in the table. You'll return to the PivotTable report to see the effect of this change.

> **3.** Switch to the **Appraised Value Summary** worksheet. The appraised value totals for the East Pavilion are still $606,414, $135,225, and $3,350, respectively. The PivotTable is not updated when the data in its source table is updated, so you need to refresh the PivotTable manually.

> **4.** Click any cell in the PivotTable.

> **5.** Click the **PivotTable Tools Options** tab on the Ribbon, and then click the **Refresh** button in the Data group. The PivotTable report is updated. The appraised value totals are now $609,414, $138,225, and $6,350.

> **6.** In the Show group, click the **Field List** button. See Figure 5-49.

| Figure 5-49 | Refreshed PivotTable |
| --- | --- |

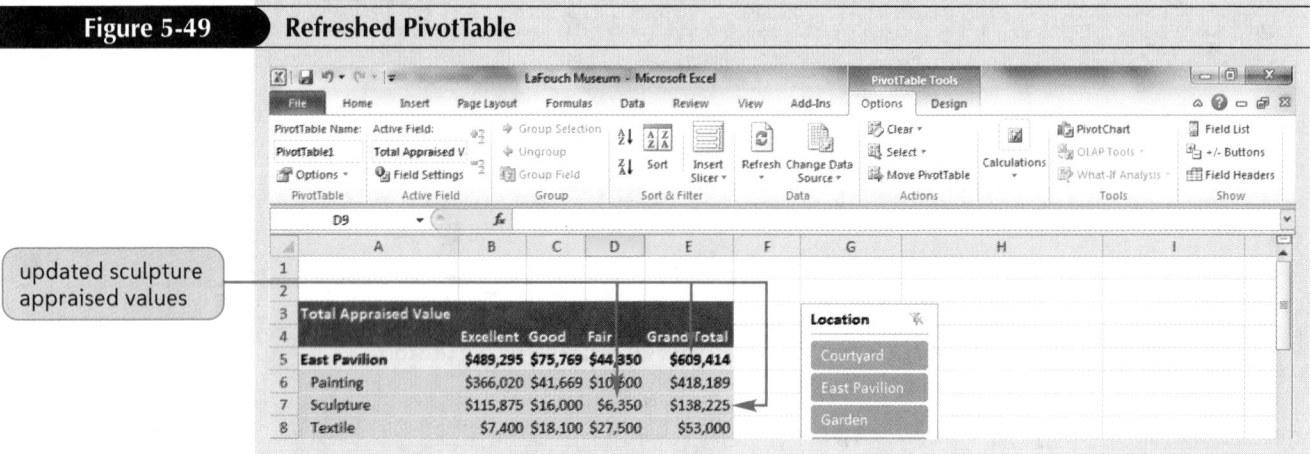

**Grouping PivotTable Items**

When a field contains numbers, dates, or times, you can combine items in the rows of a PivotTable and combine them into groups automatically. Mary thinks a PivotTable that displays the number of objects acquired each year would be of interest to the board of directors. This report involves using the Date Acquired field as a row label and ArtID as the values field, although you could use any field as the values field. When using a date field as a row label in a PivotTable, each date initially appears as a separate item.

Typically, you want to analyze date data by month, quarter, or year. To do that, you need to group the data in the Date Acquired field. Grouping items combines dates into larger groups such as months, quarters, or years so that the PivotTable can include the desired level of summarization. You can also group numeric items, typically into equal ranges. For example, you can calculate the number of art objects in appraised value groups based on increments of any amount you specify (for example, 1–25,000, 25,001–50,000, and so on).

You'll add a second PivotTable in a new worksheet.

**To create a PivotTable based on the Date Acquired field:**

> **1.** Switch to the **Art Collection** worksheet, and then click any cell in the Excel table. The table is active.

2. Click the **Insert** tab on the Ribbon, and then click the **PivotTable** button in the Tables group. The Create PivotTable dialog box opens.

3. Verify that the Table/Range box shows **ArtObjects** and the **New Worksheet** option button is selected, and then click the **OK** button. The PivotTable report area and PivotTable Field List appear in a new worksheet.

4. In the PivotTable Field List, click the **Date Acquired** check box. The Date Acquired field appears in the Row Labels box. Each unique date appears in the PivotTable report area. Mary wants each year to appear as a row label. You will correct that shortly.

5. Click the **ArtID** check box in the PivotTable Field List. "Sum of ArtID" appears in the Values box in the layout area because the ArtID field contains numeric data. See Figure 5-50.

| Figure 5-50 | PivotTable with Sum of ArtID for each date |

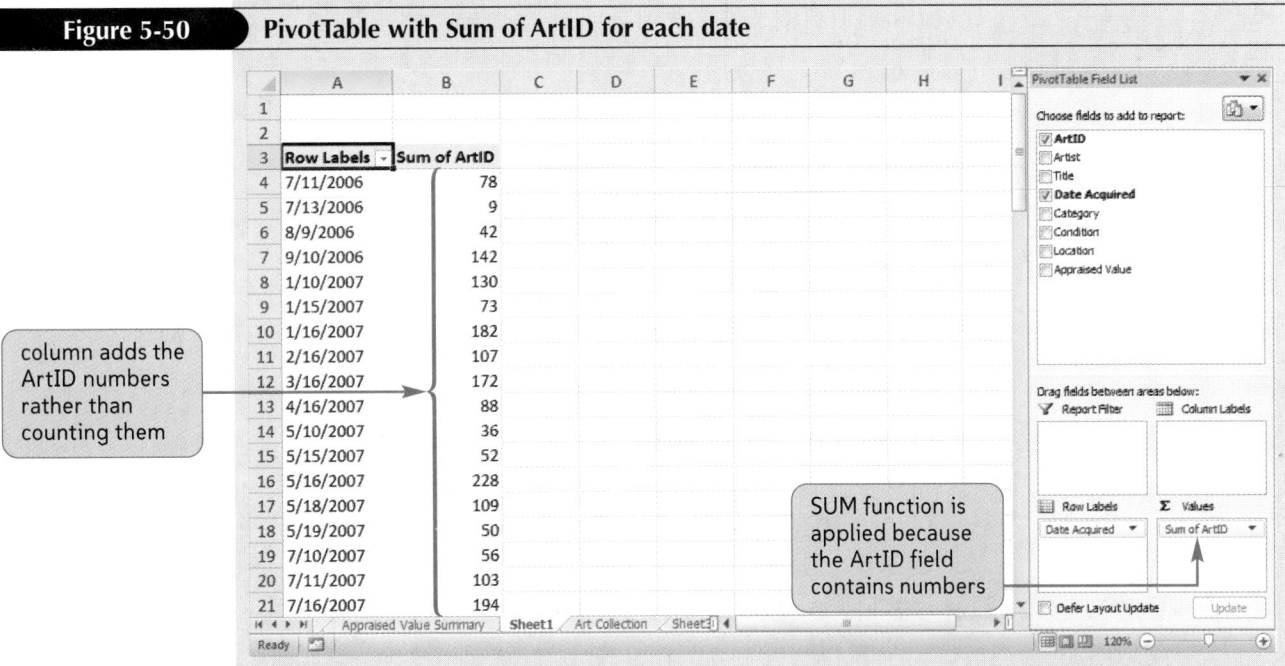

column adds the ArtID numbers rather than counting them

SUM function is applied because the ArtID field contains numbers

The PivotTable includes the sum of ArtIDs instead of a count of art objects, as Mary requested. This occurs because fields that contain numbers placed in the Values area are summed. Adding all the ArtIDs together to get a total is meaningless; you need to count the number of ArtIDs in each year. To do this, you need to change the SUM function to the COUNT function so Excel will *count* the number of objects in each group.

### To count the number of objects in each group:

1. Click any value in the **Sum of ArtID** column, and then click the **PivotTable Tools Options** tab on the Ribbon.

2. Click the **Calculations button arrow**, click the **Summarize Values By** button, and then click **Count**. The label indicating the type of summary in the PivotTable changes to Count of ArtID, and the PivotTable report displays the number of art objects acquired by date. See Figure 5-51.

| Figure 5-51 | PivotTable report with count |
|---|---|

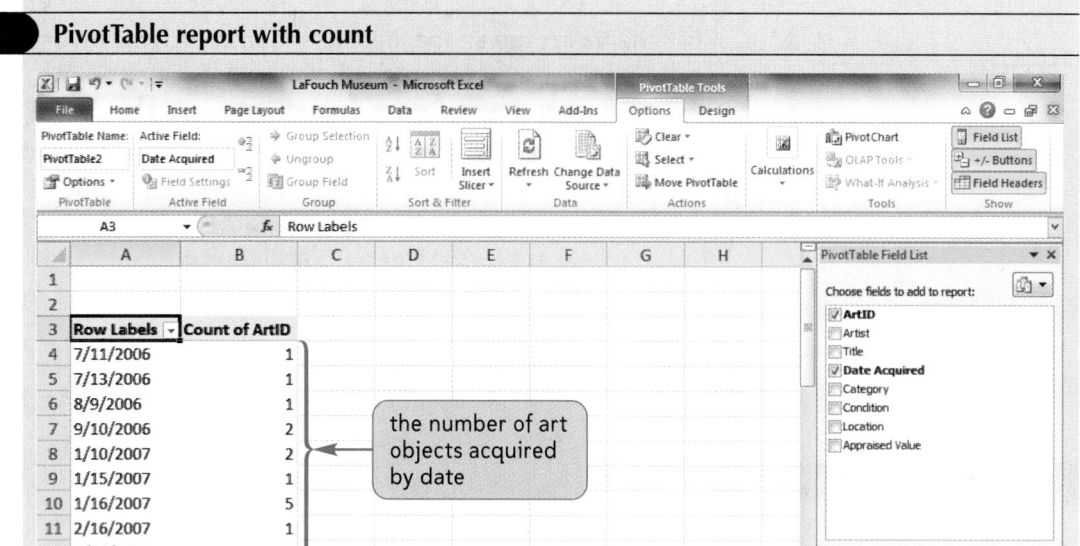

## Grouping Date Fields

Mary wants the PivotTable layout to show a count of acquisitions by year, not by date. You can group a range of dates into periods such as months, quarters, or years using the Group Field command. You will group the Date Acquired dates by year.

### To group acquisitions by year:

1. Click any date value in the Row Labels column of the PivotTable.

2. In the Group group on the PivotTable Tools Options tab, click the **Group Field** button. The Grouping dialog box opens.

3. Click **Months** to deselect it, and then click **Years** to select it.

4. Click the **OK** button. The PivotTable report is grouped by year, displaying the number of art acquisitions in each year. See Figure 5-52.

| Figure 5-52 | PivotTable report of annual acquisitions |
|---|---|

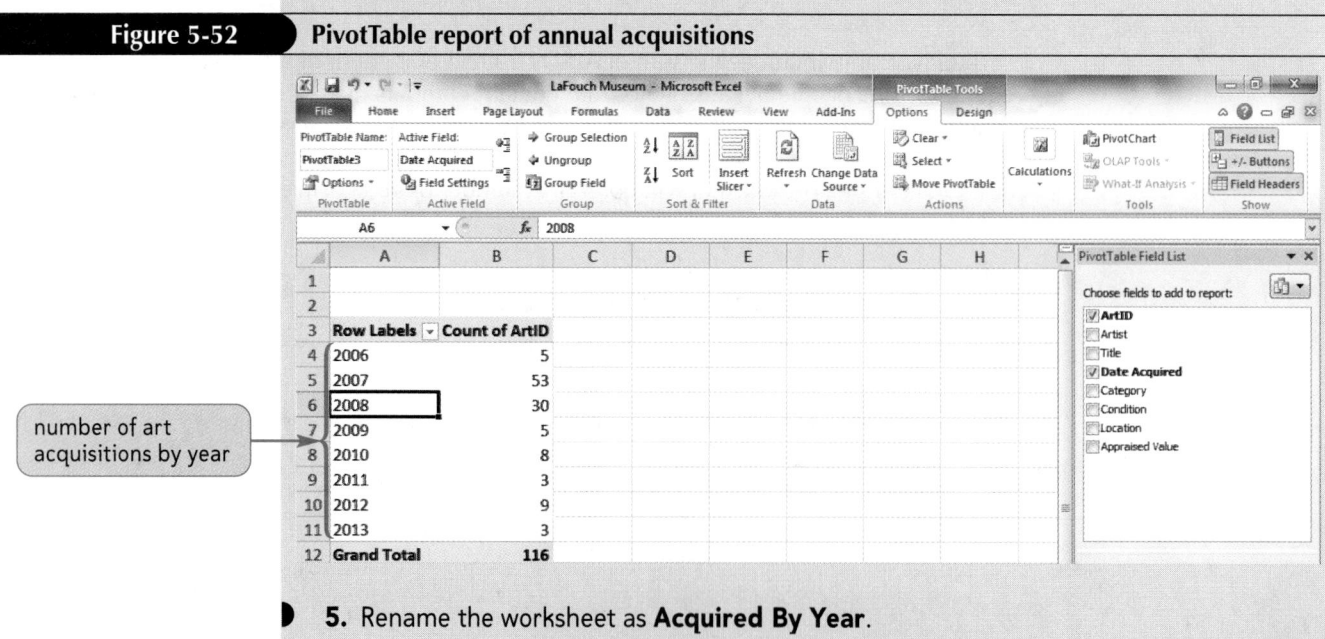

5. Rename the worksheet as **Acquired By Year**.

### Creating Different Types of PivotTable Reports

This tutorial only scratched the surface of the variety of PivotTable reports you can create. Here are a few more examples:

- Most PivotTable summaries are based on numeric data, but PivotTables can also contain only nonnumeric data. You cannot add nonnumeric data, so you must use the COUNT function to produce summaries. For example, you could count the number of art objects by Location and Category.
- You can use PivotTables to combine items into groups. Items that appear as row labels or column labels can be grouped. If items are numbers or dates, they can be grouped automatically using the Grouping dialog box, or they can be grouped manually using the Ctrl key to select items in a group and choosing Group from the shortcut menu. For example, you can manually combine the Courtyard and Garden locations into an Outdoor group, combine the three pavilion locations into an Indoor group, and then provide counts or total appraised values by these groups within the PivotTable. Being able to combine categories that aren't part of your original data using the grouping feature gives you flexibility to summarize your PivotTables in a way that meets your analysis requirements.
- You can develop PivotTables using the value filter, which allows you to filter one of your row or column fields in the PivotTable based on numbers that appear in the Values area of the PivotTable. For example, a PivotTable can show the total value of art objects for each artist and be filtered to display only artists whose total is greater than $25,000. Filtering provides you with a more precise way to view the PivotTable results by enabling you to include or remove data from the report.

## Creating a PivotChart

Mary wants you to add a PivotChart next to the PivotTable. A PivotChart allows you to interactively add, remove, filter, and refresh data fields in the PivotChart similar to working with a PivotTable. PivotCharts can have all the same formatting as other charts, including layouts and styles. You can move and resize chart elements, or change formatting of individual data points.

You will prepare a clustered column chart next to the new PivotTable report. You can create a PivotChart from the PivotTable.

### To create the PivotChart:

**TIP**

You can also create a PivotChart based directly on an Excel table, in which case both a PivotTable and a PivotChart are created.

1. Click any cell in the PivotTable.

2. In the Tools group on the PivotTable Tools Options tab, click the **PivotChart** button. The Insert Chart dialog box opens.

3. Click the **Clustered Column** chart (the first chart in the first row of the Column section), if necessary, and then click the **OK** button. A PivotChart appears next to the PivotTable along with the PivotTable Field List.

4. Click the **PivotChart Tools Layout** tab, click the **Legend button arrow** in the Labels group, and then click **None**. The legend is removed from the PivotChart. You do not need a legend because the PivotChart has only one series.

5. In the PivotChart, right-click the **chart title**, and then click **Edit Text**. The insertion point appears in the title so you can edit it.

6. Select the title, type **Number Acquired By Year** as the new title, and then click the chart area to deselect the title.

> **7.** Drag the **PivotChart** so its upper-left corner is in cell C3. The PivotChart is aligned with the PivotTable. See Figure 5-53.

**Figure 5-53**  **PivotChart added to the PivotTable report**

The PivotChart Tools contextual tabs enable you to manipulate and format the selected PivotChart the same way as an ordinary chart. A PivotChart and its associated PivotTable are linked. When you modify one, the other also changes.

You can quickly display different chart views of the PivotChart using the chart filter button on the PivotChart to filter the data. Mary wants you to display only art acquisitions after 2009.

### To filter items in the PivotChart:

> **1.** Make sure the PivotChart is selected, and then click the **Date Acquired** axis field button in the PivotChart. The AutoFilter menu opens.

> **2.** Click the **Select All** check box. All the check boxes are deselected.

> **3.** Click the **2010**, **2011**, **2012**, and **2013** check boxes. The years after 2009 are selected.

> **4.** Click the **OK** button. The PivotChart displays only art objects acquired after 2009. The PivotTable is also filtered to display the same results.

> **5.** Click cell **A1**. See Figure 5-54.

| Figure 5-54 | **Filtered PivotChart** |

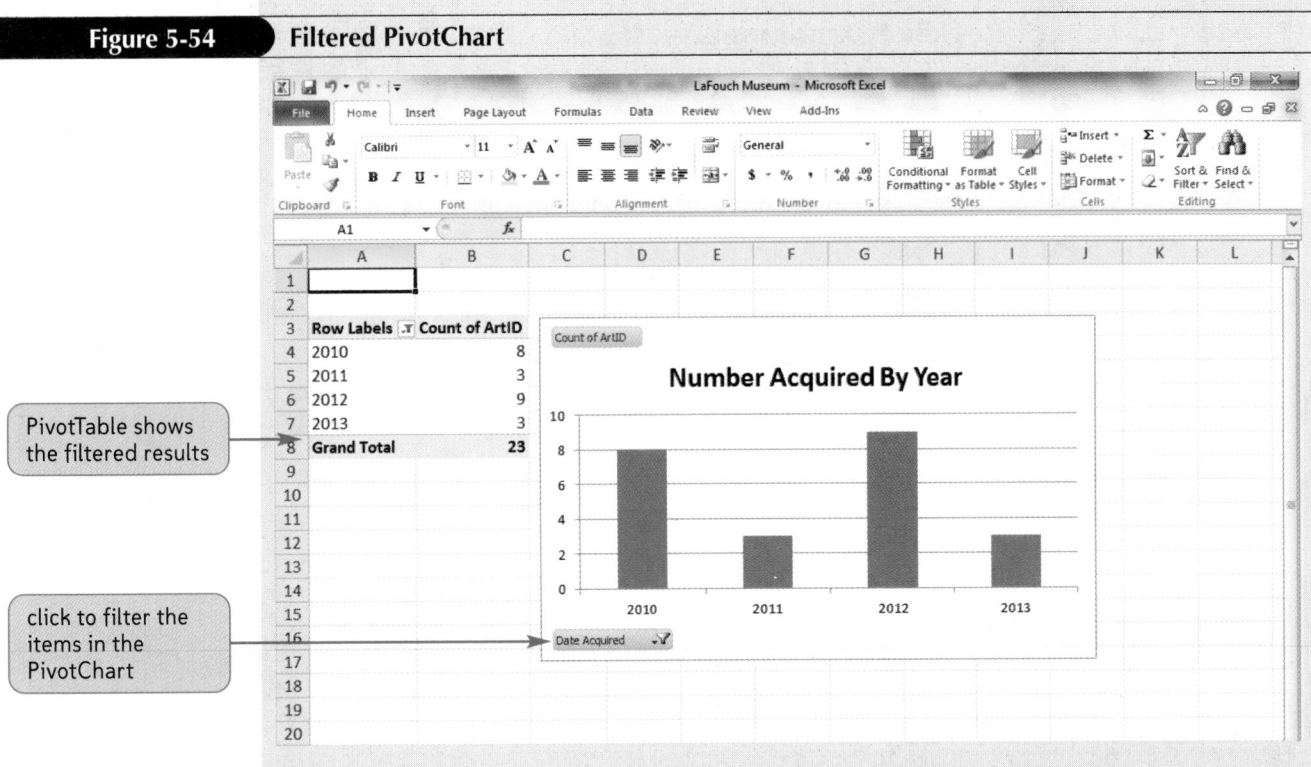

PivotTable shows the filtered results

click to filter the items in the PivotChart

▶ **6.** Save the LaFouch Museum workbook, and then close it.

Mary is pleased with the PivotTable and PivotChart. Both show the number of art objects acquired by year, which will be important information for her upcoming board meeting.

## Session 5.3 Quick Check

**REVIEW**

1. What is the default summary function for numeric data in a PivotTable?
2. When creating a PivotTable, what do you use to lay out the fields in the PivotTable report?
3. After you update data in an Excel table, what must you do to a PivotTable based on that Excel table?
4. How are fields such as region, state, and country most likely to appear in a PivotTable?
5. How are fields such as revenue, costs, and profits most likely to appear in a PivotTable?
6. A list of college students includes a code to indicate the student's gender (male or female) and a field to identify the student's major. Which tool—Filter or PivotTable—would you use to (a) create a list of all females majoring in history, and (b) count the number of males and females in each major?
7. When the Date Acquired field is displayed in a row of a PivotTable by month or year, you have _____ the Date Acquired field.
8. A PivotChart displays the number of art objects in each Location. How would you exclude the art objects in the Courtyard from the PivotTable?

*Practice the skills you learned in the tutorial using the same case scenario.*

**PRACTICE**

# Review Assignments

**Data File needed for the Review Assignments: Art.xlsx**

Mary has another art object to enter in the art objects list. She wants to sort the data by the date acquired. She wants to filter data to retrieve all art with the word "cowboy" in the title. She wants to use a PivotTable to determine the average value of the artwork for each artist. Complete the following:

1. Open the **Art** workbook located in the Excel5\Review folder included with your Data Files, and then save the workbook as **Art Museum** in the same folder.

2. In the Documentation sheet, enter your name and the date.

3. Switch to the ArtObjects worksheet. Create an Excel table for the art objects data, and then change the table style to Medium 25. Format the Appraised Value field using the Accounting number format with no decimal places.

4. Rename the Excel table as **Collection**.

5. Make a copy of the ArtObjects worksheet, and then rename the copied worksheet as **Q5** (for "Question 5"). (*Hint*: To make a copy of the worksheet, press and hold the Ctrl key and drag the sheet tab to the right of the ArtObjects sheet tab.) Sort the art objects by date acquired to display the newest objects first.

6. Make a copy of the ArtObjects worksheet, and then rename the copied worksheet as **Q6**. Sort art objects by category (Z to A), location (A to Z), artist (A to Z), and date acquired (showing the oldest first).

7. Make a copy of the ArtObjects worksheet, and then rename the copied worksheet as **Q7**. Filter the Collection table to produce a list of art objects with the word "cowboy" in the title.

8. Make a copy of the ArtObjects worksheet, and then rename the copied worksheet as **Q8**. Use the Total row to calculate the average value of objects acquired between 2009 and 2013. Change the label in the Total row from Total to **Average**. Sort the filtered data by date acquired (newest first).

9. Make a copy of the ArtObjects worksheet, and then rename the copied worksheet as **Q9**. Use the Subtotal command to count how many art objects there are in each location, displaying the count in the ArtID column.

10. Create a PivotTable to show the average value of art objects by artist. Format the Value column appropriately. Rename the worksheet with the PivotTable as **Q10-11**.

11. Sort the PivotTable showing the artist with the highest average value first.

12. Create a PivotTable to show the number of art objects and the total value by category. Include location as a Report Filter field, and then filter the report so the number and total value by category is based on the Courtyard location. Rename the worksheet with the PivotTable as **Q12**.

13. Save and close the workbook. Submit the finished workbook to your instructor, either in printed or electronic form, as requested.

*Use the skills you learned to analyze and summarize donation data.*

**APPLY**

# Case Problem 1

**Data File needed for this Case Problem: Pledges.xlsx**

***Hewart Zoo*** Marvis Chennard is the director of fund-raising for the Hewart Zoo. The zoo relies on donations to fund operations, temporary exhibits, and special programs. Marvis created an Excel table to track information about donors and their pledges. You will analyze the data in the list. Complete the following:

1. Open the **Pledges** workbook located in the Excel5\Case1 folder included with your Data Files, and then save the workbook as **Zoo Pledges** in the same folder.

2. In the Documentation worksheet, enter your name and the date, and then switch to the Pledges worksheet.

3. Create an Excel table, apply the Medium 7 table style, and then rename the table as **PledgeData**.

4. Make a copy of the Pledges worksheet, and then rename the copied worksheet as **Q4-6** (for "Question 4-6"). (*Hint*: Press the Ctrl key and drag the sheet tab to the right of the Pledges sheet tab to make a copy of the worksheet.) Sort the data in ascending order by donor type and fund name, and in descending order by amt pledged (largest first).

5. In the Q4-6 worksheet, insert a Total row. Display the number of pledges in the Donor Name column, the average pledge in the Amt Pledged column, the total received in the Amt Received column, and the total owed in the Amt Owed column.

6. In the Q4-6 worksheet, split the worksheet into two horizontal panes at row 23. In the top pane, display the pledge transactions. In the bottom pane, display the Total row.

7. Make a copy of the Pledges worksheet, and then rename the copied worksheet as **Q7**. Filter the data to display individual donors whose amt owed is greater than zero. Sort the filtered data by pledge date, with the oldest date displayed first.

8. Make a copy of the Pledges worksheet, and then rename the copied worksheet as **Q8**. Filter the data to display records that have a pledge date in October through December. Sort the filtered data by amt pledged (largest first).

9. Make a copy of the Pledges worksheet, and then rename the copied worksheet as **Q9**. Filter the data to display only records with an amt received greater than zero. Then use the Subtotal command (SUM) to display the total amt received by fund name.

10. Create a PivotTable that displays the total and average amt owed by each donor type and fund name. Place the PivotTable in a new worksheet, and then rename the worksheet as **Q10**. Select an appropriate report layout and format. Insert a Donor Type slicer and filter using the Organization donor type.

11. Using Figure 5-55 as a guide, create a PivotTable in a new worksheet that shows the amt pledged by month and fund name. Format the PivotTable appropriately, and then rename the worksheet as **Q11**.

| **Figure 5-55** | **PivotTable for the amount pledged** |
| --- | --- |

| | A | B | C | D | E | F |
| --- | --- | --- | --- | --- | --- | --- |
| 1 | | | | | | |
| 2 | | | | | | |
| 3 | Total Pledged | | | | | |
| 4 | | Bird Sanctuary | Children's Zoo | General Support | ZooMobile | Grand Total |
| 5 | Jan | | $  100.00 | $  1,000.00 | | $  1,100.00 |
| 6 | Feb | | $  1,100.00 | | $  150.00 | $  1,250.00 |
| 7 | Mar | | $  100.00 | | $  1,000.00 | $  1,100.00 |
| 8 | Apr | $  75.00 | $  425.00 | $  500.00 | | $  1,000.00 |
| 9 | Jun | | $  1,000.00 | | $  50.00 | $  1,050.00 |
| 10 | Jul | $  1,000.00 | | $  1,000.00 | | $  2,000.00 |
| 11 | Sep | $  100.00 | $  250.00 | $  25.00 | $  150.00 | $  525.00 |
| 12 | Oct | $  200.00 | | $  200.00 | | $  400.00 |
| 13 | Nov | | | $  250.00 | | $  250.00 |
| 14 | Dec | | $  150.00 | | $  750.00 | $  900.00 |
| 15 | Grand Total | $  1,375.00 | $  3,125.00 | $  2,975.00 | $ 2,100.00 | $ 9,575.00 |

12. Save and close the workbook. Submit the finished workbook to your instructor, either in printed or electronic form, as requested.

*Use the skills you learned to analyze and summarize expenditure data.*

APPLY

## Case Problem 2

**Data File needed for this Case Problem: Ring.xlsx**

***Ring Family Farm***    Fred and Alesia Ring own a small family farm outside Abita Springs, Louisiana. The couple wants to better organize their financial records. They created an Excel workbook to record their expenses. Typical expenses include those associated with hay production (seed, fertilizer, and irrigation), animal husbandry, fence maintenance, veterinary services, vehicles and maintenance, and so forth. The workbook includes categories associated with these expenses as well as an area to record how much is spent, the purpose of the expenditure, the check number, and the date paid. Complete the following:

1. Open the **Ring** workbook located in the Excel5\Case2 folder included with your Data Files, and then save the workbook as **Ring Farm** in the same folder.

2. Insert a new worksheet. Enter the company name, your name, the date, and a purpose statement, and then rename the worksheet as **Documentation**.

3. Create an Excel table in the Expenditures worksheet. Rename the table as **Checkbook**.

4. Replace the category code "Farm" in each record with **Payroll**.

5. Make a copy of the Expenditures worksheet, and then rename the copied worksheet as **Q5**. (*Hint*: Press the Ctrl key and drag the Expenditures sheet tab to the right of the Expenditures sheet tab to make a copy of the worksheet.) Sort the Checkbook table in ascending order by category, then by payee, and then by date paid (newest first).

6. Make a copy of the Expenditures worksheet, and then rename the copied worksheet as **Q6**. Filter the Checkbook table to display all expenditures for equipment and repairs in December, and then sort by amount (smallest first).

7. Make a copy of the Expenditures worksheet, and then rename the copied worksheet as **Q7**. Filter the Checkbook table to display all checks that include the word "vet" in the payee's name. Include the total amount at the bottom of the table.

8. Make a copy of the Expenditures worksheet, and then rename the copied worksheet as **Q8**. Use conditional formatting to apply a yellow fill with dark yellow text to all outstanding checks. (*Hint*: "Yes" appears in the Outstanding column.)

9. Make a copy of the Expenditures worksheet, and then rename the copied worksheet as **Q9**. Use the Subtotal command to display the total amount for each category, displaying the subtotal in the Amount column.

10. Create a PivotTable that summarizes expenditures by category and month. Place the PivotTable in a new worksheet, and then rename the worksheet as **Q10-11**. Format the PivotTable appropriately and choose a layout.

11. Insert a PivotChart with the Clustered Column chart type on the Q10-11 worksheet.

12. Create the PivotTable shown in Figure 5-56 in a new worksheet, rename the worksheet as **Q12**, and then sort the Total Amount column in descending order. (*Hint*: Click the Show Values As button in the Calculations group on the PivotTable Tools Options tab on the Ribbon to calculate the Pct Of Total column.)

**Figure 5-56**    **PivotTable for the amount by category**

| | A | B | C |
|---|---|---|---|
| 1 | Category | Total Amount | Pct Of Total |
| 2 | Equipment | $6,575.00 | 37.05% |
| 3 | Payroll | $2,638.27 | 14.87% |
| 4 | Vet | $2,320.57 | 13.08% |
| 5 | Repairs | $2,003.44 | 11.29% |
| 6 | Feed | $2,002.24 | 11.28% |
| 7 | Medicine | $1,249.32 | 7.04% |
| 8 | Administration | $958.09 | 5.40% |
| 9 | Grand Total | $17,746.93 | 100.00% |

13. Save and close the workbook. Submit the finished workbook to your instructor, either in printed or electronic form, as requested.

*Use the skills you learned to analyze and summarize loan data for a bank.*

**APPLY**

## Case Problem 3

**Data File needed for this Case Problem: CustLoans.xlsx**

***High Desert Bank***   Eleanor Chimayo, loan manager for High Desert Bank, is getting ready for the bank's quarterly meeting. Eleanor is expected to present data on the status of different types of loans within three New Mexican cities. Eleanor asks you to summarize and analyze the data for her presentation. Complete the following:

1. Open the **CustLoans** workbook located in the Excel5\Case3 folder included with your Data Files, and then save the workbook as **High Desert Bank** in the same folder.

2. In the Documentation sheet, enter your name and the date.

3. In the Loans worksheet, create an Excel table, and then rename the table as **LoanData**.

4. Format the Amount and Interest Rate fields so that it is clear that these fields contain dollars and percentages, respectively.

5. Format the table using the table style of your choice.

6. To the right of the Type column, insert a new column named **Monthly Payment**. Use the PMT function to calculate the monthly payment for each loan. Adjust the formula so that each loan is displayed as a positive amount, and then improve the formatting.

7. Make a copy of the Loans worksheet, and then rename the copied worksheet as **Q7-8**. (*Hint*: Press the Ctrl key and drag the sheet tab to the right of the current sheet tab to make a copy of the worksheet.) Sort the loan data in ascending order by type, within type by city, and within city by last name.

8. Use conditional formatting to display all loans in Taos using a format of your choice to highlight these loans.

9. Make a copy of the Loans worksheet, and then rename the copied worksheet as **Q9-10**. Filter the LoanData table to display loans made during April and May of 2013.

10. Insert a Total row in the Q9-10 worksheet. Display the average amount of loans and the total monthly payment for the filtered data in Question 9.

11. Make a copy of the Loans worksheet, and then rename the copied worksheet as **Q11**. Sort the loans in ascending order by city, then by type of loan, and then by amount of loan (largest loan first). Insert subtotals (Average) for the loan amount and monthly payment by city and type of loan. Prepare the worksheet for printing. Include the worksheet name in the center of the custom header. Include your name in the left section of the custom footer and page numbers in the right section of the custom footer. Fit all columns on one page.

12. Create a PivotTable that displays the number (Count) and average loan by type and city. Place the PivotTable in a new worksheet, and then rename the PivotTable worksheet as **Q12 Loans-Type And City**. Remove the Other loan type from the PivotTable. Format the PivotTable appropriately.

13. Create a second PivotTable, as shown in Figure 5-57, in a new worksheet, and then rename the PivotTable worksheet as **Q13 Loans-Type and Date**. The PivotTable shows three calculations: number of loans, total loan amount, and average monthly payment categorized by type of loan. Insert a report filter based on the loan date, grouped so you can filter by month. Insert a Loan Date slicer and filter the PivotTable report for March and April.

| Figure 5-57 | PivotTable for loans by type and date |
| --- | --- |

14. Save and close the workbook. Submit the finished workbook to your instructor, either in printed or electronic form, as requested.

## Case Problem 4

*Explore how to summarize data by creating subtotals, PivotTables, and PivotCharts.*

**CHALLENGE**

Data File needed for this Case Problem: Bowls.xlsx

**Bowls Department Stores**   Bowls Department Stores, with corporate headquarters in Portland, Oregon, operates department stores in midsize towns in selected areas of the Northwest. Although the organization maintains a large computer system for its accounting operations, the sales department often downloads data to complete additional analysis of its operations. Daniel Partner, analyst for the corporate sales department, regularly downloads data by territories and product areas including automotive, electronics, garden centers, and sporting goods. He often presents reports based on his analysis of sales by product areas and territory, best- and worst-performing product group periods, and total sales for certain regions and product groups. You will help Daniel compile and summarize the data. Complete the following:

1. Open the **Bowls** workbook located in the Excel5\Case4 folder included with your Data Files, and then save the workbook as **Bowls Stores** in the same folder.

2. In the Documentation sheet, enter your name, the date, and an appropriate purpose statement.

3. In the SalesData worksheet, create an Excel table. Rename the table as **ProductSales**. Format the Sales column in the Currency number format with no decimal places.

4. Make a copy of the SalesData worksheet, and then rename the copied worksheet as **Q4**. (*Hint*: Press the Ctrl key and drag the sheet tab to the right of the SalesData sheet tab to make a copy of the worksheet.) Sort the table in ascending order by territories, then by product group, then by year, and then by month. Month should be sorted in chronological order (Jan, Feb, Mar, ...), not in alphabetical order.

5. Make a copy of the SalesData worksheet, and then rename the copied worksheet as **Q5**. Display records for Automotive and Electronics products in 2013, excluding sales in Vancouver. Sort this data by sales in descending order. Add a Total row and calculate the average sales for the filtered data. Change the label in the Total row to **Average**. Split the worksheet into two panes. In the top pane, display all the rows except the last row on your screen. In the bottom pane, display the Total row.

⊕ **EXPLORE** 6. Make a copy of the SalesData worksheet, and then rename the copied worksheet as **Q6**. Display subtotals for sales (Sum) by year, month (Jan, Feb, Mar, ...), and territory.

7. Make a copy of the SalesData worksheet, and then rename the copied worksheet as **Q7**. Display the five lowest periods based on sales. Assume each row represents a period. Sort the sales so lowest sales appears first.

**⊕ EXPLORE**

8. Create a PivotTable similar to the one shown in Figure 5-58, displaying percentage of sales by product group, territories, and year. Omit the columnar grand totals. Use a tabular layout, inserting subtotals at the bottom of each product group and excluding the Toy product group. Rename the worksheet as **Q8**.

**Figure 5-58     Sample PivotTable showing percentage of sales**

| | A | B | C | D |
|---|---|---|---|---|
| 1 | | | | |
| 2 | | | | |
| 3 | **Pct of Sales** | | **Year** ▾ | |
| 4 | **Product Group** ▾ | **Territories** ▾ | **2012** | **2013** |
| 5 | ⊟ **Automotive** | Oregon | 10.05% | 8.85% |
| 6 | | Vancouver | 7.32% | 9.71% |
| 7 | | Washington | 6.88% | 9.94% |
| 8 | **Automotive Total** | | **24.25%** | **28.50%** |
| 9 | ⊟ **Electronics** | Oregon | 7.53% | 8.67% |
| 10 | | Vancouver | 7.61% | 6.88% |
| 11 | | Washington | 8.05% | 9.22% |
| 12 | **Electronics Total** | | **23.20%** | **24.78%** |
| 13 | ⊟ **Gardening** | Oregon | 8.19% | 6.85% |
| 14 | | Vancouver | 8.46% | 5.89% |
| 15 | | Washington | 9.77% | 9.91% |
| 16 | **Gardening Total** | | **26.42%** | **22.66%** |
| 17 | ⊟ **Houseware** | Oregon | 6.86% | 5.01% |
| 18 | | Vancouver | 8.20% | 7.67% |
| 19 | | Washington | 11.07% | 11.39% |
| 20 | **Houseware Total** | | **26.14%** | **24.07%** |
| 21 | **Grand Total** | | **100.00%** | **100.00%** |

**⊕ EXPLORE**

9. Using Figure 5-59 as a guide, create a PivotChart of total sales by product group. Create a second PivotChart of total sales by territory in the same worksheet. Rename the worksheet as **Q9**.

**Figure 5-59     Sample PivotChart of total sales by product group**

EXPLORE 10. Using Figure 5-60 as a guide, create a PivotTable to show four calculations: average, total, minimum, and maximum sales, categorized by territories and product group, and filtered by year and territories using two slicer filters. Display the results for 2013 and the Vancouver and Washington territories. Rename the worksheet as **Q10**.

| Figure 5-60 | Sample PivotTable showing calculations |
|---|---|

| | A | B | C | D | E | F | G | H | I |
|---|---|---|---|---|---|---|---|---|---|
| 1 | Year | 2013 ⏷ | | | | | | | |
| 2 | | | | | | | | | |
| 3 | **Territories** ⏷ | **Product Group** ⏷ | **Average** | **Sum** | **Minimum** | **Maximum** | | **Year** 🔽 | |
| 4 | ⊟Vancouver | Automotive | $ 55,074 | $ 660,886 | $ 865 | $ 99,526 | | | |
| 5 | | Electronics | $ 39,033 | $ 468,391 | $ 2,141 | $ 98,044 | | 2012 | |
| 6 | | Gardening | $ 33,419 | $ 401,027 | $ 467 | $ 97,793 | | | |
| 7 | | Houseware | $ 43,473 | $ 521,678 | $ 4,046 | $ 80,035 | | 2013 | |
| 8 | | Toys | $ 60,199 | $ 722,385 | $ 29,824 | $ 94,129 | | | |
| 9 | **Vancouver Total** | | **$ 46,239** | **$ 2,774,367** | **$ 467** | **$ 99,526** | | | |
| 10 | ⊟Washington | Automotive | $ 56,359 | $ 676,304 | $ 3,893 | $ 99,258 | | **Territories** 🔽 | |
| 11 | | Electronics | $ 52,307 | $ 627,680 | $ 15,485 | $ 84,624 | | | |
| 12 | | Gardening | $ 56,206 | $ 674,471 | $ 5,507 | $ 94,166 | | Oregon | |
| 13 | | Houseware | $ 64,579 | $ 774,942 | $ 27,164 | $ 94,725 | | | |
| 14 | | Toys | $ 63,189 | $ 758,272 | $ 17,919 | $ 90,879 | | Vancouver | |
| 15 | **Washington Total** | | **$ 58,528** | **$ 3,511,669** | **$ 3,893** | **$ 99,258** | | | |
| 16 | **Grand Total** | | **$ 52,384** | **$ 6,286,036** | **$ 467** | **$ 99,526** | | Washington | |

11. Save and close the workbook. Submit the finished workbook to your instructor, either in printed or electronic form, as requested.

## SAM: Skills Assessment Manager

For current SAM information, including versions and content details, visit SAM Central (http://samcentral.course.com). If you have a SAM user profile, you may have access to hands-on instruction, practice, and assessment of the skills covered in this tutorial. Because various versions of SAM are supported throughout the life of this text, check with your instructor for the correct instructions and URL/Web site for accessing assignments.

**ASSESS**

## ENDING DATA FILES

Excel5 → Tutorial
LaFouch Museum.xlsx

Review
Art Museum.xlsx

Case1
Zoo Pledges.xlsx

Case2
Ring Farm.xlsx

Case3
High Desert Bank.xlsx

Case4
Bowls Stores.xlsx

## OBJECTIVES

**Session 6.1**
- Create a worksheet group
- Format and edit multiple worksheets at once
- Create cell references to other worksheets
- Consolidate information from multiple worksheets using 3-D references
- Create and print a worksheet group

**Session 6.2**
- Create a link to data in another workbook
- Create a workbook reference
- Learn how to edit links
- Create and use an Excel workspace

**Session 6.3**
- Insert a hyperlink in a cell
- Create a custom template
- Save a workbook to SkyDrive and use the Excel Web App

# Managing Multiple Worksheets and Workbooks

*Summarizing Ticket Sales*

## Case | *Global Travel*

Global Travel, a member-owned organization, provides a variety of services ranging from travel assistance to insurance programs to discounted vacation packages. The company also offers special services and discounts to one-time entertainment events. Global Travel purchases tickets to selected theme and amusement parks to resell to its members. Each local office of Global Travel markets and sells these tickets to its members. Theme and amusement park sales account for more than 10 percent of Global Travel's sales.

Rhohit Gupta, accountant for Global Travel in New Mexico, is responsible for tracking ticket sales within the state and preparing an analysis for Alvin Alton, the corporate controller. Rhohit asks you to create a summary report that shows the quarterly sales in New Mexico for the past year. He already entered each quarter's values in separate worksheets, but wants you to summarize all the quarterly information in one worksheet.

Alvin has already received workbooks with the quarterly sales for Colorado and Utah. After Alvin receives the New Mexico workbook, you will create a workbook that summarizes the annual totals from each state workbook in the Southwest region.

## STARTING DATA FILES

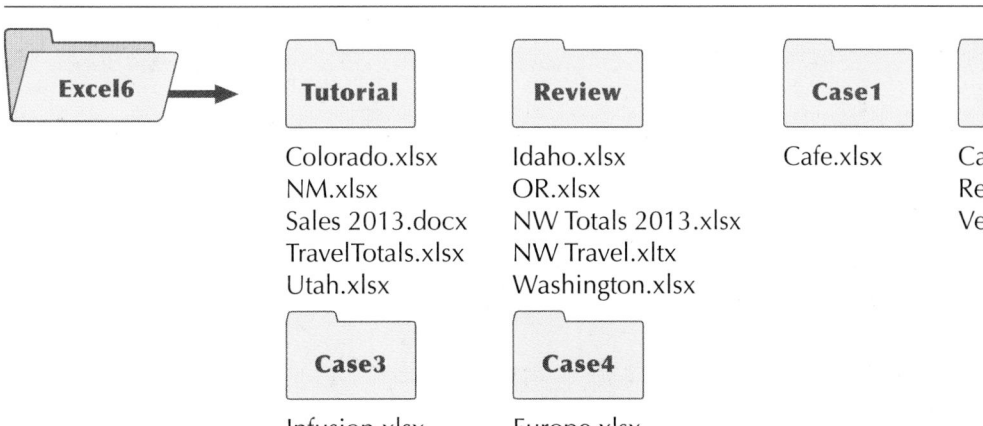

**Excel6** →

**Tutorial**
Colorado.xlsx
NM.xlsx
Sales 2013.docx
TravelTotals.xlsx
Utah.xlsx

**Review**
Idaho.xlsx
OR.xlsx
NW Totals 2013.xlsx
NW Travel.xltx
Washington.xlsx

**Case1**
Cafe.xlsx

**Case2**
Carson.xlsx
Reno.xlsx
Vegas.xlsx

**Case3**
Infusion.xlsx

**Case4**
Europe.xlsx
North America.xlsx
Pluto Template.xltx
South America.xlsx

# SESSION 6.1 VISUAL OVERVIEW

Anything you do in the active sheet—such as entering formulas, adding labels, and formatting—is automatically done to all sheets in the worksheet group, saving you time and ensuring consistency.

When worksheets are grouped, the workbook is in group-editing mode and "[Group]" appears in the title bar.

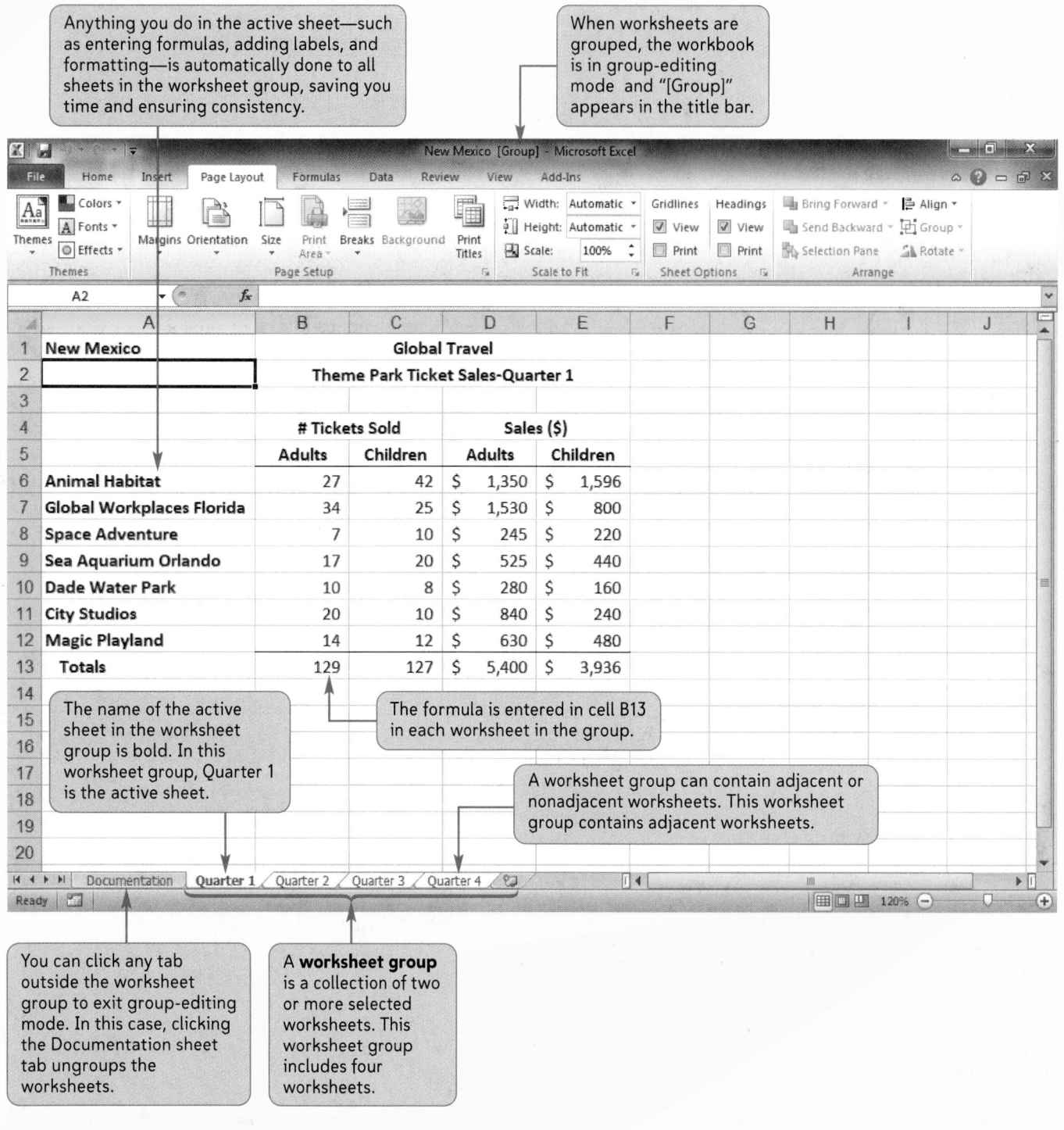

The name of the active sheet in the worksheet group is bold. In this worksheet group, Quarter 1 is the active sheet.

The formula is entered in cell B13 in each worksheet in the group.

A worksheet group can contain adjacent or nonadjacent worksheets. This worksheet group contains adjacent worksheets.

You can click any tab outside the worksheet group to exit group-editing mode. In this case, clicking the Documentation sheet tab ungroups the worksheets.

A **worksheet group** is a collection of two or more selected worksheets. This worksheet group includes four worksheets.

# WORKSHEET GROUPS AND 3-D REFERENCES

A **3-D reference** is a reference to the same cell or range in multiple worksheets in the same workbook. This 3-D reference refers to cell B6 in the Quarter 1, Quarter 2, Quarter 3, and Quarter 4 worksheets.

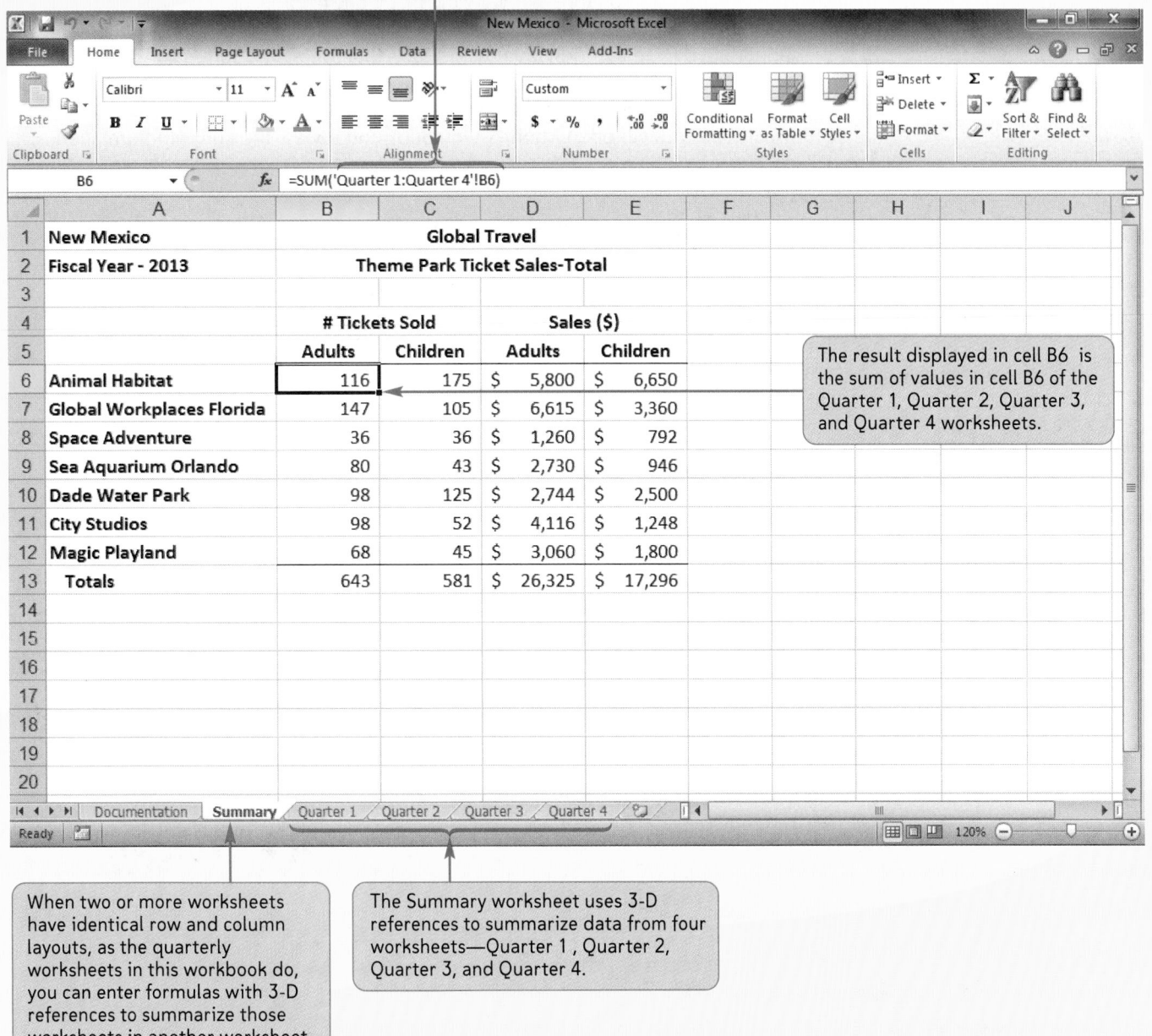

The result displayed in cell B6 is the sum of values in cell B6 of the Quarter 1, Quarter 2, Quarter 3, and Quarter 4 worksheets.

B6    =SUM('Quarter 1:Quarter 4'!B6)

| | # Tickets Sold | | Sales ($) | |
| --- | --- | --- | --- | --- |
| | **Adults** | **Children** | **Adults** | **Children** |
| **Animal Habitat** | 116 | 175 | $ 5,800 | $ 6,650 |
| **Global Workplaces Florida** | 147 | 105 | $ 6,615 | $ 3,360 |
| **Space Adventure** | 36 | 36 | $ 1,260 | $ 792 |
| **Sea Aquarium Orlando** | 80 | 43 | $ 2,730 | $ 946 |
| **Dade Water Park** | 98 | 125 | $ 2,744 | $ 2,500 |
| **City Studios** | 98 | 52 | $ 4,116 | $ 1,248 |
| **Magic Playland** | 68 | 45 | $ 3,060 | $ 1,800 |
| Totals | 643 | 581 | $ 26,325 | $ 17,296 |

New Mexico — Global Travel
Fiscal Year - 2013 — Theme Park Ticket Sales-Total

When two or more worksheets have identical row and column layouts, as the quarterly worksheets in this workbook do, you can enter formulas with 3-D references to summarize those worksheets in another worksheet.

The Summary worksheet uses 3-D references to summarize data from four worksheets—Quarter 1, Quarter 2, Quarter 3, and Quarter 4.

# Grouping Worksheets

Workbook data is often placed in several worksheets. Using multiple worksheets makes it easier to group and summarize data. For example, a company such as Global Travel with branches in different geographic regions can place sales information for each region in separate worksheets. Rather than scrolling through one large and complex worksheet that contains data for all regions, users can access sales information for a specific region simply by clicking a sheet tab in the workbook.

Using multiple worksheets enables you to place summarized data first. Managers interested only in an overall picture can view the first worksheet of summary data without looking at the details available in the other worksheets. Others, of course, might want to view the supporting data in the individual worksheets that follow the summary worksheet. In the case of Global Travel, Rhohit used separate worksheets to summarize the number of tickets sold and sales in dollars for the New Mexico branch offices for each quarter of the 2013 fiscal year. You will open Rhohit's workbook and review the current information.

**TIP**

If a worksheet group includes all the worksheets in a workbook, you can edit only the active worksheet; any changes will be made to all the worksheets in the group. Clicking another sheet tab ungroups the worksheets.

### To open and review the Global Travel workbook:

1. Open the **NM** workbook located in the Excel6\Tutorial folder included with your Data Files, and then save the workbook as **New Mexico** in the same folder.

2. In the **Documentation** worksheet, enter your name and the date.

3. Switch to the **Quarter 1** worksheet, and then view the number of tickets sold and sales for the first quarter of the year. See Figure 6-1.

**Figure 6-1**   Quarter 1 worksheet for Global Travel – New Mexico

each quarter's data is entered on a different worksheet

ticket and sales data for the first quarter

4. Review the **Quarter 2**, **Quarter 3**, and **Quarter 4** worksheets. The layout for all four worksheets is identical.

Rhohit didn't enter any formulas in the workbook. You need to enter formulas to calculate the total number of tickets and sales for each column (B through E) in all four worksheets. Rather than retyping the formulas in each worksheet, you can enter them all at once by creating a worksheet group. A worksheet group, like a range, can contain adjacent or nonadjacent worksheets. In group-editing mode, most editing tasks that you do to the active worksheet also affect the other worksheets in the group. By forming a worksheet group, you can:

- Enter or edit data and formulas in the active worksheet to enter or edit the data and formulas in the same cells in all the worksheets in the group. Find and replace can also be used with a worksheet group.
- Apply formatting to the active worksheet to format all the worksheets in the group, including changing row heights or column widths and applying conditional formatting.
- Insert or delete rows and columns of the active worksheet to make the same changes to all the worksheets in the group.
- Set the page layout options in one worksheet to apply the settings to all worksheets in the group, such as changing the orientation, scaling to fit, and inserting headers and footers.
- Apply view options such as zooming, showing and hiding worksheets, and so forth to all worksheets in the group.
- Print all the worksheets in the worksheet group at the same time.

Worksheet groups save you time and help improve consistency among the worksheets because you can perform an action once, yet affect multiple worksheets.

**REFERENCE**

### Grouping and Ungrouping Worksheets

- To select an adjacent group, click the sheet tab of the first worksheet in the group, press and hold the Shift key, click the sheet tab of the last worksheet in the group, and then release the Shift key.
- To select a nonadjacent group, click the sheet tab of one worksheet in the group, press and hold the Ctrl key, click the sheet tabs of the remaining worksheets in the group, and then release the Ctrl key.
- To ungroup the worksheets, click the sheet tab of a worksheet not in the group.
  or
- Right-click the sheet tab of one worksheet in the group, and then click Ungroup Sheets on the shortcut menu.

In the New Mexico workbook, you'll group an adjacent range of worksheets: the Quarter 1 worksheet through the Quarter 4 worksheet.

### To group the quarterly worksheets:

**TIP**

If you cannot see the sheet tab of a worksheet you want to include in a group, use the sheet navigation controls to display it.

1. Click the **Quarter 1** sheet tab to make the worksheet active. This is the first worksheet you want to include in the group.

2. Press and hold the **Shift** key, and then click the **Quarter 4** sheet tab. This is the last worksheet you want to include in the group.

3. Release the **Shift** key. The sheet tabs for Quarter 1 through Quarter 4 are white, indicating they are all selected. The text "[Group]" appears in the title bar to remind you that a worksheet group is selected in the workbook. See Figure 6-2.

**Figure 6-2** | **Grouped worksheets**

## Entering Formulas in a Worksheet Group

When you enter a formula in the active worksheet (in this case, the Quarter 1 work-sheet), the formula is entered in the same cells in all the worksheets in the group. The grouped worksheets must have the exact same organization and layout (rows and columns) for this to work. Otherwise, any formulas you enter in the active sheet will be incorrect in the other worksheets in the group and could overwrite existing data. With the quarterly sheets grouped, you will enter the formulas to calculate the total number of tickets sold and total sales.

**To enter formulas in the worksheet group:**

1. Click cell **B13**. You want to enter the formula in cell B13 in each of the four work-sheets in the group.

2. In the Editing group on the Home tab, click the **Sum** button $\Sigma$, and then press the **Enter** key. The formula =SUM(B6:B12) is entered in the cell, adding the total number of adult tickets sold in the quarter, which is 127.

3. Copy the formula in cell B13 to the range **C13:E13**. The formula calculates the total number of children's tickets sold (127), the total adult ticket sales ($5400), as well as the total children's ticket sales ($3936).

4. In cell A13, enter **Totals**, and then click the **Increase Indent** button in the Alignment group on the Home tab. The label shifts to the right.

   The formulas and label you entered in the Quarter 1 worksheet were entered in the Quarter 2, 3, and 4 worksheets at the same time.

▶ **5.** Click the **Quarter 2** sheet tab, and then click cell **B13**. The value 174 appears in the cell and the formula =SUM(B6:B12), which adds the number of adult tickets sold in Quarter 2, appears in the formula bar.

▶ **6.** Click the **Quarter 4** sheet tab, and then make sure that cell **B13** is the active cell. The value 177 appears in the cell, and the same formula used in cell B13 in the Quarter 1 and Quarter 2 worksheets appears in the formula bar. See Figure 6-3.

| Figure 6-3 | Formulas entered in all worksheets in the group |

formula in cell B13 is the same in all the grouped worksheets

Quarter 4 worksheet has same layout as the Quarter 1, 2, and 3 worksheets

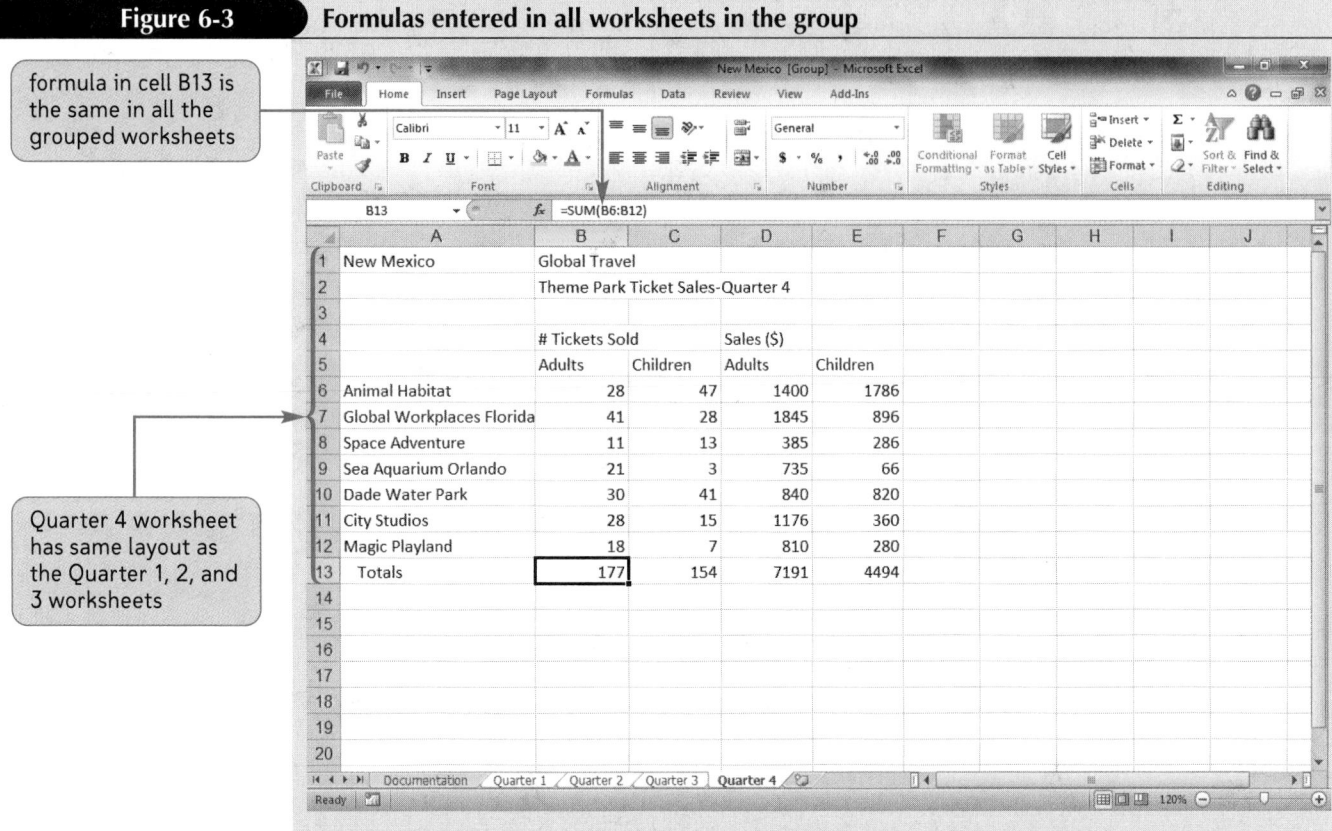

B13    =SUM(B6:B12)

|  | A | B | C | D | E |
|---|---|---|---|---|---|
| 1 | New Mexico | Global Travel | | | |
| 2 | | Theme Park Ticket Sales-Quarter 4 | | | |
| 3 | | | | | |
| 4 | | # Tickets Sold | | Sales ($) | |
| 5 | | Adults | Children | Adults | Children |
| 6 | Animal Habitat | 28 | 47 | 1400 | 1786 |
| 7 | Global Workplaces Florida | 41 | 28 | 1845 | 896 |
| 8 | Space Adventure | 11 | 13 | 385 | 286 |
| 9 | Sea Aquarium Orlando | 21 | 3 | 735 | 66 |
| 10 | Dade Water Park | 30 | 41 | 840 | 820 |
| 11 | City Studios | 28 | 15 | 1176 | 360 |
| 12 | Magic Playland | 18 | 7 | 810 | 280 |
| 13 | Totals | 177 | 154 | 7191 | 4494 |

Documentation / Quarter 1 / Quarter 2 / Quarter 3 / **Quarter 4**

▶ **7.** Click the **Quarter 1** sheet tab to redisplay the Quarter 1 results.

## Editing Grouped Worksheets

**INSIGHT**

When you enter, edit, or format cells in a worksheet group, the changes you make to one worksheet are automatically applied to the other worksheets in the group. For example, if you delete a value from one cell, the content is also deleted from the same cell in all the worksheets in the group. Be cautious when editing a worksheet that is part of a group. If the layout and structure of the other grouped worksheets are not exactly the same, you may inadvertently overwrite data in some of the worksheets. Also, remember to ungroup the worksheet group after you finish entering data, formulas, and formatting. Otherwise, changes you intend to make in one worksheet will be made to all the worksheets in the group, potentially producing incorrect results.

## Formatting a Worksheet Group

As with inserting formulas and text, any formatting changes you make to the active sheet are applied to all sheets in the group. You will format the quarterly worksheets.

### To apply formatting to the worksheet group:

1. Bold the text in the nonadjacent range **A1:B2;A6:A13;B4:E5**.

2. Increase the width of column A to **24**.

3. Merge and center each of the following ranges: **B1:E1**, **B2:E2**, **B4:C4**, and **D4:E4**.

4. Center the text in the range **B5:E5**.

5. Apply the **Comma Style** number format with no decimal places to the range B6:C13. No change is visible because all the numbers are less than 1000.

6. Apply the **Accounting** number format with no decimal places to the range D6:E13 so the values appear with a dollar sign and no decimal places.

7. Add a **bottom border** to the ranges B5:E5 and B12:E12.

8. Click cell **A1**. All the worksheets in the group are formatted. See Figure 6-4.

| Figure 6-4 | Formatting applied to the worksheet group |
| --- | --- |

9. Click each sheet tab in the worksheet group and review the formatting changes, and then click the **Quarter 1** sheet tab.

## Ungrouping Worksheets

When you ungroup the worksheets, each worksheet functions independently again. If you forget to ungroup the worksheets, any changes you make in one worksheet will be applied to all the worksheets in the group. So be sure to ungroup worksheets when you are finished with changes that apply to multiple worksheets.

You will ungroup the quarterly worksheets so you can work in each worksheet separately.

**To ungroup the quarterly worksheets:**

Be sure to ungroup the worksheets; otherwise, any changes you make will affect all worksheets in the group.

1. Click the **Documentation** sheet tab. The worksheets are ungrouped because the Documentation worksheet was not part of the worksheet group. The text "[Group]" no longer appears in the Excel title bar.

2. Verify that the worksheets are ungrouped and the word "[Group]" no longer appears in the title bar.

## PROSKILLS

*Written Communication: Using Multiple Worksheets with Identical Layouts*

Using multiple worksheets to organize complex data can help make it simpler to understand and analyze as well as to navigate to specific data. For example, a workbook that contains data about a variety of products, stores, or regions could use a different worksheet for each product, store, or region. This organization provides a way to view discrete units of data that can be combined and summarized in another worksheet.

When you use multiple worksheets to organize similar types of data, the worksheets should have identical layouts. You can quickly group the worksheets with the identical layouts, and then enter the formulas, formatting, and labels in all of the grouped worksheets at once. This helps to ensure consistency and accuracy among the worksheets as well as make it faster to create the different worksheets needed.

Using multiple worksheets with identical layouts enables you to use 3-D references to quickly summarize the data in another worksheet. The summary worksheet provides an overall picture of the data that is detailed in the other worksheets. Often, managers are more interested in this big picture view. However, the supporting data is still available in the individual worksheets when a deeper analysis is needed.

So, when you are working with a large and complex worksheet filled with data, consider the different ways to organize it in multiple worksheets. Not only will you save time when entering and finding data, but also the data becomes more understandable, and connections and results become clearer.

# Working with Multiple Worksheets

Rhohit wants the workbook to include a Summary worksheet that adds the annual totals of tickets and sales from the quarterly worksheets. Rather than starting from scratch, you will copy one of the quarterly worksheets as a starting point. The formulas you create in the Summary worksheet will reference cells in each quarterly worksheet using 3-D references. You can then group the completed worksheets to develop a consistent page setup in all worksheets and then print them all at once.

## Copying Worksheets

Often, after spending a lot of time developing a worksheet, you can use the existing worksheet as a starting point for creating another, saving you time and energy compared to building a new worksheet from scratch. Copying a worksheet duplicates all the values, formulas, and formats into the new worksheet, leaving the original worksheet intact. You can then edit, reformat, and enter new content as needed to create the exact worksheet you need.

Next, you'll create the Summary worksheet to provide an overall picture of the data included in the detailed quarterly worksheets. The Summary worksheet needs the same formatting and structure as the quarterly worksheets. To ensure consistency among worksheets, you will copy the Quarter 1 worksheet, and then modify its contents.

**REFERENCE**

### Copying Worksheets

- Select the sheet tabs of the worksheets you want to copy.
- Right-click the sheet tabs, and then click Move or Copy on the shortcut menu.
- Click the To book arrow, and then click the name of an existing workbook or click (new book) to create a new workbook for the worksheets.
- In the Before sheet box, click the worksheet you want to insert the new worksheet before.
- Click the Create a copy check box to insert a check mark to copy the worksheets.
- Click the OK button.

*or*

- Select the sheet tabs of the worksheets you want to copy.
- Press and hold the Ctrl key as you drag the selected sheet tabs to a new location in the sheet tabs, and then release the Ctrl key.

You'll copy the Quarter 1 worksheet to the beginning of the workbook, and then modify the new copy to create the Summary worksheet.

### To copy the Quarter 1 worksheet and create the Summary worksheet:

**TIP**

To move a worksheet or worksheet group to another location in the same workbook, select the worksheets and then drag and drop them by the selected sheet tabs.

1. Click the **Quarter 1** sheet tab, and then press and hold the **Ctrl** key as you drag the worksheet to the left of the Documentation sheet. The pointer changes to �k and a triangle indicates the drop location.

2. Release the mouse button, and then release the **Ctrl** key. An identical copy of the Quarter 1 worksheet appears in the new location. The sheet tab shows "Quarter 1 (2)" to indicate that this is the copied sheet.

3. Rename the Quarter 1 (2) worksheet as **Summary**.

4. Move the **Summary** worksheet between the Documentation worksheet and the Quarter 1 worksheet.

5. Make sure the **Summary** worksheet is the active sheet. You will modify the Summary worksheet.

6. In cell A2, enter **2013**. This is the year to which the summary refers.

7. In cell B2, enter **Theme Park Ticket Sales-Total**. The new title reflects this worksheet's content.

8. Select the range **B6:E12**, and then press the **Delete** key. The Quarter 1 sales data is removed, but the formatting remains intact and will apply to the combined sales data for all four quarters that you will enter shortly.

## Referencing Cells and Ranges in Other Worksheets

When you use multiple worksheets to organize related data, you can reference a cell or range in another worksheet in the same workbook. For example, the Summary worksheet references cells in the four quarterly worksheets to calculate the total sales for the entire year. The syntax to reference a cell or range in a different worksheet is as follows:

```
=SheetName!CellRange
```

In this formula, *SheetName* is the worksheet's name as listed on the sheet tab and *CellRange* is the reference for the cell or range in that worksheet. An exclamation mark (!) separates the worksheet reference from the cell or range reference. For example, you could enter the following formula in the Summary worksheet to reference cell D10 in the Quarter1 worksheet:

```
=Quarter1!D10
```

If the worksheet name contains spaces, you must enclose the sheet name in single quotation marks. For example, the following formula references cell D10 in the Quarter 1 worksheet:

```
='Quarter 1'!D10
```

You can use these references to create formulas that reference cells in different locations in different worksheets. For example, to add sales from two worksheets—cell E12 in the Quarter 1 worksheet and cell D12 in the Quarter 2 worksheet—you would enter the following formula:

```
='Quarter 1'!E12+'Quarter 2'!D12
```

You could type the formula directly in the cell, but it is faster and more accurate to use the point-and-click method to enter references to other worksheets.

---

**REFERENCE**

*Entering a Formula with References to Another Worksheet*

- Click the cell where you want to enter the formula.
- Type = and begin entering the formula.
- To insert a reference from another worksheet, click the sheet tab for the worksheet, and then click the cell or select the range you want to reference.
- When the formula is complete, press the Enter key.

---

Rhohit wants you to enter a formula in cell A2 in each quarterly worksheet that displays the fiscal year from cell A2 in the Summary worksheet. All four quarterly worksheets will use the formula =Summary!A2 to reference the fiscal year in cell A2 of the Summary sheet.

### To enter the formula that references the Summary worksheet:

1. Click the **Quarter 1** sheet tab, press and hold the **Shift** key, and then click the **Quarter 4** worksheet. The Quarter 1 through Quarter 4 worksheets are grouped.

2. Click cell **A2**. This is the cell in which you want to enter the formula to display the fiscal year.

3. Type **=** to begin the formula, click the **Summary** sheet tab, and then click cell **A2**. The reference to cell A2 in the Summary worksheet is added to the formula in cell A2 in the grouped worksheets.

4. On the formula bar, click the **Enter** button ✔. The formula =Summary!A2 is entered in cell A2 in all the worksheets in the group. The formula appears in the formula bar and 2013 appears in cell A2. See Figure 6-5.

**Figure 6-5**    Formula with a worksheet reference

formula references cell A2 in the Summary worksheet

cell displays the contents of cell A2 from the Summary worksheet

5. In each worksheet in the group, verify that the formula =Summary!A2 appears in the formula bar and 2013 appears in cell A2.

6. Switch to the **Summary** worksheet. The quarterly worksheets are ungrouped.

7. In cell A2, enter **Fiscal Year - 2013**. The descriptive label in cell A2 is entered in the Summary worksheet, and is also displayed in the quarterly worksheets because of the formula you entered.

8. Verify that the label "Fiscal Year - 2013" appears in cell A2 in the Quarter 1 through Quarter 4 worksheets.

## Using 3-D References to Add Values Across Worksheets

You need to calculate the number of tickets sold and the total sales for each theme park for the year, and display the totals for the fiscal year in the Summary worksheet. To calculate the totals for the year, you can add the results from each quarterly worksheet and place the sum in the Summary worksheet. For example, in cell B6 of the Summary worksheet, you can enter the formula:

```
='Quarter 1'!B6+'Quarter 2'!B6+'Quarter 3'!B6+'Quarter 4'!B6
```

This formula calculates the number of Adult tickets sold to Animal Habitat by adding the values in cell B6 in each of the quarterly worksheets. Continuing this approach for the entire worksheet is time consuming and error prone.

Instead, when two or more worksheets have *identical* row and column layouts, as do the quarterly worksheets in the New Mexico workbook, you can enter formulas with 3-D references to summarize those worksheets in another worksheet. The 3-D reference specifies not only the range of rows and columns, but also the range of worksheet names in which the cells appear. The general syntax of a 3-D cell reference is:

*WorksheetRange!CellRange*

In this syntax, *WorksheetRange* is the range of worksheets you want to reference and is entered as *FirstSheetName:LastSheetName* with a colon separating the first and last worksheets in the worksheet range. *CellRange* is the same cell or range in each of those worksheets that you want to reference. An exclamation mark (!) separates the worksheet range from the cell or range. For example, the following formula adds the values in cell E13 in the worksheets between Quarter1 and Quarter4, including Quarter1 and Quarter4:

```
=SUM(Quarter1:Quarter4!E13)
```

If worksheets named Quarter1, Quarter2, Quarter3, and Quarter4 are included in the workbook, the worksheet range Quarter1:Quarter4 references all four worksheets. Although the Quarter2 and Quarter3 worksheets aren't specifically mentioned in this 3-D reference, all worksheets positioned within the starting and ending names are included in the calculation.

**INSIGHT**

### Managing 3-D References

The results of a formula using a 3-D reference reflect the current worksheets in the worksheet range. If you move a worksheet outside the referenced worksheet range or remove a worksheet from the workbook, the formula results will change. For example, consider a workbook with four worksheets named Quarter1, Quarter2, Quarter3, and Quarter4. If you move the Quarter3 worksheet after the Quarter4 worksheet, the worksheet range Quarter1:Quarter4 includes only the Quarter1, Quarter2, and Quarter4 worksheets. Similarly, if you insert a new worksheet or move an existing worksheet within the worksheet range, the formula results reflect the change. To continue the example, if you insert a Quarter5 worksheet before the Quarter4 worksheet, the 3-D reference Quarter1:Quarter4 includes the Quarter5 worksheet.

When you create a formula, make sure that the 3-D cell reference reflects the appropriate worksheets. Also, if you later insert or delete a worksheet within the 3-D reference, be aware of how doing so will affect the formula results.

3-D references are often used in formulas that contain Excel functions, including SUM, AVERAGE, COUNT, MAX, MIN, STD, and VAR.

**REFERENCE**

### Entering a Function That Contains a 3-D Reference

- Click the cell where you want to enter the formula.
- Type = to begin the formula, type the name of the function, and then type ( to indicate the beginning of the argument.
- Click the sheet tab for the first worksheet in the worksheet range, press and hold the Shift key, and then click the tab for the last worksheet in the worksheet range.
- Select the cell or range to reference, and then press the Enter key.

In the New Mexico workbook, you'll use 3-D references in the Summary worksheet to add the total number of tickets sold and sales for the year. You will begin by entering a formula to add the number of tickets sold to adults for the Animal Habitat theme park in all four quarters of the year. Then, you'll copy this formula to calculate the tickets sold to adults and children for each theme park as well as the sales generated.

### To enter a formula with a 3-D reference to the quarterly worksheets:

▶ **1.** In the Summary worksheet, click cell **B6**, and then type **=SUM(** to begin the formula. A ScreenTip shows the SUM function syntax. See Figure 6-6. You'll enter a 3-D reference to cell B6 in the four quarterly worksheets.

**Figure 6-6** **Formula for the 3-D reference**

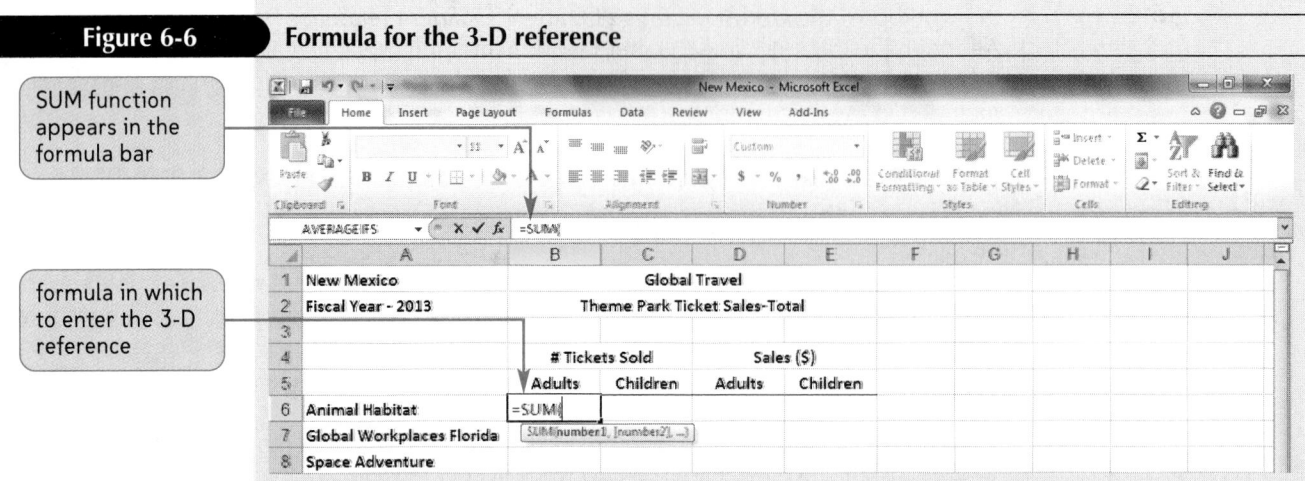

SUM function appears in the formula bar

formula in which to enter the 3-D reference

▶ **2.** Click the **Quarter 1** sheet tab, press and hold the **Shift** key, click the **Quarter 4** sheet tab, and then release the **Shift** key. The worksheet range is selected and added to the SUM function as 'Quarter 1:Quarter 4'. Single quotation marks appear around the worksheet range because the worksheet names include spaces.

▶ **3.** In the Quarter 1 worksheet, click cell **B6**. The cell is selected and added to the function. See Figure 6-7.

**Figure 6-7** **SUM function with a 3-D reference**

3-D reference in the SUM function references cell B6 in the worksheet range Quarter1:Quarter4

cell selected for the 3-D reference

worksheet range selected for the 3-D reference

▶ **4.** Press the **Enter** key to complete the formula. The closing right parenthesis is automatically inserted at the end of the formula.

**5.** In the Summary worksheet, click cell **B6**. The completed formula =SUM('Quarter 1:Quarter 4'!B6) appears in the formula bar. The total number of tickets for Animal Habitat sold to adults in 2013—116—appears in cell B6.

You'll repeat the process to enter a 3-D reference in cell C6 that adds the total number of tickets sold to children for Animal Habitat in 2013.

### To enter another formula with a 3-D reference:

**1.** In the Summary worksheet, click cell **C6**, and then type **=SUM(** to begin the formula.

**2.** Click the **Quarter 1** sheet tab, press and hold the **Shift** key, click the **Quarter 4** sheet tab, and then release the **Shift** key. The quarterly worksheets are grouped.

**3.** In the Quarter 1 worksheet, click cell **C6** to select the cell, and then press the **Enter** key to complete the formula and return to the Summary worksheet.

**4.** In the Summary worksheet, click cell **C6**. The formula =SUM('Quarter 1:Quarter 4'!C6) appears in the formula bar. Also, the value 175—the total number of tickets sold to children for Animal Habitat in 2013—appears in cell C6.

In cells D6 and E6, you'll enter the SUM function with a 3-D reference to calculate the total revenue from tickets sales for Animal Habitat.

### To calculate total sales revenue for Animal Habitat:

**1.** In the Summary worksheet, click cell **D6**, and then type **=SUM(** to begin the formula.

**2.** Group the **Quarter 1** through **Quarter 4** worksheets, and then click cell **D6**.

**3.** Press the **Enter** key. The SUM function with a 3-D reference to cell D6 in the quarterly worksheets is entered. The completed formula is =SUM('Quarter 1:Quarter 4'!D6) and the total revenue from ticket sales to adults for Animal Habitat in 2013 is $5,800.

**4.** In the Summary worksheet, click cell **E6**, and then enter the SUM function formula with a 3-D reference to cell **E6** in the quarterly worksheets. The completed formula is =SUM('Quarter 1:Quarter 4'!E6) and the total revenue from ticket sales to children for Animal Habitat in 2013 is $6,650.

Instead of entering the SUM function to create the totals for the remaining theme parks, you can copy the formulas to the rest of the range. You copy formulas with 3-D references the same way you copy other formulas—using copy and paste or AutoFill. You'll copy the formulas in the range B6:E6 to the range B7:E12 so you can calculate the total ticket sales and revenue in 2013 for the remaining theme parks.

### To copy the formulas with 3-D cell references:

**1.** Select the range **B6:E6**. This range contains the SUM functions with the 3-D references you already entered.

▶ **2.** Drag the fill handle over the range B7:E12. The formulas are copied for the rest of the theme park rows. The Auto Fill Options button appears below the copied range.

▶ **3.** Click the **Auto Fill Options** button 📴, and then click the **Fill Without Formatting** option button. You don't want to copy the formatting in this case because you want to keep the bottom border formatting in the range B12:E12. The total values for the year appear in the range.

▶ **4.** Click cell **B6** to deselect the range. The Summary worksheet now shows the totals for 2013 in New Mexico for each theme park as well as statewide totals. See Figure 6-8.

| Figure 6-8 | **Summary worksheet with all the 3-D reference formulas** |

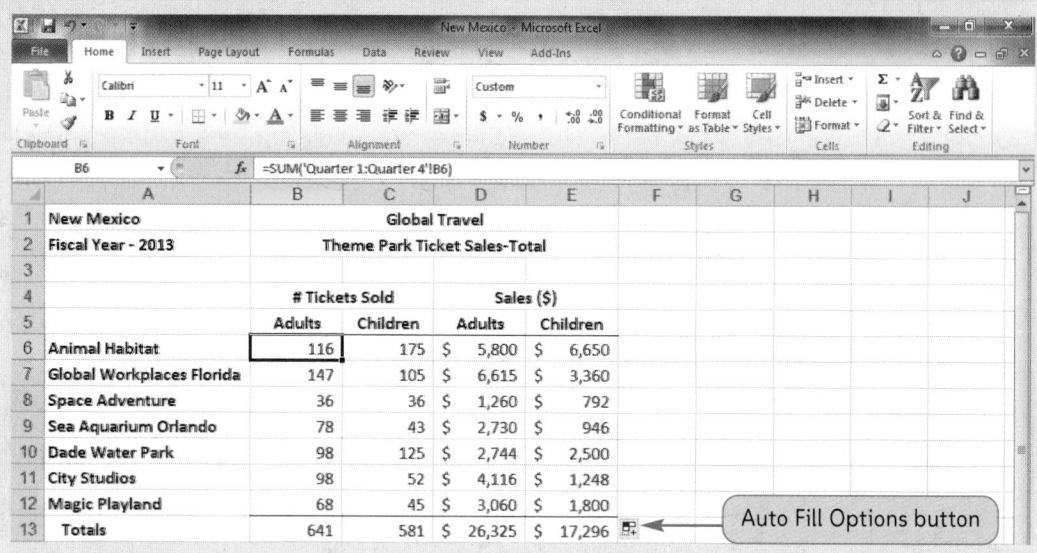

One benefit of summarizing data using 3-D reference formulas, like any other formula, is that if you change the value in one worksheet, the results of formulas that reference that cell reflect the change. Rhohit has discovered an error in the ticket sales data. Sea Aquarium Orlando sold 17 adult tickets in Quarter 1, not 15. You will correct the number of tickets sold for Sea Aquarium Orlando in Quarter 1.

### To change the ticket value in the Quarter 1 worksheet:

▶ **1.** In the Summary worksheet, note that 78 adult tickets were sold for Sea Aquarium Orlando in 2013 and 641 total adult tickets were sold.

▶ **2.** Switch to the **Quarter 1** worksheet, and then, in cell B9, enter **17**. The total adult tickets sold in Quarter 1 is now 129.

The results in the Summary worksheet are also updated because of the 3-D references in the formulas.

▶ **3.** Switch to the **Summary** worksheet. The total number of tickets sold to adults for Sea Aquarium Orlando in 2013 is now 80, and the total number of tickets sold to adults for all theme parks in 2013 is now 643. See Figure 6-9.

**Figure 6-9**    **Summary worksheet with the updated ticket data**

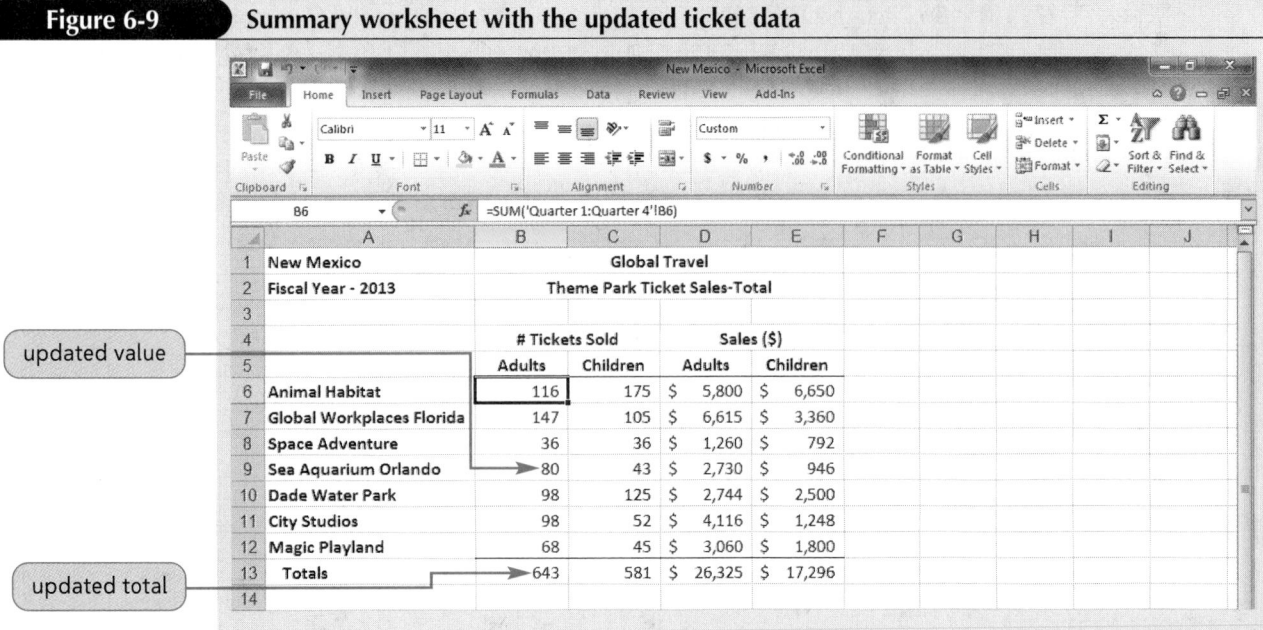

Printing a Worksheet Group

By creating a worksheet group, you apply the same page layout settings to all the worksheets in the group at the same time. You can also print all the worksheets in the group at once.

Rhohit wants a printed copy of the five ticket sales worksheets to include in his report. Each page should have the same setup. Because the layout will be the same for all the quarterly worksheets in the New Mexico workbook, you can speed the page layout setup by creating a worksheet group before selecting settings.

**To print the Summary and quarterly worksheets with a custom header and footer:**

Be sure to include all five worksheets in the group so that you can apply page layout settings and print the worksheets at once.

1. Group the **Summary**, **Quarter 1**, **Quarter 2**, **Quarter 3**, and **Quarter 4** worksheets. The five worksheets are grouped.

2. Click the **Page Layout** tab on the Ribbon, and then, in the Page Setup group, click the **Dialog Box Launcher**. The Page Setup dialog box opens with the Page tab active.

3. Click the **Margins** tab, and then, in the Center on page section, click the **Horizontally** check box to insert a check mark. The printed content will be centered horizontally on the page.

4. Click the **Header/Footer** tab, click the **Custom Header** button to open the Header dialog box, click in the **Center section** box, click the **Insert Sheet Name** button 🔲 to add the &[Tab] code in the section box to insert the sheet tab name in the center section of the header, and then click the **OK** button. A preview of the header appears in the upper portion of the dialog box.

5. Click the **Custom Footer** button to open the Footer dialog box, type your name in the Left section box, click in the Right section box, click the **Insert Date** button 🔲 to add the &[Date] code in the section box to insert the current date in the right section of the footer, and then click the **OK** button.

6. Click the **Print Preview** button. The preview of the Summary worksheet, the first worksheet in the group, appears on the Print tab in Backstage view. See Figure 6-10.

**Figure 6-10**    **Preview of the worksheet group**

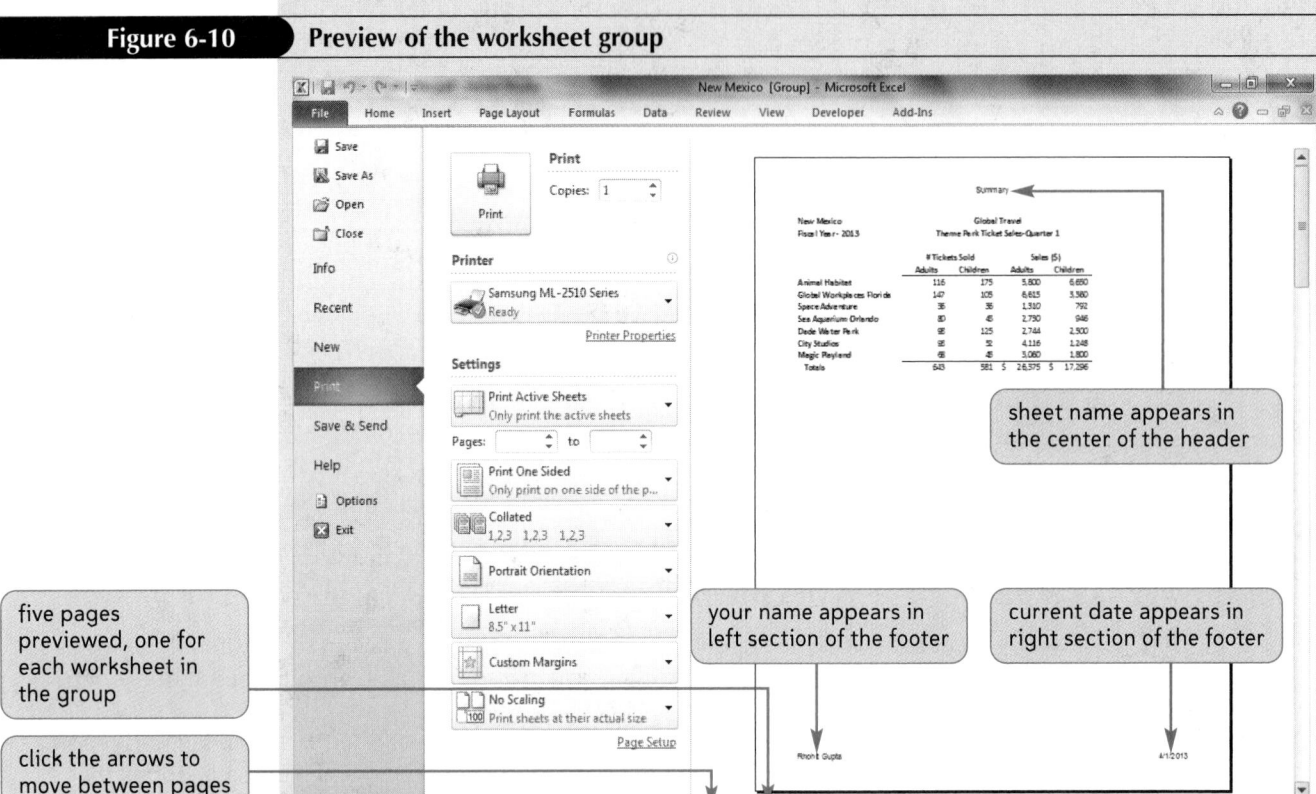

sheet name appears in the center of the header

five pages previewed, one for each worksheet in the group

click the arrows to move between pages

your name appears in left section of the footer

current date appears in right section of the footer

7. Below the preview, click the **Next Page** button ▶ four times to view the other worksheets in the group. Each page has the same page layout but the header shows the sheet tab names.

    **Trouble?** If only one page appears in the preview, the worksheets are not grouped. Click the File tab to exit Backstage view, and then repeat Steps 1 through 7.

8. Unless you are instructed to print, click the **Home** tab to exit Backstage view without printing the worksheet group. Otherwise, click the **Print** button 🖨.

9. Switch to the **Documentation** sheet to ungroup the worksheets, and then switch to the **Summary** worksheet.

In this session, you consolidated the data in Global Travel's New Mexico workbook in a Summary sheet, so that Rhohit and Alvin can quickly see the totals for the theme park sales. In the next session, you will help Alvin determine the annual totals for all of Global Travel's Southwest locations—New Mexico, Utah, and Colorado.

**REVIEW**

## Session 6.1 Quick Check

1. What is a worksheet group?
2. How do you select an adjacent worksheet group? How do you select a non-adjacent worksheet group? How do you deselect a worksheet group?
3. What formula would you enter in the Summary worksheet to reference cell A10 in the Quarter 2 worksheet?
4. What is the 3-D cell reference to cell A10 in the adjacent Summary 1, Summary 2, and Summary 3 worksheets?
5. Explain what the formula =MAX(Sheet1:Sheet4!B1) calculates.
6. If you insert a new worksheet named Sheet5 after Sheet4, how would you change the formula =MAX(Sheet1:Sheet4!B1) to include Sheet5 in the calculation?
7. If you insert a new worksheet named Sheet5 before Sheet4, how would you change the formula =MAX(Sheet1:Sheet4!B1) to include Sheet5 in the calculation?
8. How do you apply the same page layout to all of the worksheets in a workbook at one time?

# SESSION 6.2 VISUAL OVERVIEW

An **external reference** is a reference to cells or ranges in a worksheet from another workbook. For example, *'[New Mexico.xlsx]Summary'!$B6* references cell B6 in the Summary worksheet in the New Mexico workbook.

When two workbooks are linked, the **destination file** (sometimes referred to as the dependent file) is the workbook that receives data from another workbook. In this case, the Totals 2013 workbook is the destination file.

The total value shown in the destination file is calculated from values in the three source files.

Whenever a value in a source file changes, the destination is also updated to reflect the most recent information. For example, if Animal Habitat sales in New Mexico increase by four tickets, the changes are also reflected in the Totals 2013 workbook.

| File | Home | Insert | Page Layout | Formulas | Data | Review | View |

Microsoft

**Workbook Views:** Normal, Page Layout, Page Break Preview, Custom Views, Full Screen

**Show:** Ruler, Formula Bar, Gridlines, Headings

**Zoom:** Zoom, 100%, Zoom to Selection

B6    *fx*    ='[New Mexico.xlsx]Summary'!$B6+[Colorad

**Totals 2013**

| | A | B | C | D |
|---|---|---|---|---|
| 1 | All States | | Global Travel | |
| 2 | | | Theme Park Ticket Sale | |
| 3 | | | | |
| 4 | | # Tickets Sold | | |
| 5 | | Adults | Children | Adul |
| 6 | Animal Habitat | 346 | 499 | $ 17, |
| 7 | Global Workplaces Florida | 451 | 376 | $ 20, |
| 8 | Space Adventure | 115 | 97 | $ 4.0 |

Documentation    Summary

**New Mexico**

| | A | B | C | D |
|---|---|---|---|---|
| 1 | New Mexico | | Global Travel | |
| 2 | Fiscal Year - 2013 | | Theme Park Ticket Sales- | |
| 3 | | | | |
| 4 | | # Tickets Sold | | Sa |
| 5 | | Adults | Children | Adults |
| 6 | Animal Habitat | 116 | 175 | $ 5,80 |
| 7 | Global Workplaces Florida | 147 | 105 | $ 6,61 |
| 8 | Space Adventure | 36 | 36 | $ 1.31 |

Documentation    Summary    Quarter 1    Quarter 2    Quarter 3    Qu

Ready

# LINKS AND EXTERNAL REFERENCES

The Arrange All button displays all of the open workbooks in a tiled configuration within the program window.

The Switch Windows button lists each open workbook so you can change which workbook is active.

A **workspace** is an Excel file that saves information about all of the currently opened workbooks, such as their locations, window sizes, zoom level, and other settings. This workspace opens four workbooks in a tiled configuration.

When two or more workbooks are linked, the **source file** is a workbook that contains data to be used in the destination file. In this case, the New Mexico, Utah, and Colorado workbooks are source files.

These windows are arranged in a tiled configuration. Other options are horizontal, vertical, and cascade.

A **link** is a connection between files that allows data to be transferred from one file to the other.

# Linking Workbooks

Alvin has workbooks from the Colorado and Utah accountants similar to the one you helped Rhohit prepare. These three travel workbooks (named New Mexico, Colorado, and Utah) contain the number of tickets sold and sales for 2013. Alvin wants to create a company-wide workbook that summarizes the annual totals from each state workbook.

When creating formulas in a workbook, you can reference data in other workbooks. To do so, you must create a link between the workbooks. When two files are linked, the source file contains the data, and the destination file (sometimes called the *dependent* file) receives the data. In this case, as illustrated in Figure 6-11, the New Mexico, Utah, and Colorado workbooks are the source files because they contain the data from the three states. The Totals 2013 workbook is the destination file because it receives the data from the three state workbooks to calculate the company totals for 2013. The Totals 2013 workbook will always have access to the most recent information in the state workbooks because it can be updated whenever any of the linked values change.

| Figure 6-11 | Source and destination files |
| --- | --- |

destination file

source file

To create the link between destination and source files, you need to insert a formula in the Totals 2013 workbook that references a specific cell or range in the three state workbooks. That reference, called an external reference, has the syntax

[*WorkbookName*]*WorksheetName*!*CellRange*

where *WorkbookName* is the filename of the workbook (including the file extension) enclosed in square brackets; *WorksheetName* is the name of the worksheet that contains the data followed by an exclamation mark; and *CellRange* is the cell or range that contains the data. For example, the following formula references cell B6 in the Summary worksheet of the Colorado.xlsx workbook:

=[Colorado.xlsx]Summary!B6

If the workbook name or the worksheet name contains one or more spaces, you must enclose the entire workbook name and worksheet name in single quotation marks. For example, the following formula references cell B6 in the Summary worksheet of the New Mexico.xlsx workbook:

='[New Mexico.xlsx]Summary'!B6

**TIP**

When you use the point-and-click method to build formulas with external references, Excel enters all of the required punctuation, including quotation marks.

When the source and destination workbooks are stored in the same folder, you need to include only the workbook name in the external reference. However, when the source and destination workbooks are located in different folders, the workbook reference must include the file's complete location (also called the path). For example, if the destination file is stored in C:\TicketSales and the source file is stored in C:\TicketSales\Domestic Sales, the complete reference in the destination file would be:

```
='C:\TicketSales\Domestic Sales\[New Mexico.xlsx]Summary'!B6
```

The single quotation marks start at the beginning of the path and end immediately before the exclamation mark.

**PROSKILLS**

### Decision Making: Understanding When to Link Workbooks

More than one person is usually involved in developing information that will be used in an organization's decision-making process. If each person has access to only part of the data, everyone's ability to see the whole picture and make good decisions is limited. Linking workbooks provides one way to pull together all of the data being compiled by different people or departments to support the decision-making process.

When deciding whether to link workbooks, consider the following questions:

- **Can separate workbooks have the same purpose and structure?** With linked workbooks, each workbook can focus on a different store, branch office, or department with the same products or expenditure types and reporting periods (such as weekly, monthly, and quarterly).
- **Is a large workbook too unwieldy to use?** A large workbook can be divided into smaller workbooks for each quarter, division, or product and then linked to provide the summary information.
- **Can information from different workbooks be summarized?** Linked workbooks provide a way to quickly and accurately consolidate information from multiple source workbooks, and the summary worksheet will always contain the most current information even when information is later updated.
- **Are source workbooks received from another person or group continually updated?** With linked workbooks, an outdated source workbook can be replaced and the destination workbook will then reflect the latest information.

If you can answer yes to these questions, then linked workbooks are the way to go. Creating linked workbooks can help you analyze data better, leading to better decision making. It also provides greater flexibility as data becomes more expansive and complex.

## Navigating Multiple Workbooks

You'll combine the three state worksheets into one regional summary. You'll open all the workbooks you need to reference. Then, you'll switch between them to make each Summary worksheet the active sheet in preparation for creating the external references.

### To open the workbooks needed to create the regional summary:

1. If you took a break after the previous session, make sure the New Mexico workbook is open and the Summary worksheet is active.

2. Open the **TravelTotals** workbook located in the Excel6\Tutorial folder included with your Data Files, and then save the workbook as **Totals 2013**.

3. In the Documentation sheet, enter your name and the date, and then make the **Summary** worksheet active.

4. Open the **Utah** and **Colorado** workbooks located in the Excel6\Tutorial folder included with your Data Files.

You'll need to move between open workbooks when you create the external reference formulas in the Totals 2013 workbook. The Switch Windows button in the Window group on the View tab lists each open workbook so you can change which workbook is active. Another method is to click the Excel program button on the taskbar and then click the thumbnail of the workbook you want to make active.

**To switch between the open workbooks:**

▶ **1.** Click the **View** tab on the Ribbon, and then, in the Window group, click the **Switch Windows** button to display a list of all the workbooks that are currently open.

▶ **2.** Click **Utah** to make it the active workbook, and then make the **Summary** sheet active.

▶ **3.** In the Window group, click the **Switch Windows** button, click **Colorado** to switch to the Colorado workbook, and then make the **Summary** worksheet active.

▶ **4.** Make the **Totals 2013** workbook the active workbook.

## Arranging Multiple Workbooks

You might also want to display all the open workbooks on your screen at the same time. This way, you can easily click among the open workbooks to create links without having to continually change the active workbook, as well as quickly compare the contents of worksheets in different workbooks. You can arrange workbooks in the following layouts:

• **Tiled**, which divides the open workbooks evenly on the screen.
• **Horizontal**, which divides the open workbooks into horizontal bands.
• **Vertical**, which divides the open workbooks into vertical bands.
• **Cascade**, which layers the open workbooks on the screen.

The layout you select will depend on the contents being displayed and your purpose.

**REFERENCE**

*Arranging Workbooks*

• On the View tab, in the Window group, click the Arrange All button.
• Select the layout in which you want to arrange the open workbooks.
• When arranging multiple workbooks, uncheck the Windows of active workbook option. When arranging multiple worksheets within one workbook, check the option.
• Click the OK button.

Currently, four workbooks are open but only one is visible. You'll arrange the workbooks using the tiled arrangement.

**To tile the open workbooks:**

▶ **1.** In the Window group on the View tab, click the **Arrange All** button. The Arrange Windows dialog box opens so you can select the layout arrangement you want.

▶ **2.** Click the **Tiled** option button, if necessary. The Tiled option arranges the four Global Travel workbooks evenly on the screen.

▶ **3.** Click the **OK** button. The four open workbooks appear in a tiled layout.

**4.** Click in the **Totals 2013** workbook to make it the active workbook, if necessary. In the tiled layout, the active workbook has darker text in the title bar, a gray background, scroll bars, and the active cell. See Figure 6-12.

**Figure 6-12** ▶ **Four workbooks arranged in a tiled layout**

active workbook's title bar has Excel icon and dark text

active cell is in the active workbook

scroll bars appear in the active workbook

inactive workbooks (your workbook locations might differ)

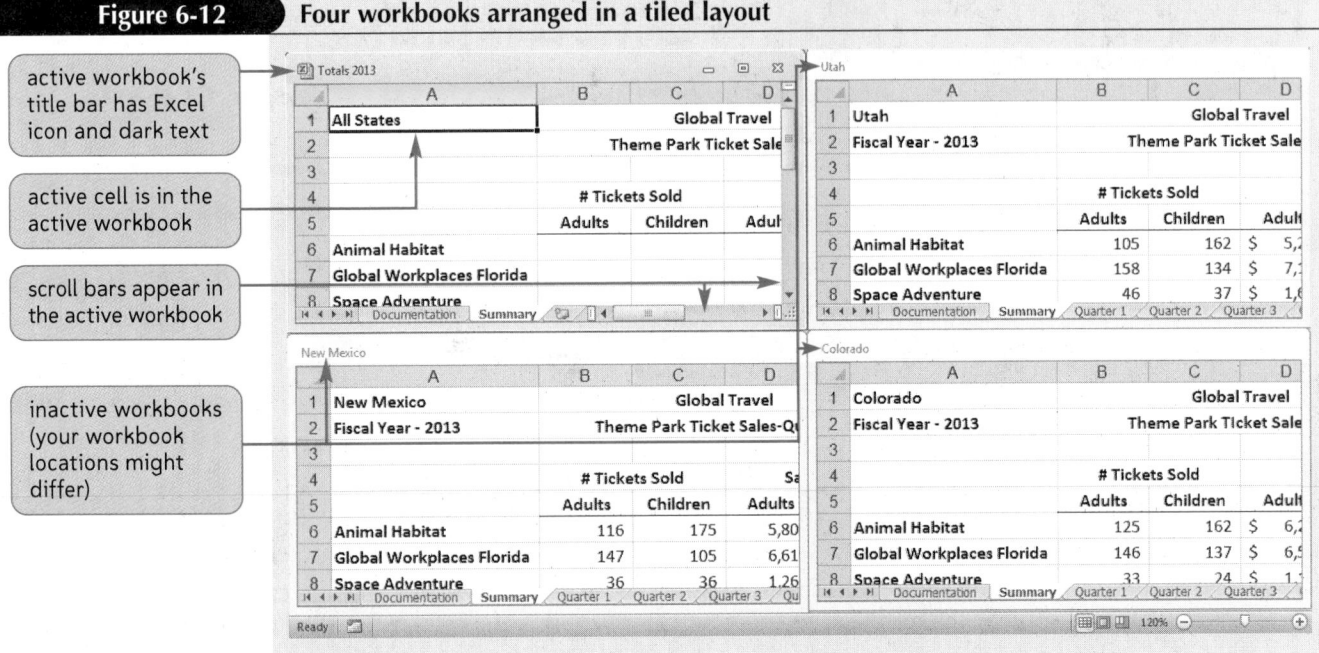

## Creating Formulas with External References

A formula can include a reference to another workbook (called an external reference), which creates a set of linked workbooks. The process for entering a formula with an external reference is the same as entering any other formula using references within the same worksheet or workbook. You can enter the formulas by typing them or using the point-and-click method. In most situations, you will use the point-and-click method to switch between the source files and destination files so that Excel enters the references to the workbook, worksheet, and cell using the correct syntax.

You need to enter the external reference formulas in the Totals 2013 workbook to summarize the states' totals into one workbook for Alvin. You'll start by creating the formula that adds the total number of adult tickets to Animal Habitat sold in New Mexico, Utah, and Colorado. You cannot use the SUM function with 3-D references here because you are referencing multiple workbooks and 3-D references can only be used to reference multiple worksheets in the same workbook.

### To create the external reference formula to total adult tickets for Animal Habitat:

**1.** In the Summary worksheet in the Totals 2013 workbook, click cell **B6**, and then type **=** to begin the formula.

As you create the formula, be sure to verify each external reference before going to the next step.

**2.** Click anywhere in the **New Mexico** workbook, and then, in the Summary worksheet, click cell **B6**. The external reference to cell B6 in the Summary worksheet of the New Mexico workbook—'[New Mexico.xlsx]Summary'!$B$6—is added to the formula in the Totals 2013 workbook. See Figure 6-13.

**Figure 6-13** | **External reference entered in the formula**

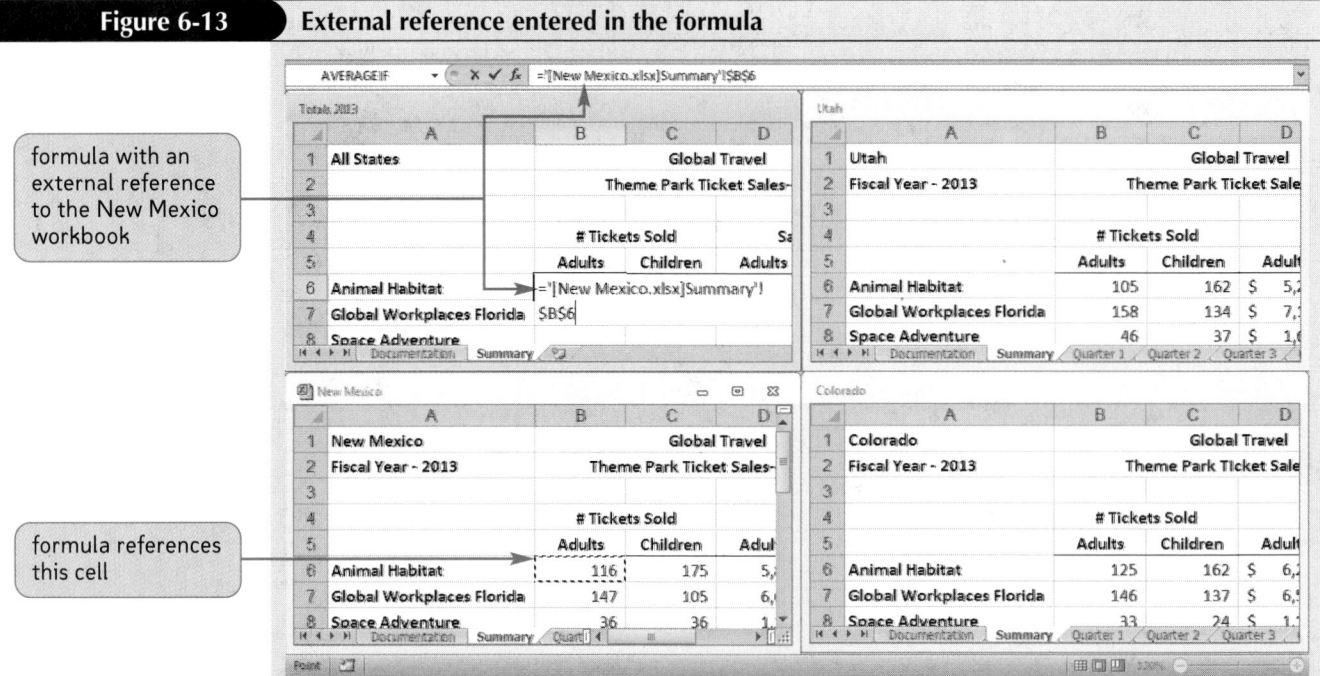

formula with an external reference to the New Mexico workbook

formula references this cell

▶ **3.** Type **+**. The Totals 2013 workbook becomes active and you can continue entering the formula. You need to create an external reference to the Colorado workbook.

▶ **4.** Click anywhere in the **Colorado** workbook, click cell **B6** in the Summary worksheet, and then type **+**. The formula in the Totals 2013 workbook includes the external reference to the cell that has the total number of adult tickets to Animal Habitat sold in Colorado.

▶ **5.** Click anywhere in the **Utah** workbook, click cell **B6** in the Summary worksheet, and then press the **Enter** key. The formula with three external references is entered in the Summary sheet in the Totals 2013 workbook.

▶ **6.** In the Totals 2013 workbook, in the Summary sheet, click cell **B6**. The complete formula appears in the formula bar and the formula results appear in cell B6, showing that 346 adult tickets to Animal Habitat were sold in the three states: 116 in New Mexico, 105 in Utah, and 125 in Colorado. See Figure 6-14.

**Figure 6-14** | **Complete formula with external references**

external references in the formula entered in cell B6

formula results appear in the cell

**Trouble?** If 346 doesn't appear in cell B6 in the Summary sheet in the Totals 2013 workbook, you might have clicked an incorrect cell for an external reference in the formula. Repeat Steps 1 through 6 to correct the formula.

You'll use the same process to enter the external reference formula for cell C6, which is the number of children's tickets to Animal Habitat sold in the three states. Then you'll do the same to create the formulas to calculate the total sales from all three states.

### To create the remaining external reference formulas:

1. In the Totals 2013 workbook, in the Summary worksheet, click cell **C6**, and then type **=** to begin the formula.

2. Click the **New Mexico** workbook, click cell **C6** in the Summary worksheet, and then type **+**. The formula in the Totals 2013 workbook includes the external reference to cell C6 in the Summary worksheet in the New Mexico workbook.

3. Click the **Colorado** workbook, click cell **C6** in the Summary worksheet, and then type **+**. The formula includes an external reference to cell C6 in the Summary worksheet in the Colorado workbook.

4. Click the **Utah** workbook, click cell **C6** in the Summary worksheet, and then press the **Enter** key. The external reference formula is complete.

5. In the Totals 2013 workbook, click cell **C6** in the Summary sheet. Cell C6 displays 499, the total children's tickets sold to Animal Habitat, and the following formula appears in the formula bar: ='[New Mexico.xlsx]Summary'!$C$6+[Colorado.xlsx]Summary!$C$6+[Utah.xlsx]Summary!$C$6.

   Next, you'll enter the external reference formulas in cells D6 and E6 to add the total sales from adult and children's tickets to Animal Habitat.

6. Use the same procedure in Steps 1 through 4 to enter the formula in cell **D6** in the Summary worksheet in the Totals 2013 workbook. The formula results displayed in cell D6 are 17300—the total sales from adult tickets to Animal Habitat in New Mexico, Colorado, and Utah.

7. Use the same procedure in Steps 1 through 4 to enter the formula in cell **E6** in the Summary worksheet in the Totals 2013 workbook. You may need to scroll each worksheet to see cell E6. The formula results displayed in cell E6 are 18962—the total sales from children's tickets to Animal Habitat in New Mexico, Colorado, and Utah.

You need to enter the remaining formulas for the other six theme parks. Rather than creating the rest of the external reference formulas manually, you can copy the formulas in row 6 to rows 7 through 12. The formulas created using the point-and-click method contain absolute references. Before you copy them to other cells, you need to change them to use mixed references because the rows in the formula need to change.

### To edit the external reference formulas to use mixed references:

1. Maximize the Totals 2013 workbook. The Totals 2013 workbook fills the program window. The other workbooks are still open but are not visible.

2. In the Summary worksheet, double-click cell **B6** to enter Edit mode and display the formula in the cell.

**TIP**

You can also create the mixed reference by deleting the $ symbol from the row references in the formula.

> 3. Click in the first absolute reference in the formula, and then press the **F4** key twice to change the absolute reference $B$6 to the mixed reference $B6.

> 4. Edit the other two absolute references in the formula to be mixed references with absolute column references and relative row references.

> 5. Press the **Enter** key. The formula is updated to include mixed references, but the formula results aren't affected. Cell B6 still displays 346, which is correct.

> 6. Edit the formulas in cells C6, D6, and E6 to change the absolute references to the mixed references $C6, $D6, and $E6, respectively. The formulas are updated, but the cells in the range C6:E6 still correctly display 499, 17300, and 18962, respectively.

With the formulas corrected to include mixed references, you can now copy the external reference formulas in cells B6:E6 to the other rows. Then, you'll enter the SUM function to total the values in each column.

### To copy and paste the external reference formulas:

> 1. Select the range **B6:E6**, and then drag the fill handle to select the range **B7:E12**. The formulas are copied to the range B7:E12 and the formula results appear in the cells. The Auto Fill Options button appears in the lower-right corner of the selected range, but you do not need to use it.

> 2. In cell B13, enter the SUM function to add the range **B6:B12**. A total of 2035 adult tickets were sold for all theme parks.

> 3. Copy the formula in cell B13 to the range **C13:E13**. The totals are 1855, 81889, and 55704, respectively.

> 4. Format the range B6:C13 with the **Comma** style and no decimal places, and then format the range D6:E13 with the **Accounting** number format and no decimal place.

> 5. Format the range B12:E12 with a **bottom border**, and then click cell **A1** to deselect the range. See Figure 6-15.

| Figure 6-15 | Completed formulas in the Summary worksheet in the Totals 2013 workbook |

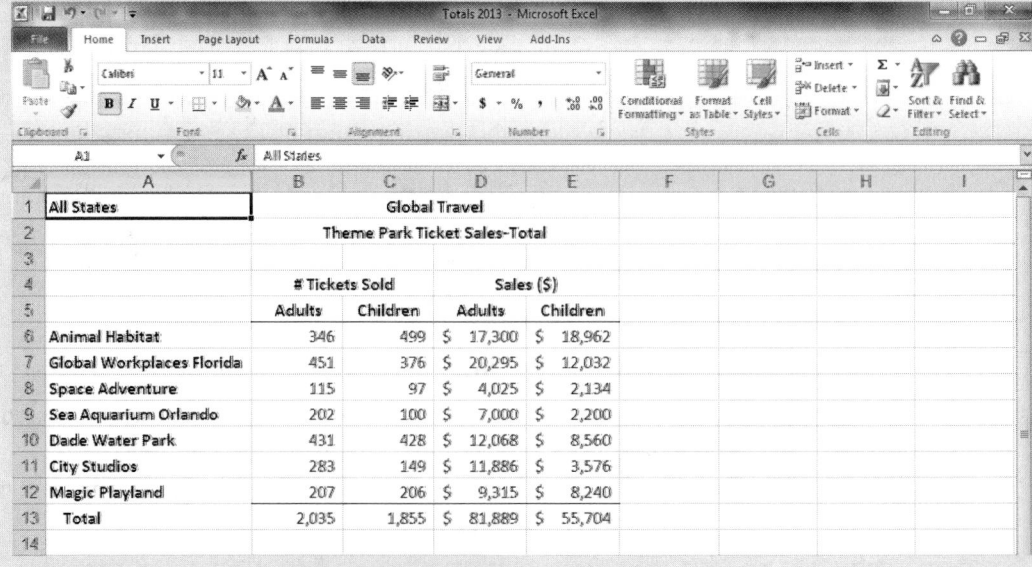

Alvin is pleased; the regional summary results match the executive team's expectations.

### Managing Linked Workbooks

As you work with a linked workbook, you might need to replace a source file or change where you stored the source and destination files. However, replacing or moving a file can affect the linked workbook. Keep in mind the following guidelines to manage your linked workbooks:

- If you rename a source file, the destination workbook won't be able to find it. A dialog box opens, indicating "This workbook contains one or more links that cannot be updated." Click the Continue button to open the workbook with the most recent values, or click the Change Source button in the Edit Links dialog box to specify the new name of that linked source file.
- If you move a source file to a different folder, the link breaks between the destination and source files. Click the Change Source button in the Edit Links dialog box to specify the new location of the linked workbook.
- If you receive a replacement source file, you can swap the original source file with the replacement file. No additional changes are needed.
- If you receive a destination workbook but the source files are not included, Excel will not be able to find the source files, and a dialog box opens with the message "This workbook contains one or more links that cannot be updated." Click the Continue button to open the workbook with the most recent values, or click the Break Link button in the Edit Links dialog box to replace the external references with the existing values.
- If you change the name of a destination file, you can open that renamed version destination file without affecting the source files or the original destination file.

# Updating Linked Workbooks

When workbooks are linked, it is important that the data in the destination file accurately reflects the contents of the source file. When data in a source file changes, you want the destination file to reflect those changes. If both the source and destination files are open when you make a change, the destination file is updated automatically. If the destination file is closed when you make a change in a source file, you choose whether to update the link to display the current values, or continue to display the older values from the destination file when you open the destination file.

## Updating a Destination Workbook with Source Workbooks Open

When both the destination and source workbooks are open, any changes you make in a source workbook appear in the destination workbook. Rhohit tells Alvin that the total New Mexico children's sales for Animal Habitat in Quarter 4 is actually $1,000 more than recorded. After you correct the value in the Quarter 4 worksheet, the amount in the Summary worksheet of the New Mexico workbook and the regional total in the Totals 2013 workbook also change if both the source and destination files are open.

**To update the source workbook with the destination file open:**

▶ 1. Switch to the **New Mexico** workbook, and then make the **Quarter 4** worksheet active. You'll update the value of the Animal Habitat children's dollar amount in this worksheet.

▶ **2.** In cell E6, enter **2786**. The Animal Habitat children's sales are updated.

▶ **3.** Switch to the **Summary** worksheet in the New Mexico workbook, and then verify that the total Animal Habitat children's sales is now $7,650.

▶ **4.** Switch to the **Totals 2013** workbook, and then, in the Summary worksheet, verify that the value in cell E6 is $19,962 and the total dollar amount from sales of children's tickets is $56,704, reflecting the new value you entered in the New Mexico workbook. Because both the destination and source files are open, Excel updated the destination file automatically.

▶ **5.** Save the New Mexico and Totals 2013 workbooks, and then close the Utah, Colorado, and Totals 2013 workbooks. The New Mexico workbook remains open.

## Updating a Destination Workbook with Source Workbooks Closed

When you save a workbook that contains external reference formulas, such as Totals 2013, Excel stores the most recent results of those formulas in the destination file. Source files, such as the New Mexico, Colorado, and Utah workbooks, are often updated while the destination file is closed. In that case, the values in the destination file are not updated at the same time the source files are updated. The next time you open the destination file, the cells containing external reference formulas still display the old values. Therefore, some of the values in the edited source workbooks are different from the values in the destination workbook.

To update the destination workbook with the current data, you must specify that you want the update to occur. As part of the Excel security system that attempts to protect against malicious software, links to other workbooks are not updated without your permission. When you open a workbook with external reference formulas (the destination file), a Security Warning appears in the Information Bar, notifying you that the automatic update of links has been disabled. If you "trust" the provider of the source file(s), you can enable the content, which allows the external reference formulas to function and updates the links in the destination workbook. If you do not "trust" the provider of the source files or do not want the destination file updated at that time, do not enable the content. The old values in the destination workbook are displayed and the links to the source files remain disabled.

Rhohit informs Alvin that the New Mexico workbook needs a second correction. Space Adventure adult sales in Quarter 4 are $435, not $385, which is the current value in the New Mexico workbook. You will increase the amount of the Space Adventure adult sales in Quarter 4 by $50. As a result, sales in the Summary sheet of the New Mexico workbook and the regional total in the Totals 2013 workbook will both increase by $50. You'll edit the source file, the New Mexico workbook, while the destination file is closed.

### To update the source workbook with the destination file closed:

▶ **1.** In the New Mexico workbook, make the **Quarter 4** worksheet active.

▶ **2.** In cell D8, enter **435**. The sales total for adults in Quarter 4 increases to $7,241.

▶ **3.** Switch to the **Summary** worksheet. The sales total for 2013 in cell D8 is $1,310 and the adult sales total is $26,375. See Figure 6-16.

**Figure 6-16** | **Summary worksheet with revised Quarter 4 sales for Space Adventure**

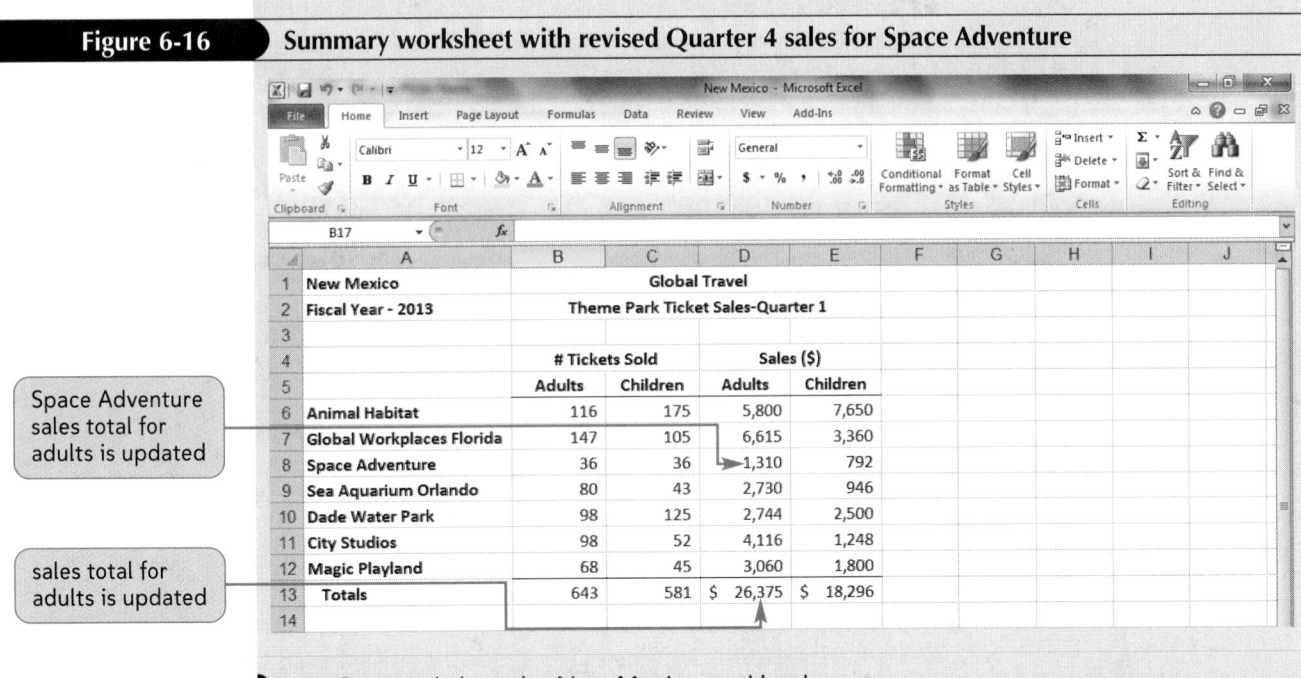

Space Adventure sales total for adults is updated

sales total for adults is updated

> **4.** Save and close the New Mexico workbook.

Now you'll open the destination file (the Totals 2013 workbook). The total adult sales calculated from the source workbooks won't be updated until you specify that they should. When the destination file is open and the source files are closed, the complete file path is included as part of the external reference formula that appears in the formula bar.

## To open and update the destination workbook:

> **1.** Open the **Totals 2013** workbook, and then switch to the **Summary** worksheet, if necessary. The value in cell D8 has *not* changed; it still is $4,025. A Security Warning message appears in the Information Bar, indicating that automatic update of links has been disabled. See Figure 6-17.

**Figure 6-17** | **Security Warning in the Information Bar**

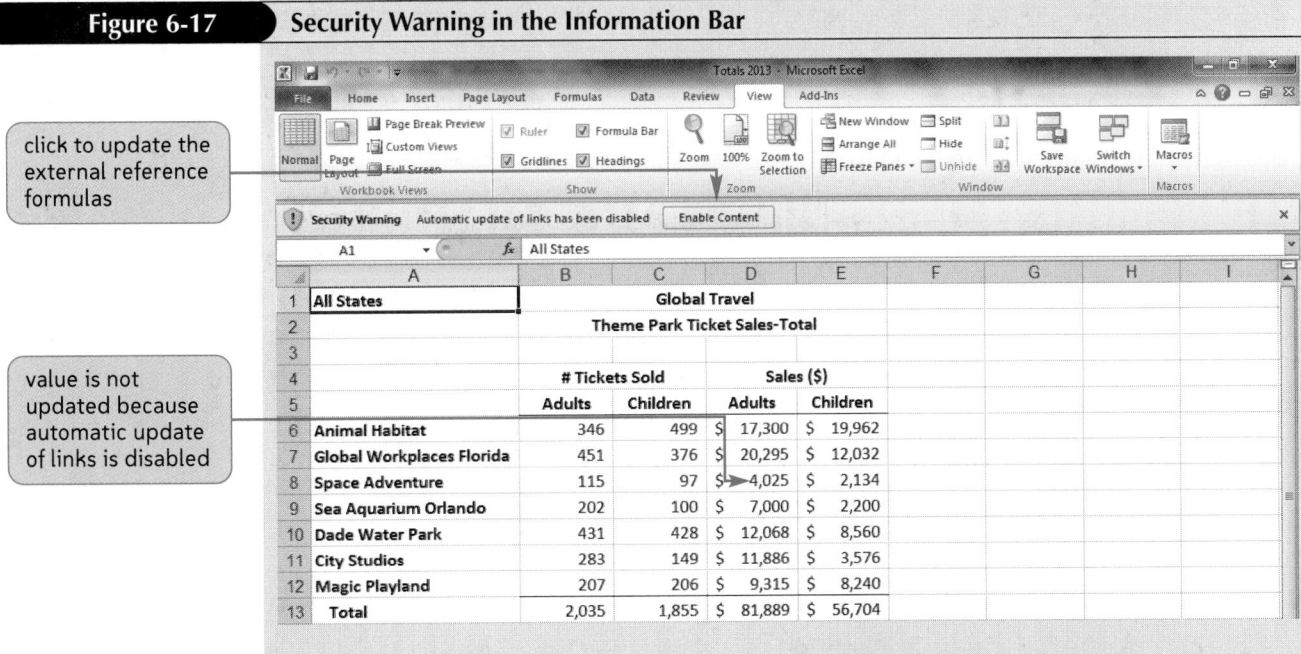

click to update the external reference formulas

value is not updated because automatic update of links is disabled

You want the current values in the source files to appear in the destination workbook.

▶ 2. In the Information Bar, click the **Enable Content** button. The values in the destination file are updated. The sales total in cell D8 of the Totals 2013 workbook increases to $4,075 and the total in cell D13 increases to $81,939.

▶ 3. Click cell **D8**, and then look at the complete file path for each external reference in the formula. The full path appears because the source workbooks are closed.

▶ 4. Save the workbook.

## Managing Links

When workbooks are linked, the Edit Links dialog box provides ways to manage the links. You can review the status of the links, update the data in the files, repair broken links, open the source file, and break the links, which converts all external reference formulas to their most recent values.

After the fiscal year audit is completed and the source workbooks are final, Alvin will archive the summary workbook and move the files to an off-site storage location as part of his year-end backup process. You will save a copy of the Totals 2013 workbook and then break the links to the source files in the copy.

### To save a copy of the Totals 2013 workbook and open the Edit Links dialog box:

▶ 1. Save the Totals 2013 workbook as **Audited 2013** in the Excel6\Tutorial folder included with your Data Files. The Totals 2013 workbook closes and the Audited 2013 workbook remains open.

▶ 2. Click the **Data** tab on the Ribbon.

▶ 3. In the Connections group, click the **Edit Links** button. The Edit Links dialog box opens. See Figure 6-18.

| Figure 6-18 | Edit Links dialog box |

updates the destination file with data from the latest saved version of the selected source file

locates the source file and repairs broken links

click to update the external reference formulas

replaces the links to source files with the current values of the linked cells

checks the status of all links in the dialog box

opens the selected source file

The Edit Links dialog box lists all of the files that the destination workbook is linked to so that you can update, change, open, or remove the links. You can see that the destination workbook, Audited 2013, has links to the Colorado, New Mexico, and Utah workbooks. The dialog box shows the following information about each link:

- **Source** indicates the file to which the link points. The Audited 2013 workbook contains three links pointing to the New Mexico.xlsx, Colorado.xlsx, and Utah.xlsx workbooks.
- **Type** identifies the type of each source file. In this case, the type is an Excel worksheet but it could also be a Word document, a PowerPoint presentation, or some other type of file.
- **Update** specifies the way values are updated from the source file. The letter *A* indicates the link is updated automatically when you open the workbook or when both the source and destination files are open simultaneously. The letter *M* indicates the link must be updated manually by the user, which is useful when you want to see the older data values before updating to the new data. To manually update the link and see the new data values, click the Update Values button.
- **Status** shows whether Excel successfully accessed the link and updated the values from the source document (status is OK), or Excel has not attempted to update the links in this session (status is Unknown). The status of the three links in the Audited 2013 workbook is Unknown.

You'll break the links so that the Audited 2013 workbook contains only the updated values (and is no longer affected by changes in the source files). Then you'll save the Audited 2013 workbook for Alvin to archive. This allows Alvin to store a "snapshot" of the data at the end of the fiscal year.

### To convert all external reference formulas to their current values:

1. Click the **Break Link** button. A dialog box opens, alerting you that breaking links in the workbook permanently converts formulas and external references to their existing values.

2. Click the **Break Links** button. No links appear in the Edit Links dialog box.

3. Click the **Close** button. The Audited 2013 workbook now contains values instead of formulas with external references.

4. Click cell **B6**. The value 346 appears in the cell and the formula bar; the link (the external reference formula) was replaced with the data value. All cells in the range B6:E12 contain values rather than external reference formulas.

5. Save and close the Audited 2013 workbook. The Totals 2013 workbook has external reference formulas, and the Audited 2013 workbook has current values.

## Creating an Excel Workspace

When working with multiple related workbooks, such as Alvin's four workbooks that contain the ticket sales data, you may want to access all of the workbooks at one time. Rather than having to open each workbook individually, you can create a workspace to open multiple workbooks at one time, saving time and avoiding having to remember all the filenames and folder locations.

A workspace is an Excel file that saves information about all of the currently opened workbooks, such as their locations, window sizes, zoom magnifications, and other settings. The workspace file has the file extension .xlw. The workspace does not contain the workbooks themselves—only information about them. To use that set of workbooks, you open the workspace file. Excel then opens the workbooks and settings in the same configuration they were in when you saved the workspace file. Even if a workbook is included in a workspace file, you can still open that workbook separately.

You will create a workspace file for Alvin that includes the four workbooks in a cascade layout, which arranges the open workbooks so that they overlap each other with all the title bars visible. Alvin prefers this layout because he can see more of the active workbook.

### To create the Theme Parks workspace file:

**TIP**

The workspace file contains only the location and name of each file, not the actual workbooks and worksheets. To use the workspace on another computer, you must copy the workspace file *and* the workbook files.

1. Open the **Colorado**, **New Mexico**, **Utah**, and **Totals 2013** workbooks located in the Excel6\Tutorial folder included with your Data Files, clicking the **Don't Update** button in the dialog that opens indicating that the workbook contains links. Four workbooks are open.

2. Make sure the **Summary** worksheet is the active worksheet in each workbook.

3. Switch to the **Totals 2013** workbook.

4. Click the **View** tab on the Ribbon, and then click the **Arrange All** button in the Window group. The Arrange Windows dialog box opens.

5. Click the **Cascade** option button, and then click the **OK** button. The four workbooks overlap each other, with the title bars visible. See Figure 6-19.

**Figure 6-19**    Workbooks arranged in cascade layout

cascade arrangement (your workbook order might differ)

6. In the Window group, click the **Save Workspace** button. The Save Workspace dialog box opens and functions similarly to the Save As dialog box.

7. Type **Theme Parks** in the File name box, verify that **Workspaces** is selected in the Save as type box, verify that the save location is the Excel6\Tutorial folder, and then click the **Save** button. A dialog box might open, prompting you to save your changes to the open workbook files, if you haven't already done so.

8. If prompted to save changes, click the **Save** button. The Theme Parks workspace file is saved. The workspace file has the file extension .xlw.

You will test the workspace file you created to make sure it opens all four Global Travel workbooks.

**To open the Theme Parks workspace:**

▶ **1.** Close all four workbooks.

▶ **2.** Click the **File** tab on the Ribbon, and then click the **Open** command in the navigation bar. The Open dialog box opens, displaying the Excel6\Tutorial folder. The icon for the Theme Parks workspace file is different from the Excel workbook file icon.

▶ **3.** Click the **Theme Parks** workspace file, and then click the **Open** button. A dialog box opens, indicating that the workbook contains links.

▶ **4.** Click the **Don't Update** button. The four travel workbooks open and are arranged in a cascade layout, the same layout in which you saved them. You can work with the workbooks as usual.

▶ **5.** Click the **Colorado** workbook title bar to bring it to the front of the cascaded workbooks. Colorado is now the active workbook.

The workspace file provides a quick way to open a series of workbooks in a specific display. Because it doesn't actually contain the workbooks, you must close each workbook separately, saving as needed.

▶ **6.** Close the New Mexico, Utah, Colorado, and Totals 2013 workbooks without saving any changes.

In this session, you worked with multiple worksheets and workbooks, summarizing data and linking workbooks. This ensures that the data in the summary workbook is accurate and remains updated with the latest data in the source files. In the next session, you will create templates, hyperlinks, and a Web page.

## REVIEW

### Session 6.2 Quick Check

1. What is the external reference to the range A1:A10 in the Sales Info worksheet in the Product Report workbook located in the Reports folder on drive D?
2. What is a source file?
3. What is a destination file?
4. How are linked workbooks updated when both the destination and source files are open?
5. How are linked workbooks updated when the source file is changed and the destination file is closed?
6. How would you determine to what workbooks a destination file is linked?
7. What is a workspace?
8. Explain how creating a workspace file can help you organize your work.

# SESSION 6.3 VISUAL OVERVIEW

This Travel expense report workbook was created from one of the templates available from Office.com. Microsoft provides many other templates that you can download.

From Backstage view, you can save the open workbook to your SkyDrive and then use the Exel Web App to work on that file from any computer with an Internet connection.

A **template** is a workbook with labels, formats, and formulas already built into it with data removed. In other words, a template includes everything but the variable data.

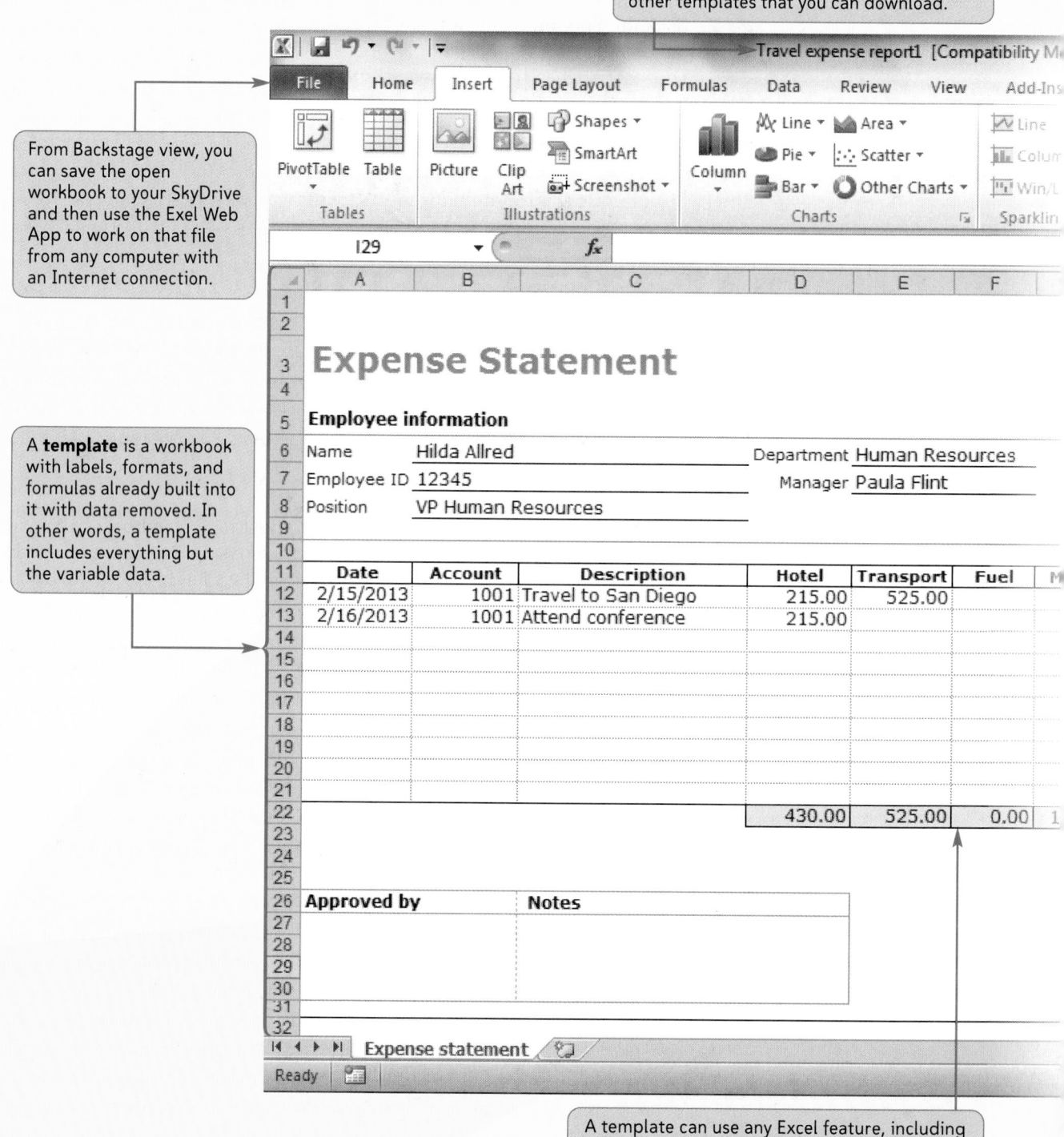

A template can use any Excel feature, including formatting, formulas, charts, data validation, cell protection, and macros. The template used to create this workbook includes labels, formatting, and formulas.

# TEMPLATES AND HYPERLINKS

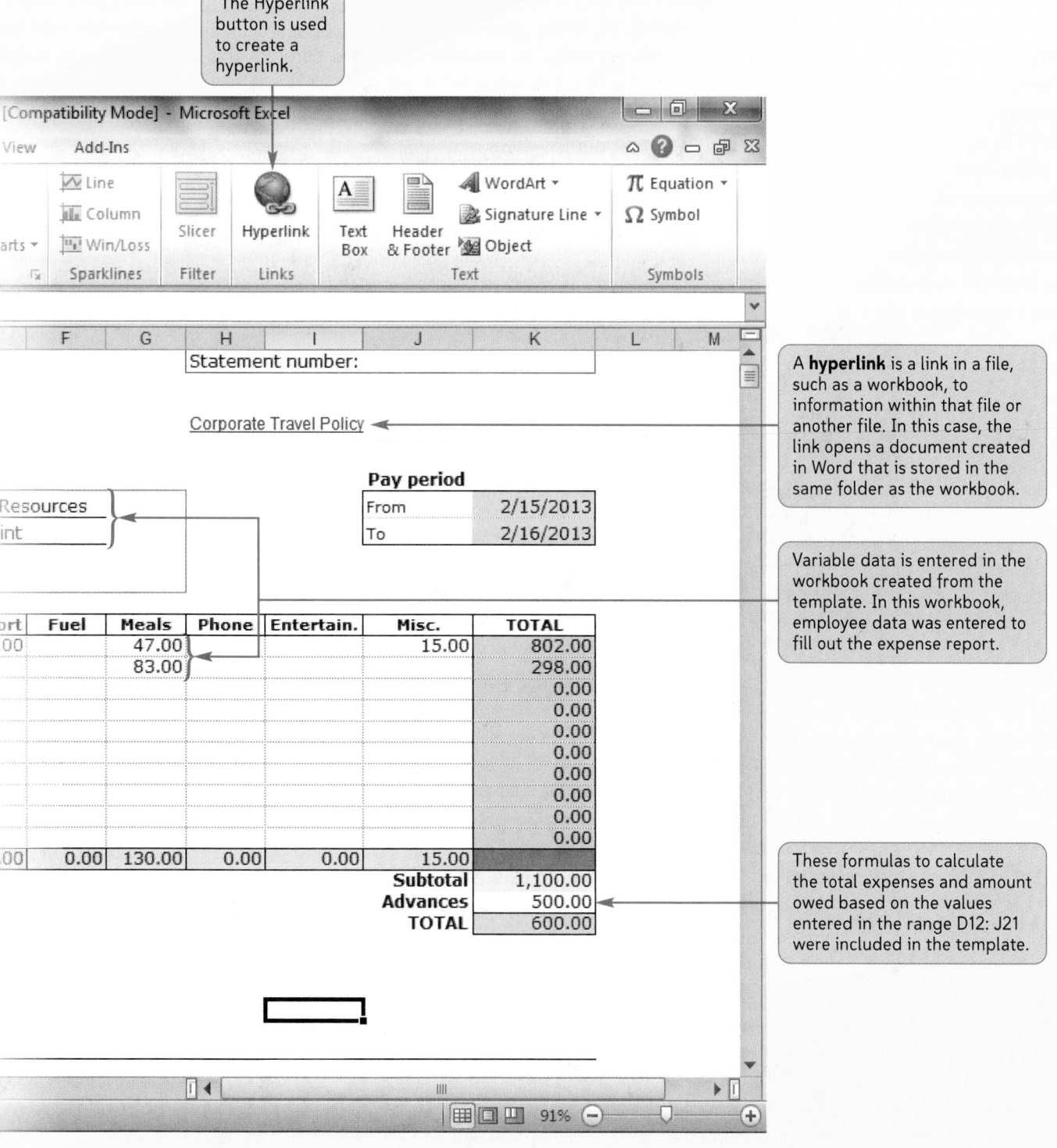

The Hyperlink button is used to create a hyperlink.

A **hyperlink** is a link in a file, such as a workbook, to information within that file or another file. In this case, the link opens a document created in Word that is stored in the same folder as the workbook.

Variable data is entered in the workbook created from the template. In this workbook, employee data was entered to fill out the expense report.

These formulas to calculate the total expenses and amount owed based on the values entered in the range D12: J21 were included in the template.

| | Fuel | Meals | Phone | Entertain. | Misc. | TOTAL |
|---|---|---|---|---|---|---|
| .00 | | 47.00 | | | 15.00 | 802.00 |
| | | 83.00 | | | | 298.00 |
| | | | | | | 0.00 |
| | | | | | | 0.00 |
| | | | | | | 0.00 |
| | | | | | | 0.00 |
| | | | | | | 0.00 |
| | | | | | | 0.00 |
| | | | | | | 0.00 |
| | | | | | | 0.00 |
| .00 | 0.00 | 130.00 | 0.00 | 0.00 | 15.00 | |
| | | | | | Subtotal | 1,100.00 |
| | | | | | Advances | 500.00 |
| | | | | | TOTAL | 600.00 |

Statement number:

Corporate Travel Policy

**Pay period**

| From | 2/15/2013 |
|---|---|
| To | 2/16/2013 |

Resources
int

# Creating a Hyperlink

A hyperlink is a link in a file, such as a workbook, to information within that file or another file. Although hyperlinks are most often found on Web pages, they can also be placed in a worksheet and used to quickly jump to a specific cell or range within the active worksheet, another worksheet, or another workbook. Hyperlinks can also be used to jump to other files, such as a Word document or a PowerPoint presentation, or sites on the Web.

## Inserting a Hyperlink

You can insert a hyperlink directly in a workbook file to link to information in that workbook, another workbook, or a file associated with another application on your computer, a shared file on a network, or a Web site. Hyperlinks are usually represented by colored words with underlines or images. When you click a hyperlink, the computer switches to the file or portion of the file referenced by the hyperlink.

**REFERENCE**

*Inserting a Hyperlink*

- Select the text, graphic, or cell in which you want to insert the hyperlink.
- In the Links group on the Insert tab, click the Hyperlink button.
- To link to a file or Web page, click Existing File or Web Page in the Link to list, and then select the file or Web page from the Look in box.
- To link to a location in the current workbook, click Place in This Document in the Link to list, and then select the worksheet, cell, or range in the current workbook.
- To link to a new document, click Create New Document in the Link to list, and then specify the filename and path of the new document.
- To link to an email address, click E-mail Address in the Link to list, and then enter the email address of the recipient and a subject line for the message.
- Click the OK button.

Alvin wrote a memo summarizing the sales results for New Mexico, Utah, and Colorado in 2013. He wants the Totals 2013 workbook to include a link to this memo that points to the Sales 2013 Word document.

**To insert a hyperlink into the Totals 2013 workbook:**

▶ **1.** Open the **Totals 2013** workbook located in the Excel6\Tutorial folder included with your Data Files, but don't update the links.

▶ **2.** Maximize the Totals 2013 worksheet window.

▶ **3.** Switch to the **Documentation** worksheet, and then click cell **A8**. You want to create the hyperlink in this cell.

▶ **4.** Click the **Insert** tab on the Ribbon, and then click the **Hyperlink** button in the Links group. The Insert Hyperlink dialog box opens. You use this dialog box to define the hyperlink.

**5.** If necessary, click the **Existing File or Web Page** button in the Link to bar and click the **Current Folder** button in the Look in area. All the existing files and folders in the Tutorial folder, which is the folder where the Totals 2013 workbook is stored, are displayed. See Figure 6-20.

**Figure 6-20**    **Insert Hyperlink dialog box**

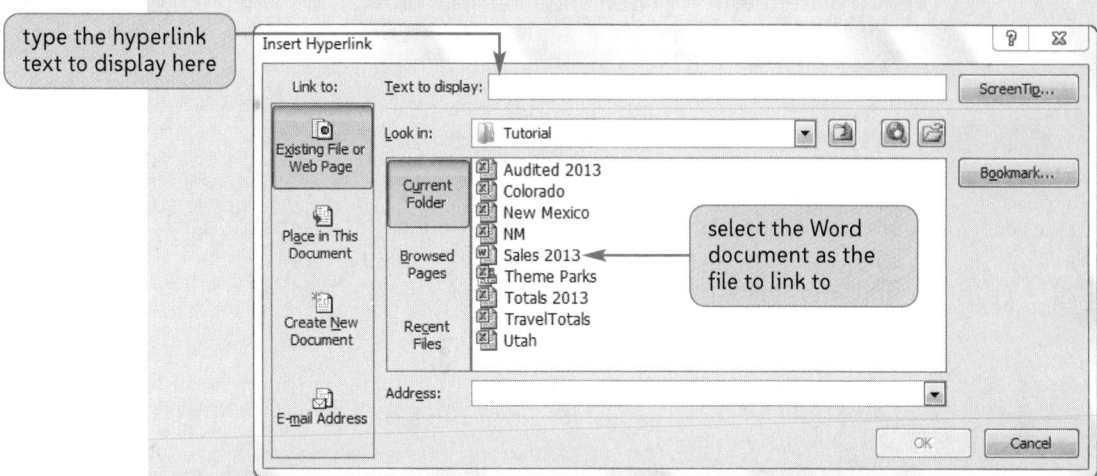

**6.** Click the **Text to display** box, and then type **Click here to read Executive Memo**. This is the hyperlink text that will appear in cell A8 in the Documentation worksheet.

**7.** Click the **Sales 2013** Word document in the list of files. This is the file you want to open when the hyperlink is clicked.

**8.** Click the **OK** button. As shown in Figure 6-21, the hyperlink text entered in cell A8 is underlined and in a blue font, indicating that the text within the cell is a hyperlink.

**Figure 6-21**    **Hyperlink to the Sales 2013 document**

You will test the hyperlink that you just created to ensure it works correctly. To use a hyperlink in a worksheet, you must click the text inside the cell that contains the link. If you click white space in the cell or any text that flows into an adjacent cell, the hyperlink does not work.

**To test the hyperlink:**

▶ **1.** Point to the text in cell **A8** until the pointer changes to 🖑, and then click the hyperlink. The Sales 2013 document opens in Word.

   **Trouble?** If the hyperlink doesn't work, you might have clicked the text that overflows cell A8. Point to the text within cell A8, and then click the hyperlink.

▶ **2.** Close the Word document and exit Word. The Documentation worksheet in the Totals 2013 workbook is active. The hyperlink in cell A8 changed color to indicate that you used the link.

**TIP**

To delete a hyperlink, right-click the hyperlink cell and then click Clear Contents. To delete the hyperlink but keep the text, right-click the hyperlink cell, and then click Remove Hyperlink.

## Editing a Hyperlink

You can modify an existing hyperlink by changing its target file or Web page, modifying the text that is displayed, or changing the ScreenTip for the hyperlink. ScreenTips, which appear whenever you place the pointer over a hyperlink, provide additional information about the target of the link. The default ScreenTip is the folder location and filename of the file you will link to, which isn't very helpful. You can insert a more descriptive ScreenTip when you create a hyperlink or edit an existing hyperlink.

You will edit the hyperlink to the memo so that it has a more descriptive ScreenTip.

**To edit the hyperlink:**

▶ **1.** In the Documentation worksheet, right-click cell **A8**, and then click **Edit Hyperlink** on the shortcut menu. The Edit Hyperlink dialog box opens; it has the same layout and information as the Insert Hyperlink dialog box.

▶ **2.** Click the **ScreenTip** button. The Set Hyperlink ScreenTip dialog box opens.

▶ **3.** Type **Click to view sales analysis for 2013** in the ScreenTip text box, and then click the **OK** button.

▶ **4.** Click the **OK** button to close the Edit Hyperlink dialog box.

▶ **5.** Point to the text in cell **A8**, and then confirm that the ScreenTip "Click to view sales analysis for 2013" appears just below the cell.

▶ **6.** Save and close the Totals 2013 workbook.

# Creating Templates

If you want to create a new workbook that has the same format as an existing workbook, you could save the existing workbook with a new name and replace the values with new data or blank cells. The potential drawback to this method is that you might forget to rename the original file and overwrite data you intended to keep. A better method is to create a template workbook that includes all the text (row and column labels), formatting, and formulas but does not contain any data. The template workbook is a model from which you create new workbooks. When you create a new workbook from a template, an unnamed copy of the template opens. You can then enter data as well as modify the existing content or structure as needed. Any changes or additions you make to the new workbook do not affect the template file; the next time you create a workbook based on the template, the original text, formatting, and formulas will be present.

The three state workbooks for 2013 have the same format. Alvin wants to use this workbook format for data collection and analysis for next year. You will create a template from one of the state workbooks.

**PROSKILLS**

### Teamwork: Using Excel Templates

A team working together will often need to create the same types of workbooks. Rather than each person or group designing a different workbook, each team member should create a workbook from the same template. The completed workbooks will then all have the same structure with identical formatting and formulas. Not only does this ensure consistency and accuracy, it also makes it easier to compile and summarize the results. Templates help teams work better together and avoid misunderstandings.

For example, a large organization may need to collect the same information from several regions. By creating and distributing a workbook template, each region knows what data to track and where to enter it. The template already includes the formulas, so the results are calculated consistently.

The following are just some of the advantages of building and using templates to create multiple workbooks with the same features:

- Templates save time and ensure consistency in the design and content of workbooks because all labels, formatting, and formulas are entered once.
- Templates ensure accuracy because formulas can be entered and verified once, and then be used with confidence in all workbooks.
- Templates standardize the appearance and content of workbooks.
- Templates prevent data from being overwritten when an existing workbook is inadvertently saved with new data rather than saved as a new workbook.

If you are part of a team that needs to create the same type of workbook repeatedly, it's a good idea to use a template to both save time and ensure consistency in the design and content of the workbooks.

## Creating a Workbook Based on an Existing Template

The blank Book1 workbook that opens when you start Excel is based on the **default template**. The default template contains no text or formulas, but it includes all the formatting available in every new workbook: General number format applied to numbers, Calibri 11-point font, labels aligned to the left side of a cell, values and the formula results aligned to the right side of a cell, column width set to 8.43 characters, three worksheets inserted in the workbook, and so forth.

Excel has many other templates available. Some are automatically installed on your hard drive when you install Excel. Other templates are available to download from the Office.com site. These templates provide commonly used worksheet formats, saving you from "reinventing the wheel." Some of the task-specific templates available from the Office.com site include:

- **Monthly Family Budget.** This template builds projections and actual expenditures for items such as housing, transportation, and insurance.
- **Inventory List.** This template tracks the cost and quantity reorder levels of inventory.
- **Team Roster.** This template organizes a list with each player's name, phone number, email address, and so forth.
- **Time sheets.** This template creates an online time card to track employees' work hours.

You will create a new workbook based on one of the Excel templates provided by Microsoft.

REFERENCE

### Creating a Workbook Based on a Template

- Click the File tab on the Ribbon, and then click the New tab in the navigation bar.
- In the center pane, click a template category for the type of workbook you want to create, and then click a template.
- In the right pane, check the preview, and then click the Download button.
- Save the workbook with a new filename.

You'll download the Employee Timecard template. Note that you need an Internet connection to complete the following set of steps. If you don't have an Internet connection, you should read but not complete the steps involving creating and using the online template.

**To create a workbook based on the Employee Timecard template:**

1. Click the **File** tab on the Ribbon, and then click the **New** tab in the navigation bar. The center pane shows the available templates on your computer and template categories on Office.com.

2. Click the **Time sheets** folder. All the available templates in this category appear in the center pane. There are several time sheet templates.

   **Trouble?** If you cannot find the Time sheets folder, you can search for the folder. In the search box to the ri ght of the Office.com Templates header, type **Employee timecard**, and then click the Start searching arrow.

3. Click the **Employee timecard (daily, weekly, monthly, and yearly)** template. A preview of a worksheet based on the selected template appears in the right pane. See Figure 6-22.

| Figure 6-22 | Preview of the Employee timecard template |

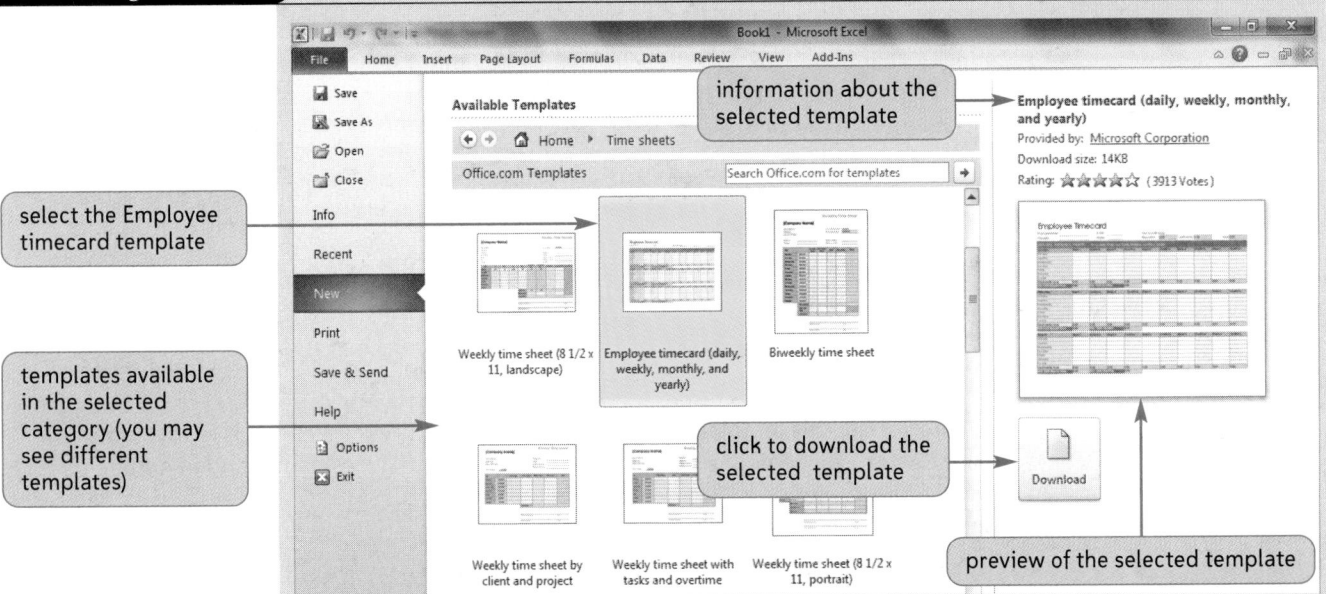

4. Click the **Download** button in the right pane. A new workbook based on the selected template opens. See Figure 6-23.

**Figure 6-23**  **Workbook created from the Employee timecard template**

A workbook based on a specific template always displays the name of the template followed by a sequential number. Just as a blank workbook that you open is named Book1, Book2, and so forth, the workbook based on the Employee timecard template is named "Employee timecard1" in the title bar, not "Employee timecard." Any changes or additions to data, formatting, or formulas that you make affect only this workbook and not the template (in this case, the Employee timecard template). If you want to save your changes, you must save the workbook with a new name, the same way you save any new workbook.

Look at the labels and formatting already included in the Employee timecard workbook. Some cells have descriptive labels, others are blank so you can enter data in them, and still other cells contain formulas where calculations for total hours worked each day and pay category will be automatically displayed as data is entered.

You'll enter data for Ed Hoot, the student assisting Alvin, in the worksheet based on the Employee timecard template.

### To enter data in the Employee timecard1 workbook:

1. In cell C3, enter **Ed Hoot**.

2. In cell D8, enter **8**. This is the total regular hours Ed worked on Monday. Totals appear in cells D15, D16, I4, and M4 because formulas are already entered into these cells. Cell D15 shows 8 hours worked that week, cell D16 shows the number of hours worked in January, cell I4 shows the number of regular hours worked that year, and cell M4 shows the number of total hours worked that year.

3. In cell D9, enter **8** as the regular hours Ed worked on Tuesday, and then, in cell E9, enter **2** as the overtime hours Ed worked on Tuesday. The totals are updated to 16 regular hours worked that week, 2 overtime hours worked that week, and 18 total hours worked that year.

▶  **4.** Save the workbook as **Hoot Time Card** in the Excel6\Tutorial folder included with your Data Files. The Hoot Time Card workbook, like any other workbook, is saved with the .xlsx file extension. It does not overwrite the template file.

▶  **5.** Close the workbook.

Each day Ed Hoot works at Global Travel, he or his supervisor can open the Hoot Time Card workbook and enter the hours Ed worked that day. The total hours are automatically updated. You can see how useful templates with formulas can produce a weekly time card that is fully formatted.

## Creating a Custom Workbook Template

A **custom template** is a workbook template you create that is ready to run with the formulas for all calculations included as well as all formatting. A template can use any Excel feature, including formulas, charts, data validation, cell protection, and macros. To create a custom template, you build the workbook with all the necessary labels, formatting, and data, and then you save the workbook as a template. The template includes everything but the variable data.

Before you create a template from an existing workbook, you should make sure that all the formulas work as intended, the numbers and text are entered correctly, and the worksheet is formatted appropriately. You should also remove any values and text that will change in each workbook created from the custom template. Be careful not to delete the formulas. When you are sure the workbook is complete and accurate, you save it as an Excel template file. You can store template files in any folder, but keep in mind that custom template files stored in the Templates folder are available on the New tab in Backstage view.

**REFERENCE**

### Creating a Custom Template

- Prepare the workbook: enter values, text, and formulas as needed; apply formatting; and replace data values with zeros or blank cells.
- Click the File tab on the Ribbon, and then click the Save As command in the navigation bar.
- In the File name box, enter the template name.
- Click the Save as type button, and then click Excel Template.
- Save the file in the Templates folder or select an alternative folder location.
- Click the Save button.

Alvin wants you to use the New Mexico workbook as the basis for creating a custom template. Then, Alvin can create new workbooks based on that template and distribute them to the accountants preparing the state workbooks. You'll reopen the workbook and clear the data values in the worksheets, leaving all of the formulas intact. After completing these modifications, you will save the workbook as a template.

### To replace the data values in the New Mexico workbook:

▶  **1.** Open the **New Mexico** workbook located in the Excel6\Tutorial folder included with your Data Files.

▶  **2.** Group the **Quarter 1** through **Quarter 4** worksheets. The worksheet group includes the four quarterly worksheets but not the Summary and Documentation worksheets.

> **3.** Select the range **B6:E12**. This range includes the specific ticket and sales data for each theme park. You want to delete these values.

> **4.** Right-click the selected range, and then click **Clear Contents** on the shortcut menu. The data values are cleared from the selected range in each of the quarterly worksheets, but the formulas and formatting remain intact. The cleared cells are blank. The range B13:E13 displays dashes, representing zeros, where there are formulas.

**TIP**

To delete the data values, you can also click the Clear button in the Editing group on the Home tab, and then click Clear Contents.

> **5.** Apply an orange fill color (the third color in the Standard Colors section of the Fill Color gallery) to the selected range. The range B6:E12 has an orange fill to indicate where users should enter data for the number of tickets sold and the sales amount in the quarterly worksheets.

> **6.** In cell A1, enter **=Summary!A1**. This formula inserts the contents of cell A1 in the Summary worksheet into cell A1 in the quarterly worksheets. The text "New Mexico" is still displayed because that text is currently in cell A1 in the Summary worksheet.

> **7.** Switch to the **Summary** worksheet. The quarterly worksheets are ungrouped, and dashes, representing zeros, appear in the cells in the range B6:E13, which contain formulas.

> **8.** In cell A1, enter **Enter state name here** and then, in cell A2, enter **Enter Fiscal Year – yyyy**. This text will remind users to enter the correct state name and year. See Figure 6-24.

**Figure 6-24**   **Worksheet with formatting and formulas but no data**

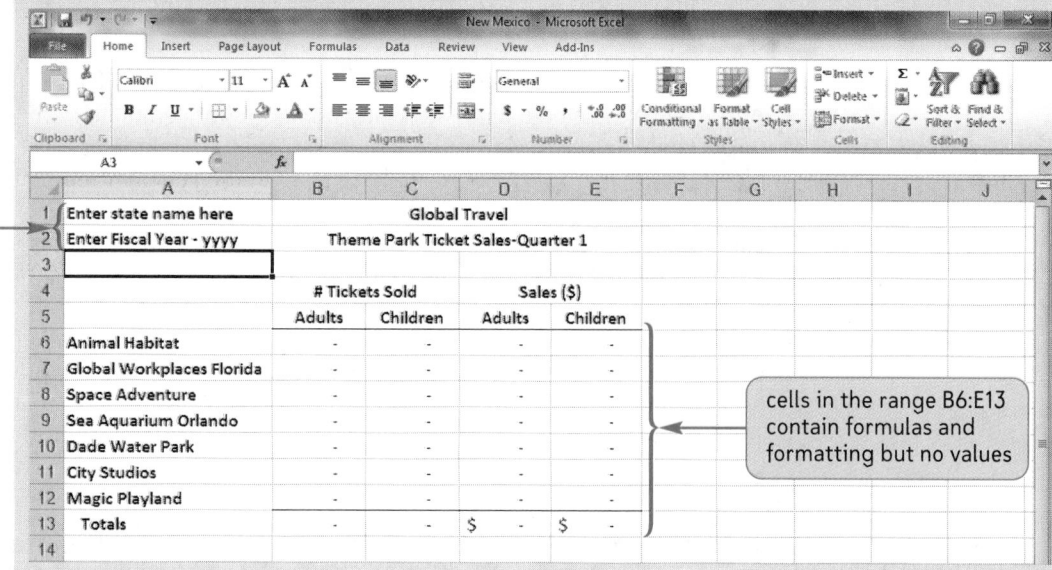

text reminds users to enter data in these cells

cells in the range B6:E13 contain formulas and formatting but no values

> **9.** Switch to the **Documentation** worksheet, delete your name and the date from the range B3:B4, enter **Theme park ticket sales** in cell B6, and then click cell **A1**. The Documentation sheet is updated to reflect the purpose of the workbook.

When you save the workbook as a template, the save location opens to the Templates folder, which is where custom template files are often stored. Excel, by default, looks for template files in this folder. However, you can store templates in other folders as well. Because you might not have access to the Templates folder, you will save the template file with the other Data Files. All template files have the .xltx file extension. This extension differentiates template files from workbook files, which have the .xlsx file extension.

After you have saved a workbook in a template format, you can make the template accessible to other users.

The New Mexico workbook no longer contains any specific data, but the formulas and formatting will still be in effect when new data is entered. It is ready to save in template format.

---

### To save the New Mexico workbook as a template:

▶ **1.** Click the **File** tab on the Ribbon to open Backstage view, and then click the **Save As** command in the navigation bar. The Save As dialog box opens.

▶ **2.** Type **Travel Template** in the File name box.

▶ **3.** Click the **Save as type** button, and then click **Excel Template**. The Address bar displays the Templates folder on your computer. You will change this location.

Make sure the save location and save as type are accurate so that you can locate and use the template file later in this session.

▶ **4.** Navigate to the **Excel6\Tutorial** folder included with your Data Files.

▶ **5.** Click the **Save** button. The Travel Template is saved in the same folder as your Data Files.

▶ **6.** Close the Travel Template workbook template.

---

Alvin will use the Travel Template file to create the workbooks to track next year's sales for each state and then distribute the workbooks via email to each accountant. By basing these new workbooks on the template file, Alvin has a standard workbook with identical formatting and formulas for each accountant to use. He also avoids the risk of accidentally changing the workbook containing the 2013 data when preparing for 2014.

## Creating a New Workbook from a Template

After you have saved a template, you can access the template from the New tab in Backstage view. If you saved the template file in the Templates folder, click the My templates button to open the New dialog box with the Personal Templates tab displayed to select the template you want to use. If you saved the template to another location, you can use the New from existing button to create a new workbook from the file, much like creating a workbook based on a template found in the Templates folder. The New from existing button opens a copy of the selected file, not the selected file. Also, the copy of the workbook that opens has a number at the end of the filename, and is considered an unnamed file, which prevents anyone from inadvertently overwriting the original file.

You will use the New from existing button to create a workbook from the Travel Template file because you saved the template in your Excel6\Tutorial folder.

---

### To create a new workbook based on the Travel Template file:

▶ **1.** Click the **File** tab on the Ribbon to open Backstage view, and then click the **New** tab in the navigation bar. The New tab appears in Backstage view.

▶ **2.** Click the **New from existing** button. The New from Existing Workbook dialog box opens, with All Excel Files displayed.

**TIP**

The active worksheet in the new workbook is the same worksheet that was active when you saved the template file.

3. Click **Travel Template** located in the Excel6\Tutorial folder included with your Data Files, and then click the **Create New** button. A copy of the Travel Template workbook opens named "Travel Template1" to indicate this is the first copy of the Travel Template workbook created during the current Excel session.

4. Click the **Summary** sheet tab, enter **New Mexico** in cell A1, and then enter **Fiscal Year - 2014** in cell A2.

5. Switch to the **Quarter 1** worksheet. The text "New Mexico" appears in cell A1, and the text "Fiscal Year - 2014" appears in cell A2.

6. Enter the following test data in the data area (range B6:E6, which has the orange background fill color), and then review the column totals in the range B13:E13 (the cells that contain formulas to sum each column):

   cell B6: **120**
   cell C6: **150**
   cell D6: **3000**
   cell E6: **2850**

7. Enter the following test data in the range B7:E7, and then notice that the formulas in the range B13:E13 are updated. See Figure 6-25.

   cell B7: **180**
   cell C7: **200**
   cell D7: **3500**
   cell E7: **3150**

**Figure 6-25**    **New workbook based on the Travel Template**

default workbook name is based on the template filename

formulas display the state name and year entered in the Summary worksheet

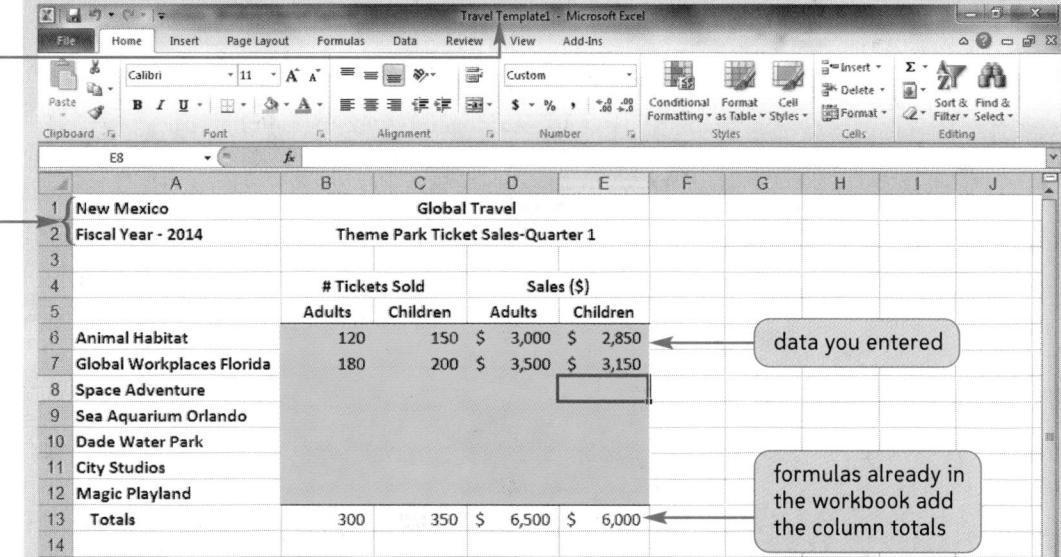

data you entered

formulas already in the workbook add the column totals

8. Switch to the **Summary** worksheet. Totals appear in the ranges B6:E7 and B13:E13 as a result of the formulas in this worksheet. See Figure 6-26.

**Figure 6-26**    **Summary worksheet after data is entered**

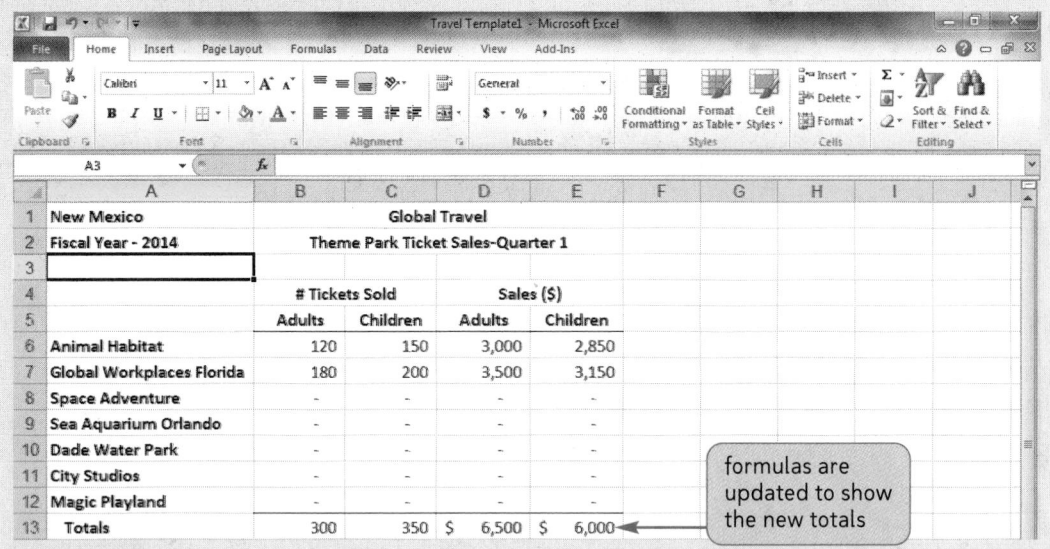

9. Save the workbook as **New Mexico 2014** in the Excel6\Tutorial folder included with your Data Files, and then close the workbook. The copy of the template is saved as a workbook with the .xlsx file extension. The original template file is not changed.

You'll add data to the Quarter 2, Quarter 3, and Quarter 4 worksheets to verify that the Summary worksheet is correctly adding numbers from the four worksheets.

**To test the New Mexico 2014 workbook:**

1. Open the **New Mexico 2014** workbook located in the Excel6\Tutorial folder included with your Data Files.

2. Group the **Quarter 2**, **Quarter 3**, and **Quarter 4** worksheets, enter **120** in cell B6, and then, enter **150** in cell C6.

3. Switch to the **Summary** worksheet. The total in cell B6 is 480 and the total in cell C6 is 600. The formulas in the Summary worksheet correctly add values from all the quarterly worksheets. The template workbook is functioning as intended.

4. Save and close the workbook.

# Using the Excel Web App and SkyDrive

**Office Web Apps** are Web-based versions of Microsoft Excel, Word, PowerPoint, and OneNote. These Web apps allow you to create, view, and edit Office files directly from a Web browser as well as share files and collaborate with other users online. Office Web Apps are a part of **Windows Live**, which is a collection of services and Web applications that you can use to be more productive. For example, you can use Windows Live to upload Office files to an online storage and file sharing service called SkyDrive. The service requires a Windows Live ID, allowing you to keep your files private, share them with individuals you specify, or make the files public. You can save your files directly from Microsoft Office 2010 onto SkyDrive from Backstage view.

Note: SkyDrive and Office Web Apps are dynamic Web pages, and might change over time, including the way they are organized and how commands are performed. The steps and figures in this tutorial were accurate at the time this book was published.

## Obtaining a Windows Live ID

To save files to SkyDrive or use the Office Web Apps, you need a Windows Live ID. You obtain a Windows Live ID by going to the Windows Live Web site and creating a new account. Once you have a Windows Live ID, you can access your SkyDrive and use it to store files, create new files, and share your files with others.

*Note:* If you already have a Windows Live ID, you can skip this set of steps.

### To obtain a Windows Live ID:

▶ 1. Start your Web browser, and then go to **www.windowslive.com**. The page where you can sign into Windows Live opens.

   **Trouble?** If the URL doesn't bring you to the page where you can sign into Windows Live, use a search engine to search for "Windows Live."

▶ 2. Click the **Sign up** button. The Create your Windows Live ID page opens.

▶ 3. Follow the instructions on the screen to create a Windows Live ID.

▶ 4. Sign out of Windows Live, exit your browser, and return to Excel.

## Saving a Workbook to SkyDrive

After you have a Windows Live ID, you can access your SkyDrive and the Office Web Apps. You can access your SkyDrive from the Windows Live page in your browser after you signed in with your Windows Live ID, or from Backstage view in Excel. You can save a file to a private or public folder on your SkyDrive.

**REFERENCE**

*Saving a Workbook to SkyDrive*

- Open the workbook you want to save to SkyDrive.
- Click the File tab, click Save & Send in the navigation pane, and then click the Save to Web command in the center pane.
- In the right pane, click the Sign In button, and then complete the sign-in process.
- Click the folder in which to save the workbook, and then click the Save As button.
- Enter a filename in the File name box, and then click the Save button.

You'll save the New Mexico 2014 workbook to the My Documents folder on your SkyDrive. This is a private folder that only you can access.

### To save the workbook from Excel to the My Documents folder on your SkyDrive:

▶ 1. In Excel, open the **New Mexico 2014** workbook located in the Excel6/Tutorial folder.

▶ 2. Click the **File** tab, and then click **Save & Send** in the navigation bar. The Save & Send options appear in Backstage view.

▶ 3. Under Save & Send, click the **Save to Web** button. A Sign in button appears that you use to sign in to your Windows Live account. See Figure 6-27.

| Figure 6-27 | Save to Web options on the Save & Send tab in Backstage view |
| --- | --- |

Save to Web command

Save & Send tab

button to open the dialog box to sign in to Windows Live ID

**Trouble?** If you're already signed into Windows Live, you'll see the folders in your SkyDrive account and the Save As button (see Figure 6-28). Continue with Step 8.

4. Click the **Sign In** button. The Connecting to docs.live.net dialog box opens.

5. In the E-mail address box, type the email address associated with your Windows Live ID, and then press the **Tab** key.

6. In the Password box, type the password associated with your Windows Live ID.

7. Click the **OK** button. The dialog box closes, and another dialog box appears while you connect to the Windows Live server. After you connect to Windows Live, the right pane in Backstage view lists the folders on your SkyDrive and a Save As button appears. See Figure 6-28.

| Figure 6-28 | Save & Send tab after connecting to Windows Live |
| --- | --- |

default folders available on SkyDrive (you might not have a shared folder)

8. In the right pane, click the **My Documents** folder, if necessary, and then click the Save As button. Backstage view closes, and the **Save As** dialog box opens.

9. Click the **Save** button. The workbook is saved in the My Documents folder on your SkyDrive. In Excel, close the workbook.

## Editing a Workbook with the Excel Web App

You can view and edit workbooks in the Excel Web App. The interface for the Excel Web App is similar to the interface of the full-featured program on your computer; however, only a limited number of commands are available.

You'll sign in to your Windows Live account and use the Excel Web App to update the New Mexico 2014 workbook on your SkyDrive.

### To edit the workbook using the Excel Web App:

1. Start your browser, and then go to **www.windowslive.com** and sign in to your SkyDrive using your Windows Live ID.

2. If your SkyDrive account is not open, click the **Office** link at the top of the Windows Live page, and then click **Your documents**.

3. Click **My Documents**, and then point to **New Mexico 2014**. See Figure 6-29.

| Figure 6-29 | New Mexico 2014 Information page on SkyDrive |
| --- | --- |

click to open the workbook in the Excel Web App in Edit mode

name of the open workbook

link to sign out of Windows Live

indicates the workbook is not a shared file

4. Click the **Edit in browser** link. The New Mexico 2014 workbook opens in the Excel Web App in Edit mode so you can make changes to the file.

   **Trouble?** If this is the first time you have opened a file in SkyDrive file, you might be asked to read and accept the user agreement in order to continue. Accept the user agreement, and then continue with Step 5.

5. Click the **Quarter 1** sheet tab, and then enter **200** in cell B8, **1500** in cell C8, **1500** in cell D8, and **4000** in cell E8. See Figure 6-30.

| Figure 6-30 | Edited New Mexico 2014 workbook in the Excel Web App |
| --- | --- |

commands available on the Home tab in the Excel Web App

click to sign out of Windows Live

click to close the Excel Web App

click to open the workbook in Excel on your computer

new data entered

totals updated to include the new data

▶ **6.** Switch to the **Summary** worksheet and verify that the data on the Summary worksheet was also updated.

**TIP**

To open the file in Excel on your computer, click the Open in Excel button in the Office group on the Home tab of the Excel Web App (refer to Figure 6-30).

The Excel Web App in Edit mode does not have all of the features of the program installed on your computer available. To use the other features, you need to open the workbook in the full-featured program on your computer. You can save a workbook from SkyDrive to your computer and then continue working in the full version of Excel. You'll save the updated version of the New Mexico 2014 workbook to your computer.

### To save the workbook from SkyDrive to your computer:

▶ **1.** Click the **File** tab on the Ribbon, and then click **Download a Copy** in the navigation bar. The File Download dialog box opens.

▶ **2.** Click the **Save** button. The Save As dialog box opens.

▶ **3.** Save the workbook as **SkyDrive New Mexico 2014** in the Excel6/Tutorial folder, closing the dialog box when the download is complete.

▶ **4.** Click the **File** tab on the Ribbon, and then **click** Close in the navigation bar. The New Mexico 2014 workbook closes. Files are automatically updated as you enter data in the workbook on your SkyDrive. As a result, you do not need to save your workbook in SkyDrive.

▶ **5.** In the upper-right corner of the Web page, click the **sign out** link. You are no longer connected to your Windows Live account.

▶ **6.** Close your Web browser.

With the ability to edit a workbook from any computer, Rhohit can be sure that his workbooks are always updated. The templates you created will ensure that all regions enter data consistently, making it simpler for Alvin to track ticket sales for Global Travel.

**REVIEW**

### Session 6.3 Quick Check

1. How do you insert a hyperlink into a worksheet cell?
2. True or False. A hyperlink in a worksheet cell can be used to jump to another worksheet in the same workbook.
3. What is a template?
4. What is one advantage of using a custom template rather than simply using the original workbook file to create a new workbook?
5. How do you save a file as a template?
6. You can use Windows Live to upload your Office files to an online storage and file sharing service called _____.
7. True or False. You need a Windows Live ID to save files to your SkyDrive and use the Office Web Apps.

*Practice the skills you learned in the tutorial using the same case scenario.*

**PRACTICE**

## Review Assignments

**Data Files needed for the Review Assignments: OR.xlsx, Idaho.xlsx, Washington.xlsx, NW Totals 2013.xlsx, and NW Travel.xltx**

Elaine Dennerson, accountant for Global Travel in Oregon, needs your help. Global Travel has added Oregon to its Northwest territory, which already includes Washington and Idaho. You will complete the Summary worksheet in the Oregon workbook, and then enter the formulas in the NW Totals 2013 workbook to summarize the regional totals in one workbook. Complete the following:

1. Open the **OR** workbook located in the Excel6\Review folder included with your Data Files, and then save the workbook as **Oregon** in the same folder.

2. In the Documentation sheet, enter your name and the date, and then review the worksheets in the workbook.

3. Create a worksheet group that contains the Qtr 1 through Qtr 4 worksheets.

4. In the worksheet group, insert formulas in the range B13:E13 to total each column.

5. Format the quarterly worksheets as specified below, and then ungroup the worksheets:

   a. Bold the range A1:B2;A6:A13; and B4:E5.

   b. Merge and center the ranges B1:E1, B2:E2, B4:C4, and D4:E4.

   c. Format the range A6:A12 in italic.

   d. Add a top and double bottom border to the range B13:E13.

   e. Add a fill color to the range B1:E2 using the Orange color in the Standard Colors section.

   f. Apply the Accounting number format with no decimal places to the range D6:E13.

6. Make a copy of the Qtr 1 worksheet, rename it as **Summary**, and place it after the Documentation worksheet.

7. In the Summary worksheet, remove the data from the range B6:E12, change the heading in cell B2 to **Theme Park Ticket Sales – Total** and then enter the label **Fiscal Year – 2013** in cell A2.

8. In worksheets Qtr 1 through Qtr 4, enter formulas to reference the labels in cells A1 and A2 of the Summary worksheet.

9. In the Summary worksheet, create 3-D reference formulas to calculate annual totals for theme park tickets sold and sales.

10. Prepare all worksheets except the Documentation sheet for printing. Display the name of the workbook and the name of the worksheet on separate lines in the right section of the header. Display your name and the date on separate lines in the right section of the footer. Preview the five worksheets.

11. Ungroup the worksheets and save the workbook.

12. Open the regional **NW Totals 2013** workbook located in the Excel6\Review folder included with your Data Files, and then save the workbook as **Northwest Totals 2013**. In the Documentation worksheet, enter your name and the date.

13. In the Summary worksheet, enter external reference formulas to create a set of linked workbooks to summarize the totals for Oregon, Washington, and Idaho in the Northwest Totals 2013 workbook.

14. In the Northwest Totals 2013 workbook, switch to the Documentation sheet. In the range A10:A12, enter the name of each state (**Idaho**, **Oregon**, and **Washington**). Create hyperlinks from each state label to its corresponding workbook. Add appropriate text for the ScreenTip to each hyperlink. Test each hyperlink.

15. Create a workspace with the following four workbooks in a tiled layout: Idaho, Oregon, Washington, and Northwest Totals 2013. Make the Summary worksheet in each workbook the active worksheet, and make the Northwest Totals 2013 workbook the active workbook. Save the workspace as **NW Workspace**.

16. Create a new workbook based on the **NW Travel** template located in the Excel6\Review folder included with your Data Files. Save the workbook as **Oregon 2014** in the same folder. In the Documentation worksheet, enter your name and the date.

17. In the Summary worksheet, enter **Oregon** in cell A1 and **Fiscal Year – 2014** in cell A2. In the Qtr 1 worksheet, enter **2000** in each cell of the range B6:C12. In the Qtr 2 worksheet, enter **3000** in each cell of the range B6:C12. Confirm that the values entered in this step were correctly totaled in the Summary worksheet. Save the Oregon 2014 workbook.

18. Save the Oregon 2014 workbook to the My Documents folder on your SkyDrive using the same name. In the Qtr 3 worksheet, enter **4000** in each cell in the range B6:C12. Download the file to your computer using the name **SkyDrive Oregon 2014**.

19. Close all the workbooks. Submit the finished files to your instructor, either in printed or electronic form, as requested.

---

*Use the skills you learned to summarize sales data.*

**APPLY**

## Case Problem 1

**Data File needed for this Case Problem: Cafe.xlsx**

*Java Café*   Java Café currently has three stores in the Southwest: Tucson, Arizona; Las Cruces, New Mexico; and Dallas, Texas. Jayne Mitchell manages the three stores and uses Excel to summarize sales data from these stores. She asks you to total the sales by product group and store for each quarter and then format each worksheet. Jayne also needs you to add another worksheet to calculate Summary sales for the stores and product groups. Complete the following:

1. Open the **Cafe** workbook located in the Excel6\Case1 folder included with your Data Files, and then save the workbook as **Java Cafe** in the same folder.

2. In the Documentation worksheet, enter your name and the date, and then switch to the Quarter 1 worksheet.

3. Group the four quarterly worksheets. For each quarter, calculate the product totals in the range B8:F8 and the store locations in the range F5:F7. Improve the look of the quarterly worksheets using the formatting of your choice. Ungroup the worksheets.

4. Place a copy of one of the quarterly worksheets between the Documentation and Quarter 1 worksheets, rename the new worksheet as **Summary Sales**, and then delete the values in the range B5:E7. The Summary Sales worksheet is identical in appearance to the quarterly worksheets.

5. In the Summary Sales worksheet, in the range B5:E7, insert the formulas that add the sales in the corresponding cells of the four quarterly worksheets. Use 3-D references to calculate the totals for each product group and store.

6. Set up the Summary Sales and four quarterly worksheets for printing. Each worksheet should be centered horizontally, fit on one page, display the name of the worksheet centered in the header, and display your name and the date on separate lines in the right section of the footer.

7. Save the Java Cafe workbook, and then remove the sales data, but not the formulas, from each of the quarterly worksheets.

8. Return to the Documentation worksheet, and then save the workbook as an Excel template with the name **Java Template** in the Excel6\Case1 folder included with your Data Files.

9. Use the Java Template file to create a new workbook. Save the workbook as **Java Cafe 2014** in the Excel6\Case1 folder. In the range B5:E7 of all four quarterly worksheets, enter **1**. Verify that the formulas in each worksheet summarize the data accurately.

10. Save the Java Cafe 2014 workbook to the My Documents folder on your SkyDrive using the same name. In the Quarter 1 worksheet, change coffee sales in Tucson to **$30,000**. Download the file to your computer using the name **SkyDrive Java Cafe 2014**.

11. Save and close the workbook. Submit the finished files to your instructor, either in printed or electronic form, as requested.

*Link workbooks to summarize sales data for a car dealership.*

**APPLY**

## Case Problem 2

**Data Files needed for this Case Problem: Carson.xlsx, Reno.xlsx, and Vegas.xlsx**

*UTE Auto Sales & Services*    Hardy Ute is founder and operator of UTE Auto Sales & Services, which has dealerships in Las Vegas, Reno, and Carson City, Nevada. His dealerships sell new and used cars, hybrids, SUVs, and trucks, as well as service customers' vehicles. To analyze sales and service at each of his three dealerships, Hardy wants his staff to prepare a report that shows the unit and dollar sales of new and used vehicles by type as well as service by vehicle type. Complete the following:

1. Open the **Carson** workbook located in the Excel6\Case2 folder included with your Data Files, and then save the workbook as **UTE Carson City** in the same folder.

2. In the Documentation worksheet, enter your name, the date, and an appropriate purpose statement, and then switch to the Quarter 1 worksheet.

3. Group the four quarterly worksheets. For each quarter, calculate the totals in the range B10:G10, and then improve the formatting of the quarterly worksheets by merging and centering cells B4:C4, cells D4:E4, and cells F4:G4, and then center aligning the range B5:G5. Ungroup the worksheets.

4. Insert a new worksheet between the Documentation and Quarter 1 worksheets, and then rename this worksheet as **Summary**. Format the worksheet identically to the quarterly worksheets except leave the range B6:G9 blank. (*Hint*: Copy one of the quarterly worksheets, and then modify it as needed.)

5. In the Summary worksheet, in the range B6:G9, insert formulas that add the sales in the corresponding cells of the four quarterly worksheets.

6. Prepare the Summary and four quarterly sales worksheets for printing. Center the worksheets horizontally, center the worksheet name in the header, and place your name and the current date on separate lines in the right section of the footer.

7. Save and close the workbook.

8. Open the **Reno** workbook located in the Excel6\Case2 folder included with your Data Files, and then save the workbook as **UTE Reno**. Repeat Steps 2 through 7 for this workbook.

9. Open the **Vegas** workbook located in the Excel6\Case2 folder, and then save the workbook as **UTE Vegas**. Repeat Steps 2 through 7 for this workbook.

10. Create a new workbook, and then use Figure 6-31 as a guide to create a summary of the three dealerships' workbooks. Save the workbook as **UTE Summary**.

| Figure 6-31 | UTE sales for all dealers |
| --- | --- |

| ▲ | A | B | C | D | E | F | G |
| --- | --- | --- | --- | --- | --- | --- | --- |
| 1 | | | UTE Auto Sales & Service | | | | |
| 2 | | | Sales - All Dealers | | | | |
| 3 | | | | | | | |
| 4 | | | New | | Pre-owned | | Service |
| 5 | | Units | Sales ($) | Units | Sales ($) | Units | Sales ($) |
| 6 | Cars | 733 | $ 14,940,828 | 203 | $ 1,476,397 | 5405 | $ 1,058,958 |
| 7 | Hybrids | 288 | $ 7,979,268 | 76 | $ 478,632 | 1798 | $ 492,525 |
| 8 | SUVs | 166 | $ 3,928,990 | 87 | $ 750,758 | 1007 | $ 328,662 |
| 9 | Trucks | 113 | $ 1,639,386 | 64 | $ 341,907 | 691 | $ 117,874 |
| 10 | Totals | 1300 | $ 28,488,472 | 430 | $ 3,047,694 | 8901 | $ 1,998,019 |

11. Use the UTE Carson City workbook to create an Excel template with the name **UTE Template** in the Excel6\Case2 folder included with your Data Files. Add appropriate formatting of your choice and remove the date in cell B4 from the Documentation worksheet.

12. Create a new workbook using the UTE Template. Add appropriate test data for Quarter 1. Save the workbook as **Carson City 2014** in the Excel6\Case2 folder included with your Data Files. In the Documentation sheet, enter the date in cell B4.

13. Save the Carson City 2014 workbook to the My Documents folder on your SkyDrive using the same name. In the Quarter 2 worksheet, enter **75** new cars at a value of **$825,000**. Download the file to your computer using the name **SkyDrive Carson City 2014**.

14. Close any open workbooks. Submit the finished files to your instructor, either in printed or electronic form, as requested.

*Create a worksheet to summarize sales data.*

**CREATE**

## Case Problem 3

**Data File needed for this Case Problem: Infusion.xlsx**

*Infusion Blend*   Micki Goldstein is a sales representative for Infusion Blend, a specialty soft drink producer. Micki is based in Tampa, and she travels around Florida to meet and make product presentations to managers of stores ranging from major supermarket chains to small corner markets. Although Micki does not personally make the deliveries, she often works closely with the delivery staff to assure quality service to her customers.

Micki must report her sales progress to her regional manager in Atlanta, Georgia. These reports include the overall sales volume, the types of products sold, locations, and stores where the products were delivered. For the larger markets, she must prepare a separate workbook for each chain store. Complete the following:

1. Open the **Infusion** workbook located in the Excel6\Case3 folder included with your Data Files, and then save the workbook as **Infusion 2013** in the same folder.

2. In the Documentation worksheet, enter your name and the date, and then switch to the January worksheet.

3. Group the 12 monthly worksheets. For each month (January through December), enter formulas to calculate the total sales for each product and store, and then improve the formatting of the monthly worksheets using the formatting of your choice. Ungroup the worksheets.

4. Insert a new worksheet between the Documentation and January worksheets that has the same content as the monthly worksheets except the range B6:G12 is blank, rename the worksheet as **YTD Summary**, and then format this worksheet identically to the monthly worksheets.

5. Use 3-D reference formulas to calculate the total number of cases sold for each product by store from January through December. For example, in cell B6, the formula results in 1335 cases of the Popgo product sold in the Elteron store.

6. Insert formulas that calculate total cases sold by product for all stores in column G, and total cases of all products sold by store in row 12. Calculate the Summary total for all products sold in all stores.

⊕ **EXPLORE**

7. Insert a new worksheet following the Documentation worksheet, and then rename this worksheet as **Annual Recap**. Using Figure 6-32 as a guide, create three summaries on this worksheet by product, store, and month, using the following formulas:

   a. Insert formulas that add the total cases sold of each product in the range C7:C12 (column G in the monthly worksheets). Calculate the total for all products.

   b. Insert formulas that add the total cases sold at each store in the range G7:G11 (row 12 in the monthly worksheets). Calculate the total for all stores.

   c. Insert formulas that add the total cases sold each month in the range K7:K18 (cell G12 in each monthly worksheet). Calculate the total for all months.

   d. Insert formulas in column D to calculate the percentage of cases sold for each product to the total cases sold for all products. Calculate the percentage of each product's total to the total cases sold for all products.

   e. Insert formulas in column H to calculate the percentage of cases sold by each store total to the total cases sold by all stores. Calculate the percentage of each store's total to the total for all stores.

   f. Insert formulas in column L to calculate the percentage of cases sold each month to the total cases sold for the year. Calculate the percentage of each month's total to the total for the year.

**Figure 6-32**     **Infusion Blend's sales by product, store, and month**

| | A | B | C | D | E | F | G | H | I | J | K | L |
|---|---|---|---|---|---|---|---|---|---|---|---|---|
| 1 | | | | | | Infusion Blend Sales by Product, Store and Month | | | | | | |
| 2 | | | | | | Cases Sold | | | | | | |
| 3 | | | | | | | | | | | | |
| 4 | | | | | | | | | | | | |
| 5 | | | Breakdown by Product | | | | Breakdown by Store | | | | Breakdown by Month | |
| 6 | | Products | Cases Sold | Percent | | Store | Cases Sold | Percent | | Month | Cases Sold | Percent |
| 7 | | Popgo | 7,065 | 30.7% | | Elteron | 4,700 | 20.5% | | January | 8,975 | 39.1% |
| 8 | | Diet Popgo | 4,760 | 20.7% | | Everett | 4,600 | 20.0% | | February | 7,120 | 31.0% |
| 9 | | Mt. Spring | 3,360 | 14.6% | | Franklin | 4,700 | 20.5% | | March | 3,905 | 17.0% |
| 10 | | Red Burst | 1,675 | 7.3% | | Grant | 4,625 | 20.1% | | April | 2,980 | 13.0% |
| 11 | | Dr Selsa | 3,135 | 13.6% | | Grover | 4,355 | 19.0% | | May | - | 0.0% |
| 12 | | L & L | 2,985 | 13.0% | | Totals | 22,980 | 100.0% | | June | - | 0.0% |
| 13 | | Totals | 22,980 | 100% | | | | | | July | - | 0.0% |
| 14 | | | | | | | | | | August | - | 0.0% |
| 15 | | | | | | | | | | September | - | 0.0% |
| 16 | | | | | | | | | | October | - | 0.0% |
| 17 | | | | | | | | | | November | - | 0.0% |
| 18 | | | | | | | | | | December | - | 0.0% |
| 19 | | | | | | | | | | Totals | 22,980 | 100.0% |

8. Save the Infusion 2013 workbook, and then use the Save As command to save a copy of the Infusion 2013 workbook with the name **Infusion with May 2013**.

9. In the Infusion with May 2013 workbook, insert the May results, shown in Figure 6-33, into the May worksheet.

**Figure 6-33** | **Infusion Blend's May sales**

| | A | B | C | D | E | F | G |
|---|---|---|---|---|---|---|---|
| 1 | Infusion Blend Sales by Store and Product | | | | | | |
| 2 | Cases Sold | | | | | | |
| 3 | | | | | | | |
| 4 | | | | Stores | | | |
| 5 | Products | Elteron | Everett | Franklin | Grant | Grover | Totals |
| 6 | Popgo | 515 | 545 | 560 | 670 | 510 | 2,800 |
| 7 | Diet Popgo | 435 | 445 | 435 | 430 | 410 | 2,155 |
| 8 | Mt. Spring | 235 | 275 | 240 | 240 | 205 | 1,195 |
| 9 | Red Burst | 125 | 125 | 150 | 150 | 325 | 875 |
| 10 | Dr Selsa | 160 | 145 | 150 | 160 | 125 | 740 |
| 11 | L & L | 325 | 240 | 175 | 245 | 225 | 1,210 |
| 12 | Totals | 1,795 | 1,775 | 1,710 | 1,895 | 1,800 | 8,975 |

10. In the Documentation worksheet, in the range A8:A19, type the months **January** through **December**. Create hyperlinks from each cell to its corresponding worksheet. Test the hyperlinks.

11. Save and close the workbook. Submit the finished workbooks to your instructor, either in printed or electronic form, as requested.

*Explore using worksheet groups, 3-D and external references, workspaces, and templates.*

**CHALLENGE**

## Case Problem 4

Data Files needed for this Case Problem: Europe.xlsx, North America.xlsx, South America.xlsx, and PlutoTemplate.xltx

***Pluto Pharmaceuticals*** Pluto Pharmaceuticals is a multinational manufacturer of healthcare products. The chief financial analyst, Kevin Cross, asks you to prepare the first quarter revenue summary based on workbooks from the regions of North America, South America, and Europe. Each workbook has monthly worksheets displaying forecasted and actual revenues of the major product groups for the first quarter. Kevin wants you to calculate the difference between forecasted and actual sales (Difference) and the percent change between forecasted and actual sales (% Change). He also wants you to summarize each workbook, reporting the quarterly forecasted and actual totals for revenues in a new worksheet. After you have added this information to each workbook, Kevin wants you to consolidate the information from the three regional workbooks, reporting in a single workbook the summarized information for each region. Complete the following:

1. Open the **Europe**, **North America**, and **South America** workbooks located in the Excel6\Case4 folder included with your Data Files. Save the Europe workbook as **PlutoEU**, save the North America workbook as **PlutoNA**, and save the South America workbook as **PlutoSA**. In the Documentation worksheet in each regional revenue workbook, enter your name and the date.

2. Each regional workbook contains a Documentation worksheet, a first quarter summary worksheet, and three monthly worksheets. Complete the monthly worksheets in each region's workbook by doing the following:

a. Calculate the difference for each product group: Actual–Forecast.

b. Calculate the % change for each product group: Difference/Forecast.

c. Calculate the total revenue for the Forecast, Actual, and Difference columns, and then calculate the total % change.

d. Format the numbers to improve the appearance of the worksheets.

3. In each workbook, complete the Quarter 1 worksheet by first summarizing the forecasted and actual totals for product groups for the first three months of the year, then calculating the difference and the % change, and, finally, summarizing the forecasted, actual, difference, and % change values for the quarter. (*Hint*: The Total Revenue % change in cell E10 is not the sum of the column; it is the percent change between the forecasted and actual totals.) Use Figure 6-34 as a guide as you complete the worksheet.

**Figure 6-34**    First quarter North America revenue

| | A | B | C | D | E |
|---|---|---|---|---|---|
| 1 | | Pluto Pharmaceuticals-North America | | | |
| 2 | | Revenue - Quarter 1 | | | |
| 3 | | | | | |
| 4 | Product Group | Forecast | Actual | Difference | % Change |
| 5 | Personal Care | $ 2,295,600 | $ 2,363,891 | $ 68,291 | 3.0% |
| 6 | Beauty | $ 340,500 | $ 363,536 | $ 23,036 | 6.8% |
| 7 | Animal Healthcare | $ 2,079,100 | $ 2,101,693 | $ 22,593 | 1.1% |
| 8 | Prescription Medicine | $ 522,300 | $ 526,672 | $ 4,372 | 0.8% |
| 9 | Photo | $ 1,006,200 | $ 976,096 | $ (30,104) | -3.0% |
| 10 | Total Revenue | $ 6,243,700 | $ 6,331,888 | $ 88,188 | 1.4% |

4. Format the Quarter 1 worksheet for each regional workbook with the same formatting used for the monthly worksheets, and then save the workbooks.

5. Create a new workbook, and save it as **PlutoSummary** in the Excel6\Case4 folder included with your Data Files. Rename the Sheet1 worksheet as **Documentation**, and in column A enter the same labels used in the Documentation worksheets in the other workbooks. In column B, enter **Corporate** as the region, your name as the author, the current date as the date created, and **To report on revenue for all regions** as the purpose. Format the Documentation worksheet to match the Documentation worksheet formatting in the PlutoNA, PlutoSA, and PlutoEU workbooks.

6. Switch to the Sheet2 worksheet, and then enter the text shown in Figure 6-35. Enter formulas to total the Forecasted and Actual revenue for each product group. Compute the difference and % change for each product group. Include the totals for the Forecast, Actual, and Difference columns, and calculate the % change for the total revenue for the quarter. Rename the worksheet as **Quarter 1**.

**Figure 6-35**    First quarter corporate revenue

| | A | B | C | D | E |
|---|---|---|---|---|---|
| 1 | | Pluto Pharmaceuticals-Corporate | | | |
| 2 | | Revenue - Quarter 1 | | | |
| 3 | | | | | |
| 4 | Product Group | Forecast | Actual | Difference | % Change |
| 5 | Personal Care | $ 5,670,800 | $ 5,913,673 | $ 242,873 | 4.3% |
| 6 | Beauty | $ 1,210,500 | $ 1,250,000 | $ 39,500 | 3.3% |
| 7 | Animal Healthcare | $ 4,632,300 | $ 4,662,070 | $ 29,770 | 0.6% |
| 8 | Prescription Medicine | $ 1,432,900 | $ 1,507,357 | $ 74,457 | 5.2% |
| 9 | Photo | $ 2,707,600 | $ 2,657,288 | $ (50,312) | -1.9% |
| 10 | Total Revenue | $ 15,654,100 | $ 15,990,388 | $ 336,288 | 2.1% |

⊕ EXPLORE

7. Insert a bar chart similar to Figure 6-36 that compares the actual and forecast sales by product group. Place the chart beneath the data you entered in the Quarter 1 worksheet. Change the axis so the sales (Displayed Units) are displayed in millions of dollars.

**Figure 6-36** **Chart of first quarter corporate revenue**

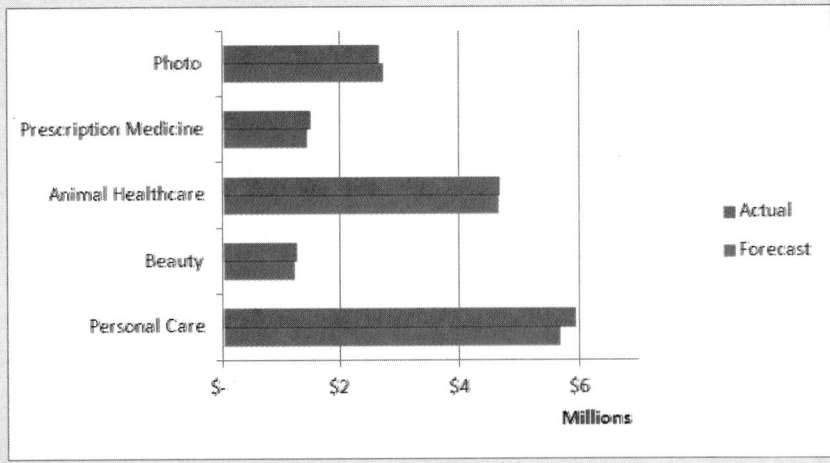

8. Prepare the three regional and corporate workbooks for printing. On each page, include the worksheet name in the center section of the header and your name in the left section of the footer.

9. Create a workspace that opens with the Quarter 1 worksheet active in each of the four workbooks using a horizontal layout for the four workbooks, and then save it as **Quarter1 Files** in the Excel6\Case4 folder included with your Data Files.

10. Save a copy of the **PlutoSummary** workbook located in the Excel6\Case4 folder as **Pluto Yearend** in the same folder. For year-end backup, break the links in the Pluto Yearend workbook.

**EXPLORE** 11. You receive a new source file to substitute for the original source file. The new source file has a different name.

  a. Open the **PlutoSummary** workbook, save the workbook as **PlutoSummaryTest** in the Excel6\Case4 folder, and then close the workbook.

  b. Open the **PlutoNA** workbook, and then save the workbook as **PlutoNorth**. In the PlutoNorth workbook in the March worksheet, change the actual personal care revenue in cell C5 to **$863,298**. Save and close the PlutoNorth workbook.

  c. Open the **PlutoSummaryTest** workbook, and change the link to the source workbook from PlutoNA to **PlutoNorth**. (*Hint*: Use the Edit Links dialog box.) Save and close the PlutoSummaryTest workbook.

**EXPLORE** 12. Update the source file but not the destination file.

  a. Open the **PlutoEU** workbook, and then save the workbook as **PlutoEurope**.

  b. Open the **PlutoSummaryTest** workbook, and change the link to the source workbook from PlutoEU to **PlutoEurope**. Note the actual total revenue in the Quarter 1 worksheet (cell C10). Close the PlutoSummaryTest workbook.

  c. In the PlutoEurope workbook, switch to the March worksheet and change the actual animal healthcare revenue in cell C7 to **$275,569**. Save and close the PlutoEurope workbook.

  d. Open the **PlutoSummaryTest** workbook and click the Don't Update button. How does this affect the Quarter 1 total actual revenue (cell C10) in the PlutoSummaryTest workbook (compare the current value to the value you noted in Step b)?

  e. Use the Edit Links dialog box to update the PlutoSummaryTest workbook. How does this affect the Quarter 1 total actual revenue (cell C10) in the PlutoSummaryTest workbook (compare the current value to the value you noted in Step d)?

**EXPLORE**

13. Modify the template named **PlutoTemplate** located in the Excel6\Case4 folder. Make the following two changes to the template, and then save the modified template as **PlutoTemplateRevised**:

   a. In the quarterly and monthly worksheets, change the formula in column E to display 0.0% when no values are entered in column B (Forecast) instead of #DIV/0!.

   b. In the monthly worksheets, apply a fill color of your choice to the range B5:C9 to identify where to enter data.

14. Create a new workbook from the PlutoTemplateRevised template. In the Documentation worksheet, enter your name and the date. In each monthly worksheet, enter **$500,000** in the range B5:B9 and enter **$550,000** in the range C5:C9. Save the workbook as **Pluto2014**.

15. Save and close all workbooks. Submit the finished workbooks to your instructor, either in printed or electronic form, as requested.

**SAM: Skills Assessment Manager**

For current SAM information, including versions and content details, visit SAM Central (http://samcentral.course.com). If you have a SAM user profile, you may have access to hands-on instruction, practice, and assessment of the skills covered in this tutorial. Since various versions of SAM are supported throughout the life of this text, check with your instructor for the correct instructions and URL/Web site for accessing assignments.

**ENDING DATA FILES**

**Tutorial**

Audited 2013.xlsx
Colorado.xlsx
Hoot Time Card.xlsx
New Mexico.xlsx
New Mexico 2014.xlsx
Sales 2013.docx
SkyDrive New Mexico
  2014.xlsx
Theme Parks.xlw
Totals 2013.xlsx
Travel Template.xltx
Utah.xlsx

**Review**

Idaho.xlsx
Northwest Totals 2013.xlsx
NW Workspace.xlw
Oregon.xlsx
Oregon 2014.xlsx
SkyDrive Oregon 2014.xlsx
Washington.xlsx

**Case1**

Java Cafe.xlsx
Java Cafe 2014.xlsx
Java Template.xltx
SkyDrive Java Cafe
  2014.xlsx

**Case2**

Carson City 2014.xlsx
SkyDrive Carson City
  2014.xlsx
UTE Carson City.xlsx
UTE Reno.xlsx
UTE Summary.xlsx
UTE Template.xltx
UTE Vegas.xlsx

**Case3**

Infusion 2013.xlsx
Infusion with May
  2013.xlsx

**Case4**

Pluto2014.xlsx
PlutoEU.xlsx
PlutoEurope.xlsx
PlutoNA.xlsx
PlutoNorth.xlsx
PlutoSA.xlsx
PlutoSummary.xlsx
PlutoSummaryTest.xlsx
PlutoTemplateRevised.xltx
PlutoYearend.xlsx
Quarter1 Files.xlw

TUTORIAL 7

EXCEL

## OBJECTIVES

**Session 7.1**
- Use the IF function
- Use the AND function
- Use the OR function
- Use structured references in formulas

**Session 7.2**
- Nest the IF function
- Use the VLOOKUP function
- Review the HLOOKUP function
- Use the IFERROR function

**Session 7.3**
- Use conditional formatting to highlight duplicate values
- Summarize data using the COUNTIF, SUMIF, and AVERAGEIF functions

# Using Advanced Functions and Conditional Formatting

*Calculating Employee Benefits*

## Case | *Talent Tracs*

Rita Corvales started Talent Tracs, a software development company for the music and entertainment business that is located in Austin, Texas. Talent Tracs sells EasyTracs, a software program that matches venues with artists, and then schedules the performances. As the company's reputation grew, the business expanded rapidly. Today, Talent Tracs has nearly 100 employees, ranging from software developers to online customer relations staff. Rita uses Excel to track basic employee information such as each employee's name, gender, birth date, hire date, health plan, job status, pay type (hourly or salaried), pay grade, and annual salary.

Rita needs to track employee enrollment in and costs related to the benefit programs offered by the company. She wants to calculate each employee's life insurance premium and how much the company contributes to each employee's 401(k) retirement account and health plan. Rita also needs to calculate the amount Talent Tracs spends on bonuses, which are based on employee pay grades and performance. To provide Rita with all this information, you'll use a variety of logical functions, filters, and conditional formatting. After you calculate those values, Rita wants you to summarize information in the Employee Summary worksheet so she can quickly see the impact of the compensation and benefits package on the company. You will use functions to calculate counts, sums, and averages based on search criteria.

## STARTING DATA FILES

Excel7 → Tutorial | Review | Case1 | Case2 | Case3 | Case4

Employees.xlsx  Tracs.xlsx  Modem.xlsx  Leave.xlsx  M-Fresh.xlsx  Rock Island.xlsx

# SESSION 7.1 VISUAL OVERVIEW

> When you create a formula that references all or parts of an Excel table, you can replace a specific cell or range address with a **structured reference**, which is the actual table name or column header.

Talent Tracs - Microsoft Excel

| File | Home | Insert | Page Layout | Formulas | Data | Review | View | Add-In |

Calibri  11  A A  | Accounting
B I U | | $ % ,

Clipboard | Font | Alignment | Number

**P2** | *fx* | =IF(OR([Location]="Home",[Job Status]="FT"),[An

| | D | E | F | G | H | I | J | K |
|---|---|---|---|---|---|---|---|---|
| 1 | Birth Date | Sex | Location | Job Status | Add Life Ins | Pay Grade | Pay Type | Annual Salary |
| 2 | 9/6/1966 | M | Austin | FT | Y | 3 | S | $ 85,00 |
| 3 | 2/15/1986 | F | Home | FT | N | 2 | S | $ 40,00 |
| 4 | 9/24/1968 | M | New Orleans | FT | Y | 2 | S | $ 37,24 |
| 5 | 8/9/1959 | F | Austin | FT | N | 3 | S | $ 80,00 |
| 6 | | | | | | | | $ 65,00 |
| 7 | | | | | | | | $125,00 |
| 8 | | | | | | | | $ 95,00 |
| 9 | | | | | | | | $ 36,00 |
| 10 | | | | | | | | $ 33,50 |
| 11 | | | | | | | | $ 21,84 |
| 12 | | | | | | | | $ 25,79 |
| 13 | | | | | | | | $ 32,01 |
| 14 | | | | | | | | $ 23,92 |
| 15 | | | | | | | | $ 32,01 |
| 16 | 1/4/1960 | F | Nashville | FT | Y | 1 | H | $ 21,84 |
| 17 | 1/16/1970 | F | Austin | FT | Y | 2 | S | $ 55,00 |
| 18 | 12/2/1985 | M | Nashville | FT | Y | 2 | S | $ 65,00 |
| 19 | 5/9/1959 | F | New Orleans | FT | Y | 3 | S | $125,00 |

> The **AND function** is a logical function that returns a TRUE value if all of the logical conditions are true, and a FALSE value if any or all of the logical conditions are false.

> The Function Arguments dialog box makes it simpler to build an IF function with a nested AND function (shown here) or a nested OR function for the logical test.

**Function Arguments**

IF

Logical_test | AND(G2="FT",M2>=1) | = TRUE
Value_if_true | K2*.03 | = 2550
Value_if_false | 0 | = 0

= 2550

Checks whether a condition is met, and returns one value if TRUE, and another value if FALSE.

**Value_if_false** is the value that is returned if Logical_test is FALSE. If omitted, FALSE is returned.

Formula result = 2550

Help on this function | OK | Cancel

| Documentation | Employee Data | Employee Summary | Lookup Tables |

Ready

# LOGICAL FUNCTIONS

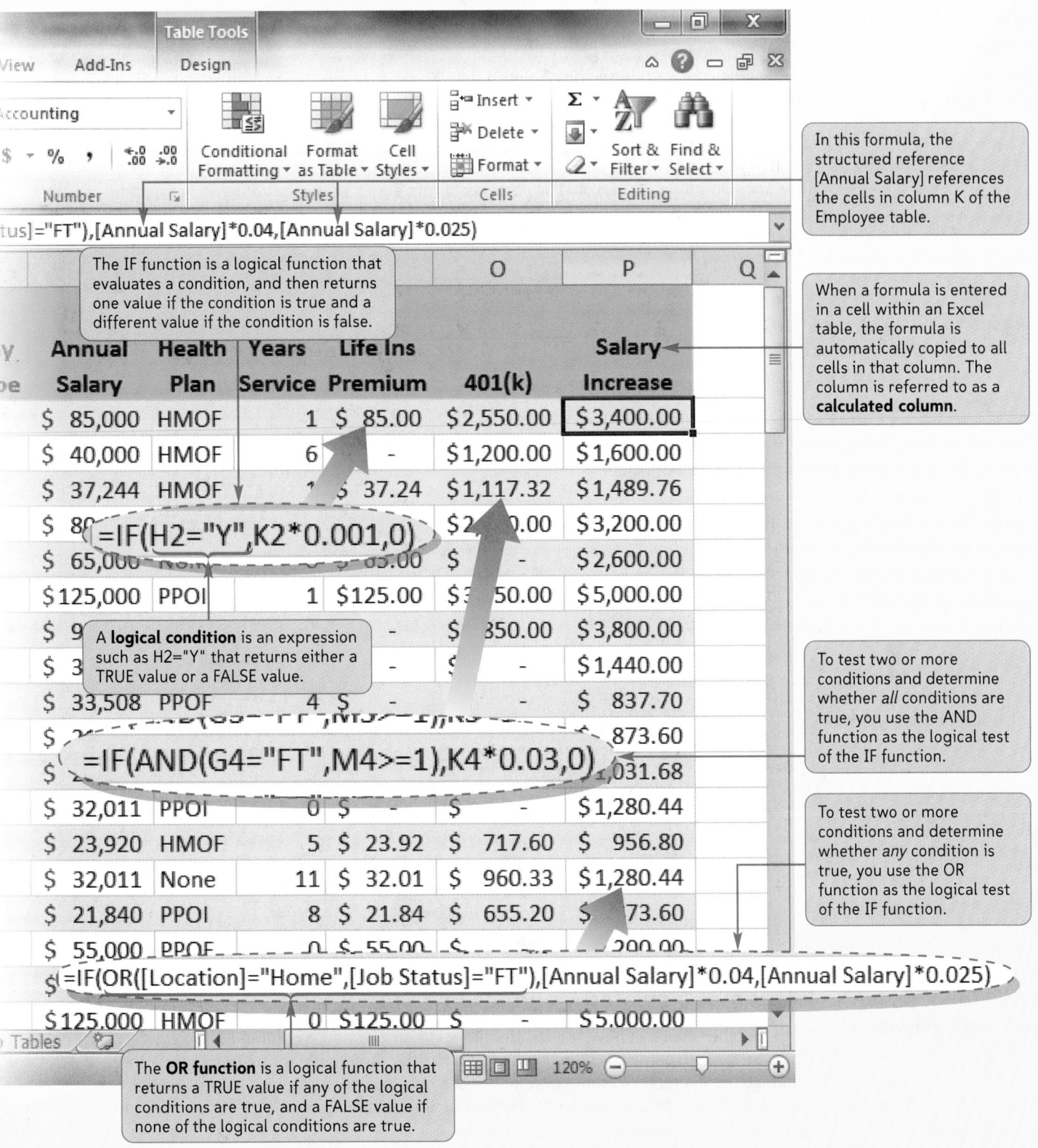

In this formula, the structured reference [Annual Salary] references the cells in column K of the Employee table.

The IF function is a logical function that evaluates a condition, and then returns one value if the condition is true and a different value if the condition is false.

When a formula is entered in a cell within an Excel table, the formula is automatically copied to all cells in that column. The column is referred to as a **calculated column**.

A **logical condition** is an expression such as H2="Y" that returns either a TRUE value or a FALSE value.

To test two or more conditions and determine whether *all* conditions are true, you use the AND function as the logical test of the IF function.

To test two or more conditions and determine whether *any* condition is true, you use the OR function as the logical test of the IF function.

The **OR function** is a logical function that returns a TRUE value if any of the logical conditions are true, and a FALSE value if none of the logical conditions are true.

=IF(H2="Y",K2*0.001,0)

=IF(AND(G4="FT",M4>=1),K4*0.03,0)

=IF(OR([Location]="Home",[Job Status]="FT"),[Annual Salary]*0.04,[Annual Salary]*0.025)

# Working with Logical Functions

Logical functions such as IF, AND, and OR determine whether a condition is true or false. The condition uses one of the comparison operators <, <=, =, <>, >, or >= to compare two values. You can combine two or more functions in one formula, creating more complex conditions.

Rita created a workbook that contains data for each Talent Tracs employee. She stored this information in an Excel table. The table includes each employee's ID, last name, hire date, birth date, gender, location, job status, additional life insurance coverage, pay grade, pay type, annual salary, health plan, and years of service at Talent Tracs. You will use IF, AND, and OR functions to calculate each Talent Tracs employee's additional life insurance premium (if any), 401(k) cost, health plan cost, proposed salary increase, and bonus amount. You will open Rita's workbook and review the employee data.

### To open the Talent Tracs workbook:

▶ 1. Open the **Employees** workbook located in the Excel7\Tutorial folder included with your Data Files, and then save the workbook as **Talent Tracs**.

▶ 2. In the Documentation worksheet, enter your name and the date.

▶ 3. Switch to the **Employee Data** worksheet. See Figure 7-1.

| Figure 7-1 | Employee Data worksheet |
|---|---|

| | A | B | C | D | E | F | G | H | I | J | K | L | M |
|---|---|---|---|---|---|---|---|---|---|---|---|---|---|
| 1 | Emp ID | Last Name | Hire Date | Birth Date | Sex | Location | Job Status | Add Life Ins | Pay Grade | Pay Type | Annual Salary | Health Plan | Years Service |
| 2 | 1024 | Hovey | 8/28/2011 | 9/6/1966 | M | Austin | FT | Y | 3 | S | $ 85,000 | HMOF | 1 |
| 3 | 1025 | Overton | 5/24/2007 | 2/15/1986 | F | Home | FT | N | 2 | S | $ 40,000 | HMOF | 6 |
| 4 | 1026 | Fetherston | 4/24/2012 | 9/24/1968 | M | New Orleans | FT | Y | 2 | S | $ 37,244 | HMOF | 1 |
| 5 | 1027 | Lebrun | 7/18/2011 | 8/9/1959 | F | Austin | FT | N | 3 | S | $ 80,000 | None | 1 |
| 6 | 1028 | Hanson | 8/21/2012 | 7/15/1950 | M | Austin | FT | Y | 3 | S | $ 65,000 | None | 0 |
| 7 | 1029 | Philo | 3/5/2012 | 5/2/1958 | M | New Orleans | FT | Y | 3 | S | $125,000 | PPOI | 1 |
| 8 | 1030 | Stolt | 3/1/2010 | 12/7/1977 | M | New Orleans | FT | N | 3 | S | $ 95,000 | HMOI | 3 |
| 9 | 1031 | Akhalaghi | 12/8/2012 | 12/4/1961 | M | Austin | FT | N | 2 | S | $ 36,000 | None | 0 |
| 10 | 1032 | Vankeuren | 8/11/2008 | 1/10/1959 | F | Austin | PT | N | 1 | H | $ 33,508 | PPOF | 4 |
| 11 | 1033 | Mccorkle | 6/12/2006 | 1/30/1942 | F | Nashville | FT | N | 1 | H | $ 21,840 | None | 7 |
| 12 | 1034 | Nightingale | 5/4/2009 | 8/27/1989 | M | Nashville | FT | N | 1 | H | $ 25,792 | PPOF | 4 |
| 13 | 1035 | Croasdale | 12/18/2012 | 1/6/1968 | F | Austin | FT | N | 1 | H | $ 32,011 | PPOI | 0 |
| 14 | 1036 | Lambrechts | 5/4/2008 | 4/28/1958 | F | Nashville | FT | Y | 1 | H | $ 23,920 | HMOF | 5 |
| 15 | 1037 | Palmer | 11/26/2001 | 10/4/1971 | F | Austin | FT | Y | 1 | H | $ 32,011 | None | 11 |
| 16 | 1038 | Tetreault | 2/22/2005 | 1/4/1960 | F | Nashville | FT | Y | 1 | H | $ 21,840 | PPOI | 8 |
| 17 | 1039 | Cugini | 12/4/2012 | 1/16/1970 | F | Austin | FT | Y | 2 | S | $ 55,000 | PPOF | 0 |
| 18 | 1040 | Dash | 10/12/2012 | 12/2/1985 | M | Nashville | FT | Y | 2 | S | $ 65,000 | HMOF | 0 |
| 19 | 1041 | Donnelly | 12/4/2012 | 5/9/1959 | F | New Orleans | FT | Y | 3 | S | $125,000 | HMOF | 0 |

## Inserting Calculated Columns in an Excel Table

An Excel table does not have a fixed structure. When you add a column to an Excel table, the table expands and the new column has the same table formatting as the other columns. If you enter a formula in one cell of a column, the formula is automatically copied to all cells in that column. These calculated columns are helpful as you add formulas to an Excel table.

If you need to modify the formula in a calculated column, you edit the formula in any cell in the column and the formulas in all the cells in that table column are also modified. If you want to edit only one cell in a calculated column, you need to enter a value or a formula that is different from all the others in that column. A green triangle appears in the upper-left corner of the cell with the custom formula in the calculated column, making the inconsistency easy to find. After a calculated column contains one inconsistent formula or value, any other edits you make to that column are no longer automatically copied to the rest of the cells in that column. Excel does not overwrite custom values.

**PROSKILLS**

### *Written Communication: Creating Excel Table Fields*

Excel tables should be easy to use as well as understand. This requires labeling and entering data in a way that effectively communicates a table's content or purpose. If a field is entered in a way that is difficult to use and understand, it becomes more difficult to find and present data in a meaningful way.

To effectively communicate a table's function, keep the following guidelines in mind when creating fields in an Excel table:

- **Create fields that require the least maintenance.** For example, hire date and birth date require no maintenance after entered, unlike age and years of service, whose values change each year. If you need to know the specific age or years of service, use calculations to determine them based on values in the Hire Date and Birth Date columns.
- **Store the smallest unit of data possible in a field.** For example, use three separate fields for City, State, and Zip code rather than one field. Using separate fields for each unit of data enables you to sort or filter each field. If you want to display data from two or more fields in one column, you can use a formula to reference the City, State, and Zip code columns. For example, you can use the & operator to combine the city, state, and zip code in one cell as follows: =C2&D2&E2.
- **Apply a text format to fields with numerical text data.** For example, formatting fields such as zip codes and Social Security numbers as text ensures that leading zeros are stored as part of the data. Otherwise, the zip code 02892 is stored as a number and displayed as 2892.

Using these guidelines means that you and others will spend less time interpreting data and more time analyzing results. This lets you more effectively communicate the data in an Excel table.

## Using the IF Function

In many situations, the value you store in a cell depends on certain conditions. Consider the following examples:

- An employee's gross pay depends on whether that employee worked overtime.
- An income tax rate depends on the taxpayer's adjusted taxable income.
- A shipping charge depends on the size of an order.

To evaluate these types of conditions, you use the IF function. Recall that the IF function is a logical function that evaluates a condition, and then returns one value if the condition is true and another value if the condition is false. The IF function has the syntax

```
IF(logical_test, [value_if_true,] [value_if_false])
```

where *logical_test* is a condition that is either true or false, *value_if_true* is the value returned by the function if the condition is true, and *value_if_false* is the value returned by the function if the condition is false. The IF function results in only one value—either the *value_if_true* or the *value_if_false*.

For example, the following IF function tests whether the value in cell A5 is equal to "Yes." If it is, the *value_if_true* argument, C5+B5, is calculated and its value is displayed in the cell. Otherwise, the *value_if_false* argument, B5–C5, is calculated and its value is displayed in the cell.

```
=IF(A5="Yes",C5+B5,B5-C5)
```

You will use the IF function to calculate the additional life insurance premiums in the Employee table. Talent Tracs employees can elect to purchase additional life insurance coverage. This is indicated in the Add Life Ins column with Y for yes and N for no. The premium amount is equal to the employee's annual salary multiplied by the premium rate (.001). Rita sketched the flowchart shown in Figure 7-2 to illustrate the logic for calculating an employee's additional life insurance premium. The flowchart shows that if the employee elected additional life insurance (Add Life Ins = "Y" is True), the premium is calculated using the formula Salary*.001. If the employee did not elect additional life insurance (Add Life Ins = "Y" is False), the premium is 0.

**Figure 7-2**   **Flowchart with logic for the additional life insurance premium**

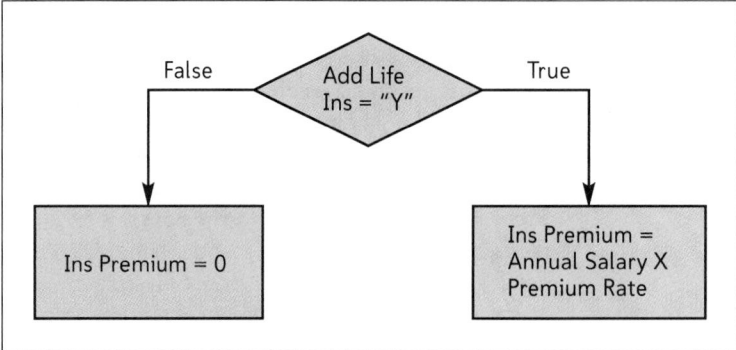

You'll add a column to the Employee table to display the results of the IF function that calculates the premium employees will pay if they elect additional life insurance coverage.

### To calculate the life insurance premium using an IF function:

1. In cell N1, enter **Life Ins Premium**. The Excel table expands to include this column and applies the table formatting to all the rows in the new column.

2. Make sure cell **N2** is the active cell, and then click the **Insert Function** button $f_x$ in the formula bar. The Insert Function dialog box opens.

3. Click **Logical** in the Or select a category list, click **IF** in the Select a function box, and then click the **OK** button. The Function Arguments dialog box for the IF function opens.

4. In the Logical_test box, type **H2="Y"** and then press the **Tab** key. This sets the logical test to evaluate whether the employee wants additional life insurance, indicated by "Y" for Yes or "N" for No in cell H2. TRUE appears to the right of the Logical_test argument box, indicating the result for the employee in row 2 is true. That is, the employee wants additional life insurance.

5. In the Value_if_true box, type **K2*0.001**. This argument specifies that if the condition is true (the employee wants additional life insurance), the result of the employee's current salary (listed in cell K2) is multiplied by 0.1% and displayed in cell N2. The value to the right of the Value_if_true argument box is 85, which is the premium the employee will pay for additional life insurance if the condition is true.

6. In the Value_if_false box, type **0**. This argument specifies that if the condition is false (the employee does not want additional life insurance), 0 is displayed in cell N2. The value to the right of the Value_if_false argument box is 0, which is the value that will appear in cell N2 if the condition is false. See Figure 7-3.

**Figure 7-3**    **Function Arguments dialog box for the IF Function**

function arguments applied to the employee in the current row of the table

> **Function Arguments**
>
> IF
>
> Logical_test    H2="Y"        = TRUE
> Value_if_true    K2*0.001        = 85
> Value_if_false    0        = 0
>
>                      = 85
>
> Checks whether a condition is met, and returns one value if TRUE, and another value if FALSE.
>
> **Value_if_false**  is the value that is returned if Logical_test is FALSE. If omitted, FALSE is returned.
>
> Formula result = 85
>
> Help on this function        OK    Cancel

**7.** Click the **OK** button. The formula =IF(H2="Y",K2*0.001,0) appears in the formula bar, and 85 appears in cell N2 because the condition is true. The formula is automatically copied to all the cells in column N of the table.

**TIP**

Click just above a cell in the header row of an Excel table (not the worksheet column heading) to select the column data but not the header; double-click to select the entire column including the column header.

**8.** Position the pointer just above cell **N1** until the pointer changes to ⬇, and then click to select the range N2:N101. The data in the Life Ins Premium column is selected, but not the column header.

**9.** Format the selected range N2:N101 with the **Accounting** number format, which includes the dollar sign and two decimal places. The Life Ins Premium column shows the additional life insurance premiums employees will pay formatted as currency.

**10.** Click cell **N2** to deselect the column. See Figure 7-4.

**Figure 7-4**    **Life Ins Premium column added to the Employee table**

formula to calculate the life insurance premium

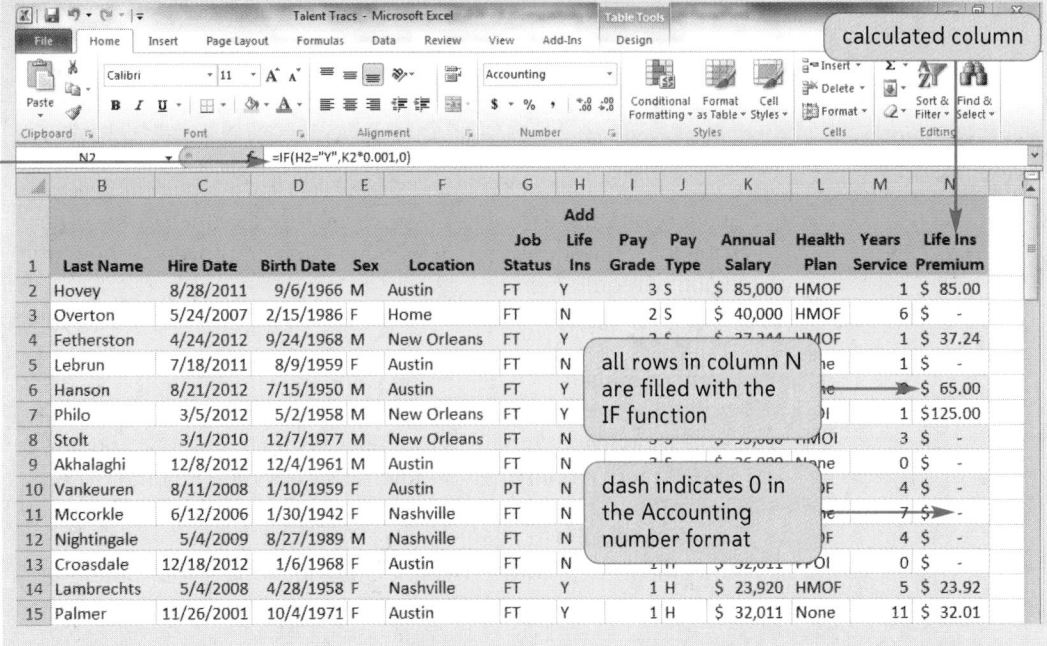

calculated column

N2    =IF(H2="Y",K2*0.001,0)

| | Last Name | Hire Date | Birth Date | Sex | Location | Job Status | Add Life Ins | Pay Grade | Pay Type | Annual Salary | Health Plan | Years Service | Life Ins Premium |
|---|---|---|---|---|---|---|---|---|---|---|---|---|---|
| 2 | Hovey | 8/28/2011 | 9/6/1966 | M | Austin | FT | Y | 3 | S | $ 85,000 | HMOF | 1 | $ 85.00 |
| 3 | Overton | 5/24/2007 | 2/15/1986 | F | Home | FT | N | 2 | S | $ 40,000 | HMOF | 6 | $  - |
| 4 | Fetherston | 4/24/2012 | 9/24/1968 | M | New Orleans | FT | Y | | | | HMOF | 1 | $ 37.24 |
| 5 | Lebrun | 7/18/2011 | 8/9/1959 | F | Austin | FT | N | | | | | 1 | $  - |
| 6 | Hanson | 8/21/2012 | 7/15/1950 | M | Austin | FT | Y | | | | | | $ 65.00 |
| 7 | Philo | 3/5/2012 | 5/2/1958 | M | New Orleans | FT | Y | | | | | 1 | $125.00 |
| 8 | Stolt | 3/1/2010 | 12/7/1977 | M | New Orleans | FT | N | | | | | 3 | $  - |
| 9 | Akhalaghi | 12/8/2012 | 12/4/1961 | M | Austin | FT | N | | | | None | 0 | $  - |
| 10 | Vankeuren | 8/11/2008 | 1/10/1959 | F | Austin | PT | N | | | | | 4 | $  - |
| 11 | Mccorkle | 6/12/2006 | 1/30/1942 | F | Nashville | FT | N | | | | | 7 | $  - |
| 12 | Nightingale | 5/4/2009 | 8/27/1989 | M | Nashville | FT | N | | | | | 4 | $  - |
| 13 | Croasdale | 12/18/2012 | 1/6/1968 | F | Austin | FT | N | | | | | 0 | $  - |
| 14 | Lambrechts | 5/4/2008 | 4/28/1958 | F | Nashville | FT | Y | | 1 | H | $ 23,920 | HMOF | 5 | $ 23.92 |
| 15 | Palmer | 11/26/2001 | 10/4/1971 | F | Austin | FT | Y | | 1 | H | $ 32,011 | None | 11 | $ 32.01 |

all rows in column N are filled with the IF function

dash indicates 0 in the Accounting number format

## Using the AND Function

The IF function evaluates a single condition. However, you often need to test two or more conditions and determine whether *all* conditions are true. You can do this with the AND function. The AND function is a logical function that returns the value TRUE if all the logical conditions are true and the value FALSE if any or all of the logical conditions are false. The syntax of the AND function is

```
AND(logical1 [,logical2,]...)
```

where *logical1* and *logical2* are conditions that can be either true or false. If all of the logical conditions are true, the AND function returns the logical value TRUE; otherwise, the function returns the logical value FALSE. You can include up to 255 logical conditions in an AND function. However, keep in mind that *all* the logical conditions listed in the AND function must be true for the AND function to return a TRUE value.

Talent Tracs employees are eligible for the 401(k) benefit if they are full-time employees (FT in Job Status) *and* have worked for the company for one or more years (1 or greater in Years Service). As long as *both* conditions are true, the company contributes an amount equal to 3 percent of the employee's salary to the employee's 401(k). If neither condition is true or if only one condition is true, the employee is not eligible for the 401(k) benefit and the company's contribution is 0. Rita outlined these eligibility conditions in the flowchart shown in Figure 7-5.

---

**Figure 7-5**     **Flowchart illustrating AND logic for the 401(k) benefit**

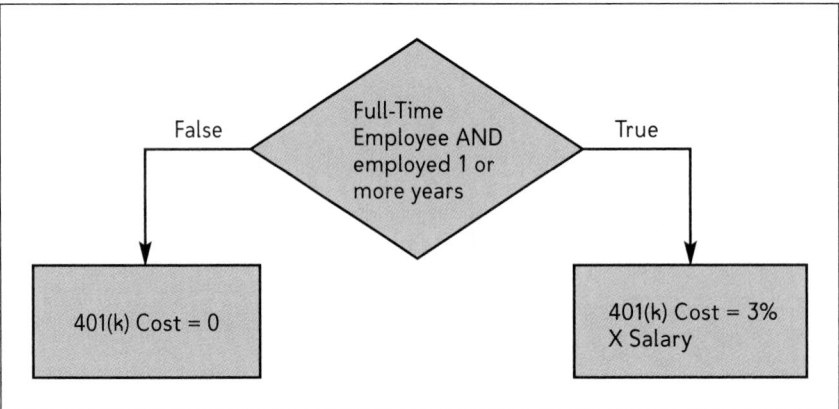

To calculate the cost of the 401(k) plan for each employee, you need to use the AND function with the IF function. You use the AND function shown in the following formula as the logical test to evaluate whether each employee in the Employee table fulfills the eligibility requirements:

```
=AND(G2="FT",M2>=1)
```

This formula tests whether the value in cell G2 (the job status for the first employee) is equal to FT (an abbreviation for full time) and whether the value in cell M2 (the years of service for the first employee) is greater than or equal to one (indicating one or more years of employment at Talent Tracs). When an employee is a full-time employee (G2="FT") *and* has worked one or more years at Talent Tracs (M2>=1), the AND function returns the value TRUE; otherwise, the AND function returns the value FALSE. Figure 7-6 shows the result returned by the AND function for four different sets of employee values for job status and years of service.

| Figure 7-6 | **Example of AND function results** |

**Purpose:**    To determine employee eligibility for the company's 401(k) plan

**Logic Scenario:** An employee is eligible for the 401(k) plan if the employee's status is full time (FT) AND the employee's years of service total one or more years.

**Formula:**    AND function with two conditions
=AND(G2="FT",M2>=1)

**Data:**    cell G2 stores Employee Status
cell M2 stores Years Service

**Example:**

| Data | | Condition1 | Condition2 | Results |
|------|------|------------|------------|---------|
| **Cell G2** | **Cell M2** | **G2="FT"** | **M2>=1** | **(Eligible?)** |
| FT | 1 | True | True | True |
| FT | 0 | True | False | False |
| PT | 5 | False | True | False |
| PT | 0 | False | False | False |

The AND function shows only whether an employee is eligible for the 401(k) plan. It does not calculate how much Talent Tracs will contribute to that employee's 401(k) plan if the employee is eligible. To determine whether an employee is eligible *and* to calculate the amount of the 401(k) contribution, you use this AND function within an IF function. When the results of one function are used as the argument of another function, the functions are nested. In the following formula, the AND function (shown in red) is nested within the IF function and is used as the logical test that determines whether the employee is eligible for a 401(k) contribution. If the employee is eligible, the AND function returns the logical value TRUE and the IF function multiplies the employee's annual salary by 3 percent. If the AND function returns the logical value FALSE, the IF function displays the value 0.

=IF(AND(G2="FT",M2>=1),K2*0.03,0)

Figure 7-7 illustrates how the AND function is used to determine student eligibility for the dean's list. In this scenario, when students have 12 or more credits (stored in cell B1) *and* their GPA is greater than 3.25 (stored in cell B2), they are placed on the dean's list. Both conditions must be true for the AND function to return the logical value TRUE.

**Figure 7-7**    Additional AND function example

**Purpose:**    To determine dean's list requirements

**Logic Scenario:** 12 or more semester credits and GPA above 3.25

**Formula:**    AND function with two conditions
=AND(B1>=12,B2>3.25)

**Data:**    cell B1 stores number of credits
cell B2 stores student's GPA

**Example:**

| Data | | Condition1 | Condition2 | Results |
|---|---|---|---|---|
| Cell B1 | Cell B2 | B1>=12 | B2>3.25 | (Dean's List?) |
| 15 | 3.5 | True | True | True |
| 12 | 3.25 | True | False | False |
| 6 | 3.4 | False | True | False |
| 10 | 3.0 | False | False | False |

You'll insert a new column in the Employee table, and then enter the formula to calculate the 401(k) contribution.

**To use the IF and AND functions to calculate the 401(k) contribution:**

1. In cell O1, enter **401(k)** as the column header. The Excel table expands to include the new column, and cell O2 is the active cell.

2. Make sure cell O2 is the active cell, and then click the **Insert Function** button $f_x$ in the formula bar. The Insert Function dialog box opens.

3. Click **IF** in the Select a function box, and then click the **OK** button. The Function Arguments dialog box opens.

4. In the Logical_test box, type **AND(G2="FT",M2>=1)** and then press the **Tab** key. This logical test evaluates whether the employee is full time, indicated by "FT" in cell G2, and has worked at Talent Tracs for one year or more. TRUE appears to the right of the Logical_test box, indicating the result for the employee in row 2 is true. This employee is eligible for the 401(k) plan.

5. In the Value_if_true box, type **K2*0.03** and then press the **Tab** key. This argument specifies that if the condition is true (the employee is eligible for the 401(k) plan as determined by the AND function), the amount in the employee's salary cell is multiplied by 3 percent. The amount of this employee's 401(k) contribution, 2550, appears to the right of the Value_if_true box.

6. In the Value_if_false box, type **0**. This argument specifies that if the condition is false (the employee is not eligible for the 401(k) as determined by the AND function), the amount displayed in cell O2 is 0, which appears to the right of the Value_if_false box. See Figure 7-8.

**Figure 7-8**  ▶  **Function Arguments dialog box for the IF function with the AND function**

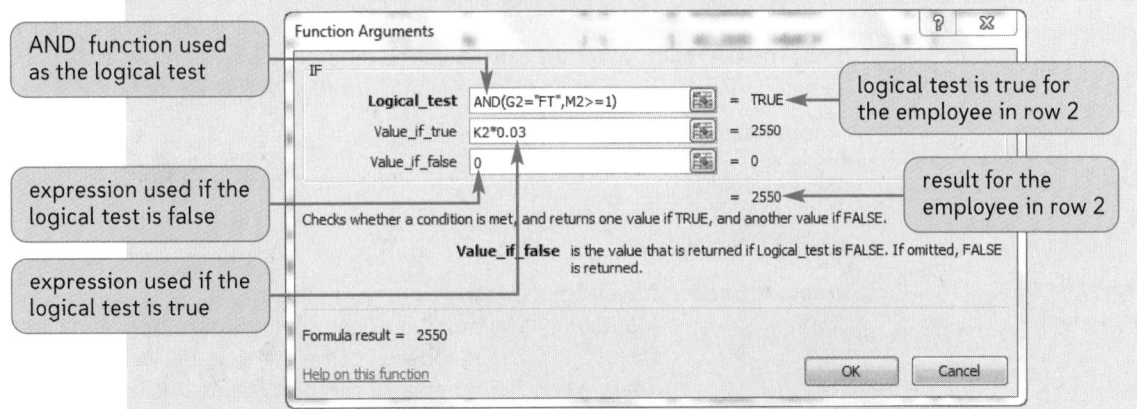

AND function used as the logical test

expression used if the logical test is false

expression used if the logical test is true

logical test is true for the employee in row 2

result for the employee in row 2

7. Click the **OK** button. The formula with the IF function that you just created is entered in cell O2 and copied to all rows in column O of the table.

8. Position the pointer at the top of cell **O1** until the pointer changes to ↓, click to select the 401(k) data values, and then format the range using the **Accounting** number format.

9. Click cell **O2** to make it the active cell. The formula =IF(AND(G2="FT",M2>=1),K2*0.03,0) appears in the formula bar and $2,550.00 appears in cell O2 because the condition is true. See Figure 7-9.

**Figure 7-9**  ▶  **IF function with the AND function to calculate 401(k)**

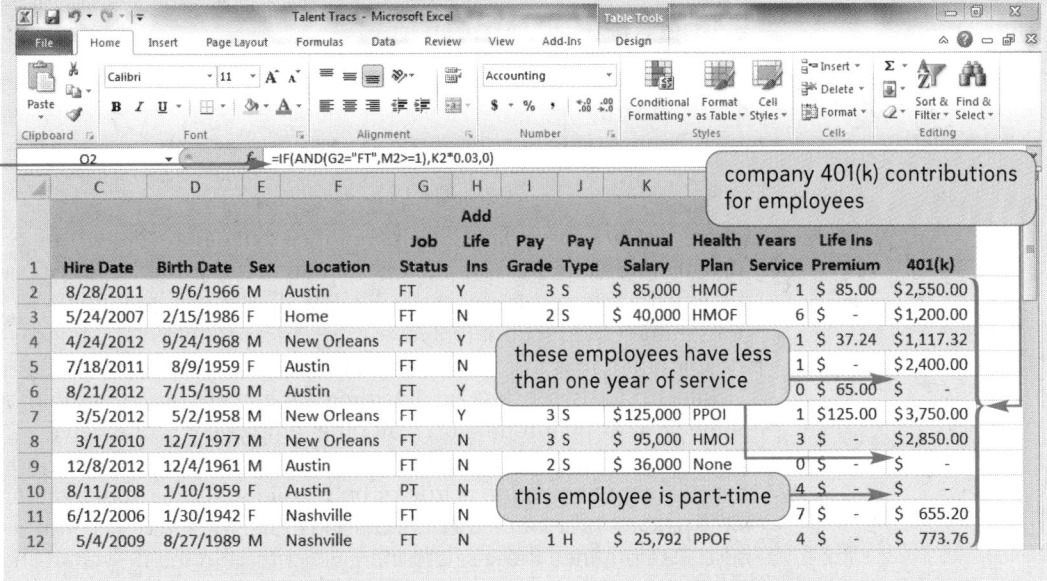

formula in cell O2 uses the IF and AND functions

company 401(k) contributions for employees

O2  =IF(AND(G2="FT",M2>=1),K2*0.03,0)

| | Hire Date | Birth Date | Sex | Location | Job Status | Life Ins | Pay Grade | Pay Type | Annual Salary | Health Plan | Years Service | Life Ins Premium | 401(k) |
|---|---|---|---|---|---|---|---|---|---|---|---|---|---|
| 1 | **Hire Date** | **Birth Date** | **Sex** | **Location** | **Status** | **Ins** | **Grade** | **Type** | **Salary** | **Plan** | **Service** | **Premium** | **401(k)** |
| 2 | 8/28/2011 | 9/6/1966 | M | Austin | FT | Y | 3 | S | $ 85,000 | HMOF | 1 | $ 85.00 | $2,550.00 |
| 3 | 5/24/2007 | 2/15/1986 | F | Home | FT | N | 2 | S | $ 40,000 | HMOF | 6 | $ - | $1,200.00 |
| 4 | 4/24/2012 | 9/24/1968 | M | New Orleans | FT | Y | | | 1 | $ 37.24 | $1,117.32 | | |
| 5 | 7/18/2011 | 8/9/1959 | F | Austin | FT | N | | | 1 | $ - | $2,400.00 | | |
| 6 | 8/21/2012 | 7/15/1950 | M | Austin | FT | Y | | | 0 | $ 65.00 | $ - | | |
| 7 | 3/5/2012 | 5/2/1958 | M | New Orleans | FT | Y | 3 | S | $125,000 | PPOI | 1 | $125.00 | $3,750.00 |
| 8 | 3/1/2010 | 12/7/1977 | M | New Orleans | FT | N | 3 | S | $ 95,000 | HMOI | 3 | $ - | $2,850.00 |
| 9 | 12/8/2012 | 12/4/1961 | M | Austin | FT | N | 2 | S | $ 36,000 | None | 0 | $ - | $ - |
| 10 | 8/11/2008 | 1/10/1959 | F | Austin | PT | N | | | 4 | $ - | $ - | | |
| 11 | 6/12/2006 | 1/30/1942 | F | Nashville | FT | N | | | 7 | $ - | $ 655.20 | | |
| 12 | 5/4/2009 | 8/27/1989 | M | Nashville | FT | N | 1 | H | $ 25,792 | PPOF | 4 | $ - | $ 773.76 |

these employees have less than one year of service

this employee is part-time

### Using the DATEDIF Function to Calculate Years of Service

In the Employee table, the Years Service column was calculated using the DATEDIF function. The **DATEDIF function** calculates the difference between two dates and shows the result in months, days, or years. The syntax for the DATEDIF function is

```
DATEDIF(Date1,Date2,Interval)
```

where *Date1* is the earliest date, *Date2* is the latest date, and *Interval* is the unit of time the DATEDIF function will use in the result. You specify the *Interval* with one of the following interval codes:

| Interval Code | Meaning | Description |
|---|---|---|
| "m" | Months | The number of complete months between Date1 and Date2 |
| "d" | Days | The number of complete days between Date1 and Date2 |
| "y" | Years | The number of complete years between Date1 and Date2 |

For example, the following formula calculates years of service at Talent Tracs in complete years:

```
=DATEDIF(C2,$AB$1,"y")
```

The earliest date is located in cell C2, the hire date. The latest date is in cell $AB$1, which shows the date used to compare against the hire date—years of service as of a cut-off date. The Interval "y" indicates that you want to display the number of complete years between these two dates.

The DATEDIF function is undocumented in Excel, but it has been available since Excel 97. To learn more about this function, search the Web using "DATEDIF function in Excel" as the search text in your favorite search engine.

## Using the OR Function

The OR function is a logical function that returns a TRUE value if any of the logical conditions are true and a FALSE value if all of the logical conditions are false. The syntax of the OR function is

```
OR(logical1 [,logical2,]...)
```

where *logical1* and *logical2* are conditions that can be either true or false. If any of the logical conditions are true, the OR function returns the logical value TRUE; otherwise, the function returns the logical value FALSE. You can include up to 255 logical conditions in the OR function. However, keep in mind that if *any* logical condition listed in the OR function is true, the OR function returns a TRUE value.

Talent Tracs is considering awarding a 4 percent raise to employees working from home *or* working full-time (FT); all other employees will receive a 2.5 percent increase. The criteria for awarding a salary increase is based on two conditions—location and job status. If either condition is true or both conditions are true, the employee will receive the 4 percent raise. If neither condition is true, the employee will receive the 2.5 percent raise. Rita outlined these salary increase criteria in the flowchart shown in Figure 7-10.

| Figure 7-10 | Flowchart of the OR function |

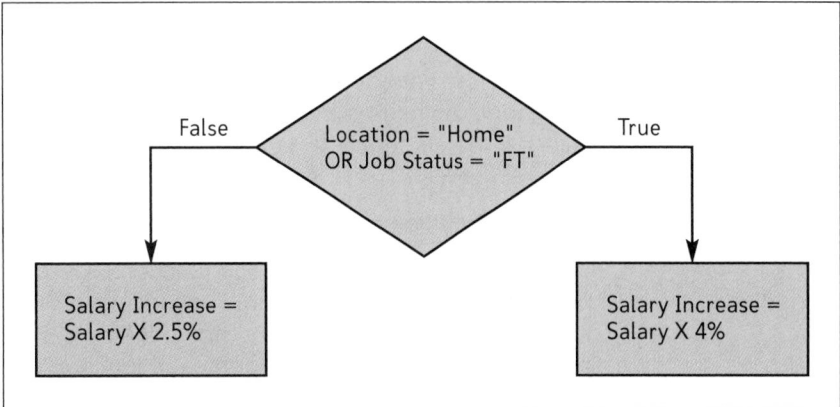

You need to use the OR function to test whether an employee meets the criteria for the 4 percent or 2.5 percent salary increase. The following formula uses the OR function to test whether the value in cell F2 (the work location for the first employee) is equal to "Home" or whether the value in cell G2 (the job status for the first employee) is equal to "FT." If the employee works from home *or* the employee works full time *or* the employee both works from home and works full time, the OR function returns the value TRUE; otherwise, the OR function returns the value FALSE.

`=OR(F2="Home", G2="FT")`

Figure 7-11 shows the results returned using the OR function for four different sets of values for employee work location and job status.

| Figure 7-11 | Examples of OR function results |

**Purpose:**    To determine an employee's salary increase percentage

**Logic Scenario**: Proposed 4 percent salary increase to full-time (FT) employees or employees working from home

**Formula:**    OR function with two conditions
`=OR(F2="Home",G2="FT")`

**Data**:    cell F2 stores Location
cell G2 stores Job Status

**Example**:

| Data | | Condition1 | Condition2 | Results |
|---|---|---|---|---|
| **Cell F2** | **Cell G2** | F2="Home" | G2="FT" | (4% increase) |
| Home | FT | True | True | True |
| Austin | FT | False | True | True |
| Home | PT | True | False | True |
| Nashville | PT | False | False | False |

The OR function only determines which raise an employee is eligible for. It does not calculate the amount of the salary increase. To determine the amount of the salary increase, the OR function must be nested within an IF function. In the following formula, the logical test of the IF function uses the OR function (shown in red) to determine whether an employee is either working from home or working full-time or both. If the OR function returns a TRUE value, the IF function multiplies the annual salary by 4 percent. If the OR function returns a FALSE value, the IF function multiplies the annual salary by 2.5 percent.

```
=IF(OR(F2="Home",G2="FT"),K2*0.04,K2*0.025)
```

Figure 7-12 illustrates how the OR function is used to determine eligibility for a 10 percent discount. In this scenario, anyone who is 65 years or older (stored in cell B1) *or* anyone who is a college student (stored in cell B2) receives a 10 percent discount. At least one condition must be true for the OR function to return the logical value TRUE.

| Figure 7-12 | Additional example of the OR function |
| --- | --- |

**Purpose:** To determine who is eligible for a discount

**Logic Scenario:** Discount is 10 percent for seniors (65 or older) or college students (Status = STU)

**Formula:** OR function with two conditions
=OR(B1>=65,B2="STU")

**Data:** cell B1 stores Age
cell B2 stores Status (STU, FAC, STF)

**Example:**

| Data | | Condition1 | Condition2 | Results |
| --- | --- | --- | --- | --- |
| Cell B1 | Cell B2 | B1>=65 | B2="STU" | (Discount?) |
| 22 | STU | False | True | True |
| 65 | FAC | True | False | True |
| 67 | STU | True | True | True |
| 45 | STF | False | False | False |

# Using Structured References to Create Formulas in Excel Tables

When you create a formula that references all or parts of an Excel table, you can replace the specific cell or range address with a structured reference, the actual table name or column header. This makes the formula easier to create and understand. The default Excel table name is Table1, Table2, and so forth unless you entered a more descriptive table name, as you did for the Employee table. Column headers provide a description of the data entered in each column. Structured references make it easier to create formulas that use portions or all of an Excel table because the names or headers are usually simpler to identify than cell addresses. For example, in the Employee table, the table name

**TIP**

If you are not sure of a table's name, click in the table, click the Table Tools Design tab on the Ribbon, and then check the Table Name box in the Properties group.

"Employee" refers to the range A2:N101, which is the range of data in the table excluding the header row and the Total row. When you want to reference an entire column of data in a table, you create a column qualifier, which has the syntax

`Tablename[qualifier]`

where *Tablename* is the name entered in the Table Name box in the Properties group on the Table Tools Design tab, and *qualifier* is the column header enclosed in square brackets. For example, the structured reference Employee[Annual Salary] references the annual salary data in the range K2:K101 of the Employee table.

You use structured references in formulas. The following formula adds the annual salary data in the range K2:K101 of the Employee table; in this case, [Annual Salary] is the column qualifier:

`=SUM(Employee[Annual Salary])`

When you create a calculated column, as you did to calculate life insurance premiums and 401(k) contributions in the Employee table, you can use structured references to create the formula. A formula that includes a structured reference can be fully qualified or unqualified. In a fully qualified structured reference, the table name precedes the column qualifier. In an unqualified structured reference, only the column qualifier appears in the reference. For example, you could have used either of the following formulas with structured references to calculate Life Ins Premium in the calculated column you added to the Employee table:

**Fully qualified**
`=IF(Employee[Add Life Ins]="Y",Employee[Annual Salary]*.001,0)`

**Unqualified**
`=IF([Add Life Ins]="Y",[Annual Salary]*.001,0)`

If you are creating a calculated column or formula within an Excel table, you can use either the fully qualified structured reference or the unqualified structured reference in the formula. If you use a structured reference outside the table or in another worksheet to reference an Excel table or portion of the table, you must use a fully qualified reference.

You'll use structured references to calculate the salary increases for Talent Tracs employees.

### To calculate the salary increase:

1. In cell P1, enter **Salary Increase** as the column header. The Excel table expands to include the new column, and cell P2 is the active cell.

2. Make sure cell P2 is the active cell, and then click the **Insert Function** button $f_x$ in the formula bar. The Insert Function dialog box opens.

3. Click **IF** in the Select a function box, and then click the **OK** button. The Function Arguments dialog box opens.

4. Next to the Logical_test box, click the **Collapse Dialog Box** button. The Function Arguments dialog box reduces to show only the Logical_test box.

5. In the Logical_test box, type **OR([Location]="Home",[Job Status]="FT")** to enter the OR function with structured references. This logical test evaluates whether the employee works from home or works full-time or both. See Figure 7-13.

Be sure to type square brackets around the structured references and use the exact spelling and location shown. Otherwise, the formula will return an error.

**Figure 7-13**  **Logical_test argument for the OR function**

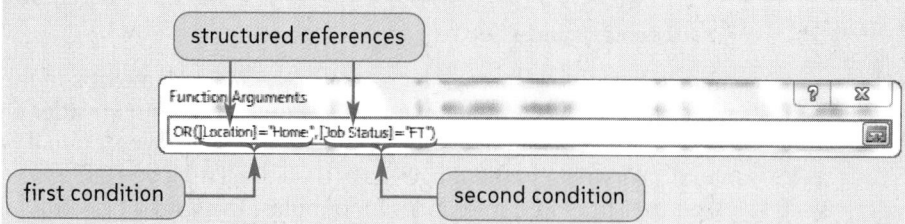

structured references

Function Arguments

OR([Location]="Home",[Job Status]="FT")

first condition

second condition

▶ **6.** Click the **Expand Dialog Box** button to show the full Function Arguments dialog box, and then press the **Tab** key. TRUE appears to the right of the Logical_test box, indicating the result for the employee in the active row, row 2, is true. This employee is eligible for the 4 percent salary increase.

**Trouble?** If "Invalid" appears instead of "TRUE" as the logical test results, you probably mistyped the logical test. Compare the function in your Logical_test box to the one shown in Figure 7-13, confirming that you used square brackets around the structured references [Location] and [Job Status] and typed all the text correctly.

▶ **7.** In the Value_if_true box, type **[Annual Salary]*0.04** and then press the **Tab** key. This argument specifies that if the logical test is true (the employee is eligible for the 4 percent increase), the amount in the employee's salary cell is multiplied by 4 percent. The salary increases for all employees, beginning in row 2, whose logical test is true appear to the right of the Value_if_true box.

▶ **8.** In the Value_if_false box, type **[Annual Salary]*0.025**. This argument specifies that if the logical test is false (the employee is not eligible for the 4 percent increase), the amount in the employee's salary cell is multiplied by 2.5 percent. The salary increases for all employees, beginning in row 2, whose logical test is false appear to the right of the Value_if_false box. See Figure 7-14.

**Figure 7-14**  **Function Arguments dialog box for the IF function with an OR function**

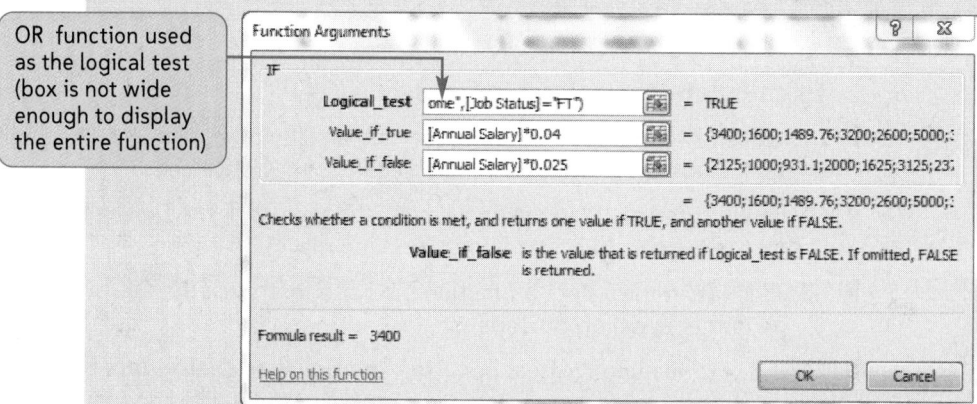

OR function used as the logical test (box is not wide enough to display the entire function)

Function Arguments

IF

Logical_test  ome",[Job Status]="FT")  = TRUE

Value_if_true  [Annual Salary]*0.04  = {3400;1600;1489.76;3200;2600;5000;

Value_if_false  [Annual Salary]*0.025  = {2125;1000;931.1;2000;1625;3125;23;

= {3400;1600;1489.76;3200;2600;5000;

Checks whether a condition is met, and returns one value if TRUE, and another value if FALSE.

Value_if_false  is the value that is returned if Logical_test is FALSE. If omitted, FALSE is returned.

Formula result = 3400

Help on this function  OK  Cancel

▶ **9.** Click the **OK** button. The formula =IF(OR([Location]="Home",[Job Status]="FT"), [Annual Salary]*0.04,[Annual Salary]*0.025) appears in the formula bar and the value 3400 appears in cell P2 because the condition is true. The results are automatically copied to all rows in column P of the table.

▶ **10.** Position the pointer at the top of cell **P1** until the pointer changes to ↓, click to select the Salary Increase data values, and then format the range using the **Accounting** number format.

> **11.** Click cell **P2** to deselect the column. See Figure 7-15.

**Figure 7-15**    IF function with the OR function calculates salary increase

formula uses structured references to calculate the salary increases

salary increases for employees

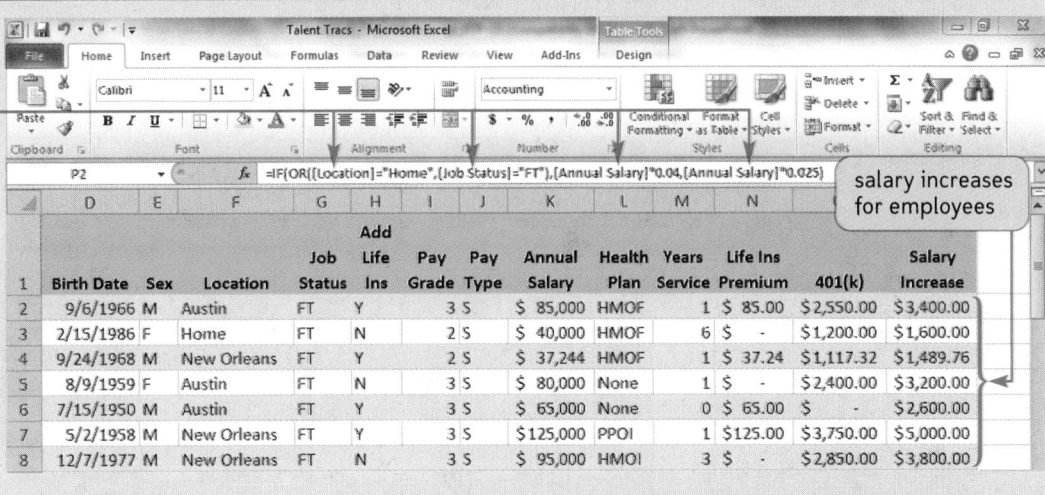

P2    fx =IF(OR([Location]="Home",[Job Status]="FT"),[Annual Salary]*0.04,[Annual Salary]*0.025)

| | Birth Date | Sex | Location | Job Status | Add Life Ins | Pay Grade | Pay Type | Annual Salary | Health Plan | Years Service | Life Ins Premium | 401(k) | Salary Increase |
|---|---|---|---|---|---|---|---|---|---|---|---|---|---|
| 1 | Birth Date | Sex | Location | Status | Ins | Grade | Type | Salary | Plan | Service | Premium | 401(k) | Increase |
| 2 | 9/6/1966 | M | Austin | FT | Y | 3 | S | $ 85,000 | HMOF | 1 | $ 85.00 | $2,550.00 | $3,400.00 |
| 3 | 2/15/1986 | F | Home | FT | N | 2 | S | $ 40,000 | HMOF | 6 | $ - | $1,200.00 | $1,600.00 |
| 4 | 9/24/1968 | M | New Orleans | FT | Y | 2 | S | $ 37,244 | HMOF | 1 | $ 37.24 | $1,117.32 | $1,489.76 |
| 5 | 8/9/1959 | F | Austin | FT | N | 3 | S | $ 80,000 | None | 1 | $ - | $2,400.00 | $3,200.00 |
| 6 | 7/15/1950 | M | Austin | FT | Y | 3 | S | $ 65,000 | None | 0 | $ 65.00 | $ - | $2,600.00 |
| 7 | 5/2/1958 | M | New Orleans | FT | Y | 3 | S | $125,000 | PPOI | 1 | $125.00 | $3,750.00 | $5,000.00 |
| 8 | 12/7/1977 | M | New Orleans | FT | N | 3 | S | $ 95,000 | HMOI | 3 | $ - | $2,850.00 | $3,800.00 |

In this session, you used the IF, AND, and OR functions to calculate the additional life insurance premiums, 401(k) benefits, and next year's salary increases for Talent Tracs employees. Rita still needs to calculate the employee bonuses, health plan costs, and the employee recognition award for each employee. In the next session, you will create formulas with functions to perform these calculations.

**REVIEW**

## Section 7.1 Quick Check

1. What changes occur in the appearance and size of an Excel table after you enter a new column header named "Phone"?
2. Whenever you enter a formula in an empty column of an Excel table, Excel automatically fills the column with the same formula. What is this called?
3. If an Excel worksheet stores the cost per meal in cell Q5, the number of attendees in cell Q6, and the total cost of meals in cell Q7, what IF function would you enter in cell Q7 to calculate the total cost of meals (cost per meal times the number of attendees) with a minimum cost of $10,000?
4. True or False. The AND function is a logical function that returns a TRUE value if any of the logical conditions are true and a FALSE value if all of the logical conditions are false.
5. Write the formula that displays the label "Outstanding" if the amount owed (cell X5) is greater than 0 and the transaction date (cell R5) is before 3/15/2013, but otherwise leaves the cell blank.
6. When you create a formula that references all or parts of an Excel table, you can use _____ to replace the specific cell or range addresses with the actual table or column header names.
7. If the formula `=IF(OR(B25="NY",B25="CA",B25="TX"),"Select","Ignore")` is entered in cell B26, and "PA" is entered in cell B25, what is displayed in cell B26?
8. What OR function represents the rule, "A potential enlistee in the Army is not eligible to enlist if younger than 17 or older than 42." The age is stored in cell B25.

# SESSION 7.2 VISUAL OVERVIEW

A **nested IF function** is when one IF function is placed inside another IF function to test an additional condition, such as calculating employee bonuses based on pay grade.

The **lookup value** is the value you are trying to find. In this case, the lookup value is the code in the Health Plan column.

The invalid code in the Health Plan column causes the IFERROR message to appear in the Health Cost column.

Talent Tracs - Microsoft Excel

File    Home    Insert    Page Layout    Formulas    Data    Review    View    Add-Ins

Calibri    11    A A    Custom

B  I  U    A    $  %

Paste

Clipboard    Font    Alignment    Number

Q2    fx    =IF([Pay Grade]=1,$Y$2,IF([Pay Grade]=2,$Y$3,$Y$4

| | G | H | I | J | K | L | M | N | |
|---|---|---|---|---|---|---|---|---|---|
| 1 | Job Status | Add Life Ins | Pay Grade | Pay Type | Annual Salary | Health Plan | Years Service | Life Ins Premium | 40 |
| 2 | FT | Y | 3 | S | $ 85,000 | HMOF | 1 | $ 85.00 | $2,5 |
| 3 | FT | N | 2 | S | $ 40,000 | HMOF | 6 | $ - | $1,2 |
| 4 | FT | Y | 2 | S | $ 37,244 | HMOF | 1 | 37.24 | $1,1 |
| 5 | FT | N | 3 | S | $ 80,000 | None | 1 | $ | $2,4 |
| 6 | FT | Y | 3 | S | $ 65,000 | None | 0 | $ 65.00 | |
| 7 | FT | Y | 3 | S | $125,000 | PPOI | 1 | $125.00 | $3, |
| 8 | FT | N | 3 | S | $ 95,000 | HMOI | 3 | $ - | $2,8 |
| 9 | FT | N | 2 | S | $ 36,000 | None | 0 | $ - | $ |
| 10 | PT | N | 1 | H | | | | $ - | $ |
| 11 | FT | N | 1 | H | | | | | $ 6 |
| 12 | FT | N | 1 | H | | | | $ - | $ 7 |
| 13 | FT | N | 1 | H | $ 32,011 | PPOI | 0 | $ - | $ |
| 14 | FT | Y | 1 | H | $ 23,920 | HMOH | 5 | $ 23.92 | $ 7 |
| 15 | FT | Y | 1 | H | $ 32,011 | None | 11 | $ 32.01 | $ 9 |
| 16 | FT | Y | 1 | H | $ 21,840 | PPOI | 8 | $ 21.84 | $ 6 |
| 17 | FT | Y | 2 | S | | | | 55.00 | $ |
| 18 | FT | Y | 2 | S | | | | 65.00 | $ |
| 19 | FT | Y | 3 | S | $125,000 | HMOF | 0 | $125.00 | $ |

A **lookup table** is a table that organizes data that you want to retrieve into different categories, such as health plan codes. This lookup table is named "HealthPlanRates" and is used in the VLOOKUP function.

The **compare values**, the categories for a lookup table, are located in the table's first column or row.

Documentation    Employee Data    Employee Summary    Lookup Tables

Ready

# NESTED IFS AND LOOKUP TABLES

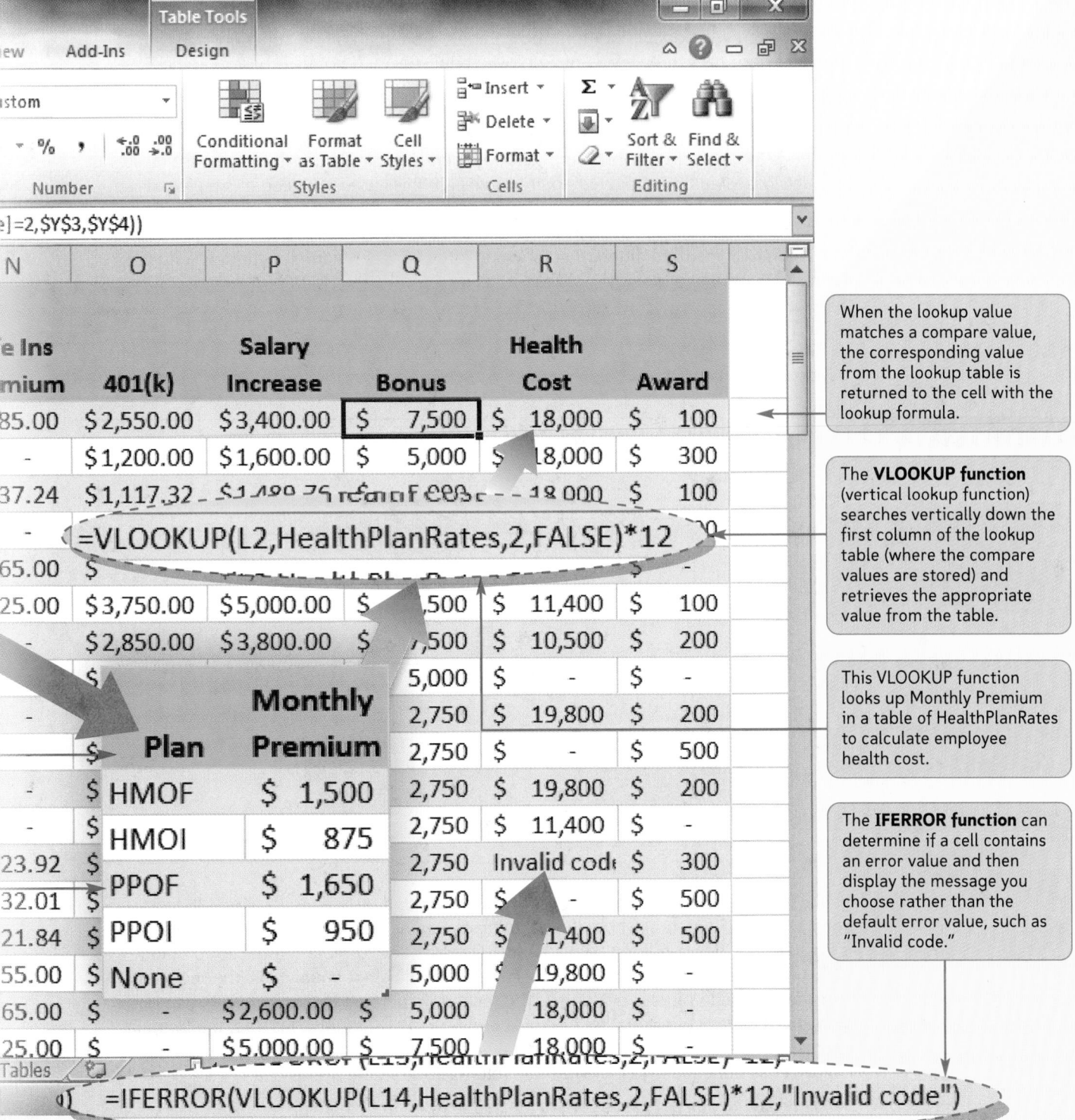

When the lookup value matches a compare value, the corresponding value from the lookup table is returned to the cell with the lookup formula.

The **VLOOKUP function** (vertical lookup function) searches vertically down the first column of the lookup table (where the compare values are stored) and retrieves the appropriate value from the table.

This VLOOKUP function looks up Monthly Premium in a table of HealthPlanRates to calculate employee health cost.

The **IFERROR function** can determine if a cell contains an error value and then display the message you choose rather than the default error value, such as "Invalid code."

=VLOOKUP(L2,HealthPlanRates,2,FALSE)*12

| Plan | Monthly Premium |
|------|-----------------|
| HMOF | $ 1,500 |
| HMOI | $ 875 |
| PPOF | $ 1,650 |
| PPOI | $ 950 |
| None | $ - |

=IFERROR(VLOOKUP(L14,HealthPlanRates,2,FALSE)*12,"Invalid code")

# Creating Nested IFs

The IF function can choose between only two outcomes; it cannot choose from among three or more outcomes. However, you can nest IF functions to allow for three or more outcomes. A nested IF function is when one IF function is placed inside another IF function to test an additional condition. You can nest more than one IF function.

Talent Tracs pays three levels of employee bonuses. Each bonus is based on the employee's pay grade, which is a system Talent Tracs uses to group jobs based on difficulty and responsibility. Talent Tracs has three pay grade codes (1, 2, and 3). Pay grade 1 has a starting bonus of $2,500, pay grade 2 has a starting bonus of $5,000, and pay grade 3 has a starting bonus of $7,500. Supervisors can increase or decrease these amounts based on the employee's performance. In this case, you need to nest two IF functions to calculate the different series of outcomes for the employee bonuses.

Rita created the flowchart shown in Figure 7-16 to illustrate the logic for determining bonus awards. She used different colors to identify each nested IF function. The flowchart shows that if an employee's pay grade equals 1, the bonus amount equals 2500 and the IF function (shown in green) is finished. If the employee's pay grade does not equal 1, then the second IF function (shown in blue) is evaluated. If the employee's pay grade equals 2, then the bonus amount equals 5000 and the IF function is finished. If the employee's pay grade does not equal 2, then the bonus amount equals 7500.

**Figure 7-16** | **Flowchart illustrating nested IF functions to determine the bonus amount**

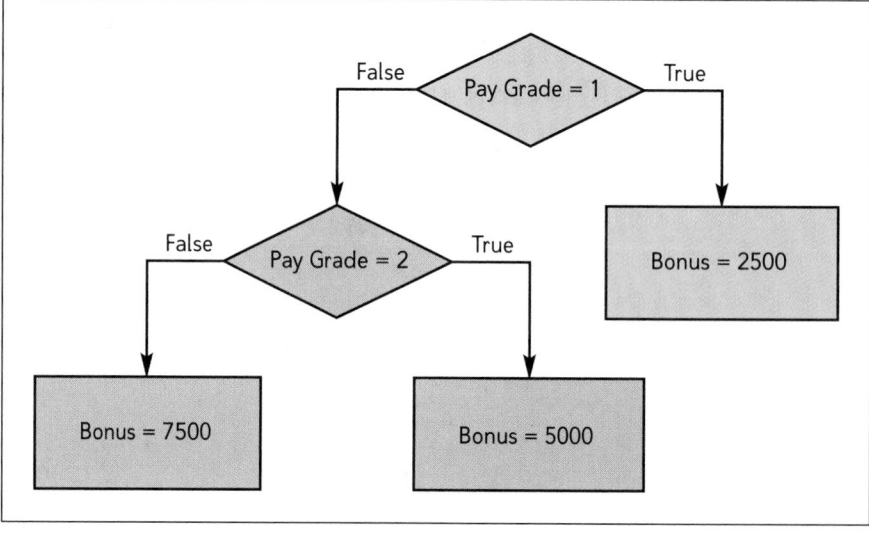

The following formula converts Rita's flowchart into a formula with nested IF functions. The first IF function (shown in green) tests whether the value in the Pay Grade cell is equal to 1. If this condition ([Pay Grade]=1) is true, the formula returns 2500 in the Bonus cell. If this condition is false (the Pay Grade cell is not equal to 1), the second IF function (shown in blue) is evaluated. The second IF function tests whether the value in the Pay Grade cell is equal to 2. If this condition ([Pay Grade]=2) is true, the formula returns 5000 in the Bonus cell. If this condition is false (the value in the current Pay Grade cell is not equal to 2), the formula returns 7500 in the Bonus cell.

```
=IF([Pay Grade]=1,2500,IF([Pay Grade]=2,5000,7500))
```

Figure 7-17 illustrates how one nested IF function is used to determine among three outcomes—whether the home football team won, lost, or tied a game. The first IF function evaluates whether the home team score (stored in cell B1) is greater than the visiting team score (stored in cell B2). If the home team score is higher, "Won" appears in the cell. If not, the nested IF function evaluates whether the visiting team score is greater than the home team score. If the visiting team score is higher, "Lost" appears in the cell. Otherwise, "Tie" appears in the cell.

**Figure 7-17**    **Additional example of nested IF functions**

**Purpose:**    To determine the outcome of football games for the home team

**Logic Scenario:**  Display Won, Lost, or Tie based on home team and visitor team scores

**Formula:**    Nested IF functions
               =IF(B1>B2,"Won",IF(B2>B1,"Lost","Tie"))

**Data:**       cell B1 stores the home team score
               cell B2 stores the visitor team score

**Example:**

| Data | | Condition1 | Condition2 | Results |
|---|---|---|---|---|
| Cell B1 | Cell B2 | B1>B2 | B2>B1 | (Outcome) |
| 21 | 18 | True | Not evaluated | Won |
| 17 | 24 | False | True | Lost |
| 9 | 9 | False | False | Tie |

Figure 7-18 illustrates how two nested IFs are used to determine among four possible outcomes for a driver's license based on the applicant's age (stored in cell B1). The first IF function evaluates whether the applicant is less than 16 years old. If the applicant is younger than 16, "Too Young" appears in the cell. If not, the first nested IF function evaluates whether the applicant is 45 years old or younger. If so, 30 appears in the cell as the fee. If not, the second nested IF function evaluates whether the applicant is 60 years old or younger. If so, 25 appears in the cell as the fee. Otherwise, 20 appears in the cell as the fee.

**Figure 7-18**   **Additional example of nested IF functions**

**Purpose:**   To determine the fee for a driver's license

**Logic Scenario:** Driver's license fee varies by age

| | |
|---|---|
| Below 16 | "Too Young" |
| 16–45 | $30 |
| 46–60 | $25 |
| 61 and older | $20 |

**Formula:**   Nested IF functions
=IF(B1<16,"Too Young",IF(B1<=45,30,IF(B1<=60,25,20)))

**Data:**   cell B1 stores the driver's age

**Example:**

| Data | Condition1 | Condition2 | Condition3 | Results |
|---|---|---|---|---|
| **Cell B1** | **B1<16** | **B1<=45** | **B1<=60** | **(Fee)** |
| 15 | True | Not evaluated | Not evaluated | Too Young |
| 25 | False | True | Not evaluated | 30 |
| 55 | False | False | True | 25 |
| 65 | False | False | False | 20 |

**PROSKILLS**

*Problem Solving: Finding and Fixing Errors in Formulas*

Errors occur in spreadsheets as illustrated in the following real-life incident: "City officials miscalculated the amount of sales taxes generated from a local sporting goods store. The mistake inflated the tax figures by tens of thousands of dollars, which, in turn, meant the total sales estimate was overblown by millions of dollars. The city believed the mistake was a result of an error in a spreadsheet formula...."

If formulas in a worksheet are returning errors or not working as expected, you need to find and fix the problems. Two common categories of formula errors in Excel are syntax errors and logic errors. A syntax error is an error in a statement that violates the rules of Excel. A syntax error might occur due to unmatched parentheses or a required argument that is omitted in a function. Logic errors occur in formulas that work but return an incorrect result. A logic error could occur because the formula uses the wrong calculation, the formula references the wrong cell, or the formula uses faulty reasoning, leading to incorrect results.

Some problem-solving approaches can help resolve these types of errors. First, examine the formulas in worksheet cells instead of the results by pressing the Ctrl+~ keys to show the formulas in each cell. Next, troubleshoot problem areas in the worksheet by pressing the F9 key to highlight part of a formula and temporarily display the actual value in the cell so you can check intermediate results. Press the Esc key to return the cell references. Finally, you can use the Formula Auditing tools on the Formulas tab to visually identify and trace cells used in a formula. This can help you locate and fix inaccurate cell references and faulty logic.

Carefully evaluating formulas and fixing any problems help to ensure that a worksheet is error-free and returns accurate results.

Next, you'll add a Bonus column to the Employee table and enter the formula to calculate the bonus amount. The bonus amounts for each pay grade are not yet final. To make the bonus calculation more flexible, Rita stored the three bonus amounts (2500, 5000, and 7500) in the Employee worksheet. You will reference these cells in the formula to calculate the employee bonus. This approach enables you to quickly update the calculated bonus amounts in the Employee worksheet without having to edit the bonus formula.

### To enter nested IFs to calculate employee bonuses:

1. If you took a break at the end of the previous session, make sure the Talent Tracs workbook is open and the Employee Data worksheet is active.

2. In cell Q1, enter **Bonus** as the column header. The Excel table expands to include the new column, and cell Q2 is the active cell.

3. Make sure cell Q2 is the active cell, and then click the **Insert Function** button $f_x$ in the formula bar. The Insert Function dialog box opens.

4. Click **IF** in the Select a function box, and then click the **OK** button. The Function Arguments dialog box opens.

5. In the Logical_test box, type **[Pay Grade]=1** and then press the **Tab** key to enter the logical test using a structured reference. This logical test evaluates whether the employee has a pay grade equal to 1. The values to the right of the Logical_test box are {False;False;..., indicating that the pay grades for the first few employees are not equal to 1.

   **Trouble?** If the value to the right of the Logical_test box is "Invalid," you probably mistyped the logical test. Select the text in the Logical_test box, and then repeat Step 5, typing the logical test exactly as shown, being sure to use square brackets around the structured reference.

6. In the Value_if_true box, type **$Y$2** and then press the **Tab** key. The value to the right of the Value_if_true argument box is 2500, which is the value in cell Y2. This argument specifies that if the logical test is true (the Pay Grade cell is equal to 1), the value stored in cell Y2 (the 2500 bonus amount) is displayed.

7. In the Value_if_false box, type **IF([Pay Grade]=2,$Y$3,$Y$4)**. This argument is a nested IF function that specifies if the logical condition is true (the Pay Grade cell is equal to 2), the value stored in cell Y3 (the 5000 bonus amount) is displayed; otherwise, the value stored in cell Y4 (the 7500 bonus amount) is displayed. The values to the right of the Value_if_false box are {7500;5000;5000;... indicating the bonus amounts for the employees in the first few rows. See Figure 7-19.

| Figure 7-19 | Function Arguments dialog box with a nested IF |

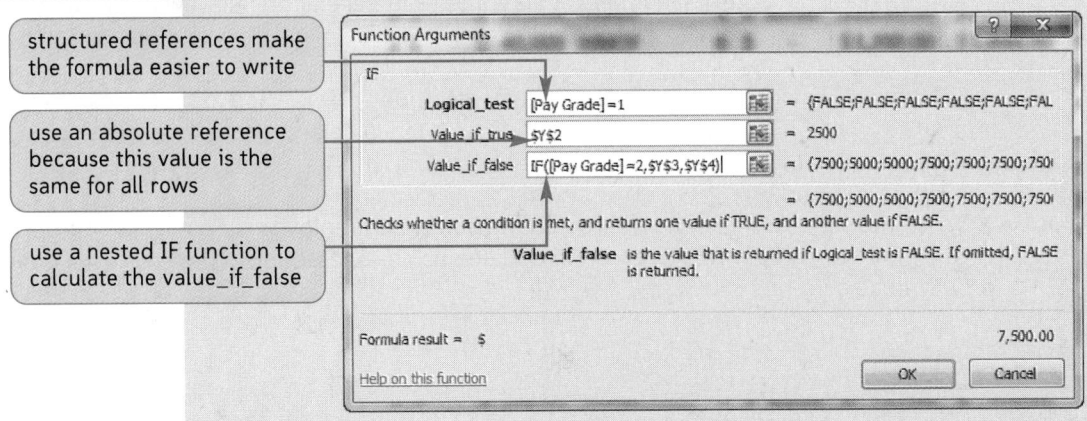

structured references make the formula easier to write

use an absolute reference because this value is the same for all rows

use a nested IF function to calculate the value_if_false

8. Click the **OK** button. The formula =IF([Pay Grade]=1,$Y$2,IF([Pay Grade]=2,$Y$3, $Y$4)) appears in the formula bar, and the value 7500 appears in cell Q2 because this employee has a pay grade of 3. The bonus formula is automatically copied to all other rows in the Bonus column. The references to cells Y2, Y3, and Y4 are absolute references and do not change from cell to cell in the Bonus column.

9. Select the Bonus values, and then format the selected range using the **Accounting** number format with no decimal places.

10. Click cell **Q2** to deselect the column. See Figure 7-20.

**Figure 7-20** — **Nested IF function calculating the employee bonus amounts**

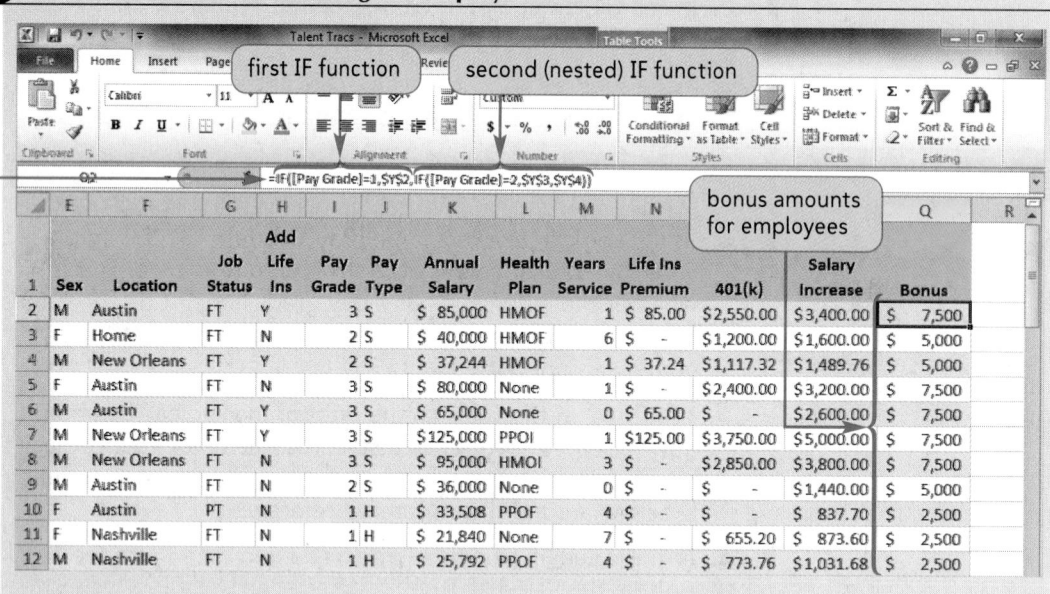

formula uses a nested IF function and structured references to calculate the bonus amount

## Checking Formulas for Matching Parentheses

A common problem when creating formulas is mismatched parentheses. As you write a formula, you should verify that you enclosed the correct argument, function, or term within the parentheses of the formula you are creating. This is especially important when you develop a complex formula that includes many parentheses, such as a nested IF function. Excel color-codes the parentheses as you build a formula so you can quickly determine whether you have complete pairs of them. You can also verify that the formula includes matching pairs of parentheses by selecting the cell with the formula and then clicking in the formula bar. Press the → key to move the insertion point through the formula one character at a time. When the insertion point moves across one parenthesis, its matching parenthesis is also highlighted briefly. This color coding helps you ensure that all parentheses in a formula are paired (opening and closing parentheses).

The executive team has increased the bonus for employees in pay grade 1 from $2,500 to $2,750. Rita asks you to update this bonus amount so the employee bonuses will be current.

**TIP**

Placing cell references to input values rather than constants in formulas makes a worksheet more flexible and easier to update.

**To update the bonus amount for Pay Grade 1:**

▶ **1.** In cell Y2, enter **2750**.

▶ **2.** Scroll to the **Bonus** column and observe that all employees with a pay grade equal to 1 show a bonus amount of $2,750.

# Using Lookup Tables and Functions

**Lookup functions** allow you to use tables of data to "look up" values and insert them in another worksheet location. For example, you might enter a product table in a worksheet that includes the product ID, product name, and price of all products a company sells. You could then use this product table to build an invoice in another worksheet by entering a product ID and having Excel look up the product name and price, and insert these values in the invoice.

The table that stores the data you want to retrieve is called a lookup table, and it organizes the data you want to retrieve into different categories, such as by product ID. The categories for the lookup table, called compare values, are located in the table's first column or row. To retrieve a particular value from the table, a lookup value (the value you are trying to find) needs to match one of the compare values. When a match is found, the corresponding value in the lookup table is displayed in the cell where the lookup formula is entered. Lookup values can also be used as part of a formula.

At Talent Tracs, all employees are eligible for the company's health plan. Employees can choose one of four health plans: an HMO for individuals (HMOI), an HMO for families (HMOF), a PPO for individuals (PPOI), or a PPO for families (PPOF). Each plan has a different cost, and Talent Tracs pays the entire health plan cost. If an employee shows evidence of coverage elsewhere, there is no health plan cost. You could calculate the health plan costs for each employee using several nested IF functions. However, a simpler approach is to use a lookup function.

You can use the HealthPlanRates table shown in Figure 7-21 as a lookup table. The lookup table shows the available plans and the corresponding monthly premiums. The health plan cost for each eligible employee is based on the plan the employee selected. The lookup value is the employee's health plan code, which is entered in column L of the Employee table. The compare values come from the first column of the HealthPlanRates table, which is in the range B3:C8 in the Lookup Tables worksheet. To retrieve the monthly cost for an employee, Excel moves down the first column in the HealthPlanRates lookup table until it finds the health plan code that matches the lookup value. Then it moves to the second column in the lookup table to locate the monthly cost, which is displayed in the cell where the lookup formula is entered or used as part of a calculation.

**Figure 7-21**    **HealthPlanRates table used for an exact match lookup**

|   | A | B | C |
|---|---|---|---|
| 1 |   |   |   |
| 2 |   |   |   |
| 3 |   | Plan | Monthly Premium |
| 4 |   | HMOF | $ 1,500 |
| 5 |   | HMOI | $   875 |
| 6 |   | PPOF | $ 1,650 |
| 7 |   | PPOI | $   950 |
| 8 |   | None | $    - |
| 9 |   |   |   |

Lookup tables can be constructed as either exact match or approximate match lookups. An **exact match lookup** occurs when the value entered must match one of the values in the first column of the lookup table. The HealthPlanRates table in Figure 7-21 is an example of an exact match lookup because the health plan code must match one of the values in the HealthPlanRates table or a value is not returned. An **approximate match lookup** occurs when the value entered falls within a range of values in the first column of the lookup table. A discount based on the quantity of items purchased where each discount covers a range of units purchased is an example of an approximate match lookup. Figure 7-22 shows the approximate match lookup table for these quantity discounts. In this example, purchases of fewer than 25 units receive no discount, purchases of between 25 and 99 units receive a 2 percent discount, purchases of between 100 and 499 units receive a 3 percent discount, and purchases of 500 or more units receive a 4 percent discount.

**Figure 7-22**    **Approximate match lookup table**

| Quantity | Discount Rate |
| --- | --- |
| 0 | 0% |
| 25 | 2% |
| 100 | 3% |
| 500 | 4% |

## Using the VLOOKUP Function to Find an Exact Match

To retrieve the correct value from the lookup table, you use the VLOOKUP function. This function searches a lookup table and, based on what you entered, retrieves the appropriate value from that table. The VLOOKUP function searches vertically down the first column of the lookup table. The VLOOKUP function has the syntax

```
VLOOKUP(lookup_value, table_array, col_index_num, [range_lookup])
```

where *lookup_value* is the value you want to use to search the first column of the lookup table, *table_array* is the range reference of the lookup table or its table name, *col_index_num* is the number of the column in the lookup table that contains the value you want to return, and *range_lookup* indicates whether the compare values are a range of values (for an approximate match) or an exact match. When you use a range of values (such as in a tax rate table), you set the *range_lookup* value to TRUE; when you want the *lookup_value* to exactly match a value in the first column of the *table_array* (such as in the HealthPlanRates table), you set the *range_lookup* value to FALSE. The *range_lookup* argument is optional; if you don't include a *range_lookup* value, the value is considered TRUE (an approximate match).

You'll use the VLOOKUP function to calculate the annual health plan cost for Talent Tracs because you want to search the values in the first column of the lookup table. You can use range references or structured references when you create the formula for the annual health plan cost for an employee from the HealthPlanRates table, as follows:

**Range references**    `=VLOOKUP(L2,'Lookup Tables'!$B$4:$C$8,2,FALSE)*12`

**Structured references**    `=VLOOKUP([HealthPlan],HealthPlanRates,2,FALSE)*12`

Both of these formulas use the VLOOKUP function to search for the code in the Health Plan column (column L) of the Employee table, in the first column of the lookup table (the HealthPlanRates table in the range B4:C8 in the Lookup Tables worksheet), and then return the value in the second column of the HealthPlanRates lookup table, which shows the monthly cost. The formulas use FALSE as the *range_lookup* argument because you want the lookup value to exactly match a value in the first column of the HealthPlanRates table.

## To find an exact match in the HealthPlanRates table:

1. In cell R1, enter **Health Cost**. The table expands to include the new column.

2. Make sure cell R2 is the active cell, and then click the **Insert Function** button $f_x$ in the formula bar. The Insert Function dialog box opens.

3. Click the **Or select a category** arrow, click **Lookup & Reference**, and then double-click **VLOOKUP** in the Select a function box. The Function Arguments dialog box opens.

4. Drag the Function Arguments dialog box below row 2 so you can see the column headers.

5. In the Lookup_value box, enter **L2** and then press the **Tab** key. The lookup value is the employee's health plan code, which is located in column L.

6. In the Table_array box, type **HealthPlanRates** and then press the **Tab** key. HealthPlanRates is the table name assigned to the range B4:C8 in the Lookup Tables worksheet. If the HealthPlanRates data was entered in a range of cells, the table_array argument would be entered as 'Lookup Tables'!B4:C8, and you would need to change the range to absolute references ('Lookup Tables'!$B$4:$C$8) so the formula would copy correctly to other cells.

7. In the Col_index_num box, type **2** and then press the **Tab** key. The number 2 indicates the monthly cost is stored in the second column of the HealthPlanRates lookup table.

8. In the Range_lookup box, type **FALSE**. This sets the function to find an exact match in the lookup table. See Figure 7-23.

**TIP**

For the col_index_num value, be sure to enter the number that corresponds to the column's position rather than its column letter; otherwise, the VLOOKUP formula may return #NAME? or #VALUE! as the result.

**Figure 7-23**     Function Arguments dialog box for the VLOOKUP function

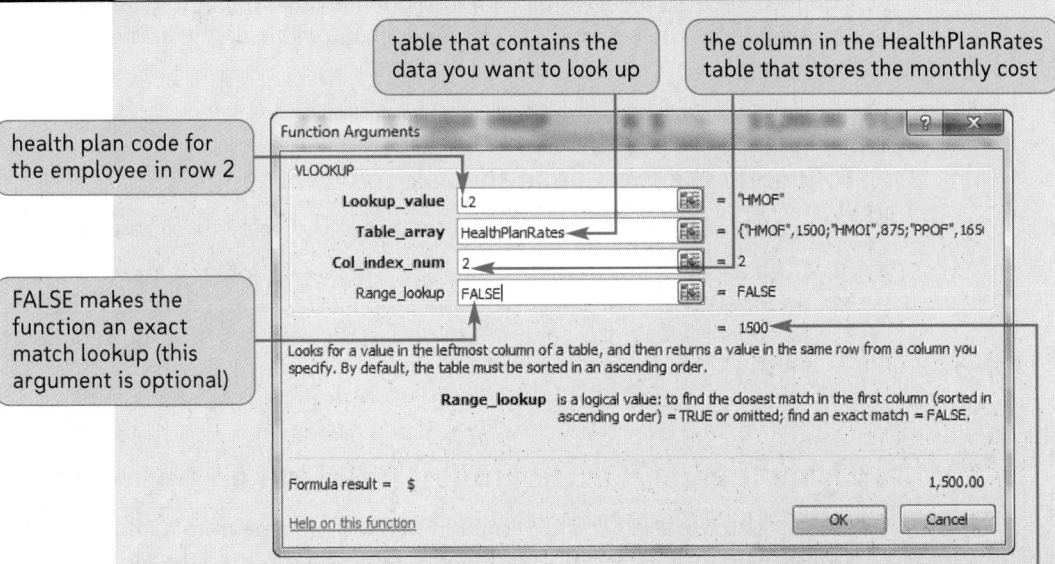

table that contains the data you want to look up

the column in the HealthPlanRates table that stores the monthly cost

health plan code for the employee in row 2

FALSE makes the function an exact match lookup (this argument is optional)

cost of the health plan for the employee in row 2 of the Employee table

9. Click the **OK** button. The dialog box closes, 1500 appears in cell R2, and the formula VLOOKUP(L2,HealthPlanRates,2,FALSE) appears in the formula bar. The remaining rows in the Health Cost column are filled with the VLOOKUP function. If the value in column L does not match a value in the first column of the HealthPlanRates table, an exact match does not exist and the function returns #N/A in the cell.

▶ **10.** Select the Health Cost values, and then format the range using the **Accounting** number format with no decimal places.

▶ **11.** Click cell **R2** to deselect the column. See Figure 7-24.

---

**Figure 7-24** | **VLOOKUP function calculating employee health costs**

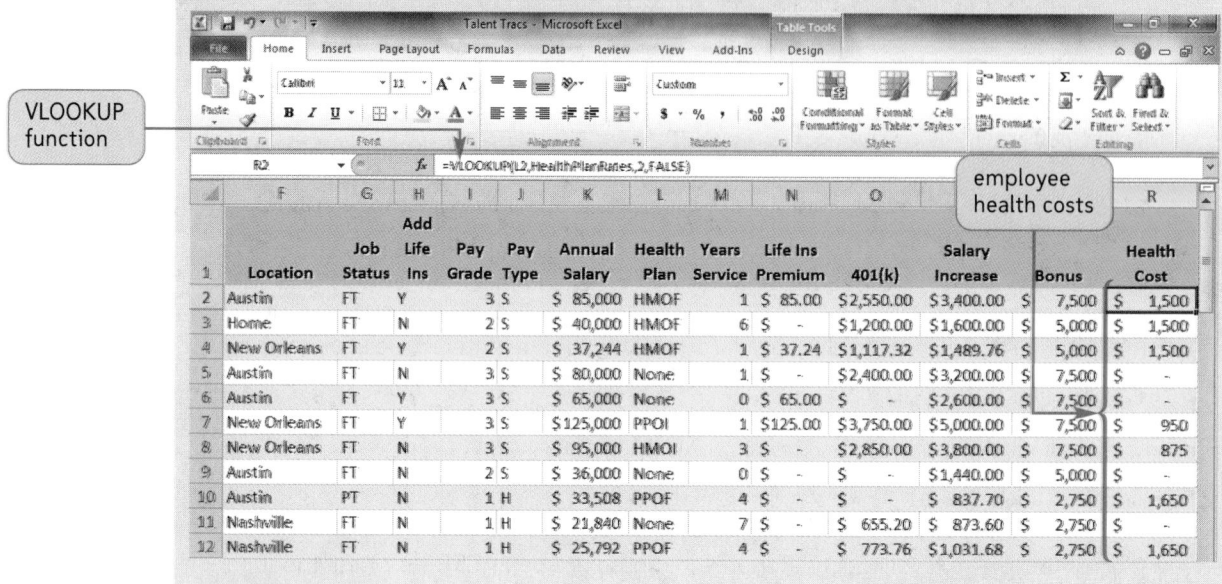

The health plan costs in the Employee table are monthly amounts rather than annual amounts. You need to modify the formula in the Health Cost column to reflect the annual amounts. Because the formula is in a calculated table column, you need to make the change in only one cell and the change will automatically be copied to all the cells in the column.

### To modify the formula in the calculated column:

▶ **1.** Double-click cell **R2** to enter Edit mode and display the formula in the cell.

▶ **2.** Click at the end of the formula, type **\*12** to multiply the monthly amount by 12, and then press the **Enter** key. The amount in cell R2 changes to $18,000 and all the other cells in the column are updated with the revised formula and display the annual cost.

## Using the VLOOKUP Function to Find an Approximate Match

You can also use a VLOOKUP function to return a value from a table that is based on an approximate match lookup. The previous table lookup used the HealthPlanRates table to return a value only if Excel found an exact match in the first column of the lookup table. The categories in the first column or row of a lookup table can also represent a range of values. Quantity discounts, shipping charges, and income tax rates are a few examples of approximate match lookups.

As part of Talent Tracs' 10-year anniversary, management plans to give employee-recognition awards based on the number of years individuals have worked for Talent Tracs. Rita developed the criteria shown in Figure 7-25 to summarize how the company plans to distribute the recognition awards.

**Figure 7-25**    **Recognition Awards table**

| Years of Service | Award |
| --- | --- |
| >=0 years and <1 year | 0 |
| >=1 year and <3 years | 100 |
| >=3 years and <5 years | 200 |
| >=5 years and <7 years | 300 |
| 7 years or more | 500 |

In the Recognition Awards table, you are not looking for an exact match for the lookup value. Instead, you need to use an approximate match lookup, which determines whether the lookup value falls within a range of values. You want to use the table lookup to determine what service range an employee falls into, and then return the recognition award based on the appropriate row. To accomplish this, you must rearrange the first column of the lookup table so that each compare value (row) in the table represents the low end of the category range, as shown in Figure 7-26.

**Figure 7-26**    **Recognition Awards table**

| | F | G | H |
| --- | --- | --- | --- |
| 1 | | | |
| 2 | | | |
| 3 | | Years of Service | Recognition Award |
| 4 | | 0 | $  - |
| 5 | | 1 | $  100 |
| 6 | | 3 | $  200 |
| 7 | | 5 | $  300 |
| 8 | | 7 | $  500 |

To determine whether a lookup value falls within a range of values in the revised lookup table, Excel searches the first column of the table until it locates the largest value that is less than the lookup value. Then Excel moves across the row in the table to retrieve the corresponding value. For an employee working at Talent Tracs for six years, Excel would search the lookup table until the compare value is 5 (the largest value less than the lookup value) and retrieve 300 from column 2 of the corresponding row.

When a lookup table is used with a range of values, the compare values must be sorted in alphabetical order if they are text and in low-to-high order if they are numbers. When the compare values are arranged in a different order, Excel may not retrieve the correct value, leading to incorrect results. Even though the VLOOKUP function is accurate, the data in the lookup table is not organized the right way. The setup of the lookup table in an approximate match is critical for a VLOOKUP formula to work.

INSIGHT

## Setting Up an Approximate Match Lookup Table

Approximate lookup tables are commonly used to find a taxpayer's tax rate in a tax table, find a shipping charge based on the weight of a package in a shipping charges table, or determine a student's letter grade from a table of grading criteria. Setting up the lookup tables for an approximate match lookup can be tricky. Consider the following example, in which an instructor uses Excel to calculate grades. The instructor assigns final grades based on the following grading policy table:

| Score | Grade |
| --- | --- |
| 90–100 | A |
| 80–89 | B |
| 70–79 | C |
| 60–69 | D |
| 0–59 | F |

To set up the lookup table so it works in Excel, the leftmost column in the lookup table must represent the lower end of the range for each category, and the lookup table must be sorted in ascending order based on the value in the first column. Otherwise, Excel cannot retrieve the correct result. Following this structure, the lookup table for the instructor's grading policy would be arranged as follows:

| Score | Grade |
| --- | --- |
| 0 | F |
| 60 | D |
| 70 | C |
| 80 | B |
| 90 | A |

You'll create a formula in the Employee table to determine the recognition award for each employee. You will use an approximate match VLOOKUP formula because the years of service in the lookup table have a range of values.

### To insert an approximate match VLOOKUP formula:

1. In cell S1, enter **Award**. A new column is added to the table, and cell S2 is the active cell.

2. Click the **Insert Function** button $f_x$ in the formula bar. The Insert Function dialog box opens with the Lookup & Reference category active.

3. In the Select a function box, double-click **VLOOKUP**. The Function Arguments dialog box opens.

4. In the Lookup_value box, type **[Years Service]** and then press the **Tab** key. The lookup value is entered using the column header (structured reference) for the employee's years of service, which is located in column M. You can also enter the lookup value as M2. The number 1 appears as the lookup value for the current row.

5. In the Table_array box, type **Recognition** and then press the **Tab** key. Recognition is the table name assigned to the range G4:H8 in the Lookup Tables worksheet. If the Recognition data was entered in a range of cells, the table_array argument would be entered as 'Lookup Tables'!G4:H8, and you would need to change the range to absolute references ('Lookup Tables'!$G$4:$H$8) so that the formula would copy correctly to other cells.

> **6.** In the Col_index_num box, type **2**. The number 2 indicates the column where the amount of the award is stored—in the second column of the Recognition table. See Figure 7-27. You do not need to enter the optional fourth argument in the VLOOKUP formula because Excel assumes the value to be TRUE and will use an approximate match table lookup.

| Figure 7-27 | Function Arguments dialog box for the VLOOKUP function |
| --- | --- |

omitting the range_lookup entry makes VLOOKUP an approximate match lookup

> **7.** Click the **OK** button. All the cells in the Award calculated column are filled with the VLOOKUP formula and display the award amounts. The employee in row 2 has 1 year of service and will receive a recognition award of $100. The employee in row 3 has 6 years of service and will receive an award of $300. This second employee is a good illustration of the approximate match lookup, because 6 does not equal a value in the first column of the lookup table. Instead, it falls within two values in the table.

> **8.** Make sure that the values in the Award column are formatted with the Accounting number format and no decimal places.

> **9.** Click cell **S2** to deselect the column. See Figure 7-28.

| Figure 7-28 | Award column |
| --- | --- |

approximate match VLOOKUP function formula without the fourth argument

award amounts calculated for each employee

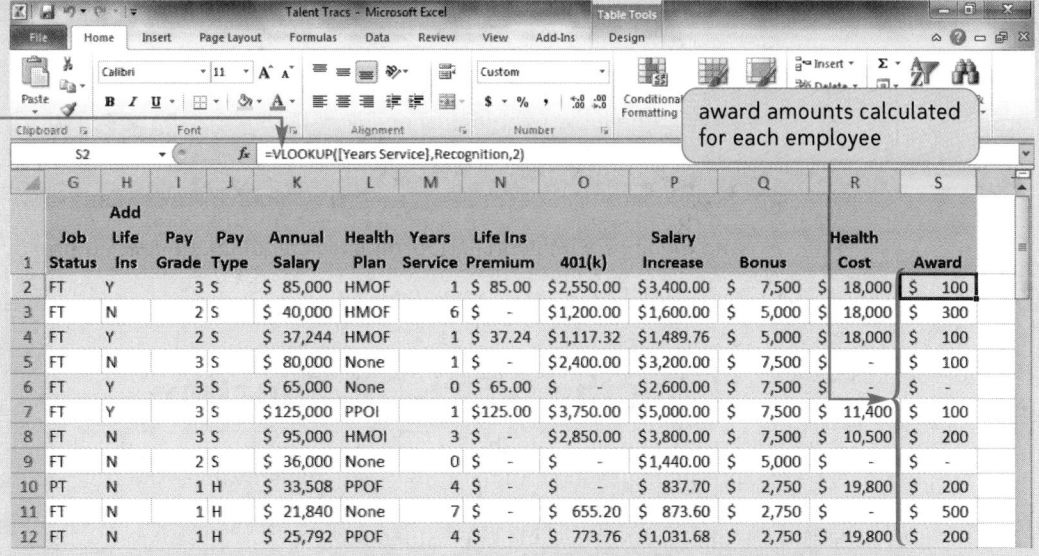

## Looking Up Values Using the HLOOKUP Function

The HLOOKUP function is very similar to the VLOOKUP function. The **HLOOKUP function** (horizontal lookup function) searches horizontally across the top row of the lookup table and retrieves the value in the column you specify. You use the HLOOKUP function when the comparison values are located in the first row of the lookup table and you want to look down a specified number of rows to find the data to enter in another cell.

The HLOOKUP function has the syntax

HLOOKUP(lookup_value, table_array, row_index_num, [range_lookup])

where *lookup_value* is the value you want to use to search the first row of the lookup table, *table_array* is the range reference of the lookup table or its table name, *row_index_num* is the number of the row in the lookup table that contains the value you want to return, and *range_lookup* indicates whether the compare values are a range of values or an exact match. When you use a range of values (such as in a tax rate table), you set the *range_lookup* value to TRUE; when you want the *lookup_value* to exactly match a value in the first row of the *table_array*, you set the *range_lookup* value to FALSE. The *range_lookup* argument is optional; if you don't include a *range_lookup* value, the value is considered TRUE (an approximate match).

The major difference between HLOOKUP and VLOOKUP functions is the way the lookup tables are organized. Figure 7-28 shows how the HealthPlanRates and Recognition tables would be arranged for a lookup using the HLOOKUP function.

**Figure 7-29** **Lookup tables for the HLOOKUP function**

| | A | B | C | D | E | F | G |
|---|---|---|---|---|---|---|---|
| 1 | | Health Rate Plans | | | | | |
| 2 | | | | | | | |
| 3 | | Plan | HMOF | HMOI | PPOF | PPOI | None |
| 4 | | Monthly Premium | $ 1,500 | $ 875 | $ 1,650 | $ 950 | $  - |
| 5 | | | | | | | |
| 6 | | | | | | | |
| 7 | | Recognition Award | | | | | |
| 8 | | | | | | | |
| 9 | | Years of Service | 0 | 1 | 3 | 5 | 7 |
| 10 | | Recognition Award | $  - | $ 100 | $ 200 | $ 300 | $ 500 |
| 11 | | | | | | | |

With the lookup tables arranged as shown in Figure 7-29, the exact match formula to calculate the annual health plan cost is

=HLOOKUP([HealthPlan],HealthPlanRates,2,FALSE)*12

and the approximate match formula to calculate the recognition award is

=HLOOKUP([Years Service],Recognition,2)

# Using the IFERROR Function

**Error values** indicate that some element in a formula or a cell referenced in a formula is preventing Excel from returning a calculated value. An error value begins with a number sign (#) followed by an error name that indicates the type of error. For instance, the error value #N/A appears in a Health Cost cell when the VLOOKUP function cannot find the health plan code in the HealthPlanRates lookup table because it was entered incorrectly. Figure 7-30 describes common error values you might see in workbooks.

| Figure 7-30 | Excel error values |
| --- | --- |

| Error Value | Description of Error |
| --- | --- |
| #DIV/0! | The formula or function contains a number divided by 0. |
| #NAME? | Excel doesn't recognize text in the formula or function, such as when the function name is misspelled. |
| #N/A | A value is not available to a function or formula, which can occur when an invalid value is specified in the LOOKUP function. |
| #NULL! | A formula or function requires two cell ranges to intersect, but they don't. |
| #NUM! | Invalid numbers are used in a formula or function, such as text entered in a function that requires a number. |
| #REF! | A cell reference used in a formula or function is no longer valid, which can occur when the cell used by the function was deleted from the worksheet. |
| #VALUE! | The wrong type of argument is used in a function or formula. This can occur when you supply a range of values to a function that requires a single value. |

These error value messages are not particularly descriptive or helpful. To display a more descriptive message that helps users fix the problem, you can use the IFERROR function. The IFERROR function can determine if a cell contains an error value and then display the message you choose rather than the default error value. The IFERROR function has the syntax

```
IFERROR(expression, valueIfError)
```

where *expression* is the formula you want to check for an error, and *valueIfError* is the message you want displayed if Excel detects an error in the formula you are checking. If Excel does not detect an error, the result of the *expression* is displayed.

The IFERROR function enables you to easily find and handle formula errors. For example, you can enter the following formula to determine whether an invalid code was entered in the Health Plan column of the Employee table and then display a more descriptive message if Excel detects an error:

```
=IFERROR(VLOOKUP(L2,HealthPlanRates,2,False)*12,"Invalid code")
```

Based on this formula, if the value in cell L2 is HMOF, the result of the VLOOKUP formula is $1,500 (the corresponding value from the HealthPlanRates table), the first argument in the IFERROR function (shown in purple) is executed, and the health cost is displayed. On the other hand, if cell L2 has an invalid health plan code, such as HMOG, the VLOOKUP function returns the error value #N/A, the second argument in the IFERROR function (shown in red) is executed, and "Invalid code" is displayed.

You will scroll the Health Cost column to verify that all employees have an amount assigned to Health Cost.

### To check for an error value in the Health Cost column:

1. Scroll to row **54** of the Health Plan column to see the error value #N/A in cell R54.

2. Click cell **R54**. See Figure 7-31.

**Figure 7-31** **Error value in the Health Cost column**

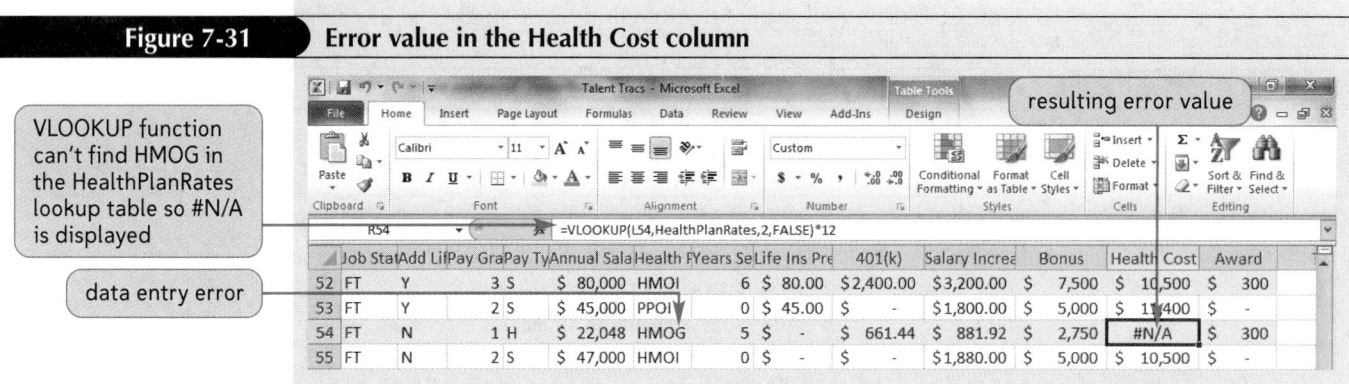

VLOOKUP function can't find HMOG in the HealthPlanRates lookup table so #N/A is displayed

data entry error

R54    =VLOOKUP(L54,HealthPlanRates,2,FALSE)*12

| | Job Stat | Add Lif | Pay Gra | Pay Ty | Annual Sala | Health P | Years Se | Life Ins Pre | 401(k) | Salary Increa | Bonus | Health Cost | Award |
|---|---|---|---|---|---|---|---|---|---|---|---|---|---|
| 52 | FT | Y | 3 | S | $ 80,000 | HMOI | 6 | $ 80.00 | $2,400.00 | $3,200.00 | $ 7,500 | $ 10,500 | $ 300 |
| 53 | FT | Y | 2 | S | $ 45,000 | PPOI | 0 | $ 45.00 | $ - | $1,800.00 | $ 5,000 | $ 11,400 | $ - |
| 54 | FT | N | 1 | H | $ 22,048 | HMOG | 5 | $ - | $ 661.44 | $ 881.92 | $ 2,750 | #N/A | $ 300 |
| 55 | FT | N | 2 | S | $ 47,000 | HMOI | 0 | $ - | $ - | $1,880.00 | $ 5,000 | $ 10,500 | $ - |

resulting error value

**3.** In row 54 in the Health Plan column, observe that the health plan code is HMOG, which is an invalid code.

Rita asks you to modify the formulas in the Health Cost column so that the descriptive error message "Invalid code" appears rather than the error value. The IFERROR function will check for errors in the formula, and display the error message you create rather than the error value if it finds an error.

You'll nest the VLOOKUP function within the IFERROR function to display the message "Invalid code" in the Health Cost column if Excel detects an error value.

## To nest the VLOOKUP function within the IFERROR function:

**1.** Double-click cell **R54** (the cell in row 54 of the Health Cost column) to enter Edit mode. The formula =VLOOKUP(L54,HealthPlanRates,2,False)*12 appears in the cell and the formula bar. You'll nest this formula within the IFERROR function.

**2.** Click to the right of **=** (the equal sign), and then type **IFERROR(** to begin entering the IFERROR function. The first argument in the IFERROR function is the formula you want to use if no error value is found; this is the VLOOKUP function already entered in the cell.

**3.** Move the insertion point to the right of the VLOOKUP formula, and then type **,"Invalid code")** to add the text you want to display if an error is found.

**4.** Press the **Enter** key. The error message "Invalid code" appears in cell R54, and the revised formula is automatically copied to all cells in the column. See Figure 7-32.

**Figure 7-32** **Invalid code message in the Health Cost column**

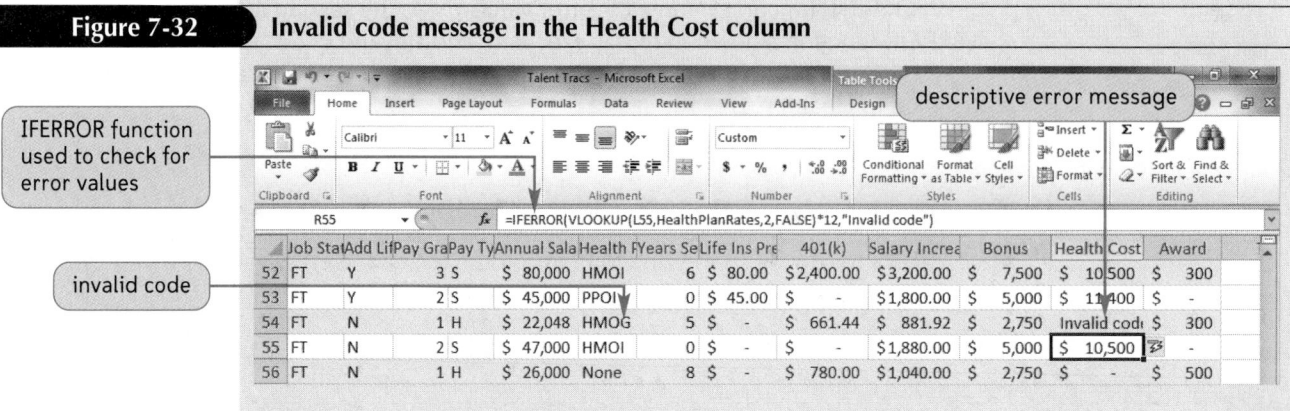

IFERROR function used to check for error values

invalid code

R55    fx =IFERROR(VLOOKUP(L55,HealthPlanRates,2,FALSE)*12,"Invalid code")

descriptive error message

| | Job Stat | Add Lif | Pay Gra | Pay Ty | Annual Sala | Health P | Years Se | Life Ins Pre | 401(k) | Salary Increa | Bonus | Health Cost | Award |
|---|---|---|---|---|---|---|---|---|---|---|---|---|---|
| 52 | FT | Y | 3 | S | $ 80,000 | HMOI | 6 | $ 80.00 | $2,400.00 | $3,200.00 | $ 7,500 | $ 10,500 | $ 300 |
| 53 | FT | Y | 2 | S | $ 45,000 | PPOI | 0 | $ 45.00 | $ - | $1,800.00 | $ 5,000 | $ 11,400 | $ - |
| 54 | FT | N | 1 | H | $ 22,048 | HMOG | 5 | $ - | $ 661.44 | $ 881.92 | $ 2,750 | Invalid code | $ 300 |
| 55 | FT | N | 2 | S | $ 47,000 | HMOI | 0 | $ - | $ - | $1,880.00 | $ 5,000 | $ 10,500 | $ - |
| 56 | FT | N | 1 | H | $ 26,000 | None | 8 | $ - | $ 780.00 | $1,040.00 | $ 2,750 | $ - | $ 500 |

**Trouble?** If the error #NAME? appears in cell R54, you may have omitted quotation marks around the descriptive error message, "Invalid code." Correct the formula, and then continue with Step 5.

5. In cell L54 (the cell in row 54 of the Health Plan column), enter **HMOF**. The health plan code you entered is valid, so the health cost value $18,000 appears in cell R54.

6. Scroll to the top of the table, click cell **R2**, and observe in the formula bar that the IFERROR formula was copied to this cell.

In this session, you used nested IF functions to determine employee bonuses, the VLOOKUP function to calculate health cost and recognition award amounts, and the IFERROR function to display a descriptive message if invalid health plan codes are entered in the Employee table. In the next session, you will use conditional formatting and the COUNTIF, SUMIF, and AVERAGEIF functions to report on employee salaries.

**REVIEW**

## Session 7.2 Quick Check

1. When you include one IF function inside another IF function, you have created a(n) _____.
2. If cell Y5 displays the value 24, cell Y6 displays the value 27, and cell Y7 contains the following formula, what is displayed in cell Y7?
   `=IF(Y5>Y6,"Older",IF(Y5<Y6,"Younger","Same Age"))`
3. Explain the difference between an exact match and an approximate match table lookup.
4. A customer table includes columns for name, street address, city, state abbreviation, and zip. A second table includes state abbreviations and state names from all 50 states (one state per row). You need to add a new column to the customer table with the state name. What is the most appropriate function to use to display the state name in this new column?
5. Convert the following table that shows the criteria used to determine a student's level to a table that can be used in a VLOOKUP function to display the level of each student:

   | Earned Credits | Level |
   |---|---|
   | 0 but < 30 | Freshman |
   | 30 but < 60 | Sophomore |
   | 60 but < 90 | Junior |
   | 90 or more | Senior |

6. In cell X5, the error value #DIV/0! appears when you divide by 0. Use the IFERROR function with the formula =W5/W25 so that instead of the error value #DIV/0! being displayed, the message "Dividing by zero" appears in the cell.
7. The following Sales Tax Rate table and the _____ function could be used to display the sales tax rate for a customer in one of these four states.

   | State | AZ | NM | OK | TX |
   |---|---|---|---|---|
   | Sales Tax Rate | 8.5% | 7% | 9% | 9.25% |

# SESSION 7.3 VISUAL OVERVIEW

Highlighting duplicate values adds formatting to cells that have the same entry. In this instance, a yellow fill highlights cells with the same employee ID.

The Conditional Formatting button provides access to the Duplicate Values conditional format and the Manage Rules option, which opens the Conditional Formatting Rules Manager dialog box.

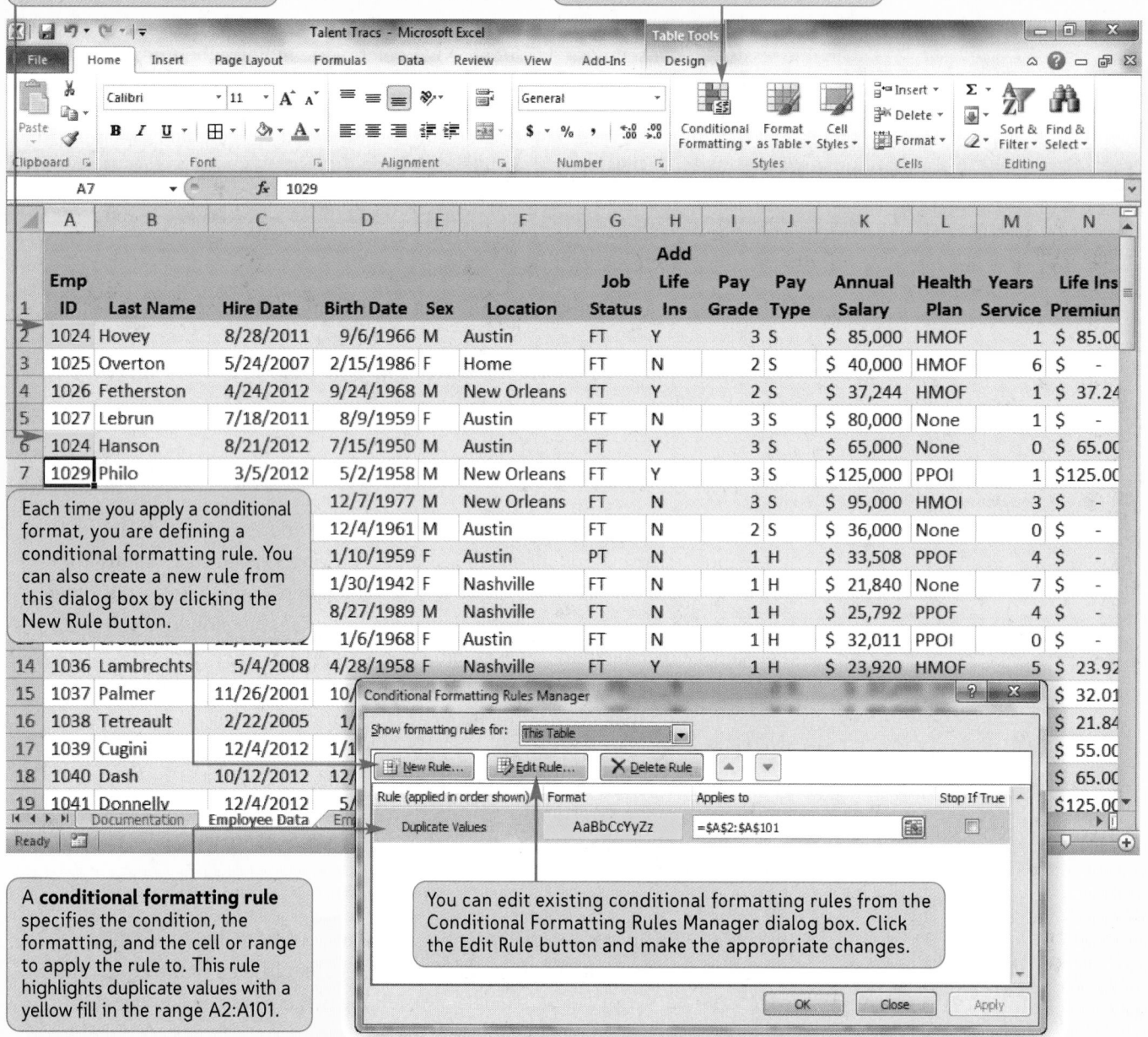

Each time you apply a conditional format, you are defining a conditional formatting rule. You can also create a new rule from this dialog box by clicking the New Rule button.

A **conditional formatting rule** specifies the condition, the formatting, and the cell or range to apply the rule to. This rule highlights duplicate values with a yellow fill in the range A2:A101.

You can edit existing conditional formatting rules from the Conditional Formatting Rules Manager dialog box. Click the Edit Rule button and make the appropriate changes.

# CONDITIONAL FORMATTING

This formula must be fully qualified because the Employee table is located in a different worksheet.

These formulas use fully qualified structured references to make them easier to create and understand.

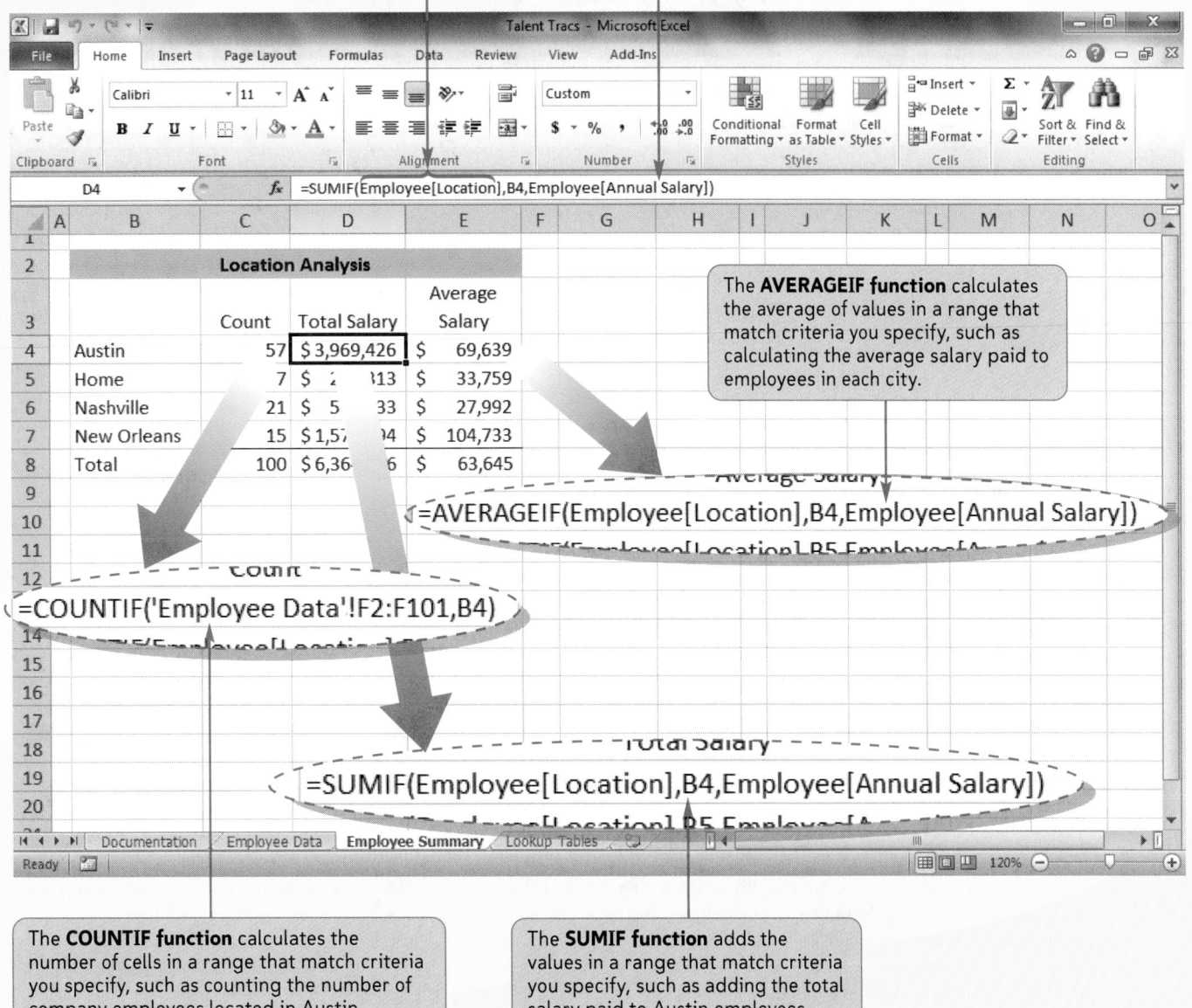

The **AVERAGEIF function** calculates the average of values in a range that match criteria you specify, such as calculating the average salary paid to employees in each city.

=AVERAGEIF(Employee[Location],B4,Employee[Annual Salary])

=COUNTIF('Employee Data'!F2:F101,B4)

=SUMIF(Employee[Location],B4,Employee[Annual Salary])

The **COUNTIF function** calculates the number of cells in a range that match criteria you specify, such as counting the number of company employees located in Austin.

The **SUMIF function** adds the values in a range that match criteria you specify, such as adding the total salary paid to Austin employees.

# Conditional Formatting

Conditional formatting changes a cell's formatting when its contents match a specified condition. You've already used conditional formatting to highlight cells based on their values and to add data bars that graph the relative values in a range. You can also use conditional formatting to highlight duplicate values in a column of data.

**PROSKILLS**

### Decision Making: Using Conditional Formatting to Evaluate Data

Decisions are made by evaluating data. However, this becomes complex when large quantities of data or dynamic data are involved. In these instances, conditional formatting can be a useful tool to help with your decision making. Conditional formatting is designed to make searching a data range both simple and efficient. For instance, you can quickly find the latest market prices in a real-time stock quote spreadsheet by using conditional formatting to highlight them. You can use conditional formatting to find stocks whose price drops below the target buy price by highlighting the row of any stock that meets the buy criteria. You can use conditional formatting to quickly identify bank accounts with a bank balance that is overdrawn by highlighting accounts with a negative balance. Mastering the art of conditional formatting will help you make better decisions.

## Highlighting Duplicate Values

Excel is often used to manage lists of data, such as employee information, inventory, or phone numbers. These types of lists often include data that repeats in different records, such as the employee's state in his or her mailing address, a warehouse location for inventory, or an area code for phone numbers. On the other hand, some of the data is usually unique for each record, such as an employee ID or a product number. As the list of data becomes more extensive, duplicate entries may inadvertently occur. One way to identify unintended duplicate entries is to use conditional formatting to highlight duplicate values in a range with a font and/or fill color. This color coding makes it easier to identify the duplicates so you can then determine whether an entry needs to be corrected. In addition to the colors provided, you can create a custom format for the highlighting.

**REFERENCE**

### Highlighting Duplicate Values

- Select the range in which to highlight duplicate values.
- In the Styles group on the Home tab, click the Conditional Formatting button, point to Highlight Cells Rules, and then click Duplicate Values.
- Select the appropriate formatting option.
- Click the OK button.

You will use duplicate value highlighting to verify that each cell in the employee ID column has a unique entry. Rita believes the current employee ID data in the Employee table is accurate, but wants you to use conditional formatting to ensure that there are no duplicate entries.

### To highlight duplicate employee IDs:

▶ **1.** If you took a break at the end of the previous session, make sure the Talent Tracs workbook is open and the Employee Data worksheet is active.

> **2.** Scroll to column **A**, and then select the data in the Emp ID column. Rows 2 through 101 in the Emp ID column are selected.

> **3.** Click the **Home** tab on the Ribbon, if necessary, and then click the **Conditional Formatting** button in the Styles group.

> **4.** Point to **Highlight Cells Rules**, and then click **Duplicate Values**. The Duplicate Values dialog box opens.

> **5.** Click the **values with** arrow to display a list of formatting options, and then click **Custom Format** to create a format that is not in the list. The Format Cells dialog box opens. You'll change the background fill color to red.

> **6.** Click the **Fill** tab, and then, in the Background Color palette, click **red** (the second color in the last row).

> **7.** Click the **OK** button in the Format Cells dialog box, and then click the **OK** button in the Duplicate Values dialog box. Any duplicate values in the ID column appear in a red cell.

> **8.** Scroll the table to ensure that no duplicate values are found.

After you enter a formula, you should test all situations to verify how the formula performs in each case. In this case, you should test the column both with duplicate values and without duplicate values. No duplicate records appear in the Employee table, so you'll change the ID of the last record from 1123 to 1024, which is the ID of the first employee. The backgrounds of the cells with the duplicate IDs should turn red, which will confirm that the conditional formatting is working as intended. Then, you will return the ID to its original value and confirm that the duplicate value highlighting disappears.

### To test the duplicate value conditional formatting:

> **1.** Click in the **Name** box, and then enter **A101**. The active cell moves to the last record in the Employee table.

> **2.** In cell A101, enter **1024**. The ID changes from 1123 to 1024 and cell A101 is filled with a red background because it contains a duplicate ID. See Figure 7-33.

| **Figure 7-33** | **Duplicate record highlighted** |

duplicate value is highlighted in red

> **3.** Press the **Ctrl+Home** keys. Cell A1 becomes the active cell. Cell A2 has a red background fill because it has the same ID that you entered in cell A101. The conditional formatting correctly identified the duplicate values.

## Using the Conditional Formatting Rules Manager

Each time you apply a conditional format, you are defining a conditional formatting rule. A rule specifies the type of condition (such as formatting cells greater than a specified value), the type of formatting when that condition occurs (such as light red fill with dark red text), and the cell or range the formatting is applied to. You can edit existing conditional formatting rules from the Conditional Formatting Rules Manager dialog box.

**REFERENCE**

*Editing a Conditional Formatting Rule*

- Select the range with the conditional formatting you want to edit.
- In the Styles group on the Home tab, click the Conditional Formatting button, and then click Manage Rules.
- Select the rule you want to edit, and then click the Edit Rule button.
- In the Select a Rule Type box, click a rule type, and then make the appropriate changes in the Edit the Rule Description section.
- Click the OK button in each dialog box.

The red background fill makes the cell content difficult to read. Rita asks you to use a yellow fill color to better contrast with the black text. You'll use the Conditional Formatting Rules Manager dialog box to edit the rule that specifies the formatting applied to duplicate values in the ID column.

**To change the duplicate values background fill color:**

▶ 1. In the Styles group on the Home tab, click the **Conditional Formatting** button, and then click **Manage Rules**. The Conditional Formatting Rules Manager dialog box opens, listing all the formatting rules for the current selection, which, in this case, is the Employee table.

▶ 2. Verify that the Show formatting rules for box shows **This Table**. All the rules currently in effect in the Employee table are displayed. You can add new rules and edit or delete existing rules. You also can control which formatting rules are displayed in the dialog box, such as all rules in a specific worksheet or table. See Figure 7-34.

| **Figure 7-34** | **Conditional Formatting Rules Manager dialog box** |

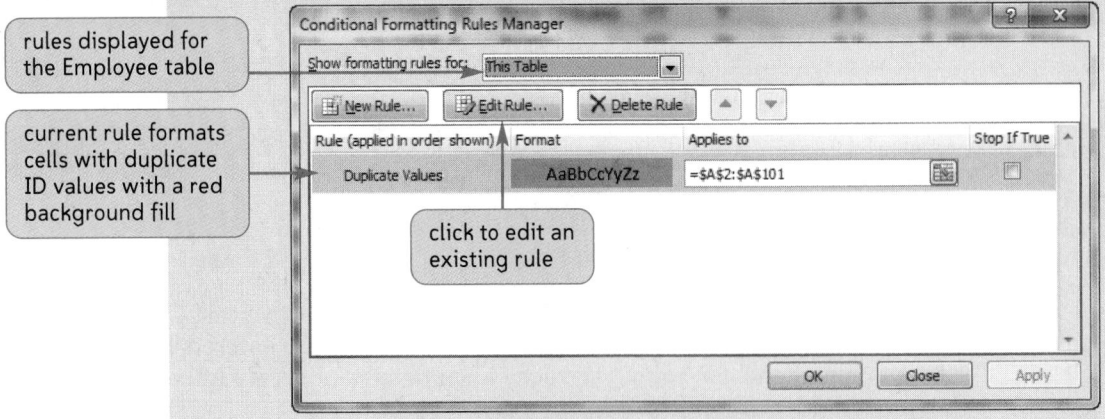

rules displayed for the Employee table

current rule formats cells with duplicate ID values with a red background fill

click to edit an existing rule

3. Click **Duplicate Values** in the Rule list to select the rule, and then click the **Edit Rule** button. The Edit Formatting Rule dialog box opens. See Figure 7-35.

| Figure 7-35 | Edit Formatting Rule dialog box |
| --- | --- |

selected rule type

preview of the formatting for the selected rule type

click to open the Format Cells dialog box

4. Click the **Format** button. The Format Cells dialog box opens.

5. Click the **Fill** tab, if necessary, and then, in the Background Color palette, click **yellow** (the fourth color in the last row).

6. Click the **OK** button in each dialog box. The duplicate records in the table are formatted with a yellow background color. See Figure 7-36.

| Figure 7-36 | Revised conditional formatting for duplicate records |
| --- | --- |

background color of duplicate value is yellow

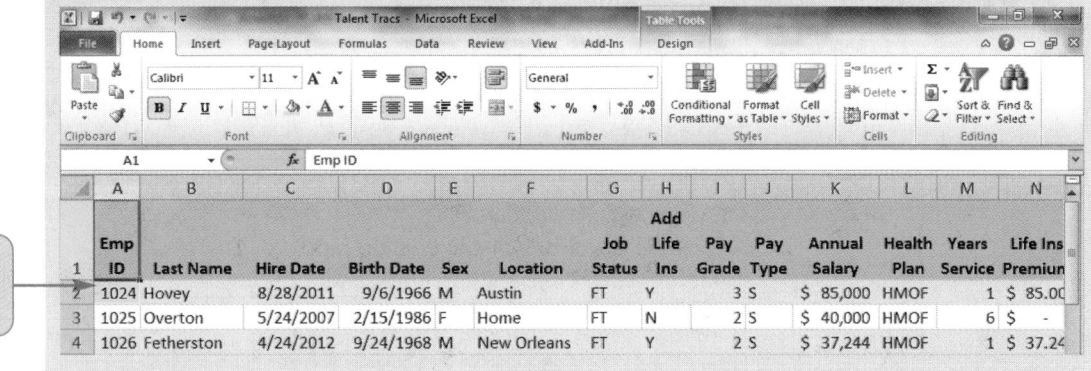

The cell text is easier to read on the yellow background. You'll correct the duplicate ID in cell A101 by entering the employee's actual ID number. The conditional format will remain active, and apply to any new records that Rita adds to the Employee table. Keep in mind that the Duplicate Values rule enables you to verify that each entry in the ID column is unique, but it does not ensure that each unique value is accurate.

**To correct the duplicate ID:**

1. Make cell **A101** the active cell, and then enter **1123**. The employee's ID is updated and the conditional formatting disappears because the value in the ID column is no longer a duplicate.

2. Scroll to the top of the Employee table, and verify that the conditional formatting no longer appears in cell A2.

INSIGHT

*Creating a Formula to Conditionally Format Cells*

Sometimes the built-in conditional formatting rules do not apply the formatting you need. In these instances, you may be able to create a conditional formatting rule based on a formula that uses a logical expression to describe the condition you want. For example, you can create a formula that uses conditional formatting to compare cells in different columns or to highlight an entire row.

When you create the formula, keep in mind the following guidelines:
- The formula must start with an equal sign.
- The formula must be in the form of a logical test that results in a True or False value.
- In most cases, the formula should use relative references and point to the first row of data in the table. If the formula references a cell or range outside the table, use an absolute reference.
- After you create the formula, enter test values to ensure the conditional formatting works in all situations that you intended.

For example, to use conditional formatting to highlight whether the hire date entered in column C is less than the birth date entered in column D, you need to enter a formula that applies conditional formatting that compares cells in different columns of a table. The following steps describe how to create this formula:

1. Select the range you want to format (in this case, the Hire Date column).
2. Click the Conditional Formatting button in the Styles group on the Home tab, and then click New Rule.
3. In the Select a Rule Type box, click the "Use a formula to determine which cells to format" rule.
4. In the Format values where this formula is true box, enter the appropriate formula (in this case, =C2<D2).
5. Click the Format button to open the Format Cells dialog box, and select the formatting you want to apply.
6. Click the OK button in each dialog box.

Another example is to highlight the entire row if an employee has 10 or more years of service. In this case, you would select the range of data, such as A2:S101, and enter =M$2>=10 in the Format values where this formula is true box. The other steps remain the same.

# Summarizing Data Conditionally

The COUNT function tallies the number of data values in a range, the SUM function adds the values in a range, and the AVERAGE function calculates the average of the values in a range. However, sometimes you need to calculate a conditional count, sum, or average using only those cells that meet a particular condition. In those cases, you need to use the COUNTIF, SUMIF, and AVERAGEIF functions. Rita wants you to create a report that shows the number, total, and average salaries for employees in Austin, New Orleans, and Nashville as well as for those employees who work from home.

## Using the COUNTIF Function

You can calculate the number of cells in a range that match criteria you specify using the COUNTIF function, which is sometimes referred to as a **conditional count**. The COUNTIF function has the syntax

```
COUNTIF(range, criteria)
```

where *range* is the range of cells you want to count, and *criteria* is an expression that defines which cells to count.

Rita wants to know how many employees are located in Austin. You can use the COUNTIF function to find this answer because you want a conditional count (a count of employees who meet a specified criterion; in this case, employees located in Austin). The location information is stored in column F of the Employee table. To count the number of employees in Austin, you can use either one of the following formulas:

**Cell references**   =COUNTIF('Employee Data'!F2:F101,"Austin")

**Fully qualified structured references**   =COUNTIF(Employee[Location],"Austin")

With either formula, Excel counts all the cells in the Location column of the Employee table that contain the text "Austin". Because Austin is text, you must enclose it within quotation marks. Numbers are not enclosed in quotation marks.

You will enter this formula using the COUNTIF function in the Employee Summary worksheet. You will use the Insert Function dialog box to help you build the formula using worksheet and range references to calculate the number of employees who work in Austin.

### To count employees located in Austin:

1. Switch to the **Employee Summary** worksheet.

2. Click cell **C4**, and then click the **Insert Function** button $f_x$ in the formula bar. The Insert Function dialog box opens.

3. Click the **Or select a category** arrow, and then click **Statistical**.

4. In the Select a function box, double-click **COUNTIF**. The Function Arguments dialog box opens.

5. In the Range box, type **'Employee Data'!F2:F101** to enter the range to search, and then press the **Tab** key. The range 'Employee Data'!F2:F101 refers to all data values in the range F2:F101 (Location column) in the Employee Data worksheet.

6. In the Criteria box, type **B4**. Cell B4 contains "Austin," which is the criterion you want Excel to use to determine which employee records to count. See Figure 7-37.

**Figure 7-37**    Function Arguments dialog box for the COUNTIF function

beginning values in
the Location column

number of cells in the
range that contain
the criterion "Austin"

criterion to determine
which employee
records to count

> **7.** Click the **OK** button. Cell C4 remains active. The formula =COUNTIF('Employee Data'!F2:F101,B4) appears in the formula bar and 57 appears in cell C4, indicating that the company employs 57 workers in Austin. See Figure 7-38.

**Figure 7-38**    Location Analysis with Austin workers

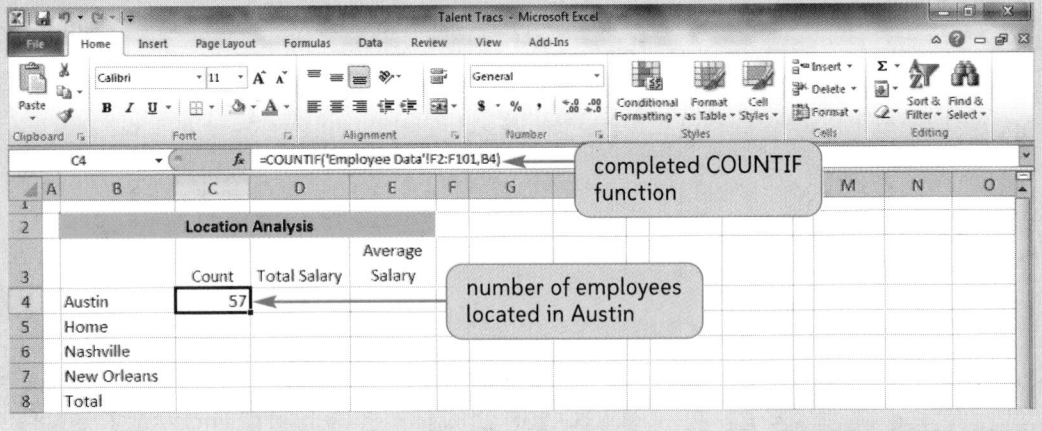

completed COUNTIF
function

number of employees
located in Austin

You will enter a similar formula to calculate the number of employees who work from home. This time, however, you will use structured references to specify the range to search.

## To count the number of employees who work from home:

> **1.** Click cell **C5**, and then click the **Insert Function** button $f_x$ in the formula bar. The Insert Function dialog box opens with the Statistical category still selected.

> **2.** In the Select a function box, double-click **COUNTIF**. The Function Arguments dialog box opens.

> **3.** In the Range box, type **Employee[Location]** to enter the range to search, and then press the **Tab** key. The range Employee[Location] is a structured reference that refers to all data values in the Location column in the Employee table (range F2:F101). The beginning values in the Location column appear to the right of the Range box.

**4.** In the Criteria box, type **B5**. Cell B5 contains "Home" (the value shown to the right of the Criteria box), which is the criterion Excel will use to determine which employee records to count.

**5.** Click the **OK** button. Cell C5 remains active. The formula =COUNTIF(Employee[Location],B5) appears in the formula bar and 7 appears in cell C5, indicating 7 employees work from home.

You need to count employees at two other locations—Nashville and New Orleans. Rather than enter the COUNTIF formula, you'll copy the formula in cell C5 to cells C6 and C7.

**To copy the COUNTIF formula:**

**1.** Copy the formula in cell **C5** to cell **C6** and cell **C7** to calculate the number of employees for Nashville (cell B6) and New Orleans (cell B7). Talent Tracs has 21 employees working in Nashville and 15 employees working in New Orleans.

**2.** In cell C8, enter the **SUM** function to calculate the total number of employees working at Talent Tracs. Talent Tracs has a total of 100 employees.

## Using the SUMIF Function

The SUMIF function adds the values in a range that meet criteria you specify. The SUMIF function is also called a **conditional sum**. The syntax of the SUMIF function is

```
SUMIF(range, criteria [, sum_range])
```

where *range* is the range of cells you want to filter before calculating a sum, *criteria* is the condition used to filter the range, and *sum_range* is the range of cells to total. The *sum_range* is optional; if you omit it, Excel will total the values specified in the *range* argument. For example, if you want to total the salaries for all employees with salaries greater than $50,000, you do not use the optional third argument.

Rita wants to know the total salaries paid to employees at each location. She can use the SUMIF function to do this, because she wants to conditionally add salaries of employees at a specified location. Location is recorded in column F of the Employee Data worksheet, and the salary data is stored in column K. You can use either of the following formulas to calculate this value:

**Cell references**
```
=SUMIF('Employee Data'!F2:F101,"Austin", 'Employee Data'!K2:K101)
```

**Fully qualified structured references**
```
=SUMIF(Employee[Location],"Austin",Employee[Annual Salary])
```

Both of these formulas state that the salary of any employee whose location is Austin will be added to the total. Using the SUMIF function, you will insert the formula with structured references into the Employee Summary worksheet.

**To sum employee salaries in different locations:**

**1.** Click cell **D4**, and then click the **Insert Function** button $f_x$ in the formula bar. The Insert Function dialog box opens.

**2.** Click the **Or select a category** arrow, and then click **Math & Trig**.

▶ **3.** In the Select a function box, double-click **SUMIF**. The Function Arguments dialog box opens.

▶ **4.** In the Range box, type **Employee[Location]** to specify the range of data to filter, and then press the **Tab** key. The range Employee[Location] is a structured reference that refers to all data values in the Location column in the Employee table (range F2:F101).

▶ **5.** In the Criteria box, type **B4** and then press the **Tab** key. Cell B4 contains "Austin" (shown to the right of the Criteria box), which is the criterion Excel will use to determine which employee records to sum.

▶ **6.** In the Sum_range box, type the structured reference **Employee[Annual Salary]** to indicate that the Annual Salary column in the Employee table contains the data to sum in the filtered rows. The values to the right of the Sum_range box are the amounts in the filtered Annual Salary column. See Figure 7-39.

| Figure 7-39 | Function Arguments dialog box for the SUMIF function |
|---|---|

▶ **7.** Click the **OK** button. Cell D4 is active. The formula =SUMIF(Employee[Location], B4,Employee[Annual Salary]) appears in the formula bar and $3,969,426 appears in cell D4, indicating the total annual salaries paid to Austin employees.

▶ **8.** Copy the SUMIF formula in cell D4 to the range **D5:D7**. The total annual salary for employees working from home is $236,313. The total annual salary for Nashville employees is $587,833. The total annual salary for New Orleans employees is $1,570,994.

▶ **9.** In cell D8, enter a SUM function to calculate the total salaries of all employees. The total salary of all Talent Tracs employees is $6,364,566.

## Using the AVERAGEIF Function

The AVERAGEIF function is similar to the SUMIF function. You use the AVERAGEIF function to calculate the average of values in a range that meet criteria you specify. The syntax of the AVERAGEIF function is

```
AVERAGEIF(range, criteria [, average_range])
```

where *range* is the range of cells you want to filter before calculating the average, *criteria* is the condition used to filter the range, and *average_range* is the range of cells to average. The *average_range* is optional; if you omit it, Excel will average the values specified in the *range* argument.

Rita wants to know the average salaries paid to employees at each location. Location is recorded in column F of the Employee Data worksheet, and the annual salary data is stored in column K. The formula to calculate this value is:

**Cell references**

`=AVERAGEIF('Employee Data'!F2:F101,"Austin", 'Employee Data'!K2:K101)`

**Fully qualified structured references**

`=AVERAGEIF(Employee[Location],"Austin",Employee[Annual Salary])`

Both of these formulas state that the annual salary of any employee whose location is Austin will be included in the average. You will enter the formula using the AVERAGEIF function with structured references into the Employee Summary worksheet.

### To average employee salaries in different locations:

▶ 1. Click cell **E4**, and then click the **Insert Function** button $f_x$ in the formula bar. The Insert Function dialog box opens.

▶ 2. Click the **Or select a category** arrow, and then click **Statistical**.

▶ 3. In the Select a function box, double-click **AVERAGEIF**. The Function Arguments dialog box opens.

▶ 4. In the Range box, type the structured reference **Employee[Location]** to specify the range of data to filter, and then press the **Tab** key. The range Employee[Location] is a structured reference that refers to all data values in the Location column in the Employee table (range F2:F101).

▶ 5. In the Criteria box, type **B4** and then press the **Tab** key. Cell B4 contains "Austin" (shown to the right of the Criteria box), which is the criterion Excel will use to determine which employee records to average.

▶ 6. In the Average_range box, type **Employee[Annual Salary]** to indicate that the Annual Salary column in the Employee table contains the data to average in the filtered rows. See Figure 7-40.

| **Figure 7-40** | **Function Arguments dialog box for the AVERAGEIF function** |

▶ 7. Click the **OK** button. Cell E4 remains active. The formula =AVERAGEIF(Employee [Location],B4,Employee[Annual Salary]) appears in the formula bar and $69,639 appears in cell E4, indicating the average salary paid to Austin employees.

▶ 8. Copy the formula in cell E4 to the range **E5:E7**. Talent Tracs pays an average of $33,759 to employees working at home, $27,992 to employees working in Nashville, and $104,733 to employees working in New Orleans.

9. In cell E8, enter **=D8/C8** to calculate the average salary at Talent Tracs by dividing the total salaries at Talent Tracs by the number of employees at the company. The average salary for all Talent Tracs employees is $63,646.

10. If necessary, format the range E4:E8 in the **Accounting** number format with no decimal places.

11. Add a bottom border to the range C7:E7, and then click cell **E4** to deselect the range. See Figure 7-41.

**Figure 7-41** | **Completed Location Analysis report**

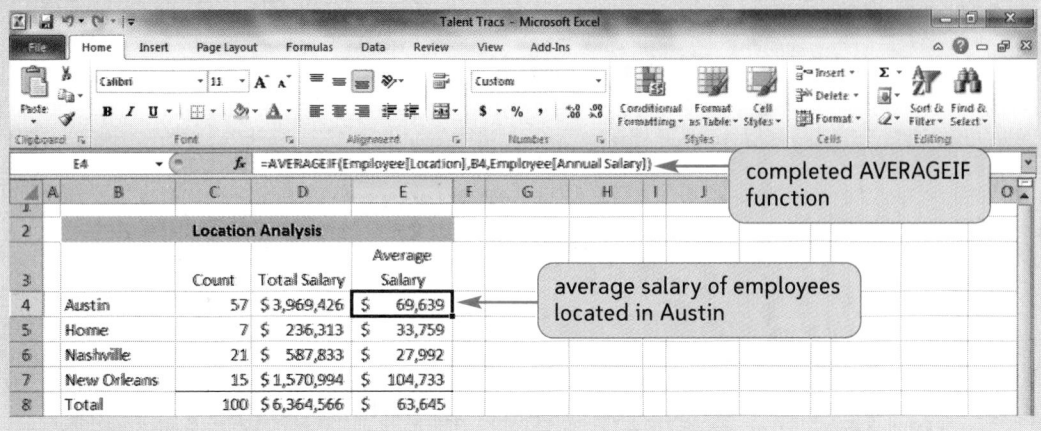

As Rita enters new employees or edits the location or annual salary values of current employees, the values in the Employee Summary worksheet will be automatically updated because the formulas reference the Employee table.

Rita has recently hired a new employee and asks you to add the new record to the Excel table.

## To add a record to the Employee table:

1. Switch to the **Employee Data** worksheet, and then click cell **A102**. You will enter the new employee record in this row.

2. In the range A102:L102 enter **1124** for Emp ID, **Joplin** for last name, **4/1/2013** for hire date, **11/15/1970** for birth date, **M** for sex, **Home** for location, **PT** for job status, **N** for Add Life Ins, **1** for pay grade, **H** for pay type, **23000** for annual salary, and **None** for health plan, and then click cell **A103**. The new employee record is added to the Employee table.

3. Switch to the **Employee Summary** worksheet. The Location Analysis report has been updated to reflect the new employee. See Figure 7-42.

**Figure 7-42**    **Updated Location Analysis report**

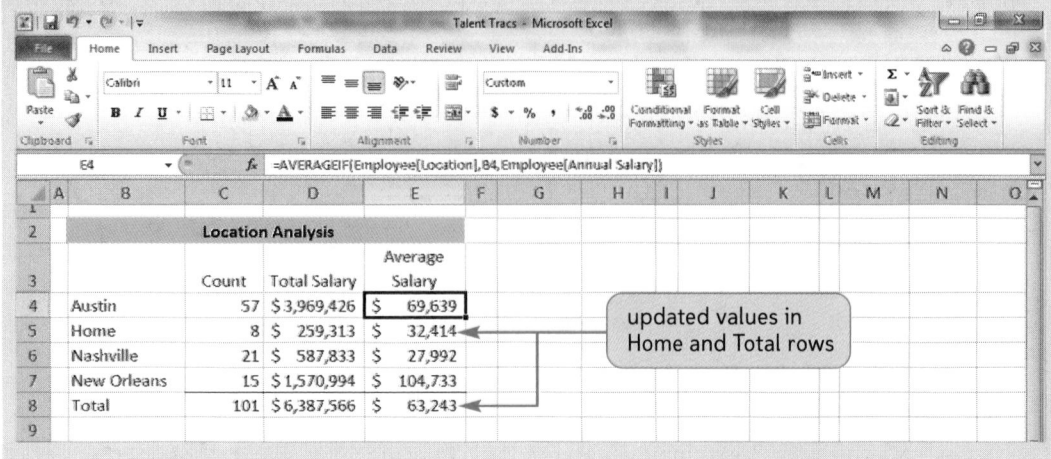

If the employee data had been stored as a range of data instead of an Excel table, the Location Analysis report would not have been automatically updated. Instead, you would have had to modify all the formulas in the report to reflect the expanded range of employee data. Rita is pleased with the formulas you added to the Employee Data and Employee Summary worksheets.

## Session 7.3 Quick Check

REVIEW

1. Would you apply the duplicate value conditional formatting rule to a table column of last names? Why or why not?
2. If you receive a worksheet that includes conditional formatting, which dialog box would you use to find out what criteria were used for the formatting?
3. Explain what the formula =COUNTIF(Employee[Sex],"F") calculates.
4. Explain what the formula =AVERAGEIF(Employee[Pay Type],"H",Employee[Annual Salary]) calculates.
5. Explain what the formula =SUMIF(Employee[Job Status],"FT",Employee[Annual Salary]) calculates.
6. Explain what the formula =COUNTIF(Employee[Annual Salary],">100000") calculates.
7. True or False. To display the number of females working from home, you could use the COUNTIF function.
8. True or False. Applying the duplicate value conditional formatting rule deletes the duplicate record.

*Practice the skills you learned in the tutorial using the same case scenario.*

**PRACTICE**

## Review Assignments

**Data File needed for the Review Assignments: Tracs.xlsx**

Rita wants you to try some alternative calculations for bonuses and benefits for the Talent Tracs employees. Complete the following:

1. Open the **Tracs** workbook located in the Excel7\Review folder included with your Data Files, save the workbook as **Tracs Employees** in the same folder, and then, in the Documentation worksheet, enter your name and the date.

2. Go to the Employee Data worksheet, and then rename the Excel table as **EmpData**.

3. Employees who elect additional life insurance coverage (Add Life Ins) pay 0.1 percent times their annual salary. The life insurance premium rate of 0.1 percent is entered in cell Y5. Employees who do not elect additional coverage pay nothing. In the Life Ins Premium column, enter an IF function to calculate the life insurance premiums; use a reference to cell **Y5** to obtain the life insurance rate and enter **0** for employees who do not elect coverage.

4. All full-time (Job Status) employees over the age of 30 (Age) are eligible for the 401(k) benefit. In the 401(k) column, enter the IF and AND functions to calculate the 401(k) benefit as 3 percent of annual salary; use a reference to cell **Y6** to obtain the 401(k) matching percent rate (3 percent). If the employee is not eligible, enter **0**.

5. All employees with one or more years of service (Years Service) are eligible for a bonus. Pay Grade 1 employees receive $3,000 (cell Y2), Pay Grade 2 employees receive $6,000 (cell Y3), and Pay Grade 3 employees receive $8,000 (cell Y4). In the Bonus column, enter nested IF functions to calculate the bonus. For employees not eligible for a bonus, display the label **NE**.

6. In the Salary Increase column, enter IF and OR functions to insert the text **Not Eligible** if the individual's job status is a consultant (CN) or the pay grade is 4. Leave the cell blank if the individual is eligible for a salary increase.

7. In the Health Cost column, enter the HLOOKUP function to do an exact match lookup to calculate the health plan cost. The layout of HealthPlanRates data ($B$2:$F$3) in the Lookup Tables worksheet has been revised to work with the HLOOKUP function. Use the range address reference in the HLOOKUP function to reference HealthPlanRates data.

8. In the Award column, modify the VLOOKUP function to incorporate the IFERROR function and display the message **Invalid hire date**. Test the modified formula by changing the date in cell C2 from 3/13/2008 to **13/13/2008**. Increase the column width to view the entire message.

9. In the Emp ID column, change the format color of the duplicate value conditional formatting rule to Green (the sixth color in the last row of the Background Color palette) using the Conditional Formatting Rules Manager dialog box.

10. Go to the Reports worksheet, and then enter the COUNTIF function in cells C4 and C5 to count the number of female and male employees.

11. In cells D4 and D5, enter the AVERAGEIF function to calculate the average salary of female employees and the average salary of male employees.

12. Save and close the workbook. Submit the finished workbook to your instructor, either in printed or electronic form, as requested.

Apply the skills
you learned to
analyze and
summarize
sales data.

APPLY

## Case Problem 1

**Data File needed for this Case Problem: Modem.xlsx**

*PC-Market Distribution*   Linda Klaussen works for PC-Market Distribution, a computer supply store. She needs your help with designing an Excel workbook to enter purchase order information. She has already entered the product information on PC-Market's line of modems. She wants you to insert a lookup function to look up data from the product table. The company also offers three shipping options—Standard, Express, and Overnight—that vary in price. She wants the purchase order worksheet to be able to calculate the total cost of the order, including the type of shipping the customer requests. Complete the following:

1. Open the **Modem** workbook located in the Excel7\Case1 folder included with your Data Files, save the workbook as **PC Modem** in the same folder, and then, in the Documentation worksheet, enter your name and the date.

2. Go to the Purchase Order worksheet. In cell B5, enter the Product ID **1050**. In cell C7, create a lookup function to display the product type. In cell C8, create a lookup function to display the model name. In cell C9, create a lookup function to display the price. Product information is displayed in the Product List worksheet.

3. If an incorrect Product ID is entered in cell B5, cells C7, C8, and C9 will display the #N/A error value. Modify the formula in these cells so that **Product ID not found** is displayed in the cell if the ID entered is not found.

4. In the range D40:E42, enter labels and shipping costs based on the following information: **Standard**, **$9.50**; **Express**, **$14.50**; and **Overnight**, **$18.50**. In cell B15, enter **Express**.

5. In cell C17, use nested IF functions to display the shipping costs for the option entered in cell B15. If the shipping option in cell B15 is blank, then cell C17 should be blank. (*Hint:* The IF functions should reference the cells in the range D40:E42.)

6. In cell C19, enter a formula to display the total cost of the product (price times quantity) plus shipping. In cell B12, enter **4**.

7. In cell C19, modify the formula so that if the cell equals an error value (#Value!), the message **Check Product ID, Quantity, or Shipping option** is displayed.

8. Go to the Product List worksheet, and then use conditional formatting to highlight all duplicate values in the ID column with the formatting you choose. To test that conditional formatting is working, temporarily change the Product ID in cell A119 to **1121**. When the test is completed, return the value in cell A119 to **1122**.

9. In the Product List worksheet, use conditional formatting to highlight all prices above $300 with the formatting you choose.

10. Go to the Summary worksheet, and then enter appropriate functions in the range B5:C7 to determine the average modem price and count for each modem type.

11. Save and close the workbook. Submit the finished workbook to your instructor, either in printed or electronic form, as requested.

Apply the skills
you learned to
track employee
vacation and
family leave.

APPLY

## Case Problem 2

**Data File needed for this Case Problem: Leave.xlsx**

*Town of Baltic Administrative Office*   Alan Welton, HR Generalist at the Town of Baltic Administrative Office in Baltic, Indiana, wants to create a workbook that tracks the amount of vacation time and family leave used by each employee of the town. The workbook needs to calculate how much vacation and family leave each employee is eligible for. Then it should subtract the time already used from that amount. It should also calculate the total number of vacation and family leave days used by all employees, as well as the total number of days remaining. The eligibility requirements for the different vacation and family leave plans are as follows:

For vacation:

- 15 days for full-time employees
- 10 days for part-time employees
- 0 days for everyone else

For family leave:

- 5 days for full-time employees who have worked 1 or more years
- 0 days for everyone else

Use these eligibility requirements to calculate the available vacation and family leave time for each employee. Complete the following:

1. Open the **Leave** workbook located in the Excel7\Case2 folder included with your Data Files, save the workbook as **Baltic Leave** in the same folder, and then, in the Documentation worksheet, enter your name and the date.
2. Go to the LeaveData worksheet. Create an Excel table in the range A5:J107, name the Excel table **Leave**, and then remove the filter arrows. Set the column width for columns B through J to **10**.
3. In column D, enter a formula to calculate Years Employed. Use the Date Hired cell and the current date (assume 7/1/2013, which is stored in cell Z6), and express the length of time employed in years. (*Hint*: Use the formula **(current date–Date Hired)/365**.)
4. In column E, enter a formula using a nested IF function to determine the number of vacation days (based on the vacation rules above) each employee is eligible for based on the employee's job status in column B.
5. In column G, enter a formula to subtract the amount of vacation used from the available vacation time, which displays the remaining vacation time for each employee.
6. In column H, enter a formula to determine each employee's total family leave time (based on the Family leave rules above).
7. In column J, enter a formula to subtract used family leave from the total family leave to determine the remaining family leave available for each employee.
8. In column J, apply conditional formatting that highlights the remaining family leave of any employee who has not used any family leave days. You decide the formatting.
9. Go to the Leave Summary worksheet. In the range C4:C6, use a function to count the total number of employees eligible for each vacation plan. (*Hint*: Any employee who is eligible for 15 vacation days will have the value 15 in column E of the LeaveData worksheet.)
10. In the range D4:D6, use functions to calculate the total number of vacation days for each vacation plan.
11. In the range E4:E6, use functions to calculate the total vacation days remaining for each vacation plan.
12. In the range C7:E7, calculate totals for Number Eligible, Total Days, and Days Remaining.
13. Save and close the workbook. Submit the finished workbook to your instructor, either in printed or electronic form, as requested.

*Create reports for a water company that determine different billing plans.*

**CHALLENGE**

## Case Problem 3

Data File needed for this Case Problem: M-Fresh.xlsx

**M-Fresh Water Company**   M-Fresh Water Company is a small independent water company in Miami, Oklahoma, that provides water to commercial customers throughout the region, delivering the water supply through pipelines, on-demand storage tanks, and bottles. Customers of M-Fresh Water range from government offices to nonprofit organizations to commercial retail shops and markets. Town regulations tax the latter group of commercial customers based on their usage, whereas nonprofit and government offices are not taxed. Furthermore, M-Fresh Water will occasionally waive a water bill based on its charitable-giving policy. Dawes Cado is in charge of the billing system that must take into account these business rules and assure accurate and on-time billing, which occurs quarterly. Complete the following:

1. Open the **M-Fresh** workbook located in the Excel7\Case3 folder included with your Data Files, save the workbook as **Water Bill** in the same folder, and then, in the Documentation worksheet, enter your name and the date.

2. In the Quarterly Data worksheet, create an Excel table for the range A1:F73, and name the table **WaterData**. Remove the filter arrows. Format the data in the Gal Used column with the Comma Style number format and no decimal places.

3. Add a column named **Gal Billed** to the table, and then enter a formula to calculate the number of gallons billed based on the following rules: If a customer's bill is waived (Bill Waived column) or the number of gallons used is less than 25,000 (Gal Used column), display **0** in Gal Billed column; otherwise, display the value from the Gal Used column in the Gal Billed column.

4. Add a column named **Water Bill** to the table, and then enter a formula to calculate the water bill based on the following rules: The billing rate varies based on the type of customer (Cust Type column). The billing rate is $3, $2, or $1.50 per *thousand* gallons billed, depending on the customer type (see the lookup table in cells B2:C5 of the Billing Rate worksheet). For example, a commercial customer using 75,000 gallons has a water bill of $225 (75 X $3), whereas a government customer using 100,000 gallons pays $150 (100 X $1.50). A commercial customer using 15,000 gallons has a water bill of $0 (see Gal Used rule in question 3).

5. Add a column named **Tax** to the table, and then enter a formula to calculate the tax based on the following rule: If a customer pays tax (Taxable column), then multiply the Water Bill by 3.5 percent; otherwise, the tax is 0. The tax rate is stored in cell T1.

6. Add a column named **Total Bill** to the table, and then enter a formula to calculate the bill amount by adding the Water Bill column and the Tax column.

7. Improve the formatting of the number fields in the WaterData table.

8. Make a copy of the Quarterly Data worksheet, rename the copied worksheet as **Q2-Q8**, and then add a Totals row to the Excel table displaying totals for the Gal Used, Gal Billed, Tax, and Total Bill columns.

**✛ EXPLORE**

9. Make another copy of the Quarterly Data worksheet, rename the copied worksheet as **Q9**, and then use conditional formatting to highlight the top 15 percent of the Total Bill amounts with a yellow background color. Filter the table so that only the top 15 percent are displayed. Sort the filtered table by largest to smallest.

10. Insert a new worksheet, rename the worksheet as **Billing Summary**, and then create the report shown in Figure 7-43, using COUNTIF, AVERAGEIF, and SUMIF functions to prepare the report.

**Figure 7-43**    **Water usage and billing by customer type**

| | A | B | C | D | E |
|---|---|---|---|---|---|
| 1 | | | | | |
| 2 | | | | | |
| 3 | | | | | |
| 4 | | | | | |
| 5 | | Customer Type | Nbr Customers | Avg Gallons Used | Total Billed |
| 6 | | Commercial | 37 | 322,437 | $37,043.12 |
| 7 | | Nonprofit | 11 | 87,661 | $ 224.18 |
| 8 | | Government | 24 | 774,532 | $27,901.44 |
| 9 | | Total | 72 | 437,267 | $65,168.74 |

✦ EXPLORE    11. Make another copy of the Quarterly Data worksheet, and then rename the copied worksheet as **Q11**. Add a custom filter to the table to display only those organizations that have "church" or "center" as part of the customer name.

✦ EXPLORE    12. Make another copy of the Quarterly Data worksheet, and then rename the copied worksheet as **Q12**. Use the lookup table in cells E2:H3 of the Billing Rate worksheet and the HLOOKUP function to modify the formula to calculate the Water Bill column (column H).

13. Save and close the workbook. Submit the finished workbook to your instructor, either in printed or electronic form, as requested.

*Create a worksheet that compiles and summarizes reports for a newspaper.*

**CREATE**

## Case Problem 4

**Data File needed for this Case Problem: Rock Island.xlsx**

*Rock Island Home Sales*    Tim Derkson is a reporter for *Rock Island Times*, a newspaper in Rock Island, Illinois. He is compiling a quarterly real estate sales analysis for his newspaper. He obtained data on home sales from the local real estate association and county records. He wants to create a worksheet that will display summary information on the home sales in Rock Island. Tim has already set up and formatted the workbook, but he wants you to insert the correct formulas. Tim stored the housing data in the Home Sales Data worksheet. He wants to use the Home Summary worksheet to search for information about the homes. Complete the following:

1. Open the **Rock Island** workbook located in the Excel7\Case4 folder included with your Data Files, save the workbook as **Home Sales** in the same folder, and then, in the Documentation worksheet, enter your name and the date.

2. In the Home Sales Data worksheet, create an Excel table in the range A1:K118. Remove the filter arrows. Rename the Excel table as **SalesData**.

3. In column L, add a calculated column named **Days on Market**, and then enter a formula to verify that the date sold occurs after the date listed. If it does not, display the message **Check Dates**; otherwise, calculate the number of days on the market. (*Hint:* You might need to format this column in the General number format.)

4. An incentive bonus of $1,000 is awarded if the sales price is above the asking price or the number of days on the market is less than 25 days. In column M, add a calculated column named **Incentive**, and then enter a formula to calculate the bonus amount.

5. Use conditional formatting to highlight records in the Days on Market column where the house was on the market for 300 or more days.

6. Display the Total row in the SalesData table. In this row, display a count of homes sold (place in Listing ID), average asking price, average taxes, average sales price, and average days on the market.

7. Split the Home Sales Data worksheet so that the top pane shows rows in the SalesData table and the bottom pane displays the Total row.

8. Insert a new worksheet, and then rename it as **Sales Summary**. Create a report on home sales based on the style sold and the average sales price, as shown in Figure 7-44.

**Figure 7-44**    Home sales by type of home

| | Style | Number Sold | Average Sales Price |
|---|---|---|---|
| | Rock Island Home Sales | | |
| | Overall Data | | |
| | | | |
| | By Style of Home | | |
| | | | |
| | | | |
| Condo | | 23 | $ 90,347.83 |
| Ranch | | 46 | $ 91,842.39 |
| Victorian | | 48 | $113,567.71 |
| Total | | 117 | $100,461.54 |

**EXPLORE**    9. Create a PivotTable report with the information shown in Figure 7-45. Rename the worksheet as **DaysOnMarket**.

**Figure 7-45**    Days on Market PivotTable report

| Days | Values Number Sold | Average Sales Price |
|---|---|---|
| Days on Market | | |
| 1-100 | 31 | $ 94,452 |
| 101-200 | 27 | $ 106,880 |
| 201-300 | 37 | $ 103,939 |
| 301-400 | 22 | $ 95,205 |
| Grand Total | 117 | $ 100,462 |

**EXPLORE**    10. Make a copy of the Home Sales Data worksheet, and then rename the worksheet as **Q10**. Remove the current conditional formatting, and then add conditional formatting to highlight records in the Sales Price column where the sales price was above the asking price. Use appropriate formatting. (*Hint*: Create a new rule by selecting the Use formula to determine which cells to format rule type, and then editing the rule description to enter a formula with a conditional statement that compares the first data row between the two columns of interest.)

11. Save and close the workbook. Submit the finished workbook to your instructor, either in printed or electronic form, as requested.

### ENDING DATA FILES

Excel7 → Tutorial — Talent Tracs.xlsx

Review — Tracs Employees.xlsx

Case1 — PC Modem.xlsx

Case2 — Baltic Leave.xlsx

Case3 — Water Bill.xlsx

Case4 — Home Sales.xlsx

EXCEL

# Developing an Excel Application

*Creating an Invoice*

## Case | *Eugene Community Theatre*

Ellen Jefferson, business manager for the Eugene Community Theatre in Eugene, Oregon, is automating several processes for the theatre's business office. Each year, the theatre mails a brochure to patrons and other interested individuals showcasing the upcoming season's offerings. Then, theatre-goers make their selections and mail in the order form. Ellen wants to automate the process of invoicing, capturing the order, calculating the charges, and printing an invoice. She also wants the invoice system to reflect specific requests for tickets (number, series, and location in theatre).

Many of these tasks can be accomplished in Excel. But without validating data entry, protecting cells with formulas from accidental deletion, and reducing repetitive keystrokes and mouse clicks, Ellen realizes too many opportunities for errors exist. In addition, as a nonprofit organization, the theatre relies on numerous volunteers who have varying degrees of computer experience and skill. To accommodate these varying skill levels and reduce potential errors, Ellen wants to create a custom interface for this project that does not rely exclusively on the Ribbon, galleries, and so forth. You will help Ellen create a unique Excel application that can resolve these issues and help ensure accurate data entry.

**STARTING DATA FILES**

| | Tutorial | Review | Case1 | Case2 | Case3 | Case4 |
|---|---|---|---|---|---|---|
| Excel8 | Theatre.xlsx | Rentals.xlsx | MediTrax.xlsx | Popcorn.xlsx | Cookin.xlsx | (none) |

# SESSION 8.1 VISUAL OVERVIEW

A **defined name** (often called a **range name**) is a word or string of characters associated with a single cell or a range.

The Name box displays the cell reference or the defined name of the selected cell.

Click the Name box to display a list of all the defined names in the workbook.

An application includes an input area to enter and edit data. You can set what types of values can be entered and where the user can enter data.

An **Excel application** is a spreadsheet written or tailored to meet specific needs. It typically includes reports and charts, a data entry area, a custom interface, as well as instructions and documentation.

TicketCost

Name box list:
- Address
- City_State_Zip
- Decals
- Donation
- HandlingCost
- Invoice_Date
- Location
- ParkingFee
- Phone
- Series
- Subscriber
- Ticket_Quantity
- TicketCost
- TicketPrices
- TotalInvoice

Formula bar: =IF(Location="Orchestra",VLOOKUP(Series,Tic... FALSE))*Ticket_Quantity

### Invoice Data

| Invoice Date | 7/15/2013 |
| Subscriber | Michael Keller |
| Address | 4321 Main Street |
| City State Zip | Eugene, OR 70777 |
| Phone | (806)555-1111 |
| Ticket Quantity | 4 |
| Series | C |
| Location | Balcony |
| No. Parking Decals | 2 |
| Donation | 50 |

### Ticket Price Table

| Series | Orchestra | Balcony |
| --- | --- | --- |
| A | 225 | 175 |
| B | 200 | 165 |
| C | 175 | 150 |
| D | 150 | 125 |

Documentation | Invoice | Ticket Data

Ready

# EXCEL APPLICATION AND DEFINED NAMES

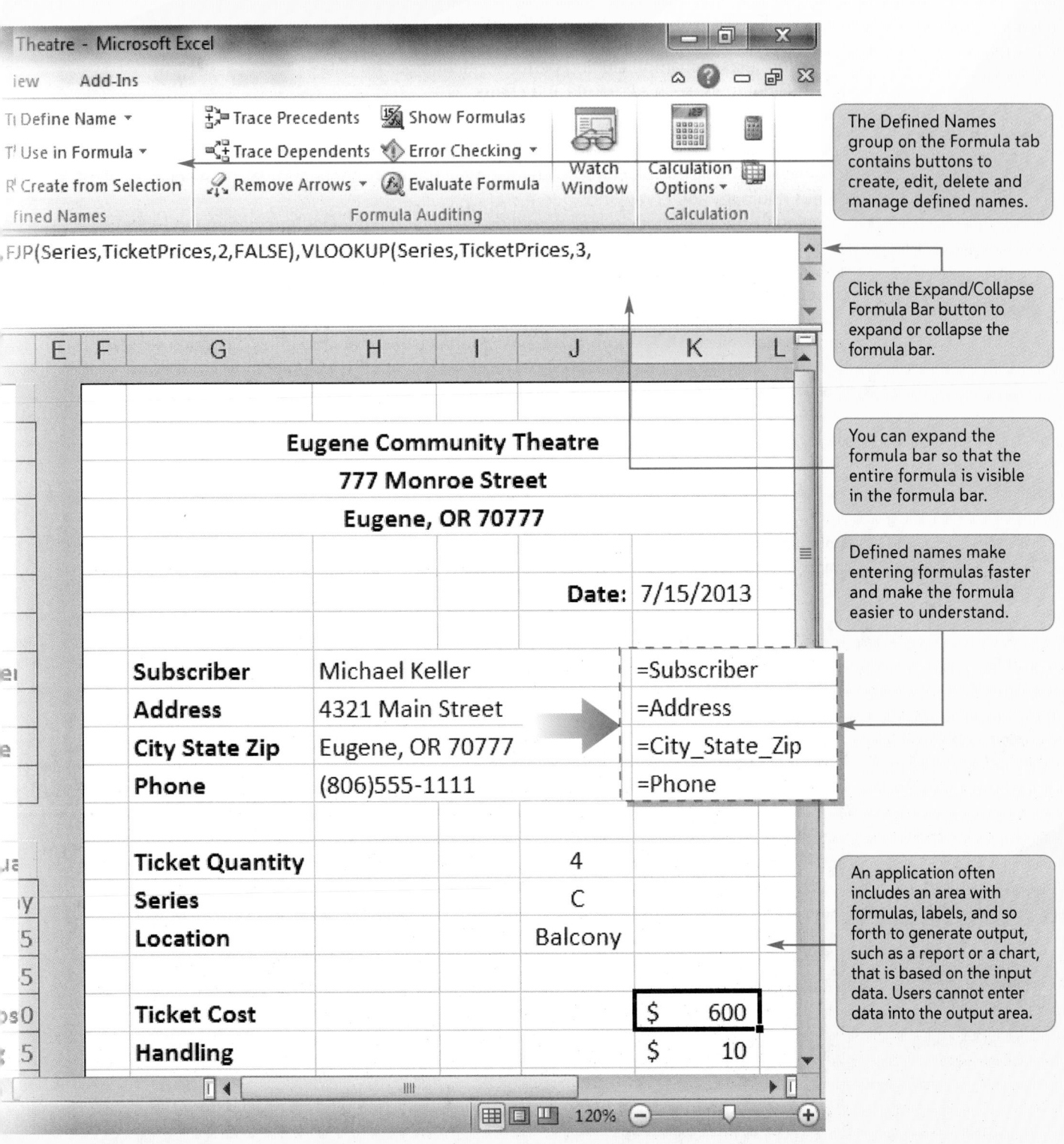

The Defined Names group on the Formula tab contains buttons to create, edit, delete and manage defined names.

Click the Expand/Collapse Formula Bar button to expand or collapse the formula bar.

You can expand the formula bar so that the entire formula is visible in the formula bar.

Defined names make entering formulas faster and make the formula easier to understand.

An application often includes an area with formulas, labels, and so forth to generate output, such as a report or a chart, that is based on the input data. Users cannot enter data into the output area.

# Planning an Excel Application

Planning an Excel application includes designing how the worksheet(s) will be organized. You can include different sections for each function, depending on the complexity of the project. For example, an application often includes separate sections to:

- Enter and edit data (setting where and what types of data can be entered)
- Store data after it has been entered
- Use formulas to manipulate and perform calculations on data
- Display outputs, such as reports and charts

An application's interface helps others use it. For example, you can have separate sections for inputting data and displaying outputs. You can create special buttons for performing specific tasks. You can also change the entire Excel interface by adding custom menus, toolbars, and commands.

An application often includes internal documentation in a Documentation worksheet as well as comments to explain cell contents and provide instructions. It can also include a set of clearly written instructions. All of these help you and others use the workbook correctly and accurately.

Ellen wants to be able to easily print the invoice and transfer the invoice items to another worksheet. In addition, she wants volunteers to be able to enter data for a season ticket in a specific area of the worksheet reserved for input. The application would use this data to automatically generate and print the invoice. To keep the process simple, she wants users to be able to click buttons to print a single invoice, print the entire worksheet, and transfer the data from one worksheet to another. You'll open the workbook Ellen created.

## To open and review the Theatre workbook:

1. Open the **Theatre** workbook located in the Excel8\Tutorial folder included with your Data Files, and then save the workbook as **Community Theatre**.

2. In the Documentation worksheet, enter your name and the date.

3. Review the contents of the workbook, and then switch to the **Invoice** worksheet. See Figure 8-1.

**Figure 8-1** | **Initial Invoice worksheet**

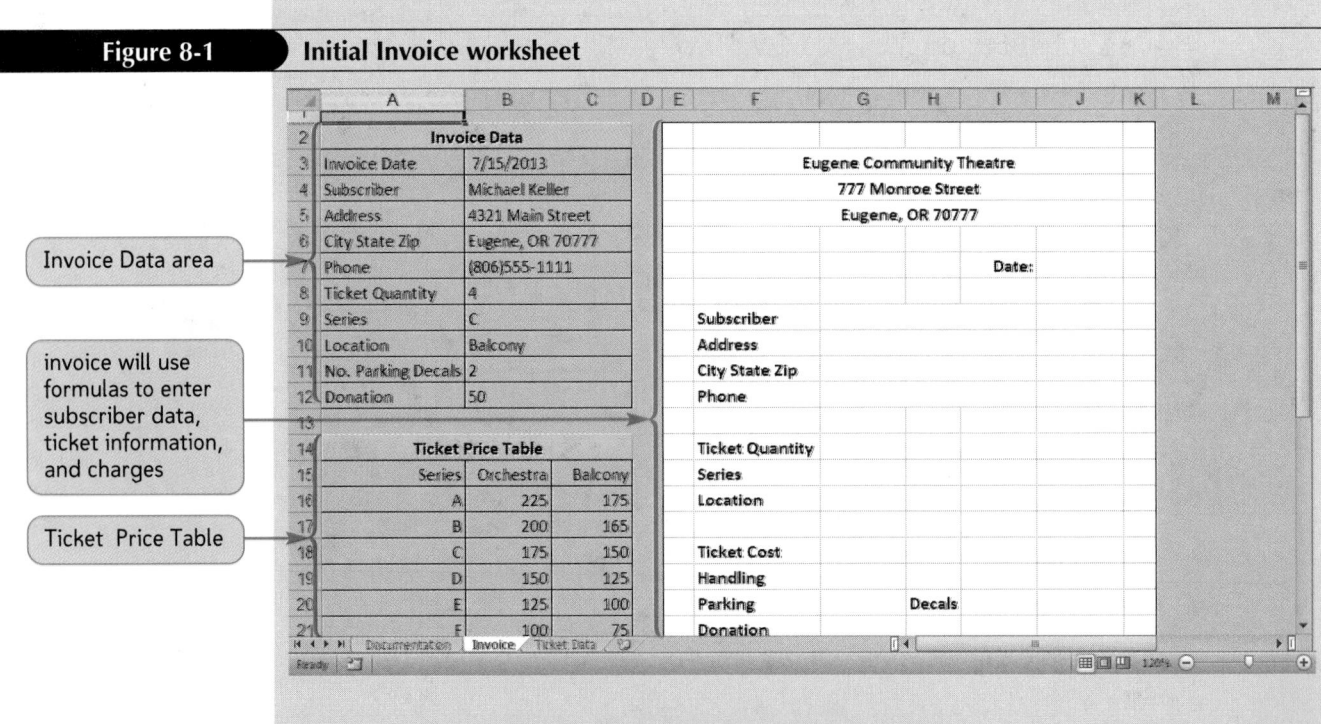

**TIP**

Larger and more complex applications often place the input and output sections in separate worksheets.

In addition to the Documentation worksheet, the Community Theatre workbook includes two other worksheets: Invoice and Ticket Data. The Invoice worksheet contains input, output, and transfer sections. The input section is divided into the following three areas:

- Invoice Data contains items that change for each subscriber transaction such as the subscriber name, address, phone number, ticket quantity, series, and location of seats.
- Ticket Price Table contains the table with ticket prices for the upcoming season.
- Invoice Constants contains charges for items that will not change during the upcoming season, such as the cost for parking ($15/decal) and the handling charge ($10/invoice).

The output section contains formulas and labels used to generate the invoice based on data in the input section. The invoice in the output section will be printed. The transfer section gathers selected data from the invoice in one area before the data is transferred to the Ticket Data worksheet for storage. The transfer section makes it simpler to move the data to the Ticket Data worksheet.

# Naming Cells and Ranges

So far, you have referred to a cell or range by its address except when you entered formulas within an Excel table. Cell and range references do not indicate what data is stored in those cells. Instead, you can use a defined name to assign a meaningful, descriptive name to a cell or range. For example, if the range D1:D100 contains sales data for 100 transactions, you can define the name "Sales" to refer to the range of sales data.

A defined name enables you to quickly navigate within a workbook to the cell with the defined name. You can also use defined names to create more descriptive formulas.

In the Invoice worksheet, the range B3:B12 contains the data values for each request for season tickets. As you can see, this range includes many variables. It will be simpler to remember where different data is stored by assigning a descriptive name to each cell or range rather than using its cell address. For example, the name Subscriber better identifies what is stored in the cell than cell B4.

**Written Communication: Saving Time with Defined Names**

Words can be more descriptive than numbers. This is especially true in cell references. Instead of using the letter and number references for cells, you can create defined names to provide more intuitive references. Defined names have several advantages over cell references, especially as a worksheet becomes longer and more complex. Some advantages include:

- Names, such as TaxRate and TotalSales, are more descriptive than cell references, making it easier to remember what a cell or range contains.
- Names can be used in formulas, making it easier for users to understand the calculations being performed. For example, =GrossPay–Deductions is more understandable than =C15–C16.
- When you move a named cell or range within a worksheet, its name moves with it. Any formulas that contain the name automatically reference the new location.
- In a formula, referencing a named cell or range is the same as referencing the cell or range's absolute reference. So, if you move a formula that includes a defined name, the reference remains pointed to the correct cell or range.

By using defined names, you'll often save time and everyone reviewing the worksheet will have a clearer understanding of what a formula is calculating.

## Creating Defined Names

Creating defined names for cells or ranges makes building an application more intuitive and easier to document. When you define a name for a cell or range, keep in mind the following rules:

- The name must begin with a letter or _ (an underscore).
- The name can include letters and numbers as well as periods and underscores, but not other symbols or spaces. To distinguish multiword names, use an underscore between the words or capitalize the first letter of each word. For example, the names *Net_Income* and *NetIncome* are valid, but *Net Income* and *Net-Income* are not.
- The name cannot be a valid cell address (such as FY2013), function name, or reserved word (such as *Print_Area*).
- The name can include as many as 255 characters, although short, meaningful names of 5 to 15 characters are more practical.
- The name is not case sensitive. For example, both *Sales* and *SALES* refer to the same cell or range.

### Creating a Defined Name for a Cell or Range

- Select the cell or range to which you want to assign a name.
- Click in the Name box on the formula bar, type the name, and then press the Enter key.

  *or*

  In the Defined Names group on the Formulas tab, click the Define Name button, type a name in the Name box, and then click the OK button.

  *or*

- Select the range with labels to which you want to assign a name.
- In the Defined Names group on the Formulas tab, click the Create from Selection button.
- Specify whether to create the ranges based on the top row, bottom row, left column, or right column in the list.
- Click the OK button.

The fastest way to create a defined name is to use the Name box. You'll use the Name box to define names for the cells and ranges in the worksheet.

### To create defined names using the Name box:

1. Click cell **B24** to make it active, and then click the **Name box** on the formula bar. The cell reference for the active cell, B24, is selected in the Name box.

2. Type **HandlingCost** and then press the **Enter** key. Cell B24 remains active, and "HandlingCost" appears in the Name box instead of the cell reference. See Figure 8-2.

**Figure 8-2**    **Defined name for cell B24**

defined name for the active cell appears in the Name box

**Trouble?** If "HandlingCost" appears in cell B24, you probably did not click the Name box before typing the name. On the Quick Access Toolbar, click the Undo button , and then repeat Steps 1 and 2.

**Trouble?** If "cell B24" appears in the Name box instead of "HandlingCost," you probably didn't press the Enter key. Repeat Steps 1 and 2 being sure to press the Enter key to assign the defined name to cell B24.

3. Click cell **B25** to make it active, click the **Name box** to select the cell reference, type **ParkingFee** and then press the **Enter** key. Cell B25 remains active, and ParkingFee appears in the Name box instead of the cell reference.

4. Select the range **A16:C21**. The cell reference for the active cell in the range appears in the Name box.

5. Click the **Name box**, type **TicketPrices** and then press the **Enter** key. The name TicketPrices is assigned to the range A16:C21.

6. Select the range **F25:J25**, click the **Name box**, type **TransferArea** and then press the **Enter** key. The name TransferArea is assigned to the range F25:J25.

7. Click cell **J18** to make it active, click the **Name box** to select the cell reference, type **TicketCost** and then press the **Enter** key. Cell J18 remains active, and TicketCost appears in the Name box instead of the cell reference.

8. Click cell **J22** to make it active, click the **Name box** to select the cell reference, type **TotalInvoice** and then press the **Enter** key. Cell J22 remains active, and TotalInvoice appears in the Name box instead of the cell reference.

The Name box displays all of the names in a workbook. You can select a name in the Name box to quickly select the cell or range referenced by the name. You'll view the defined names you added to the workbook.

### To select cells and ranges with the Name box:

▶ **1.** Click the **Name box arrow** to open a list of defined names in the workbook. Six names appear in the list. See Figure 8-3.

Figure 8-3 | **Name box with the defined names in the workbook**

▶ **2.** Click **ParkingFee**. The active cell moves to cell B25.

▶ **3.** Click the **Name box arrow**, and then click **TicketPrices**. The range A16:C21 is selected in the worksheet, and cell A16 is the active cell.

You can quickly define names without typing them if the data is organized in a table format with labels in the first or last column or top or bottom row. The names are based on the row or column labels. Any blank or parenthesis in the labels are changed to an underscore (_) in the defined name. You will create names for each cell in the Invoice Data area, using the labels in the range A3:A11.

### To create defined names by selection for the Invoice Data area:

> Select only the range A3:B12 though text extends into column C; otherwise, formulas you create later in this tutorial will not work.

▶ **1.** Select the range **A3:B12**. In this range, column A contains the labels you want to use as the defined names, and column B contains the cells you want to name.

▶ **2.** Click the **Formulas** tab on the Ribbon, and then click the **Create from Selection** button in the Defined Names group. The Create Names from Selection dialog box opens. See Figure 8-4.

Figure 8-4 | **Create Names from Selection dialog box**

▶ **3.** Click the **Top row** check box to remove the check mark because this range doesn't include labels at the top, and then verify that the **Left column** check box contains a check mark. The labels in the left column will be used to create the defined names.

▶ **4.** Click the **OK** button. Each cell in the range B3:B12 is named based on its label in column A.

  **5.** Click the **Name box arrow** to see the 16 defined names in the list.

  **6.** Press the **Esc** key to close the list of defined names.

Although you can use the Name box to verify the names were created, the Name Manager dialog box lists all of the names currently defined in the workbook, including Excel table names. You can also use the Name Manager dialog box to create a new name, edit or delete existing names, and filter the list of names.

The name No._Parking_Decals is too long, so you'll change it to Decals. You will also delete the TransferData defined name, which Ellen decides is not needed.

### To edit and delete defined names with the Name Manager dialog box:

**TIP**

The Name Manager dialog box also lists Excel table names.

  **1.** In the Defined Names group on the Formulas tab, click the **Name Manager** button. The Name Manager dialog box opens, listing the 16 defined names based on the labels in the range A3:A12 in the Invoice Data area, as well as the six names you defined with the Name box. See Figure 8-5.

**Figure 8-5**    Name Manager dialog box

opens the New Name dialog box to create a new defined name

opens the Edit Name dialog box to modify the selected defined name

underscores replace spaces in the label name

deletes the selected defined name

location in the workbook

current value in the cell

  **2.** Click **No._Parking_Decals** in the Name list, and then click the **Edit** button. The Edit Name dialog box opens. See Figure 8-6.

**Figure 8-6**    Edit Name dialog box

type a new name

type or select a new cell or range

▶ **3.** In the Name box, type **Decals** and then click the **OK** button. The edited name appears in the list in the Name Manager dialog box.

▶ **4.** Scroll to find the TransferArea name, click **TransferArea**, and then click the **Delete** button. A dialog box opens to confirm that you want to delete the selected name.

▶ **5.** Click the **OK** button. The name is removed from the list.

▶ **6.** Click the **Close** button. The Name Manager dialog box closes.

## Using the Paste Names Command

When a workbook contains many defined names, it can be helpful to list all of the defined names and their corresponding cell addresses in the workbook's documentation. You can generate a list of names using the Paste Names command.

### To create a list of defined names in the Documentation worksheet:

▶ **1.** Switch to the **Documentation** worksheet.

▶ **2.** Click in cell **A10**, type **Defined Names** and then press the **Enter** key. The label for the list of defined names appears in cell A10, and cell A11 is the active cell.

▶ **3.** In the Defined Names group on the Formulas tab, click the **Use in Formula** button. The list includes all of the defined names in the workbook followed by the Paste Names command.

▶ **4.** Click **Paste Names**. The Paste Name dialog box opens. You can paste any selected name, or you can paste the entire list of names.

▶ **5.** Click the **Paste List** button. The defined names and their associated cell references are pasted into the range A11:B25.

▶ **6.** Deselect the range. See Figure 8-7.

| Figure 8-7 | Defined names in the Community Theatre workbook |

list of defined names used in the workbook

worksheet and cell or range location in the workbook

▶ **7.** Switch to the **Invoice** worksheet.

If you edit a defined name or add a new defined name, the list of defined names and their addresses in the Documentation worksheet is not updated. You must paste the list again to update the names and locations. Usually, it is a good idea to wait until the workbook is complete before pasting defined names in the Documentation worksheet.

## Using Defined Names in Formulas

You can create more descriptive formulas by using defined names instead of cell or range references in formulas. For example, in the following formulas, the defined name Sales replaces the range reference D1:D100 in a formula to calculate average sales:

**Range reference**    `=AVERAGE(D1:D100)`
**Defined name**    `=AVERAGE(Sales)`

Keep in mind that if you enter a formula using a range reference rather than a defined name, the defined names do *not* automatically replace the range reference in the formula.

You need to enter the formulas required to generate the invoice. You'll start by entering formulas to display the invoice date, the subscriber's name, and the subscriber's address entered in the Invoice Data area in the invoice.

### To enter formulas to display the subscriber's name and address:

▶ **1.** In cell J7, enter **=B3**. The invoice date recorded in the Invoice Data area, 7/15/2013, appears in the cell.

▶ **2.** In cell G9, enter **=B4**. Michael Keller, the subscriber's name, appears in the cell.

▶ **3.** In cell G10, enter **=B5**. The subscriber's address, 4321 Main Street, appears in the cell.

▶ **4.** Click cell **G10**. The formula =B5 appears in the formula bar.

You entered these formulas using cell addresses rather than defined names. Although you defined names for cells B3, B4, and B5, the names do not automatically replace the cell addresses in the formula. Because defined names make formulas simpler to enter and understand, you will use named cells and ranges in the remaining formulas.

As you type a defined name in a formula, the Formula AutoComplete box lists functions and defined names that begin with the letters you typed. As you type additional letters, the list narrows. You can double-click the name you want in the Formula AutoComplete box or press the Tab key to enter the selected name. You can also just continue to type the rest of the name.

### To type defined names in formulas:

▶ **1.** In cell G11, type **=C** to display a list of functions and defined names that begin with the letter "C."

▶ **2.** Type **i** to narrow the list to the defined name =City_State_Zip.

▶ **3.** Press the **Tab** key to enter the defined name in the formula, and then press the **Enter** key. The subscriber's city, state, and zip code appear in the cell.

▶ **4.** Click cell **G11**. The data from cell B6 appears in the cell, and the formula with the defined name, =City_State_Zip, appears in the formula bar.

▶ **5.** In cell G12, enter **=Phone** and then click cell **G12**. The sample data from cell B7 appears in the cell, and the formula with the defined name, =Phone, appears in the formula bar.

You can also use the point-and-click method to create a formula with defined names. When you click a cell or select a range, Excel substitutes the defined name for the cell reference in the formula. You'll use this method to enter formulas that display the ticket quantity, series, and theatre location from the input area in the invoice.

### To enter formulas with defined names using the point-and-click method:

▶ **1.** Click cell **I14**, type **=** and then click cell **B8**. The formula uses the defined name Ticket_Quantity rather than the cell reference B8.

▶ **2.** Click the **Enter** button ✓ on the formula bar. The number 4, which is the number of tickets the subscriber ordered, appears in cell I14. See Figure 8-8.

**Figure 8-8** **Formula with a defined name**

▶ **3.** In cell I15, type **=** and then click cell **B9**. The formula uses the defined name Series rather than the cell reference B9.

▶ **4.** Press the **Enter** key. The letter "C," indicating the series the subscriber selected, appears in cell I15.

▶ **5.** In cell I16, type **=**, click **B10**, and then click the **Enter** button ✓ on the formula bar. The subscriber's preferred seat location, Balcony, appears in cell I16, and the formula with the defined name, =Location, appears in the formula bar.

Next, you will enter the formula to calculate the ticket cost to the subscriber. You need to combine two VLOOKUP functions within an IF function to create the formula to calculate ticket costs. The VLOOKUP functions will find the ticket price. The lookup value is the Series the subscriber selects (A, B, C, D, E, or F). Recall that the lookup value searches the first column of the lookup table to find the appropriate row. In this case, the lookup table is the Ticket Price Table (the range you earlier named TicketPrices), which contains two columns of ticket prices. Column 2 of the table lists the prices for the Orchestra, and column 3 of the table lists the prices for the Balcony. The column used to return the ticket prices depends on the Location the subscriber selected. You need to use an IF function to determine whether to search the second or third column for the ticket price.

## To enter the formula to determine ticket cost:

▶ **1.** Click cell **J18** to make it the active cell. The defined name, TicketCost, appears in the Name box.

▶ **2.** In the Function Library group on the Formulas tab, click the **Logical** button, and then click **IF**. The Function Arguments dialog box opens.

▶ **3.** In the Logical_test box, type **Location="Orchestra"**. This logical test evaluates whether the subscriber wants to sit in the Orchestra. If the value in cell B10 equals Orchestra, then the condition is true. False appears to the right of the Logical_test box, indicating the subscriber wants to sit in the Balcony.

▶ **4.** In the Value_if_true box, type **VLOOKUP(Series,TicketPrices,2,FALSE)**. This argument specifies that if the logical_test is true (the customer wants to sit in the Orchestra), the ticket price is determined using a VLOOKUP function, return-ing a value from column 2 (Orchestra prices) in the TicketPrices range. The first argument of the VLOOKUP function, Series, is the defined name that stores the Series code (A, B, C, and so on) used to look up a value in the second argument, TicketPrices (range A16:C21). The third argument, 2, returns a ticket price from the second column (Orchestra) of the TicketPrices table. The fourth argument, FALSE, indicates an exact match lookup.

▶ **5.** In the Value_if_false box, type **VLOOKUP(Series,TicketPrices,3,FALSE)**. This argument specifies that if the logical_test is false (the customer wants to sit in the Balcony), the ticket price is determined using a VLOOKUP function, returning a value from column 3 (Balcony prices) in the TicketPrices range.

▶ **6.** Click the **OK** button. The following formula appears in the formula bar, and 150 appears in cell J18 because the condition is false: =IF(Location="Orchestra", VLOOKUP(Series,TicketPrices,2,FALSE),VLOOKUP(Series,TicketPrices,3,FALSE)).

**Trouble?** If #Name?, #Value?, or VLOOKUP appears in cell J18, you probably mistyped the formula. Click cell J18, compare the formula you entered with the complete formula in Step 6, and then edit the formula in the formula bar as needed. Also, make sure the references in your defined names are correct (refer to Figure 8-7 for the list of defined names used in the workbook).

Next, you will complete the formula by multiplying the cost for one ticket by the number of tickets purchased.

▶ **7.** Double-click cell **J18** to enter Edit mode and display the formula in the cell.

▶ **8.** Click at the end of the formula, type **\*Ticket_Quantity** and then press the **Enter** key. The amount in cell J18 changes to $600.

▶ **9.** Click cell **J18**, and then click the **Expand Formula Bar** button ⌄ on the right side of the formula bar. The entire formula is visible in the expanded formula bar. The IF function determines which column in the TicketPrices range to use to return the ticket price. If Location in the Invoice Data area is Orchestra, then the condi-tion Location="Orchestra" is TRUE and the VLOOKUP function returns a ticket price from column 2. If the Location in the Invoice Data area is Balcony, then the VLOOKUP function searches column 3 for the ticket price. The price for one ticket, as determined by the IF and VLOOKUP functions, is then multiplied by the ticket quantity to calculate the total ticket cost for this transaction. See Figure 8-9.

**Figure 8-9** Formula to calculate the ticket cost

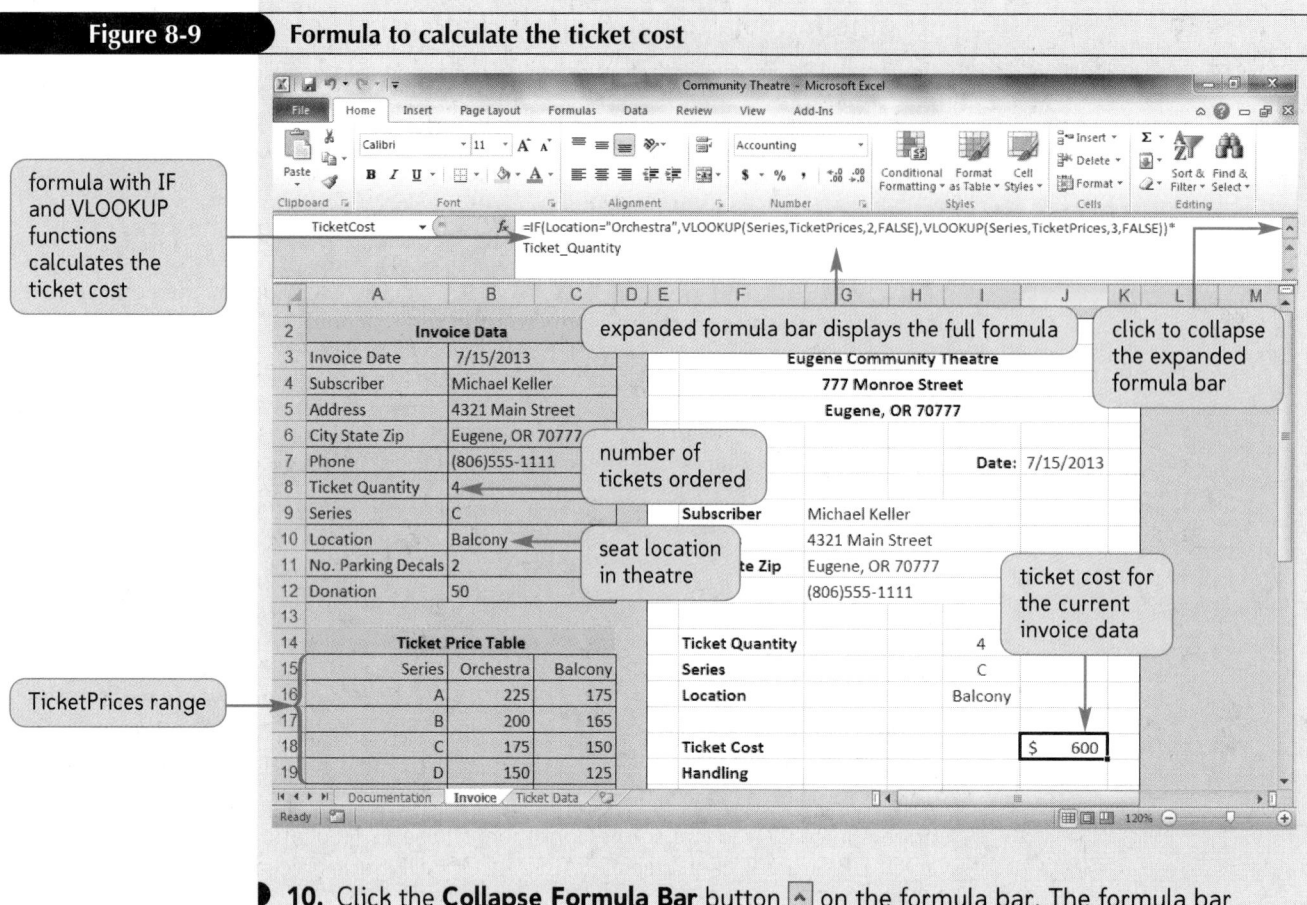

formula with IF and VLOOKUP functions calculates the ticket cost

expanded formula bar displays the full formula

click to collapse the expanded formula bar

number of tickets ordered

seat location in theatre

ticket cost for the current invoice data

TicketPrices range

10. Click the **Collapse Formula Bar** button ⌃ on the formula bar. The formula bar returns to its usual height.

You'll enter the remaining formulas needed to complete the invoice.

### To enter the remaining formulas in the invoice:

**TIP**

If a formula uses a defined name that doesn't exist, #NAME? appears in the cell. Verify the defined name spelling and that the name wasn't deleted from the worksheet.

1. In cell J19, enter **=HandlingCost**. The handling cost is $10, which is the amount in cell B24 in the Invoice Constants area.

2. In cell I20, enter **=Decals**. The number of parking decals ordered is 2, which is the number listed in cell B11 in the Invoice Data area.

3. In cell J20, enter **=Decals*ParkingFee**. The parking cost is $30, which is the number of parking decals listed in cell B11 multiplied by the parking fee in cell B25. The defined names make entering this calculation faster and the formula easier to understand.

4. In cell J21, enter **=Donation**. The donation amount is $50, which is listed in cell B12.

5. In cell J22, enter **=SUM(J18:J21)**. The SUM function adds all of the costs to determine the total invoice amount of $690. See Figure 8-10.

**Figure 8-10**    **Invoice with all formulas entered**

*handling cost equals the amount in cell B24*

*number of decals equals the value in cell B11*

*donation equals the amount in cell B12*

*parking fee equals the number of decals times the fee in cell B25*

## Adding Defined Names to Existing Formulas

Sometimes, you might name cells after creating formulas in the worksheet. Other times, you might not use the defined names when you create formulas (as with the first three formulas you created in the invoice for the invoice date, subscriber name, and address). Because defined names are not automatically substituted for the cell addresses in a formula, you can replace cell addresses in existing formulas in the worksheet with their defined names to make the formulas more understandable.

**REFERENCE**

### Adding Defined Names to Existing Formulas

- In the Defined Names group on the Formulas tab, click the Define Name button arrow, and then click Apply Names (if the cell reference and defined name are in the same worksheet).
- In the Apply Names dialog box, select the names you want to apply.
- Click the OK button.

*or*

- Edit the formula by selecting the cell reference and typing the defined name or clicking the appropriate cell.

You'll change the two formulas you created to display the subscriber name and address in the invoice to use defined names instead of cell references.

### To add defined names to existing formulas in the invoice:

▶ 1. In the Defined Names group on the Formulas tab, click the **Define Name button arrow**, and then click **Apply Names**. The Apply Names dialog box opens. See Figure 8-11.

**Figure 8-11** Apply Names dialog box

list of defined names in the workbook

You want to select only the names you need for the existing formulas with cell references.

▶ 2. If any name is selected in the Apply names list, click that name to deselect it.

▶ 3. In the Apply names list, click **Address**, **Invoice_Date**, and **Subscriber**. The three names you want to apply to the formulas are selected.

▶ 4. Click the **OK** button. The three selected names are applied to the formulas.

▶ 5. Click cell **J7** and verify that the formula changed to =Invoice_Date.

▶ 6. Click cell **G9** and verify that the formula changed to =Subscriber.

▶ 7. Click cell **G10** and verify that the formula changed to =Address.

Ellen wants to store the following items in the Ticket Data worksheet: subscriber name, transaction date, ticket quantity, ticket cost, and total amount owed from the invoice. Displaying these data items in the Transfer Area enables you to copy and paste all of the items to the Ticket Data worksheet at once. You'll enter formulas to display the appropriate items in this section of the worksheet.

### To enter formulas to display data in the Transfer Area:

▶ 1. In cell F25, enter **=Subscriber**. The formula displays the subscriber name in this cell.

▶ 2. In cell G25, enter **=Invoice_Date**. The formula displays the current date.

▶ 3. In cell H25, enter **=Ticket_Quantity**. The formula displays the number of tickets.

▶ 4. In cell I25, enter **=TicketCost**. The formula displays the ticket cost.

▶ 5. In cell J25, enter **=TotalInvoice**. The formula displays the total cost.

The worksheet contains all of the formulas required to create the invoice based on the subscriber information. Because Ellen relies on volunteers to enter season ticket requests into the worksheet and print invoices, she wants to be sure the values entered are correct. You will continue to work on Ellen's application by creating validation checks, which are designed to prevent users from inserting incorrect data values. You will also protect cells so that volunteers cannot accidentally overwrite or delete the formulas. You'll do both of these tasks in the next session.

**REVIEW**

## Session 8.1 Quick Check

1. What is a defined name?
2. What are two advantages of using names in workbooks?
3. Describe three ways to create a name.
4. Which of the following is a valid defined name?
    a. Annual_Total
    b. 3rdQtr
    c. Annual total
5. How can you quickly select a cell or range using its name?
6. In the Report workbook, the defined name "Expenses" refers to a list of expenses stored in the range D2:D100. Currently, the total expenses are calculated by the formula =SUM(D2:D100). Change this formula to use the defined name.
7. True or False. If you create a defined name for a range referenced in an existing formula, you cannot change the formula to use the new name.

# SESSION 8.2 VISUAL OVERVIEW

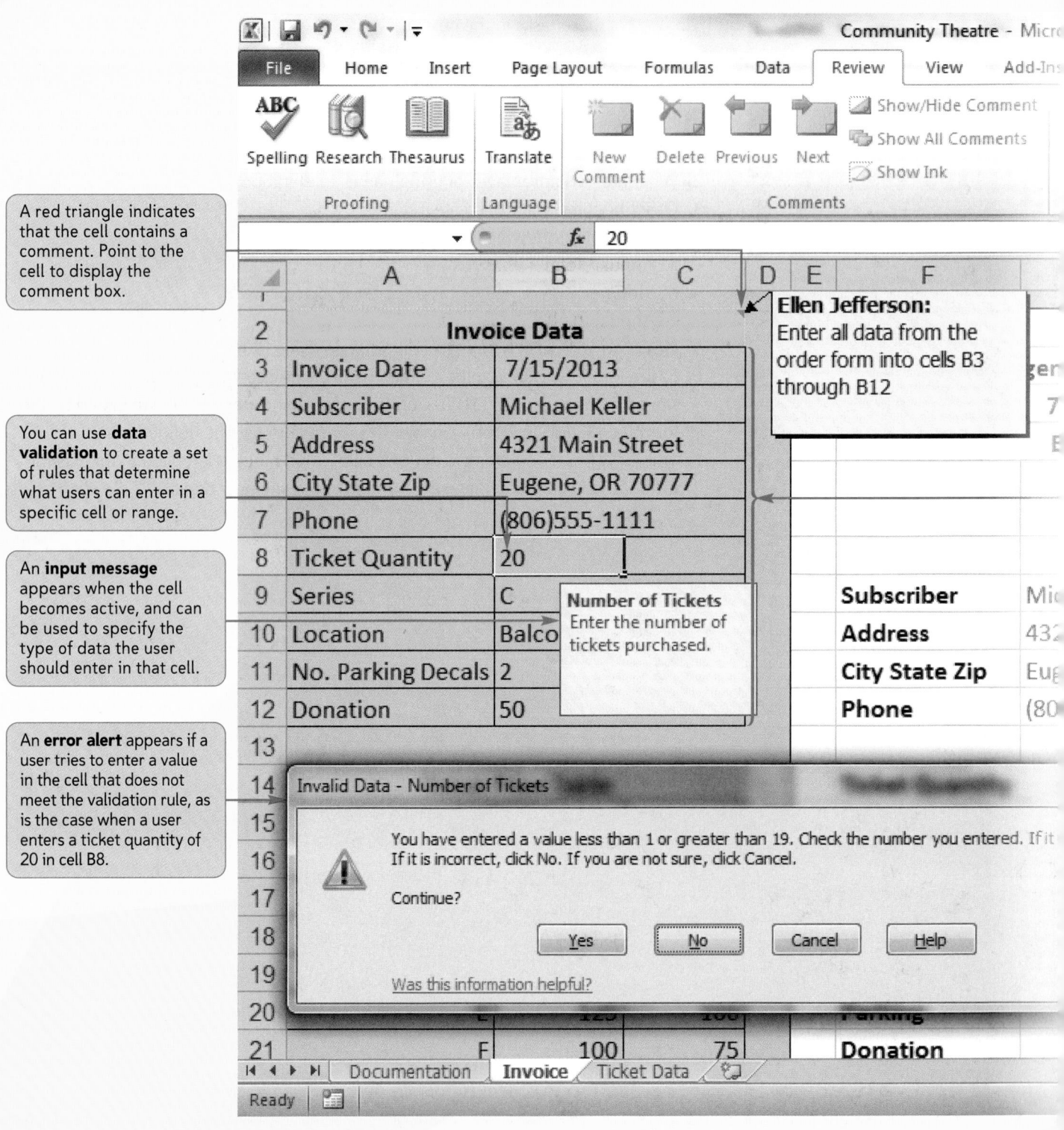

A red triangle indicates that the cell contains a comment. Point to the cell to display the comment box.

You can use **data validation** to create a set of rules that determine what users can enter in a specific cell or range.

An **input message** appears when the cell becomes active, and can be used to specify the type of data the user should enter in that cell.

An **error alert** appears if a user tries to enter a value in the cell that does not meet the validation rule, as is the case when a user enters a ticket quantity of 20 in cell B8.

**Ellen Jefferson:**
Enter all data from the order form into cells B3 through B12

**Number of Tickets**
Enter the number of tickets purchased.

**Invalid Data - Number of Tickets**

You have entered a value less than 1 or greater than 19. Check the number you entered. If it
If it is incorrect, click No. If you are not sure, click Cancel.

Continue?

Yes    No    Cancel    Help

Was this information helpful?

# DATA VALIDATION AND PROTECTION

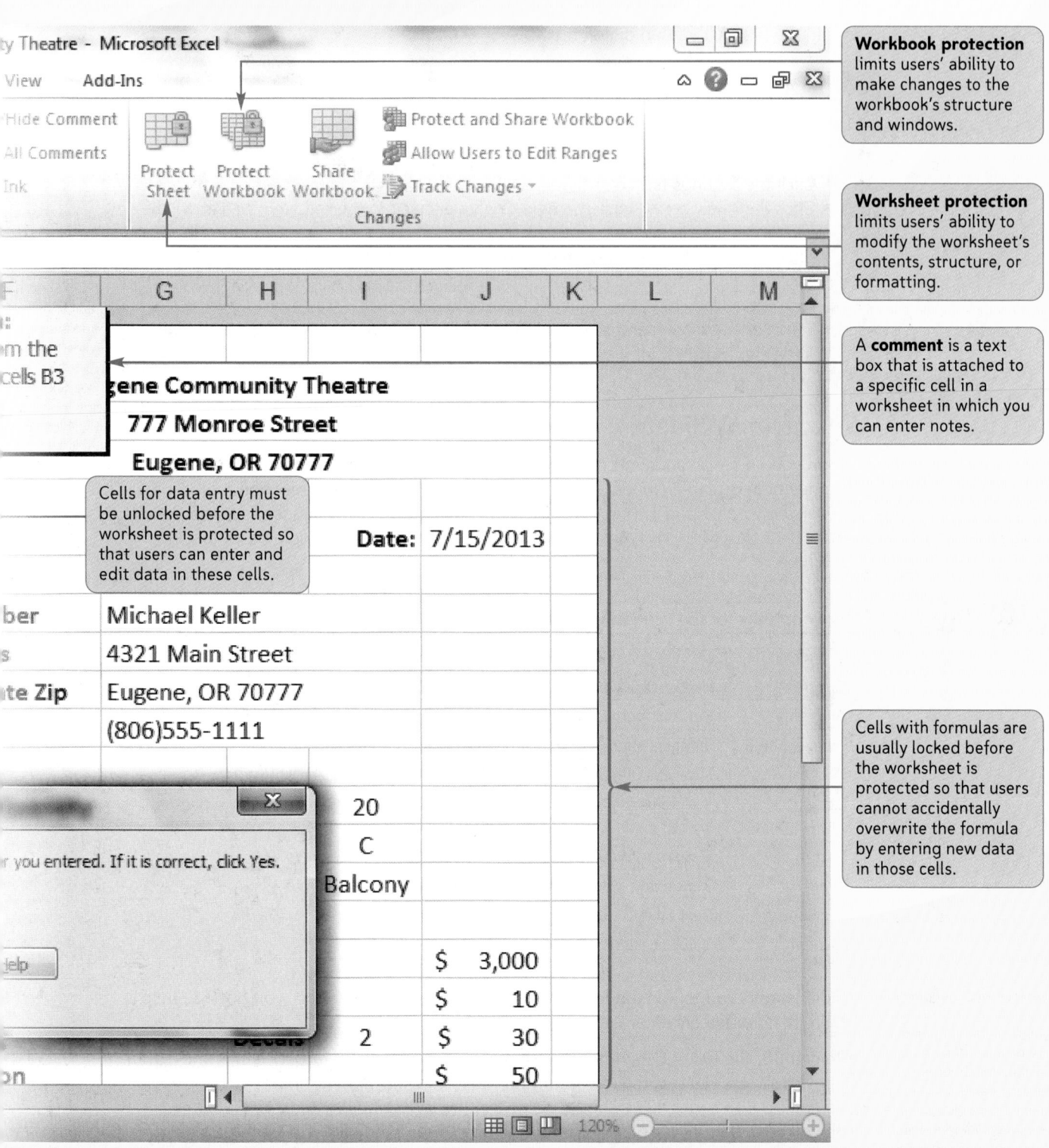

**Workbook protection** limits users' ability to make changes to the workbook's structure and windows.

**Worksheet protection** limits users' ability to modify the worksheet's contents, structure, or formatting.

A **comment** is a text box that is attached to a specific cell in a worksheet in which you can enter notes.

Cells for data entry must be unlocked before the worksheet is protected so that users can enter and edit data in these cells.

Cells with formulas are usually locked before the worksheet is protected so that users cannot accidentally overwrite the formula by entering new data in those cells.

ty Theatre - Microsoft Excel

View    Add-Ins

Hide Comment
All Comments
Ink

Protect    Protect    Share    Protect and Share Workbook
Sheet    Workbook    Workbook    Allow Users to Edit Ranges
Track Changes

Changes

gene Community Theatre

777 Monroe Street

Eugene, OR 70777

Date: 7/15/2013

ber    Michael Keller

s    4321 Main Street

te Zip    Eugene, OR 70777

(806)555-1111

you entered. If it is correct, click Yes.

elp

20

C

Balcony

$    3,000

$    10

2    $    30

$    50

# Validating Data Entry

**TIP**

Each cell can have only one validation rule. Creating a second validation rule for a cell replaces the existing rule.

To ensure that correct data is entered and stored in a worksheet, you can use data validation. Each **validation rule** defines criteria for the data that can be stored in a cell or range. You can also add input and error alert messages for the user to that cell or range. You specify the validation criteria, the input message, and the error alert for the active cell in the Data Validation dialog box.

**REFERENCE**

*Validating Data*

- In the Data Tools group on the Data tab, click the Data Validation button.
- Click the Settings tab.
- Click the Allow arrow, click the type of data allowed in the cell, and then enter the validation criteria for that data.
- Click the Input Message tab, and then enter a title and text for the input message.
- Click the Error Alert tab, and then, if necessary, click the Show error alert after invalid data is entered check box to insert a check mark.
- Select an alert style, and then enter the title and text for the error alert message.
- Click the OK button.

## Specifying Validation Criteria

When you create a validation rule, you specify the type of data allowed as well as a list or range of acceptable values (called validation criteria). For example, you might specify integers between 1 and 100, or a list of codes such as Excellent, Good, Fair, and Poor. Figure 8-12 describes the types of data you can allow and the acceptable values for each type.

**Figure 8-12**    **Allow options for the validation**

| Type | Acceptable Values |
|---|---|
| Any value | Any number, text, or date; removes any existing data validation |
| Whole number | Integers only; you can specify the range of acceptable integers |
| Decimal | Any type of number; you can specify the range of acceptable numbers |
| List | Any value in a range or entered in the Data Validation dialog box separated by commas |
| Date | Dates only; you can specify the range of acceptable dates |
| Time | Times only; you can specify the range of acceptable times |
| Text length | Text limited to a specified number of characters |
| Custom | Values based on the results of a logical formula |

**TIP**

To apply a validation rule to all of the cells in an Excel table column, select the column of data to which the validation rule will be applied, and then create the validation rule.

Ellen wants you to add the following three validation rules to the workbook to help ensure that volunteers enter valid data in the Invoice worksheet:

- In cell B8, the Ticket Quantity value should be a whole number between 1 and 19. In previous years, 19 was the maximum number of tickets purchased.
- In cell B9, the Series value should be one of the following list: A, B, C, D, E, or F.
- In cell B10, the Location value should be one of the following list: Orchestra or Balcony.

You will define the validation rule for the number of season tickets. Cell B8, which records the ticket quantity, requires an integer that is greater than 0 and less than 20.

## To create the validation rule for the Ticket Quantity cell:

1. If you took a break after the previous session, make sure the Community Theatre workbook is open and the Invoice worksheet is active.

2. Click cell **B8**. You will enter a whole number validation rule for this cell.

3. Click the **Data** tab on the Ribbon, and then click the **Data Validation** button in the Data Tools group. The Data Validation dialog box opens. You use the Settings tab to enter the validation rule for the active cell.

4. On the Settings tab, click the **Allow** arrow, and then click **Whole number**. The Data Validation dialog box expands to display the options specific to whole numbers. The Ignore blank check box is checked, which means the validation rule is not applied when the cell is empty. If you uncheck the option, users are required to make an entry in the cell.

5. If necessary, click the **Data** arrow, and then click **between**. The dialog box reflects the selected criteria.

6. Click the **Minimum** box, and then type **1** to specify the smallest value a user can enter.

7. Press the **Tab** key to move to the Maximum box, and then type **19** to specify the largest value a user can enter. See Figure 8-13.

---

**Figure 8-13**     **Settings tab in the Data Validation dialog box**

select the type of value you want to allow in the cell

these options change to reflect the allowed value

uncheck to apply the validation rule to empty cells (which means that the cell cannot be left blank)

---

**INSIGHT**

### Validating Existing Data

Validation rules come into play only during data entry. If you add validation rules to a workbook that already contains data with erroneous values, Excel does not determine if any existing data is invalid. Instead, you can use the Circle Invalid Data command to help identify invalid data that is already in the workbook. (You'll learn about the Circle Invalid Data command later in this tutorial.)

## Creating an Input Message

One way to reduce the chance of a data-entry error is to display an input message when a user makes the cell active. An input message provides additional information about the type of data allowed for that cell. Input messages appear as ScreenTips next to the cell when the cell is selected. You can add an input message to a cell even if you don't set up a rule to validate the data in that cell.

Before volunteers enter a value for the ticket quantity, Ellen wants them to see the acceptable values that can be entered in the cell. The input message will help minimize the chance of a volunteer entering an invalid value. You will create an input message for cell B8.

### To create an input message for the Ticket Quantity cell:

▸ **1.** In the Data Validation dialog box, click the **Input Message** tab. You enter the input message title and text on this tab.

▸ **2.** Verify that the **Show input message when cell is selected** check box contains a check mark. If you uncheck this option, you cannot enter a new input message and any existing input message will not be displayed when the selected cell becomes active.

> **TIP**
>
> The maximum number of characters allowed in the Title box is 32.

▸ **3.** Click in the **Title** box, and then type **Number of Tickets**. This title will appear in bold at the top of the ScreenTip above the text of the input message.

▸ **4.** Press the **Tab** key to move the insertion point to the Input message box, and then type **Enter the number of tickets purchased.** This text will appear in the ScreenTip when the cell becomes active. See Figure 8-14.

**Figure 8-14**　　**Input Message tab in the Data Validation dialog box**

uncheck to hide the input message even when the cell is selected

title of the input message

text of the input message

## Creating an Error Alert Style and Message

An error alert determines what happens after a user attempts to make an invalid entry in a cell that has a validation rule defined. The three error alert styles are Stop, Warning, and Information. The Stop alert prevents the entry from being stored in the cell. The Warning alert prevents the entry from being stored in the cell unless the user overrides the rejection and decides to continue using the data. The Information alert accepts the data value entered, but allows the user to choose to cancel the data entry.

Ellen wants to display an error alert if a volunteer enters data that violates the validation rule. Although ticket quantities between 1 and 19 are the norm for the theatre, occasionally a subscriber may want to purchase 20 or more tickets, and those entries should be allowed. To account for this possibility, you will create a Warning error alert that appears when a user enters a ticket quantity value greater than 20 or less than 1. The user can then verify the number entered. If the entry is correct, the user can accept the entry. If the entry is incorrect, the user can reenter the correct number.

You'll create the Warning error alert for the Ticket Quantity cell.

### To create the Warning error alert for the Ticket Quantity cell:

▶ **1.** In the Data Validation dialog box, click the **Error Alert** tab. You use this tab to select the type of error alert and enter the message you want to appear.

▶ **2.** Make sure that the **Show error alert after invalid data is entered** check box is checked. If unchecked, the error alert won't appear when an invalid value is entered in the cell.

▶ **3.** Click the **Style** arrow, and then click **Warning**. This style allows the user to accept the invalid value, return to the cell and reenter a valid value, or cancel the data entry and restore the previous value to the cell.

▶ **4.** Click in the **Title** box, and then type **Invalid Data - Number of Tickets**. This text will appear as the title of the error alert box.

▶ **5.** Press the **Tab** key to move the insertion point to the Error message box, and then type **You have entered a value less than 1 or greater than 19. Check the number you entered. If it is correct, click Yes. If it is incorrect, click No. If you are not sure, click Cancel.** See Figure 8-15.

**TIP**

You might hide the input and error alert messages when only experienced users will enter data in the workbook by unchecking the Show check box. You can show them again if a new user will enter data.

| Figure 8-15 | Error Alert tab in the Data Validation dialog box |

▶ **6.** Click the **OK** button. The input message appears below cell B8 because the cell is active. See Figure 8-16.

**Figure 8-16**    Input message for cell B8

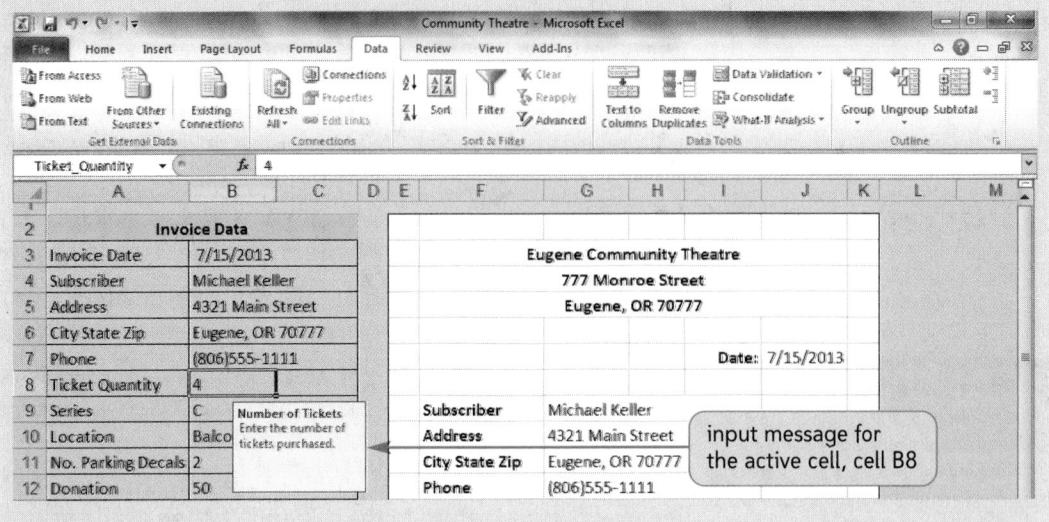

## Using Formulas to Define Complex Validation Criteria

**INSIGHT**

The built-in data validation rules are adequate for most simple needs. Sometimes, however, those rules just don't fit your specific worksheet. In those cases, you need to create a custom validation rule that includes a formula. To create a custom validation rule, open the Data Validation dialog box. On the Settings tab, click the Allow arrow, and then click Custom. You can then create the data validation formula.

The formula you specify must be in the form of a condition that returns either True or False. If True is returned, the data entered is considered valid and accepted. If False is returned, the entry is considered invalid and an error alert message is displayed. Consider two data validation examples.

The first example uses data validation to prevent the entry of dates that fall on Saturday or Sunday. The WEEKDAY function returns a number (1 to 7) for the date entered in the cell, and then you create a formula to display an error alert if values of 1 (Sunday) or 7 (Saturday) are detected. Assuming the date is entered in cell B2, the following formula returns False if either Saturday or Sunday is entered in cell B2:

```
=AND(WEEKDAY(B2)<>1,WEEKDAY(B2)<>7)
```

The second example uses data validation to ensure all product codes begin with the letter "C." To prevent any letter except a "C" from being entered as the first character in cell A2, you would use the LEFT function to extract the first character in the cell. The following formula returns True if the first character entered in cell A2 begins with a "C"; otherwise, an error alert message is displayed:

```
=LEFT(A2,1) = "C"
```

## Creating a List Validation Rule

You can use the data validation feature to restrict a cell to accept only entries that are on a list you create. You can create the list of valid entries in the Data Validation dialog box, or you can use a list of valid entries in a single column or row.

You will enter the validation rule for the Series being requested, which is one of the following six values: A, B, C, D, E, and F.

## To restrict the Series values to a list of entries:

▶ **1.** Click cell **B9**. You will create a list validation rule for this cell.

▶ **2.** In the Data Tools group on the Data tab, click the **Data Validation** button to open the Data Validation dialog box, and then click the **Settings** tab.

▶ **3.** Click the **Allow** arrow, and then click **List**. The dialog box expands to display the Source box. You can enter values separated by commas directly in the Source box, or you can select a range of valid entries in the worksheet.

▶ **4.** Click the **Collapse** button [icon] next to the Source box so you can see the entire worksheet.

▶ **5.** Select the range **A16:A21**, which lists the valid six entry values, and then click the **Expand** button [icon]. The Data Validation dialog box returns to its full size and displays =$A$16:$A$21. Next, you'll enter an input message.

▶ **6.** Click the **Input Message** tab, click in the **Title** box, and then type **Series** to enter the title of the input message.

▶ **7.** Click in the Input message box, and then type **Click the arrow and select one of the choices listed.** to enter the text of the input message.

▶ **8.** Click the **Error Alert** tab, and then verify that **Stop** appears in the Style box. You want to prevent a user from entering a value that is not included in the list of values you specified.

▶ **9.** In the Title text box, type **Invalid Series** to enter the title of the error alert.

▶ **10.** In the Error message box, type **An invalid series has been entered. Click Retry. Press the Esc key, and click the arrow to the right of cell B9. Select A, B, C, D, E, or F.** to enter the text of the error message.

▶ **11.** Click the **OK** button. An arrow appears to the right of cell B9 and the input message appears in a ScreenTip.

You need to enter a data validation rule for cell B10, which indicates the subscriber's choice of seat location. This list validation rule will allow a user to select either Orchestra or Balcony and will include an error alert.

## To create a list validation rule for the Location cell:

▶ **1.** Click cell **B10**. You will create a list validation rule for this cell.

▶ **2.** In the Data Tools group on the Data tab, click the **Data Validation** button. The Data Validation dialog box opens.

▶ **3.** Click the **Settings** tab, select **List** in the Allow box, click the **Source** box, and then select the range **B15:C15**. This range contains the two values you want to allow users to select for the seat location.

▶ **4.** Click the **Input Message** tab, type **Location** in the Title box, and then type **Click the arrow and select Orchestra or Balcony.** in the Input message box.

▶ **5.** Click the **Error Alert** tab, verify that **Stop** appears in the Style box, type **Invalid Location** in the Title box, and then type **An invalid location has been entered. Click Retry, press Esc, and click the arrow to the right of cell B10. Select Orchestra or Balcony.** in the Error message box.

▶ **6.** Click the **OK** button. An arrow appears to the right of cell B10 and the input message appears in a ScreenTip.

After you create validation rules, you should test them. You do this by entering incorrect values that violate the validation rules. Keep in mind that the only way an error occurs in cells that have a list validation is if an incorrect entry is *typed* in the cell. Entering invalid data will ensure that validation rules work as expected. You will test the validation rules you've just created.

## To test the data validation rules:

1. Click cell **B8**. The input message appears in a ScreenTip, indicating the type of data allowed in the cell. You will enter an invalid value to test the validation rule for the Ticket Quantity field.

2. Type **30** and then press the **Tab** key. The Invalid Data - Number of Tickets message box opens, informing you that the value you entered might be incorrect. The entry 30 is incorrect; you'll enter a valid number.

3. Click the **No** button, type **4** in cell B8, and then press the **Enter** key. The data is entered in cell B8. Cell B9 is the active cell and the input message for Series appears.

4. Click the **arrow** to the right of cell B9, and then click **B**. The value is accepted. The only way an error occurs in cells that have a list validation is if an incorrect entry is *typed* in the cell. You'll try that method.

5. In cell B9, enter **G**. The Invalid Series message box opens.

6. Click the **Retry** button to close the message box, and then press the **Esc** key to return the original value from the cell.

7. Click the **arrow** to the right of cell B9, and then click **C**.

8. In cell B10, enter **Mezzanine**. The Invalid Location message box opens, indicating that the location must be Orchestra or Balcony.

9. Click the **Retry** button, and then press the **Esc** key to return the original value entered. The three validation rules you entered work as you intended.

---

**TIP**

After the error alert appears, you must press the Esc key to return the original value to the cell; otherwise, the error alert will reappear when you click the arrow to make another selection.

---

**INSIGHT**

### Using the Circle Invalid Data Command

Validation rules come into play only during data entry. If you add validation rules to a workbook that already contains data with erroneous values, Excel does not determine if any existing data is invalid.

To ensure the entire workbook contains valid data, you need to also verify any data previously entered in the workbook. You can use the Circle Invalid Data command to find and mark cells that contain invalid data. Red circles appear around any data that does not meet the validation criteria, making it simple to scan a worksheet for errors. After you correct the data in a cell, the circle disappears.

To display circles around invalid data, perform the following steps:
1. Apply validation rules to existing range.
2. In the Data Tools group on the Data tab, click the Data Validation button arrow, and then click Circle Invalid Data. Red circles appear around cells that contain invalid data.
3. To remove the circle from a single cell, enter valid data in the cell.
4. To hide all circles, in the Data Tools group on the Data tab, click the Data Validation button arrow, and then click Clear Validation Circles.

To ensure an error-free workbook, you should use the Circle Invalid Data command to verify data entered before you set up the validation criteria or to verify data in a workbook you inherited from someone else, such as a coworker.

# Protecting a Worksheet and a Workbook

Another way to reduce data-entry errors is to limit access to certain parts of the workbook. Worksheet protection prevents users from changing cell contents, such as editing formulas in a worksheet. Workbook protection prevents users from changing the workbook's organization, such as inserting or deleting worksheets in the workbook. You can even keep users from viewing the formulas used in the workbook.

Ellen wants to protect the contents of the Invoice and Ticket Data worksheets. She wants volunteers to have access only to the range B3:B12 in the Invoice worksheet, where new invoice data is entered. She wants to prevent volunteers from editing the contents of any cells in the Ticket Data worksheet.

## Locking and Unlocking Cells

Every cell in a workbook has a **locked property** that determines whether changes can be made to that cell. The locked property has no impact as long as the worksheet is unprotected. However, after you protect a worksheet, the locked property controls whether the cell can be edited. You unlock a cell by turning off the locked property. By default, the locked property is turned on for each cell, and worksheet protection is turned off.

So, unless you unlock cells in a worksheet *before* protecting the worksheet, all of the cells in the worksheet will be locked, and you won't be able to make any changes in the worksheet. Usually, you will want to protect the worksheet, but leave some cells unlocked. For example, you might want to lock cells that contain formulas and formatting so they cannot be changed, but unlock cells in which you want to enter data.

To protect some—but not all—cells in a worksheet, you first turn off the locked property of cells in which data can be entered. Then, you protect the worksheet to activate the locked property for the remaining cells.

In the Invoice worksheet, users should be able to enter data in the range B3:B12 but not any other cell. To do this, you must unlock the cells in the range B3:B12.

### To unlock the cells in the range B3:B12:

1. In the Invoice worksheet, select the range **B3:B12**. You want to unlock the cells in this range before you protect the worksheet.

2. Click the **Home** tab on the Ribbon, and then click the **Dialog Box Launcher** in the Font group. The Format Cells dialog box opens with the Font tab active.

3. Click the **Protection** tab, and then click the **Locked** check box to remove the check mark.

4. Click the **OK** button. The cells in the range B3:B12 are unlocked.

5. Click cell **A1** to deselect the range.

## Protecting a Worksheet

When you set up worksheet protection, you specify which actions are still available to users in the protected worksheet. For example, you can choose to allow users to insert new rows or columns, or to delete rows and columns. You can limit the user to selecting only unlocked cells, or allow the user to select any cell in the worksheet. These choices remain active as long as the worksheet is protected.

A protected worksheet can always be unprotected. You can also add a password to the protected worksheet that users must enter in order to turn off the protection. If you are concerned that users will turn off protection and make changes to formulas, you should use a password; otherwise, it's probably best to not specify a password.

*Protecting a Worksheet*

- Select the cells and ranges to unlock so that users can enter data in them.
- In the Font group on the Home tab, click the Dialog Box Launcher.
- In the Format Cells dialog box, click the Protection tab, click the Locked check box to remove the check mark, and then click the OK button.
- In the Changes group on the Review tab, click the Protect Sheet button.
- Enter a password (optional).
- Select all of the actions you want to allow users to take when the worksheet is protected.
- Click the OK button.

Ellen wants to protect the Invoice and Ticket Data worksheets, but she doesn't want a password specified. You will enable worksheet protection that will allow users to select any cell in those worksheets, but enter data only in the unlocked cells.

### To protect the Invoice worksheet:

1. Click the **Review** tab on the Ribbon, and then click the **Protect Sheet** button in the Changes group. The Protect Sheet dialog box opens. See Figure 8-17.

**Figure 8-17** | Protect Sheet dialog box

check the actions you want users to be able to perform in the protected worksheet

You will leave the Password to unprotect sheet box blank because you do not want to use a password. By default, users can select locked and unlocked cells, which are all of the cells in the worksheet, but they can enter or edit values only in unlocked cells.

2. Click the **OK** button. The Protect Sheet dialog box closes.

Any time you modify a worksheet, you should test the worksheet to ensure that changes work as intended. You'll test the protection you added to the Invoice worksheet by trying to edit a locked cell and then trying to edit an unlocked cell in the Invoice worksheet.

### To test the Invoice worksheet protection:

▶  1. Click cell **I14**, and then type **8**. As soon as you press any key, a dialog box opens, indicating that the cell is protected and cannot be modified. See Figure 8-18.

**Figure 8-18**    Message displayed after trying to change a protected cell

▶  2. Click the **OK** button.

▶  3. Click cell **B8**, type **8** and then press the **Enter** key. The ticket quantity is updated because you allowed editing in the range B3:B12. A user can enter and edit values in these cells. Although users can select any cell in the worksheet, they cannot make an entry in any other cell.

▶  4. On the Quick Access Toolbar, click the **Undo** button ↺ to return the ticket quantity to 4.

You will repeat this process to protect all of the cells in the Ticket Data worksheet. Then you will test to see what would happen if someone tried to edit one of the cells in the Ticket Data worksheet.

### To protect and test the Ticket Data worksheet:

▶  1. Switch to the **Ticket Data** worksheet.

▶  2. In the Changes group on the Review tab, click the **Protect Sheet** button. The Protect Sheet dialog box opens.

▶  3. Click the **OK** button to accept the default set of user actions.

▶  4. Click cell **A2**, and then type **B**. A dialog box opens, indicating that the cell is protected and cannot be modified. All of the cells in this worksheet are protected because no cells have been unlocked.

▶  5. Click the **OK** button to close the dialog box.

## Protecting a Workbook

Worksheet protection applies only to the contents of a worksheet, not to the worksheet itself. To keep a worksheet from being modified, you need to protect the workbook. You can protect both the structure and the windows of a workbook. Protecting the structure prohibits users from renaming, deleting, hiding, or inserting worksheets. Protecting the windows prohibits users from moving, resizing, closing, or hiding parts of the Excel window. The default is to protect only the structure of the workbook, not the windows used to display it.

You can also add a password to the workbook protection. However, the same guideline applies here as for protecting worksheets. Add a password only if you are concerned that others might unprotect the workbook and modify it. If you add a password, keep in mind that it is case sensitive and you cannot unprotect the workbook without it.

### Protecting a Workbook

- In the Changes group on the Review tab, click the Protect Workbook button.
- Click the check boxes to indicate whether you want to protect the workbook's structure, windows, or both.
- Enter a password (optional).
- Click the OK button.

The contents of the Invoice and Ticket Data worksheets, with the exception of the range B3:B12 in the Invoice worksheet, cannot be changed. However, a theatre volunteer could inadvertently rename or delete the protected worksheet. To keep the worksheets themselves from being modified, you will protect the workbook. Ellen doesn't want users to be able to change the structure of the workbook, so you will set workbook protection for the structure, but not the window.

### To protect the Community Theatre workbook:

1. In the Changes group on the Review tab, click the **Protect Workbook** button. The Protect Structure and Windows dialog box opens. You can choose to protect the structure, protect the windows, or both. See Figure 8-19.

| Figure 8-19 | Protect Structure and Windows dialog box |

2. Make sure the **Structure** check box is checked, the **Windows** check box is unchecked, and the **Password** box is blank.

3. Click the **OK** button to protect the workbook without specifying a password.

4. Right-click the **Ticket Data** sheet tab. On the shortcut menu, notice that the Insert, Delete, Rename, Move or Copy, Tab Color, Hide, and Unhide commands are gray, indicating that the options that modify the worksheets are no longer available for the Ticket Data worksheet.

5. Press the **Esc** key to close the shortcut menu.

## Unprotecting a Worksheet and a Workbook

You can turn off worksheet protection at any time. This is often referred to as unprotecting the worksheet. You need to unprotect a worksheet to edit its contents. If you assigned a password when you protected the worksheet, you would need to enter the password to remove worksheet protection. Likewise, you can unprotect the workbook. If you need to insert a new worksheet or rename an existing worksheet, you can unprotect the protected workbook, make the changes to the structure, and apply workbook protection again.

At this point, you still have a lot of editing to do in the Invoice worksheet, so you'll turn off worksheet protection in that worksheet. Later, when you've completed your modifications, Ellen can turn worksheet protection back on.

**TIP**

To remove workbook protection, click the Protect Workbook button in the Changes group on the Review tab.

### To turn off worksheet protection for the Invoice worksheet:

1. Switch to the **Invoice** worksheet.

2. In the Changes group on the Review tab, click the **Unprotect Sheet** button. Worksheet protection is removed from the Invoice worksheet. The button changes back to the Protect Sheet button.

## Inserting Comments

Comments are often used in workbooks to: (a) explain the contents of a particular cell, such as a complex formula; (b) provide instructions to users; and (c) share ideas and notes from several users collaborating on a project. The username for your installation of Excel appears in bold at the top of the comments box. If you collaborate on a workbook, the top of the comments boxes would show the name of each user who created that comment. A small red triangle appears in the upper-right corner of a cell with a comment. The comment box appears when you point to a cell with a comment.

**REFERENCE**

*Inserting a Comment*

- Click the cell to which you want to attach a comment.
- Right-click the cell, and then click Insert Comment on the shortcut menu.
  *or*
  In the Comments group on the Review tab, click the New Comment button.
- Type the comment into the box.

Ellen wants you to insert a note in cell A2 about entering data from the order form into the input section, and a note in cell J18 explaining how the IF and VLOOKUP functions are used to determine the cost of theatre tickets.

**TIP**

You can also add a comment by right-clicking the cell, and then clicking Insert Comment on the shortcut menu.

### To insert comments in cells A2 and J18:

1. In the Invoice worksheet, click cell **A2**.

2. In the Comments group on the Review tab, click the **New Comment** button. A box opens to the right of cell A2. The username for your installation of Excel appears in bold at the top of the box. A small red triangle appears in the upper-right corner of the cell.

3. Type **Enter all data from the order form into cells B3 through B11** in the box. An arrow points from the box to cell A2, which contains the comment. A selection box with sizing handles appears around the box. See Figure 8-20.

| Figure 8-20 | Comment added to cell A2 |

red triangle indicates this cell has a comment

drag a sizing handle to resize the box

username for your installation of Excel appears here

drag the selection box to move the comment

4. Click cell **B12** to hide the comment. The comment disappears. A small red triangle remains in the upper-right corner of cell A2 to indicate this cell contains a comment.

5. Move the pointer over cell **A2**. The comment appears.

6. Click cell **A2**.

7. In the Comments group on the Review tab, click the **Edit Comment** button. The comment appears with the insertion point at the end of the comment text, so you can edit the incorrect cell reference.

8. Select **B11** in the comment box, and then type **B12**. The comment in cell A2 now correctly references the range B3:B12.

9. Click any cell to hide the comment, and then point to cell **A2** to view the edited comment.

10. Click cell **J18**, and then click the **New Comment** button in the Comments group on the Review tab. A comment box opens to the right of cell J18.

11. Type **This IF function determines whether to use a VLOOKUP function referencing column 2 or 3 of the Ticket Price Table** in the box.

12. Drag the lower-right sizing handle down to increase the size of the box to fit the comment.

13. Click cell **I17** to hide the comment. A small red triangle remains in the upper-right corner of cell J18 to indicate it contains a comment.

14. Point to cell **J18** to see the comment. Ellen decides that the volunteers don't need to know how the ticket cost is calculated. You'll delete the comment in cell J18.

15. Click cell **J18**, and then click the **Delete** button in the Comments group on the Review tab. The comment is deleted, and the red triangle in the upper-right corner of cell J18 is removed.

**TIP**

To keep an active cell's comment on-screen, click the Show/Hide Comment button in the Comments group on the Review tab. Click the button again to hide the active cell's comment.

## PROSKILLS

### Written Communication: Documenting a Spreadsheet

Providing documentation for a spreasheet is important because it provides instructions on the spreadsheet's use, defines technical terms, explains complex formulas, and identifies assumptions. By documenting a spreadsheet, you help users work more effectively. In addition, documentation helps you recall months or years from now what is in the spreadsheet that might otherwise be forgotten. Furthermore, when someone else becomes responsible for modifying the spreadsheet in the future, the documentation will help that person get up to speed quickly.

It is helpful for you to create a Documentation worksheet to provide an overview, definitions, assumptions, and instructions on how to use various parts of a workbook. Excel also offers many tools to help you document spreadsheets, including:

- Defined names and structured references to make formulas easier to create and understand
- Data validation including input messages specifying what to enter in a cell, and error messages providing instructions on what to do if the data entered is incorrect
- Cell comments to explain complex formulas, give reminders, and so on
- Formula mode to view all formulas in a worksheet at one time

Providing documentation will help users get a better understanding of the application, saving time and frustration.

In this session, you used data validation to help ensure that all values entered in the Invoice worksheet are valid. You created validation rules that included input messages and error alert messages. You learned how to protect and unprotect both the worksheet and the workbook. In addition, you used comments to add notes to specific cells. In the next session, you'll automate some of the steps in the application by recording macros.

## REVIEW

### Session 8.2 Quick Check

1. Why do you want to validate data?
2. What is the purpose of the input message in the Data Validation command?
3. Describe the three types of error alert messages Excel can display when a user violates a validation rule.
4. What is a locked cell?
5. What is the difference between worksheet protection and workbook protection?
6. Can you rename a protected worksheet? Explain why or why not.
7. Give two reasons for adding a comment to a worksheet cell.

# SESSION 8.3 VISUAL OVERVIEW

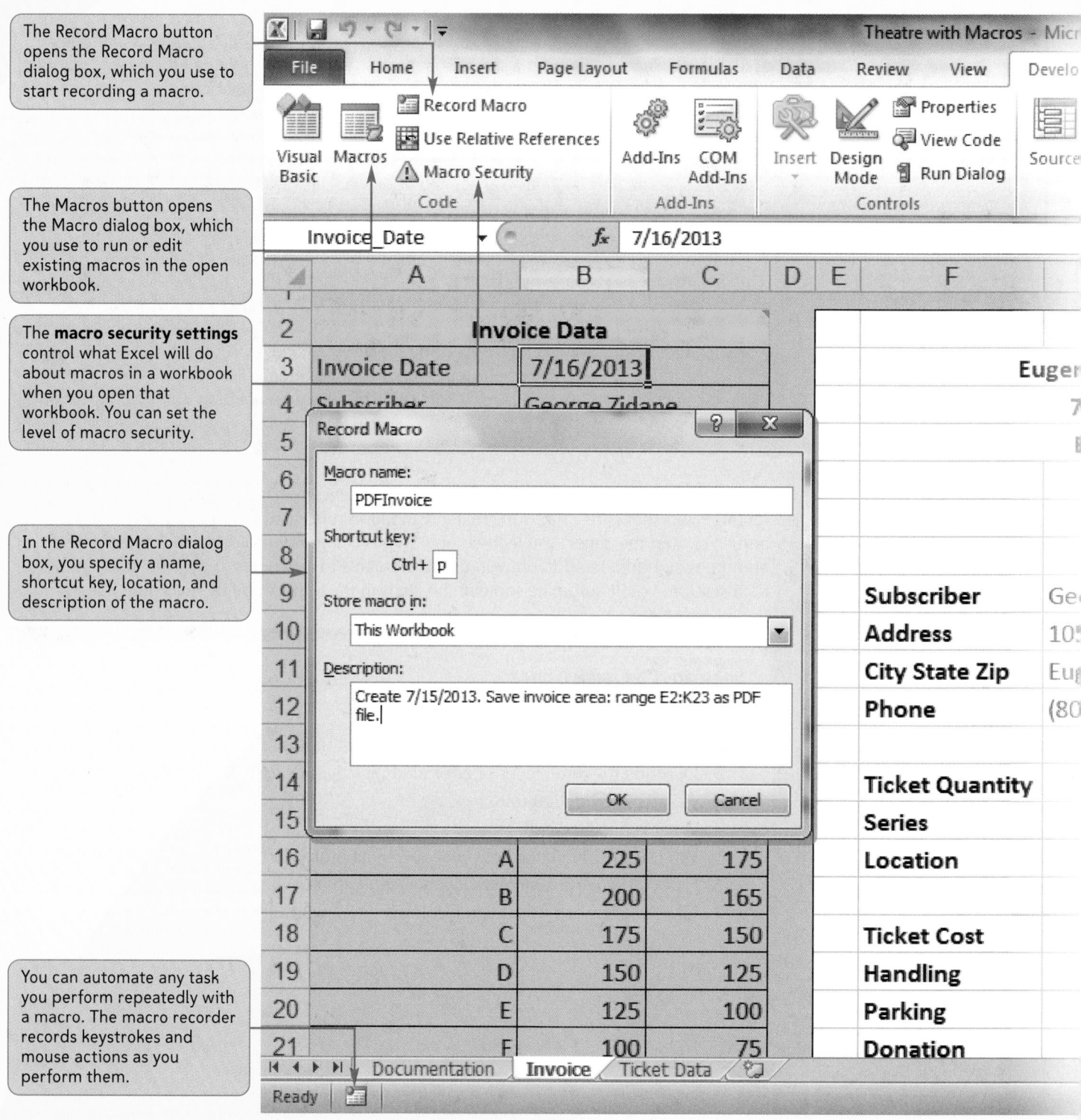

The Record Macro button opens the Record Macro dialog box, which you use to start recording a macro.

The Macros button opens the Macro dialog box, which you use to run or edit existing macros in the open workbook.

The **macro security settings** control what Excel will do about macros in a workbook when you open that workbook. You can set the level of macro security.

In the Record Macro dialog box, you specify a name, shortcut key, location, and description of the macro.

You can automate any task you perform repeatedly with a macro. The macro recorder records keystrokes and mouse actions as you perform them.

**Record Macro**

Macro name:
PDFInvoice

Shortcut key:
Ctrl+ p

Store macro in:
This Workbook

Description:
Create 7/15/2013. Save invoice area: range E2:K23 as PDF file.

# WORKING WITH MACROS

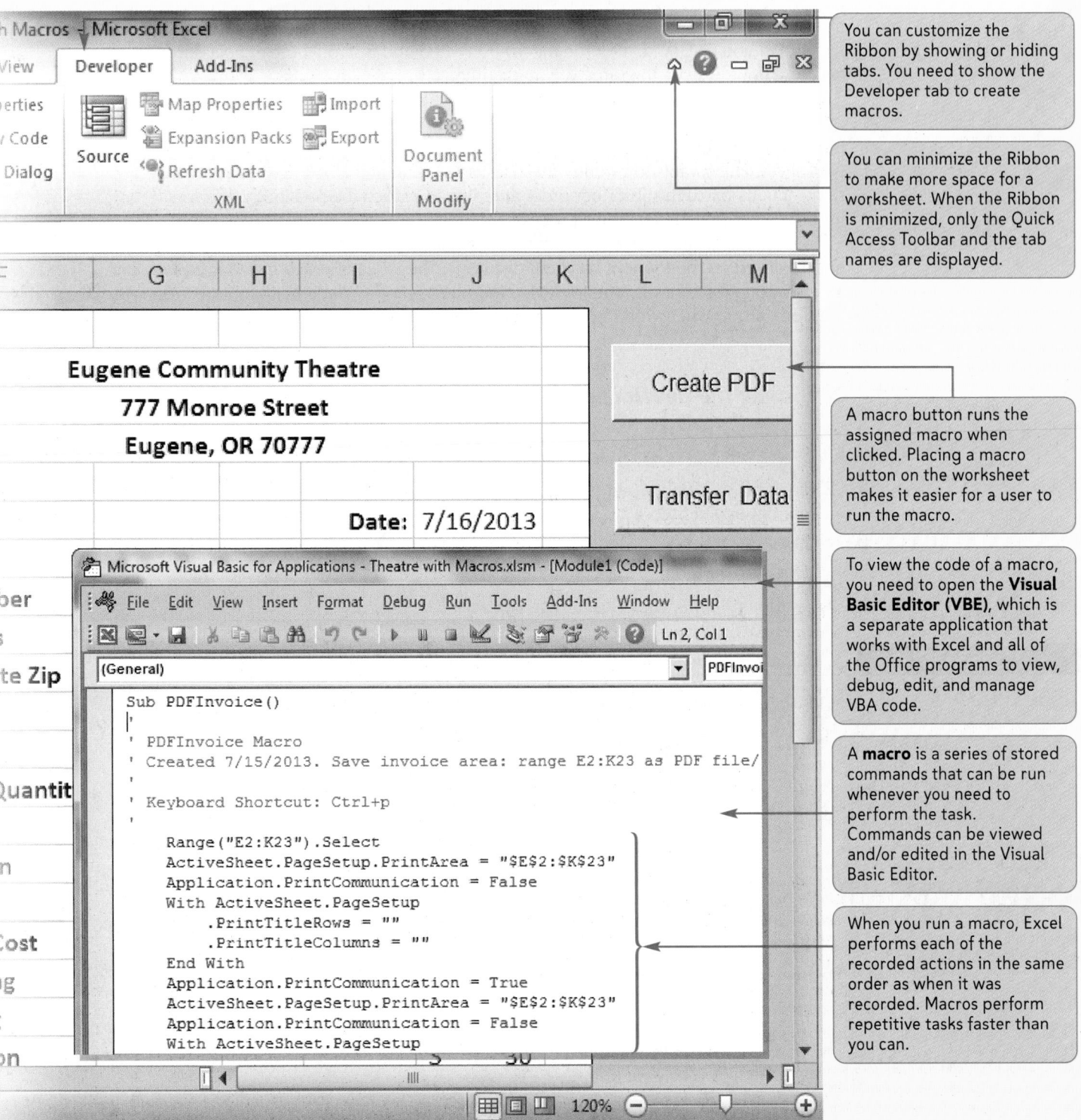

You can customize the Ribbon by showing or hiding tabs. You need to show the Developer tab to create macros.

You can minimize the Ribbon to make more space for a worksheet. When the Ribbon is minimized, only the Quick Access Toolbar and the tab names are displayed.

A macro button runs the assigned macro when clicked. Placing a macro button on the worksheet makes it easier for a user to run the macro.

To view the code of a macro, you need to open the **Visual Basic Editor (VBE)**, which is a separate application that works with Excel and all of the Office programs to view, debug, edit, and manage VBA code.

A **macro** is a series of stored commands that can be run whenever you need to perform the task. Commands can be viewed and/or edited in the Visual Basic Editor.

When you run a macro, Excel performs each of the recorded actions in the same order as when it was recorded. Macros perform repetitive tasks faster than you can.

# Automating Tasks with Macros

Using a macro, you can automate any task you perform repeatedly. For example, you can create a macro to print a worksheet, insert a set of dates and values, or import data from a text file and store it in Excel. Macros perform repetitive tasks consistently and faster than you can. And, after the macro is created and tested, you can be assured the tasks are done exactly the same way each time.

Ellen needs to save only the invoice as a PDF file so she can later send it as an attachment to the season subscriber along with an email confirming the ticket purchase transaction. In addition, data from the invoice needs to be transferred to the Ticket Data worksheet. Ellen wants to simplify these tasks so volunteers don't need to repeat the same actions for each subscriber order and also to reduce the possibility of errors being introduced during the repetitive process. You will create a macro for each action.

To create and run macros, you need to use the Developer tab. By default, this tab is not displayed on the Ribbon, so you'll display it. The Developer tab has four groups: one for code, one for controls, one for XML, and one to modify document controls. You'll use the Code group when working with macros. You'll add the Developer tab to the Ribbon.

## To display the Developer tab on the Ribbon:

1. If you took a break after the previous session, make sure the Community Theatre workbook is open and the Invoice worksheet is active.

2. Look for the **Developer** tab on the Ribbon. If you do not see the Developer tab, continue with Step 3. If you see the Developer tab, continue with Step 7.

3. Click the **File** tab on the Ribbon to open Backstage view, and then click the **Options** button in the navigation bar. The Excel Options dialog box opens.

4. In the left pane, click **Customize Ribbon**. See Figure 8-21.

**Figure 8-21** | Customize Ribbon options in the Excel Options dialog box

5. In the right pane, click the **Developer** check box to insert a check mark.

6. Click the **OK** button. The Developer tab appears on the Ribbon.

> **7.** Click the **Developer** tab. See Figure 8-22.

| **Figure 8-22** | **Developer tab on the Ribbon** |

Developer tab added to the Ribbon

# Protecting Against Macro Viruses

In recent years, viruses have been attached as macros to files created in Excel and other Office programs. A **virus** is a computer program designed to copy itself into other programs with the intention of causing mischief or harm. When unsuspecting users opened these infected workbooks, Excel automatically ran the attached virus-infected macro. **Macro viruses** are a type of virus that uses a program's own macro programming language to distribute the virus. Most macro viruses are not harmful and do not affect data in any way. For example, one macro virus changed the title bar text from *Microsoft Excel* to *Microsofa Excel*. Occasionally, macro viruses are destructive and can modify or delete files that may not be recoverable. Because it is possible for a macro to contain a virus, Microsoft Office 2010 provides several options from which you can choose to set a security level you feel comfortable with.

## Macro Security Settings

The macro security settings control what Excel will do about macros in a workbook when you open that workbook. For example, one user may choose to run macros only if they are "digitally signed" by a developer who is on a list of trusted sources. Another user might want to disable all macros in workbooks and see a notification when a workbook contains macros. The user can then elect to enable the macros. Excel has four macro security settings, which are described in Figure 8-23.

| **Figure 8-23** | **Macro security settings** |

| Setting | Description |
| --- | --- |
| Disable all macros without notification | All macros in all workbooks are disabled and no security alerts about macros are displayed. Use this setting if you don't want macros to run. |
| Disable all macros with notification | All macros in all workbooks are disabled, but security alerts appear when the workbook contains a macro. Use this default setting to choose on a case-by-case basis whether to run a macro. |
| Disable all macros except digitally signed macros | The same as the Disable all macros with notification setting except any macro signed by a trusted publisher runs if you have already trusted the publisher. Otherwise, security alerts appear when a workbook contains a macro. |
| Enable all macros | All macros in all workbooks run. Use this setting temporarily in such cases as when developing an application that contains macros. This setting is not recommended for regular use. |

You set macro security in the Trust Center. The **Trust Center** is a central location for all of the security settings in Office 2010. By default, all potentially dangerous content, such as macros and workbooks with external links, is blocked without warning. If content is blocked, the Message Bar (also called the trust bar) located under the Ribbon appears, notifying you that some content was disabled. You can click the Message Bar to enable that content.

In Office 2010, you can define a set of locations (file paths) where you can place files you consider trustworthy. This feature is known as Trusted Locations. Any workbook opened from a trusted location is considered safe, and content such as macros will work without having to respond to additional security questions to use the workbook.

**REFERENCE**

*Setting Macro Security in Excel*

- In the Code group on the Developer tab, click the Macro Security button.
- Click the option button for the macro setting you want.
- Click the OK button.

*or*

- Click the File tab, and then click the Options button in the navigation bar.
- Click the Trust Center category, and then click the Trust Center Settings button.
- Click the Macro Settings category, and then click the option button for a macro setting.
- Click the OK button.

Ellen wants some protection against macro viruses, so she suggests you set the security level to "Disable all macros with notification." When you open a file with macros, this macro security level disables the macros and displays a security alert, allowing you to enable the macros if you believe the workbook comes from a trusted source. After the macros are enabled, you can run them.

**To set the macro security level:**

▶ **1.** In the Code group on the Developer tab, click the **Macro Security** button. The Trust Center dialog box opens with the Macro Settings category displayed.

▶ **2.** In the Macro Settings section, click the **Disable all macros with notification** option button if it is not selected. See Figure 8-24.

| Figure 8-24 | Macro Settings in the Trust Center dialog box |
| --- | --- |

▶ **3.** Click the **OK** button.

Each time you open a workbook that contains a macro detected by the Trust Center, the macro is disabled and a Message Bar containing the Security Warning that macros have been disabled appears below the Ribbon. If you developed the workbook or trust the person who sent you the workbook, click the Enable Content button to run the macros in the workbook. If you do not click the Enable Content button, you cannot run the macros in the workbook, but you can use the rest of the workbook.

---

**INSIGHT**

### Using Digital Signatures with Macros

A **digital signature** is like a seal of approval. It's often used to identify the author of a workbook that contains macros. You add a digital signature as the last step before you distribute a file. Before you can add a digital signature to a workbook, you need to obtain a digital ID (also called a digital certificate) that proves your identity. Digital certificates are typically issued by a certificate authority. After you have a digital certificate, do the following to digitally sign a workbook:

1. Click the File tab on the Ribbon, and then, in the navigation bar, click Info.
2. On the Info tab, click the Protect Workbook button, and then click the Add a Digital Signature button.
3. If a message dialog box opens, click the OK button. The Sign dialog box opens.
4. In the Purpose for signing this document box, enter a reason why you are adding a digital signature to this workbook.
5. Click the Sign button, and then click the OK button. The invisible digital signature does not appear within the workbook, but users will see the Signatures button on the status bar.

By digitally signing a workbook that contains a macro you intend to publicly distribute, you assure others of two things: (1) the identity of the creator of the macro, and (2) the macro has not been altered since the digital signature was created.

When you open a digitally signed file, you can see who the author is and decide whether the information in the file is authentic and whether you trust that the macros in the workbook are safe to run.

The digital signature is removed any time a file is saved after the signature has been added to the file. Therefore, no one (including the original workbook author) can open a digitally signed file, make changes to the workbook, save the workbook, and then send the file to another user with the digital signature intact. The original author must digitally sign the modified workbook.

---

# Recording a Macro

You can create an Excel macro in one of two ways: You can use the macro recorder to record keystrokes and mouse actions as you perform them, or you can enter a series of commands in the **Visual Basic for Applications (VBA)** programming language. The macro recorder can record only those actions you perform with the keyboard or mouse. The macro recorder is a good choice for creating simple macros. For more sophisticated macros, you might need to write VBA code directly in the Visual Basic Editor.

For Ellen's application, the tasks you need to perform can all be done with the keyboard and the mouse, so you will use the macro recorder to record the two macros. One macro will save the invoice as a PDF file, which is a file format created by Adobe Systems for document exchange. The second macro will transfer data from the Invoice worksheet to the Ticket Data worksheet.

**PROSKILLS**

*Decision Making: Planning and Recording a Macro*

Advance planning and practice help to ensure you create an error-free macro. First, decide what you want to accomplish. Then, consider the best way to achieve those results. Next, practice the keystrokes and mouse actions before you actually record the macro. This may seem like extra work, but it reduces the chance of error when you actually record the macro. As you set up the macro, consider the following:

- Choose a descriptive name that helps you recognize the macro's purpose.
- Weigh the benefits of selecting a shortcut key against its drawbacks. Although a shortcut key is an easy way to run a macro, you are limited to one-letter shortcuts, which can make it difficult to remember the purpose of each shortcut key. In addition, the macro shortcut keys will override the standard Office shortcuts for the workbook.
- Store the macro with the current workbook unless the macro can be used with other workbooks.
- Include a description that provides an overview of the macro and perhaps your name and contact information.

    Good decision making includes thinking about what to do and what *not* to do as you progress to your goals. This is true when developing a macro as well.

Each macro must have a unique name that begins with a letter. The macro name can contain up to 255 characters, including letters, numbers, and the underscore symbol. The macro name cannot include spaces or special characters. It is helpful to use a descriptive name that describes the macro's purpose.

You can assign a shortcut key to run the macro directly from the keyboard. Macro shortcut keys are used to run a macro. Assigning a shortcut key overrides the equivalent default Excel shortcut for the open workbook. For example, using the Ctrl+p keys to run a macro overrides the default Excel 2010 shortcut for printing a selected area while the workbook containing the macro is open. Some people find macro shortcut keys a quick way to run a macro; others dislike them because they override the original function of the shortcut key. It's a personal preference.

A macro needs to be stored somewhere. By default, the macro is stored in the current workbook, making the macro available in only that workbook when it is open. Another option is to store the macro in the **Personal Macro workbook**, a hidden workbook named Personal.xlsb that opens whenever you start Excel, making the macro available any time you use Excel. The Personal Macro workbook stores commonly used macros that apply to many workbooks. It is most convenient for users on stand-alone computers. Finally, you can store the macro in a new workbook. Keep in mind that the new workbook must be open to use the macro. For example, an accountant might store a set of macros that help with end-of-the-month tasks in a separate workbook.

You can also add a description of the macro to briefly explain what it does. You can also include the name of the person to contact and the date it was created.

**TIP**

You can also use Ctrl+Shift+*letter* as the shortcut by entering the uppercase letter for the key.

**REFERENCE**

*Recording a Macro*

- In the Code group on the Developer tab, click the Record Macro button.
- Enter a name for the macro, and then specify the location to store the macro.
- Specify a shortcut key (optional).
- Enter a description of the macro (optional).
- Click the OK button to start the macro recorder.
- Perform the tasks you want to automate.
- Click the Stop Recording button.

Ellen provides you with the following outline of the actions needed for the macro to save the invoice as a PDF file:

1. Set the range E2:K23 as the print area.
2. Define the Page Layout setting with the custom heading "Customer Invoice."
3. Create the PDF file and name the PDF file "Invoice."
4. Make cell A1 the active cell.

You'll record the steps for this macro using a macro named "PDFInvoice" that is assigned a keyboard shortcut, has a description, and is stored in the Community Theatre workbook. You'll start the macro recorder.

### To start the macro recorder:

If you make a mistake when recording the macro, you can close the workbook without saving, reopen the workbook, and then record the macro again.

1. Save your workbook.

2. In the Code group on the Developer tab, click the **Record Macro** button. The Record Macro dialog box opens. The Macro name box displays a default name for the macro that consists of the word "Macro" followed by a number that is one greater than the number of macros already recorded in the workbook during the current Excel session. See Figure 8-25.

| Figure 8-25 | Record Macro dialog box |
| --- | --- |

3. In the Macro name box, type **PDFInvoice** to change the default name to a more descriptive one, and then press the **Tab** key.

4. In the Shortcut key box, type **p** to set Ctrl+p as the shortcut to run the macro from the keyboard, and then press the **Tab** key.

5. Verify that the Store macro in box is set to **This Workbook** to store the macro in the Community Theatre workbook, and then press the **Tab** key.

6. In the Description box, type **Created 7/15/2013. Save invoice area: range E2:K23 as PDF file.** to enter notes about the macro.

7. Click the **OK** button. The workbook enters macro record mode. The Record Macro button in the Code group on the Developer tab changes to the Stop Recording button ▪, which also appears on the status bar.

From this point on, *every* mouse click and keystroke you perform will be recorded and stored as part of the PDFInvoice macro. For that reason, it's very important to follow the instructions in the next steps precisely. Take your time as you perform each step, reading the entire step carefully first. After you finish recording the keystrokes, click the Stop Recording button to turn off the macro recorder.

**To record the PDFInvoice macro:**

1. Click the **Page Layout** tab on the Ribbon.

2. Select the range **E2:K23**. This range contains the invoice area.

3. In the Page Setup group, click the **Print Area** button, and then click **Set Print Area**. The invoice area is set as the print area. Next, you'll insert a custom header.

4. In the Page Setup group, click the **Dialog Box Launcher** to open the Page Setup dialog box.

5. Click the **Header/Footer** tab, and then click the **Custom Header** button to open the Header dialog box.

6. Click in the **Center section** box, type **Customer Invoice** and then click the **OK** button to close the Header dialog box.

7. In the Page Setup dialog box, click the **Margins** tab, click the **Horizontally** check box to center the invoice on the page, and then click the **OK** button.

8. Click the **File** tab on the Ribbon to open Backstage view, and then click **Save & Send** in the navigation bar.

9. In the File Types area, click **Create PDF/XPS Document**.

10. In the right pane, click the **Create PDF/XPS** button to open the Publish as PDF or XPS dialog box.

11. Type **Invoice** in the File name box, make sure the "Open file after publishing" check box is checked, and then click the **Publish** button. The invoice is saved as a PDF file in the same location as the Excel workbook, and automatically opens in Adobe Reader.

12. Close the PDF file, and then, in the Invoice worksheet, click cell **A1**.

    You've completed all of the steps in the PDFInvoice macro. You'll turn off the macro recorder.

13. Click the **Stop Recording** button ▪ on the status bar. The macro recorder turns off, and the button changes to the Record Macro button ▦.

    **Trouble?** If you made a mistake while recording the macro, close the Community Theatre workbook without saving your changes. Reopen the workbook, and then repeat all of the steps beginning with the "To start the macro recorder" steps.

Be sure to turn off the macro recorder; otherwise, you'll continue to record your keystrokes and mouse clicks, leading to unintended consequences.

Be aware that the process for saving a workbook with a macro is different from saving one that does not contain a macro. If you need to save the workbook before you complete this session, refer to the section "Saving Workbooks with Macros" later in this session.

## Running a Macro

After you record a macro, you should run it to test whether it works as intended. Running a macro means Excel performs each of the steps in the same order as when it was recorded. To run the macro you created, you can either use the shortcut key you specified or select the macro in the Macro dialog box. The Macro dialog box lists all of the macros in the open workbooks. From this dialog box, you can select and run a macro, edit the macro with VBA, run the macro one step at a time so you can determine in which step an error occurs, or delete it.

*Running a Macro*

- Press the shortcut key assigned to the macro.

*or*

- In the Code group on the Developer tab, click the Macros button.
- Select the macro from the list of macros.
- Click the Run button.

You will test the PDFInvoice macro.

### To run the PDFInvoice macro:

**1.** Click the **Developer** tab on the Ribbon, and then click the **Macros** button in the Code group. The Macro dialog box opens, listing all of the macros in the open workbooks. See Figure 8-26.

**Figure 8-26** Macro dialog box

all macros in the workbook(s) open on your computer are listed

click to run the selected macro

click to edit the macro with VBA

click to delete the selected macro

**2.** Verify that **PDFInvoice** is selected in the Macro name box, and then click the **Run** button. The PDFInvoice macro runs. The invoice is saved as a PDF file and the file is opened in Adobe Reader.

**3.** Close Adobe Reader. Cell A1 is the active cell in the Invoice worksheet.

**Trouble?** If the PDFInvoice macro did not run properly, you might have made a mistake in the steps while recording the macro. Click the Developer tab, and then click the Macros button in the Code group. Select the PDFInvoice macro, and then click the Delete button. Click the OK button to confirm the deletion, and then repeat all of the steps beginning with the "To start the macro recorder" steps.

Next, you will test the shortcut keys you used for the PDFInvoice macro.

**4.** Press the **Ctrl+p** keys. The PDFInvoice macro runs. The invoice is saved as a PDF file, and cell A1 in the Invoice worksheet is the active cell.

> **5.** Close Adobe Reader.
>
> **Trouble?** If your macro doesn't end on its own, you need to end it. Press the Ctrl+Break keys to stop the macro from running.

### How Edits Can Affect Macros

Be careful when making seemingly small changes to a workbook, as these can have a great impact on macros. If a run-time error (an error that occurs while running a macro) appears when you run a macro that has worked in the past, some part of the macro code no longer makes sense to Excel. For example, simply adding a space to a worksheet name can affect a macro that references the worksheet. If you recorded a macro that referenced a worksheet named "TicketData" (no spaces in the name) that you later changed to "Ticket Data" (space added to the name), the macro no longer works because the TicketData worksheet no longer exists. You could record the macro again, or you could edit the macro in VBA by changing "TicketData" to "Ticket Data."

## Creating the TransferData Macro

You need to record one more macro. The data you entered earlier in the input section of the Invoice worksheet was never added to the Ticket Data worksheet. Ellen wants to add this data from the purchase of season tickets to the next available blank row in the Ticket Data worksheet. The macro that you'll record will do this. The actions of this macro will be as follows:

1.  Switch to the Ticket Data worksheet.
2.  Turn off worksheet protection in the Ticket Data worksheet.
3.  Switch to the Invoice worksheet.
4.  Select and copy the Transfer Area to the Clipboard.
5.  Switch to the Ticket Data worksheet.
6.  Go to cell A1, and then go to the last row in the ticket data table.
7.  Turn on Relative References. The Relative Reference button controls how Excel records the act of selecting a range in the worksheet. By default, the macro will select the same cells regardless of which cell is first selected because the macro records a selection using absolute cell references. If you want a macro to select cells regardless of the position of the active cell when you run the macro, set the macro recorder to record relative cell references.
8.  Move down one row.
9.  Turn off Relative References.
10.  Paste values to the Ticket Data worksheet.
11.  Go to cell A1.
12.  Turn on worksheet protection.
13.  Switch to the Invoice worksheet, and then make cell B3 the active cell.

Ellen wants you to name this new macro "TransferData" and assign the Ctrl+t keys as the shortcut.

## To record the TransferData macro:

▶ **1.** Click the **Record Macro** button on the status bar to open the Record Macro dialog box, type **TransferData** in the Macro name box, type **t** in the Shortcut key box, type **Created 7/15/2013. Copy values in the transfer area in the Invoice worksheet to the Ticket Data worksheet.** in the Description box, and then click the **OK** button. The macro recorder is on.

▶ **2.** Click the **Ticket Data** sheet tab, click the **Review** tab on the Ribbon, and then click the **Unprotect Sheet** button in the Changes group to turn off protection.

▶ **3.** Click the **Invoice** sheet tab, and then select the range **F25:J25** in the Transfer Area.

▶ **4.** Click the **Home** tab on the Ribbon, and then click the **Copy** button 📋 in the Clipboard group.

▶ **5.** Click the **Ticket Data** sheet tab, click cell **A1**, and then press the **End+↓** keys to go to the last row with values.

▶ **6.** Click the **Developer** tab on the Ribbon, and then click the **Use Relative References** button in the Code group. Relative references ensure that the invoice data being transferred is inserted in the next blank row (in this case, row 6) and not always in row 5 in the Ticket Data worksheet.

▶ **7.** Click the ↓ key to move to the first blank cell in the worksheet.

▶ **8.** In the Code group on the Developer tab, click the **Use Relative References** button. The Use Relative References button is toggled off.

▶ **9.** Click the **Home** tab on the Ribbon.

▶ **10.** In the Clipboard group, click the **Paste button arrow**, and then click the **Values** button 🔢 in the Paste Values section. This option pastes the values rather than the formulas from the Transfer Area.

   **Trouble?** If #REF! appears in row 6 of the Ticket Data worksheet, you clicked the Paste button instead of the Paste Values button. Stop recording the macro. Delete the macro and begin recording the macro again.

▶ **11.** Click cell **A1**, click the **Review** tab on the Ribbon, click the **Protect Sheet** button in the Changes group, and then click the **OK** button in the Protect Sheet dialog box.

▶ **12.** Click the **Invoice** sheet tab, and then click cell **B3**.

▶ **13.** Click the **Stop Recording** button 🔲 on the status bar. The macro recorder turns off, and the button changes to the Record Macro button 🖾.

### TIP
You can also turn off the macro recorder by clicking the Stop Recording button in the Code group on the Developer tab.

You've completed recording the TransferData macro. Next, you'll test whether it works. Ellen has a new season ticket subscription to add to the worksheet. You'll enter this data as you test the TransferData macro.

**To test the TransferData macro:**

▶ **1.** Enter the following data into the range B3:B12, pressing the **Enter** key after each entry:

**7/15/2013**
**Kate Holland**
**186 Pinetop Drive**
**Eugene, OR 70777**
**(888) 555–1234**
**2 tickets, D series, Balcony**
**1 decal, 40 donation**

▶ **2.** Press the **Ctrl+t** keys. The TransferData macro runs and the data transfers to the Ticket Data worksheet.

▶ **3.** Switch to the **Ticket Data** worksheet, verify that the data for Kate Holland appears in row 7, and then return to the **Invoice** worksheet.

### Fixing Macro Errors

If a macro does not work correctly, you can fix it. Sometimes, you'll find a mistake when you test a macro you just created. Other times, you might not discover that error until later. No matter when you find an error in a macro, you have the following options:

- Rerecord the macro using the same macro name.
- Delete the recorded macro, and then record the macro again.
- Run the macro one step at a time to locate the problem, and then use one of the previous methods to correct the problem.

You can delete or edit a macro by opening the Macro dialog box (shown earlier in Figure 8-26), selecting the macro from the list, and then clicking the appropriate button. To rerecord the macro, simply restart the macro recorder and enter the same macro name you used earlier. Excel overwrites the previous version of the macro.

## Working with the Visual Basic Editor

To view the code of a macro, you need to open the Visual Basic Editor (VBE), which is a separate application that works with Excel and all of the Office programs to view, debug, edit, and manage VBA code. The VBE consists of several components, including the Code window that contains the VBA code, the Project Explorer window that displays a tree-like diagram consisting of every open workbook, and a menu bar with menus of commands you use to edit, debug, and run VBA statements. You can access the Visual Basic Editor through the Macro dialog box or the Visual Basic button in the Code group on the Developer tab.

REFERENCE

*Editing a Macro*

- In the Code group on the Developer tab, click the Macros button, select the macro in the Macro name list, and then click the Edit button.
  *or*
  In the Code group on the Developer tab, click the Visual Basic button.
- Use the Visual Basic Editor to edit the macro code.
- Click File on the menu bar, and then click Close and Return to Microsoft Excel.

Ellen wants the PDFInvoice macro to stop in cell B3 of the Invoice worksheet. Right now, the macro stops with cell A1 selected. Although you can delete the PDFInvoice macro and record it again, it is simpler to edit the existing macro. You will edit the VBA command in the macro.

### To view the code for the PDFInvoice macro:

1. Click the **Developer** tab on the Ribbon, and then click the **Macros** button in the Code group. The Macro dialog box opens.

2. Click **PDFInvoice** in the Macro name list, and then click the **Edit** button. The Visual Basic Editor opens as a separate program, consisting of two windows—the Project Explorer and the Code window.

3. If the Code window is not maximized, click the **Maximize** button ▣ on the Code window title bar. The Code window contains the VBA code generated by the macro recorder. See Figure 8-27 (your window may differ).

---

**Figure 8-27**   Code window in the Visual Basic Editor

- Project Explorer
- Sub and the macro name indicate first line of a macro
- comments appear in green
- Code window for Module1
- command to select the range E2:K23
- command to set the center section of the custom header
- command that creates the PDF file
- file path and filename (your path will differ)
- end of the PDFInvoice macro

**Trouble?** If you see a different number of windows in the Visual Basic Editor, your computer is configured differently. You will be working with the Code window, so you can ignore any other windows.

## Understanding the Structure of Macros

The VBA code in the Code window lists all of the actions you performed when recording the PDFInvoice macro. In VBA, macros are called **sub procedures**. Each sub procedure begins with the keyword *Sub* followed by the name of the sub procedure and a set of parentheses. In this example, the code begins with

```
Sub PDFInvoice()
```

which provides the name of this sub procedure, PDFInvoice—the name you gave the macro. The parentheses are used to include any arguments in the procedure. These arguments pass information to the sub procedure and have roughly the same purpose as the arguments in an Excel function. If you write your own VBA code, sub procedure arguments are an important part of the programming process. However, they are not used when you create macros with the macro recorder.

Following the Sub PDFInvoice() statement are comments about the macro, taken from the macro name, shortcut key, and description you entered in the Record New Macro dialog box. Each line appears in green and is preceded by an apostrophe ('). The apostrophe indicates that the line is a comment and does not include any actions Excel needs to perform.

After the comments is the body of the macro, a listing of all of the commands performed by the PDFInvoice macro as written in the language of VBA. Your list of commands might look slightly different, depending on the exact actions you performed when recording the macro. Even though you might not know VBA, some of the commands are easy to interpret. For example, near the top of the PDFInvoice macro you should see the following command, which tells Excel to select the range E2:K23:

```
Range("E2:K23").Select
```

Several lines below this command you see the following command, which sets the words "Customer Invoice" at the top of the print page in the center of the custom header:

```
.CenterHeader = "Customer Invoice"
```

At the bottom of the macro is the following statement, which indicates the end of the PDFInvoice sub procedure:

```
End Sub
```

A Code window can contain several sub procedures, with each procedure separated from the others by the Sub*ProcedureName*() statement at the beginning, and the End Sub statement at the end. Sub procedures are organized into **modules**. As shown in Figure 8-27, all of the macros that have been recorded are stored in the Module1 module (your window may differ).

## Editing a Macro Using the Visual Basic Editor

The Visual Basic Editor provides tools to assist you in writing error-free code. As you type a command, the editor will provide pop-up windows and text to help you insert the correct code.

Ellen wants you to edit the following command in the PDFInvoice sub procedure, which sets the active cell to cell A1:

```
Range("A1").Select
```

You'll edit the command to the following to change the active cell from cell A1 to cell B3:

```
Range("B3").Select
```

## To edit a command in the macro:

▶ **1.** Scroll down the Code window to the line immediately before End Sub in the PDFInvoice macro.

▶ **2.** In the line with the command `Range("A1")`, select **A1**, and then type **B3**. The command in the macro is edited to select a different cell. See Figure 8-28.

| Figure 8-28 | Edited line in the PDFInvoice macro |
| --- | --- |

cell reference changed

▶ **3.** On the menu bar, click **File**, and then click **Close and Return to Microsoft Excel**. The Visual Basic Editor closes, and the Community Theatre workbook is displayed.

Ellen wants you to test the macro. You'll check to see whether cell B3 is the active cell once the macro has run.

## To test the edited PDFInvoice macro:

▶ **1.** Press the **Ctrl+p** keys. The PDFInvoice macro runs.

**Trouble?** If a Microsoft Visual Basic message box appears with a run-time error, click the End button, click the Macros button, click PDFInvoice in the Macro name box, and then click the Edit button. In the Code window, find the line you edited (one line above End Sub), and then correct it to **Range("B3").Select**. On the menu bar, click File, and then click Close and Return to Microsoft Excel.

▶ **2.** Close Adobe Reader. Cell B3 is the active cell.

# Creating Macro Buttons

Another way to run a macro is to assign it to a button placed directly in the worksheet. Macro buttons are often a better way to run macros than shortcut keys. Clicking a button (with a descriptive label) is often more intuitive and simpler for users than trying to remember different combinations of keystrokes.

**REFERENCE**

*Creating a Macro Button*

- In the Controls group on the Developer tab, click the Insert button.
- In the Form Controls section, click the Button (Form Control) button.
- Click the worksheet where you want the macro button to be located, drag the pointer until the button is the size and shape you want, and then release the mouse button.
- In the Assign Macro dialog box, select the macro you want to assign to the button.
- With the button still selected, type a new label.

Ellen wants you to add two macro buttons to the Invoice worksheet, one for each of the macros you've created.

## To insert a macro button in the worksheet:

▶ **1.** Scroll to the right so that columns L and M are completely visible.

▶ **2.** In the Controls group on the Developer tab, click the **Insert** button. The Form Controls appear, with a variety of objects that can be placed in the worksheet. You'll insert the Button form control. See Figure 8-29.

| Figure 8-29 | Form Controls |

click to insert a button on the worksheet

**Trouble?** If the Insert button is unavailable, the worksheet is protected. Click the Review tab on the Ribbon, click the Unprotect Sheet button in the Changes group to unprotect the Invoice worksheet, and then repeat Step 2.

▶ **3.** In the Form Controls section, click the **Button (Form Control)** button ▭, and then point to cell **L3**. The pointer changes to **+**.

▶ **4.** Click and drag the pointer over the range **L3:M4**, and then release the mouse button. A button appears on the worksheet, and the Assign Macro dialog box opens with the button's default name in the Macro name box. See Figure 8-30.

| Figure 8-30 | Assign Macro dialog box |

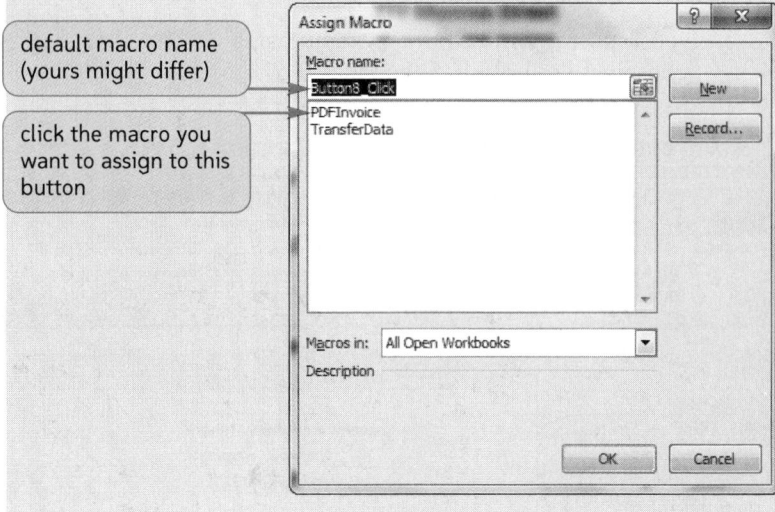

**default macro name (yours might differ)**

**click the macro you want to assign to this button**

From the Assign Macro dialog box, you can assign a macro to the button. After you assign a macro to the button, the button appears with a default label. You can change the default label to a descriptive one that will indicate which macro will run when the button is clicked.

Ellen wants you to assign the PDFInvoice macro to this new button, and then rename the button with a label that reflects the PDFInvoice macro.

### To assign the PDFInvoice macro to the new button:

1. Click **PDFInvoice** in the Macro name box, and then click the **OK** button. The PDFInvoice macro is assigned to the selected button.

2. With the sizing handles still displayed around the button, type **Create PDF** (do not press the Enter key). The new label replaces the default label.

   **Trouble?** If no sizing handles appear around the button, the button is not selected. Right-click the button, click Edit Text to place the insertion point within the button, and then repeat Step 2.

   **Trouble?** If you pressed the Enter key after entering the label on the button, you created a new line in the button. Press the Backspace key to delete the line, and then continue with Step 3.

3. Click any cell in the worksheet to deselect the macro button.

At this point, if you click the Create PDF button, the PDFInvoice macro will run. Before you test the PDFInvoice button, you will add the other button.

### To add another macro button to the Invoice worksheet:

1. In the Controls group on the Developer tab, click the **Insert** button, click the **Button (Form Control)** button , and then drag the pointer over the range **L6:M7**.

**2.** Click **TransferData** in the Macro name box in the Assign Macro dialog box, and then click the **OK** button.

**3.** Type **Transfer Data** as the button label, and then click any cell in the worksheet to deselect the button. See Figure 8-31.

**Figure 8-31**    **Macro buttons in the Invoice worksheet**

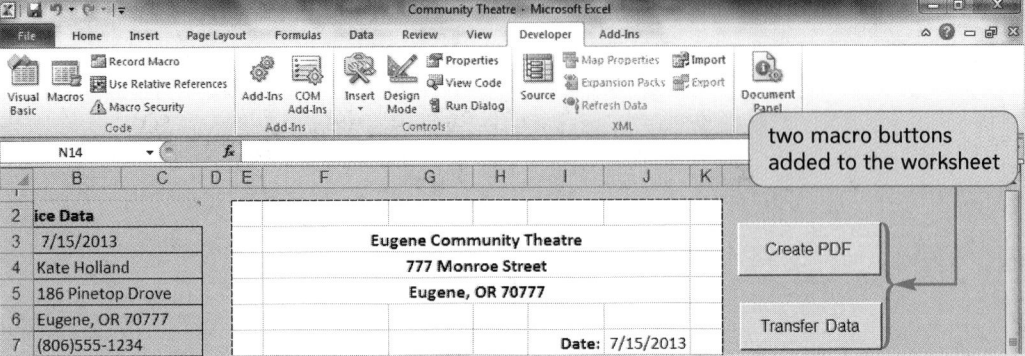

**TIP**

To move or resize a macro button, right-click the button to select it, press the Esc key to close the shortcut menu, and then drag a sizing handle or the selection box.

**Trouble?** If the macro buttons on your screen do not match the size and location of the buttons shown in the figure, right-click a button to select it, press the Esc key to close the shortcut menu, and then resize or reposition the button on the worksheet.

You have completed the application so you will reset worksheet protection.

**4.** Click the **Review** tab on the Ribbon, and then click the **Protect Sheet** button in the Changes group. The Protect Sheet dialog box opens.

**5.** Click the **OK** button to turn on worksheet protection.

Next, you will test the macro buttons to verify that they run the macros. Ellen received another subscriber order. You will use the new macro buttons as you enter this data.

**To test the macro buttons:**

**1.** In the range B3:B12, enter the following subscriber order:

**7/16/2013**
**George Zidane**
**105 Central Ave.**
**Eugene, OR 70777**
**(808) 555-5555**
**3 tickets, E series, Balcony**
**2 parking decals, 30 donation**

**2.** Click the **Create PDF** button to save the current invoice as a PDF file.

**3.** Close Adobe Reader to return to the Invoice worksheet.

**4.** Click the **Transfer Data** button to transfer data to the Ticket Data worksheet. Excel inserts the new transaction in the table.

▶ **5.** Switch to the **Ticket Data** worksheet, and then verify the data was transferred. See Figure 8-32.

**Figure 8-32** | **Ticket Data worksheet with the new transaction record**

new record inserted

▶ **6.** Switch to the **Documentation** worksheet.

# Saving Workbooks with Macros

When you save a workbook that contains macros, a dialog box opens indicating that the workbook you are trying to save contains features that cannot be saved in a macro-free workbook. The default Excel workbook does not allow macros to be stored as part of the file. If you want to save the workbook without the macros, click the Yes button. The workbook will be saved as a macro-free workbook, which means the macros you created will be lost. If you want to save the workbook with the macros, click the No button, and then save the workbook as a new file—one that allows macros to be saved as part of the file. The default Excel Workbook format, which is a macro-free workbook, has the .xlsx file extension. You need to change this to a macro-enabled workbook, which has the .xlsm file extension.

You've completed your work on the Excel application, so you will save and close the workbook and then exit Excel.

### To save the workbook with macros:

▶ **1.** On the Quick Access Toolbar, click the **Save** button 💾. A dialog box opens, indicating that the workbook you are trying to save contains features that cannot be saved in a macro-free workbook. See Figure 8-33.

**Figure 8-33** | **Macro warning dialog box**

2. Click the **No** button. The Save As dialog box opens so you can save the workbook as a macro-enabled workbook.

3. In the File name box, type **Theatre with Macros** so you can easily determine which workbook contains macros.

4. Click the **Save as type** button, and then click **Excel Macro-Enabled Workbook**.

5. Click the **Save** button. The workbook is saved with the macros.

6. Close the workbook.

## Opening a Workbook with Macros

When you open a file with macros, Excel checks the opening workbook to see if it contains any macros. The response you see is based on the security level set on the computer. Earlier, you disabled all macros with notification. So, all of the macros will be disabled when the workbook opens. When the workbook opens the first time, a Security Warning appears in the Message Bar providing the option to enable the macros so they can be run, or to open the workbook with the macros disabled. If you know a workbook contains macros that you or a coworker created, you can enable them, which adds the filename to a list of trusted files so that you won't see the Security Warning when you open this file again. If you do not click the Enable Content button, the macros remain disabled and unavailable during the current session, but the other features of the workbook are still available.

You'll open the Theatre with Macros workbook and enable the macros.

**To open the Theatre with Macros workbook:**

1. Open the **Theatre with Macros** workbook. The workbook opens, and "Security Warning: Macros have been disabled" appears in the Message Bar below the Ribbon. See Figure 8-34.

**Figure 8-34**    Security Warning appears when opening a workbook with macros

Security Warning that this workbook contains macros

2. In the Message Bar, click the **Enable Content** button. The macros in the workbook are available for use.

3. Switch to the **Invoice** worksheet.

## Customizing the Ribbon

Excel 2010 enables you to change the Ribbon to fit your work style. Among many other customization features, you can minimize the Ribbon, create new tabs and groups, hide tabs or commands, and rename tabs or commands.

## Minimize the Ribbon

You can minimize the Ribbon to make more space for a worksheet. When the Ribbon is minimized, only the Quick Access Toolbar and the tab names are displayed. To access a command from the Ribbon, click the appropriate tab. The Ribbon expands to show all of the groups and buttons on that tab. After you click a button on the Ribbon or a cell in the worksheet, the Ribbon returns to its minimized state.

Now that the application is complete, Ellen wants to provide more screen space for the input and output sections of the worksheet.

**TIP**

You can also minimize the Ribbon by double-clicking any tab on the Ribbon. Repeat to maximize the Ribbon.

### To minimize the Ribbon:

1. Near the upper-right corner of the Excel window, click the **Minimize the Ribbon** button ⌃. The Ribbon is minimized, leaving more room for the Invoice worksheet. See Figure 8-35.

**Figure 8-35**    **Minimized Ribbon**

only the tab names appear on the minimized Ribbon

click to expand or collapse the Ribbon

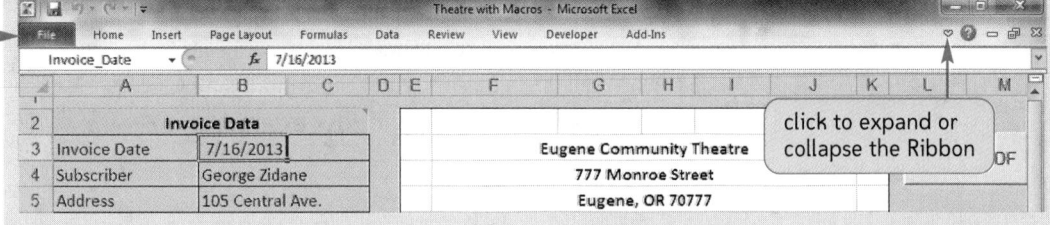

2. Click the **Home** tab. All of the buttons for this tab appear on the Ribbon.

3. Click cell **B3**. The Ribbon returns to its minimized state.

## Removing a Tab from the Ribbon

If you decide you don't want a tab displayed on the Ribbon, you can remove it. Now that the macros are completed, Ellen doesn't need the Developer tab to appear on the Ribbon. You will remove the Developer tab from the Ribbon.

### To remove the Developer tab from the Ribbon:

1. Click the **File** tab on the Ribbon, and then click the **Options** button in the navigation bar. The Excel Options dialog box opens.

2. Click **Customize Ribbon** in the left pane, and then click the **Developer** check box in the Customize the Ribbon box to remove the check mark.

3. Click the **OK** button. The Developer tab is removed from the Ribbon.

## Expanding the Ribbon

If worksheet space is not an issue and you prefer to view the maximized Ribbon, you can expand the Ribbon to show the tabs with all of the options displayed. You will expand the Ribbon so that all tab contents are visible.

### To expand the Ribbon:

▶ **1.** Near the upper-right corner of the Excel window, click the **Expand the Ribbon** button ⊡. The Ribbon is maximized.

▶ **2.** Save and close the workbook.

Ellen is pleased with the Community Theatre workbook. The workbook protection and macros will streamline the data entry process for theatre volunteers.

**REVIEW**

*Session 8.3 Quick Check*

1. The _____ tab on the Ribbon is necessary to record a macro.
2. Discuss two ways of creating a macro.
3. What are the three places in which you can store a macro?
4. Identify two ways to run a macro.
5. What are the steps you follow to edit a macro?
6. How do you insert a macro button into your worksheet?
7. True or False. A workbook that contains a macro can be saved using the Excel Workbook format with the .xlsx extension.
8. How do you minimize the Ribbon?

*Practice the skills you learned in the tutorial using the same case scenario.*

**PRACTICE**

## Review Assignments

**Data File needed for the Review Assignments: Rentals.xlsx**

You did such a good job helping Ellen with the Community Theatre application that she recommended you to a friend who has a similar project. Ellen's friend wants to create an invoice system for his new car rental company, Eugene Discount Car Rental. Complete the following:

1. Open the **Rentals** workbook located in the Excel8\Review folder included with your Data Files, and then save the workbook as **Discount Rentals**.
2. In the Documentation worksheet, enter your name and the date.
3. In the Customer worksheet, define names for cells as follows:

   | Cell | Defined Name | Cell | Defined Name |
   |------|--------------|------|--------------|
   | B4 | **Customer** | H9 | **ChargePerDay** |
   | B5 | **TypeCar** | H10 | **ChargePerMile** |
   | B6 | **DaysRented** | A12:C16 | **RentalRates** |
   | B7 | **MilesDriven** | B19 | **SalesTaxRate** |

4. Create the validation rules for cells B5, B6, and B7 shown in Figure 8-36.

**Figure 8-36**    **Validation rules for cells B5, B6, and B7**

| Cell | Settings | Input Message | Error Alert |
|------|----------|---------------|-------------|
| B5 | List Source (A12:A16) | Title: Type of Car<br>Message: Click arrow to select the type of car. | Style: Stop<br>Title: Invalid Type<br>Message: Invalid Type. Use arrow to select Type. |
| B6 | Whole number between 1 and 29 | Title: Number of Days Rented<br>Message: Enter a whole number between 1 and 29. | Style: Warning<br>Title: Warning Days Rented<br>Message: Invalid entry. Enter whole number between 1 and 29. |
| B7 | Whole number between 1 and 5000 | Title: Number of Miles Driven<br>Message: Enter a whole number between 1 and 5000. | Style: Warning<br>Title: Warning Miles<br>Message: Invalid entry. Enter a value between 1 and 5000. |

5. Enter formulas based on the following using the defined names you created in Step 3 to calculate the Rental Bill:
   - Cell F6 is equal to the value in cell B4.
   - Cell F7 is equal to the value in cell B5.
   - Cell F9 is equal to the value in cell B6.
   - Cell F10 is equal to the value in cell B7.
   - Cell H9 is equal to the charge per day, which depends on the type of car entered in cell B5 and the rate table. (*Hint*: Use the VLOOKUP function.)
   - Cell H10 is equal to the charge per mile, which depends on the type of car entered in cell B5 and the rate table. (*Hint*: Use the VLOOKUP function.)

- Cell F12 is equal to the rental amount, which equals the number of days rented multiplied by the charge per day plus the miles driven multiplied by the charge per mile.
- Cell F13 is equal to the sales tax rate multiplied by the rental amount.
- Cell F14 is equal to the rental amount plus the sales tax.
- Use the IFERROR function in cells H9, H10, F12, F13, and F14 to test for an error value. If an error value is found, display a blank cell; otherwise, use the appropriate formula.

6. Test the worksheet using the following data: **Myles Fast**, **Intermediate**, **4**, **450**.

7. Protect the worksheet so a user can enter data only in the range B4:B7. Do not use a password to enable protection. Save the workbook.

   *Note:* In the following steps, you'll create one macro. Save your workbook before recording the macro. That way, if you make a mistake when recording the macro, you can close the workbook without saving the changes, and then reopen the workbook and try again. Be sure to read the list of tasks before you begin recording them.

8. Remove worksheet protection from the Customer worksheet.

9. Add the Developer tab to the Ribbon.

10. Save the workbook, then create a macro named **PDFBill** with the shortcut key **Ctrl+p** and the description **Created 7/15/2013. Macro saves the customer bill as a PDF file.**

11. Record the following macro steps to create a PDF file that displays only the bill portion of the worksheet:

    a. Select the range E3:H15, and set the range as the print area.

    b. Open the Page Layout dialog box, and then center the output horizontally on the page and insert your name in the right section of the custom footer.

    c. Create a PDF file using the Save & Send tab in Backstage view with **CustomerBill** as the filename.

    d. Close Adobe Reader.

    e. Stop the Macro Recorder.

12. Edit the PDFBill macro to set cell A1 in the Customer worksheet as the active cell when the macro stops running. Insert the following command immediately before the End Sub command:

    `Range("A1").Select`

13. Create a macro button, assign the PDFBill macro to the button, and then change the default label to **Create PDF**. Place the macro button in the range J3:K4.

14. Enter the following data for a new customer: **Ed Elders**, **Full**, **3** days, **2000** miles.

15. Test the PDFBill macro button using the customer bill for Ed Elders.

16. In the Documentation worksheet, use the Paste List command to document the defined names and their locations.

17. Turn on worksheet protection for the Customer worksheet. Do not assign a password.

18. Turn on workbook protection. Do not assign a password.

19. Remove the Developer tab from the Ribbon.

20. Save the workbook as **Rentals with Macros** in the macro-enabled workbook format, and then close it.

21. Submit the finished workbook to your instructor, either in printed or electronic form, as requested.

*Apply the macro skills you learned to produce monthly reports.*

## Case Problem 1

**Data File needed for this Case Problem: MediTrax.xlsx**

*MediTrax Controls*   MediTrax Controls, a U.S. subsidiary of a European multinational corporation, is testing an HVAC system designed to eliminate large temperature variances in its medical storage rooms. Lisa Goodman is a product tester for MediTrax. Each week, she records 25 temperature readings, five samples each day, in an Excel workbook. At the end of the month, Lisa sends the results to the parent company's Quality Department. Because many repetitive steps occur in developing the output requested by the parent company, Lisa asks you to create a macro to speed the creation of the report and reduce chances for error. Complete the following:

1. Open the **MediTrax** workbook located in the Excel8\Case1 folder included with your Data Files, and then save the workbook as **MediTrax Controls**.

2. In the Documentation sheet, enter your name and the date, and then review all of the worksheets in the workbook. Make Week 1 the active worksheet.

3. Create a macro to convert the worksheet to the one shown in Figure 8-37. Name the macro **ConvertData**, assign the shortcut key **Ctrl+d** to run the macro, and insert the macro description **Automate the weekly temperature reading report**. The macro performs the following steps:

    a. Formats the dates in the Date column using the date format type (3/14/2013).

    b. Formats the times in the Time column so they are displayed in 24-hour notation (format type 13:30).

    c. Types the title **Celsius** in cell D1.

    d. Converts the Fahrenheit temperatures to Celsius by entering the following formula in cell D2, and then copying the formula down the column: **=5/9*(C2–32)**.

    e. Formats the cells in column D using the Number format to 1 decimal place.

    f. Bolds the column heading and resizes the column to fully display Fahrenheit.

    g. Places the label **Average** in cell A27, computes the average Celsius temperature for the week in cell D27, and then bolds the row.

    h. Makes cell F1 the active cell.

    i. Stops recording the macro.

4. Switch to the Week 2 worksheet and test the macro using the shortcut key.

5. Edit the macro so that you end at cell A1 instead of ending at cell F1.

6. Switch to the Week 3 worksheet and test the revised macro using the shortcut key.

7. In the Week 1 worksheet, add the following comment to cell A1: **Use macro shortcut Ctrl+d to prepare a formatted report.**

8. Save the workbook as **MTC with Macros** as an Excel Macro-Enabled workbook, and then close it.

9. Submit the finished workbook to your instructor, either in printed or electronic form, as requested.

**Figure 8-37**    **Worksheet formatted by a macro**

| | A | B | C | D |
|---|---|---|---|---|
| 1 | Date | Time | Fahrenheit | Celsius |
| 2 | 4/1/2013 | 1:05 | 60.5 | 15.8 |
| 3 | 4/1/2013 | 2:02 | 64.5 | 18.1 |
| 4 | 4/1/2013 | 6:42 | 63.8 | 17.7 |
| 5 | 4/1/2013 | 14:45 | 61.1 | 16.2 |
| 6 | 4/1/2013 | 21:12 | 60.2 | 15.7 |
| 7 | 4/2/2013 | 1:33 | 61.2 | 16.2 |
| 8 | 4/2/2013 | 2:25 | 62.9 | 17.2 |
| 9 | 4/2/2013 | 6:12 | 64.4 | 18.0 |
| 10 | 4/2/2013 | 15:35 | 62.3 | 16.8 |
| 11 | 4/2/2013 | 20:32 | 61.9 | 16.6 |
| 12 | 4/3/2013 | 1:56 | 63.9 | 17.7 |
| 13 | 4/3/2013 | 2:51 | 60.6 | 15.9 |
| 14 | 4/3/2013 | 6:55 | 62.6 | 17.0 |
| 15 | 4/3/2013 | 14:30 | 64.5 | 18.1 |
| 16 | 4/3/2013 | 22:18 | 63.2 | 17.3 |
| 17 | 4/4/2013 | 1:32 | 62.6 | 17.0 |
| 18 | 4/4/2013 | 2:58 | 62.7 | 17.1 |
| 19 | 4/4/2013 | 7:05 | 62.4 | 16.9 |
| 20 | 4/4/2013 | 14:12 | 63.5 | 17.5 |
| 21 | 4/4/2013 | 21:45 | 62.6 | 17.0 |
| 22 | 4/5/2013 | 1:22 | 64.8 | 18.2 |
| 23 | 4/5/2013 | 2:18 | 62.4 | 16.9 |
| 24 | 4/5/2013 | 6:50 | 61.9 | 16.6 |
| 25 | 4/5/2013 | 13:59 | 63.4 | 17.4 |
| 26 | 4/5/2013 | 22:03 | 64.2 | 17.9 |
| 27 | Average | | | 17.1 |

*Apply the skills you've learned to create a profit analysis workbook.*

**APPLY**

## Case Problem 2

**Data File needed for this Case Problem: Popcorn.xlsx**

***Seattle Popcorn***    Seattle Popcorn is a small company located in Tacoma, Washington, that produces gourmet popcorn distributed in the Northwest. Steve Wilkes has developed a workbook that will allow him to perform a profit analysis for the company. Using this workbook, he wants to create formulas to determine the break-even point for the company—the sales volume needed so that revenues will match the anticipated monthly expenses. Three factors determine the break-even point: the sales price of each unit of Seattle Popcorn, the variable manufacturing cost to the company for each unit, and the fixed expenses (salaries, rent, insurance, and so on) that the company must pay each month. Steve wants to be able to explore a range of possible values for each of these factors, as follows:

- The sales price of each unit of Seattle Popcorn can vary from $5 to $15 (in whole numbers).
- The variable manufacturing cost of each unit can vary from $5 to $15 (in whole numbers).
- The fixed monthly expense for the company can vary from $15,000 to $30,000 (in whole numbers).

Complete the following:

1. Open the **Popcorn** workbook located in the Excel8\Case2 folder included with your Data Files, and then save the workbook as **Seattle Popcorn**. In the Documentation sheet, enter your name and the date.

2. Switch to the Profit Analysis worksheet, and then define names for cells, as follows:
   cell C15: **PricePerUnit**
   cell C16: **CostPerUnit**
   cell C17: **MonthlyExpenses**

3. In the range H3:H43, enter a formula using defined names to calculate the revenue, which is determined by the units sold multiplied by the price per unit.

4. In the range I3:I43, enter a formula using defined names to calculate the expenses, which are determined by the units sold multiplied by the cost per unit plus the fixed monthly expense.

5. In cell C18, enter a formula to calculate the break-even point, which is determined by the fixed monthly expense divided by the difference between the price per unit and the number of units. Use the IFERROR function to display a blank cell instead of an error value.

6. In cell C19, enter a formula to calculate the revenue at the break-even point, which is determined by the break-even point multiplied by the sales price per unit. Use the IFERROR function to display a blank cell instead of an error value.

7. Create the validation rules for cells C15, C16, and C17, as shown in Figure 8-38.

**Figure 8-38**    Validation rules for cells C15, C16, and C17

| Cell | Settings | Input Message | Error Alert |
|------|----------|---------------|-------------|
| C15 | Whole numbers between 5 and 15 | Title: Price per Unit<br>Message: *Enter an appropriate message.* | Style: Warning<br>Title: Invalid Price per Unit<br>Message: *Enter an appropriate message.* |
| C16 | Whole numbers between 5 and 15 | Title: Cost per Unit<br>Message: *Enter an appropriate message.* | Style: Warning<br>Title: Invalid Cost per Unit<br>Message: *Enter an appropriate message.* |
| C17 | Whole numbers between 15000 and 30000 | Title: Monthly Expenses<br>Message: *Enter an appropriate message.* | Style: Warning<br>Title: Invalid Monthly Expense<br>Message: *Enter an appropriate message.* |

8. Protect the worksheet so the user can enter data only in cells C15, C16, and C17. Everything else in the worksheet should remain locked.

9. Enter the following values in the worksheet to determine how many units Seattle Popcorn must sell each month in order to break even:
   - Sales Price per Unit = **$13**
   - Manufacturing Cost per Unit = **$10**
   - Fixed Monthly Expense = **$30,000**

10. In cell C16, add the following comment: **Call Joe Heller in Cost Accounting for unit cost data.**

    *Note:* In the following steps, you'll create a macro. Save your workbook before recording the macro. That way, if you make a mistake while recording the macro, you can close the workbook without saving the changes, and then reopen the workbook and try again. Also, read the list of tasks before you begin recording them.

11. Save the workbook.

12. Create a macro named **PrintChart** with the shortcut key **Ctrl+a** and an appropriate macro description that performs the following tasks:

    a. Set the print area to include the chart and input/output area (range A1:E20).

    b. Set the page layout to landscape orientation, centered horizontally on the page, with the text **Break-even Analysis** in the center section of the header, and your name in the right section of the footer.

    c. Print the chart and input area.

    d. Make cell A1 the active cell.

    e. Stop recording the macro.

13. Test the PrintChart macro by pressing the Ctrl+a keys. If the macro doesn't work, close the workbook without saving your changes, reopen the workbook, and record the macro again.

14. Edit the PrintChart macro, replacing the line `ActiveWindow.SelectedSheets.PrintOut Copies:=1, Collate:=True, IgnorePrintAreas:=False` with `ActiveSheet.PrintPreview`. (*Hint*: The line to edit is four lines above the end of the macro.)

15. Create a button in the range A22:B23, assign the PrintChart macro to the button, and change the default label to a more descriptive one.

16. Run the PrintChart macro to test the button and the revised macro.

17. Save the workbook as a macro-enabled workbook using the name **SP with Macros**, and then close it.

18. Submit the finished workbook to your instructor, either in printed or electronic form, as requested.

*Go beyond what you learned to design an Excel workbook to use as a data entry form.*

## Case Problem 3

**Data File needed for this Case Problem: Cookin.xlsx**

***Cookin Good***   Cookin Good sells specialized home cooking products. The company employs individuals to organize "Cookin Good Parties" at which the company's products are sold. Cleo Benard is responsible for entering sales data from various Cookin Good Parties. She wants to design an Excel workbook to act as a data entry form. She has already created the workbook, but she needs your help with setting up data validation rules, creating a table lookup, and writing the macros to enter the data. Complete the following:

1. Open the **Cookin** workbook located in the Excel8\Case3 folder included with your Data Files, and then save the workbook as **Cookin Good**. In the Documentation sheet, enter your name and the date.

2. Go to the Sales Form worksheet. Create appropriate defined names for each cell in the range C3:C8. Assign the name **ProductInfo** to the range E4:G15.

3. In the Sales Form worksheet, create the following validation rules:

   a. The criteria allows only one of five regions (represented by the numbers 1, 2, 3, 4, and 5) to be entered in cell C3. Enter an appropriate input message and error alert.

   b. The criteria provides the list of 12 products (found in range E4:E15) in cell C4. Enter an appropriate input message and error alert.

   c. The criteria allows only whole numbers greater than 0 to be entered as the number of units sold in cell C7. Enter an appropriate input message and error alert.

4. In cells C5 and C6, enter a VLOOKUP function that automatically enters the product name and price into the sales form when the ProductID is entered. (*Hint*: Cells should be blank if an error value appears in a cell.)

5. In cell C8, enter a formula that automatically calculates the total sale for the order, which is determined by the number of units sold multiplied by the price of the product. Use the IFERROR function to display a blank cell if an error value occurs during the calculation of Total Sale.

6. Prevent users from entering data into any cell in the Sales Form worksheet other than cells C3, C4, and C7, and then protect the Sales Form worksheet.

7. Test the data entry form by entering the following new record: Region = **1**, Product ID = **CW**, Units Sold = **8**.

8. Save the workbook, and then create a macro named **AddData** with the shortcut key **Ctrl+d** that performs the following tasks:

   a. In the Sales Form worksheet, copy the values in the range C3:C8. (*Hint*: You'll paste later in the macro.)

   b. Switch from the Sales Form worksheet to the Sales Record worksheet. Click cell A1.

   c. Turn on Relative References.

   d. Use the End+↓ keys to locate the last used row in the first column. Then, press the ↓ key to move to the next row in the first column.

   e. Turn off Relative References.

   f. Paste the copied values from Step a into the blank row. (*Hint*: Use the Paste button arrow, and then click Paste Transpose button.)

   g. Switch to the Sales Table worksheet.

   h. Click inside the PivotTable and refresh the contents of the PivotTable to include the new data.

   i. Switch to the Sales Form worksheet and clear the values in cells C3, C4, and C7.

⊕ **EXPLORE**

j. Make C3 the active cell.

k. Stop recording the macro.

9. Create a button in the range C11:C12 on the Sales Form worksheet and assign the AddData macro to the button. Change the button label to **Transfer Sales Data**.

10. Test the data entry form and AddData macro by entering the following new records:

| Region | Product ID | Units Sold |
|--------|-----------|-----------|
| 3 | HR | 4 |
| 4 | OEG | 2 |

11. Create a macro named **ViewTable** with the **Ctrl+t** shortcut key that displays the contents of the Sales Table worksheet.

12. Create a macro named **ViewChart** with the **Ctrl+c** shortcut key that displays the Sales Chart worksheet.

13. Create a macro named **ViewForm** with the **Ctrl+f** shortcut key that displays the Sales Form worksheet. Test each macro using its shortcut keys.

14. In the Documentation worksheet, create three macro buttons below row 13 to view the Sales Table worksheet (Step 11), the Sales Chart worksheet (Step 12), and the Sales Form worksheet (Step 13). Assign the appropriate macro to each button, and change the labels on the buttons to be more descriptive.

✦ EXPLORE 15. The Sales Table worksheet displays the total product sales in each region. Change the PivotTable to show the values in the cells as percentages of the Column Total. (*Hint*: On the Options tab, in the Calculations group, click the Show Values As button, and then click % of Column Total. You can return the original value by clicking No calculation.)

✦ EXPLORE 16. Create two macros. The first displays the PivotTable as percentages of column totals (Step 15). Name this macro **ShowAsPercent**. The second macro displays the PivotTable as numbers (values shown as No Calculation). Name this macro **ShowAsNumber**.

17. Edit the ShowAsPercent macro to display the results with a percent style by adding the following three commands immediately before the End Sub statement:

```
Range("C5:H17").Select
Selection.Style = "Percent"
Range("A1").Select
```

18. Create two macro buttons below the PivotTable in the Sales Table worksheet to run each macro. Assign a macro to each button, and then change the button labels to be more descriptive.

19. Save the workbook as **CG with Macros**, and then close it. Submit the finished workbook to your instructor, either in printed or electronic form, as requested.

---

*Define names, apply worksheet protection, and create macros to prepare an invoice.*

CREATE

## Case Problem 4

**There are no Data Files needed for this Case Problem.**

*Alia's Senior Living Supplies*    Alia Moh left her job at a Chicago hospital to establish Alia's Senior Living Supplies, which provides products and services designed for seniors. Products offered by Alia on her Web site range from safety step ladders, doorknob grippers, and skid resistant surfaces to wheelchair ponchos. Alia has built up a large, steady client base—mainly seniors who find these uniquely designed products a great help in their daily lives. To ensure timely receipt of payments, Alia wants a billing/invoicing system to expedite that work. Figure 8-39 shows the finished application she has asked you to create.

**Figure 8-39**    **Completed Invoice worksheet**

| | A | B | C | D | E | F | G | H | I | J | K | L |
|---|---|---|---|---|---|---|---|---|---|---|---|---|
| 1 | | | | | | | | | | | | |
| 2 | | | **Alia's Senior Living Supplies** | | | | | | | | Print Invoice | |
| 3 | | | 2256 Central Avenue | | | | | | | | | |
| 4 | | | Arlington, Illinois 60005 | | | | | | | | | |
| 5 | | | (555) 555-1212 | | | | | | | | Clear Inputs | |
| 6 | | | | | | | | | | | | |
| 7 | | | | | | | February 15, 2013 | | | | | |
| 8 | | | | | | | | | | | | |
| 9 | | | Sold to: | | | | | | | | | |
| 10 | | | Mark Kipper | | | | | | | | | |
| 11 | | | 123 Central Road | | | | | | | | | |
| 12 | | | Arlington | IL | | 60005 | | | | | | |
| 13 | | | | | | | | | | | | |
| 14 | | | | | | | | | | | | |
| 15 | | | Item | | | | Qty | Per Unit | Total | | | |
| 16 | | | Economy Patient Gowns | | | | 4 | $ 6.95 | $ 27.80 | | | |
| 17 | | | Doorknob Gripper | | | | 5 | $ 4.95 | $ 24.75 | | | |
| 18 | | | Giant TV Remote | | | | 3 | $ 34.95 | $ 104.85 | | | |
| 19 | | | | | | | | | | | | |
| 20 | | | | | | | | | | | | |

| | A | B | C | D | E | F | G | H | I | J | K | L |
|---|---|---|---|---|---|---|---|---|---|---|---|---|
| 36 | | | | | | | | | | | | |
| 37 | | | | | | | Subtotal | $ 157.40 | | | | |
| 38 | | | | | | | Sales Tax | $ 11.81 | | | | |
| 39 | | | | | | | Shipping | $ 16.00 | | | | |
| 40 | | | | | | | **Total Due** | **$ 185.21** | | | | |
| 41 | | | | | | | | | | | | |

Complete the following:

1. Open a new workbook, and then save it as **AliaSupplies** in the Excel8\Case4 folder included with your Data Files.

2. Rename the first sheet as **Documentation**, and then enter the company name, your name, the date, and a purpose statement. Rename the second sheet as **Invoice**. Rename the third sheet as **Product Pricing and Shipping**.

3. In the Product Pricing and Shipping worksheet, enter the data for product pricing and shipping costs shown in Figure 8-40.

**Figure 8-40**    **Product pricing and shipping costs**

| | A | B | C | D | E | F |
|---|---|---|---|---|---|---|
| 1 | **Product Pricing** | | | | | |
| 2 | | | | Subtotal | Shipping Cost | |
| 3 | Adjustable Home Bed Rail | 89.95 | | 0 | 6.00 | |
| 4 | Bed Cane | 81.95 | | 55 | 9.50 | |
| 5 | Doorknob Gripper | 4.95 | | 100 | 12.50 | |
| 6 | Easy Grip Utensils | 32.95 | | 150 | 16.00 | |
| 7 | Economy Patient Gowns | 6.95 | | | | |
| 8 | Full-Page Magnifier | 4.99 | | | | |
| 9 | Giant TV Remote | 34.95 | | | | |
| 10 | Inflatable Shampoo Basin | 39.95 | | | | |
| 11 | Jar Opener | 5.95 | | | | |
| 12 | Lamp Switch Enlarger | 4.95 | | | | |
| 13 | Medication Dispenser | 135.95 | | | | |
| 14 | No Rinse Shampoo | 34.95 | | | | |
| 15 | Tilting Overbed Table | 114.95 | | | | |
| 16 | Trolley Walker | 139.95 | | | | |
| 17 | Wheelchair Poncho | 51.95 | | | | |

4. Complete the following to build the invoice shown in Figure 8-39 on the Invoice worksheet. Use defined names and structured referencing to assist in creating formulas. (*Hint*: Review the steps below before you begin to enter the tables, labels, and formulas to build the invoice.)

   a. Adjust the column widths so column A is 2.57; column B is 6.14; column C is 20.86; column D is 6.14; column E is 13.57; column F is 8.71; column G is 12.71; column H is 13.71; column I is 3.43; and column J is 2.29.

   b. Insert labels with the company's name and contact information in rows 2 through 5, and then merge and center the ranges C2:H2, C3:H3, C4:H4, and C5:H5.

   c. Enter the current date in cell G7, merge and center G7:H7, and then format the cell with bold.

   d. Insert comments as a reminder as to what data should be entered in cells C10, C11, C12, D12, and E12.

   e. Enter the column headers in row 15.

   f. Create an Excel table in the range C15:H35. Remove the filter arrows.

   g. Enter the appropriate labels in the range G37:G40, and then format the range G40:H40 as bold.

   h. Use defined names for Product Pricing and Shipping Cost data.

   i. In the Item column (the range C16:C35), create a list of the different items, which are listed in the Product Pricing table in the Product Pricing and Shipping worksheet, that users might order. (*Hint*: Use the data validation list feature.)

   j. In the Qty column, create an error alert warning message that appears if the quantity entered is more than 50.

   k. In the Per Unit column, enter a formula that uses a table lookup in the Product Pricing table based on the value selected in the Item column. Use the IFERROR function to display a blank cell instead of the error value.

   l. In the Total column, enter a formula to calculate the total charge for that row: Qty × Per Unit. Use the IFERROR function to display a blank cell instead of the error value. Format the column appropriately.

   m. In the Subtotal cell (cell H37), enter a formula to sum the Total column. Format this cell appropriately.

   n. In the Sales Tax cell, enter a formula to calculate 7.5% of the subtotal in cell H37 if the customer's state is IL (cell D12); otherwise, enter 0 for the sales tax. Format this cell appropriately.

   o. In the Shipping cell, enter a formula that does the following: If the subtotal is $200 or more, the shipping cost is 0; otherwise, look up the shipping cost (from the Shipping Cost table in the Product Pricing and Shipping worksheet) based on the subtotal in cell H37. Format this cell appropriately.

   p. In the Total Due cell, calculate the invoice total by entering a formula that adds the values in the Subtotal, Sales Tax, and Shipping cells. Format this cell appropriately.

5. Protect the worksheet so a user can enter data in cells C10, C11, C12, D12, and E12; items in the range C16:C35; and quantities in the range F16:F35 but not in any other cells. Do not use a password.

6. Save the workbook.

7. Create a macro named **PrintInvoice** that prints the invoice. Assign the **Ctrl+p** shortcut key and type a macro description as you begin recording this macro. Center the worksheet horizontally and scale it to fit on one printed page. The heading has the label **I N V O I C E** in the center of the page. Create a macro button on the Invoice worksheet in column K, assign the PrintInvoice macro to the button, and then enter a descriptive label for the button.

8. Create a macro named **ClearInputs** that deletes the values from cells C10, C11, C12, D12, and E12; items in the range C16:C35; and quantities in the range F16:F35. Assign the **Ctrl+c** shortcut key and type a macro description as you begin recording this macro. Create a macro button on the Invoice worksheet in column K, assign the ClearInputs macro to the button, and then enter a descriptive label for the button. (*Hint*: Use the Delete key to clear a value from a cell.)

9. In the Documentation worksheet, paste a list of the defined names with their locations, and below this entry type a list of the macro names and their shortcut keys.

10. Test the worksheet using the data in Figure 8-39.

11. Use the PrintInvoice macro button to print the bill for the data you entered in Step 10, and then use the ClearInputs macro button to remove the input data.

12. Save the workbook as **Alia with Macros**, and then close it. Submit the finished workbook to your instructor, either in printed or electronic form, as requested.

**ASSESS**

## SAM: Skills Assessment Manager

For current SAM information, including versions and content details, visit SAM Central (http://samcentral.course.com). If you have a SAM user profile, you may have access to hands-on instruction, practice, and assessment of the skills covered in this tutorial. Since various versions of SAM are supported throughout the life of this text, check with your instructor for the correct instructions and URL/Web site for accessing assignments.

## ENDING DATA FILES

**Excel8** →

**Tutorial**
Community
  Theatre.xlsx
Theatre with
  Macros.xlsm

**Review**
Discount
  Rentals.xlsx
Rentals with
  Macros.xlsm

**Case1**
MediTrax
  Controls.xlsx
MTC with
  Macros.xlsm

**Case2**
Seattle
  Popcorn.xlsx
SP with
  Macros.xlsm

**Case3**
CG with
  Macros.xlsm
Cookin
  Good.xlsx

**Case4**
Alia with
  Macros.xlsm
AliaSupplies.xlsx

# Problem Solving

## Solving a Problem Using an Excel Table

Problem solving is the ability to identify a gap between an existing state and a desired state of being. A problem can be a one-time issue such as which car to purchase or a process-oriented dilemma such as how to track orders. The process of solving a problem follows a logical progression that consists of (1) recognizing and defining the problem, (2) determining feasible courses of action, (3) collecting information about those actions, and (4) evaluating the merits and drawbacks of each one in order to make a choice. Problem solving leads to decision making, and enables you to evaluate different courses of action and make an informed decision or select a good solution.

## Recognize and Define the Problem

A problem is the gap between a desired state and reality. In order to recognize and define a problem, ask questions to determine the real issue and identify your ultimate goal. For example, ask such questions as: Why do I think there is a problem? Where is it occurring? When and how frequently is it occurring? What is causing the problem? Who is involved? Why is it occurring? The answers to these questions help you define the problem and determine what information you need to solve the problem. For instance, a company might want to make sure that employee benefits and overtime payments don't exceed a certain amount, and needs to track the cost of each employee's benefit package, salary, and overtime as well as determine that the total costs fall within the intended levels.

## Determine Feasible Alternatives

With the problem defined, you can brainstorm possible solutions by collecting as many ideas as possible about how to correct the problem or achieve your goal. Write them all down. Don't discount any ideas as too radical, expensive, or impossible to achieve. Think creatively. Ask what-if questions, such as what if we had unlimited resources? What if we had new skills? What if our competitors or suppliers or customers acted in a certain way? What if I do nothing? For instance, a company might want to create a consistent way to track employee data, collecting the same data each time, categorizing the data by department or employee type, and then ensuring that paid benefits and overtime don't exceed a certain amount.

## Collect Information Needed to Evaluate the Alternatives

Data is crucial to problem solving. Collect data and information related to each possible solution or alternative. This information can include data expressed as currency or numbers, as well as data that cannot be measured numerically. All collected data should be organized in a way that provides information for effective decision-making and follow-up. For example, a business needs to collect data that enables it to write checks to employees, prepare reports about overtime, report payroll taxes to government agencies, provide premiums to health insurance companies, track Social Security payments, and so on. This requires an organized system to capture the appropriate data such as employee IDs, employee names, hours worked each day, salary or hourly rate, and insurance premium. You'll likely start to see relationships between the collected information that can provide insights into the feasibility of the possible solutions.

ProSkills

## Evaluate and Choose an Alternative

Document both the benefits and costs of all alternatives, whether numerical (cost savings) or other (employee morale). Spreadsheet software often helps problem solvers track and quantify merits and drawbacks. Consider the resources required—financial, human, equipment, and so on. Are they affordable? Is there enough time to implement the different solutions? What risks are associated with an alternative? What consequences would result if the solution didn't work? The best choice is to go with the solution that offers the greatest reward for the least amount of risk. In some cases, the solution may require developing a "Plan B" to fall back on in case the chosen solution fails to solve the problem. For instance, when collecting payroll data, it may become apparent that insurance premiums are higher percentage of payroll than previously thought, which requires further investigation and an alternative solution.

Don't try to select a solution that addresses every aspect of a problem, especially if it is complex. Solutions are rarely perfect. Instead, consider the overall effect each alternative may have. Will the resulting change generate positive results while solving the problem? Will the chosen alternative resolve the problem long-term? What is realistic, given the merits and drawbacks identified?

**PROSKILLS**

## Develop an Excel Table

In daily life, you solve all sorts of problems, such as which car purchase makes the most economic sense when comparing purchase price, mileage, and maintenance, or which software package will help your biking club manage its funds, plan road trips, and keep memberships up-to-date. To solve these and other problems, you need to collect data that tracks the current situation, determine your ultimate goal, and then follow a logical progression to the best solution. Developing an Excel table can help you to track the data you need to solve such problems.

In this exercise, you need to select an activity you participate in or an organization you belong to and identify a one-time or process-oriented problem that needs to be solved. Then, create a worksheet and develop an Excel table to track relevant data and create a solution to the problem, using the Excel skills and features presented in Tutorials 5 through 8.

**Note:** Please be sure *not* to include any personal information of a sensitive nature in any worksheets you create to submit to your instructor. Later, you can update the worksheets with such information for your own personal use.

1. Identify a problem to solve. This can be a one-time problem, such as a car purchase, or a process-oriented problem, such as tracking membership data for a club you belong to. Determine feasible alternatives to solve the problem, and then collect the data you need to evaluate these alternatives.

2. Plan the organization of your workbook and the Excel table you will develop based on how you will use the data. Consider the outputs you want to create, and the fields needed to produce those outputs. Decide what each record represents (such as data on a participant) and then identify the fields and field names (such as last name, first name, birth date, as so on) within each record. What calculations will you need to perform? How do you want to format the information?

3. Create a Documentation worksheet that includes your name, the date, and the purpose of your workbook. Format it appropriately.

4. Create an Excel table to track the data needed to solve the problem you identified. Enter an appropriate table name and column headers to track the data needed to create a solution to the problem. Add one or more calculated columns to the table to perform calculations on the data that you will use to solve the problem.

5. Improve the appearance of the table using appropriate formatting.

6. Apply validity checks to improve the accuracy of data entry.

7. Add records to the table.

8. Apply conditional formatting to at least one column in the table to highlight some aspect of the data that will help you evaluate and solve the problem.

9. Add a comment to the column with the conditional formatting to explain what the conditional formatting shows and how it will help you to evaluate and solve the problem.

10. Insert a Total row in the table and make appropriate summary calculations that you can use to evaluate and solve the problem.

11. Divide the table into two horizontal panes—one for the data and the second for the Total row.

12. Sort the data in a logical way.

13. Use a filter to answer a question about the data that you can use to evaluate and solve the problem.

14. Create a PivotTable and a PivotChart to analyze the data. Format, filter, and sort the PivotTable appropriately.

15. In a Word document, explain the problem you solved, identify the alternatives you considered, document the data you collected to evaluate the alternatives, and then describe the results of your analysis. Include the PivotChart in the Word document.

16. In an appropriate worksheet, insert a hyperlink that links to the Word document you created.

17. If you have a Windows Live ID, save the workbook to the My Documents folder on your SkyDrive. Modify the workbook by editing cell content. Save the workbook to your computer using a new filename.

18. Create at least one macro to automate a repetitive task you need to perform in the workbook, such as printing or saving a worksheet as a PDF file.

19. Prepare your workbook for printing. Include headers and footers that indicate the filename of your workbook, the workbook's author, and the date on which the report is printed. If a printed worksheet will extend across several pages, repeat appropriate print titles across all of the pages and include page numbers and the total number of pages on each printed page.

20. Save the workbook. Submit the completed files to your instructor in printed or electronic form, as requested.

EXCEL

## OBJECTIVES

- Open a workbook in Compatibility Mode
- Use the LEN function
- Use the LEFT function
- Use the Paste Values command
- Use the PROPER function
- Use the & operator
- Use the Text to Columns command
- USE the UPPER function
- Use the SUBSTITUTE function
- Use a special format for phone numbers
- Create custom formats for numbers and dates
- Using the Compatibility Checker

# Working with Text Functions and Creating Custom Formats

*Cleaning Data in a Spreadsheet*

## Case | *Zeus Engineering*

Growth in the town of Bayville has strained the capacity of local roads. Traffic increases have created delays, vehicular hazards, and pedestrian safety concerns. To address these issues, the town has contracted Zeus Engineering to develop a Transportation Improvement Program (TIP).

Myron Londale, traffic analyst at Zeus Engineering, will analyze data on private homes and commercial buildings located along the route being analyzed. He received the data from the Bayville Assessor's Office, which transferred the data to Excel. Before Myron begins his analysis, he needs to "clean" the data, and has asked for your help.

## STARTING DATA FILES

| ExcelA | Tutorial | Review | Case1 | Case2 |
|--------|----------|--------|-------|-------|
| | County Records.xls | Assessor.xls | Mesa.xls | Research.xls |

# Opening and Saving Workbooks Created in Earlier Versions of Excel

**TIP**

In the Open dialog box, point to a workbook file; the ScreenTip "Microsoft Excel Worksheet" appears for Excel 2007/2010 files and "Microsoft Excel 97-2003 Worksheet" appears for earlier files.

When you open a workbook that was created in an earlier version of Excel (Excel 2003 or earlier), Excel 2010 opens the workbook in Compatibility Mode. **Compatibility Mode** keeps the workbook in the older file format, making the workbook accessible for users who do not have the current version of Excel installed. The words "[Compatibility Mode]" appear in the title bar, indicating the file is not in the latest Excel format. You can work in Compatibility Mode, which keeps the workbook in the older file format with the .xls file extension. However, to have access to all the latest features and tools in Excel 2010, the workbook must be converted to the current file format, which has the .xlsx file extension. This is the file format you have used to save all workbooks in the tutorials.

The workbook Myron received from the Bayville Assessor's Office was created in Excel 2003. Myron wants you to convert the workbook to the current format.

### To save the workbook in the Excel 2007/2010 file format:

▶ **1.** Open the **County Records** workbook located in the ExcelA\Tutorial folder included with your Data Files. The workbook opens in Compatibility Mode because the workbook was created in an earlier version of Excel. See Figure A-1.

| Figure A-1 | Workbook in Compatibility Mode |
| --- | --- |

workbook was created in an earlier version of Excel

▶ **2.** Click the **File** tab on the Ribbon to open Backstage view, and then click the **Save As** command in the navigation bar. The Save As dialog box opens.

▶ **3.** In the File name box, type **Bayville County**. The Save as type box shows that the current file format is Excel 97-2003 Workbook, which is the earlier file format. You'll change this to the latest file format.

▶ **4.** Click the **Save as type** button, and then click **Excel Workbook**. This is the file format for Excel 2007 and 2010.

▶ **5.** Click the **Save** button. The workbook is saved with the new name and file type.

The workbook remains in Compatibility Mode, as you can see from the title bar. You can continue to work in Compatibility Mode, or you can close and then reopen the workbook in the new file format. You will open the workbook in the current file format.

### To open the Bayville County workbook in the current file format:

▶ **1.** Close the **Bayville County** workbook.

▶ **2.** Open the **Bayville County** workbook. The title bar no longer has "[Compatibility Mode]", indicating that the workbook is in the Excel 2007/2010 file format.

▶ **3.** In the Documentation sheet, enter your name and the date.

The Data worksheet contains data obtained from the county assessor's office. Myron wants you to convert this data to an Excel table.

**To create an Excel table from the county records:**

▶ **1.** Switch to the **Data** worksheet.

▶ **2.** Click the **Insert** tab on the Ribbon, and then click the **Table** button in the Tables group. The Create Table dialog box opens with the range A1:H51 selected.

▶ **3.** Click the **OK** button to create the Excel table.

▶ **4.** In the Properties group on the Table Tools Design tab, enter **TIPData** in the Table Name box to rename the table.

▶ **5.** Click the **Data** tab on the Ribbon, and then click the **Filter** button in the Sort & Filter group. The filter arrows are removed from the column headers.

▶ **6.** Click any cell in the Excel table.

# Using Text Functions

If you receive a workbook from a coworker or obtain data from other software packages, you often have to edit (sometimes referred to as *clean* or *scrub*) and manipulate the data before it is ready to use. Many Text functions help users edit and correct the text values in their workbooks. Text, also referred to as a *text string* or *string*, contains one or more characters and can include spaces, symbols, and numbers as well as uppercase and lowercase letters. For example, Text functions are used to return the number of characters, remove extra spaces, and change the case of text strings. Figure A-2 reviews some of the common Text functions available in Excel.

**Figure A-2**    **Text functions**

| Function | Syntax | Description | Example |
|---|---|---|---|
| LEFT | =LEFT(*text,nbr chars*) | Returns a specified number of characters at the left of the string | =LEFT("Michael",3) returns Mic |
| RIGHT | =RIGHT(*text,nbr chars*) | Returns a specified number of characters at the right of the string | =RIGHT("Michael",3) returns ael |
| MID | =MID(*text,start nbr, nbr chars*) | Returns a specified number of characters from a string, starting at a position you specify | =MID("Net Income",5,3) returns Inc |
| UPPER | =UPPER(*text*) | Converts all lowercase characters in a string to uppercase | =UPPER("kim") returns KIM |
| LOWER | =LOWER(*text*) | Converts all uppercase characters in a string to lowercase | =LOWER("KIM") returns kim |
| PROPER | =PROPER(*text*) | Capitalizes the first letter of each word in a string | =PROPER("JASON BAKER") returns Jason Baker |
| LEN | =LEN(*text*) | Returns the number of characters in a string | =LEN("Judith Tinker") returns 13 |
| SEARCH | =SEARCH(*find_text, within_text, start_nbr*) | Returns the number of the character at which the find_text is first found reading from left to right | =SEARCH("Main", "1234 Main St",1) returns 6 |
| TEXT | =TEXT(*value, format_text_code*) | Formats numbers within text using a specific number format | ="Total Revenue " & TEXT(SUM(D5:D75),"$#,0.00") returns Total Revenue $1,052.00 |
| TRIM | =TRIM(*text*) | Removes all spaces from a string except for single spaces between words | =TRIM("   Mary Eck") returns Mary Eck |

## Using the LEN and LEFT Functions

The Zip column includes zip codes in both five-digit and 10-digit formats. Myron wants only the five-digit component of the zip code. You will use the LEN and LEFT functions to convert all of the zip codes to the shorter form.

The **LEN function** returns the number of characters (length) of the specified string. Cell D4 stores the text *Narragansett, ri* so the formula =LEN(D4) returns the value 16, the number of characters, including spaces, in *Narragansett, ri*. You will use the LEN function to determine how many characters are in each cell of the Zip column.

The **LEFT function** returns a specified number of characters from the beginning of the string. To extract the five-digit zip code from the zip code 92975-0999 stored in cell G3, you use the formula =LEFT(G3,5) to return 92975.

You can use the IF function in the formula =IF(LEN([Zip])=10,LEFT([Zip],5),[Zip]) to display a five-digit zip code. The IF function uses the LEN function to test whether the zip code has 10 digits. If true (the zip code is 10 digits), the LEFT function displays the first five digits in the cell. If false (the code is not 10 digits), all the digits in the cell are displayed.

You'll insert a new column to the left of the Phone column in which to display the results.

### To extract the five-digit zip code from the Zip column:

1. Click cell **F2**. You'll insert the table column to the left of this column.

2. Click the **Home** tab on the Ribbon.

3. In the Cells group, click the **Insert button arrow**, and then click **Insert Table Columns to the Left**. A new column named Column1 is inserted with the Text number format, which is the same format as the Zip column (column E).

4. Select the range **F2:F51**. This range is formatted as Text.

> **TIP**
>
> You cannot enter a formula in a cell formatted as Text.

5. In the Number group on the Home tab, click the **Number Format arrow**, and then click **General**. Now, you can enter the formula in cell F2.

6. Make sure cell **F2** is the active cell, and then click the **Insert Function** button $f_x$ on the formula bar. The Insert Function dialog box opens.

7. Click **Logical** in the Or select a category list, click **IF** in the Select a function box, and then click the **OK** button. The Function Arguments dialog box opens.

8. In the Logical_test box, type **LEN([Zip])=10**. The logical test tests whether the number of characters in the current cell of the Zip column equals 10.

9. In the Value_if_true box, type **LEFT([Zip],5)**. This argument specifies that if the condition is true, the first five characters from the cell are displayed.

10. In the Value_if_false box, type **[Zip]**. This argument specifies that if the condition is false, all the characters from the cell are displayed. See Figure A-3.

**Figure A-3** | **IF function with the LEN and LEFT functions**

▶ **11.** Click the **OK** button. The formula =IF(LEN([Zip])=10,LEFT([Zip],5),[Zip]) appears in the formula bar, and the value 02975 appears in cell F2 because the condition is false. The results are automatically copied to all rows in column F of the table. Each cell in column F displays the five-digit zip code. See Figure A-4.

| Figure A-4 | Table column with five-digit zip codes |
| --- | --- |

**formula to display five-digit zip codes**

**five- and 10-digit zip codes**

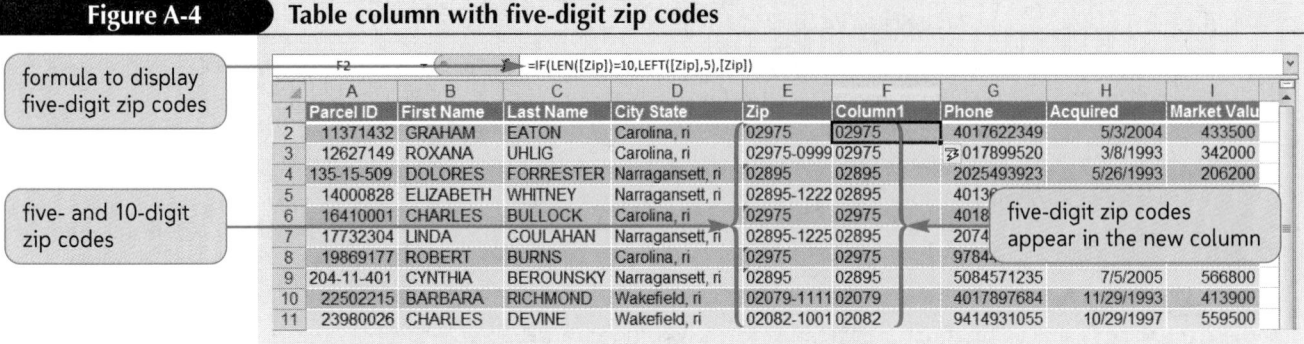

F2    =IF(LEN([Zip])=10,LEFT([Zip],5),[Zip])

| | A | B | C | D | E | F | G | H | I |
| --- | --- | --- | --- | --- | --- | --- | --- | --- | --- |
| 1 | Parcel ID | First Name | Last Name | City State | Zip | Column1 | Phone | Acquired | Market Valu |
| 2 | 11371432 | GRAHAM | EATON | Carolina, ri | 02975 | 02975 | 4017622349 | 5/3/2004 | 433500 |
| 3 | 12627149 | ROXANA | UHLIG | Carolina, ri | 02975-0999 | 02975 | 017899520 | 3/8/1993 | 342000 |
| 4 | 135-15-509 | DOLORES | FORRESTER | Narragansett, ri | 02895 | 02895 | 2025493923 | 5/26/1993 | 206200 |
| 5 | 14000828 | ELIZABETH | WHITNEY | Narragansett, ri | 02895-1222 | 02895 | 4013 | | |
| 6 | 16410001 | CHARLES | BULLOCK | Carolina, ri | 02975 | 02975 | 4018 | five-digit zip codes | |
| 7 | 17732304 | LINDA | COULAHAN | Narragansett, ri | 02895-1225 | 02895 | 2074 | appear in the new column | |
| 8 | 19869177 | ROBERT | BURNS | Carolina, ri | 02975 | 02975 | 9784 | | |
| 9 | 204-11-401 | CYNTHIA | BEROUNSKY | Narragansett, ri | 02895 | 02895 | 5084571235 | 7/5/2005 | 566800 |
| 10 | 22502215 | BARBARA | RICHMOND | Wakefield, ri | 02079-1111 | 02079 | 4017897684 | 11/29/1993 | 413900 |
| 11 | 23980026 | CHARLES | DEVINE | Wakefield, ri | 02082-1001 | 02082 | 9414931055 | 10/29/1997 | 559500 |

## Using the Paste Values Command

You now have two columns with zip codes (columns E and F). You need to keep only the column that displays the five-digit zip code. However, the data in column F is dependent on column E. If you delete column E, column F displays the #REF! error value. Therefore, before you delete column E, you need to convert the data in column F, which is based on a formula, to values. The easiest way to do that is to copy and paste the formula results, but not the actual formula, to a new column using the Paste Values command. Then, you can delete columns E and F.

### To convert the five-digit zip code formula results to values:

▶ **1.** Click cell **G2**. In the Cells group on the Home tab, click the **Insert button arrow**, and then click **Insert Table Columns to the Left**. A new column named Column2 is inserted to the left of the Phone column.

▶ **2.** Select the range **F2:F51**, which contains the formula results you want to convert to values.

▶ **3.** In the Clipboard group on the Home tab, click the **Copy** button 🗐, and then click cell **G2**.

▶ **4.** In the Clipboard group, click the **Paste button arrow**, and then click the **Values** button 🗐 in the Paste gallery. The values from Column1 are pasted into Column2. The error button that appears indicates that the numbers in column G are stored as text; you want this to display leading zeros for zip codes.

▶ **5.** Press the **Esc** key, and then click cell **F2**. The formula appears in the formula bar and the formula results appear in the cell.

▶ **6.** Click cell **G2**. Both the formula bar and the cell display values because you pasted the range using the Paste Values command.

▶ **7.** Select columns **E** and **F**, right-click the selected columns, and then click **Delete**. The two columns are removed.

▶ **8.** In cell E1, enter **Zip**. Column E, which stores the five-digit zip code values, now has a descriptive column header.

▶ **9.** Autofit the Zip column to fit the five-digit length.

# Using the PROPER Function and the & Operator

The **PROPER function** converts the first letter of each word to uppercase, capitalizes any letter that does not follow another letter, and changes all other letters to lowercase. The formula =PROPER("BOOTH") changes the word *BOOTH* to *Booth*.

The **& operator**, also called the Concatenation operator, concatenates or joins two or more text values. The syntax of the & operator is

```
Value1 & Value2 [& Value3 …]
```

where *Value1*, *Value2*, and *Value3* are string constants or cells storing text or numbers, and the & operator joins (or concatenates) these values to produce a single string. For example, if the last name "Eaton" is in cell B2 and the first name "Graham" is in cell C2, you can use the formula =B2 & C2 to join the contents of the two cells (last name and first name) to display the full name in cell D2.

However, this formula returns "EatonGraham" in cell D2. To include a comma and a space between the two names, you must change the formula to =B2 & ", " & C2 which uses two & operators and a string constant (a comma and a space enclosed in quotation marks) to display "Eaton, Graham" in the cell.

Myron wants to combine the First Name and Last Name columns into one column. Because the names were entered in all uppercase letters, you need to combine the PROPER function and the & operator into the formula =PROPER(B2)& ", " & PROPER(C2).

**To combine the names in one column with standard capitalization:**

1. Click cell **D2**, and then insert a table column to the left. A new column named Column1 is inserted to the left of the Zip column.

2. In cell D2, type **=PR** and then double-click **PROPER** in the list of functions. The beginning of the formula, =PROPER(, appears in the cell and the formula bar, and a ScreenTip shows the function's syntax.

3. Type **[** to begin the column specifier, double-click **Last Name** in the list of the column qualifiers, type **]** to end the column specifier, and then type **)** to complete the PROPER function that converts the last name to uppercase and lowercase letters.

4. Type **&** to enter the operator, and then type **", "** to join the contents of cell D2 with a comma and space.

5. Type **&** to enter the operator, type **PR** and then double-click **PROPER** in the list of functions to begin the second PROPER function.

6. Type **[** to begin the column specifier, double-click **First Name** in the list of the column qualifiers, type **]** to end the column specifier, and then type **)** to complete the second PROPER function. The complete formula =PROPER([Last Name]) & ", "& PROPER([First Name]) appears in the cell and the formula bar.

7. Press the **Enter** key. Each cell in column D displays the owner's name in the form *Last name, First name* with the first letter of each name capitalized. See Figure A-5.

| Figure A-5 | Owner's name displayed in one column |

formula displays the owners' names in one column

full names listed last name, first name with standard capitalization

& (Concatenation) operator

B3  =PROPER([Last Name]) & ", " & PROPER([First Name])

| | A | B | C | Column1 | E City St | F Zip | G Phone | Acquired | Market Valu |
|---|---|---|---|---|---|---|---|---|---|
| 1 | Parcel ID | First Name | Last Name | Column1 | City St | Zip | Phone | Acquired | Market Valu |
| 2 | 11371432 | GRAHAM | EATON | Eaton, Graham | Carolin | 02975 | 4017622349 | 5/3/2004 | 433500 |
| 3 | 12627149 | ROXANA | UHLIG | Uhlig, Roxana | arolin | 02975 | 4017899520 | 3/8/1993 | 342000 |
| 4 | 135-15-509 | DOLORES | FORRESTER | Forrester, Dolores | Narrag | 02895 | 2025493923 | 5/26/1993 | 206200 |
| 5 | 14000028 | ELIZABETH | WHITNEY | Whitney, Elizabett | Narrag | 02895 | 4013643409 | 10/23/2009 | 474300 |
| 6 | 16410001 | CHARLES | BULLOCK | Bullock, Charles | Carolin | 02975 | 4018840669 | 6/2/2010 | 238500 |
| 7 | 17732304 | LINDA | COULAHAN | Coulahan, Linda | Narrag | 02895 | 2074834659 | 4/10/2001 | 358400 |
| 8 | 19869177 | ROBERT | BURNS | Burns, Robert | Carolin | 02975 | 9784486934 | 10/4/2006 | 1279700 |
| 9 | 204-11-401 | CYNTHIA | BEROUNSKY | Berounsky, Cynthi | Narrag | 02895 | 5084571235 | 7/5/2005 | 566800 |
| 10 | 22502215 | BARBARA | RICHMOND | Richmond, Barbai | Wakefi | 02079 | 4017897684 | 11/29/1993 | 413900 |
| 11 | 23980026 | CHARLES | DEVINE | Devine, Charles | Wakefi | 02082 | 9414931055 | 10/29/1997 | 559500 |

Now that the owners' names data is stored in column D, you no longer need the data in column B (Last Name) and column C (First Name). Because the results in column D are based on a formula, you need to convert the formula in column D to values before you delete columns B and C.

---

### To paste the formula results as values and delete the original data:

▶ **1.** Click cell **E2**, and then insert a table column to the left. A new column named Column2 is added to the table.

▶ **2.** Select the range **D2:D51**, and then copy the range to the Clipboard.

▶ **3.** Click cell **E2**, and then paste the values from the Clipboard to Column2.

▶ **4.** Press the **Esc** key, and then autofit column E so you can see the owners' full names.

▶ **5.** In cell E1, enter **Owners** as the column header.

▶ **6.** Delete columns **B, C**, and **D**. The Owner column remains in the Excel table.

---

## Using the Text to Columns Command

When multiple pieces of data are stored in one cell, you can separate each piece of data into a different column using the Text to Columns command. This command starts the Convert Text to Column Wizard. You specify how to split the data based on how the data is stored. You can select what **delimits**, or separates, the data, such as a tab, a semicolon, a comma, or a space. For fixed-width data, you specify break locations. Each entry in a fixed-width field is the same length no matter how many characters are entered in the field. For example, a Last Name field with a fixed width of 20 characters always takes up 20 spaces in the record even though some last names contain a few characters and others contain many characters.

You'll split the city and state data into different columns.

---

### To split the city and state data into separate columns:

▶ **1.** Click cell **D2**, and then insert a table column to the left. A new column named Column1 is inserted to the left of the Zip column.

▶ **2.** Select the range **C2:C51**. These cells contain the values you want to split.

▶ **3.** Click the **Data** tab on the Ribbon, and then click the **Text to Columns** button in the Data Tools group. The Convert Text to Columns Wizard - Step 1 of 3 dialog box opens. You select how the data is organized in this step—delimited or a fixed width.

▶ **4.** In the Original data type area, verify that the **Delimited** option button is selected, and then click the **Next** button. The Convert Text to Columns Wizard - Step 2 of 3 dialog box opens. You select the delimiter character in this step.

▶ **5.** Click any check box with a check mark in the Delimiters section to remove the check mark, and then click the **Comma** check box. The data in the City State column is separated by a comma. The Data preview box shows the City and State data in separate columns. See Figure A-6.

| Figure A-6 | Convert Text to Columns Wizard – Step 2 of 3 dialog box |
|---|---|

6. Click the **Next** button. The Convert Text to Columns Wizard - Step 3 of 3 dialog box opens so you can set the data format for each column. The Data preview box shows that each column is set to the General number format, which you want.

7. Click the **Finish** button. Cities remain in column C; states move to column D.

8. In cell C1, enter **City** and then, in cell D1, enter **State**.

9. Autofit the widths of columns C and D. See Figure A-7.

| Figure A-7 | City and State in separate columns |
|---|---|

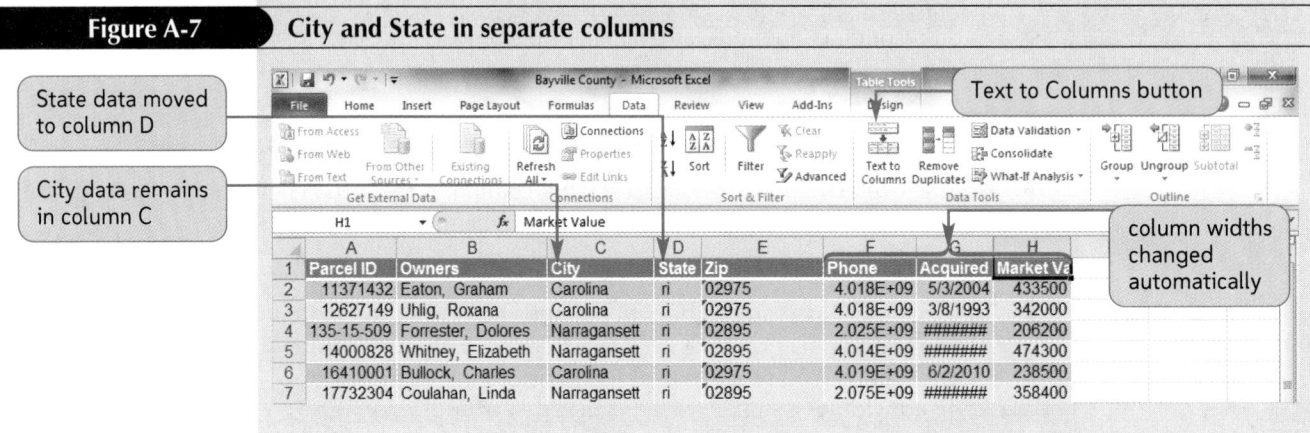

## Using the UPPER Function to Convert Case

The **UPPER function** converts all letters of each word in a text string to uppercase. The formula =UPPER("ri") returns RI. You'll use the UPPER function to change state abbreviations in column D from lowercase to uppercase.

### To use the UPPER function to capitalize the state abbreviations:

1. Click cell **E2**, and then insert a table column to the left. A new column named Column1 is inserted to the left of the Zip column.

2. In cell E2, type **=U** and then press the **Tab** key to select the UPPER function in the list. The beginning of the formula =UPPER( is in the cell and the formula bar.

3. Type **[** to begin the column specifier, double-click **State** in the list of the column qualifiers, type **]** to end the column specifier, and then type **)**. The formula =UPPER([State]) appears in the formula bar.

4. Press the **Enter** key. The state abbreviation appears in all uppercase letters in column E. See Figure A-8.

| Figure A-8 | UPPER function converted state abbreviations to uppercase |

state abbreviations are capitalized

You want to keep only the data in column E. Because the results of column E are based on a formula, you again will convert the formula in column E to values before you delete columns D and E.

### To paste the state abbreviations as values:

1. Click cell **F2**, and then insert a table column to the left. A new column named Column2 is inserted to the left of the Zip column.

2. Select the range **E2:E51**, and then copy the range to the Clipboard.

3. Click cell **F2**, and then paste the values from the Clipboard. Verify that the formula bar displays a value and not a formula.

4. Delete columns **D** and **E**. Column D remains in the Excel table.

5. In cell D1, enter **State**. The column is renamed with a more descriptive header.

## Using the SUBSTITUTE Function

The **SUBSTITUTE function** replaces existing text with new text. The SUBSTITUTE function has the syntax

```
SUBSTITUTE (text,old_text,new_text,instance_num)
```

where *text* is a string constant or reference to a cell containing text you want to replace, *old_text* is the existing text you want to replace, *new_text* is the text you want to replace *old_text* with, and *instance_num* specifies which occurrence of *old_text* you want to replace. If you omit *instance_num*, every instance of *old_text* is replaced. The formula =SUBSTITUTE("164-45-890","-","") returns 16445890.

The entries in Parcel ID, column A, are inconsistent. Sometimes they are an eight-digit value, and other times hyphens separate the components of the Parcel (Book No., Map No., and Parcel No.). Myron wants you to remove the hyphens from the Parcel ID. You'll enter a formula with the SUBSTITUTE function to remove the hyphens from the Parcel ID data.

**To remove hyphens from the Parcel ID data and paste the values:**

▶ 1. Click cell **B2**, and then insert a table column to the left. A new column named Column1 is inserted to the left of the Owners column.

▶ 2. Click the **Insert Function** button 𝑓ₓ on the formula bar. The Insert Function dialog box opens.

▶ 3. Click the **Or select a category** arrow, click **Text** to display the Text functions, and then double-click **SUBSTITUTE** in the Select a function box. The Function Arguments dialog box opens.

▶ 4. In the Text box, type **A2**. The text in cell A2 is displayed.

▶ 5. In the Old_text box, type **"-"**. The hyphen is the text you want to remove.

▶ 6. In the New_text box, type **""**. You want to replace the old text with nothing. You do not need to enter anything in the Instance_num box because you want to replace every instance of a hyphen.

▶ 7. Click the **OK** button. All of the Parcel IDs are changed to eight-digit numbers. The hyphens were replaced with an empty string (a blank, or nothing).

▶ 8. Click cell **B2**. See Figure A-9.

| Figure A-9 | SUBSTITUTE function removed hyphens from the Parcel IDs |
| --- | --- |

original IDs sometimes include hyphens

all IDs are numbers only

| | A | B | C | D | E | F | G | H | I | J | K |
| --- | --- | --- | --- | --- | --- | --- | --- | --- | --- | --- | --- |
| 1 | Parcel ID | Column1 | Owners | City | State | | | | Market Va | | |
| 2 | 11371432 | 11371432 | Eaton, Grahan | Carolina | RI | | | | 433500 | | |
| 3 | 12627149 | 12627149 | Uhlig, Roxana | Carolina | RI | | | | 342000 | | |
| 4 | 135-15-509 | 13515509 | Forrester, Dok | Narraganset | RI | | | | 206200 | | |
| 5 | 14000828 | 14000828 | Whitney, Elizal | Narraganset | RI | | | | 474300 | | |
| 6 | 16410001 | 16410001 | Bullock, Charle | Carolina | RI | | | | 238500 | | |
| 7 | 17732304 | 17732304 | Coulahan, Linc | Narraganset | RI | | | | 358400 | | |
| 8 | 19869177 | 19869177 | Burns, Robert | Carolina | RI | 02975 | 9.8E+09 | ####### | 1279700 | | |
| 9 | 204-11-401 | 20411401 | Berounsky, Cy | Narraganset | RI | '02895 | 5.1E+09 | 7/5/2005 | 566800 | | |
| 10 | 22502215 | 22502215 | Richmond, Bai | Wakefield | RI | '02079 | 4E+09 | ####### | 413900 | | |
| 11 | 23980026 | 23980026 | Devine, Charle | Wakefield | RI | '02082 | 9.4E+09 | ####### | 559500 | | |

SUBSTITUTE function replaces hyphens with an empty string, converting the Parcel IDs to eight digits

▶ 9. Click cell **C2**, and then insert a table column to the left. A new column named Column2 is inserted to the left of the Owners column.

▶ 10. Select the range **B2:B51**, and then copy this range to the Clipboard.

▶ 11. Click cell **C2**, and then paste the values from the Clipboard.

▶ 12. Delete columns **A** and **B**. The Parcel ID column remains in the Excel table.

▶ 13. In cell A1, enter **Parcel ID**.

▶ 14. Autofit the Parcel ID, Owners, City, State, Zip, Phone, Acquired, and Market Value columns.

# Using Special Formats

Four commonly used formats, referred to as special formats, are available: two zip code formats (five-digit and 10-digit), a phone number format (with the area code in parentheses and a hyphen between the prefix and the last four digits), and a Social Security number format. Using these special formats allows you to type a number without punctuation, yet still display that number in its common format.

Myron wants you to display the phone number using the common format of area code in parentheses and a hyphen between the prefix and the last four digits.

### To format the phone number with the Phone Number format:

▶ 1. Select the range **F2:F51**. In the Number group on the Home tab, click the **Dialog Box Launcher**. The Format Cells dialog box opens with the Number tab active.

▶ 2. In the Category box, click **Special**. Four special formats appear in the Type list: Zip Code, Zip Code + 4, Phone Number, and Social Security Number.

▶ 3. In the Type box, click **Phone Number**. See Figure A-10.

| Figure A-10 | Special category on the Number tab |
|---|---|

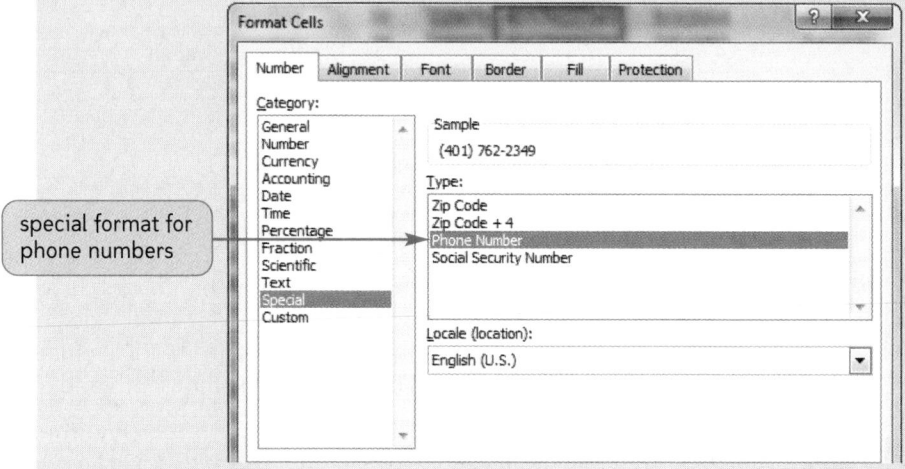

special format for phone numbers

▶ 4. Click the **OK** button. The phone numbers are formatted in a standard format.

# Creating Custom Formats

**TIP**

Any custom format you create is stored only in the workbook in which it was created. To use it in another workbook, you must reenter it.

Excel supplies a generous collection of formats and styles to improve the appearance and readability of worksheets. However, sometimes you will need a format and style to accommodate a specific requirement. In these cases, you can create your own formats, called **custom formats**. Custom formats use **format codes**, a series of symbols, to describe exactly how Excel should display a number, date, time, or text string. You can use format codes to display text strings and spaces, and determine how many decimal places to display in a cell.

## Creating a Custom Number Format

Each number is composed of digits. In displaying these digits, Excel makes special note of **insignificant zeros**, which are zeros whose omission from the number does not change the number's value. For example, the number 0.1 is displayed in the General number format but changes to 0.10 when the cell is formatted as a number. To format a value, Excel uses the **placeholders** shown in Figure A-11 to represent individual digits.

| Figure A-11 | Description of digit placeholders |
|---|---|

| Placeholder | Description |
|---|---|
| # | Displays only significant digits; insignificant zeros are omitted. |
| 0 (zero) | Displays significant digits as well as insignificant zeros. |
| ? | Replaces insignificant zeros with spaces on either side of the decimal point so that decimal points align when formatted with a fixed-width font, such as Courier. |

A custom format can use combinations of these placeholders. For example, the custom format #.00 displays the value 8.9 as 8.90. If a value has more digits than placeholders in the custom format, Excel rounds the value to match the number of placeholders. Thus, the value 8.938 formatted with the custom format #.## is displayed as 8.94. Figure A-12 shows how the same series of numbers appears with different custom number formats.

**Figure A-12** **Examples of digit placeholders**

| | Custom Formats | | | |
|---|---|---|---|---|
| Cell Value | #.## | 0.00 | ?.?? | #.#0 |
| 0.57 | .57 | 0.57 | .57 | .57 |
| 123.4 | 123.4 | 123.40 | 123.4 | 123.40 |
| 3.45 | 3.45 | 3.45 | 3.45 | 3.45 |

Number formats also include the decimal point separator (.), the thousands separator (,), and the fraction separator (/). The thousands separator can be used to separate the number in groups of 1000 or to scale a number by a multiple of 1000.

The fraction separator displays decimal values as fractions. The general syntax is *placeholder/placeholder*, where *placeholder* is one or more of the custom format placeholders. Excel displays the fraction that best approximates the decimal value. You can also specify the denominator for the fraction to convert the decimals to halves, quarters, and so forth. Figure A-13 provides examples of the thousands and fraction separators.

**Figure A-13** **Examples of thousands and fraction separators**

| Value | Custom Format | Appearance |
|---|---|---|
| 12000 | #,### | 12,000 |
| 12000 | #, | 12 |
| 12200000 | 0.0,, | 12.2 |
| 5.4 | # #/# | 5 2/5 |

All of the numeric format codes can be combined in a single custom format. If you don't specify a numeric code for data values, Excel uses the General format code, which hides all insignificant zeros.

You'll create a custom format to display the market values to the nearest thousand.

### To create a custom format for the market values:

1. Select the range **H2:H51**.

2. In the Number group on the Home tab, click the **Dialog Box Launcher**. The Format Cells dialog box opens with the Number tab active.

3. In the Category box, click **Custom**. You will enter a custom format to display the numbers to the nearest thousand.

4. In the Type box, double-click **General** to select it, and then type **#,###,** as the custom format code. See Figure A-14.

Be sure to type a comma at the end of the format code so that the numbers will be displayed to the nearest thousand.

| Figure A-14 | Custom category on the Number tab |

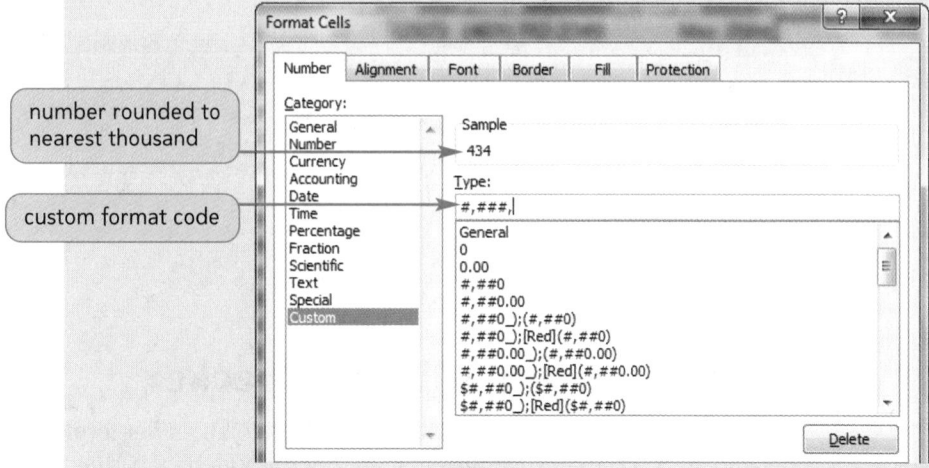

number rounded to nearest thousand

custom format code

**5.** Click the **OK** button. The market values are displayed to the nearest thousand.

## Creating a Custom Date Format

When you have dates, times, or both in a workbook, you can use a predefined date and time format to display this information in a readable format. Although the predefined time and date formats are usually fine, you can also create your own custom date formats. Figure A-15 describes the format codes used for dates and times.

| Figure A-15 | Date and Time format codes |

| Symbol | To Display | Symbol | To Display |
|--------|------------|--------|------------|
| m | Months as 1 through 12 | dddd | Days as Sunday through Saturday |
| mm | Months as 01 through 12 | yy | Years as 00 through 99 |
| mmm | Months as Jan through Dec | yyyy | Years as 1900 through 9999 |
| mmmm | Months as January through December | h | Hours as 1 through 24 |
| d | Days as 1 through 31 | mm | Minutes as 01 through 60 (when immediately following h, mm signifies minutes; otherwise, months) |
| dd | Days as 01 through 31 | | |
| ddd | Days as Sun through Sat | ss | Seconds as 01 through 60 |

Myron wants the date values in the Acquired column to show the name of the month followed by the year (for example, 7/22/2013 should be displayed as July, 2013). You need to apply the custom format code *mmmm, yyyy* to do this.

### To apply a custom date format to the Acquired dates:

**1.** Select the range **G2:G51**.

**2.** In the Number group on the Home tab, click the **Dialog Box Launcher**. The Format Cells dialog box opens with the Number tab active.

**3.** In the Category box, click **Custom**.

**4.** In the Type box, select the current format, and then type **mmmm, yyyy**. The Sample box shows an example of the custom format you entered.

**5.** Click the **OK** button, and then click cell **A1** to deselect the range. See Figure A-16.

**Figure A-16** **Final formatted workbook**

dates with
custom format

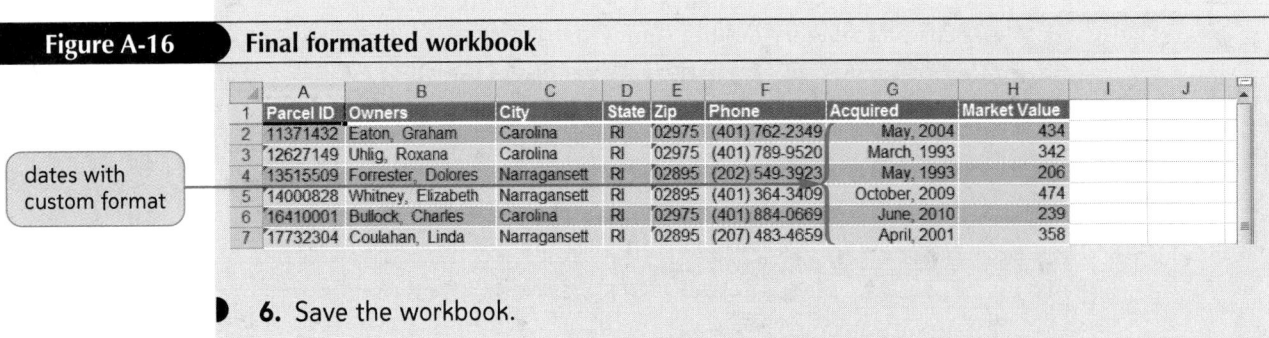

| | A | B | C | D | E | F | G | H | I | J |
|---|---|---|---|---|---|---|---|---|---|---|
| 1 | Parcel ID | Owners | City | State | Zip | Phone | Acquired | Market Value | | |
| 2 | 11371432 | Eaton, Graham | Carolina | RI | '02975 | (401) 762-2349 | May, 2004 | 434 | | |
| 3 | 12627149 | Uhlig, Roxana | Carolina | RI | '02975 | (401) 789-9520 | March, 1993 | 342 | | |
| 4 | 13515509 | Forrester, Dolores | Narragansett | RI | '02895 | (202) 549-3923 | May, 1993 | 206 | | |
| 5 | 14000828 | Whitney, Elizabeth | Narragansett | RI | '02895 | (401) 364-3409 | October, 2009 | 474 | | |
| 6 | 16410001 | Bullock, Charles | Carolina | RI | '02975 | (401) 884-0669 | June, 2010 | 239 | | |
| 7 | 17732304 | Coulahan, Linda | Narragansett | RI | '02895 | (207) 483-4659 | April, 2001 | 358 | | |

▶ **6.** Save the workbook.

# Using the Compatibility Checker

When you save an Excel 2007 or 2010 workbook to an earlier format, the **Compatibility Checker** alerts you to any features that are not supported by earlier versions of Excel. You can click the Cancel button and redo the worksheet using a different approach, or you can click the Continue button to save the workbook in the earlier format. If you save the workbook in an earlier format, unsupported features will be lost.

You'll save a copy of the workbook in the Excel 2003 format.

**To convert the workbook to the Excel 2003 file format:**

▶ **1.** Open the Save As dialog box, and then change the filename to **Bayville County 2003**.

▶ **2.** Click the **Save as type** button, and then click **Excel 97-2003 Workbook**. This is the earlier Excel file format you want to use.

▶ **3.** Click the **Save** button. The Compatibility Checker dialog box opens, alerting you to features not supported by earlier versions of Excel. See Figure A-17.

**Figure A-17** **Compatibility Checker**

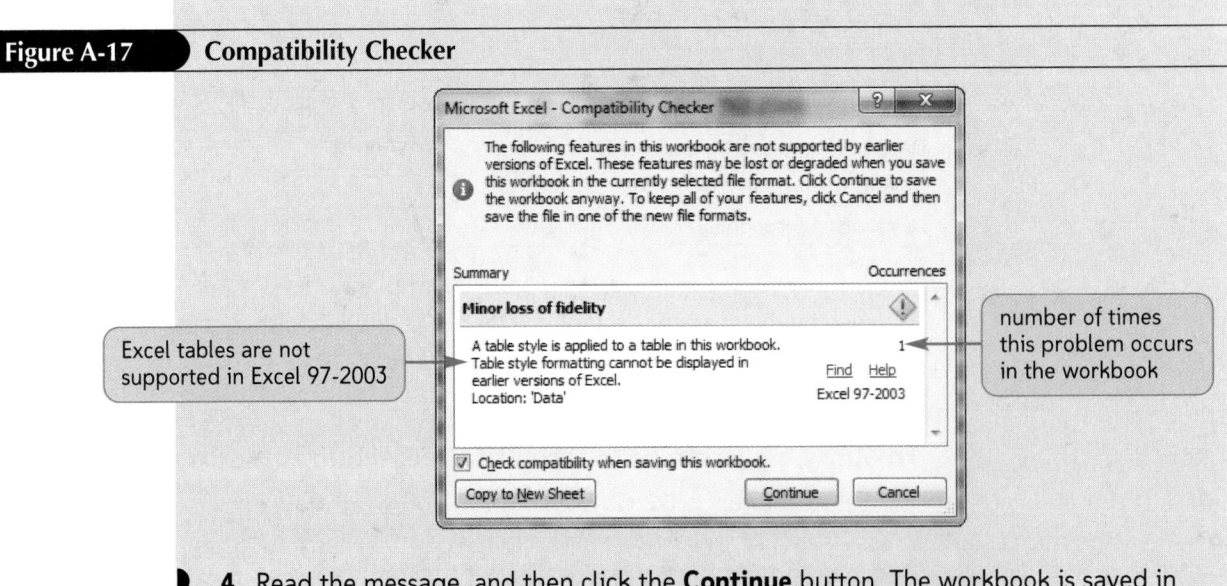

Excel tables are not
supported in Excel 97-2003

number of times
this problem occurs
in the workbook

▶ **4.** Read the message, and then click the **Continue** button. The workbook is saved in the earlier file format with the .xls file extension. Close the workbook.

The workbook data is clean and formatted in the best way for Myron. He'll analyze this data as he comes up with a proposal to address Bayville's traffic concerns.

Practice the skills you learned by using the same case scenario.

**PRACTICE**

## Review Assignments

**Data File needed for the Review Assignments: Assessor.xls**

As part of the Transportation Improvement Program (TIP) study, Myron Londale obtained a second workbook from the Bayville Assessor's Office containing data on private homes and commercial buildings located along the route being reviewed. Myron asks you to clean and format the data. Complete the following:

1. Open the **Assessor** workbook located in the ExcelA\Review folder, and then save the workbook in the Excel Workbook (2007-2010) format as **Owners**.
2. Insert a new worksheet. Enter your name, the date, and a purpose statement in the worksheet, and then rename the worksheet as **Documentation**.
3. In the Owners worksheet, create an Excel table for the data in the range A1:G51. Apply the Table Style Medium 10 table style to the Excel table.
4. Use the Text to Columns command to split the Owner column into two columns named **Last Name** and **First Name**. Insert a blank column to the left of column C to store the first name, and leave the last name in column B.
5. In cell I1, enter the column header **Status**. In the Status column, use the IF and LEFT functions to display the word **Discard** if the address is a PO Box; otherwise, leave the cell blank.
6. In cell J1, enter the column header **Twn**. In cell J2, enter a formula to convert the data in the Town column to proper case.
7. In cell K1, enter the column header **St**. In column K, enter a formula to convert the data in the State column to uppercase.
8. In cell L1, enter the column header **Town State**. In column L, combine the town and state data from columns J and K into one column using the format *town, state*.
9. Format the data in the SSN column (column A) with the Social Security Number format.
10. Save and close the workbook. Submit the finished workbook to your instructor, either in printed or electronic form, as requested.

Apply the skills you learned to clean and format data.

**APPLY**

## Case Problem 1

**Data File needed for this Case Problem: Mesa.xls**

*Mesa Senior Center*   Elliot Turner, director of the Mesa Senior Center, has begun compiling a list of its members. He's asked you to clean and format the data in the worksheet before he continues working on the project. Complete the following:

1. Open the **Mesa** workbook located in the ExcelA\Case1 folder, and then save the workbook in Excel Workbook (2007-2010) format as **Senior Center**.
2. Insert a new worksheet. Enter the company name, your name, the date, and a purpose statement in the worksheet, and then rename the worksheet as **Documentation**.
3. In the Members worksheet, apply the Social Security Number format to the data in the SSN column.
4. Split the Name data into two columns. Store the first name in column B and the last name in column C. Change the column headers to **First Name** and **Last Name**.
5. Insert two columns to the left of the CSZ column. In column D, apply the proper case to the first name data, and change the column header to **F Name**. In column E, apply the proper case to the last name data, and change the column header to **L Name**.
6. In the Member Since column, apply a custom format that displays only the year.
7. Split the CSZ column into three columns named **City**, **State**, and **Zip**. (*Hint*: Repeat the split twice.)

⊕ **EXPLORE**

8. Sort the data by City and then within City by L Name.

9. Name column J **UniqueID**. The senior center uses an ID that consists of the first three letters of the last name (L Name) followed by the first letter of first name (F Name). If the last name is fewer than three characters, the letter "Z" replaces each missing character. Use the LEN and LEFT functions and the & operator to display the proposed UniqueID.

10. Save the workbook. Submit the finished workbook to your instructor, either in printed or electronic form, as requested.

*Apply the skills you learned to calculate overhead.*

**APPLY**

## Case Problem 2

**Data File needed for this Case Problem: Research.xls**

***Steuben Institute***   Every two weeks, Elli Pjster processes payroll information for employees whose salaries are paid fully or partially from research grants. She downloads an Excel workbook from the Steuben Institute's Research and Grant Accounting system to calculate overhead. The overhead rate varies depending on the research grant. She asks you to clean and format the data in the worksheet. Complete the following:

1. Open the **Research** workbook located in the ExcelA\Case2 folder, and save the workbook in the Excel 2007/2010 format as **Grants**.

2. Insert a new worksheet. Enter the company name, your name, the date, and a purpose statement in the worksheet, and then rename the worksheet as **Documentation**.

3. In the Pay Period 10 worksheet, create an Excel table for the range A1:C51. Hide the filter arrows.

4. Split the data in column A into separate columns for the first name and the last name. Change the column headers to **First Name** and **Last Name**. Autofit the two columns, and then sort the table by the Last Name data.

⊕ **EXPLORE**

5. Use the MID function to extract the grant number from the ChartString column and display it in column E. Name the new column **Grant Nbr**. The Grant Nbr is a four-digit number that begins in position 10 of the ChartString column. (*Hint*: Research the MID function in the Help system.)

6. In the column to the right of the Grant Nbr column (column F), enter a VLOOKUP function to find the grant number in the lookup table in the Overhead Rates worksheet and display the grant name from the second column in the lookup table. Change the column header to **Grant Name**. Autofit the column.

7. In column G, enter the formula to calculate overhead (the Overhead Rate in the third column of the Overhead Rates worksheet multiplied by Salary). Use a VLOOKUP function to find the correct overhead rate for the grant. Name the column **Overhead**.

8. Format the Salary and Overhead columns using the Accounting number format.

9. Save and close the workbook. Submit the finished workbook to your instructor, either in printed or electronic form, as requested.

### ENDING DATA FILES

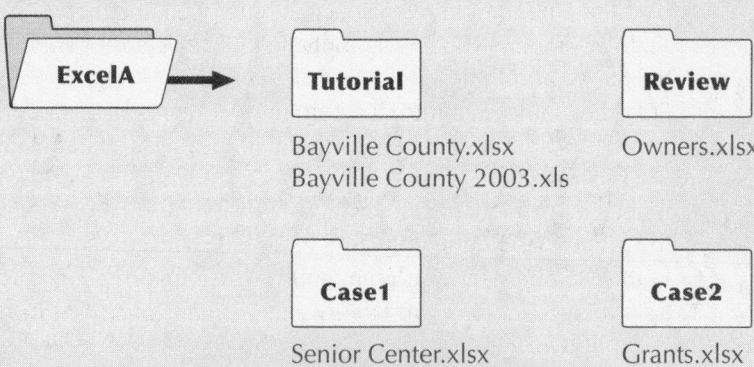

| | | |
|---|---|---|
| **ExcelA** → | **Tutorial** | **Review** |
| | Bayville County.xlsx | Owners.xlsx |
| | Bayville County 2003.xls | |
| | **Case1** | **Case2** |
| | Senior Center.xlsx | Grants.xlsx |

## OBJECTIVES

- Use advanced filters
- Create a criteria range
- Use Database functions
- Summarize data using the COUNTIFS, SUMIFS, and AVERAGEIFS functions

EXCEL

# Advanced Filters, Database, and Summary IFS Functions

*Generating a List of Eligible Employee Candidates*

## Case | *Talent Tracs*

Talent Tracs is growing rapidly and plans to hire additional full-time employees. Before searching outside the company, Rita Corvales wants to give preference to part-time employees and consultants at Talent Tracs who want to apply for the new full-time positions. Rita has established the following criteria to determine which part-time employees and consultants will be considered for full-time employment:

- Part-time employees who have worked for Talent Tracs for two or more years
- Consultants who have worked for Talent Tracs for more than three years earning less than $55,000

You will use advanced filters to generate the list of candidates who are eligible for the new positions.

## STARTING DATA FILES

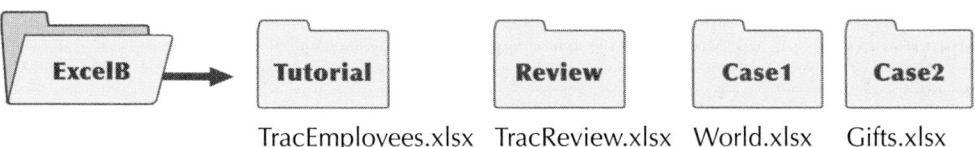

ExcelB → Tutorial | Review | Case1 | Case2

TracEmployees.xlsx    TracReview.xlsx    World.xlsx    Gifts.xlsx

# Using Advanced Filters

**Advanced filtering** displays a subset of the rows in an Excel table or a range of data that match the criteria you specify. With advanced filtering, you specify the filter criteria in a separate range, called the criteria range. Advanced filtering enables you to perform OR conditions across multiple fields, such as the criteria Rita wants you to use to find eligible candidates within Talent Tracs for the new full-time positions. You can also use advanced filtering to create complex criteria using functions and formulas. For example, Rita could use advanced filtering to find all female salaried employees whose salary falls below the median salary for all employees.

Rita created a workbook that contains data for each employee. You will open this workbook and filter the employee information to identify employees who are eligible for the new positions.

## To open the Talent Tracs workbook:

▶ **1.** Open the **TracEmployees** workbook located in the ExcelB\Tutorial folder included with your Data Files, and then save the workbook as **TracSearch**.

▶ **2.** In the Documentation worksheet, enter your name and the date.

▶ **3.** Switch to the **Employee Data** worksheet. See Figure B-1.

**Figure B-1** ▶ Employee table

| ID | Last Name | Hire Date | Birth Date | Sex | Location | Job Status | Add Life Ins | Pay Grade | Pay Type | Annual Salary | Health Plan | Years Service |
|---|---|---|---|---|---|---|---|---|---|---|---|---|
| 1024 | Hovey | 8/28/2011 | 9/6/1966 | M | Austin | FT | Y | 3 | S | $ 85,000 | HMOF | 1 |
| 1025 | Overton | 5/24/2007 | 2/15/1986 | F | Home | FT | N | 2 | S | $ 40,000 | HMOF | 6 |
| 1026 | Fetherston | 4/24/2012 | 9/24/1968 | M | New Orleans | FT | Y | 2 | S | $ 37,244 | HMOF | 1 |
| 1027 | Lebrun | 7/18/2011 | 8/9/1959 | F | Austin | FT | N | 3 | S | $ 80,000 | None | 1 |
| 1028 | Hanson | 8/21/2012 | 7/15/1950 | M | Austin | FT | Y | 3 | S | $ 65,000 | None | 0 |
| 1029 | Philo | 3/5/2012 | 5/2/1958 | M | New Orleans | FT | Y | 3 | S | $ 125,000 | PPOI | 1 |
| 1030 | Stolt | 3/1/2010 | 12/7/1977 | M | New Orleans | FT | N | 3 | S | $ 95,000 | HMOI | 3 |
| 1031 | Akhalaghi | 12/8/2012 | 12/4/1961 | M | Austin | FT | N | 2 | S | $ 36,000 | None | 0 |
| 1032 | Vankeuren | 8/11/2008 | 1/10/1959 | F | Austin | PT | N | 1 | H | $ 33,508 | PPOF | 4 |
| 1033 | Mccorkle | 6/12/2006 | 1/30/1942 | F | Nashville | FT | N | 1 | H | $ 21,840 | None | 7 |

## Understanding the Criteria Range

The **criteria range** is an area in a worksheet, separate from a range of data or an Excel table, used to specify the criteria for the data to be displayed after the filter is applied to the range or Excel table. The criteria range consists of a header row that lists field names from the table's header row, and at least one row with the specific filtering criteria for each field. The criteria range specifies which records from the data range will be included in the filtered data.

Criteria placed on the same row are considered to be connected with the logical operator AND. That means all criteria in the same row must be met before a record is included in the filtered data. Figure B-2 shows an AND criteria range filter to retrieve all employees from Nashville who earn more than $55,000.

**Figure B-2**    Example of an AND filter specified in a criteria range

| | A | B | C | D | E | F | G | H | I | J | K | L | M |
|---|---|---|---|---|---|---|---|---|---|---|---|---|---|
| 1 | ID | Last Name | Hire Date | Birth Date | Sex | Location | Job Status | Add Life Ins | Pay Grade | Pay Type | Annual Salary | Health Plan | Years Service |
| 2 | | | | | | Nashville | | | | | >55000 | | |

Criteria placed on separate rows of the criteria range are treated as being connected by the logical operator OR. That means records that meet all the criteria on either row in the criteria range will be displayed. Figure B-3 shows an example of the OR filter to retrieve female employees or employees who are working in Austin and earning less than $50,000.

**Figure B-3**    Example of an OR filter specified in a criteria range

| | A | B | C | D | E | F | G | H | I | J | K | L | M |
|---|---|---|---|---|---|---|---|---|---|---|---|---|---|
| 1 | ID | Last Name | Hire Date | Birth Date | Sex | Location | Job Status | Add Life Ins | Pay Grade | Pay Type | Annual Salary | Health Plan | Years Service |
| 2 | | | | | F | | | | | | | | |
| 3 | | | | | | Austin | | | | | <50000 | | |

To specify criteria between a range of values in the same field, you use the same field name repeated in separate cells within the same row to match a range of values (BETWEEN criteria). Figure B-4 shows a criteria range to retrieve all employees who were hired between 1/1/2008 and 12/31/2012.

**Figure B-4**    Example of a Between filter specified in a criteria range

| | A | B | C | D | E | F | G | H | I | J | K | L | M |
|---|---|---|---|---|---|---|---|---|---|---|---|---|---|
| 1 | ID | Last Name | Hire Date | Hire Date | Sex | Location | Job Status | Add Life Ins | Pay Grade | Pay Type | Annual Salary | Health Plan | Years Service |
| 2 | | | >=1/1/2008 | <=12/31/2012 | | | | | | | | | |

## Creating a Criteria Range

Typically, you place a criteria range above the data range to keep it separate from the data. If you place a criteria range next to the data range, the criteria might be hidden when the advanced filtering causes rows to be hidden. You can also place a criteria range in a separate worksheet, particularly if you need to use several criteria ranges in different cells to perform calculations based on various sets of filtered records.

You will place the criteria range in rows 1 to 4 of the Employee Data worksheet to make it easier to locate. Because the field names in the criteria range must exactly match the field names in the Excel table or range except for capitalization, you should copy and paste the field names instead of retyping them. In row 2, you will enter an AND criteria range with the criteria for consultants (code CN) who earn less than $55,000 and have worked at Talent Tracs for more than three years. In row 3, you will enter the criteria for part-time employees who have more than two years of service.

### To create the criteria range to find eligible candidates:

1. Point to the left side of cell **A6** until the pointer changes to ➡, and then click the mouse button. The column headers in row 6 are selected.

▶ **2.** Copy the field names to the Clipboard.

▶ **3.** Click cell **A1**, and then paste the field names. The field names for the criteria range appear in row 1.

▶ **4.** Press the **Esc** key to remove the copied data from the Clipboard.

▶ **5.** In cell G2, enter **CN**. The condition specifies the criteria to retrieve all consultants (Pay Type code beginning with CN).

▶ **6.** In cell K2, enter **<55000**. This condition specifies the criteria to retrieve all employees whose salaries are less than $55,000.

▶ **7.** In cell M2, enter **>3**. This condition specifies the criteria to retrieve all employees who have more than 3 years of service. The criteria in row 2 select all consultants who earn less than $55,000 and have more than three years of service at Talent Tracs.

▶ **8.** In cell G3, enter **PT**.

▶ **9.** In cell M3, enter **>=2**. The criteria in row 3 select all employees who are part-time (Job Status is equal to PT) and who have two or more years of service at Talent Tracs (Years Service is greater than or equal to 2). See Figure B-5.

| Figure B-5 | Criteria range to filter records |

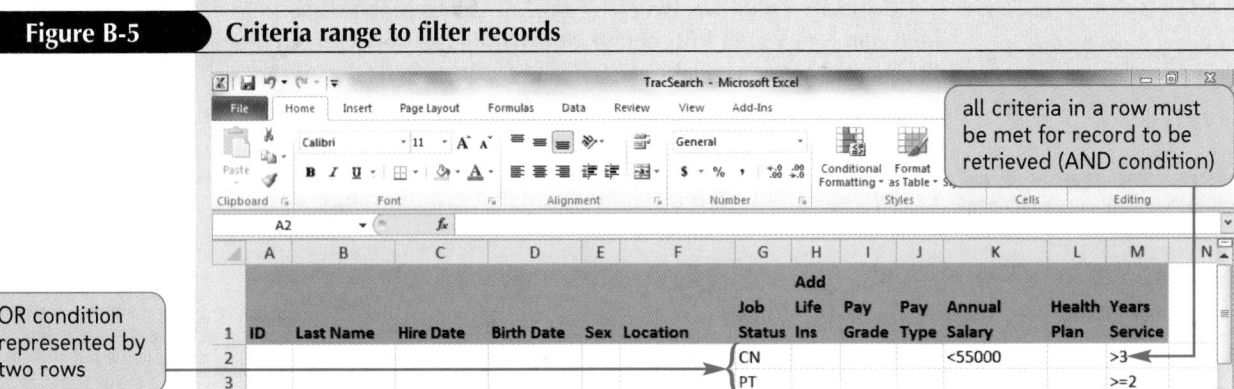

OR condition represented by two rows

all criteria in a row must be met for record to be retrieved (AND condition)

Now that the criteria range is established, you can use the Advanced Filter command to filter the Employee table. You can filter the records in their current location by hiding rows that don't match your criteria, as you have done with the Filter command. Or, you can copy the records that match your criteria to another location in the worksheet. Rita wants you to filter the records in their current location.

### To filter the Employee table in its current location:

▶ **1.** Click any cell in the Employee table to make the table active.

▶ **2.** Click the **Data** tab on the Ribbon.

▶ **3.** In the Sort & Filter group, click the **Advanced** button. The Advanced Filter dialog box opens.

▶ **4.** Make sure the **Filter the list, in-place** option button is selected and the range **$A$6:$M$106** appears in the List range box. The range $A$6:$M$106 is the current location of the Employee table, which is the table you want to filter.

▶ **5.** Make sure the Criteria range box displays **$A$1:$M$3**. This range references the criteria range. See Figure B-6.

| Figure B-6 | Completed Advanced Filter dialog box |

> **6.** Click the **OK** button, and then scroll to the top of the worksheet. The list is filtered in its current location, and nine employee records match the criteria (as shown in the status bar). See Figure B-7.

| Figure B-7 | Filtered employee data |

employees eligible to apply for the full-time position

| | A | B | C | D | E | F | G | H | I | J | K | L | M | N |
|---|---|---|---|---|---|---|---|---|---|---|---|---|---|---|
| 6 | ID | Last Name | Hire Date | Birth Date | Sex | Location | Job Status | Add Life Ins | Pay Grade | Pay Type | Annual Salary | Health Plan | Years Service | |
| 15 | 1032 | Vankeuren | 8/11/2008 | 1/10/1959 | F | Austin | PT | N | 1 | H | $ 33,508 | PPOF | 4 | |
| 41 | 1058 | Myette | 5/4/2009 | 6/28/1967 | M | Home | PT | N | 2 | S | $ 33,000 | HMOF | 4 | |
| 65 | 1082 | Steyerl | 3/13/2008 | 5/12/1969 | M | Austin | CN | N | 3 | S | $ 54,000 | None | 5 | |
| 75 | 1092 | Sherman | 11/26/2010 | 3/2/1955 | M | Austin | PT | N | 1 | H | $ 33,280 | HMOI | 2 | |
| 76 | 1093 | Mulcahey | 8/25/2001 | 5/13/1964 | F | Austin | PT | N | 2 | S | $ 45,000 | None | 11 | |
| 79 | 1096 | Silver | 9/6/2005 | 6/26/1967 | F | Austin | PT | N | 3 | S | $ 93,000 | None | 7 | |
| 82 | 1099 | Reels | 6/15/2009 | 7/31/1963 | F | Austin | PT | N | 1 | H | $ 26,520 | None | 4 | |
| 89 | 1106 | Tucker | 3/11/2007 | 3/3/1958 | F | Nashville | PT | N | 1 | H | $ 22,880 | PPOF | 6 | |
| 100 | 1117 | Zunjic | 10/12/2010 | 1/17/1970 | F | Austin | PT | N | 1 | H | $ 36,004 | HMOI | 2 | |

**Trouble?** If all of the data in the table is filtered, the list range or criteria range might be incorrect. Click the Clear button in the Sort & Filter group on the Data tab, and then repeat Steps 1 through 6, making sure the list range is $A$6:$M$106 and the criteria range is $A$1:$M$3 in the Advanced Filter dialog box.

After providing the list of eligible employees to Rita, you remove the filter to display all of the records in the Employee table.

### To show all of the records in the table:

> **1.** In the Sort & Filter group on the Data tab, click the **Clear** button. All of the records in the Employee table reappear.

# Using Database Functions to Summarize Data

**Database functions** (or **Dfunctions**) perform summary data analysis, such as sum, average, and count, on an Excel table or data range based on criteria specified in a criteria range. Although you can often use the SUMIF, AVERAGEIF, and COUNTIF functions;

the Total row of an Excel table; and PivotTables to achieve the same results as Database functions, some situations require Database functions. For example, the type of summary analysis, the placement of the summary results, or the complexity of the criteria might require using Database functions. Figure B-8 lists the Database functions.

| Figure B-8 | Database functions |

| Function | Description |
|---|---|
| DAVERAGE | Returns the average of the values that meet specified criteria |
| DCOUNT | Returns the number of cells containing numbers that meet specified criteria |
| DCOUNTA | Returns the number of nonblank cells that meet specified criteria |
| DMAX | Returns the maximum value in the search column that meets specified criteria |
| DMIN | Returns the minimum value in the search column that meets specified criteria |
| DSTDEV | Returns the estimate of standard deviation based on a sample of entries that meet the specified criteria |
| DSUM | Returns the sum of the values in the summary column that meet specified criteria |

Rita needs to prepare a report comparing the average salaries paid to employees by pay type (hourly and salaried) and by gender. To create this report, you must set up a criteria range to retrieve the appropriate records for each calculation. Consequently, a Database function is a good approach.

Database functions use a criteria range to specify the records to summarize. In a Database function, the criteria range is used as one of the arguments of the function. The general syntax for any Database function is

```
DatabaseFunctionName(table range, column to summarize, criteria range)
```

where *table range* refers to the cells where the data to summarize is located, including the column header, *column to summarize* is the column name of the field to summarize entered within quotation marks, and *criteria range* is the range where the criteria that determine which records are used in the calculation are specified.

You will use Database functions to complete the Employee Summary worksheet, summarizing the average salaries for employees by pay type and gender. First, you will set up a criteria range. Although the criteria range often includes all fields from the table, even those not needed to select records, you do not have to include all field names from the table when setting up a criteria range. In this case, you will use only the fields needed to specify the criteria.

You will create two criteria ranges for the Employee Pay Comparison report.

## To create criteria ranges for the Employee Pay Comparison report:

1. Switch to the **Employee Summary** worksheet. The column headers for the criteria range have already been copied from the Employee Data worksheet.

2. In cell G6, enter **F** and then, in cell H6, enter **S**. These are the criteria to find all salaried females.

3. In cell J6, enter **M** and then, in cell K6, enter **S**. These are the criteria to find all salaried males.

4. In cell G10, enter **F** and then, in cell H10, enter **H**. These are the criteria to find all hourly females.

5. In cell J10, enter **M** and then, in cell K10, enter **H**. These are the criteria to find all hourly males. See Figure B-9.

| Figure B-9 | Criteria ranges for the report |

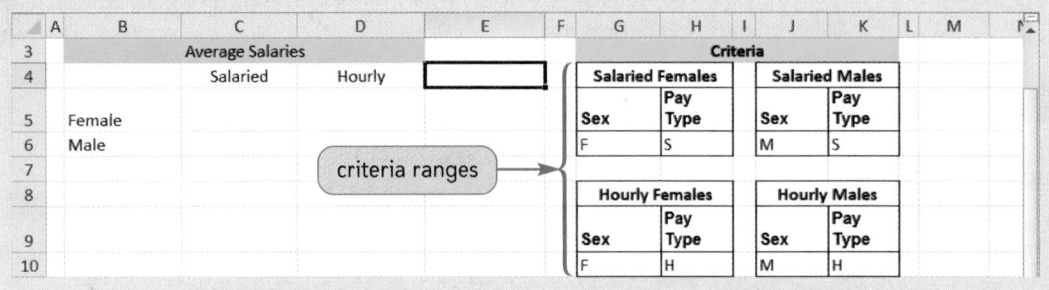

The criteria ranges are complete, so you can enter the formulas for the employee salary comparison. You will enter the DAVERAGE function to calculate the average salary in each group. In each function, the first two arguments are identical. The third argument, the criteria range, is different for each function so you can average a different subset of employees each time.

## To find average salaries for salaried males and salaried females:

1. Click cell **C5**, and then click the **Insert Function** button 𝑓ₓ on the formula bar. The Insert Function dialog box opens.

2. Click the **Or select a category arrow**, and then click **Database**.

3. In the Select a function box, select **DAVERAGE**, if necessary, and then click the **OK** button. The Function Arguments dialog box opens.

4. In the Database box, type **'Employee Data'!$A$6:$M$106** to enter the range to search, and then press the **Tab** key. In this case, 'Employee Data'!$A$6:$M$106 refers to all data values in the range A6:M106 of the Employee Data worksheet.

   **Trouble?** If the error "Invalid" appears to the right of the Database box, you probably mistyped the range to search. Make sure you typed apostrophes (') and not quotation marks (") around the Employee Data worksheet name, included a space in the Employee Data worksheet name, and typed ! (an exclamation mark) before the criteria range.

5. In the Field box, type **"Annual Salary"** and then press the **Tab** key. The field specifies the table column that contains the data to be averaged.

6. In the Criteria box, type **G5:H6** to specify the criteria for salaried females. See Figure B-10.

| Figure B-10 | DAVERAGE Function Arguments dialog box |

Function Arguments

DAVERAGE

Database  'Employee Data'!$A$6:$M$106   = {"ID","Last Name","Hire Date","Birth Dat

Field  "Annual Salary"   = "Annual Salary"

Criteria  G5:H6   = G5:H6

= 61793.91304

Averages the values in a column in a list or database that match conditions you specify.

Criteria  is the range of cells that contains the conditions you specify. The range includes a column label and one cell below the label for a condition.

Formula result = $    61,794

Help on this function          OK     Cancel

▶ 7. Click the **OK** button. The formula =DAVERAGE('Employee Data'!$A$6:$M$106, "Annual Salary",G5:H6) appears in the formula bar and $61,794 appears in cell C5, indicating the average salary paid to salaried females. See Figure B-11.

---

**Figure B-11** **DAVERAGE function**

DAVERAGE function used to calculate average salary of salaried females

criteria range for salaried females

average salary of salaried females

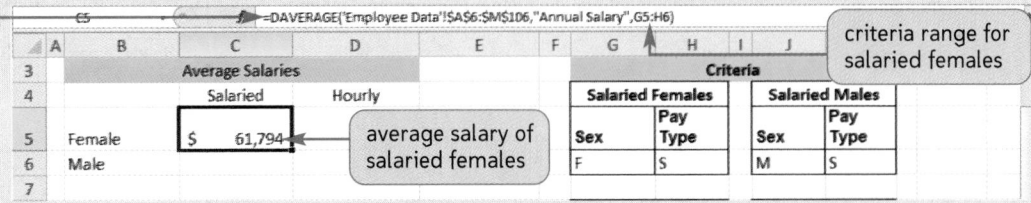

---

▶ 8. Click cell **C6**, and then click the **Insert Function** button $f_x$ on the formula bar.

▶ 9. Repeat Steps 2 through 5 to enter the first two arguments for the DAVERAGE function to calculate the average salary paid to male employees.

▶ 10. In the Criteria box, type **J5:K6** to specify the criteria for salaried males.

▶ 11. Click the **OK** button. The formula =DAVERAGE ('Employee Data'!$A$6:$M$106, "Annual Salary",J5:K6) appears in the formula bar and $95,081 appears in cell C6, indicating the average salary paid to salaried males.

For the last two cells in the salary comparison, you will copy the formulas in cells C5:C6 to cells D5 and D6 to calculate the average salaries paid to hourly females and hourly males.

---

### To find the average salaries for male and female hourly employees:

▶ 1. Copy the formula in cell **C5** to cell **D5**.

▶ 2. Click cell **D5**, and then change the criteria range (the third argument) from H5:I6 to **G9:H10**. The formula =DAVERAGE('Employee Data'!$A$6:$M$106,"Annual Salary",G9:H10) appears in the formula bar and $27,213 appears in cell D5, indicating the average salary paid to hourly females.

▶ 3. Copy the formula from cell **C6** to cell **D6**.

▶ 4. Click cell **D6**, and then change the criteria range (the third argument) from K5:L6 to **J9:K10**. The formula =DAVERAGE('Employee Data'!$A$6:$M$106,"Annual Salary",J9:K10) appears in the formula bar and $26,707 appears in cell D6, indicating the average salary paid to salaried males. See Figure B-12.

---

**Figure B-12** **Completed Average Salaries report**

location of data

criteria range for hourly males

average salaries for hourly males

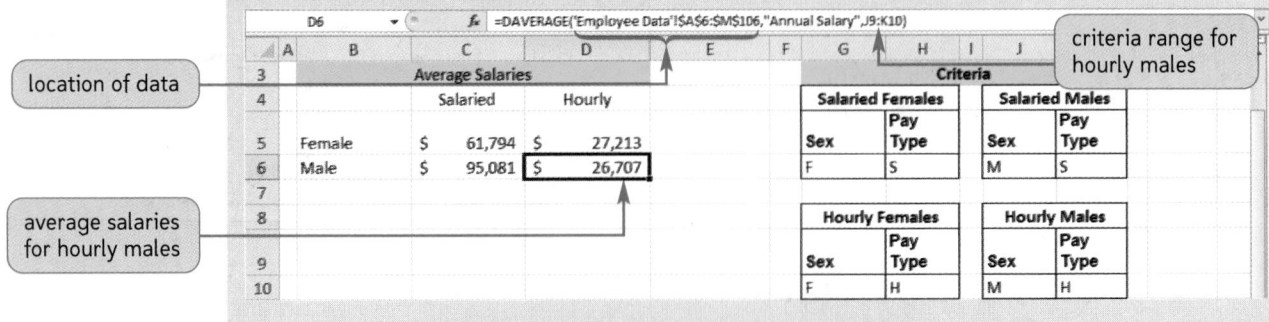

# Summarizing Data Using the COUNTIFS, SUMIFS, and AVERAGEIFS Functions

The COUNTIFS, SUMIFS, and AVERAGEIFS functions are similar to the COUNTIF, SUMIF, and AVERAGEIF functions except the latter functions enable you to specify only one condition to summarize the data, whereas the former functions enable you to summarize the data using several conditions.

The **COUNTIFS function** counts the number of cells within a range that meet multiple criteria. Its syntax is

```
COUNTIFS(,criteria_range1,criteria1[,criteria_range2,criteria2,…])
```

where *criteria_range1*, *criteria_range2*, and up represent up to 127 ranges (columns of data) in which to evaluate the associated criteria, and *criteria1*, *criteria2*, and up represent 127 criteria in the form of a number, an expression, a cell reference, or text that define which cells will be counted. Criteria can be expressed as a number such as 50 to find a number equal to 50, the expression ">10000" to find an amount greater than 10000, text such as "FT" to find a text value equal to FT, or the cell reference B4 to find the value equal to the value stored in cell B4. Each cell in a range is counted only if all of the corresponding criteria specified in the COUNTIFS function are true.

To count the number of full-time (FT) employees who are female (F) and earn more than $50,000, you can use the following function to count the full-time employees (Employee[Job Status],"FT") who are female (Employee[Sex],"F") and have a salary greater than 50,000 (Employee[Annual Salary],">50000"). The criteria are treated as if they are connected by an AND function, so all conditions must be true for a record to be counted.

```
=COUNTIFS(Employee[Job Status],"FT",Employee[Sex],"F",
Employee[Annual Salary],">50000")
```

The SUMIFS and AVERAGEIFS functions have a slightly different syntax. The **SUMIFS function** adds values in a range that meet multiple criteria using the syntax

```
SUMIFS(sum_range,criteria_range1,criteria1[,criteria_range2,
criteria2,…])
```

where *sum_range* is the range you want to add; *criteria_range1*, *criteria_range2*, and so on represent up to 127 ranges (columns of data) in which to evaluate the associated criteria; and *criteria1*, *criteria2*, and so on up to 127 criteria in the form of a number, expression, cell reference, or text define which cells will be added.

To calculate the total salary paid to full-time (FT) employees hired after 2012 who are living in Austin, you can use the following SUMIFS function to add the salaries (Employee[Annual Salary]) of employees located in Austin (Employee[Location],"Austin") who have a hire date on or later than 1/1/2012 (Employee[Hire Date],">=1/1/2012") and are full-time employees (Employee[Job Status],"FT"):

```
=SUMIFS(Employee[Annual Salary],Employee [Location],"Austin",
Employee[Hire Date],">=1/1/2012",Employee[Job Status],"FT")
```

The **AVERAGEIFS function** calculates the average of values within a range of cells that meet multiple conditions. Its syntax is

```
AVERAGEIFS(average_range,criteria_range1,criteria1[,criteria_range2,
criteria2,…])
```

where *average_range* is the range to average; *criteria_range1*, *criteria_range2*, and so on represent up to 127 ranges in which to evaluate the associated criteria; and *criteria1*, *criteria2*, and so on up to 127 criteria in the form of a number, an expression, a cell reference, or text define which cells will be averaged.

To calculate the average salary paid to males (M) who have worked at Talent Tracs for more than five years, you can use the following AVERAGEIFS function to average the salaries (Employee[Annual Salary]) of male employees (Employee[Sex],"M"), having more than five years of service (Employee[Years Service],">5"):

```
=AVERAGEIFS(Employee[Annual Salary],Employee[Sex],"M",
Employee[Years Service],">5")
```

Rita wants you to complete the Years' Service Summary report using the COUNTIFS, SUMIFS, and AVERAGEIFS functions to compute statistical information for Talent Tracs employees excluding employees working from home.

### To calculate employees with years of service between 0 and 4 years:

▶ **1.** Click cell **C16**, and then click the **Insert Function** button $f_x$ on the formula bar. The Insert Function dialog box opens.

▶ **2.** Click the **Or select a category arrow**, and then click **Statistical**.

▶ **3.** In the Select a function box, click **COUNTIFS**, and then click the **OK** button. The Function Arguments dialog box opens.

▶ **4.** In the Criteria_range1 box, enter **Employee[Location]** and then press the **Tab** key. This criterion selects employees not working from home.

▶ **5.** In the Criteria1 box, type **"<>Home"** to specify employees not working from home, and then press the **Tab** key. The first condition is complete, and 93 appears as the total count in the middle of the Function Arguments dialog box.

▶ **6.** In the Criteria_range2 box, enter **Employee[Years Service]** to enter the range referencing the number of years the employee has worked at Talent Tracs, and then press the **Tab** key.

▶ **7.** In the Criteria2 box, type **">=0"** to select employees whose years of service are greater than or equal to 0, and then press the **Tab** key. The second condition is complete, and 93 appears as the total count.

▶ **8.** In the Criteria_range3 box, enter **Employee[Years Service]** to enter the range referencing the number of years the employee has worked at Talent Tracs, and then press the **Tab** key.

▶ **9.** In the Criteria3 box, type **"<=4"** to enter the criterion that employees' years of service are less than or equal to 4. The third condition is complete, and 57 appears as the total count. See Figure B-13.

| Figure B-13 | **Function Arguments box for the COUNTIFS function** |
|---|---|

▶ **10.** Click the **OK** button. The formula =COUNTIFS(Employee[Location],"<>Home",
Employee[Years Service],">=0",Employee[Years Service],"<=4") appears in the
formula bar and the value 57 appears in cell C16. See Figure B-14.

| **Figure B-14** | **Years' Service Summary report in process** |

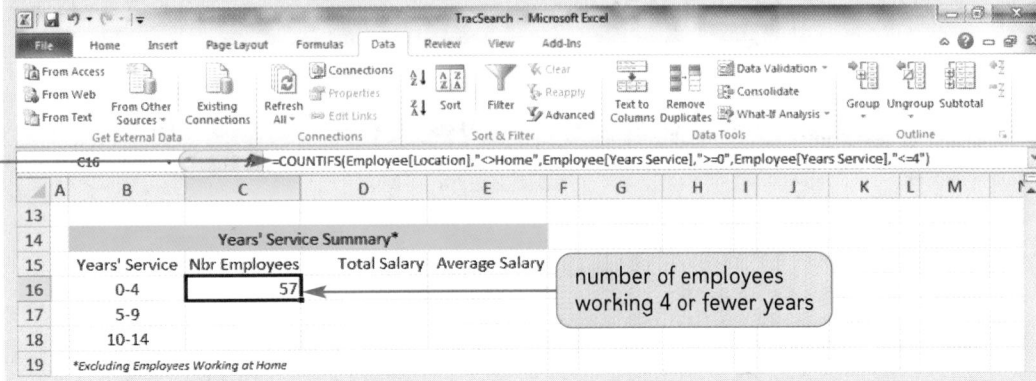

COUNTIFS function
to calculate the
number of employees
who have worked 4
or fewer years

number of employees
working 4 or fewer years

▶ **11.** Copy the formula from cell **C16** to the range **C17:C18**.

▶ **12.** In cell C17, change the second criteria argument from ">=0" to **">=5"** and change
the third criteria argument from "<=4" to **"<=9"**. The criteria specify years of
service greater than or equal to 5 and less than or equal to 9. The formula =COUNT
IFS(Employee[Location],"<>Home",Employee[Years Service],">=5",Employee[Years
Service],"<=9") appears in the formula bar and 26 appears in cell C17.

▶ **13.** In cell C18, change the second criteria argument from ">=0" to **">=10"** and
change the third criteria argument from "<=4" to **"<=14"**. The criteria specify
years of service greater than or equal to 10 and less than or equal to 14. The
formula =COUNTIFS(Employee[Location],"<>Home",Employee[Years Service],
">=10",Employee[Years Service],"<=14") appears in the formula bar and 10 appears
in cell C18.

Next, you will calculate the total salary paid to employees based on years of service.
To do this, you will use the SUMIFS function.

### To calculate the total salary paid to employees:

▶ **1.** Click cell **D16**, and then click the **Insert Function** button 𝑓𝑥 on the formula bar.
The Insert Function dialog box opens.

▶ **2.** Click the **Or select a category arrow**, and then click **Math & Trig**.

▶ **3.** In the Select a function box, click **SUMIFS**, and then click the **OK** button. The
Function Arguments dialog box opens.

▶ **4.** In the Sum_range box, type **Employee[Annual Salary]** to enter the range of data
to sum, and then press the **Tab** key. In this case, a structured reference was used
to reference all data values in the Annual Salary column.

▶ **5.** In the Criteria_range1 box, enter **Employee[Location]** and then press the
**Tab** key.

**TIP**

You could also have used
the worksheet reference
'Employee Data'!K6:K106
to reference the annual
salaries for all employees.

▶ **6.** In the Criteria1 box, type **"<>Home"** to specify employees not working from home, and then press the **Tab** key. The first condition is complete. See Figure B-15.

**Figure B-15**   **Function Arguments dialog box for the SUMIFS function**

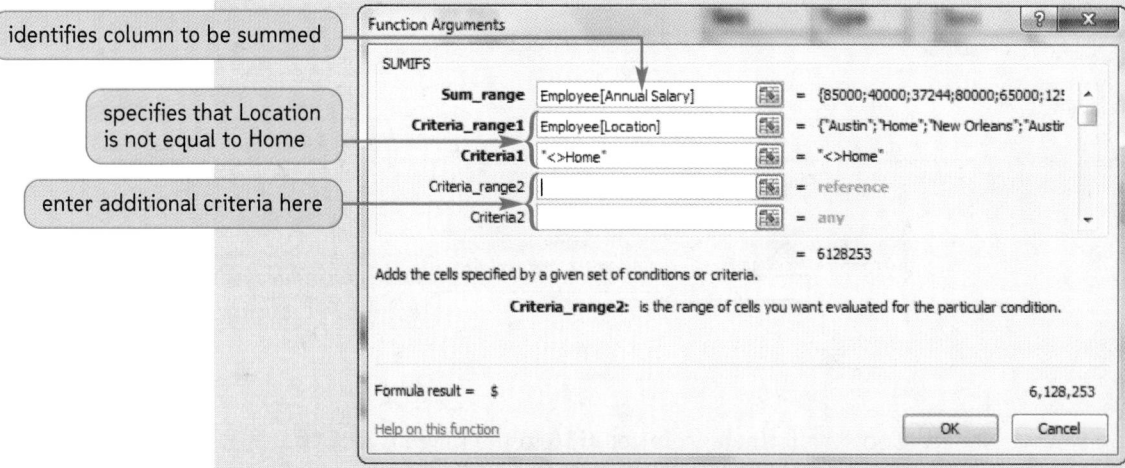

identifies column to be summed

specifies that Location is not equal to Home

enter additional criteria here

▶ **7.** In the Criteria_range2 box, enter **Employee[Years Service]** for the range referencing the number of years the employee has worked at Talent Tracs, and then press the **Tab** key.

▶ **8.** In the Criteria2 box, type **">=0"** to specify years of service that are greater than or equal to 0, and then press the **Tab** key.

▶ **9.** In the Criteria_range3 box, type **Employee[Years Service]** for the range referencing the number of years the employee has worked at Talent Tracs, and then press the **Tab** key.

▶ **10.** In the Criteria3 box, type **"<=4"** to specify years of service that are less than or equal to 4, and then press the **Tab** key.

▶ **11.** Click the **OK** button. The formula =SUMIFS(Employee[Annual Salary],Employee [Location],"<>Home",Employee[Years Service],">=0",Employee[Years Service], "<=4") appears in the formula bar and 3,868,395 appears in cell D16.

▶ **12.** Copy the formula from cell **D16** to the range **D17:D18**.

▶ **13.** In cell D17, change the second criteria argument from ">=0" to **">=5"** and change the third criteria argument from "<=4" to **"<=9"**. The criteria specify years of service greater than or equal to 5 and less than or equal to 9. The formula =SUMIFS(Employee[Annual Salary],Employee[Location],"<>Home", Employee[Years Service],">=5",Employee[Years Service],"<=9") appears in the formula bar and 1,517,799 appears in cell D17.

▶ **14.** In cell D18, change the second criteria argument from ">=0" to **">=10"** and then change the third criteria argument from "<=4" to **"<=14"**. The criteria specify years of service greater than or equal to 10 and less than or equal to 14. The formula =SUMIFS(Employee[Annual Salary],Employee[Location],"<>Home", Employee[Years Service],">=10",Employee[Years Service],"<=14") appears in the formula bar and 742,059 appears in cell D18.

Next, you will calculate the average salary paid to employees based on years of service. You will use the AVERAGEIFS function to do this.

### To calculate the average salary paid to employees:

▶ **1.** Click cell **E16**, and then click the **Insert Function** button 𝑓𝑥 on the formula bar. The Insert Function dialog box opens.

▶ **2.** Click the **Or select a category arrow**, and then click **Statistical**.

▶ **3.** In the Select a function box, click **AVERAGEIFS**, and then click the **OK** button. The Function Arguments dialog box opens.

▶ **4.** In the Average_range box, type **Employee[Annual Salary]** to enter the range to be averaged, and then press the **Tab** key.

▶ **5.** In the Criteria_range1 box, enter **Employee[Location]** and then press the **Tab** key.

▶ **6.** In the Criteria1 box, type **"<>Home"** to specify employees not working from home, and then press the **Tab** key. The first condition is complete.

▶ **7.** In the Criteria_range2 box, enter **Employee[Years Service]** for the range referencing the number of years the employee has worked at Talent Tracs, and then press the **Tab** key.

▶ **8.** In the Criteria2 box, type **">=0"** to specify years of service greater than or equal to 0, and then press the **Tab** key.

▶ **9.** In the Criteria_range3 box, enter **Employee[Years Service]** for the range referencing the number of years the employee has worked at Talent Tracs, and then press the **Tab** key.

▶ **10.** In the Criteria3 box, type **"<=4"** to specify years of service less than or equal to 4, and then press the **Tab** key.

▶ **11.** Click the **OK** button. The formula =AVERAGEIFS(Employee[Annual Salary], Employee[Location],"<>Home",Employee[Years Service],">=0",Employee[Years Service],"<=4") appears in the formula bar and 67,867 appears in cell E16.

▶ **12.** Copy the formula from cell E16 to the range **E17:E18**.

▶ **13.** In cell E17, change the second criteria argument from ">=0" to **">=5"** and change the third criteria argument from "<=4" to **"<=9"**. The criteria specify years of service greater than or equal to 5 and less than or equal to 9. The formula =AVERAGEIFS(Employee[Annual Salary],Employee[Location],"<>Home", Employee[Years Service], ">=5",Employee[Years Service],"<=9") appears in the formula bar and 58,377 appears in cell E17.

▶ **14.** In cell E18, change the second criteria argument from ">=0" to **">=10"** and change the third criteria argument from "<=4" to **"<=14"**. The criteria specify years of service greater than or equal to 10 and less than or equal to 14. The formula =AVERAGEIFS(Employee[Annual Salary],Employee[Location],"<>Home", Employee[Years Service],">=10",Employee[Years Service],"<=14") appears in the formula bar and 74,206 appears in cell E18.

▶ **15.** Click cell **E18**, and then expand the formula bar. See Figure B-16.

| Figure B-16 | Completed Years' Service Summary report |

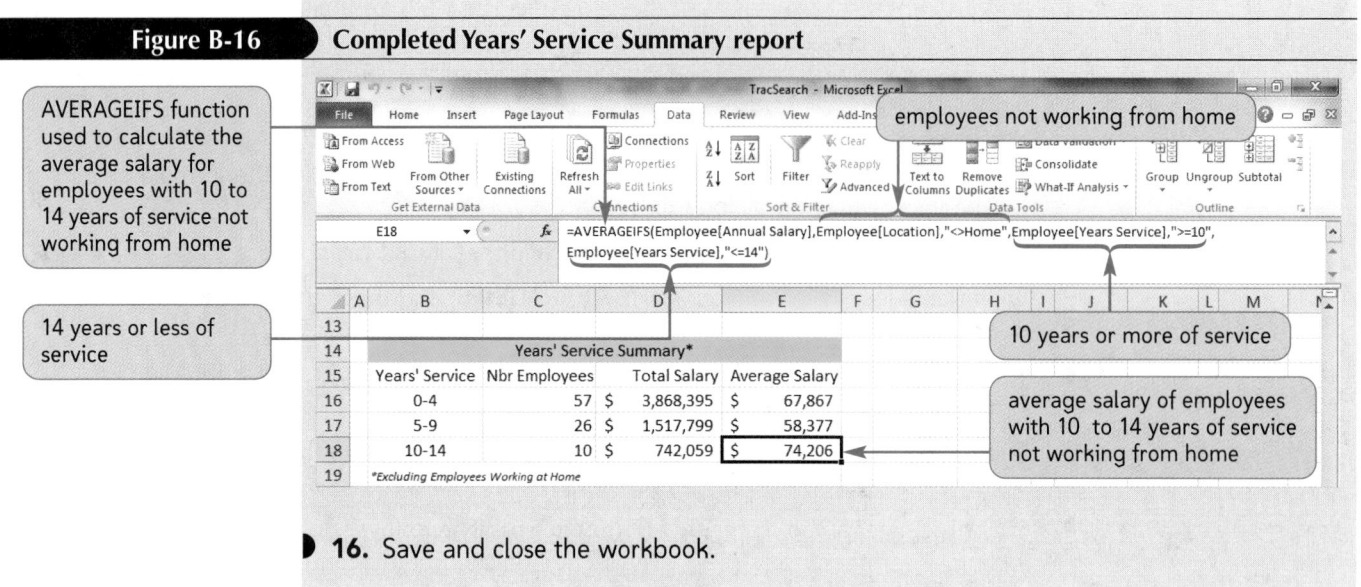

AVERAGEIFS function used to calculate the average salary for employees with 10 to 14 years of service not working from home

14 years or less of service

employees not working from home

10 years or more of service

average salary of employees with 10 to 14 years of service not working from home

=AVERAGEIFS(Employee[Annual Salary],Employee[Location],"<>Home",Employee[Years Service],">=10", Employee[Years Service],"<=14")

| Years' Service Summary* | | | |
| Years' Service | Nbr Employees | Total Salary | Average Salary |
| 0-4 | 57 | $ 3,868,395 | $ 67,867 |
| 5-9 | 26 | $ 1,517,799 | $ 58,377 |
| 10-14 | 10 | $ 742,059 | $ 74,206 |

*Excluding Employees Working at Home

▶ **16.** Save and close the workbook.

The Years' Service Summary report is complete. In this session, you used advanced filtering techniques to find potential candidates for a new full-time position. You also used the DAVERAGE and AVERAGEIFS functions to prepare a report calculating the average salary of employees broken down by pay type and gender.

*Practice the skills you learned in the tutorial using the same case scenario.*

**PRACTICE**

## Review Assignments

**Data File needed for the Review Assignments: TracReview.xlsx**

Rita wants you to perform advanced filtering tasks to create a report about employee compensation and benefits. You need to set up a criteria range to generate the report. Complete the following:

1. Open the **TracReview** workbook located in the ExcelB\Review folder included with your Data Files, and then save the workbook as **TracReviewReport**. In the Documentation sheet, enter your name and the date.

2. Make a copy of the Employee Data worksheet, and then rename the copied worksheet as **Q2**. Complete the criteria range located in the range A1:M3 of the Q2 worksheet, and then use advanced filtering to display all part-time (PT) employees who have worked 2 or more years and earned more than $60,000 or consultants (CN). Filter the Employee table.

3. Make a copy of the Employee Data worksheet, and then rename the copied worksheet as **Q3**. Complete the criteria range located in the range A1:M3 of the Q3 worksheet so you can use advanced filtering to display all part-time (PT) employees working in Austin as well as all full-time (FT) employees working at home and earning $40,000 or more. Filter the Employee table.

4. Complete the Number of Employees by Sex and Health Plan report in the Employee Summary worksheet. Complete the criteria ranges (G4:K22) and then use the DCOUNT Database function to count the number of employees found in the range C5:D9 of the report. For example, in cell C5 count the number of employees with Health Plan PPOI that are female, in cell D5 count the number of employees with Health Plan PPOI that are male, and so on. Calculate totals in row 10 and column E to complete the report.

5. Complete the Total Salaries by Years Service and Sex in the Employee Summary worksheet. Use the SUMIFS function to calculate the total salary for each cell in the range C14:D16 of the Total Salaries by Years Service and Sex report. For example, in cell C14 calculate the total salary for female employees who have worked 0 to 4 years.

6. Save and close the workbook. Submit the finished workbook to your instructor, either in printed or electronic form, as requested.

*Apply the skills you learned by summarizing order data.*

**APPLY**

## Case Problem 1

**Data File needed for this Case Problem: World.xlsx**

***World Foods***   Kerry Jeffries is analyzing orders from last year. She has already summarized orders by month for all customers. Complete the following:

1. Open the **World** workbook located in the ExcelB\Case1 folder included with your Data Files, and then save the workbook as **World Foods**.

2. In the Documentation worksheet, enter your name and the date.

3. Make a copy of the Orders worksheet, and then rename the copied worksheet as **Q3**. In the Q3 worksheet, use advanced filtering to display sales in the Scandinavian countries (Denmark, Finland, Norway, and Sweden). Set up the criteria range beginning in row 1 and use the filter the list in place option.

4. Make a copy of the Orders worksheet, and then rename the copied worksheet as **Q4**. In the Q4 worksheet, use advanced filtering to display all records for Laura Callahan with sales over $1,500 in September. Set up the criteria range beginning in row 1 and use the filter the list in place option.

5. In the Summary worksheet, complete the analysis for the South American countries (Argentina and Brazil). Use Database functions to count and sum orders totaling $150 or more in March for Argentina. Set up an appropriate criteria range in rows 1 and 2, and then build the formulas in row 11 for Argentina.

6. In the Summary worksheet, complete the analysis for the South American country Brazil. Use the COUNTIFS and SUMIFS functions to enter formulas in row 12 to count and sum orders that total $150 or more in March in Brazil.

7. Save and close the workbook. Submit the finished workbook to your instructor, either in printed or electronic form, as requested.

*Apply the skills you learned by analyzing donor gift data.*

APPLY

## Case Problem 2

**Data File needed for this Case Problem: Gifts.xlsx**

*College Fund Raising*   Elliot Fastchow, the controller at ABC University, is analyzing gifts from several hundred donors. Complete the following:

1. Open the **Gifts** workbook located in the ExcelB\Case2 folder included with your Data Files, and then save the workbook as **ABC Gifts**.

2. In the Documentation worksheet, enter your name and the date.

3. Make a copy of the FundGifts worksheet, and then rename the copied worksheet as **Q3**. In the Q3 worksheet, use advanced filtering to display records from the current operating fund (FundType C) created after the year 2000 in the College of Nursing that have gifts totaling more than $1,000.

4. Make a copy of the FundGifts worksheet, and then rename the copied worksheet as **Q4**. In the Q4 worksheet, use advanced filtering to display records for funds in the College of Engineering with gifts of either $500 or less, or more than $50,000.

5. Sort the filtered data in the Gifts column from highest to lowest, and then format the Gifts column appropriately.

6. In the Summary worksheet, complete the analysis for Gifts from Endowment Funds. Use FundType E with Gifts over $1,000 to compare the gifts to the College of Arts & Science with gifts to the College of Pharmacy. Use Database functions to calculate the results for the college of Arts & Science. Use COUNTIFS, SUMIFS, and AVERAGEIFS to calculate the results for the College of Pharmacy.

7. Save and close the workbook. Submit the finished workbook to your instructor, either in printed or electronic form, as requested.

## ENDING DATA FILES

## OBJECTIVES

- Learn about the Microsoft Office Specialist certification program
- Set document properties
- Insert multiple worksheets
- Create a custom cell style
- Print cell gridlines and row and column headers
- Set columns to repeat on each printed page
- Work with advanced header and footer print options
- Create a custom view
- View Paste Special options with Live Preview
- Use the percent symbol in a formula
- Use icon sets to format values
- Edit a defined name
- Hide and unhide worksheets
- Work with pictures and SmartArt graphics
- Customize the Excel environment

EXCEL

# Microsoft Office Specialist Certification Skills

This appendix provides information about the Microsoft Office Specialist certification program and the benefits of achieving certification. The appendix also presents coverage of additional skills related to the Microsoft Office Specialist (Core) exam for Microsoft Excel 2010 that are not covered in the main tutorials of this text. Finally, the appendix includes a grid showing where the skills for the Excel 2010 Core exam are covered in this text.

## STARTING DATA FILES

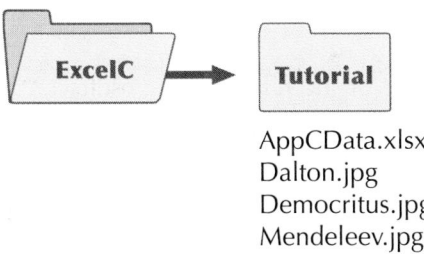

ExcelC → Tutorial

AppCData.xlsx
Dalton.jpg
Democritus.jpg
Mendeleev.jpg

# What Is Microsoft Office Specialist Certification?

Certification is a growing trend in the Information Technology industry whereby a software or hardware company devises and administers exams for users that enable them to demonstrate their ability to use the software or hardware effectively. By passing a certification exam, users prove their competence and knowledge of the software or hardware to prospective employers and colleagues.

The Microsoft Office Specialist program is the only comprehensive, performance-based certification program approved by Microsoft to validate desktop computer skills using the Microsoft Office 2010 programs, including Microsoft Excel. The program provides computer program literacy, measures proficiency, and identifies opportunities for skill enhancement. Successful candidates receive a certificate that sets them apart from their peers in the competitive job market. The certificate is a valuable credential, recognized worldwide as proof that an individual has the desktop computing skills needed to work productively and efficiently. Certification is a valuable asset to individuals who want to begin or advance their computer careers.

The Microsoft Office Specialist exams are developed, marketed, and administered by Certiport, Inc., a company that has an exclusive license from Microsoft. Exams must be taken at an authorized Certiport Center, which administers exams in a quiet room with the proper hardware and software and has trained personnel to manage and proctor the exams.

Go to www.microsoft.com/learning/en/us/certification/mos.aspx#certifications to access the Microsoft Office Specialist Certification page, as shown in Figure C-1.

| Figure C-1 | Microsoft Office Specialist Certification page |
| --- | --- |

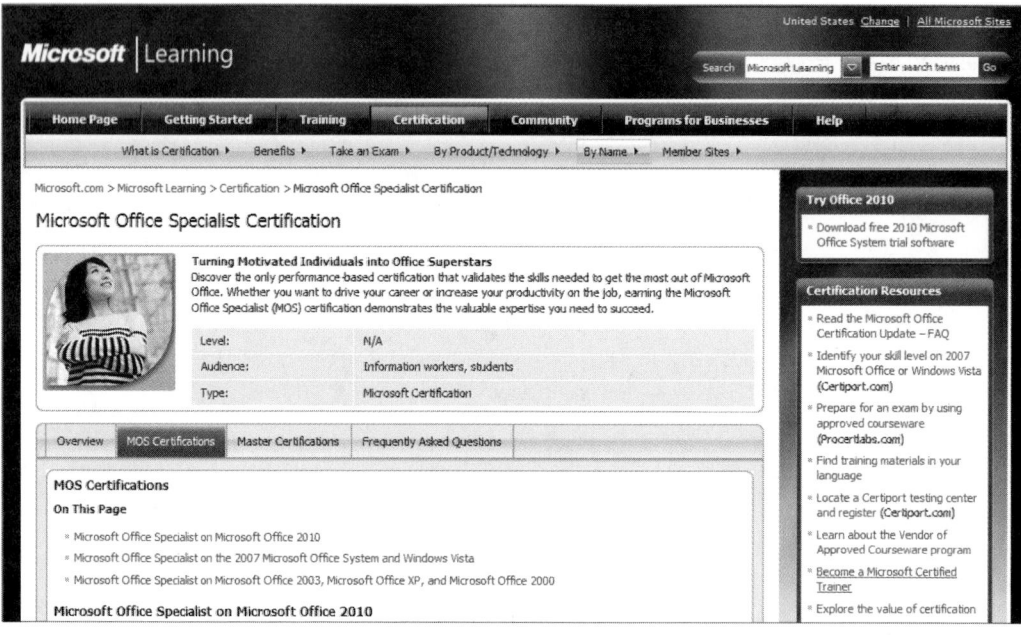

Used with permission from Microsoft.

**TIP**

For more information about the exams, view the FAQ documents at www.microsoft.com/certification or www.certiport.com/portal.

## Benefits of Achieving Certification

Achieving Microsoft Office Specialist certification in one or several of the Microsoft Office 2010 programs can be beneficial to you and your current or prospective employer. Earning certification acknowledges that you have the expertise to work with Microsoft Office programs. Individuals who are Microsoft Office Specialist certified report increased competence and productivity with Microsoft Office programs, as well as increased credibility with their employers, coworkers, and clients. Certification sets you apart in today's competitive job market, bringing employment opportunities, greater earning potential and career advancement, and increased job satisfaction.

Certification can help you increase your productivity within your current job and is a great way to enhance your skills without taking courses to obtain a new degree. Another benefit of Microsoft certification is that you gain access to a member website, career-building tools, and training. More information about the certification series can be located on the Certiport web site at www.certiport.com/portal, as shown in Figure C-2.

| Figure C-2 | Certification information on the Certiport site |
| --- | --- |

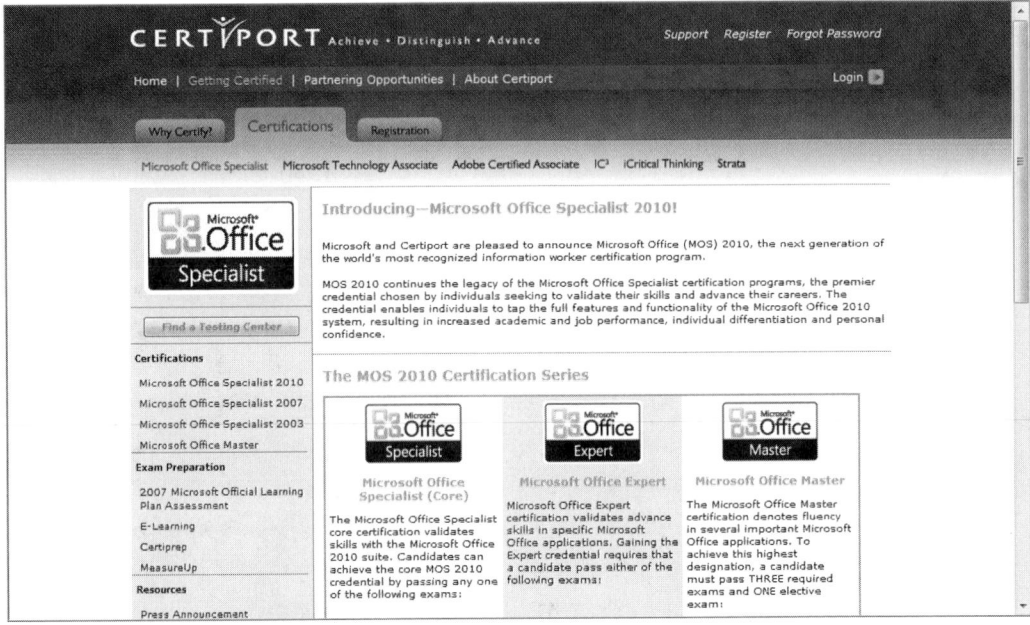

Courtesy of Certiport, Inc. www.certiport.com

## Certification Process

**TIP**

Course Technology publishes a multitude of Microsoft Office 2010 products that you can use for self-study. Visit www. cengagebrain.com to view the options. You can also purchase the texts directly from this site.

The steps to successfully completing Microsoft Office Specialist (Core) Certification for Microsoft Excel are outlined below. The core-level user should be able to create professional-looking documents for a variety of business, school, and personal situations. The core-level user should be able to use about 80% of the features of the program. Note that the Web addresses shown throughout might change. If you cannot find what you're looking for, go to the main site (www.microsoft.com or www.certiport.com) to search for a topic.

1. Find an authorized testing center near you using the Certiport Center locator at www.certiport.com/Portal/Pages/LocatorView.aspx.
2. Prepare for the exam by selecting the method that is appropriate for you, including taking a class or purchasing self-study materials.
3. Take a practice test (recommended) before taking the exam. To view the practice tests available, go to www.certiport.com/portal. Follow the online instructions for purchasing a voucher and taking the practice test.
4. Contact the Certiport Center and make an appointment for the exam you want to take. Check the organization's payment and exam policies. Purchase an exam voucher at www.certiport.com/portal. Go to the Certiport Center to take the test, and bring a printout of the exam voucher, your Certiport username and password, and a valid picture ID.
5. You will find out your results immediately. If you pass, you will receive your certificate two to three weeks after the date of the exam.

If you do not pass, refunds will not be given. But keep in mind that the exams are challenging and do not become discouraged. If you purchased a voucher with a retake, a second chance to take the exam might be all you need to pass. Check your Certiport Center's exam retake policies for more information.

# Setting Document Properties

The Documentation worksheet in a workbook includes the author's name and date created, and a description of the workbook. You can also make this information available by modifying the workbook's **document properties**, which are the descriptive details about a file, including its author, title, subject, file size, date the file was last edited, and many other items regarding the workbook.

## To add document properties to a workbook:

▶ 1. Open the **AppCData** workbook located in the ExcelC\Tutorial folder included with your Data Files, click the **Enable Editing** button if necessary to remove the workbook from Protected View, and then save the workbook as **AppCSolutions** in the same folder. The workbook contains seven worksheets that you will use as you work through the topics in this appendix.

▶ 2. In the Documentation worksheet, enter your name in cell B3 and the date in cell B4.

▶ 3. Click the **File** tab on the Ribbon to open Backstage view, and then click the **Info** tab in the navigation bar, if necessary, to display information about the workbook.

▶ 4. Click the **Show All Properties** link in the right pane to display a detailed list of properties for the file.

▶ 5. Next to "Tags" in the right pane, click **Add a tag**, and then type **Appendix C**.

▶ 6. Next to "Status" in the right pane, click **Add text**, type **Final**, next to "Categories", click **Add a category**, and then type **Solution file**.

▶ 7. Click the **Home** tab to return to the active worksheet.

Now you will insert two additional worksheets into the workbook.

# Inserting Multiple Worksheets at One Time

Although you can insert multiple new worksheets into a workbook one at a time, it's possible to insert multiple worksheets at the same time.

## To insert multiple worksheets at the same time:

▶ 1. Click the **Gridlines** worksheet, press and hold the **Shift** key, and then click the **Sales** worksheet.

▶ 2. On the Home tab, in the Cells group, click the **Insert button arrow**, and then click **Insert Sheet**. Two worksheets are added to the left of the Gridlines worksheet.

▶ 3. Rename the new Sheet1 **PasteSpc**, and then rename the new Sheet2 **Logo**.

▶ 4. Save your changes to the workbook.

You can delete multiple sheets at the same time by selecting the sheets you want to delete, clicking the Delete button arrow in the Cells group on the Home tab, and then clicking Delete Sheet.

# Creating a Custom Cell Style

A custom cell style is a cell style you create with the exact formatting you want to display in a cell. You can then apply the style to other cells. To create a custom cell style, you select and save a cell that has the formatting you want to use as the new style. The new cell style then appears in the Cell Styles gallery, ready to be applied to other worksheet cells and shared with other workbooks.

You'll create a custom cell style named ApndxTitle that formats the worksheet title in a large bold font centered over a double bottom border with orange fill.

### To create the ApndxTitle cell style:

1. Switch to the **PasteSpc** worksheet, click cell **A1** to select it (if necessary), and then change the column width in column A to **14**.

2. In cell A1, enter **Appendix C**, and then click cell **A1** to select it.

3. On the Home tab, in the Font group, click the **dialog box launcher** to open the Format Cells dialog box.

4. In the Format Cells dialog box, click the **Font** tab (if necessary), click **Bold** in the Font style box, and then click **14** in the Size box. Now you will change the cell alignment.

5. Click the **Alignment** tab, click the **Horizontal** arrow, and then click **Center**. Next, you will add a cell border.

6. Click the **Border** tab, click the **double line** in the Style box, and then click the **bottom border** in the Border preview. You can also add a fill color to the cell from the Fill tab.

7. Click the **Fill** tab, in the Background Color palette, click **orange** (last color in first row), and then click the **OK** button. The text in cell A1 appears centered, in 14-point bold font, and the cell has a bottom double-line border and an orange fill. You will make a custom cell style based upon the formatting of cell A1.

8. In the Styles group on the Home tab, click the **Cell Styles** button to open the Cell Styles gallery, and then click **New Cell Style**. The Style dialog box opens. In this dialog box, you can specify a name for the custom cell style, and you can specify which formatting options of the selected cell you want to include in the custom cell style.

9. In the Style name box, type **ApndxTitle**. Now specify the formatting elements you want to include in the custom cell style. The formatting options are currently all checked. However, you do not want to include the Number format and the Protection format.

10. Click the **Number** and **Protection** check boxes to remove the check marks, leaving the Alignment, Font, Border, and Fill style elements checked. The checked elements are included in the custom style.

11. Click the **OK** button to return to the worksheet.

The ApndxTitle cell style appears in the Cell Styles gallery and is ready to be applied to the active cell. Custom styles appear at the top of the Cell Styles gallery. Now apply the style.

### To apply the ApndxTitle cell style:

▶ **1.** Switch to the **Logo** worksheet.

▶ **2.** In column A, change the column width to 14, and then enter **Appendix C** in cell A1.

▶ **3.** Make cell **A1** the active cell.

▶ **4.** In the Styles group on the Home tab, click the **Cell Styles** button to open the Cell Styles gallery.

▶ **5.** In the Custom section, click **ApndxTitle** to apply the style to the selected cell.

▶ **6.** Click cell **A3** to deselect the cell with the formatted title. See Figure C-3.

---

**Figure C-3** Applying a custom cell style

custom style applied to cell A1

click to open the Cell Styles gallery

▶ **7.** Save your changes to the workbook.

# Printing Cell Gridlines

Normally cell gridlines, the grid of lines separating rows and columns you see on worksheets, are not printed. If you want your printout to include gridlines, you choose the Print option in the Gridlines section of the Sheet Options group on the Page Layout tab.

### To print gridlines in printed output of the Gridlines worksheet:

▶ **1.** Switch to the **Gridlines** worksheet. The worksheet contains a comparison between budgeted and actual cash flow for a budget.

▶ **2.** Click the **Page Layout** tab on the Ribbon.

▶ **3.** In the Sheet Options group, click the **Print** check box in the Gridlines section.

▶ **4.** Click the **File** tab, and then click the **Print** tab to display the print options in Backstage view. The cash budget appears with gridlines in the print preview. See Figure C-4.

| Figure C-4 | Print preview of budget with gridlines |

**5.** Click the **Print** button to print the result, and then click the **Home** tab to return to the Gridlines worksheet.

# Printing Row and Column Headers

Normally the row and column headers (column letters and row numbers) for a worksheet are not printed. If you want your printout to include these headers, you select the Print check box in the Headings section of the Sheet Options group on the Page Layout tab.

You will print the formulas used to calculate the cash budget. You will include column and row headers as part of the printout so you can see where on the worksheet these formulas are entered.

**To print row and column headers in the Gridlines worksheet:**

**1.** In the Gridlines worksheet, press the **Ctrl+`** keys. The worksheet changes to formula view.

**2.** If necessary, change the column width of column A to **14**, and then click cell **A1**.

**3.** Click the **Page Layout** tab on the Ribbon.

**4.** In the **Sheet Options** group, click the **Print** check box in the Headings section of the tab.

**5.** Click the **File** tab and then click the **Print** tab to display the print options. Notice the cash budget formulas appear in the print preview with column and row headings. See Figure C-5.

**Figure C-5** Row and column headers in print preview

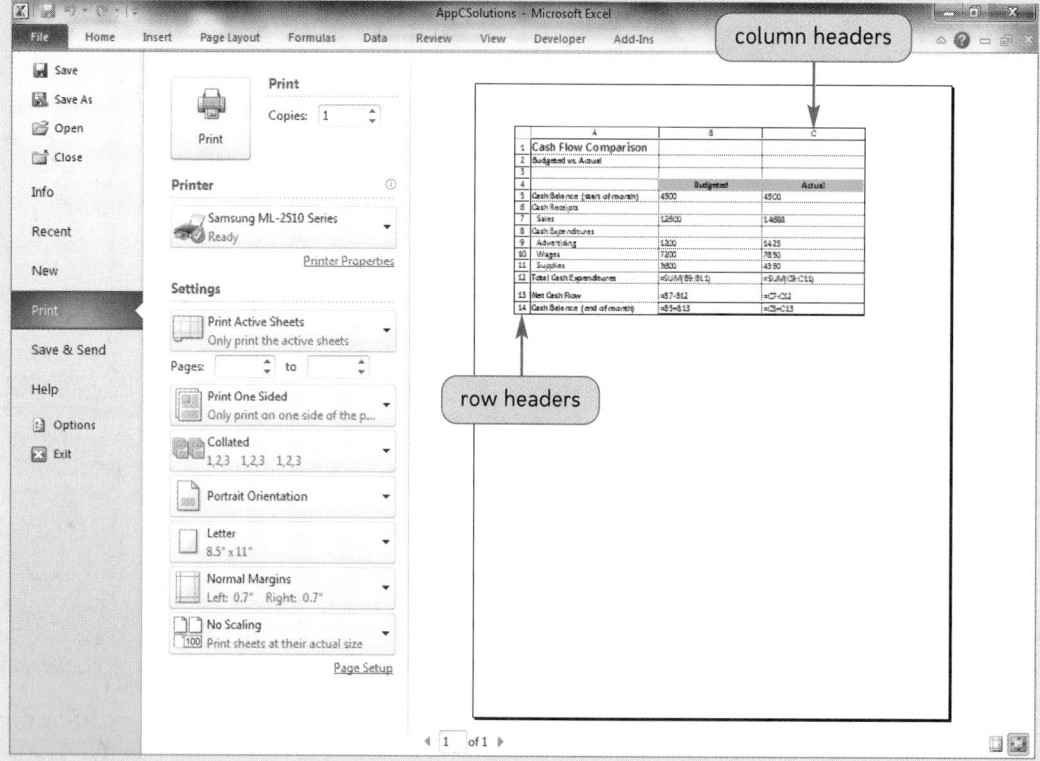

6. Click the **Print** button to print the result.

7. Click the **Home** tab to return to the Gridlines worksheet.

# Printing Columns to Repeat on Each Printed Page

Sometimes a large worksheet has too many columns to fit on one printed page. If the first column in the worksheet (which will print on the first page only) contains the row labels for the worksheet, it can make the second and subsequent pages of the printed worksheet hard to interpret. In Excel, you can set the print options to include the first column of the worksheet on each page of the printed output.

**To include column A on each page of the printed output of the Sales worksheet:**

1. Switch to the **Sales** worksheet. Notice the Sales worksheet has sales data in columns A through Y for various sales representatives. Column A contains the row labels identifying the sales representatives whose sales data appears in each row.

2. Click the **File** tab, and then click the **Print** tab to display print options in Backstage view. The first page of the worksheet appears in the print preview.

3. Click the **Next Page** button ▶ to view the second page of the worksheet. Notice on page 2 the sales rep names do not appear in the first column of this page of the printed output, making it difficult to know which rep is responsible for the sales units in each row. You want to print column A on both pages 1 and 2 of the worksheet.

4. Click the **Page Layout** tab, and then in the Page Setup group, click the **Print Titles** button. The Page Setup dialog box opens.

5. If necessary, click the **Sheet** tab, click the **Columns to repeat at left** box, and then in the Sales worksheet, click the **column A** row header. The reference $A:$A appears in the Columns to repeat at left box.

6. Click the **Print Preview** button to return to the Print tab in Backstage view, and then navigate to the second page in the print preview to verify that the sales rep names appear in the first column of the second page of the worksheet. See Figure C-6.

| Figure C-6 | Preview of printed output with repeated first column on page 2 |

7. Click the **Print** button to print the worksheet, and then click the **Home** tab to return to the Sales worksheet.

# Working with Advanced Header and Footer Print Options

In the last set of steps, you worked with the Page Setup dialog box. There are several advanced printing options available in the Page Setup dialog box on the Header/Footer tab that provide flexibility when printing headers and footers in worksheets. These include:

- **Different first page check box** – This option lets you display a different header and footer on the first page of your worksheet than on the other pages in the worksheet. Once you check this option, edit the first page's header and footer as you want. Then, edit any header or footer other than the one on the first page to display what you want on subsequent pages.
- **Different odd and even pages check box** – This option lets you create one header and footer for all even-numbered pages and one for all odd-numbered pages. This is useful if you want to print your worksheet book style and want page numbers, for example, to be at the left and right edges of the paper.
- **Scale with document check box** – This option automatically increases and decreases the size of the header and footer to properly fit the page.
- **Align with page margins check box** – As you change the page margins, this option changes the location of the header and footer so they are centered in relation to the margins.

The AppCSolutions workbook contains the TOC worksheet, with an outline for a book that will print over multiple pages. You will print it with the title "Table of Contents" as the header on the first page. On subsequent even-numbered pages, the text "New Perspectives Series" will appear in the header; and on odd-numbered pages, the text "Microsoft Excel 2010" will appear.

## To create a separate header for the first page, and different odd- and even-numbered page headers:

1. Switch to the **TOC** worksheet.

2. Click the **Page Layout** tab on the Ribbon, and then click the **Print Titles** button in the Page Setup group. The Page Setup dialog box opens.

3. If necessary, click the **Header/Footer** tab.

4. Click the **Different odd and even pages** check box, and then click the **Different first page** check box. Checks appear in both check boxes.

5. Click the **Custom Header** button to open the Header dialog box, and then, click the **First page header** tab (if necessary). See Figure C-7. Three tabs appear in this dialog box. You want the text "Table of Contents" to appear centered in the header on the first page of the printed worksheet.

**Figure C-7**    **Header dialog box**

active tab

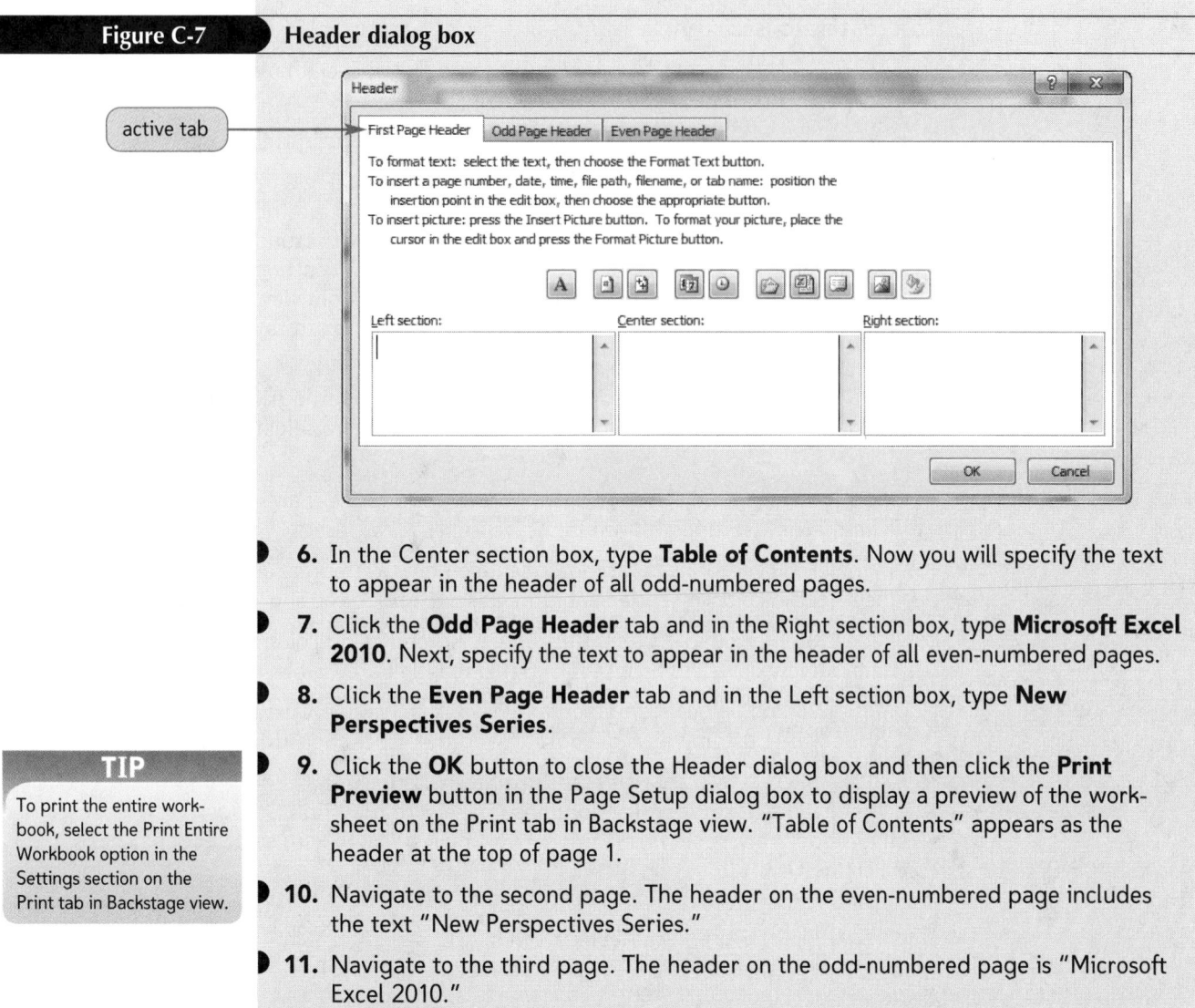

6. In the Center section box, type **Table of Contents**. Now you will specify the text to appear in the header of all odd-numbered pages.

7. Click the **Odd Page Header** tab and in the Right section box, type **Microsoft Excel 2010**. Next, specify the text to appear in the header of all even-numbered pages.

8. Click the **Even Page Header** tab and in the Left section box, type **New Perspectives Series**.

**TIP**

To print the entire workbook, select the Print Entire Workbook option in the Settings section on the Print tab in Backstage view.

9. Click the **OK** button to close the Header dialog box and then click the **Print Preview** button in the Page Setup dialog box to display a preview of the worksheet on the Print tab in Backstage view. "Table of Contents" appears as the header at the top of page 1.

10. Navigate to the second page. The header on the even-numbered page includes the text "New Perspectives Series."

11. Navigate to the third page. The header on the odd-numbered page is "Microsoft Excel 2010."

12. Click the **Home** tab to return to the TOC worksheet, and then save your changes to the workbook.

# Creating a Custom View

**Custom views** let you save a combination of view settings in a workbook, such as zoom, visible columns, and filters, so that when you want to use a particular view you select it from a list in the Custom Views dialog box, and Excel applies it to the active worksheet.

The AppCSolutions workbook contains the Employee Data worksheet. In this worksheet you want to view and edit all columns in the worksheet, but you want to be able to exclude several columns when you print this data. You will hide columns C to F, I to K, and O to T and create a custom view. Before you modify your view settings for a particular purpose, you should save the current default settings as a custom view. This provides you with an easy way to return to the unmodified default view.

### To create a custom view:

▶ **1.** Switch to the **Employee Data** worksheet, and then click the **View** tab on the Ribbon.

▶ **2.** In the Workbook Views group, click the **Custom Views** button to open the Custom Views dialog box.

▶ **3.** Click the **Add** button to open the Add View dialog box. In this dialog box, you can specify a name for the custom view, and what types of settings will be saved in the custom view. For example, you can check the Print settings check box to save the print settings for the workbook as part of the custom view. You also can click the Hidden rows, columns, and filter settings check box to save these types of settings as part of the custom view.

▶ **4.** In the Name box, type **Normal**, make sure the Print settings check box and the Hidden rows, columns, and filter settings check box are selected, and then click the **OK** button.

Now you will create a second custom view. You first need to set up the worksheet with the view settings you want to save.

▶ **5.** In the Employee Data worksheet, select column **C** through column **F**, right-click the selected column headers, and then click **Hide** on the shortcut menu.

▶ **6.** Repeat Step 5 to hide column **I** through column **K**, and column **O** through column **T**. Now only columns A, B, G, H, L, M, and N are visible with data.

▶ **7.** In the Workbook Views group on the View tab, click the **Custom Views** button to open the Custom Views dialog box, and then click the **Add** button to open the Add View dialog box.

▶ **8.** In the Name box, type **HideColumns**, make sure the Print settings check box and the Hidden rows, columns, and filter settings check box are selected, and then click the **OK** button.

Now apply the custom views you created.

### To apply a custom view:

▶ **1.** In the Workbook Views group on the Views tab, click the **Custom Views** button to open the Custom Views dialog box.

▶ **2.** In the Views box, click **Normal**, and then click the **Show** button. The default view settings are applied and all columns are now displayed.

Now apply the HideColumns custom view.

▶ **3.** In the Workbook Views group, click the **Custom Views** button to open the Custom Views dialog box.

▶ **4.** In the Views box, click **HideColumns**, and then click the **Show** button. The columns C to F, I to K, and O to T are hidden.

# Using Paste Special and Live Preview

When you use the Copy and Paste buttons to copy and paste a range of cells, Excel copies all the information in the range of cells you select—meaning both the cell contents and the formatting for the cell—and pastes this information to the new cell or range of cells. You can use Excel's Paste button arrow to open a menu of other options, such as pasting only the cell contents (without the formatting) or only the formatting (without the cell contents).

When you copy a range and click the Paste button arrow, you can view the Paste Special options. By moving your mouse over any icon, you can see a Live Preview of how each Paste Special command will appear in the worksheet before pasting the data.

## To view a Live Preview of Paste Special options in the worksheet:

▶ **1.** Switch to the **PasteSpc** worksheet.

▶ **2.** Enter the values **10, 20, 30...100** in the range **A3:A12**, and then format the range **A3:A12** with the Accounting number format.

▶ **3.** If necessary, select the range **A3:A12**, and then click the **Copy** button in the Clipboard group on the Home tab.

▶ **4.** Click cell **C3**, and then click the **Paste button arrow** to display a menu of paste options.

▶ **5.** Move the mouse over (but do not click) the **Transpose** button 🔲. The Live Preview shows the values from A3:A12 with the accounting formatting appearing in the range C3:L3. See Figure C-8.

| Figure C-8 | Live Preview of Transpose paste option |

▶ **6.** Move the mouse over the **Values** button 🔲 on the Paste button menu. The Live Preview shows the pasted values without the accounting format in the range C3:C12.

▶ **7.** Move the mouse over the **Values & Number Formatting** button 🔲. The Live Preview shows the values from A3:A12 as they would appear pasted with the accounting format in the range C3:C12.

▶ **8.** Press the **Esc** key twice.

# Using the Percent Symbol in a Formula

How does Excel perform calculations when the percent (%) symbol is encountered in a formula? Recall that if a formula contains more than one arithmetic operator, Excel performs the calculations using an order of precedence. Excel first calculates any value within parentheses, next the percent (%) operator is calculated, then the ^ operator (exponentiation) is performed, then multiplication (*) and division (/) are calculated, and finally addition (+) and subtraction (-) are calculated.

For example, the following formula

=10^2*3%

returns the value 3. First, the percent operation 3% is calculated (.03). Next, exponentiation, 10^2, is performed (100). In the final calculation, the two values (.03 and 100) are multiplied to produce the final result of 3.

# Using Icon Sets to Format Values

Excel has many conditional formatting options. One option, icon sets, allows you to assign sets of three, four, or five graphic images inside cells whose shape or color show the relationship between the cells' values.

In the AppCSolutions workbook, the CondFormat worksheet already uses data bars to format the profits data. You will use icon sets to format the sales data found in column B.

### To format sales data using icon sets:

1. Switch to the **CondFormat** worksheet and select the range **B3:B14**.

2. Click the **Home** tab on the Ribbon, click the **Conditional Formatting** button in the Styles group, and then point to **Icon Sets** to display the Icon Sets gallery.

3. In the Directional section, click **3 Arrows (Colored)** (first icon set). The icon set is added to the selected cells. The green up arrow represents higher values, the yellow right-pointing arrow represents middle values, and the red down arrow represents lower values.

4. Click cell **A2** to deselect the range. See Figure C-9.

| Figure C-9 | Conditional formatting using icon sets |
|---|---|

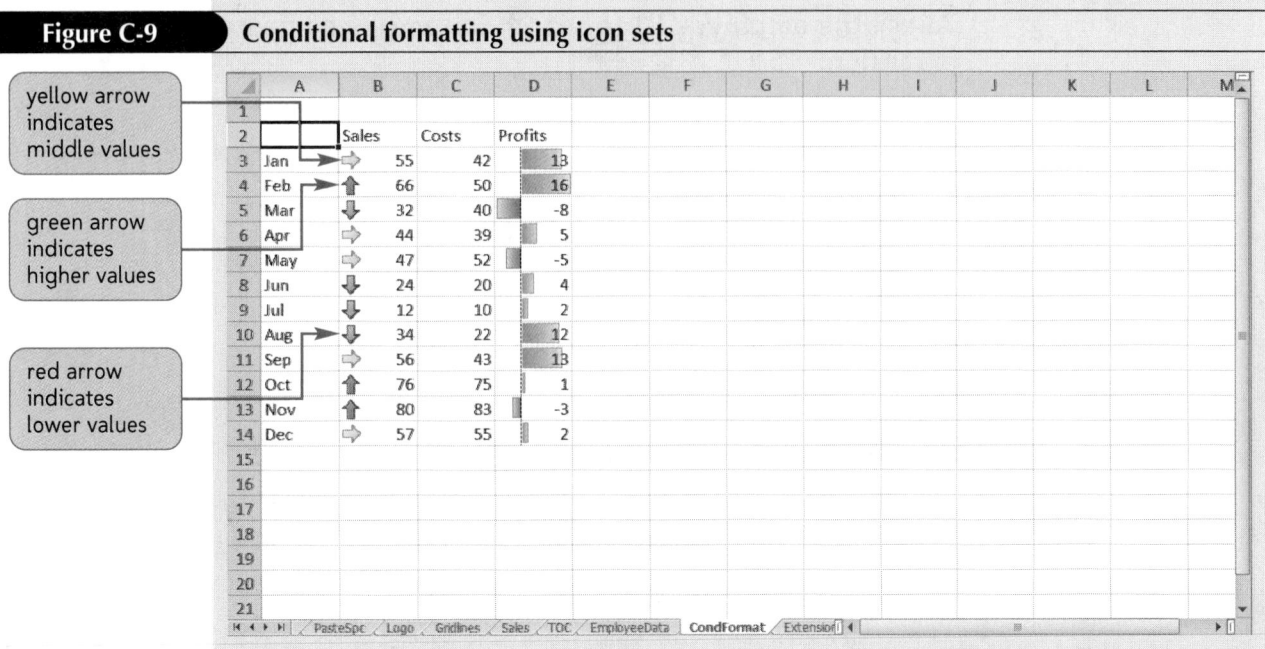

The worksheet is now too busy with the icon set and the data bars. You will remove the data bars from the profits data. You do this by clearing the conditional format in column D.

### To clear conditional formatting in column D:

1. Select the range **D3:D14**, which is the range containing the data bars.

2. In the Styles group on the Home tab, click the **Conditional Formatting** button, and then point to **Clear Rules**.

3. Click **Clear Rules from Selected Cells**. The data bars are removed from the Profits column.

4. Click cell **A1** to deselect the range, and then save your changes to the workbook.

## Editing a Defined Name

You have learned how to create and assign defined names to cells and ranges. You also can edit the defined name if the range reference changes.

In the Extension worksheet of the AppCSolutions workbook, the VLOOKUP function uses the employee ID to retrieve the employee name and phone extension from a list of employees. The data for the lookup table is referenced using a defined range name *EmployeeExt*.

### To use the employee ID to search for employee name and phone extension:

▶ **1.** Switch to the **Extension** worksheet.

▶ **2.** In cell A2, enter **3**. The employee name Charl appears in cell B2 and extension 309 appears in cell C2.

▶ **3.** Click cell **B2** and review the VLOOKUP formula in the formula bar. The defined name EmployeeExt is used to reference the employee data in the range A5:C11.

You need to add two employees to the employee list.

### To add new employees to the employee list:

▶ **1.** In cell A12, enter **8**; in cell B12, enter **Howard**; and then in cell C12, enter **678**.

▶ **2.** In A13, enter **9**; in cell B13, enter **Ireland**; and then in cell C13, enter **876**.

Now test the application.

▶ **3.** In cell A2, enter **2**. The employee name Byter appears in cell B2 and the phone extension 567 appears in cell C2.

▶ **4.** In cell A2, enter **8**. The error value, #N/A, displays in cells B2 and C2.

The error values appear in cells B2 and C2 because the defined name EmployeeExt references the range A5:C11. It needs to be modified to reference the range A5:C13, which includes the information for the two employees you added to the employee list.

### To edit the range reference of a defined name:

▶ **1.** Click the **Name Box arrow** and then click **EmployeeExt**. The range A5:C11 is highlighted in the worksheet. The defined name only references the range A5:C11; it does not reference all the employee data.

▶ **2.** Click cell **A1** to deselect the selected range, and then click the **Formulas** tab.

▶ **3.** In the Defined Names group, click the **Name Manager** button. The Name Manager dialog box opens.

▶ **4.** If necessary, select the **EmployeeExt** defined name.

▶ **5.** In the Refers to box, change =Extension!$A$5:$C$11 to **=Extension!$A$5:$C$13** and then click the **Close** button.

▶ **6.** Click the **Yes** button in the message box to confirm the changes made to the name reference. The error values in cells B2 and C2 are replaced by the employee name Howard and the phone extension 678.

▶ **7.** Click the **Name Box arrow** and then click **EmployeeExt**. The range A5:C13 is highlighted in the worksheet. The defined name now references all the employee data in the list.

▶ **8.** Click cell **A1** to deselect the range.

# Hiding and Unhiding Worksheets

There are times when information is needed in a worksheet for calculation purposes but you prefer that the worksheet is not seen by other users of the workbook. You can hide a worksheet, and when you do so, its tab is hidden but the worksheet remains within the workbook file.

Next you will hide the Extension worksheet.

**To hide and unhide the Extension worksheet:**

1. Right-click the Extension sheet tab, and then click **Hide** on the shortcut menu. The Extension tab is no longer visible. Now restore the Extension worksheet.

2. Right-click any sheet tab, and then click **Unhide** on the shortcut menu to display the Unhide dialog box.

3. In the Unhide box, click **Extension** if necessary to select it, and then click the **OK** button. The Extension sheet tab is visible again.

# Working with Pictures and SmartArt Graphics

A **SmartArt graphic** is a professionally designed business diagram, such as a flow chart, organization chart, or production cycle chart. SmartArt graphics can also be used to create graphic logos.

You will now insert the SmartArt graphic in the Logo worksheet.

**To insert the SmartArt graphic logo:**

1. Switch to the **Logo** worksheet, and then click cell **C3**.

2. Click the **Insert** tab on the Ribbon, and then click the **SmartArt** button in the Illustrations group. The Choose a SmartArt Graphic dialog box opens.

3. Click **Cycle** in the left pane, and then click **Gear** (the second graphic in the last row) as the layout.

4. Click the **OK** button. The gear SmartArt graphic is inserted in the Logo worksheet. See Figure C-10.

| Figure C-10 | SmartArt graphic inserted into the worksheet |

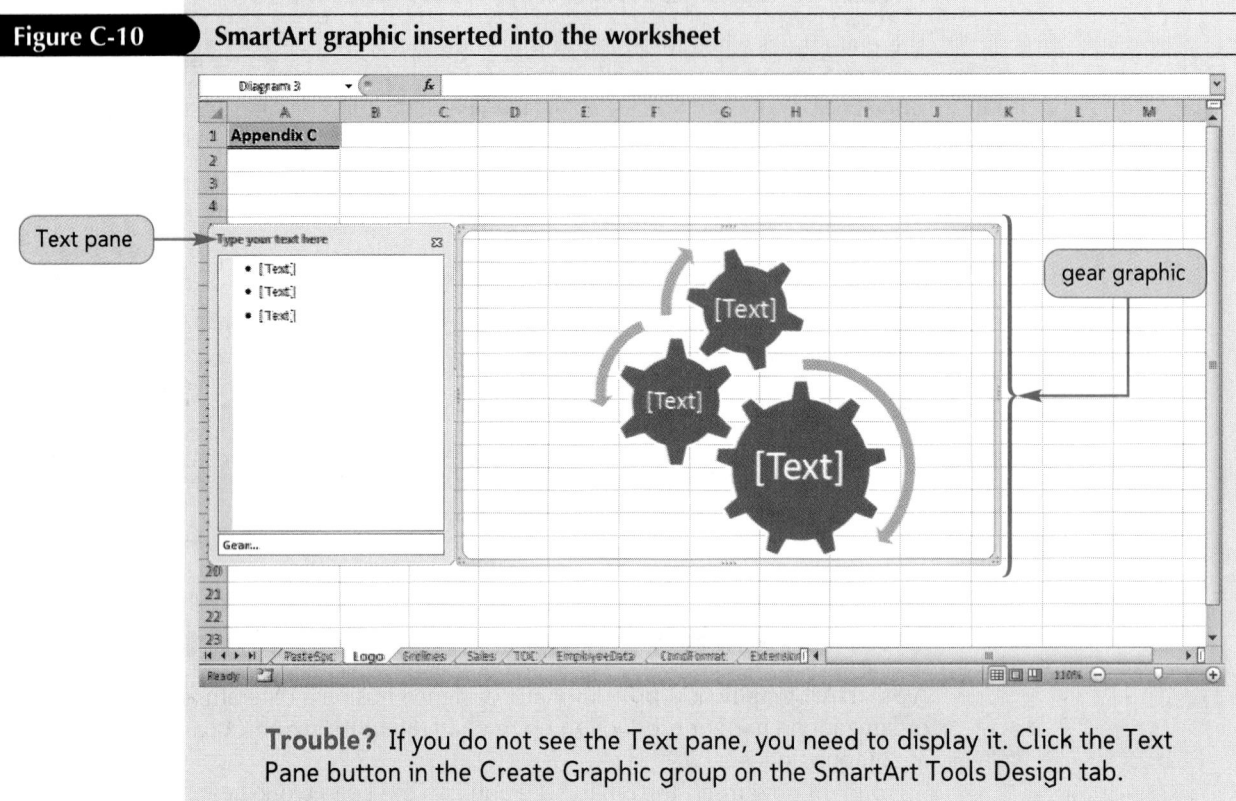

**Trouble?** If you do not see the Text pane, you need to display it. Click the Text Pane button in the Create Graphic group on the SmartArt Tools Design tab.

# Inserting Text Labels

You enter or edit text for each element of the SmartArt graphic in the Text pane.

### To enter text into the gear SmartArt graphic:

1. With the first entry selected in the Text pane, type **Chemistry** and then click the second text label entry.

2. Type **Interactive** for the second text label, and then click the third text label entry.

3. Type **Online** for the third text label. The three text labels appear in the gear graphic.

# Applying SmartArt Quick Styles

**Quick Styles** are a collection of styles you can use to quickly and easily format a SmartArt graphic's appearance. With Quick Styles you can change the color and outline style of the graphic. You can also rotate the graphic elements to give them a 3-D look.

You want the SmartArt graphic to have a 3-D or "chiseled" look, and the gear graphic color an olive green color. You'll use a Quick Style to format the Gear SmartArt graphic.

**To apply a Quick Style to the SmartArt graphic:**

▶ **1.** In the SmartArt Styles group on the SmartArt Tools Design tab, click the **More** button, and then click **Inset** (the style in the first row and second column of the 3-D section of the gallery). The style is applied to the gear graphic.

▶ **2.** In the SmartArt Styles group, click the **Change Colors** button, and then click **Gradient Loop – Accent 3** in the Accent 3 section (fourth icon). The graphic color changes to shades of olive green.

▶ **3.** Click cell **A1** to deselect the graphic. The formatted SmartArt image is shown in Figure C-11.

| Figure C-11 | Formatted SmartArt graphic |

Now insert a graphic image in each element of the gear graphic.

**To fill the gear elements of the logo with graphic images:**

▶ **1.** Click the **Chemistry** gear in the SmartArt graphic. A selection box appears around the selected element.

  **Trouble?** If the selection box is dotted, only the Chemistry label is selected. Click the gear element but not its label to select the entire gear element.

▶ **2.** Click the **SmartArt Tools Format** tab on the Ribbon, click the **Shape Fill button arrow** in the Shape Styles group, and then click **Picture**. The Insert Picture dialog box opens.

▶ **3.** Click the **Mendeleev** image file located in the ExcelC\Tutorial folder included with your Data Files, and then click the **Insert** button. The fill style of the Chemistry gear displays a portion of the Mendeleev image. The Chemistry label is difficult to read.

▶ **4.** Click the **Home** tab on the Ribbon, click the **Bold** button **B** in the Font group, and then change the font color to **Yellow** in the Standard Colors section. The Chemistry label changes to bold yellow.

▶ **5.** Click the **Interactive** gear in the SmartArt graphic, repeat Steps 2 and 3 to fill the background with the **Dalton** image file, and then repeat Step 4 to change the Interactive label to **bold yellow**.

6. Click the **Online** gear in the SmartArt graphic, repeat Steps 2 and 3 to fill the background with the **Democritus** image file, and then repeat Step 4 to change the Online label to **bold yellow**.

7. Click cell **A1** to deselect the graphic. See Figure C-12.

| Figure C-12 | Gear SmartArt graphic with pictures used as background fill |

## Editing a Picture

Imaging tools enable you to modify the appearance of pictures in a workbook. You can recolor pictures and change the picture's contrast and brightness level. For pictures inserted into a workbook as separate graphic objects (as opposed to fills), you can change the picture's shape, add a graphical border, and apply special effects such as rotating the picture in three dimensions, sharpening or softening the picture's edges, and adding a drop shadow.

You need to recolor the graphic images to make them darker, which would make the labels more readable. You'll give the Mendeleev image a green tint, the Dalton image a red tint, and the Democritus image a blue tint, and then increase the contrast to make the labels stand out.

### To edit the pictures:

1. Click the **Mendeleev** image in the Chemistry gear to select it.

2. Click the **Picture Tools Format** tab, click the **Color** button in the Adjust group, and then click **Olive Green, Accent color 3 Dark** located in the second row and fourth column of the Recolor section of the gallery to change the gear color to olive green.

3. In the Adjust group, click the **Corrections** button and then click **Brightness: -20% Contrast 0% (Normal)** located in the third row and second column of the Brightness and Contrast section of the Corrections gallery.

4. Click the **Dalton** image in the Interactive gear to select it, repeat Step 2 to apply the **Red, Accent color 2 Dark** color (located in the second row and third column of the Recolor section of the gallery) to change the gear color to red.

5. With the Dalton image still selected, click the **Corrections** button, and then click **Brightness: -40% Contrast +40%** (located in the fifth row and first column of the Brightness and Contrast section).

▶ **6.** Click the **Democritus** image in the Online gear to select it, and then repeat Step 2 to apply the **Blue, Accent color 1 Dark** color located in the second row and second column of the Recolor section of the color gallery.

▶ **7.** Click cell **A1** to deselect the SmartArt graphic.

The final task is to move and resize the SmartArt graphic.

### To position and resize the SmartArt graphic:

▶ **1.** Click the gear graphic image. The graphic border appears.

▶ **2.** Move the mouse over the border until the pointer changes to 🔆 then move the SmartArt graphic so the upper left corner of the SmartArt border is aligned with the upper left corner of cell A4.

Now resize the gear graphic.

▶ **3.** Move the mouse pointer over the middle of the right border of the SmartArt graphic, and when the pointer changes to ↔ drag the border to the right until the right border of the graphic aligns with the right edge of column F. See Figure C-13.

| **Figure C-13** | **Final SmartArt graphic** |

▶ **4.** Click cell **A1**.

# Inserting and Modifying a Screenshot

Office 2010 includes a built-in tool to capture and insert images from your computer screen. To capture a screen image, click the Insert tab on the Ribbon and then click the Screenshot button in the Illustrations group. A gallery opens displaying thumbnails of all open windows on your desktop. You can choose to take a screenshot of one of these open windows or you can click the Screen Clipping button to select a portion of an open window for the screenshot. When the screenshot is inserted into your worksheet, it is inserted as a picture. You can then modify the screenshot using the tools on the Picture Tools Format tab.

# Customizing the Quick Access Toolbar

The Quick Access Toolbar appears above the Ribbon and includes buttons for the most commonly used commands. By default, the Quick Access Toolbar contains the Save, Undo, and Redo commands but you can add or remove buttons. You add buttons to get quick access to commands you use frequently or commands from older versions of Excel not found on the Ribbon.

Next you will add the Print Preview and Print button to the Quick Access Toolbar.

**To add the Print Preview and Print button to the Quick Access Toolbar:**

▶ **1.** Click the **Customize Quick Access Toolbar** button ▾ that appears on the right end of the Quick Access Toolbar to display a list of common commands that can be added to the toolbar.

▶ **2.** Click the **Print Preview and Print** option. The Customize Quick Access Toolbar menu closes and the Print Preview and Print button appears on the Quick Access Toolbar. See Figure C-14.

| Figure C-14 | Print Preview and Print button added to the Quick Access Toolbar |

Print Preview and Print button

Now return the Quick Access Toolbar to its default state.

▶ **3.** Click the **Customize Quick Access Toolbar** button ▾ again, and then click the **Print Preview and Print** option to uncheck this option and remove the button from the Quick Access Toolbar.

# Changing the Default Font and Font Size

You can change the default font type, style, size, color, and other font effects using the options in the Excel Options dialog box, which you open by clicking the Options command in Backstage view. Once the new font style settings are set as default, all new workbooks created by Excel will use the new font settings. Workbooks created before the settings were changed will still use the previous setting.

For example, you change the default font type and font size by doing the following:

1. Click the File tab on the Ribbon to open Backstage view, and then click the Options command to open the Excel Options dialog box.
2. If necessary, click General in the left pane of the dialog box.
3. In the When creating new workbooks section of the right pane, click the Use this font arrow and select the desired font from the menu.
4. Click the Font size arrow and select the desired font size.
5. Click the OK button, and then click the OK button again in the message box informing you that you need to restart Excel so that the changes take effect. You will need to restart Excel to allow changes for default font and font size to take effect.

# Customizing Ribbon Groups

In Excel you can change the Ribbon to suit your work style. Among many other customization features, you can minimize the Ribbon, create or remove tabs and groups, hide tabs or commands, and rename tabs or commands.

Next you will remove the Symbols group from the Insert tab.

**To remove the Symbols group from the Insert tab:**

▶ **1.** Click the **File** tab on the Ribbon to open Backstage view, and then click the **Options** command to open the Excel Options dialog box.

▶ **2.** In the left pane, click **Customize Ribbon**. The right pane of the dialog box displays options for customizing the Ribbon. See Figure C-15.

| Figure C-15 | Customize Ribbon options |
| --- | --- |

▶ **3.** In the right pane, click the plus symbol to the left of **Insert tab** in the list on the right. The numerous groups included on the Insert tab are displayed.

▶ **4.** Click **Symbols** and then click the **Remove** button. The Symbols group is removed from the list of groups for the Insert tab.

▶ **5.** Click the **OK** button, and then click the **Insert** tab. Notice the Symbols group no longer appears as a group on the Insert tab.

You can return the Ribbon to its default state or restore a tab you have removed or modified to its original state.

### To restore the Symbols group to the Insert tab:

▶ **1.** Click the **File** tab on the Ribbon to open Backstage view, and then click the **Options** command to open the Excel Options dialog box.

▶ **2.** In the left pane, click **Customize Ribbon**.

▶ **3.** If necessary, click the **Insert** tab in the list on the right to select it.

▶ **4.** Click the **Reset** button at the bottom of the dialog box and then click **Reset only selected Ribbon tab**.

▶ **5.** Click the **OK** button to return to the worksheet. Notice the Symbols group appears on the Insert tab again.

## Setting AutoSave and Managed Version

It is now easier to recover an Excel file if you close your file without saving, or you want to review or return to an earlier version of the file you're currently working in.

As with earlier versions of Office, enabling *AutoRecover Excel 2010* will save versions while you are working in your file at the time interval you set. You can also choose to keep the last AutoSaved version of a file in case you accidentally close that file without saving, so that you can restore it the next time that you open the file. Also, while you are working in your file, you can access a listing of the AutoSaved files from Backstage view.

You will confirm that the AutoRecover and AutoSave features of Excel are enabled.

### To check AutoRecover and AutoSave settings:

▶ **1.** Click the **File** tab on the Ribbon to open Backstage view, and then click the **Options** command to open the Excel Options dialog box.

▶ **2.** In the left pane, click **Save** to display the Customize how workbooks are saved options. See Figure C-16.

**Figure C-16** | **Customizing how workbooks are saved**

**Excel Options**                                                                                    ?  — X

| | |
|---|---|
| General | Customize how workbooks are saved. |
| Formulas | |
| Proofing | **Save workbooks** |
| Save | Save files in this format:  Excel Workbook |
| Language | ☑ Save AutoRecover information every  10 ⟳ minutes |
| Advanced | ☑ Keep the last autosaved version if I close without saving |
| Customize Ribbon | AutoRecover file location:  C:\Users\Roy\AppData\Roaming\Microsoft\Excel\ |
| Quick Access Toolbar | Default file location:  C:\Users\Roy\Documents |
| Add-Ins | AutoRecover exceptions for:  ▣ AppCSolutions.xlsx ▾ |
| Trust Center | ☐ Disable AutoRecover for this workbook only |

if checked, Excel will save any file you don't save when closing it →

set number of minutes between saves

**Offline editing options for document management server files**

Save checked-out files to: ⓘ
 ○ The server drafts location on this computer
 ◉ The Office Document Cache
Server drafts location:  C:\Users\Roy\Documents\SharePoint Drafts\    Browse...

**Preserve visual appearance of the workbook**

Choose what colors will be seen in previous versions of Excel ⓘ  Colors...

OK    Cancel

▸ **3.** Make sure the **Keep the last autosaved version if I close without saving** check box is checked.

▸ **4.** Make sure the **Save AutoRecover Information every** check box is checked.

▸ **5.** Click the **OK** button to close the Excel Options dialog box, and then switch to the **Documentation** sheet.

▸ **6.** Save the workbook and exit Excel.

## ENDING DATA FILES

AppCSolutions.xlsx

# Microsoft Office Specialist: Excel 2010 Core Certification Skills Reference

## Managing the Worksheet Environment

| Skill | Pages Where Covered |
| --- | --- |
| Navigate through a worksheet | |
| Use hot keys | EX 6-EX 7 |
| Use the Name box | EX 424-EX 425 |
| Print a worksheet or workbook | |
| Print only selected worksheets | EX 317 |
| Print an entire workbook | EX C11 |
| Construct headers and footers | EX 105 |
| Apply printing options | |
| Scale | EX 47 |
| Print titles | EX 104 |
| Page setup | EX 101-EX 107 |
| Print area | EX 102 |
| Gridlines | EX C6-EX C7 |
| Personalize the environment using Backstage | |
| Manipulate the Quick Access Toolbar | EX C22 |
| Customize the Ribbon | |
| Tabs | EX 454, EX 472-EX 473 |
| Groups | EX C23 |
| Manipulate Excel default settings (Excel Options) | EX C22-EX C23 |
| Manipulate workbook properties (document panel) | EX C4 |
| Manipulate workbook files and folders | |
| Manage versions | EX C24 |
| AutoSave | EX C24 |

## Creating Cell Data

| Skill | Pages Where Covered |
| --- | --- |
| Construct cell data | |
| Use paste special | |
|     Formats | EX 81 |
|     Formulas | EX 81 |
|     Values | EX 81 |
|     Preview icons | EX C13 |
|     Transpose rows | EX 81, EX C13 |
|     Transpose columns | EX 81 |
|     Operations | |
|       Add | EX 81 |
|       Divide | EX 81 |
|     Comments | EX 81 |
|     Validation | EX 81 |
|     Paste as a link | EX 81 |
| Cut | EX 28 |
| Move | EX 26 |
| Select cell data | EX 24 |
| Apply AutoFill | |
| Copy data | EX 141-EX 147 |
| Fill a series | EX 143-EX 147 |
| Preserve cell format | EX 143 |
| Apply and manipulate hyperlinks | |
| Create a hyperlink in a cell | EX 338 |
| Modify hyperlinks | EX 340 |
| Modify hyperlinked cell attributes | EX 340 |
| Remove a hyperlink | EX 340 |

## Formatting Cells and Worksheets

| Skill | Pages Where Covered |
|---|---|
| Apply and modify cell formats | |
| Align cell content | EX 72-EX 73 |
| Apply a number format | EX 68-EX 71 |
| Wrapping text in a cell | EX 11-EX 12 |
| Use Format Painter | EX 79-EX 80 |
| Merge or split cells | |
| Use Merge & Center | EX 74 |
| Merge Across | EX 74 |
| Merge cells | EX 74-EX 75 |
| Unmerge cells | EX 74 |
| Create row and column titles | |
| Print row and column headings | EX C7-EX C8 |
| Print rows to repeat with titles | EX 104 |
| Print columns to repeat with titles | EX C8-EX C9 |
| Configure titles to print only on odd or even pages | EX C10-EX C11 |
| Configure titles to skip the first worksheet page | EX C10-EX C11 |
| Hide or unhide rows and columns | |
| Hide or unhide a column | EX 101 |
| Hide or unhide a row | EX 101 |
| Hide a series of columns | EX C11-EX C12 |
| Hide a series of rows | EX 101 |
| Manipulate Page Setup options for worksheets | |
| Configure page orientation | EX 44 |
| Manage page scaling | EX 47 |
| Configure page margins | EX 107 |
| Change header and footer size | EX 107 |
| Create and apply cell styles | |
| Apply cell styles | EX 84-EX 85 |
| Construct new cell styles | EX C5-EX C6 |

## Managing Worksheets and Workbooks

| Skill | Pages Where Covered |
|---|---|
| Create and format worksheets | |
| Insert worksheets | |
|     Single | EX 37 |
|     Multiple | EX C4 |
| Delete worksheets | |
|     Single | EX 38 |
|     Multiple | EX C4 |
| Reposition worksheets | EX 38 |
| Copy worksheets | EX 38 |
| Move worksheets | EX 38 |
| Rename worksheets | EX 38 |
| Group worksheets | EX 304 |
| Apply color to worksheet tabs | EX 64 |
| Hide worksheet tabs | EX C17 |
| Unhide worksheet tabs | EX C17 |
| Manipulate window views | |
| Split window views | EX 261 |
| Arrange window views | EX 324 |
| Open a new window with contents from the current worksheet | EX 324 |
| Manipulate workbook views | |
| Use Normal workbook view | EX 43 |
| Use Page Layout workbook view | EX 43-EX 44 |
| Use Page Break workbook view | EX 43-EX 44 |
| Create custom views | EX C11-EX C12 |

## Applying Formulas and Functions

| Skill | Pages Where Covered |
|---|---|
| Create formulas | |
| Use basic operators | EX 30 |
| Revise formulas | EX 390, EX 396 |
| Enforce precedence | |
| Order of evaluation | EX 30-EX 31 |
| Precedence using parentheses | EX 31 |
| Precedence of operations for percent vs. exponentiation | EX C14 |
| Apply cell references in formulas | |
| Relative and absolute references | EX 118-EX 127 |

| Skill | Pages Where Covered |
| --- | --- |
| Apply conditional logic in a formula | |
| Create a formula with values that match conditions | EX 367 |
| Edit defined conditions in a formula | EX 384, EX 396 |
| Use a series of conditional logic values in a formula | EX 382 |
| Apply named ranges in formulas | |
| Define ranges in formulas | EX 423, EX 429 |
| Edit ranges in formulas | EX C15 |
| Rename a named range | EX 427 |
| Apply cell ranges in formulas | |
| Enter a cell range definition in the formula bar | EX 431-EX 432 |
| Define a cell range | EX 431-EX 432 |

## Presenting Data Visually

| Skill | Pages Where Covered |
| --- | --- |
| Create charts based on worksheet data | EX 172-EX 175 |
| Apply and manipulate illustrations | |
| Insert | EX C17-EX C21 |
| Position | EX C17-EX C21 |
| Size | EX C17-EX C21 |
| Rotate | EX C17-EX C21 |
| Modify Clip Art SmartArt | EX C17-EX C21 |
| Modify Shape | EX C17-EX C21 |
| Modify Screenshots | EX C21 |
| Create and modify images by using the Image Editor | |
| Make corrections to an image | |
| Sharpen or soften an image | EX C20-EX C21 |
| Change brightness | EX C20-EX C21 |
| Change contrast | EX C20-EX C21 |
| Use picture color tools | EX C20-EX C21 |
| Change artistic effects on an image | EX C20-EX C21 |
| Apply Sparklines | |
| Use Line chart types | EX 211-EX 214 |
| Use Column chart types | EX 212 |
| Use Win/Loss chart types | EX 212 |
| Create a Sparkline chart | EX 211-EX 214 |
| Customize a Sparkline | EX 214-EX 215 |
| Format a Sparkline | EX 214-EX 215 |
| Show or hide data markers | EX 215 |

## Sharing Worksheet Data with Other Users

| Skill | Pages Where Covered |
| --- | --- |
| Share spreadsheets using Backstage | |
| Send a worksheet via E-mail or Skydrive | EX 348 |
| Change the file type to a different version of Excel | EX A14 |
| Save as PDF or XPS | EX 460 |
| Manage comments | |
| Insert | EX 449 |
| View | EX 450 |
| Edit | EX 450 |
| Delete comments | EX 450 |

## Analyzing and Organizing Data

| Skill | Pages Where Covered |
| --- | --- |
| Filter data | |
| Define a filter | EX 252-EX 253 |
| Apply a filter | EX 253-EX 255 |
| Remove a filter | EX 255 |
| Filter lists using AutoFilter | EX 255-EX 256 |
| Sort data | |
| Use sort options | |
| Values | EX 244-EX 249 |
| Font color | EX 246 |
| Cell color | EX 246 |
| Apply conditional formatting | |
| Apply conditional formatting to cells | EX 400-EX 404 |
| Use the Rule Manager to apply conditional formats | EX 402 |
| Use the IF function to apply conditional formatting | EX 400 |
| Clear rules | EX C15 |
| Use icon sets | EX C14-EX C15 |
| Use data bars | EX 216-EX 218 |

# GLOSSARY/INDEX

# TASK REFERENCE

| TASK | PAGE # | RECOMMENDED METHOD |
|------|--------|--------------------|
| **3-D Pie chart, rotate** | EX 210 | Select chart, click 3-D Rotation button in Background group on Chart Tools Layout tab, set rotation, click Close |
| **3-D reference, use** | EX 313 | *See* Reference box: Entering a Function That Contains a 3-D Reference |
| **Absolute reference, change to relative** | EX 118 | *See* Reference box: Entering Relative, Absolute, and Mixed References |
| **Action, undo or redo** | EX 40 | Click ↩ or ↪ on Quick Access Toolbar |
| **Advanced filter, clear** | EX B7 | Click Clear button in Sort & Filter group on Data tab |
| **Advanced filter, create** | EX B4 | Click Advanced button in Sort & Filter group on Data tab, set filter options, data, and criteria ranges in Advanced Filter dialog box, click OK |
| **AutoFill, copy formulas** | EX 142 | Select cell with formula, click and drag fill handle over adjacent range |
| **AutoFill, create series** | EX 143 | Enter first few entries in series, drag fill handle over adjacent range |
| **AutoSum feature, enter function with** | EX 35 | Click cell, click Σ ▾ in Editing group on Home tab, click function, verify range, press Enter |
| **Axis title, add** | EX 201 | Select chart, click Axis Titles button in Labels group on Chart Tools Layout tab, point to axis, select options |
| **Background image, add to worksheet** | EX 65 | Click Background button in Page Setup group on Page Layout tab, click image file, click Insert |
| **Border, add to cell** | EX 76 | Select range, click ▦ ▾ in Font group on Home tab, click border |
| **Cell, change fill color** | EX 64 | Click 🖌 ▾ in Font group on Home tab, click color |
| **Cell, clear contents of** | EX 20 | Right-click cell, range, column, or row; click Clear Contents |
| **Cell, delete** | EX 20 | Select cell or range, click Delete button in Cells group on Home tab |
| **Cell, edit** | EX 38 | Double-click cell, enter changes |
| **Cell, go to** | EX 7 | Click Find & Select button in Editing group on Home tab, click Go To |
| **Cell, move or copy** | EX 26 | *See* Reference box: Moving or Copying a Cell or Range |
| **Cell contents, align horizontally in cell** | EX 72 | Click ▤, ▤, or ▤ in Alignment group on Home tab |
| **Cell contents, increase or decrease indent of** | EX 73 | Click ▤ or ▤ in Alignment group on Home tab |
| **Cell contents, rotate** | EX 75 | Click ▨ ▾ in Alignment group on Home tab, click rotation angle |
| **Cell or range, create defined name** | EX 424 | *See* Reference box: Creating a Defined Name for a Cell or Range |
| **Cell or range, select by defined name** | EX 426 | Click Name box arrow, click defined name |
| **Cell reference, change** | EX 118 | *See* Reference box: Entering Relative, Absolute, and Mixed References |
| **Cells, lock or unlock** | EX 445 | Select cell or range, click Dialog Box Launcher in Font group on Home tab, click Protection tab, check or uncheck Locked check box, click OK |
| **Cells, merge and center** | EX 74 | Select adjacent cells, click ▦ in Alignment group on Home tab |
| **Cells, reference in other worksheets** | EX 310 | Enter reference in the format =*SheetName!CellRange* |
| **Cells, select all in worksheet** | EX 24 | *See* Reference box: Selecting Ranges |
| **Chart, add axis title to** | EX 201 | Select chart, click Axis Titles button in Labels group on Chart Tools Layout tab, point to axis, select option |

| TASK | PAGE # | RECOMMENDED METHOD |
|---|---|---|
| **Chart, add data label** | EX 182 | Select chart, click Data Labels button in Labels group on Chart Tools Layout tab, Click More Data Label Options, select options, click Close |
| **Chart, add data series** | EX 203 | *See* Reference box: Adding a Data Series to a Chart |
| **Chart, add gridlines** | EX 201 | Select chart, click Gridlines button in Axes group on Chart Tools Layout tab, select option |
| **Chart, change data** | EX 202 | Enter new values in chart's data source |
| **Chart, change layout** | EX 178 | Select chart, click layout in Chart Layout group on Chart Tools Design tab |
| **Chart, change style** | EX 177 | Select chart, click chart style in Chart Styles group on Chart Tools Design tab |
| **Chart, change to 3-D** | EX 209 | Select chart, click Change Chart Type button in Type group on Chart Tools Design tab, select 3-D chart type |
| **Chart, create** | EX172 | *See* Reference box: Inserting a Chart |
| **Chart, format data marker** | EX 207 | Click data marker, click Format Selection in Current Selection group on Chart Tools Layout tab, format as needed |
| **Chart, move within worksheet** | EX 176 | Select chart, drag to new location |
| **Chart, move to another sheet** | EX 175 | Select chart, click Move Chart button in Location group on Chart Tools Design tab |
| **Chart, resize** | EX 176 | Select chart, drag sizing handle |
| **Chart, select** | EX 176 | Click empty area of chart ("Chart Area" ScreenTip appears) |
| **Chart axis, change scale** | EX 187 | Select chart, click Axes button in Axes group on Chart Tools Layout tab, click option |
| **Chart legend, add or remove** | EX 186 | Select chart, click Legend button in Labels group on Chart Tools Layout tab, click option |
| **Chart legend, format** | EX 180 | Select chart, click Legend button in Labels group on Chart Tools Layout tab, click legend format |
| **Chart legend, overlay** | EX 199 | Double-click legend, uncheck Show the legend without overlapping the chart check box, click Close |
| **Chart sheet, create** | EX 219 | Select chart, click Move Chart button in Location group on Chart Tools Design tab, click New sheet option button, enter name, click OK |
| **Chart title, change** | EX 179 | Click chart title, type new chart title, press Enter |
| **Column, change width** | EX 15 | *See* Reference box: Changing the Column Width or Row Height |
| **Column, insert** | EX 19 | *See* Reference box: Inserting a Column or Row |
| **Column, select** | EX 17 | Click column heading |
| **Column chart, format columns** | EX 189 | Select all columns in data series, click Format Selection button in Current Selection group on Chart Tools Layout tab, specify column format |
| **Columns, select** | EX 17 | Click first column heading, hold down Shift, click last column heading |
| **Comment, delete** | EX 450 | Click cell with comment, click Delete button in Comments group on Review tab |
| **Comment, insert** | EX 449 | *See* Reference box: Inserting a Comment |
| **Comment, show or hide** | EX 450 | Click cell with comment, click Show/Hide Comment button in Comments group on Review tab |
| **Combination chart, create** | EX 206 | *See* Reference box: Creating a Combination Chart |

| TASK | PAGE # | RECOMMENDED METHOD |
|---|---|---|
| **Conditional format, clear** | EX 97 | Select cell, click Conditional Formatting button in Styles group on Home tab, point to Clear Rules, click Clear Rules from Selected Cells |
| **Conditional format, use to highlight cells** | EX 96 | *See* Reference box: Highlighting a Cell Based on Its Value |
| **Conditional formatting rule, edit** | EX 402 | *See* Reference box: Entering a Conditional Formatting Rule |
| **Criteria filter, specify complex criteria** | EX 256 | Click filter arrow, point to Number Filters, Text Filters, or Date Filters, specify filter criteria, click OK |
| **Custom format, create** | EX A11 | Select range, click Dialog Box Launcher in Number group on Home tab, click Number tab, click Custom in Category box, enter format codes in Type box, click OK |
| **Data, create input message, error alert message, or validation rule** | EX 438 | *See* Reference box: Validating Data |
| **Data, split from one column into separate columns** | EX A7 | Select range, click Text to Columns button in Data Tools group on Data tab, follow steps in wizard. |
| **Data bars, create** | EX 216 | Select range, click Conditional Formatting button in Styles group on Home tab, point to Data Bars, select data bar style |
| **Data bars, modify rule** | EX 217 | Select range with data bars, click Conditional Formatting button in Styles group on Home tab, click Manage Rules, select rule, click Edit Rule, modify rule as needed, click OK in each dialog box |
| **Data series, add to chart** | EX 203 | *See* Reference box: Adding a Data Series to a Chart |
| **Date, enter into cell** | EX 12 | Click cell, type date, press Enter or Tab |
| **Date, insert current** | EX 155 | Enter TODAY() or NOW() function in cell |
| **Dates, fill using AutoFill** | EX 144 | Enter first few dates, drag fill handle over adjacent range |
| **Defined name, create for cell or range** | EX 424 | *See* Reference box: Creating a Defined Name for a Cell or Range |
| **Defined name, edit or delete** | EX 427 | Click Name Manager button in Defined Names group on Formulas tab, select name, click Edit and modify or click Delete, click OK |
| **Defined names, add to existing formulas** | EX 433 | *See* Reference Window: Adding Defined Names to Existing Formulas |
| **Defined names, paste list in worksheet** | EX 428 | Click cell, click Use in Formula button in Defined Names group on Formulas tab, click Paste Names, click Paste List button |
| **Developer tab, display or hide** | EX 454 | Click File tab, click Options button, click Customize Ribbon, check or uncheck Developer check box, click OK |
| **Duplicate values, highlight** | EX 400 | *See* Reference box: Highlighting Duplicate Values |
| **Error Alert message, create** | EX 438 | *See* Reference box: Validating Data |
| **Excel table, add a record** | EX 242 | *See* Reference box: Adding a Record to an Excel Table |
| **Excel, start** | EX 5 | Click ⊞, click All Programs, click Microsoft Office, click Microsoft Excel 2010 |
| **Excel table, add a record** | EX 242 | *See* Reference box: Adding a Record to an Excel Table |
| **Excel table, create** | EX 239 | Click Table button in Tables group on Insert tab, verify range of data, click OK |
| **Excel table, format** | EX 241 | Click options in Table Style Options group on Table Tools Design tab |
| **Excel table, rename** | EX 240 | Click Excel table, select name in Table Name box in Properties group on Table Tools Design tab, type name |

| TASK | PAGE # | RECOMMENDED METHOD |
|------|--------|--------------------|
| **External reference formula, create** | EX 325 | Click cell in destination file, type =, click cell in source file, complete formula as usual |
| **Fill handle, use** | EX 141 | *See* Reference box: Copying Formulas and Formats with AutoFill |
| **Filter, clear from column** | EX 255 | Click filter arrow, click Clear Filter From *column* |
| **Filter, clear from Excel table** | EX 259 | Click Clear button in Sort & Filter group on Data tab |
| **Filter, select multiple items** | EX 255 | Click filter arrow, check two or more items, click OK |
| **Filter, use multiple columns** | EX 254 | Filter for one column, repeat to filter for additional columns |
| **Filter, use one column** | EX 252 | Click filter arrow, check item to filter by, click OK |
| **Filter arrows, display or hide** | EX 252 | In Sort & Filter group on Data tab, click Filter button |
| **Font, change color** | EX 62 | Click $\boxed{\mathbf{A}}$ ▾ in Font group on Home tab, click color |
| **Font, change size** | EX 61 | Click Font Size arrow in Font group on Home tab, click point size |
| **Font, change style** | EX 61 | In Font group on Home tab, click $\boxed{\mathbf{B}}$, $\boxed{\mathit{I}}$, or $\boxed{\underline{\mathbf{U}}}$ |
| **Font, change typeface** | EX 61 | Click Font arrow in Font group on Home tab, click font |
| **Format, copy using Format Painter** | EX 79 | Select range with original formatting, click 🖌 in Clipboard group on Home tab, select range to format |
| **Format, find and replace** | EX 40 | Click Find & Select in Editing group on Home tab, click Replace |
| **Format Cells dialog box, open** | EX 77 | Click Dialog Box Launcher in Number group on Home tab |
| **Formula, enter** | EX 31 | *See* Reference box: Inserting a Formula |
| **Formula, reference another worksheet** | EX 311 | *See* Reference box: Entering a Formula with References to Another Worksheet |
| **Formula results, copy and paste as values** | EX A5 | Copy range with formula results, click first cell in paste location, click Paste button arrow in Clipboard group on Home tab, click Values button |
| **Formula view, switch to** | EX 46 | Press Ctrl+` |
| **Function, insert** | EX 131 | Click function category in the Function Library group on Formulas tab, click a function, enter arguments, click OK |
| **Gridlines, add to chart** | EX 201 | Select chart, click Gridlines button in Axes group on Chart Tools Layout tab, select option |
| **Header or footer, create** | EX 105 | Click button in Header & Footer Elements group on Header & Footer Tools Design tab |
| **Hyperlink, create** | EX 338 | *See* Reference box: Inserting a Hyperlink |
| **Hyperlink, edit** | EX 340 | Right-click cell with hyperlink, click Edit Hyperlink, make edits in Edit Hyperlink dialog box, click OK |
| **Input message, create** | EX 438 | *See* Reference box: Validating Data |
| **Invalid data, circle** | EX 444 | Click Data Validation button arrow in Data Tools group on Data tab, click Circle Invalid Data |
| **Linked workbooks, update** | EX 329 | Click in source file, edit as usual |
| **Links, manage** | EX 332 | Click Edit Links button in Connections group on Data tab, select option, click OK |
| **Macro, edit** | EX 464 | *See* Reference box: Editing a Macro |
| **Macro, record** | EX 458 | *See* Reference box: Recording a Macro |

| TASK | PAGE # | RECOMMENDED METHOD |
|---|---|---|
| **Macro, run** | EX 461 | *See* Reference box: Running a Macro |
| **Macro, set security level for** | EX 456 | *See* Reference box: Setting Macro Security in Excel |
| **Macro, view code** | EX 464 | *See* Reference box: Editing a Macro |
| **Macro button, create** | EX 468 | *See* Reference box: Creating a Macro Button |
| **Macro button, move** | EX 470 | Right-click macro button, press Esc, drag button by its selection box to new location |
| **Macro button, resize** | EX 470 | Right-click macro button, press Esc, drag sizing handle |
| **Margins, set** | EX 107 | Click Margins button in Page Setup group on Page Layout tab, select margin size |
| **Number format, apply accounting number format** | EX 68 | Click $ in Number group on Home tab |
| **Number format, apply long date format** | EX 71 | Click Number Format arrow in Number group on Home tab, click Long Date |
| **Number format, apply percent number format** | EX 68 | click % in Number group on Home tab |
| **Number format, apply thousands separator** | EX 68 | Click , in Number group on Home tab |
| **Number format, increase or decrease decimal places** | EX 68 | Click or in Number group on Home tab |
| **Page break, insert or remove** | EX 103 | *See* Reference box: Inserting and Removing Page Breaks |
| **Pie chart, change slice color** | EX 183 | Click pie, click slice, click in Font group on Home tab, click color |
| **PivotChart, create** | EX 291 | Click PivotChart button in Tools group on PivotTable Tools Options tab, complete Insert Chart dialog box, click OK |
| **PivotTable, create** | EX 272 | *See* Reference box: Creating a PivotTable |
| **PivotTable, filter using slicer** | EX 286 | Click slicer button |
| **PivotTable, rearrange** | EX 277 | Drag field buttons in PivotTable Field List |
| **PivotTable, refresh** | EX 287 | click Refresh button in Data group on PivotTable Tools Options tab |
| **PivotTable field, remove** | EX 284 | Uncheck items in field area of PivotTable Field List |
| **PivotTable fields, filter** | EX 281 | Click the column or row label filter arrow in PivotTable for data to filter, check and uncheck items |
| **PivotTable items, group** | EX 288 | Click Group Field button in Group group on PivotTable Tools Options tab, select options in Grouping dialog box, click OK |
| **PivotTable report filter, add** | EX 279 | Drag field button from PivotTable Field List to Report Filter box |
| **PivotTable report filter, modify** | EX 280 | Click report filter arrow, click filter items |
| **PivotTable report layout, change** | EX 278 | Click Report Layout button in Layout group on PivotTable Tools Design tab, click layout |
| **PivotTable slicer, create** | EX 285 | Click Insert Slicer button in Sort & Filter group on PivotTable Tools Options tab, click field check box, click OK |
| **PivotTable style, apply** | EX 276 | Click More button in PivotTable Styles group on PivotTable Tools Design tab, click style |

| TASK | PAGE # | RECOMMENDED METHOD |
|------|--------|--------------------|
| **PivotTable value fields, format** | EX 276 | Click cell in PivotTable, click Field Settings button in Active Field group on PivotTable Tools Options tab, click Number Format button, select format, click OK |
| **Print area, clear** | EX 102 | Click Print Area button in Page Setup group on Page Layout tab, click Clear Print Area |
| **Print area, set** | EX 102 | Select range, click Print Area button in Page Setup group on Page Layout tab, click Set Print Area |
| **Print titles, add to printout** | EX 104 | Click Print Titles button in Page Setup group on Page Layout tab, click Rows to repeat at top, select range, click OK |
| **Range, insert or delete** | EX 29 | See Reference box: Inserting or Deleting a Range |
| **Range, move or copy** | EX 26 | See Reference box: Moving or Copying a Cell or Range |
| **Range, select adjacent or nonadjacent** | EX 24 | See Reference box: Selecting Ranges |
| **Record, delete from Excel table** | EX 244 | Select the record, click Delete button arrow in Cells group on Home tab, click Delete Table Rows |
| **Records, find and replace in Excel table** | EX 243 | Click Excel table, click the Find & Select button in Editing group on Home tab, use Find and Replace dialog box |
| **Relative reference, change to absolute or mixed** | EX 118 | See Reference box: Entering Relative, Absolute, and Mixed References |
| **Ribbon, minimize or maximize** | EX 473 | Click ⌃ or ⌄, or double-click any tab |
| **Row, change height** | EX 15 | See Reference box: Changing the Column Width or Row Height |
| **Row, hide** | EX 101 | Select rows to hide, click Format button in Cells group on Home tab, point to Hide & Unhide, click Hide Rows |
| **Row, insert** | EX 19 | See Reference box: Inserting a Column or Row |
| **Row, select one or more** | EX 20 | Click row heading, hold down Shift and click last row heading |
| **Row, unhide** | EX 101 | Select rows above and below hidden rows, click Format button in Cells group on Home tab, point to Hide & Unhide, click Unhide Rows |
| **Rows, repeat in printout** | EX 104 | Click Print Titles button in Page Setup group on Page Layout tab, click Rows to repeat at top, select range, click OK |
| **Row(s) and column(s), freeze** | EX 238 | Click cell below and to right of row(s) and column(s) to freeze, click Freeze Panes button in Window group on View tab, click option |
| **Row(s) and column(s), unfreeze** | EX 239 | Click Freeze Panes button in Window group on View tab, click Unfreeze Panes |
| **Series, create with AutoFill** | EX 144 | See Reference box: Creating a Series with AutoFill |
| **Sort, create a custom list** | EX 248 | See Reference box: Creating a Custom List |
| **Sort, multiple columns** | EX 245 | See Reference box: Sorting Data Using Multiple Sort Fields |
| **Sort, one column** | EX 244 | Click ⬇ or ⬆ |
| **Sparklines, add markers** | EX 214 | Select range with sparklines, click marker check boxes in Show group on Sparklines Tools Design tab |
| **Sparklines, create** | EX 213 | See Reference box: Creating and Editing Sparklines |
| **Special format, apply to data** | EX A10 | Select range, click Dialog Box Launcher in Number group on Home tab, click Number tab, click Special in Category box, click special format, click OK |

Microsoft Excel 2010, Introductory

REF 15

| TASK | PAGE # | RECOMMENDED METHOD |
|---|---|---|
| Spelling, check in worksheet | EX 41 | Click Spelling button in Proofing group on Review tab |
| Split panes, create or remove | Ex 261 | Click Split button in Window group on View tab |
| Style, apply to cell | EX 84 | *See* Reference box: Applying a Cell Style |
| Subtotal Outline view, use | EX 266 | Click outline button to show or hide the selected outline level |
| Subtotals, insert | EX 263 | *See* Reference box: Calculating Subtotals for a Range of Data |
| Subtotals, remove | EX 266 | Click Subtotal button in Outline group on Data tab, click Remove All button |
| Table, apply style | EX 91 | Select range, click Format as Table button in Styles group on Home tab, click style, verify range for table, click OK |
| Table, remove filter | EX 93 | Click in table, click Filter button in Sort & Filter group on Data tab |
| Table, select style options | EX 93 | Click table, select options in Table Style Options group on Design tab |
| Template, create custom | EX 344 | *See* Reference box: Creating a Custom Template |
| Text, enter multiple lines in a cell | EX 11 | Type first line of entry, press Alt+Enter, type next line |
| Text, format selection | EX 63 | Double-click cell, select text, format as needed |
| Theme, change for workbook | EX 86 | Click Themes button in Themes group on Page Layout tab, click theme |
| Total row, add or remove from Excel table | EX 259 | Check or uncheck Total Row check box in Table Style Options group on Table Tools Design tab |
| Total row, select summary statistics | EX 260 | Click arrow button in Total row cell, click summary function |
| Validation circle, clear from a cell | EX 444 | Enter valid data |
| Validation circles, clear all | EX 444 | Click Data Validation button arrow in Data Tools group on Data tab, click Clear Validation Circles |
| Validation circles, create | EX 444 | Click Data Validation button arrow in Data Tools group on Data tab, click Circle Invalid Data |
| Validation rule, create | EX 438 | *See* Reference box: Validating Data |
| VBA code, view | EX 454 | *See* Reference box: Editing a Macro |
| Visual Basic Editor, open or close | EX 454 | *See* Reference box: Editing a Macro |
| Workbook, create from template | EX 342 | *See* Reference box: Creating a Workbook Based on a Template |
| Workbook, preview and print | EX 45 | Click the File tab, click Print, click Print button |
| Workbook, protect | EX 448 | *See* Reference box: Protecting a Workbook |
| Workbook, save | EX 21 | Click File tab, click Save |
| Workbook, save earlier Excel file format in current format | EX A2 | In Save As dialog box, click Save as type button, click Excel Workbook |
| Workbook, save in earlier Excel file format | EX A14 | In Save As dialog box, click Save as type button, click Excel 97-2003 Workbook, click Save, click Continue or Cancel in Compatibility Checker |
| Workbook, save to SkyDrive | EX 349 | *See* Reference box: Saving a Workbook to SkyDrive |
| Workbook, save with macros | EX 471 | In Save As dialog box, select save location, enter filename, click the Save as type button, click Excel Macro-Enabled Workbook, click Save |
| Workbooks, arrange | EX 324 | *See* Reference box: Arranging Workbooks |
| Workbooks, link | EX 322 | Enter formula in the format =[*WorkbookName*] *WorksheetName!CellRange* |

| TASK | PAGE # | RECOMMENDED METHOD |
|---|---|---|
| **Workbooks, switch between** | EX 324 | Click Switch Windows button in Window group on View tab, click workbook to make active |
| **Worksheet, add background image** | EX 65 | Click Background button in Page Setup group on Page Layout tab, click image file, click Insert |
| **Worksheet, change orientation** | EX 44 | Click Orientation button in Page Setup group on the Page Layout tab, click Landscape or Portrait |
| **Worksheet, change view** | EX 43 | Click ▦, ▢, or ▣ on status bar |
| **Worksheet, copy** | EX 38 | Hold down Ctrl and drag sheet tab to new location |
| **Worksheet, delete** | EX 37 | Right-click sheet tab, click Delete, click Delete button |
| **Worksheet, insert** | EX 37 | Click ▣ |
| **Worksheet, move** | EX 38 | Drag sheet tab to new location |
| **Worksheet, protect** | EX 446 | *See* Reference box: Protecting a Worksheet |
| **Worksheet, rename** | EX 38 | Double-click sheet tab, type new name, press Enter |
| **Worksheet, scale for printing** | EX 47 | Set width and height in Scale to Fit group on Page Layout tab |
| **Worksheet, unprotect** | EX 449 | Make worksheet active, click Unprotect Sheet button in Changes group on Review tab |
| **Worksheet group, print** | EX 317 | Create worksheet group, apply page layout settings, print as usual |
| **Worksheets, move between** | EX 5 | Click sheet tab; or click tab scrolling button and then click sheet tab |
| **Worksheets, copy to another workbook** | EX 310 | *See* Reference box: Copying Worksheets to Another Workbook |
| **Worksheets, group or ungroup** | EX 305 | *See* Reference box: Grouping and Ungrouping Worksheets |
| **Workspace, create** | EX 333 | Open and arrange workbooks as desired, click Save Workspace button in Window group on View tab, save as usual |